ICSE Exams 2026

AF819937

All in One®

BIOLOGY

Class 10

Authors
Kavita Thareja
Rashmi Gupta

arihant
SUCCESS AND NOTHING LESS

arihant
SUCCESS AND NOTHING LESS

ARIHANT PRAKASHAN
(School Division Series)

卐 *ADMINISTRATIVE & PRODUCTION OFFICES*

Regd. Office

'Ramchhaya' 4577/15, Agarwal Road, Darya Ganj, New Delhi -110002
Tele: 011- 47630600, 43518550; Fax: 011- 23280316

卐 *Head Office*

Kalindi, TP Nagar, Meerut (UP) - 250002, Tel: 0121-7156203, 7156204

卐 *SALES & SUPPORT OFFICES*

Agra, Ahmedabad, Bengaluru, Bareilly, Chennai, Delhi, Guwahati, Hyderabad, Jaipur, Jhansi, Kolkata, Lucknow, Nagpur & Pune.

PO No : TXT-XX-XXXXXXX-X-XX

Published By Arihant Publications (India) Ltd.

For further information about the books published by Arihant, log on to www.arihantbooks.com or e-mail at info@arihantbooks.com

Follow us on

卐 *PRICE* ₹330.00

PRODUCTION TEAM

Publishing Managers	*Cover Designer*	*Inner Designer*
Mahendra Singh Rawat & Keshav Mohan	Salman Shaikh	Ankit Tyagi
Project Head	*Page Layouting*	*Proof Reader*
Neha Singh	Sachin	Nidhi, Prashant

Index *cum* Study Planner

One Book- Endless Features

to Help you Succeed

Chapter Inside

At the start of each chapter, all the Chapter topics have been listed, so that students may know what they are going to study.

CHAPTER 02

Genetics

Chapter Inside

Some Important Genetic Terms • Mendelian Inheritance • Sex-Determination in Human Beings • Sex-Linked Inheritance • Mutation

Check Your Learning

A set of 3-5 Questions given in between the text, helps students to remain connected with the text while studying. They can instantly assess themselves for their understanding.

Monohybrid Cross

This cross is performed by considering only one pair of contrasting character or one feature at a time, e.g. when a cross was made between pure tall plant (TT) and pure dwarf plant (tt) was done, only dominant feature expressed itself in the first filial generation (F_1), i.e. all tall plants were produced by masking the effect of recessive feature. After self-pollination in second filial generation (F_2), both the traits, i.e. tallness and dwarfness were expressed in the ratio 3:1.

There are 50% chances of having either a male or female child in each pregnancy. Thus, it is the phenomenon occurring by chance. So, women should not be blamed for giving birth to a girl child.

Check Your LEARNING...

1. State the law of dominance.
2. Which law of inheritance is also called law of purity of gametes?
3. What is crossing over?
4. Name the types of chromosomes which do not take part in sex-determination.
5. Write the number of chromosomes present in human body.

Simplified Theory

It contains the necessary study material well supported by Definitions, Facts, Figures, Flowcharts, etc.

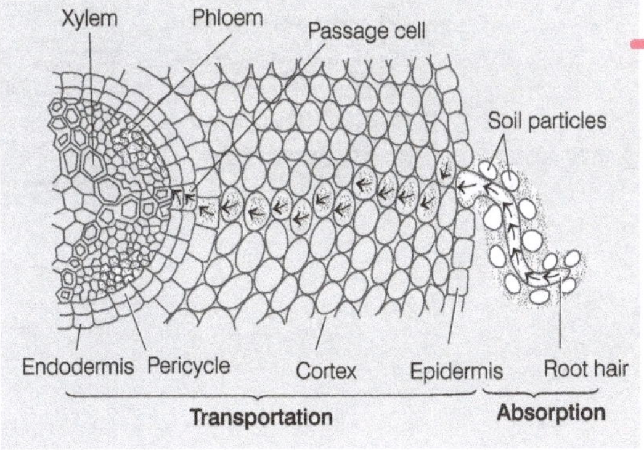

Illustrative Figures

To make the concepts completely visible, illustrative diagrams have been given at various place.

One Book- Endless Features
to Help you Succeed

QUiCK Revision

- **Genetics** is the branch of biology, which deals with the inheritance, as well as variation of characters from parents to offsprings.
- **Gregor Johann Mendel** for the first time conducted experiments to understand the pattern of inheritance and variations in living beings. He is also known as **Father of Genetics.**
- **Gene** is a unit of inheritance. It is a sequence of DNA that codes for a specific polypeptide. One gene can have slightly different forms.
- **Traits/characters** refer to the expression of genes in the form of visible physical properties, e.g. colour of flower, height of plant, shape of leaf, etc.
- **Alleles** are the alternate forms of genes in a particular gene pair, e.g. gene which codes for the colour of eyes. One of its forms code for brown and another codes for blue colour.
- **Homozygous condition** means having a pair of identical alleles (forms of gene) at a gene location (locus) on a pair of chromosomes. **Heterozygous condition** means having a pair of non-identical alleles at a gene locus on a pair of chromosomes.

(ii) **Law of segregation** (Second law) states that the alleles do not show any blending and both the characters are recovered as such in the F_2-generation. The factors or alleles of a pair segregate from each other in a way that a gamete receives only one of the two factors.

(iii) **Law of independent assortment** (Third law) states that when two pairs of traits are combined in a hybrid, segregation of one pair of character is independent of the other pair of characters at the time of gamete formation. This law was based on the result of dihybrid cross. It shows phenotypic ratio 9 : 3 : 3 : 1 and genotypic ratio 1 : 2 : 2 : 4 : 1 : 2 : 1 : 2 : 1

- **Sex-determination in human beings** Males have two types of gametes, i.e. X and Y, while females have only one type of gamete, i.e. X. If an ovum gets fertilised with a sperm carrying X-chromosome, the zygote develops into a female (XX) and if an ovum gets fertilised with a sperm carrying Y-chromosome, the zygote develops into a male. Hence, the type of sperm, which fertilises the ovum determines the sex of a child.

QUICK Revision

At the end of each chapter, QUICK Revision is given. It contains crux of the chapter in pointer form.

Chapter Practice

Section-I

1 Mark Questions

1. Name the following.
   (i) The physical expression of genes in an individual. [2013]
   (ii) An individual having dissimilar gene pairs.
   (iii) The type of gene which in the presence of contrasting allele is not expressed. [2014, 13]
   (iv) The cross between two parents having one pair of contrasting characters. [2015]
   (v) One factor that can cause mutation.

Ans. (i) Phenotype
(ii) Heterozygous
(iii) Recessive gene
(iv) Monohybrid cross
(v) Ultraviolet (UV) radiation

2. Correct and rewrite the following statements by changing the underlined words.
   (i) Peas are self-pollinated since they are unisexual.
   (ii) One of the example of X-linked inherited disease is diabetes.
   (iii) Colour blindness is inherited through Y-chromosome.
   (iv) Sudden change in genetic constitution of an individual is called genotype.

4. (i) Match the following columns.

Column I	Column II
A. Genetics	1. Chromosomes similar in size and shape
B. Recessive gene	2. Study of laws of inheritance of characters
C. Autosomes	3. A gene that can express only when in a similar pair
D. Homologous chromosomes	4. Chromosomes other than the pair of sex chromosomes

(ii) Match the following columns.

Column I	Column II
A. TT	1. Heterozygous
B. Tt	2. Homozygous dominant
C. tt	3. Recessive trait

Ans. (i) A-2, B-3, C-4, D-1 (ii) A-2, B-1, C-3

5. Choose the correct answer from each of the four options given below.
   (i) The discipline which deals with the study of transmission of characters from parents to offsprings is called
   (a) evolution (b) genetics (c) variation (d) similarity

Ans. (b)

Chapter Practice

The Exercise contains questions in that format in which these are asked in the examinations. Questions have been categorised as 1 mark questions, 2 marks questions, 3 marks questions and structured based questions. All the questions given here are fully solved.

Chapter Assessment

It is the Assessment exercise for the complete chapter. With this exercise, students can assess their understanding of the chapter and can prepare for it accordingly.

Chapter Assessment

Section-I

1 Mark Questions

1. Name the following.
   (i) A cross that considers two pairs of contrasting characters.
   (ii) Second law given by Mendel.
   (iii) A sex-linked recessive disorder that results in failure of discrimination between red and green colour.
2. Correct and rewrite the following statements by changing the underlined words.
   (i) Allele is a unit of inheritance.
   (ii) Polydactyly is an inability to straighten the little finger.
3. Give suitable biological reason for the following. Rare cases of haemophiliac males occur but no haemophiliac female is yet found.

(iii) X-linked genes can never pass from
(a) father to daughter
(b) mother to son
(c) mother to daughter
(d) father to son

(iv) In general, the possibility of a female becoming haemophilic is
(a) most (b) 50% (c) rare (d) 25%

6. Fill in the blanks by using suitable words.
   (i) The fundamental physical and functional unit of heredity is known as ....
   (ii) An organism with two copies of the same allele is .... for that trait.
   (iii) .... is the ratio of dihybrid cross.
   (iv) In humans, ... type of sex chromosomes are present.
   (v) The family pedigree of Queen Victoria shows the inheritance of ....

One Book- Endless Features

to Help you Succeed

Olympiad Section

It includes some special questions based on the pattern of Olympiad and other competitions to give the students a taste of the questions asked in competitions. These are not meant for school examinations.

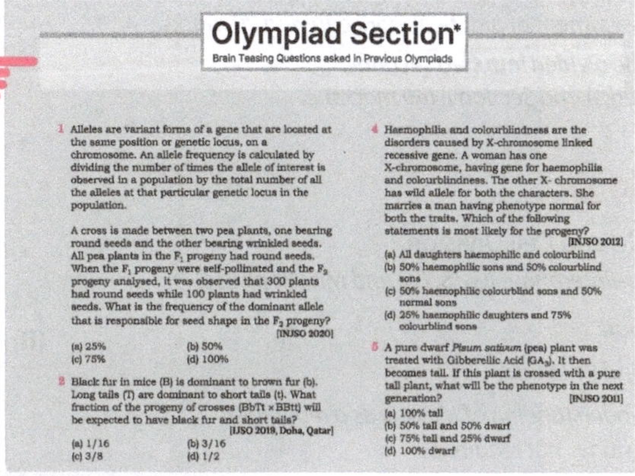

Olympiad Section*

Brain Teasing Questions asked in Previous Olympiads

1 Alleles are variant forms of a gene that are located at the same position or genetic locus, on a chromosome. An allele frequency is calculated by dividing the number of times the allele of interest is observed in a population by the total number of all the alleles at that particular genetic locus in the population.

A cross is made between two pea plants, one bearing round seeds and the other bearing wrinkled seeds. All pea plants in the F_1 progeny had round seeds. When the F_1 progeny were self-pollinated and the F_2 progeny analysed, it was observed that 300 plants had round seeds while 100 plants had wrinkled seeds. What is the frequency of the dominant allele that is responsible for seed shape in the F_2 progeny? [INJSO 2020]

(a) 25% (b) 50%
(c) 75% (d) 100%

2 Black fur in mice (B) is dominant to brown fur (b). Long tails (T) are dominant to short tails (t). What fraction of the progeny of crosses (BbTt × BBtt) will be expected to have black fur and short tails? [IJSO 2019, Doha, Qatar]

(a) 1/16 (b) 3/16
(c) 3/8 (d) 1/2

4 Haemophilia and colourblindness are the disorders caused by X-chromosome linked recessive gene. A woman has one X-chromosome, having gene for haemophilia and colourblindness. The other X- chromosome has wild allele for both the characters. She marries a man having phenotype normal for both the traits. Which of the following statements is most likely for the progeny? [INJSO 2012]

(a) All daughters haemophilic and colourblind
(b) 50% haemophilic sons and 50% colourblind sons
(c) 50% haemophilic colourblind sons and 50% normal sons
(d) 25% haemophilic daughters and 75% colourblind sons

5 A pure dwarf *Pisum sativum* (pea) plant was treated with Gibberellic Acid (GA_3). It then becomes tall. If this plant is crossed with a pure tall plant, what will be the phenotype in the next generation? [INJSO 2011]

(a) 100% tall
(b) 50% tall and 50% dwarf
(c) 75% tall and 25% dwarf
(d) 100% dwarf

Sample Question Papers

To make students practice of examination in real sense, there are 3 Sample Question Papers at the end. All these Sample Questions Papers are exactly prepared on the latest syllabus & pattern of examination.

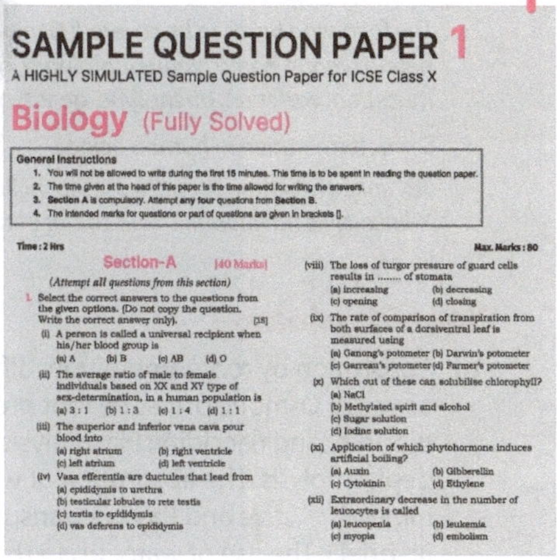

SAMPLE QUESTION PAPER 1

A HIGHLY SIMULATED Sample Question Paper for ICSE Class X

Biology (Fully Solved)

General Instructions

1. You will not be allowed to write during the first 15 minutes. This time is to be spent in reading the question paper.
2. The time given at the head of this paper is the time allowed for writing the answers.
3. Section A is compulsory. Attempt any four questions from Section B.
4. The intended marks for questions or part of questions are given in brackets [].

Time : 2 Hrs Max. Marks : 80

Section-A [40 Marks]

(Attempt all questions from this section)

1. Select the correct answers to the questions from the given options. (Do not copy the question. Write the correct answer only). [15]

(i) A person is called a universal recipient when his/her blood group is
(a) A (b) B (c) AB (d) O

(ii) The average ratio of male to female individuals based on XX and XY type of sex-determination, in a human population is
(a) 3 : 1 (b) 1 : 3 (c) 1 : 4 (d) 1 : 1

(iii) The superior and inferior vena cava pour blood into
(a) right atrium (b) right ventricle
(c) left atrium (d) left ventricle

(iv) Vasa efferentia are ductules that lead from
(a) epididymis to urethra
(b) testicular lobules to rete testis
(c) testis to epididymis
(d) vas deferens to epididymis

(viii) The loss of turgor pressure of guard cells results in .... of stomata
(a) increasing (b) decreasing
(c) opening (d) closing

(ix) The rate of comparison of transpiration from both surfaces of a dorsiventral leaf is measured using
(a) Ganong's potometer (b) Darwin's potometer
(c) Garreau's potometer (d) Farmer's potometer

(x) Which out of these can solubilise chlorophyll?
(a) NaCl
(b) Methylated spirit and alcohol
(c) Sugar solution
(d) Iodine solution

(xi) Application of which phytohormone induces artificial bolting?
(a) Auxin (b) Gibberellin
(c) Cytokinin (d) Ethylene

(xii) Extraordinary decrease in the number of leucocytes is called
(a) leucopenia (b) leukemia
(c) myopia (d) embolism

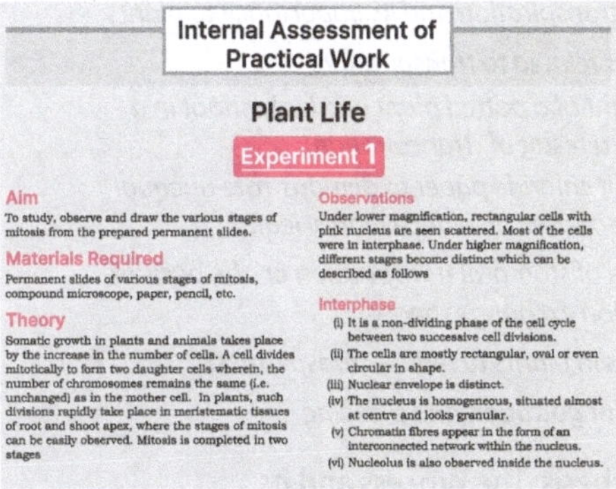

Internal Assessment of Practical Work

Plant Life

Experiment 1

Aim

To study, observe and draw the various stages of mitosis from the prepared permanent slides.

Materials Required

Permanent slides of various stages of mitosis, compound microscope, paper, pencil, etc.

Theory

Somatic growth in plants and animals takes place by the increase in the number of cells. A cell divides mitotically to form two daughter cells wherein, the number of chromosomes remains the same (i.e. unchanged) as in the mother cell. In plants, such divisions rapidly take place in meristematic tissues of root and shoot apex, where the stages of mitosis can be easily observed. Mitosis is completed in two stages

Observations

Under lower magnification, rectangular cells with pink nucleus are seen scattered. Most of the cells were in interphase. Under higher magnification, different stages become distinct which can be described as follows

Interphase

(i) It is a non-dividing phase of the cell cycle between two successive cell divisions.
(ii) The cells are mostly rectangular, oval or even circular in shape.
(iii) Nuclear envelope is distinct.
(iv) The nucleus is homogeneous, situated almost at centre and looks granular.
(v) Chromatin fibres appear in the form of an interconnected network within the nucleus.
(vi) Nucleolus is also observed inside the nucleus.

Internal Assessment of Practical Work

To make this book complete in all aspects, experiments based on latest syllabus have been given.

Latest Course *Structure*

*There will be one paper of **two hours** duration of 80 marks and Internal Assessment of practical work carrying 20 marks.*

*The paper will be divided into **two** sections, Section I (40 marks) and Section II (40 marks).*

Basic Biology

(i) Cell Cycle and Cell Division

Cell cycle – Interphase (G_1, S, G_2) and Mitotic phase.

Cell Division:

- *Mitosis and its stages.*
- *A basic understanding of Meiosis as a reduction division (stages not required).*
- *A brief idea of homologous chromosomes and crossing over leading to variations.*
- *Significance and major differences between mitotic and meiotic division.*

(ii) Structure of Chromosome

Basic structure of chromosome with elementary understanding of terms such as chromatin, chromatid, gene structure of DNA and centromere.

(iii) Genetics: Mendel's Laws of Inheritance and Sex Linked Inheritance of Diseases

- *The three laws of Mendel.*
- *Monohybrid cross – phenotype and genotype.*
- *Dihybrid cross – Only phenotype.*
- *The following terms to be covered: Gene, allele, heterozygous, homozygous, dominant, recessive, mutation, variation, phenotype, genotype.*
- *Sex determination in human beings.*

  Sex linked inheritance of diseases to include only X-linked like haemophilia and colour blindness.

Plant Physiology

(i) Absorption by roots, imbibition, diffusion and osmosis; Osmotic pressure, root pressure; turgidity and flaccidity; Plasmolysis and deplasmolysis; The absorption of water and minerals; Active and Passive transport (in brief); The rise of water up to the xylem; Forces responsible for ascent of sap.

- *Understanding of the processes related to absorption of water by the roots.*
- *Characteristics of roots, which make them suitable for absorbing water.*
- *Structure of a single full-grown root hair.*
- *A general idea of Cohesive, Adhesive forces and transpirational pull.*
- *Experiments to show the conduction of water through the xylem.*

(ii) Transpiration - process and significance. Ganong's potometer and its limitations. The factors affecting rate of transpiration. Experiments on transpiration. A brief idea of guttation and bleeding.

- *Concept of transpiration and its importance to plants*
- *Experiments related to transpiration:*

(a) *Loss in weight of a potted plant or a leafy shoot in a test tube as a result of transpiration.*

(b) *Use of cobalt chloride paper to demonstrate unequal rate of transpiration in a dorsiventral leaf.*

- *Mechanism of stomatal transpiration on the basis of potassium ion exchange theory.*
- *Adaptations in plants to reduce transpiration.*
- *A brief idea of guttation and bleeding.*

(iii) Photosynthesis: The process and its importance to life in general; Experiments to show the necessity of light, carbon dioxide, chlorophyll, formation of starch and release of oxygen; Carbon cycle.

- *The Process and Significance of Photosynthesis.*
- *The internal structure of chloroplast to be explained to give an idea of the site of light and dark reactions.*
- *Opening and closing of stomata based on potassium ion exchange theory.*
- *Overall balanced chemical equation to represent photosynthesis.*
- *Introduction of the terms "Photochemical" for light phase and "Biosynthetic" for dark phases.*
- *Light reaction - activation of chlorophyll followed by photolysis of water, release of O_2, formation of ATP (photophosphorylation) and NADPH.*
- *Dark reaction - only combination of hydrogen released by NADP with CO_2 to form glucose. (detailed equations are not required).*

- *Adaptations in plants for photosynthesis.*
- *Experiments with regard to the factors essential for photosynthesis; emphasis on destarching and the steps involved in starch test.*
- *A diagrammatic representation of "Carbon cycle".*

(iv) Chemical Coordination in Plants: A general study of plant growth regulators; Tropic movements in Plants.

- *A brief idea of the physiological effects of Auxins, Gibberellins, Cytokinins, Abscisic acid and Ethylene in regulating the growth of plants.*
- *A basic understanding of the tropic movements in plants with reference to – Phototropism, Geotropism, Hydrotropism, Thigmotropism and Chemotropism (supported with suitable examples).*

Human Anatomy and Physiology

(i) Circulatory System: Blood and lymph, the structure and working of the heart, blood vessels, circulation of blood (Only names of the main blood vessels entering and leaving the heart, liver and kidney will be required). Lymphatic system.

- *Composition of blood (Structure and functions of RBC, WBC and platelets).*
- *Brief idea of tissue fluid and lymph.*
- *Increase in efficiency of mammalian red blood cells due to absence of certain organelles; Reasons for the same.*
- *A brief idea of blood coagulation.*
- *Structure and working of the heart along with names of the main blood vessels entering and leaving the heart, the liver and the kidney.*
- *Concept of systole and diastole; Concept of double circulation.*
- *Brief idea of pulse and blood pressure.*
- *Blood vessels: artery, vein and capillary to be explained with the help of diagrams to bring out the relationship between their structure and function.*
- *Brief idea of the lymphatic organs: Spleen and tonsils.*
- *ABO blood group system, Rh factor.*
- *Significance of the hepatic portal system.*

(ii) Excretory System: A brief introduction to the excretory organs; Parts of the urinary system; Structure and function of the kidneys; Blood vessels associated with kidneys; Structure and function of nephron.

- *A brief idea of different excretory organs in the human body.*
- *External and internal structure of the kidney;*
- *Parts of the urinary system along with the blood vessels entering and leaving the kidney; Functions of various parts of the urinary system (emphasis on diagram with correct labelling). A general idea of the structure of a kidney tubule/nephron.*
- *A brief idea of ultra-filtration (emphasis on the diagram of Malpighian capsule); Selective reabsorption and tubular secretion in relation to the composition of blood plasma and urine formed.*

(iii) Nervous system: Structure of Neuron; central, autonomous and peripheral nervous system (in brief); brain and spinal cord; reflex action and how it differs from voluntary action.

Sense organs – Eye: Structure, functions, defects and corrective measures: Ear: Parts and functions of the ear.

- *Parts of a neuron.*
- *Various parts of the external structure of the brain and its primary parts: Medulla oblongata, cerebrum, cerebellum, thalamus, hypothalamus and pons; their functions.*
- *Reference to the distribution of white and gray matter in Brain and Spinal cord.*
- *Voluntary and involuntary actions – meaning with examples.*
- *Diagrammatic explanation of the reflex arc, showing the pathway from receptor to effector.*
- *A brief idea of the peripheral and autonomic nervous system in regulating body activities.*
- *Differences between natural and acquired reflex.*
- *External and Internal structure and functions of the eye and ear and their various parts.*
- *A brief idea of stereoscopic vision, adaptation and accommodation of eye.*
- *Defects of the eye (Myopia, hyperopia hypermetropia, presbiopia, astigmatism and cataract) and corrective measures (Diagrams included for myopia and hyperopia only).*

- *The course of perception of sound in human ear.*
- *Role of ear in maintaining balance of the body.*

(iv) Endocrine System: General study of the following glands: Adrenal, Pancreas, Thyroid and Pituitary. Endocrine and Exocrine glands.

- *Differences between Endocrine and Exocrine glands.*
- *Exact location and shape of the endocrine glands in the human body.*
- *Hormones secreted by the following glands: Pancreas: insulin and glucagon; Thyroid: only thyroxin; Adrenal gland: Cortical hormones and adrenaline; Pituitary: growth hormone, tropic hormones, ADH and oxytocin.*
- *Effects of hypo Secretion and hyper Secretion of hormones.*
- *A brief idea of feedback mechanism with reference to TSH.*

(v) The Reproductive System: Organs, fertilisation functions of placenta in the growth of the embryo Menstrual cycle.

- *Functions of male and female reproductive organs and male accessory glands. An idea of secondary sexual characters.*
- *Structure and functions of the various parts of the sperm and egg.*
- *Explanation of the terms: Fertilisation, implantation, placenta, gestation and parturition.*
- *A brief idea of the role of placenta in nutrition, respiration and excretion of the embryo; Its endocrinal function.*
- *Functions of Foetal membranes and amniotic fluid.*
- *Menstrual cycle, outline of menstrual cycle.*
- *Role of Sex hormones: Testosterone, oestrogen and progesterone in reproduction.*
- *Identical and fraternal twins: Meaning and differences only.*

Population

Population explosion in India; need for adopting control measures - Population control.

- *Main reasons for the sharp rise in human population in India and in the world.*
- *A brief explanation of the terms: Demography, population density, birth rate, death rate and growth rate of population.*
- *Problems faced due to population explosion: Unemployment, over exploitation of natural resources, low per capita income, price rise, pollution, unequal distribution of wealth.*
- *Methods of population control: Surgical methods – Tubectomy and vasectomy.*

Human Evolution

Basic introduction to Human evolution and Theories of evolution: Lamarck's theory of inheritance; Darwin's theory of evolution by natural selection.

- *A brief idea of human ancestors – Australopithecus, Homo habilis, Homo erectus, Neanderthals, Cro-Magnon and Homo sapiens sapiens (Modern man) with reference to the following characteristics: -*
  - *Bipedalism*
  - *Increasing cranial capacity*
  - *Reduction of size of canine teeth*
  - *Forehead and brow ridges*
  - *Development of chin*
  - *Reduction in body hair*
  - *Height and posture*
- *Lamarck's theory of inheritance of acquired characteristics – with reference to use of organs (e.g: neck and forelimbs of giraffe) and disuse of organs (e.g: vestigial organs in humans like wisdom teeth, vermiform appendix, pinnae).*
- *Darwin's theory of Natural selection: Survival of the fittest - e.g. adaptation of peppered moth.*

Pollution

(i) Types and sources of pollution; major pollutants.

- *Air: Vehicular, industrial, burning garbage, brick kilns.*
- *Water: Household detergents, sewage, industrial waste, oil spills.*
- *Thermal pollution.*
- *Soil: Industrial waste, urban commercial and domestic waste, chemical fertilisers.*
- *Biomedical waste – used and discarded needles, syringes, soiled dressings, etc.*

- *Radiation: X-rays; radioactive fallout from nuclear plants.*
- *Noise: Motor vehicles, Industrial establishments, Construction sites, Loudspeakers, etc.*

(ii) Biodegradable and Non-biodegradable Wastes

Biodegradable wastes: Meaning and example; paper, vegetable peels, etc.

Non-biodegradable wastes: meaning and example; plastics, glass, styrofoam, etc. Pesticides like DDT, etc.

(iii) Effects of pollution on climate, environment, human health and other organisms; control measures.

- *Brief explanation of: Greenhouse effect and Global warming, Acid rain, Ozone layer depletion.*
- *Measures to Control Pollution:*
  - *Use of unleaded petrol / CNG in automobiles*
  - *Switching of Engines at traffic signal lights*
  - *Social forestry*
  - *Setting of sewage treatment plants*
  - *Ban on polythene and plastics*
  - *Organic farming*
  - *Euro Bharat vehicular standard. (A brief idea of the above measures)*
- *A brief mention of "Swach Bharat Abhiyan"- A National Campaign for Clean India.*

Internal Assessment of Practical Work

The practical work is designed to test the ability of the candidates to make an accurate observation from specimens of plants and animals.

Plant Life

(i) Observation of permanent slides of stages of mitosis.

(ii) Experiments demonstrating:

- Diffusion: using potassium permanganate in water.
- Osmosis: Thistle funnel experiment and potato osmoscope,
- Absorption: using a small herbaceous plant.

(iii) Experiments on transpiration

- demonstration of the process using a Bell jar.
- demonstration of unequal transpiration in a dorsiventral leaf using cobalt chloride paper.
- demonstration of uptake of water and the rate of transpiration using Ganong's potometer.

(iii) Experiments on Photosynthesis:

- to show the necessity of light, carbon dioxide and chlorophyll for photosynthesis.
- to show the release of O_2 during photosynthesis using *Hydrilla / Elodea*.

Animal Life

(i) Identification of the structures of the urinary system, heart and kidney (Internal structure) and brain (External view) through models and charts

(ii) The identification of different types of blood cells under a microscope.

(iii) Identification of the internal structure of the ear and eye (Through models and charts).

(iv) Identification and location of selected endocrine glands: Adrenal, pancreas, thyroid and pituitary glands with the help of a model or chart.

CHAPTER

01

Cell Cycle, Cell Division and Structure of Chromosome

Chapter Inside

• Chromosomes • Cell Cycle • Cell Division

The cell is the basic structural, functional and biological unit of all living organisms. Cells were first observed by **Robert Hooke** (1665) as honeycomb-like compartments in a thin slice of cork. **Antonie van Leeuwenhoek** (1667) was the first to describe a living cell. **Rudolf Virchow** (1855) was the first to suggest that new cells are formed from the division of pre-existing cells.

Cell division is the fundamental characteristic of life in all living organisms. It helps in growth, development, repair of tissues, organs, etc., In order to understand the concept of cell cycle and division, the structure of chromosomes must be known. In this chapter, we will study about structure of chromosome, cell cycle and cell division.

Chromosomes

They are small but thick, rod-like, dark stainable structures seen in the nuclei of dividing cells at certain stages of cell division. They were first discovered by the Swiss botanist **Karl Wilhelm von Nageli** in plant cells in 1842.

In 1882, **Walther Flemming** observed chromosomes in the dividing cells of salamander's larvae.

Chromosomes were named so by **Waldeyer** (1888) because of their feature of uptaking the colour of the stain they were treated with for various studies.

Roger Kornberg in 1974 reported that chromosome is made up of DNA and proteins.

Chromosomes are the carriers of units of heredity, i.e. **genes** from one generation to the next.

Homologous Chromosomes

In our normal diploid cells, chromosomes are present as 2 sets. These chromosomes are called homologous chromosomes and counted in pairs. The chromosomes of each pair are similar in size, shape and position of centromere. Out of each pair one chromosome is shared by the male parent and other by the female parent.

Number of Chromosomes

In our body, all the cells have a specific number of chromosomes, i.e. 46 (23 pairs) in somatic cells and 23 in each sex cells i.e. ovum and sperm.

Similarly, every organism has a specific number of chromosomes that defines its identity, e.g. frog (13 pairs), rat (21 pairs), dog (39 pairs), etc.

Structure of Chromosomes

Chromosomes can be best observed at the metaphase stage of cell division. Each chromosome when present in the condensed form, consists of two exactly similar rod-like structures called **chromatids**.

Both chromatids are joined by a point of attachment known as **centromere** (primary constriction). It is located at a particular site in the chromosome and helps in attachment of the spindle fibres to the chromosome. The parts of chromatids on the two sides of the centromere, are referred to as **arms**. The chromatids consist of serially arranged swellings or bead-like aggregates called as **chromomeres**.

Some chromosomes possess a small fragment or knob-like structure called **satellite**. Such chromosomes are known as **SAT chromosomes**. The terminal regions on either sides of the chromosomes are known as **telomeres**.

> **Chromatin**
> It is a thread-like structure present in the resting state of nucleus in the cell. It is composed of DNA (40%) and proteins (60%). When the cell is not dividing, chromatin appears as long, thin and darkly stained fibre.

Types of Chromosomes

On the basis of the position of the centromere, chromosomes are classified into four main types

(i) **Metacentric chromosomes** Centromere is located in the centre. Chromosome has equal arms.

(ii) **Sub-metacentric chromosomes** Centromere is present slightly away from the centre. Thus, the chromosome has one short and one long arm.

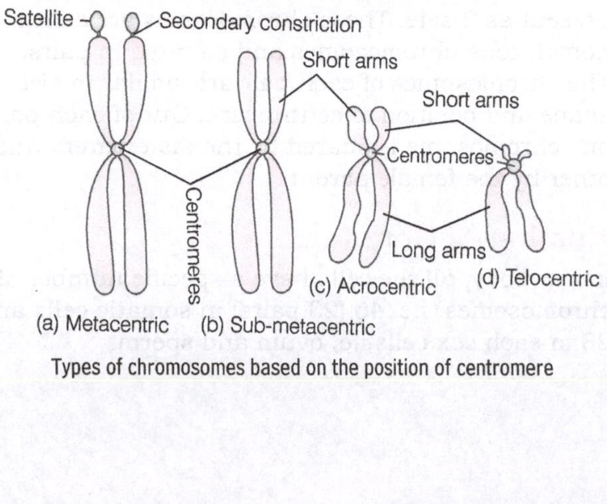

Types of chromosomes based on the position of centromere

(iii) **Acrocentric chromosomes** Centromere is located near the end of the chromosome. Thus, it has one extremely short and one very long arm.

(iv) **Telocentric chromosomes** Centromere is present at the terminal or extreme end.

Functions of Chromosomes

(i) They direct the synthesis of particular protein, enzyme, molecule, etc.

(ii) They control the cell division, growth, metabolism and differentiation.

(iii) They determine the sex of an individual.

(iv) They are responsible for evolution of species by inducing mutations, variations and crossing over.

(v) They transfer the genetic information of an organism to the next generation.

Genes

The segments of DNA responsible for transmission of characters from one generation to next generation are called genes. These are specific sequences of nucleotides which encode proteins and thus, express themselves. DNA or Deoxyribonucleic Acid is the chemical basis of gene which acts as a genetic material in most of the living organisms.

Structure of DNA

James Watson and Francis Crick (1953) proposed the double helix model for the DNA structure on the basis of X-ray diffraction data produced by **Maurice Wilkins** and **Rosalind Franklin**. The DNA molecule consists of two helical strands which are unbranched and are twisted around a common axis.

Each deoxyribonucleotide unit consists of 3 basic molecules

(i) Phosphate group (PO_4^-)

(ii) 5- carbon containing deoxyribose sugar ($C_5H_{10}O_4$)

(iii) Nitrogenous bases

Nitrogenous base may be a nine-membered, double-ringed **purine** [adenine (A) or guanine (G)] or a 6-membered, single-ringed **pyrimidine** [thymine (T) or cytosine (C)].

In a DNA molecule, adenine pairs with thymine with two hydrogen bonds (A = T) whereas guanine pairs with cytosine by three hydrogen bonds ($G \equiv C$)

The backbone of DNA chain is built up of alternating deoxyribose and phosphate group.

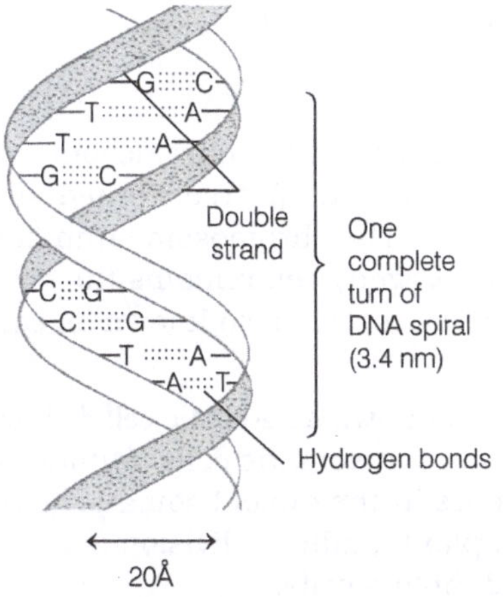

Structure of DNA

Note In nucleus the negatively charged DNA is wrapped around the positively charged histone proteins to form a structure called nucleosome. A single chromosome contains about a million nucleosomes.

Check Your LEARNING...

1 What are centromere?
2 Name the thread-like structure found in a resting state of nucleus.
3 Name the chromosome in which centromere is present at the terminal end.
4 Who proposed the double helix structure of DNA?
5 Name any two nitrogenous bases found in DNA.

Cell Cycle

It is an orderly sequence of events or a set of stages by which a cell duplicates its genome, synthesises essential constituents of the cell and eventually divides into two daughter cells.

Phases of Cell Cycle

Cell cycle consists of two main phases

1. **Interphase** or Non-dividing phase or Preparatory phase
2. **M-phase** or Division phase or Mitotic phase

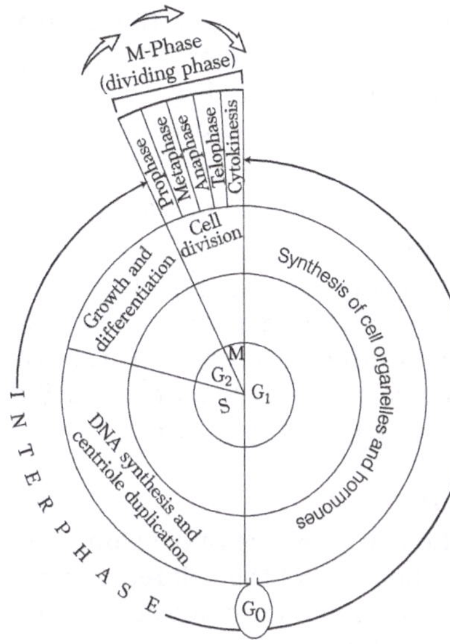

Diagrammatic representation of cell cycle

Interphase

It is the phase in a cell cycle in which the cells prepare themselves for the next cell division. Thus, it is the period between two successive cell divisions.

Interphase is the longest phase of cell cycle. Cells are metabolically active during this phase because of the biosynthesis and multiplication of various cellular components.

Interphase is further divided into three main sub-stages depending upon its synthetic activities as described below

(i) G_1-**phase** (First growth phase) In this phase, cell grows in size due to the increase in the volume of cytoplasm and becomes metabolically active. It prepares itself for DNA replication, synthesis of RNA and proteins.

Mitochondria and chloroplast are produced and divide during this phase of intensive cellular synthesis.

In the late G_1-phase, cells can enter in any one of the following two pathways

(a) Withdrawal from the cell cycle and entering into the resting phase (G_0-**phase**).

(b) Start preparation for the next cell division by entering the S-phase (**Synthesis phase**).

(ii) **S-phase** (Synthesis phase) In this phase, synthesis or replication of DNA takes place. Each chromosome contains two sister chromatids that remain attached to a common centromere. The DNA content doubles.

(iii) **G_2-phase** (Second growth phase) This phase is comparatively shorter and is also known as **pre-mitotic phase**. During this phase, the synthesis of RNA and proteins continues as they are required for mitosis. At the end of this stage, the cell is ready to start the cell division and the cycle further goes on.

M-phase or Mitotic Phase

M-phase is the actual phase of division. During this phase, all components of the cell reorganise for cell division. The duplicated chromosomes and all the other cellular contents get distributed among the two daughter cells.
It occurs in two steps, i.e. **karyokinesis** (division of nucleus) and **cytokinesis** (division of cytoplasm).

Does the cell cycle go on continuously?

The cell cycle is a continuous process. However, it stops at certain places in different cells. The stoppage of cell cycle is temporary in some cells, while permanent in others. This cycle prepares a cell for its entry into the division phase. Those cells which are not divided more than once, do not have recurring cell cycle like **nerve cells**.

Some other cells like **liver cells**, divide only once in 1-2 yrs, hence the stoppage is temporary. However, **skin cells** and **cells** of **meristems** undergo continuous cell cycle and division to replace the damaged and dead cells. A continuous cell cycle is harmful in the way, as it may cause tumours or cancers in the various parts or organs of an organism.

Check Your LEARNING...

1 Cell cycle consists of how many phases?
2 DNA replication occurs in which phase of cell cycle?
3 Which phase of cell cycle is known as pre-mitotic phase?
4 Which phase of cell cycle is actual phase of division?
5 Give example of cells which undergo continuous cell cycle and cell division.

Cell Division

It is an essential process in all living organisms. In this, processes like DNA replication and cell growth take place in a sequential and coordinated manner. Cell division ensure the correct division and formation of progeny cells with intact genomes.

The process of cell division is fundamentally similar in all living organisms and can be either of the two types, *viz*

1. Mitosis   2. Meiosis

1. Mitosis

In this type of division, the chromosomes replicate themselves and get equally distributed into daughter nuclei. The chromosome number in the parental and progeny cell remains the same (diploid). Therefore, it is also known as **equational division**.

Mitosis is also known as **somatic cell division** because it always occurs in somatic cells. Mitotic cell division occurs in the diploid somatic cells of animals. In plants, mitotic division is seen in both haploid and diploid cells.

It is known as **the phase of actual cell division**. It starts with the division of nucleus, followed by the separation of daughter chromosomes, i.e. **karyokinesis** and terminates with the cytoplasmic division, i.e. **cytokinesis**.

I. Karyokinesis

It is the division of parent nucleus into two identical daughter nuclei with same number of chromosomes as in the parents. It is further divided into four main substages which are as follows

(i) **Prophase** It is the longest and the most complex phase of mitosis. During this phase, condensation of the chromatin fibres takes place to form chromosomes.
The characteristics of this phase are as follows

- Each chromosome splits longitudinally thus duplicating itself to form two chromatids, which remain joined to each other at one point called **centromere.**
- The nuclear membrane and nucleolus disappear.
- In animal cells, the centrosome splits into two centrioles, thus initiating the division of cell.
- Centrioles develop very fine microtubular fibrils called **astral rays**. Then, they move apart from each other, towards the opposite poles.
- Between two asters, very fine proteinaceous thread-like structures called **spindle fibres**, develop.
- In plant cells, development of spindle fibres occurs without the involvement of centrioles.

(ii) **Metaphase** The second phase of mitosis starts with disintegration of nuclear membrane in the late prophase.

The characteristics of this phase are as follows

- Chromosomes start moving towards the equatorial plane of the spindle formed in prophase.
- Spindle fibres are extended towards the chromosome.
- Shortening and thickening of chromosomes occur.
- The chromosomes align or arrange themselves at the equator in one plane known as **metaphasic plate.**

Mitotic Poison : Colchicine

Colchicine, an alkaloid, extracted from the corms of autumn crocus (*Colchicum autumnale*), acts as a poison for mitosis. It does not allow the formation of mitotic spindle by preventing the assembly of microtubules. It does not affect replication of chromosomes. Thus, meristematic cells treated with this chemical show doubling of chromosomes. It usually causes the arrest of metaphase stage of mitosis.

(iii) **Anaphase** The shortest phase amongst all phases of mitosis. The characteristics of this phase are as follows

- The centromere of each chromosome divides and splits into two.
- The spindle fibres which are not connected to chromatin (non-kinetochore) elongate and the cell becomes longer.
- Two sister chromatids of each chromosome separate from each other due to the constriction of spindle fibres. As the result, they move to the opposite poles.

(iv) **Telophase** It is a long and complex phase that works just opposite to the prophase.

The characteristics of this phase are as follows

- During this phase, the spindle fibres disappear.
- The chromosomes reach their respective poles and start to decondense. They loose their individuality as discrete elements.
- Chromatids lengthen to become chromatin threads.
- Nuclear membrane starts reforming around each group of chromosomes. Golgi complex and nucleolus also reappear.

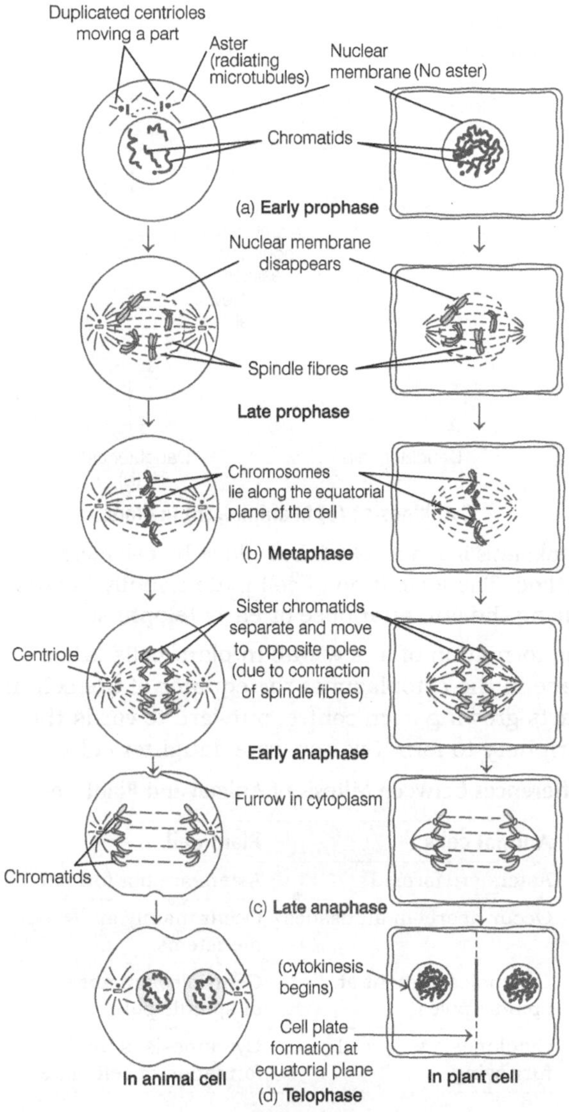

Different stages of mitosis

II. Cytokinesis

At the end of mitosis, division of cytoplasm and equal distribution of cell organelles in two daughter cells occurs by the process of cytokinesis. The process of cytokinesis occurs differently in the plant and animal cells.

Cytokinesis in animal cells takes place by **furrowing method**. A constriction or furrow appears in the cell membrane at the middle of the cell.

This furrow deepens during telophase and splits the cell into two identical daughter cells.

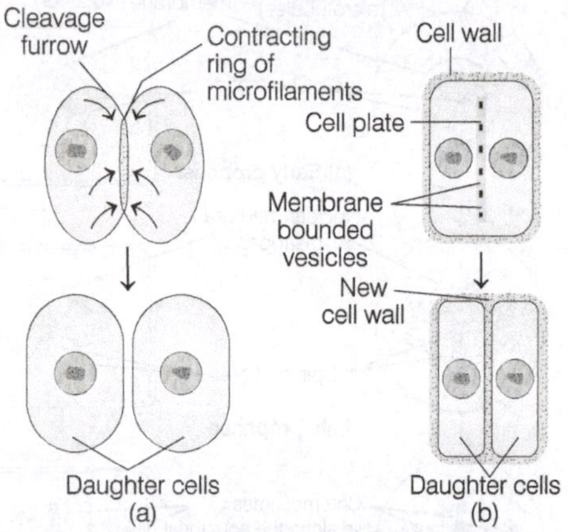

Cytokinesis : (a) In animal, (b) In plant

Cytokinesis in plant cells takes place by **cell plate method**. The formation of cell plate usually begins during the late anaphase or early telophase.

The formation of a new wall in plant cells takes place in the cytoplasm at the equator of the cell. It starts growing from centre, outward towards the periphery to form two separate daughter cells.

Differences between Mitosis of Animal and Plant Cells

Animal cells	Plant cells
Asters are formed.	Asters are not formed.
Occur nearly in all tissues.	Occur mainly at meristems.
Centrioles present at spindle poles.	Centrioles are absent at spindle poles.
Cytokinesis is by cell furrowing.	Cytokinesis is by the formation of cell plate.

Significance of Mitosis

(i) **Genetic stability** Mitosis helps in maintaining the same number of chromosomes as that of parents.

(ii) **Growth** Cell division leads to growth of a multicellular organism by forming clusters of cells. Later, these take up specific functions.

(iii) **Repair and maintenance** The wear and tear of pre-existing cells, cellular damage due to injuries, etc., are checked by new cells formed during division.

(iv) **Asexual reproduction** Single-celled unicellular organisms like *Amoeba* are able to reproduces by the mitotic division only.

(v) **Replacement** Mitosis replaces old and dead cells.

Check Your LEARNING...

1 In which cell, does mitosis occur?
2 Which stage of mitosis is considered as the longest and the most complex stage?
3 In which stage of mitosis do the spindle fibres get disappeared?
4 What is the difference between cytokinesis in animal and plant cells?
5 Mention the role of mitosis in Amoeba.

2. Meiosis

In this division, the chromosome number is reduced in such a way that each daughter cell receives only half a set of chromosomes present in the parent cell. Therefore, meiosis is also called as **reductional division**. It results in the formation of four haploid cells from a diploid cell.

Meiosis is restricted to reproductive cells (germ cells) or sex cells. It results in the formation of gametes, i.e. sperms (in testes of males) and egg (in ovaries of females).

In asexually reproducing organisms, meiosis results in the formation of asexual reproductive bodies like spores. The process of meiotic division is completed in two stages, i.e.

(i) **Meiosis-I** is a heterotypic or reductional division. Here, the parental chromosomes replicate to form identical sister chromatids. The number of chromosomes reduces from diploid ($2n$) to haploid (n).

(ii) **Meiosis-II** is a homotypic or a mitosis like equational division. Here, the haploid nuclei divide mitotically to produce four daughter nuclei.

Note
- Like mitosis, both meiosis-I and II, have four stages, i.e. prophase, metaphase, anaphase and telophase.
- Meiosis-II have same stages as in mitosis.

Significance of Meiosis

(i) **Reproduction** It produce gametes with haploid number of chromosomes in sexually reproducing organisms.

(ii) **Maintenance of chromosome number** Chromosome number gets halved in gametes due to meiosis so as to maintain the normal number, i.e. $2n$ in zygote after fertilisation. This helps in maintaining constant number of chromosomes in species.

(iii) **Variation due to crossing over** In meiosis, a mutual exchange of corresponding parts of non-sister chromatids occurs after the formation of the **chiasmata** (Latin for criss cross).

It occurs between the two members of a **homologous pair** of chromosomes and called as crossing over.

It results in genetic recombination or variations.

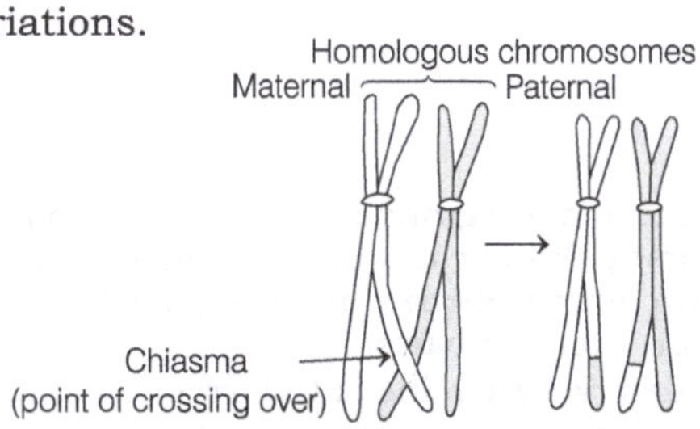

Chromatids exchange between non-sister chromatids

(iv) **Evolution** Meiosis acts as a source of producing genetic variations in species which leads to evolution.

Differences between Mitosis and Meiosis

Parameters	Mitosis	Meiosis
Occurrence	Somatic cells	Reproductive cells
Reason / Function	For growth and development of various body parts and organism as whole.	It occurs only for the formation of gametes (male and female).
Period of occurrence	Occurs repeatedly throughout the life.	Occurs only during reproductive stage.
Number of daughter cells produced	After every mitotic division, two daughter cells are formed.	Meiotic division forms four daughter cells.
Daughter cells and number of chromosomes	Daughter cells resemble each other as well as their mother cell. A full set of chromosomes is passed to each daughter cell, i.e. a diploid (2*n*) set.	Daughter cells neither resemble one another nor their mother cell. Half the number of total chromosomes, i.e. a haploid (*n*) set is passed to each daughter cell.
Nuclear divisions	After duplication of chromosome, a single nuclear division occurs.	Two nuclear divisions occur after chromosomal duplication.
Occurrence of variations	Mitosis does not introduce variations.	Meiosis generates variations in the organism.

Check Your LEARNING...

1 Which division is also called reductional division?
2 In which type of cells, does meiosis occur?
3 Why meiosis-II is called homotypic division?
4 Name four stages of meiosis.
5 Give difference between mitosis and meiosis on the basis on the period of occurrence.

QUiCK Revision

- **Cell** is the basic structural, functional and biological unit of all living organisms.
- **Chromosomes** are highly condensed and coiled chromatin fibres. They possess genes which are responsible for the transfer of traits from one generation to the next generation.
- In diploid (2*n*) cells of an organism chromosomes occur in 2 sets with pairing. Each pair among these is called homologous pair.
- **Chromatins** are the thread-like form of chromosomes. These are present in nucleus during resting stage of the cells.
- In a chromosome chromatids (arms) are present which are joined through central constrictions called centromeres.
- On the basis of the position of the centromere, chromosomes are of four types, i.e. metacentric, sub-metacentric, acrocentric and telocentric.
- **Genes** are the segments of DNA which code for particular proteins that express in the form of some features in an individual.
- The DNA molecule consists of two helical strands which are unbranched and are twisted around a common axis.
- Each deoxyribonucleotide unit consists of 3 basic molecules namely, phosphate group, deoxyribose sugar and nitrogenous base.
- **Cell cycle** involves a series of changes in a cell and cell division. It is the process of formation of new cells from the pre-existing cells.
- Cell cycle consists of two main phases, i.e. **Interphase** or **non-dividing phase** and **mitotic** (M) **phase** or **Dividing phase**.
- **Interphase** is further divided into three main stages on the basis of its synthetic activities. These are **G_1-phase** or **first growth phase** (synthesis of RNA and proteins), **S-phase** or **Synthesis phase** (DNA replication) and **G_2-phase** or **Second growth phase** (synthesis of RNA and proteins).
- The **M-phase** is the actual phase of division. It occurs in two steps, i.e. **karyokinesis** (division of nucleus) and **cytokinesis** (division of cytoplasm).
- **Cell division** is the process by which life perpetuates. It is of two types, i.e. mitosis and meiosis.
- **Mitosis** leads to the production of two identical daughter cells with the same number of chromosomes.
- **Meiosis** is a special type of cell division taking place in sex cells or gametes. In this cell division, a cell undergoes two successive divisions to produce four daughter cells. Each cell contains half the number of chromosomes as compared to the parent cell.

Chapter Practice

Section-I

1 Mark Questions

1. Name the following.
   (i) The structure responsible for transmitting characteristics from parent to offspring.
   (ii) Two symmetrical structures present in a chromosome.
   (iii) The bead-like accumulation of chromatin material.
   (iv) Nucleic acid which is the main component of chromosomes.
   (v) The complex formed by histones and DNA together.
   (vi) Cell division observed to be occurring at the tip of root and shoot systems.
   (vii) The organelle that forms the aster during cell division. [2023]
   (viii) The stage during which nuclear membrane and nucleolus reappear.
   (ix) The exchange of chromatid parts between the maternal and the paternal chromatids of a pair of homologous chromosomes during meiosis. [2016]
   (x) A pair of corresponding chromosomes of the same shape or size and derived one from each parent. [2019]

Ans. (i) Chromosomes (ii) Chromatids
(iii) Chromomeres (iv) DNA
(v) Nucleosomes (vi) Mitosis
(vii) Centrosome (viii) Telophase
(ix) Crossing over
(x) Homologous chromosomes

2. Correct and rewrite the following statements by changing the underlined words.
   (i) DNA is made up of <u>hexose</u> sugar.
   (ii) <u>Nitrogen</u> bonds are present between the complementary nitrogenous bases of DNA. [2018]
   (iii) The division which brings the chromosome number from $2n$ to n is <u>mitosis</u>.
   (iv) The region where crossing over in chromosome occurs is <u>chromomere</u>.

Ans. (i) DNA is made up of pentose sugar.
(ii) Hydrogen bonds are present between the complementary nitrogenase bases of DNA.
(iii) The division which brings the chromosome number from $2n$ to n is meiosis.
(iv) The region where crossing over in chromosome occurs is chiasmata.

3. Given below are groups of terms. In each group, the first pair indicates the relationship between the two terms. Rewrite and complete the second pair on a similar basis. [2017]
   (i) Adenine : Thymine : : Cytosine : ....
   (ii) Cytoplasm : Cytokinesis : : Nucleus : ....
   (iii) Nucleolus disappear : Prophase : : Nucleolus reappear : ....

Ans. (i) Guanine (ii) Karyokinesis
(iii) Telophase

4. Give biological reasons for the following.
   (i) Cell division is necessary for survival of a species.
   (ii) Mitosis is called as an equational division.
   (iii) Gametes have a haploid number of chromosomes.
   (iv) Different methods are used for cytokinesis in plant and animal cells.

Ans. (i) Cell division is necessary for processes like growth, repair, regeneration and reproduction of an individual which thereby help in its survival.
(ii) Mitosis is called equational division because each of the two daughter cells formed, get the same number of chromosomes as had by their parents.
(iii) Gametes are produced as a result of meiosis during which the chromosome number is reduced to half and each daughter cell receives only half the set of chromosomes. Thus, making the gametes haploid.
(iv) Different methods are used for cytokinesis in plant and animal cells because plant cells have rigid and unlike animal cells cleavage furrow cannot be formed between two daughter cells.

5. (i) Match the following columns.

	Column I		Column II
A.	Chromosomes become arranged in a horizontal plane at the equator	1.	Anaphase
B.	Daughter chromosomes move to opposite poles of the spindle	2.	Prophase
C.	Chromosomes become visible as fine-like long threads.	3.	Telophase
D.	Chromosomes lose their distinctiveness and gradually transform into chromatin network	4.	Metaphase

(ii) Match the following columns.

Column I	Column II
A. G_2-phase	1. Unit of heredity transmission
B. Anaphase	2. Synthesis of RNA and proteins
C. S-phase	3. Shortest phase of cell division
D. Adenine	4. Duplication of DNA
E. Gene	5. Guanine

Ans. (i) A–4, B–1, C–2, D–3
(ii) A–2, B–3, C–4, D–5, E–1

6. Choose the correct answer from the four options given below

(i) Among the statements given below, select the most correct option associated with a cell.
(a) The smallest entity of the living organism
(b) The structural and functional unit of life
(c) The macroscopic unit of life
(d) Both (a) and (b)

Ans. (d)

(ii) Haploid number of chromosomes are found in **[2023]**
(a) nephrons (b) neurons (c) skin cells (d) sperms

Ans. (d) sperms

(iii) The cell component visible only during cell division is **[2013]**
(a) mitochondria (b) chloroplast
(c) chromosomes (d) chromatin

Ans. (c)

(iv) A chromosome when present in condensed form, consists of
(a) four chromatids (b) two chromatids
(c) one chromatid (d) five chromatids

Ans. (b)

(v) The basic unit of heredity are .... **[Semester I 2021]**
(a) chromosomes (b) chromatids
(c) genes (d) centrosome

Ans. (c)

(vi) The nitrogenous base adenine always pairs with .... **[Semester I 2021]**
(a) thymine (b) guanine (c) cytosine (d) thiamine

Ans. (a)

(vii) During the synthesis phase of the cell cycle, more of **[2023]**
(a) RNA is synthesised
(b) RNA and proteins are synthesised
(c) DNA is synthesised
(d) Glucose is synthesised

Ans. (c)

(viii) Synthesis phase in the cell cycle is called so, because of the synthesis of more **[2017]**
(a) RNA (b) RNA and proteins
(c) DNA (d) glucose

Ans. (c)

(ix) Replication of DNA in the cell cycle occurs during the **[Semester I 2021]**
(a) G_1-phase (b) Anaphase (c) S-phase (d) G_2-phase

Ans. (c)

(x) Karyokinesis and cytokinesis are the part of which phase of the cell cycle?
(a) G_1-phase (b) S-phase (c) M-phase (d) G_2-phase

Ans. (c)

(xi) Cell division which helps in regeneration by keeping all somatic cells similar is
(a) mitosis (b) meiosis
(c) cytokinesis (d) diakinesis

Ans. (a)

(xii) Which of the following correctly explains the term karyokinesis? **[Semester I 2021]**
(a) It is the division of nucleus during cell division
(b) It is the division of cytoplasm during cell division
(c) It is the division of centrosome
(d) It is the division of nucleolus

Ans. (a)

(xiii) In which of the following are centrioles found? **[Semester I 2021]**
(a) Found only in plant cells
(b) Found inside nucleus
(c) Found only in animal cells
(d) Found in animal and plant cells

Ans. (c)

(xiv) Where are the asters found? **[Semester I 2021]**
(a) Around the centrioles in plant cells
(b) Around the centrioles in animal cells
(c) Around the chromatids in animal cells
(d) Around the chromatids in plant cells

Ans. (b)

(xv) Chromosomes get aligned at the centre of the cell during **[2015]**
(a) anaphase (b) telophase
(c) metaphase (d) prophase

Ans. (c)

(xvi) Centrioles radiate out fine microtubular fibrils called astral rays and move apart from each other towards the opposite poles. This observation is made during
(a) prophase (b) metaphase
(c) anaphase (d) telophase

Ans. (c)

(xvii) A phase said to be the reverse of prophase is
(a) interphase (b) metaphase
(c) anaphase (d) telophase

Ans. (d)

(xviii) At the end of .... cytokinesis is completed. **[Semester I 2021]**
(a) metaphase (b) prophase
(c) interphase (d) telophase

Ans. (d)

7. Fill in the blanks by using suitable words.

(i) The nitrogenous bases in DNA are .... in number. **[2011]**

(ii) The process by which a cell multiplies is called ....

(iii) Mitosis forms two daughter cells and meiosis forms .... daughter cells.

(iv) In meiosis, the parent cell is diploid whereas the daughter cell is ....

Ans. (i) four (ii) cell division (iii) four (iv) haploid

8. Choose the odd one out from the following terms given below and name the category to which other three belong.

(i) Phosphate, RNA, Sugar, Nitrogenous base **[2017]**

(ii) Thymine, Cytosine, Adenine, Pepsin **[2016]**

(iii) Centrosome, Cell wall, Cell membrane, Large vacuoles **[2018]**

Ans. (i) **Odd term** is RNA.
Other three are components of DNA.

(ii) **Odd term** is pepsin.
Other three are nitrogenous bases.

(iii) **Odd term** is centrosome.
Other three are components of plant cells.

9. Given below are the sets of five terms each. Rewrite the terms in correct order of logical sequence.

(i) Karyokinesis, S-phase, Cytokinesis, G_1-phase, G_2-phase (cell cycle) **[2012]**

(ii) Metaphase, Telophase, Prophase, Anaphase, Cytokinesis **[2013]**

Ans. (i) G_1-phase, S-phase, G_2-phase, Karyokinesis, Cytokinesis

(ii) Prophase, Metaphase, Anaphase, Telophase, Cytokinesis

10. Expand the following biological abbreviations.

(i) DNA **[2023]**

(ii) G_2-phase **[2019, 14]**

Ans. (i) Deoxyribonucleic Acid

(ii) Second Growth phase

11. State the exact location of the following.

(i) Centromere (ii) Chromatin (iii) Telomeres **[2016]**

Ans. (i) Centromere is located at a particular site on the chromosome.

(ii) Chromatin is present in nucleus.

(iii) Telomeres are terminal regions of chromosomes.

12. State the main function of the following.

(i) DNA (ii) SAT chromosome (iii) Centrosome

Ans. (i) **DNA** (Deoxyribonucleic Acid) is the carrier of genetic blueprint of an organism.

(ii) **SAT chromosome** Knob-like structures formed of non-staining regions of secondary constrictions in a chromosome. It is the main component of functional centromeres.

(iii) **Centrosome** It helps to initiate cell division in animal cells.

13. Mention one difference between each of the following pairs on the basis of what is given in the bracket.

(i) Metacentric and Telocentric chromosomes (position of centromere)

(ii) Human skin cell and Human ovum (number of chromosomes) **[2016]**

(iii) Purine base and Pyrimidine base (structure)

(iv) G_1 and G_2-phases (duration)

(v) Karyokinesis and Cytokinesis (time of occurrence) **[2023]**

(vi) Centrosome and Centromere (function)

(vii) Mitosis and Meiosis (number of daughter cells formed)

Ans. (i) Difference between metacentric and telocentric chromosomes is as follows

Metacentric	Telocentric
The chromosome with centromere in the middle.	The chromosome having a terminal centromere.

(ii) Difference between human skin cell and human ovum is as follows

Human skin cell	Human ovum
It contains 46 chromosomes.	It contains 23 chromosomes.

(iii) Difference between purine base and pyrimidine base is as follows

Purine base	Pyrimidine base
These bases have double ring structure, e.g. adenine, guanine.	These bases have a single ring structure, e.g. cytosine, thymine.

(iv) Difference between G_1-phase and G_2-phase is as follows

G_1-phase	G_2-phase
Its duration is variable.	It lasts for 2-5 years.

(v) Difference between karyokinesis and cytokinesis is as follows

Karyokinesis	Cytokinesis
It is the division of nucleus that occurs during cell division.	It is the division of cytoplasm that takes place soon after karyokinesis.

(vi) Difference between centrosome and centromere is as follows

Centrosome	Centromere
It helps in initiation of cell division in animal cells.	It is a part of chromosome that holds two sister chromatids together.

(vii) Difference between mitosis and meiosis is as follows

Mitosis	Meiosis
Two daughter cells are formed.	Four daughter cells are formed.

14. Give biological/technical terms for the following.

(i) The repeating components of each DNA strand lengthwise. **[2016]**

Or

Give technical term for repeated units of DNA molecules. **[2014]**

(ii) The complex consisting of a DNA strand and a core of histones. **[2018]**

(iii) A phase at which chromosomes are clearly outlined.

(iv) The mode of cytoplasmic division in plant cells.

Ans. (i) Nucleotides

(ii) Nucleosome

(iii) Metaphase

(iv) Cell plate method

15. Briefly explain the following terms.

(i) Purines

(ii) Pre-mitotic phase

(iii) Astral rays

Ans. (i) Purines are double-ringed, nine-membered nitrogenous bases which are found in nucleic acids like DNA or RNA.

(ii) Pre-mitotic phase is a shorter phase which occurs before the initiation of cell division or mitosis. It is also called G_2-phase.

(iii) Astral rays are fine microtubular fibrils which originate from centrioles.

16. Answer the following questions briefly.

(i) Write the number of chromosomes present in a nerve cell of a human being. **[2018]**

(ii) Write the names of four nitrogenous bases in a DNA molecule. **[2013]**

Or

Give an example of a nitrogenous base in DNA. **[2014]**

(iii) During which phase in cell cycle, proteins and RNA are synthesised for distribution to the daughter cells?

(iv) Colchicine is known to be the mitotic poison. Why?

(v) A cell having 32 chromosomes undergoes mitotic divisions. What will be the chromosome number (*n*) during metaphase? What would be the DNA content during anaphase?

(vi) The chromosome number of gametes is always *n*. Give reason.

Ans. (i) All the cells of the body except gamete cells contain 46 (23 pairs) of chromosome. The nerve cells of human beings are somatic cells and hence contain 46 chromosomes.

(ii) The four nitrogenous bases are Adenine, Guanine, Cytosine and Thymine in a DNA molecule.

(iii) RNA and proteins are synthesised in both G_1-phase and G_2-phase.

(iv) Refer to text on page no. 5.

(v) The number of chromosomes during metaphase will be 32. Also, the DNA content during anaphase will be same as in the parent cell.

(vi) The cell division that occurs in gamete cell is meiosis, which maintains the chromosome number as *n* or haploid.

2 Marks Questions

17. Mention the two pairs of nitrogenous bases which pair with each other with hydrogen bonds. **[2023]**

Ans. Adenine pairs with Thymine and Cytosine pairs with Guanine.

18. Increase in cell size is observed during certain phases of cell cycle.

(i) Identify this phase.

(ii) Give reason for this observation.

Ans. (i) G_1-phase

(ii) Increase in size is observed because the cellular contents are doubling up for equal division among two daughter cells. Due to this increase in the cellular content, the overall size of a cell is increased.

19. Can there be DNA replication without cell division?

Ans. Yes, DNA replication takes place during the synthesis stage or S-phase of interphase in the cell cycle.

It is totally independent of cell division. After G_2-phase, a cell may or may not enter into the M-phase.

20. Briefly explain cytokinesis in plant cell. **[2013]**

Ans. Refer to text on page no 5-6.

3 Marks Questions

21. Draw a well-labelled diagram to show the metaphase stage of mitosis in an animal cell having four chromosomes. **[2012]**

Ans. Refer to figure on page no. 5.

22. Draw a well-labelled diagram to show the anaphase stage of mitosis in a plant cell having four chromosomes. **[2013]**

Ans. Refer to figure on page no. 5.

23. Draw a diagram of the nucleus of a cell, having chromosome number 6, as it would appear in the metaphase stage of mitosis and label the following parts

(i) Aster rays

(ii) Achromatic spindle

(iii) Chromatid

Ans. Diagram showing metaphase stage of mitosis in the nucleus of a cell having chromosome number 6 is given below.
Refer to page no. 5.

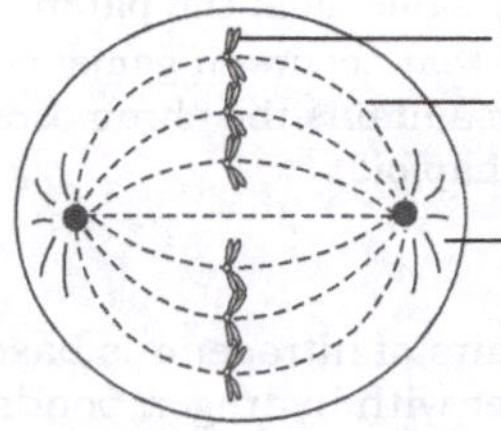

24. How is cytokinesis in plant cell different from that in animal cell ?

Ans. Cytokinesis in plant cell occurs by cell plate method whereas in animal cell, it takes place by furrowing method.

Section-II [5 Marks]

Structured Questions

1. Interphase is considered as the resting stage of a nucleus because it does not show any morphological change however, physiologically it is an active stage of a cell.

(i) Mention any three processes which occur during interphase.

(ii) Name the process/es which is/are preceded and proceded by interphase.

(iii) What will be the DNA content of a cell at G_1, S and G_2-phase, if the content after M-phase is 2C?

(iv) Which division is likely to be associated with cancer?

(v) Name the unfolded, uncondensed form of DNA found in interphase.

Ans. (i) Replication of DNA, synthesis of proteins and RNA division of centrioles or synthesis of energy rich compounds occur during interphase.

(ii) Interphase is the period between two successive mitotic divisions.

(iii) If the DNA content after M-phase is 2C, the same will be at G_1 stage because in G_1-phase, there is no division of DNA.
In S-phase, DNA gets doubled, i.e. 4 C. In G_2 phase, DNA content remains 4C.

(iv) Mitosis is likely to be associated with cancer.

(v) Chromatin is the unfolded, uncondensed form of DNA found in interphase.

2. The given diagram shows a stage during mitotic division in an animal cell. **[2016]**

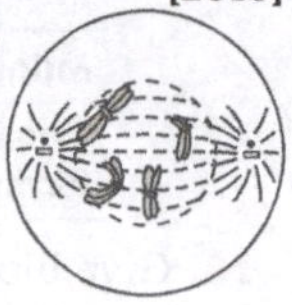

(i) Identify the stage. Give a reason to support your answer.

(ii) Draw a neat labelled diagram of the cell as it would appear in the next stage. Name the stage.

(iii) Name the type of cell division that occurs during growth of a shoot.

(iv) Name the type of cell division that occurs during formation of pollen grain.

Ans. (i) The given stage is late prophase because given chromosomes start coming in the centre of the cell. Nuclear membrane, nucleolus disappear and centriole appears which reaches at opposite pole of the cell.

(ii) The stage that appears next is **metaphase,**

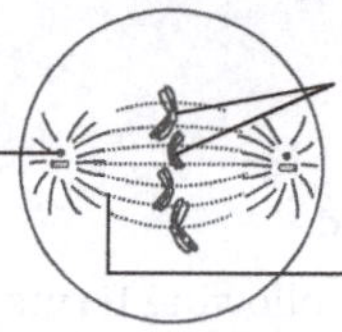

(iii) Mitosis

(iv) Meiosis

3. Given alongside is a diagram representing a stage during mitotic cell division. Study it carefully and answer the questions that follows. **[2014]**

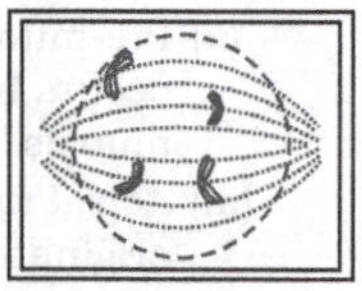

(i) Is it a plant cell or an animal cell? Give a reason to support your answer.

(ii) Identify the stage shown.

(iii) Name the stage that follows the one shown here. How is that stage identified?

(iv) How will you differentiate between mitosis and meiosis on the basis of the chromosome number in the daughter cells?

(v) Draw a duplicated chromosome and label its parts. **[2014]**

Ans. (i) It is a plant cell because cell wall is present and centrioles are absent.

(ii) The stage shown is prophase.

(iii) The stage that follows the prophase is metaphase. It is identified by the position of chromosomes that are arranged at the equator attached to the spindle fibre.

(iv) In mitosis, the chromosome number in daughter cell is same as that of the mother cell, i.e. diploid parent cell gives rise to two diploid (2 n) daughter cells. In meiosis, the chromosome number is halved in the daughter cell, i.e. the diploid mother cell gives rise to four haploid (n) daughter cells.

(v)

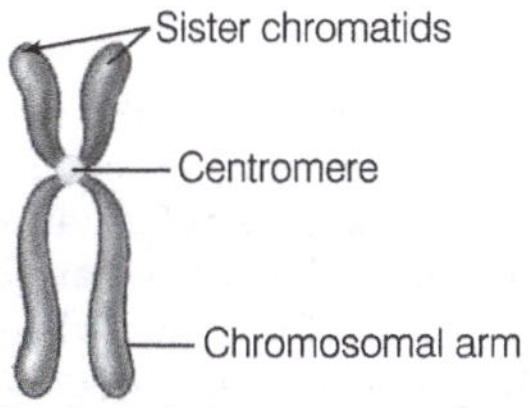

Duplicated chromosome

4. The diagram given below represents a stage during cell division.

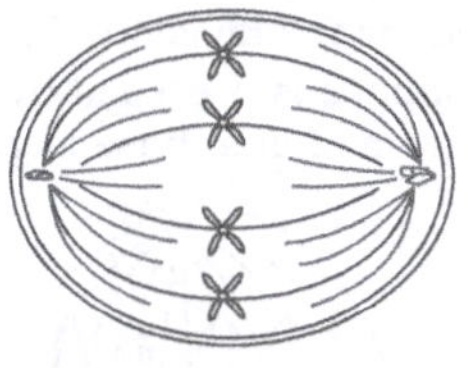

Study the same and answer the questions that follows. **[2018]**

(i) Identify whether it is a plant cell or an animal cell.
Give a reason in support of your answer.

(ii) Name the stage depicted in the diagram.
What is the unique feature observed in this stage?

(iii) Name the type of cell division that occurs during
(a) replacement of old leaves by new ones.
(b) formation of gametes.

(iv) What is the stage that comes before the stage shown in the diagram?

(v) Draw a neat, labelled diagram of the stage mentioned in (iv) above, keeping the chromosome number constant.

Ans. (i) The given cell is an animal cell as it contains centrosome and also lacks cell wall.

(ii) The metaphase stage is depicted in the diagram.
The unique feature of metaphase stage is that the chromosomes are aligned on equatorial region.

(iii) (a) Mitosis (b) Meiosis

(iv) Late prophase stage comes before the stage shown in the diagram i.e. metaphase.

(v)

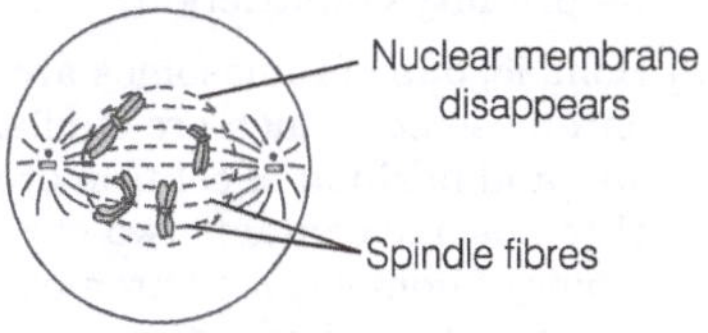

Late prophase

5. The diagram given below represents a certain stage of mitosis.

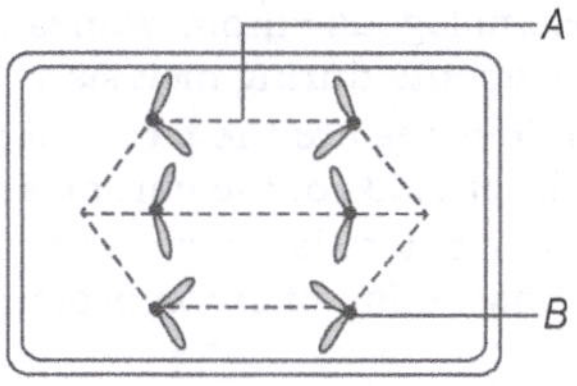

(i) Identify the stage of cell division.

(ii) Name the parts labelled as *A* and *B*.

(iii) What is the unique feature observed in this stage?

(iv) How many daughter cells are formed from this type of cell division? **[2015]**

Ans. (i) The given stage of cell division is late anaphase.

(ii) The parts labelled as *A* and *B* are
A–Spindle fibre , *B*–Centromere

(iii) The unique feature of this stage is that the chromosome gets divided into sister chromatids that move towards the opposite poles.

(iv) Two daughter cells are formed from this type of cell division.

6. The below diagram given represents a stage during cell division. Study the same and then answer the questions that follow.

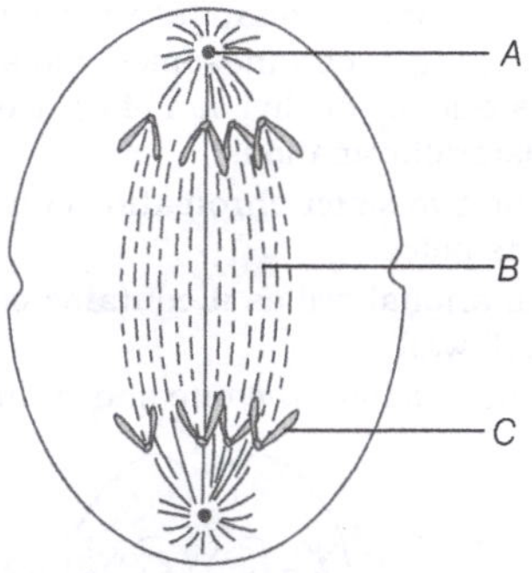

(i) Name the parts labelled as *A*, *B* and *C*.

(ii) Identify the above stage and give a reason to support your answer.

(iii) Mention where in the body this type of cell division occurs.

(iv) Name the stage prior to this stage and draw a diagram to represent the same. **[2011]**

Ans. The parts labelled as *A*, *B* and *C* are

(i) *A* – Centriole
B – Spindle fibres
C – Chromatid

(ii) The above stage is anaphase because sister chromatids are seen at the poles.

(iii) This type of cell division occurs in the somatic cells of the body.

(iv) The stage prior to anaphase is metaphase.

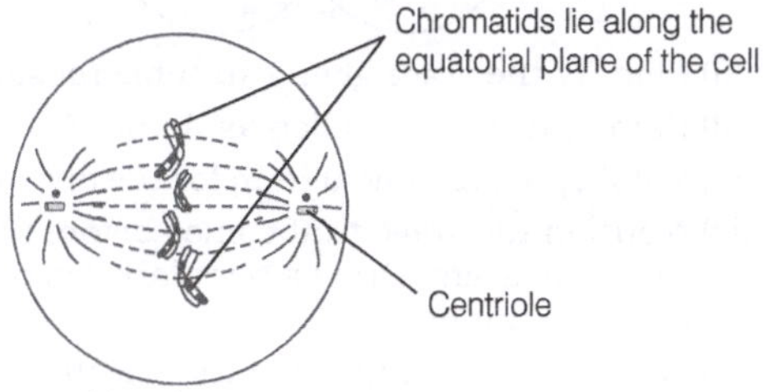

Metaphase

7. Given below is a diagram representing a stage during the mitotic cell division. Study the diagram and answer the following questions. [2019]

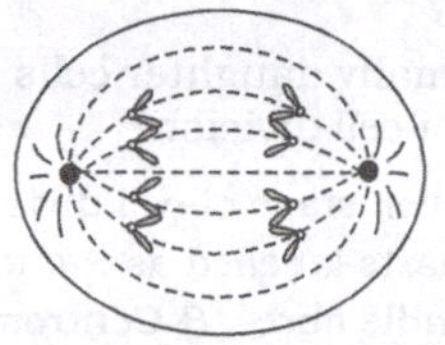

(i) Identify the stage by giving a suitable reason.

(ii) Is it a plant or an animal cell? Give a reason to support your answer.

(iii) Draw a neat, labelled diagram of the stage which follows the one shown in the diagram.

(iv) How many chromosomes will each daughter cell have after the completion of the above division?

(v) Name the four nitrogenous bases.

Ans. (i) The given stage is anaphase because during this phase, the splitting of chromosomes takes place. This splitting occurs due to the division of centromere which attaches two sister chromatids.
Also the two sister chromatids can be seen moving towards poles.

(ii) It is an animal cell as it contains centrioles and also lack cell wall.

(iii) Telophase follows the one shown in diagram.

Telophase in animal cell

(iv) Each daughter cell have four chromosomes after the completion of the above division.

(v) The four nitrogenous bases are

- Adenine
- Guanine
- Cytosine
- Thymine

8. Study the given diagram which represents a stage during the mitotic cell division and answer the questions that follow. [2017]

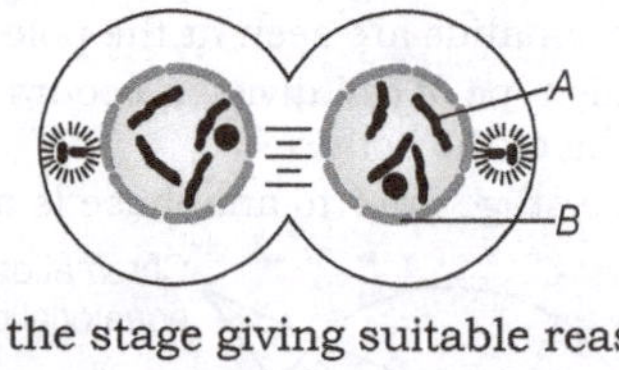

(i) Identify the stage giving suitable reasons.

(ii) Name the parts labelled as *A* and *B*.

(iii) What is the technical term for the division of nucleus?

(iv) Mention the stage that comes before the stage shown in the diagram. Draw a neat labelled diagram of the stage mentioned.

(v) Which is the cell division that results in half the number of chromosomes in daughter cells?

Ans. (i) In the given figure, the two sets of daughter chromosomes have reached to opposite poles as well as reformation of nuclear membrane has also started. Therefore, it is telophase of mitotic division.

(ii) The parts labelled as *A* and *B* are
A–Chromosome
B–Nuclear membrane (appearing)

(iii) Karyokinesis is the technical term which is used for the division of nucleus.

(iv) Telophase is preceded by anaphase. A diagram of anaphase is given below

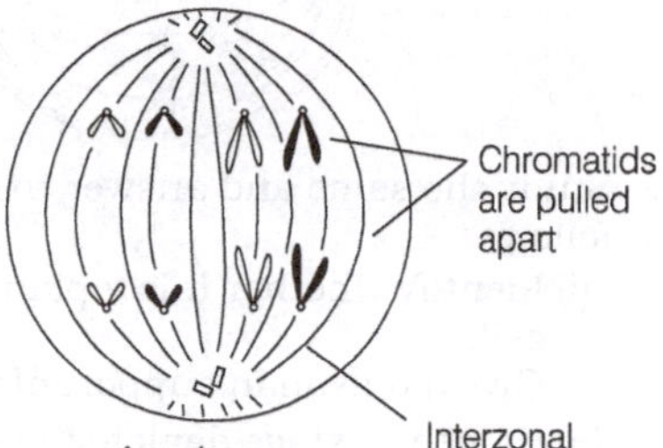

Anaphase

(v) During meiosis, the chromosome number is reduced in such a way that each daughter cell receives only half the number of chromosomes present in the parent cell.

9. Homologous chromosomes are pairs of chromosomes that have similar characteristics like size, shape, gene loci, etc. Answer the questions that follow.

(i) How many chromatids are found in homologous chromosomes?

(ii) From which parent are homologous chromosomes inherited?

(iii) What type of division requires homologous chromosomes?

(iv) What are telomeres?

(v) Which structure of chromosome is known as primary constriction?

Ans. (i) Homologous chromosomes are pair of chromosomes which are similar in shape, size and position of centromere. One chromosome contains two chromatids thus, a pair of homologous chromosomes contains four chromatids.

(ii) One chromosome in each homologous pair is inherited from father and other one from the mother.

(iii) Homologous chromosomes exchange their segments during meiosis.

(iv) Telomeres are the terminal regions on either sides of the chromosomes.

(v) Centromere is known as primary constriction of chromosome.

Chapter Assessment

Section-I

1 Mark Questions

1. Name the following.
   (i) The stage of mitotic division, where condensation of chromatin material into chromosomes occurs.
   (ii) The stage at which the sister chromosomes separate from their paired condition.
   (iii) A cell division process occurring in two parts.
2. Correct and rewrite the following statements by changing the underlined words.
   (i) Chromosomes were first observed by Strasburger.
   (ii) A chromatid is a duplicated chromosome.
   (iii) Centromere is a part of ribosomes.
   (iv) When the centromere is present at one end, the chromosome is sub-metacentric.
3. Give biological reasons for the following.
   (i) Cells require resting phase before entering cell division.
   (ii) Cell cycle is essential for perpetuation of a species.
   (iii) Interphase is the longest phase of cell cycle.
   (iv) Meiosis is reductional division.
4. Match the following columns.

Column I	Column II
A. A sequence of events occurring between the cell formation and its division.	1. G_0-phase
B. It starts with karyokinesis and ends with cytokinesis after the resting phase.	2. G_2-phase
C. Cells are metabolically active but do not proliferate.	3. M-phase
D. The pre-mitotic phase which shows increase in volume of nucleus and synthesis of RNA and proteins.	4. Cell cycle

5. Choose the correct answer from the four options given below.
   (i) At this stage of cell cycle, the cell contains $2n$ of DNA (chromosomes).
   (a) G_0-phase (b) S-phase
   (c) G_1-phase (d) All of these
   (ii) Haploid chromosome number in a cell will be
   (a) $2n$ (b) n
   (c) $4n-1$ (d) $2n+1$
   (iii) Which phase is also referred to as pre-mitotic phase?
   (a) M-phase (b) S-phase
   (c) G_2-phase (d) G_1-phase
   (iv) Duplication of DNA content is observed during
   (a) mitosis and meiosis (b) meiosis
   (c) mitosis (d) interphase
   (v) Identify the process that gives rise to daughter cells with half number of chromosomes than that of their parent cell.
   (a) Cleavage (b) Mitosis
   (c) Budding (d) Meiosis
   (vi) The cell division occurring in germ cells is
   (a) diakinesis (b) karyokinesis
   (c) mitosis (d) meiosis
6. Fill in the blanks by using suitable words.
   (i) A .... is the point at which the sister chromatids are held together.
   (ii) DNA replication occurs in the .... of interphase.
   (iii) In .... stage of interphase, synthesis of RNA and proteins occur in the cell cycle.
   (iv) During cytokinesis, a .... is formed in the plant cell in order to separate the two daughter cells.
   (v) Chromosome number is halved in gametes to restore the normal number, i.e. .... after fertilisation to form zygote.

7. Choose the odd one out from the following terms given below and name the category to which the other three belong.

   Aster formation, Spindle formation, Disappearance of nucleolus, Formation of equatorial plate

8. Expand the following biological abbreviation.
   (i) S-phase
   (ii) G_1-phase

9. State the exact location of the following.
   (i) Chromomeres
   (ii) Nucleosomes
   (iii) Meiosis

10. State the main function of the following.
    (i) Histone protein
    (ii) Genes
    (iii) Spindle fibres

11. Mention one difference in each of the following pairs on the basis of what is given in the bracket.
    (i) Mitosis and Meiosis (significance)
    (ii) Karyokinesis and Cytokinesis (purpose of occurrence)
    (iii) Mitosis in animal and plant cells (division of cytoplasm)

12. Answer the following questions briefly.
    (i) What changes do you observe during the S-phase of cell cycle?
    (ii) List any one significance of mitosis in living organisms associated with growth as a parameter.
    (iii) If two daughter cells are formed during mitosis, how are DNA and chromosomes distributed?

2 Marks Questions

13. What is a cell cycle? How many phases does a cell cycle consist of ?

14. List the events that occur during the G_1-phase of the cell cycle.

3 Marks Questions

15. Into how many sub-stages is the preparatory phase of the cell cycle divided? Explain.

16. Write any three characteristics of the prophase stage of the mitotic cell division.

17. Give a diagrammatic account of mitotic early anaphase in animal cell.

Section-II [5 Marks]

Structured Questions

18. Observe the figure given below and answer the questions that follow.

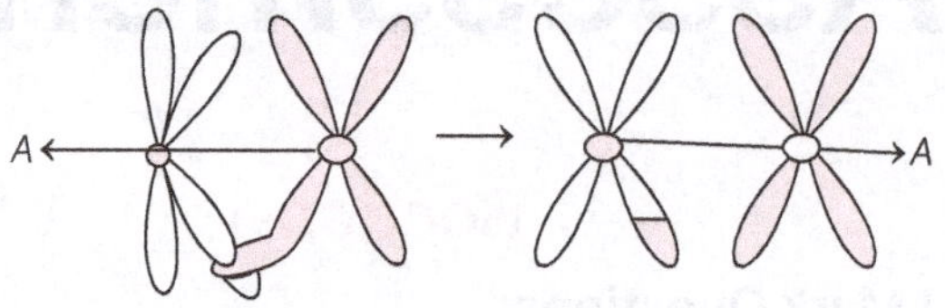

    (i) Identify the process.
    (ii) What is the purpose of this process?
    (iii) Differentiate between chromosome and chromatid.
    (iv) What is the name of structure *A* present between the chromatids?
    (v) In which type of chromosomes, is the given process seen?

19. Interphase is a period between two successive cell divisions. Answer the questions that follow.
    (i) Why are cells metabolically active during interphase?
    (ii) What are the two growth phases in interphase?
    (iii) State one characteristic feature of G_1-phase.
    (iv) What happens to cell in the late G_1-phase?
    (v) What is the other name for G_2-phase?

20. There is a diagram representing a stage during mitotic cell division in an animal cell.

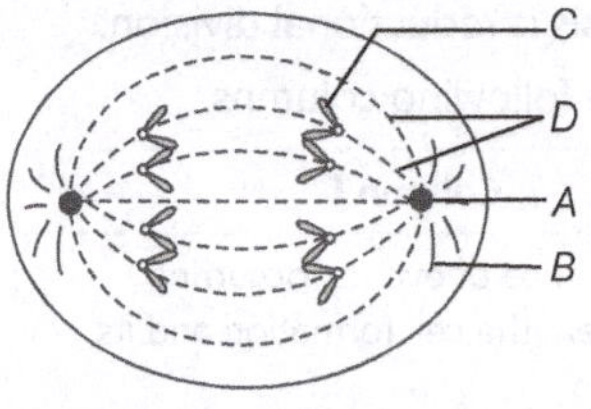

    (i) Identify the above stage. Give a reason to support your answer.
    (ii) Name the parts labelled as *A*, *B*, *C* and *D*.
    (iii) What is the function of part *D* ?
    (iv) Name the stage that comes just after the stage shown in the diagram. Draw a well-labelled diagram of this stage.

For explanations scan the given QR Code

Olympiad Section*

Brain Teasing Questions asked in Previous Olympiads

1 The figure shows the structure and condensation states of a chromosome. **[IJSO, 2015, Republic of Korea]**

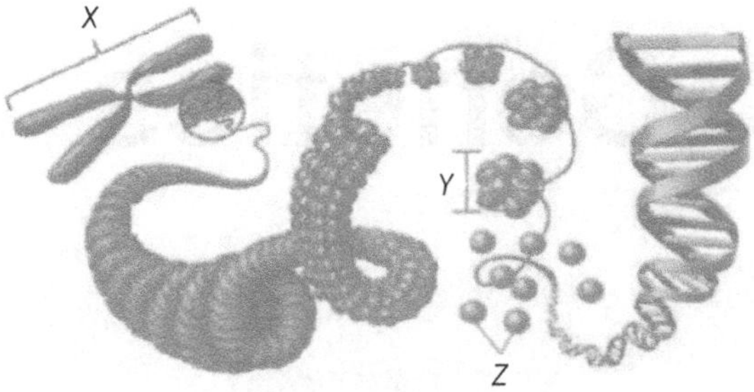

Which of the following options from *a* to *d* chooses all the correct statement(s) from the box below?

I. *X* is observed in metaphase of the cell-division cycle.
II. *Y* is a nucleosome.
III. Bacteria have Z.

(a) Only I (b) Only II (c) I and II (d) II and III

2 A short length linear DNA molecule has 110 Thymine and 110 Guanine bases. The total number of nucleotids in the DNA fragment will be **[INJSO 2014]**

(a) 110 (b) 880 (c) 440 (d) 220

3 Chromosomes in metaphase get arranged at the equatorial plate (see Fig. 1). When these cells are treated with colchicine, cell division is arrested and the cells never enter anaphase. If we were to compare a colchicine treated cell at metaphase and an untreated cell in the same phase, we notice that chromosomes are more dispersed and do not arrange themselves on the equatorial plate in the treated cells (see Fig 2.). **[INJSO 2012]**

Fig. 1; Metaphase

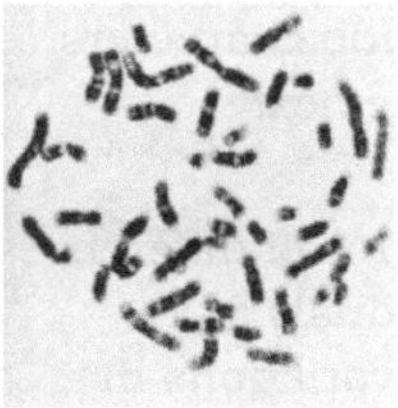

Fig. 2; Colchicine treated metaphase

Using this information, which of the following will be affected by colchicine?

(a) Centromere
(b) Spindle fibre
(c) Centriole
(d) Arms of chromosome

Answers

1. (c) **2.** (c) **3.** (b)

**These questions may or may not be asked in the examination, have been given just for additional practice required for olympiads, scholarship exams etc. For detailed explanations refer Page No. 247.*

CHAPTER 02

Genetics

Chapter Inside

Some Important Genetic Terms • Mendelian Inheritance • Sex-Determination in Human Beings • Sex-Linked Inheritance • Mutation

Genetics is the study of transmission of body features (both similarities and dissimilarities) from parents to offsprings and the laws related to their transmission. These body features are coded in the form of genetic material. The term **'Genetics'** was first used by **W Bateson** in 1905. It can be defined as the branch of science that deals with the mechanism of heredity and variation in living organisms.

Heredity is the transmission of genetic characters from one generation (parents) to the next generation, i.e. offsprings.

Variation may be defined as the degree of differences in characteristics among the individuals of a species. The greatest advantage of variations in species is that they increase the chances of survival in a changing environment.

Some Important Genetic Terms

A list of important terms used to study genetics are given below

1. **Unit factor** (Gene) **Mendel** used the word unit factor or pair factor for controlling units of various traits. Later **Johannsen** (1909) replaced the word factor with gene. A gene is a unit of inheritance. It is a piece of DNA that carries the information needed to make a specific protein. There are about 19,000 genes in humans.

   Out of these largest number of genes are found in chromosome-1 (2968) whereas the fewer number is found in chromosome-Y (231).
2. **Genome** It is the full complement of DNA, having all the genes and intergenic regions of an organism.
3. **Character** The features or characteristics of an individual like height, colour, shape, etc.
4. **Trait** An inherited character, i.e. the feature, which is normally inherited and has its detectable variant too. Thus, traits are the alternative forms of a character. For example, tall and dwarf are the two traits of a character, i.e. height.
5. **Gene locus** It is a particular position of a gene on a chromosome.
6. **Alleles or Allelomorphs** The alternate forms or varieties of genes in a particular gene pair. They occupy same locus (position) on homologous pair of chromosome. This term was given by **Bateson**.
7. **Homozygous** When a gene pair (alleles) in an organism contains two identical genes controlling similar trait of a character then the organism is considered as homozygous for that particular character, e.g. TT (tall), tt (dwarf).

8. **Heterozygous** When a gene pair (alleles) contains two different genes controlling different traits of a character in an organism then the organism is considered as heterozygous for that particular character, e.g. Tt.
9. **Phenotype** The physical appearance of an individual.
10. **Genotype** The complete genetic constitution of an individual.
11. **Gamete** A mature reproductive cell, which is specialised for amphimixis (fusion).
12. **Hybrid** The literary meaning of this word is mixture. In genetics, we define it as an offspring, which is obtained from a cross between two genetically different parents.
13. F_1- **generation** First filial (filial=offspring) generation, i.e. the generation of hybrids, which are obtained from a cross between two genetically different parents.
14. F_2- **generation** Second filial generation, i.e. individuals normally obtained after self-crossing the individuals of F_1-generation.
15. **Dominant allele** An allele which expresses itself externally whether present in homozygous (RR) or in heterozygous conditions (Rr).
16. **Recessive allele** An allele which expresses itself externally when present in homozygous condition (rr), but remains suppressed in heterozygous condition.

Dominant and Recessive Hereditary Traits in Humans

Characters	Dominant traits	Recessive traits
Eye colour	Brown	Blue
Tongue	Rolling	Non-rolling
Hand	Right handedness	Left handedness
Ear lobe	Free	Attached
Lips	Thick	Thin
Rh blood group	Positive	Negative
Colour vision (red green)	Normal	Colourblind
Cheek	Dimpled	Normal

Uncommon Hereditary Traits in Humans

- Polydactyly (Extra fingers and toes) — Dominant
- Albinism (Total absence of skin pigment) — Recessive
- Camptodactyly (Inability to straighten the little finger) — Dominant

Mendelian Inheritance

Gregor Johann Mendel (1822-1884), an Austrian Monk is known as the **Father of Genetics**. Mendel was able to formulate his laws to explain the pattern of inheritance of characters in garden pea (*Pisum sativum*). Thus, the basic principles of genetics were discovered by Mendel.

Mendel's Experiments

Mendel worked with the common garden pea plant (*Pisum sativum*). In his experiments, he choose seven visible characters represented by two contrasting forms or traits as shown below

Characters	Contrasting traits	Dominant/ Recessive
Shape of the seeds	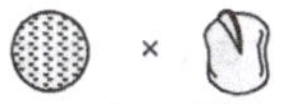 Round × Wrinkled	Round/ Wrinkled
Colour of the seeds	 Yellow × Green	Yellow/Green
Shape of the pods	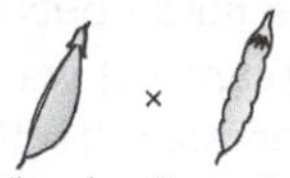 Inflated × Constricted	Inflated/Constricted
Colour of the pods	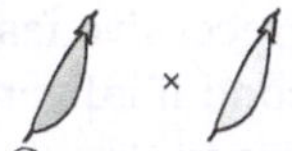 Green × Yellow	Green/Yellow
Colour of the flowers	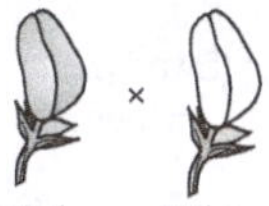 Violet × White	Violet/White
Position of the pods (Flowers)	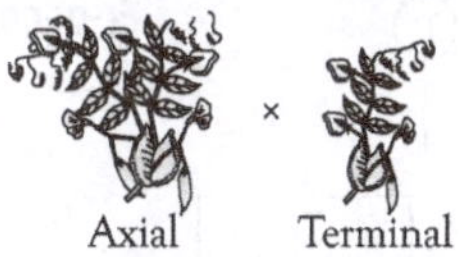 Axial × Terminal	Axial/Terminal
Height of the stem	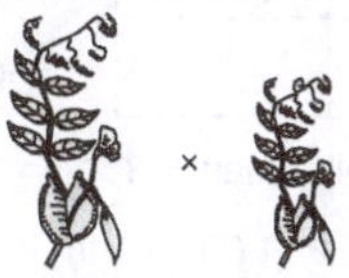 Tall × Dwarf	Tall/Dwarf

Mendel selected garden pea for his experiments due to the following reasons

(i) Varieties were available in pure forms that were true breeding, i.e. same type were produced in succeeding generations.

(ii) Many varieties were having contrasting characters.

(iii) Being bisexual, pea plants can be self-pollinated and cross-pollinated.

(iv) These are annual plants with short life cycle. So, several generations could be studied within a short period.

(v) Pea plants were readily available on large scale.

(vi) Pea plants could easily be handled, raised and maintained.

Through the selective growing of common pea plants over many generations, he discovered that certain traits appear in offspring plants without any blending of parental characteristics.
Mendel conducted his experiments for seven years (1856-1863) on garden pea, first, by taking only one character at a time (**monohybrid cross**) and then, by taking two characters together (**dihybrid cross**).

These crosses are discussed in detail below

Monohybrid Cross

This cross is performed by considering only one pair of contrasting character or one feature at a time, e.g. when a cross was made between pure tall plant (TT) and pure dwarf plant (tt) was done, only dominant feature expressed itself in the first filial generation (F_1), i.e. all tall plants were produced by masking the effect of recessive feature. After self-pollination in second filial generation (F_2), both the traits, i.e. tallness and dwarfness were expressed in the ratio 3:1.

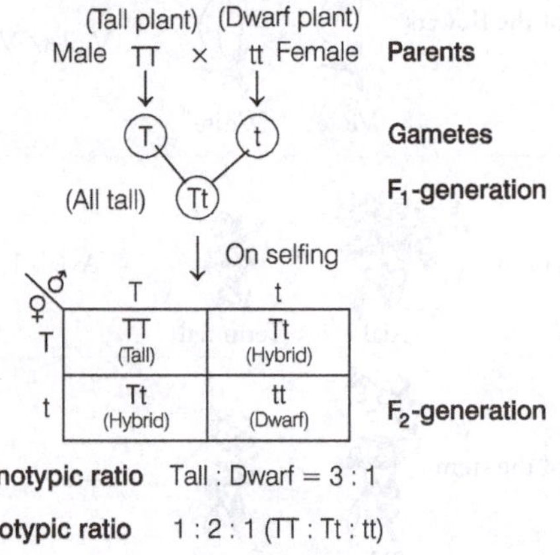

Monohybrid cross

Dihybrid Cross

This type of cross is performed by considering two pairs of contrasting characters at a time, e.g. when a cross was made between a plant having round yellow seeds (RRYY) and a plant having wrinkled green seeds (rryy), only round yellow seeds were produced in F_1-generation (as round yellow were dominant alleles).

Further, when F_1 were self-pollinated, four different types of seed combinations were obtained in F_2-generation.

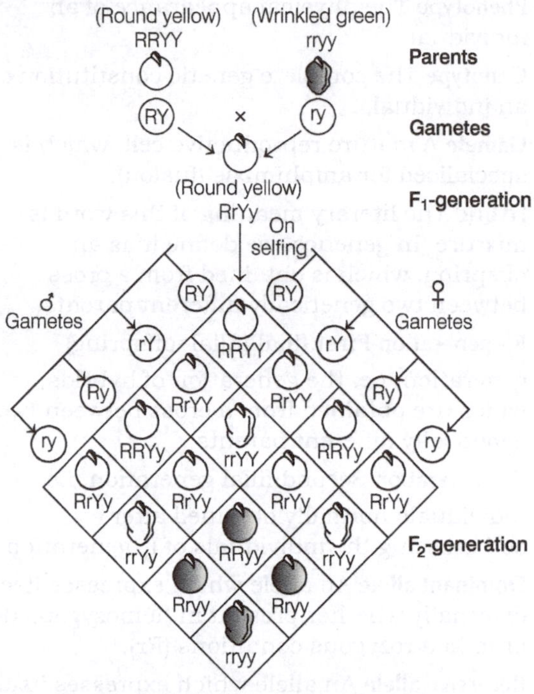

Phenotypic Ratio Round yellow : Round green : Wrinkled yellow : Wrinkled green = 9 : 3 : 3 : 1
Genotypic Ratio 1 : 2 : 2 : 4 : 1 : 2 : 1 : 2 : 1

Dihybrid cross

Note The square used in the above cross to show the cross of gametes in F_2-generation is called **Punnett square**. It is used to calculate the probability of all possible genotypes of offsprings in a genetic cross.

Check Your LEARNING...

1. Name the unit of inheritance.
2. Define alleles or allelomorphs.
3. Give any two dominant traits in pea plant.
4. What is the ratio of tallness and dwarfness in monohybrid cross?
5. Mention the phenotypic ratio of dihybrid cross in F_2-generation.

Mendel's Laws of Inheritance

On the basis of the inferences of monohybrid cross, Mendel proposed two general rules to consolidate his understanding of inheritance in monohybrid cross. These includes "law of dominance" and "law of segregation". Another law i.e. law of independent assortment was proposed by Mendel on the basis of his observation of dihybrid cross. Altogether, these three laws are called **Mendel's Principles of Inheritance** or **Mendelism**.

Law of Dominance (First Law)

This law states that 'when two alternative forms of traits or characters are present in an organism, then only one factor expresses itself in F_1-progeny and the other remains suppressed. The factor that expresses itself is called **dominant factor**, while the other factor which remains hidden is called **recessive factor**. It explains the expression of a gene in a cross. If the plants of F_1-generation are selfed than the ratio obtained in F_2-generation is 3:1.

Law of Segregation (Second Law)

This law states that 'the two factors or alleles controlling one character segregate without influencing each other during the formation of gametes, so that each gamete receives one factor for each character'.
Due to this, the gametes are pure for a character. Though, the parents contain two alleles during gamete formation, the factors or alleles of a pair segregate from each other such that a gamete receives only one of the two factors. The gametes then, combine during zygote formation. This is also called **law of purity of gametes.**

Law of Independent Assortment (Third Law)

This law states that 'when two pairs of contrasting characters are combined in a hybrid, segregation of one pair of character is independent of the other pair of character at the time of gamete formation'. It also gets randomly rearranged in the offsprings producing both parental and new combination of characters.

Exception to this phenomenon was discovered due to **linkage** i.e. tendency of the genes to remain together in their parental combination. Linkage is opposite to the phenomenon of **crossing over** i.e. exchange of chromatid segments between the homologous chromosome.

Sex-Determination in Human Beings

The establishment of sex through differential development in an individual at the time of zygote formation is called **sex-determination**. In humans, XX-XY type of sex- determination is observed.

There are 46 chromosomes (23 pairs) present in human body which can be classified into two main types

(i) **Autosomes** These are exactly similar chromosomes in both males and females (22 pairs). These are also called somatic chromosomes.

(ii) **Sex chromosome or Allosomes** These chromosomes determine the sex of a person. There are two types of sex chromosomes, i.e. X-chromosome and Y-chromosome. These are designated as 23rd pair of chromosome. Allosomes always occur in pair. In males, it is XY and in females, it is XX. Y-chromosome is much smaller than the X-chromosome.

In human beings, male gamete (sperm) contains either X or Y-chromosome, while female gamete (egg) contains only X-chromosome. Since, female produces only one type of gametes, the male gamete determines the sex of progeny. In other words, sex of a child depends upon the kind of sperm that fertilises the egg during the process of fertilisation. In case, the sperm carrying X-chromosome fertilises the egg (X) then, the resulting child will be female (XX) and if the sperm carrying Y-chromosome fertilises the egg (X), then the resulting child will be male (XY).

This can be shown by the following cross

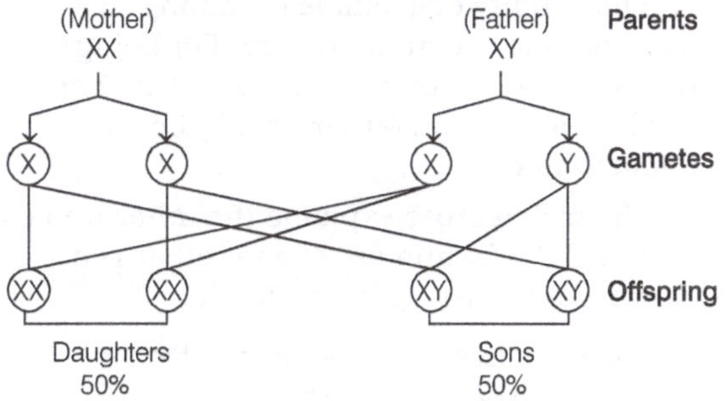

There are 50% chances of having either a male or female child in each pregnancy. Thus, it is the phenomenon occurring by chance. So, women should not be blamed for giving birth to a girl child.

Check Your LEARNING...

1. State the law of dominance.
2. Which law of inheritance is also called law of purity of gametes?
3. What is crossing over?
4. Name the types of chromosomes which do not take part in sex-determination.
5. Write the number of chromosomes present in human body.

Sex-linked Inheritance

It is the appearance of a trait due to the presence of an allele located exclusively on X-chromosome or Y-chromosome, i.e. sex chromosomes.

Types of Sex-linked Inheritance

In XX-XY type organisms including humans, sex-linked inheritance can be classified into the following types

1. X-linked

This type of inheritance is controlled by recessive genes which are localised on X-chromosome that have no corresponding allele on Y-chromosome. Examples of X-linked inheritance include **haemophilia** and **colour blindness.**

(i) **Haemophilia** It is a **sex-linked recessive disease**, which is transmitted from an unaffected carrier female to some of the male offsprings. Due to this disease, patient continues to bleed even on a minor injury because of defective blood coagulation mechanism.

The blood of haemophilic person does not contain anti-haemophilic globulin (haemophilia-A) or plasma thromboplastin (haemophilia-B) essential for blood clotting. The genes for haemophilia are located on the X-chromosome.

The possibility of a female becoming haemophilic is extremely rare. For being haemophilic, mother of such a female has to be atleast carrier and father should be haemophilic.

The following cross explains the inheritance of haemophilia in human when mother is a carrier and father is haemophilic.

(Haemophilic father) (Carrier mother) **Parents**

X^hY × X^hX

X^h Y X^h X **Gametes**

♀ \ ♂	X^h	Y
X^h	X^hX^h (Haemophilic daughter)	X^hY (Haemophilic son)
X	X^hX (Carrier daughter)	XY (Normal son)

Genotypic ratio 1 : 1 : 1 : 1

Thus, females suffer from this disease only in homozygous condition, i.e. X^hX^h. Since, it is a recessive character, a woman may carry the disease and would transmit the disease to 50% of her sons, even if the father is normal.

The family pedigree of **Queen Victoria,** who was a carrier of haemophilia, shows a number of haemophilic individuals.

(ii) **Colour blindness** It is also a **sex-linked recessive** disorder, which results in the visualisation defect of either red or green colour. It does not mean inability of seeing these colours at all. In fact, it leads to the failure in discrimination between red and green colours.

The gene for colour blindness is present on X-chromosome. The disease is more common in males (X^cY) because of the presence of only one X-chromosome as compared to two X-chromosomes in females. The cross between carrier woman and normal man explains the inheritance of colour blindness as follows

(Carrier woman) (Normal man) **Parents**

XX^c × XY

X X^c X Y **Gametes**

♀ \ ♂	X	Y
X	XX (Normal girl)	XY (Normal boy)
X^c	XX^c (Carrier girl)	X^cY (Colourblind boy)

F_1-generation

A heterozygous (carrier) female has normal vision, but it passes on the disorder to some of her sons.

Note
- X-linked characters are expressed more commonly in males than in females because males express these character in hemizygous condition.
- X-linked genes are never passed from father to son. The Y-chromosome is the only sex chromosome that passes from father to son.
- The phenomenon of transmission of sex-linked gene from mother to son and from father to daughter is called *criss-cross* **inheritance**.

2. Y-linked

The Y-chromosome linked traits (characters) occur in males but not in females, e.g. traits such as hair growing out of ears and pattern baldness. This is because the dominant genes of such traits are found only on Y-chromosome.

Mutation

It is a sudden, inheritable change in the nucleotide sequences of the genome of an individual which ultimately changes the genotype of an organism.

These mutations may or may not induce any phenotypic characteristics in an organism. The agents which cause mutation are called **mutagens**. They can be physical or chemical factors, e.g. ultraviolet (UV) radiation, certain chemicals, etc.

The mutation can be of two main types

(i) **Chromosomal mutation** Change in the number structure or arrangement of the chromosome, e.g.Down's syndrome.

(ii) **Gene mutation** Change in the sequence of DNA, e.g. sickle-cell anaemia.

Check Your LEARNING...

1 Give the genotype of a carrier haemophilic female.
2 The gene for colour blindness is located on which chromosome?
3 Name a disorder inherited through Y-chromosomes.
4 Name some mutagens.
5 Name the types of mutations.

QUiCK Revision

- **Genetics** is the branch of biology, which deals with the inheritance, as well as variation of characters from parents to offsprings.
- **Gregor Johann Mendel** for the first time conducted experiments to understand the pattern of inheritance and variations in living beings. He is also known as **Father of Genetics**.
- **Gene** is a unit of inheritance. It is a sequence of DNA that codes for a specific polypeptide. One gene can have slightly different forms.
- **Traits/characters** refer to the expression of genes in the form of visible physical properties, e.g. colour of flower, height of plant, shape of leaf, etc.
- **Alleles** are the alternate forms of genes in a particular gene pair, e.g. gene which codes for the colour of eyes. One of its forms code for brown and another codes for blue colour.
- **Homozygous condition** means having a pair of identical alleles (forms of gene) at a gene location (locus) on a pair of chromosomes. **Heterozygous condition** means having a pair of non-identical alleles at a gene locus on a pair of chromosomes.
- **Genotype** refers to the genetic constitution of an individual; a single gene pair or sum total of all the genes.
- **Phenotype** refers to observable traits or characters that result from expression of genes.
- **Mendel's Laws of Inheritance** Mendel selected garden pea (*Pisum sativum)* as an experimental material and conducted hybridisation experiments for seven years and proposed the laws of inheritance in living organisms.
  (i) **Law of dominance** (First law) states that when two alternate forms of a trait or character (genes) are present in an organism only one factor expresses itself in F_1 progeny, i.e. dominant one.
  (ii) **Law of segregation** (Second law) states that the alleles do not show any blending and both the characters are recovered as such in the F_2-generation. The factors or alleles of a pair segregate from each other in a way that a gamete receives only one of the two factors.
  (iii) **Law of independent assortment** (Third law) states that when two pairs of traits are combined in a hybrid, segregation of one pair of character is independent of the other pair of characters at the time of gamete formation. This law was based on the result of dihybrid cross. It shows phenotypic ratio 9 : 3 : 3 : 1 and genotypic ratio 1 : 2 : 2 : 4 : 1 : 2 : 1 : 2 : 1
- **Sex-determination in human beings** Males have two types of gametes, i.e. X and Y, while females have only one type of gamete, i.e. X. If an ovum gets fertilised with a sperm carrying X-chromosome, the zygote develops into a female (XX) and if an ovum gets fertilised with a sperm carrying Y-chromosome, the zygote develops into a male. Hence, the type of sperm, which fertilises the ovum determines the sex of a child.
- **Sex-linked inheritance** It is the appearance of a trait or a character due to the presence of an allele either on the X or Y-chromosome. Certain disorders in human beings are transferred to the next generation because they are associated with the inheritance of changed or altered genes or chromosomes. These are called **genetic disorders.** These disorders when occur due to change in sex-chromosomes are known as sex-linked inherited diseases.
- **Mutations** are sudden inheritable changes in the genome that alter the genotype of an individual.
- Mutations are of two types, i.e. chromosomal mutation and gene mutation.

Chapter Practice

Section-I

1 Mark Questions

1. Name the following.
   (i) The physical expression of genes in an individual. [2013]
   (ii) An individual having dissimilar gene pairs.
   (iii) The type of gene which in the presence of contrasting allele is not expressed. [2014, 13]
   (iv) The cross between two parents having one pair of contrasting characters. [2015]
   (v) One factor that can cause mutation.

Ans. (i) Phenotype
(ii) Heterozygous
(iii) Recessive gene
(iv) Monohybrid cross
(v) Ultraviolet (UV) radiation

2. Correct and rewrite the following statements by changing the underlined words.
   (i) Peas are self-pollinated since they are unisexual.
   (ii) One of the example of X-linked inherited disease is diabetes.
   (iii) Colour blindness is inherited through Y-chromosome.
   (iv) Sudden change in genetic constitution of an individual is called genotype.

Ans. (i) Peas are self-pollinated since they are bisexual.
(ii) One of the example of X-linked inherited disease is haemophilia
(iii) Baldness is inherited through Y-chromosome.
(iv) Sudden change in the genetic constitution of an individual is called mutation.

3. Give biological reasons for the following.
   (i) Colour blindness is more common in men than in women. [2016]
   (ii) The pattern of baldness is found only in males.

Ans. (i) Colour blindness is a sex-linked disease. Its gene is located on X-chromosome and not on Y-chromosome. Females can be the carriers of the disease. The male will be affected by the disease if this character is carried by its X-chromosome. So, colour blindness is more common in men than in women.
(ii) Pattern of baldness is a Y-linked disease. Due to the presence of Y-chromosome only in males, it is found only in them.

4. (i) Match the following columns.

Column I	Column II
A. Genetics	1. Chromosomes similar in size and shape
B. Recessive gene	2. Study of laws of inheritance of characters
C. Autosomes	3. A gene that can express only when in a similar pair
D. Homologous chromosomes	4. Chromosomes other than the pair of sex chromosomes

(ii) Match the following columns.

Column I	Column II
A. TT	1. Heterozygous
B. Tt	2. Homozygous dominant
C. tt	3. Recessive trait

Ans. (i) A–2, B–3, C–4, D–1 (ii) A–2, B–1, C–3

5. Choose the correct answer from each of the four options given below.
   (i) The discipline which deals with the study of transmission of characters from parents to offsprings is called
   (a) evolution (b) genetics (c) variation (d) similarity

Ans. (b)

(ii) Transfer of characters from parents to their offsprings is called
(a) heredity (b) variations (c) genetics (d) cytology

Ans. (a)

(iii) The morphological differences between parents and offsprings are called
(a) heredity (b) morphology
(c) variations (d) taxonomy

Ans. (c)

(iv) Which of the following terms represents alternate forms of a gene?
(a) Alleles (b) Phenotype
(c) Heterozygous (d) Genetics

Ans. (a)

(v) The types of gene, which in the presence of a contrasting allele is not expressed. [Semester I 2021]
(a) Homozygous (b) Heterozygous
(c) Dominant (d) Recessive

Ans. (d)

(vi) Who among the following is the 'Father of Genetics'?
(a) Khorana (b) Morgan
(c) Kornberg (d) Mendel

Ans. (d)

(vii) What is a monohybrid cross?
(a) In which only one character of an allele is studied
(b) In which both the characters of alleles are studied
(c) In which all the characters are studied
(d) In which more than two characters are studied

Ans. (a)

(viii) Which of the following states Law of dominance correctly ? **[Semester I 2021]**
(a) Out of a pair of contrasting alleles present together, only the recessive allele is able to express itself while the dominant remains suppressed
(b) Out of a pair of contrasting alleles present together, only the dominant allele is able to express itself while the recessive remains suppressed
(c) Out of a pair of contrasting alleles present together, both the dominant and recessive cannot express themselves
(d) Out of a pair of contrasting alleles present together, both the dominant and recessive can express themselves

Ans. (b)

(ix) A homozygous pea plant having purple flowers is crossed with a homozygous pea plant bearing white flowers. The phenotypic ratio of the offspring obtained in F_2-generation is **[Semester I 2021]**
(a) 2 : 1 (b) 1 : 1
(c) 1 : 2 : 1 (d) 3 : 1

Ans. (d)

(x) After mitotic cell division, a female human cell will have **[Semester I 2021, 2014]**
(a) 44 + XX-chromosome
(b) 44 + XY-chromosome
(c) 22 + X-chromosome
(d) 22 + Y-chromosome

Ans. (a)

(xi) The sex chromosome in human ovum is **[2023]**
(a) X-chromosome
(b) Y-chromosome
(c) Both X and Y-chromosomes
(d) Either X or Y-chromosome

Ans. (a)

(xii) In a human male, a sperm will contain **[2019]**
(a) Both X and Y-chromosomes
(b) Only Y-chromosome
(c) Only X-chromosome
(d) Either X or Y-chromosome

Ans. (d)

(xiii) If a colourblind woman marries a normal visioned man their sons will be
(a) all colourblind
(b) all normal visioned
(c) one-half colourblind and one-half normal
(d) three-fourth colourblind and one-fourth normal

Ans. (a) Colour blindness is expressed in males in hemizygous condition. Secondly, the male child does not receives any of its X-chromosome from his father.

(xiv) What do you understand by the term mutation? **[Semester I 2021]**
(a) It is a sudden change in one or more genes in an organism's cells which is heritable
(b) It is a change in the number of centrosomes in an organism's cells which is heritable
(c) It is a change in the structure of cell membrane in an organism's cells which is heritable
(d) It is a change in the shape of cells which is heritable

Ans. (a)

6. Fill in the blanks by using suitable words.
(i) Phenotype is the observable characteristic which is .... controlled. **[2011]**
(ii) .... is the scientific name of garden pea, which Mendel used for his experiments. **[2015]**
(iii) Mendel studied a total of .... traits in peas, each trait occurring in .... different forms.
(iv) .... is the phenotypic ratio of dihybrid cross.
(v) Law of independent assortment was proposed on the basis of observations of .... cross.
(vi) Haemophilia is caused due to .... genes.

Ans. (i) genetically (ii) *Pisum sativum*
(iii) seven, two (iv) 9:3:3: 1
(v) dihybrid (vi) X-linked recessive

7. Choose the odd one out from the following terms given below and name the category to which other three belong.
(i) Round seed, Yellow seed, Yellow pod, Axial pod
(ii) Chickenpox, Colourblindness, Haemophilia, Albinism **[2019]**
(iii) Typhoid, Haemophilia, Albinism, Colour blindness **[2016]**

Ans. (i) **Odd term** is yellow pod.
Rest three are dominant traits in pea plant.
(ii) **Odd term** is chickenpox.
Rest three are hereditary or genetic diseases.
(iii) **Odd term** is typhoid (bacterial disease).
Rest three belong to category of genetic disorders (disease).

8. State the exact location of the following.
(i) Alleles (ii) Allosomes
(iii) Autosomes

Ans. (i) Alleles are present on gene locus on the chromosome.

(ii) Allosomes are present in all the cells of an individual.

(iii) Autosomes are present in all the cells.

9. State the main function of the following.

(i) Punnett square (ii) Allosomes

(iii) Y-chromosome

Ans. (i) Punnett square predicts the genotype of genetic experiments.

(ii) Allosomes or sex chromosomes determine sex of an individual.

(iii) Y-chromosome contains the male determining gene and is responsible for male characteristics.

10. Mention one difference between each of the following pairs on the basis of what is given in the brackets.

(i) Homozygous and Heterozygous (type of alleles)

(ii) Dominant and Recessive (expression of trait)

(iii) Monohybrid cross and Dihybrid cross (phenotypic ratio) [2011]

Ans. (i) Difference between homozygous and heterozygous is as follows

Homozygous	Heterozygous
It is a condition when both alleles of a gene are similar.	It is a condition when both alleles of a gene are dissimilar.

(ii) Difference between dominant and recessive is as follows

Dominant	Recessive
When an allele expresses itself even in the presence of its recessive allele, it is called dominant trait.	It can only express itself in the absence of its dominant allele and remains masked in its presence, it is called recessive trait.

(iii) Difference between monohybrid and dihybrid cross is as follows

Monohybrid	Dihybrid
Phenotypic ratio in F_2-generation is 3 : 1.	Phenotypic ratio in F_1-generation is 9 : 3 : 3 : 1.

11. Give biological/technical terms for the following.

(i) The condition in which a pair of chromosome carries similar alleles of a particular character. [2018]

(ii) The suppressed allele of a gene. [2017]

(iii) Phenomena of crossing individuals of same generaton to obtain F_2- generation.

(iv) An alteration of the genetic material that can be inherited. [2016]

Or

Sudden, heritable change in the gene. [2014]

(v) Substances or agents that lead to mutation.

Ans. (i) Homozygous condition

(ii) Recessive allele

(iii) Selfing

(iv) Mutation

(v) Mutagens

12. Briefly explain the following terms.

(i) Gene [2013]

(ii) Allele [2012]

(iii) Phenotype

(iv) Monohybrid cross [2014]

(v) Mutation [2023]

Ans. (i) Gene is a portion or sequence of DNA that codes for a known cellular function or process. Genes are also called as the unit of inheritance containing the information required to express a trait.

(ii) The pair of genes responsible for a particular characteristic in an individual is called allele.

(iii) The observable characteristic of an organism that is genetically controlled is called a phenotype.

(iv) Monohybrid cross is a Mendelian cross taking into consideration, only one pair of contrasting character at a time.

(v) Mutation is the sudden inheritable change in sequence of DNA.

13. Given below are group of terms. In the group, the first pair indicates the relationship between the two terms. Rewrite and complete the second pair on a similar basis.

(i) TT : Homozygous :: Tt : .... [2017]

(ii) Dominant character : Green pod colour :: Recessive character : ....

(iii) Sex chromosomes : Allosomes :: Somatic chromosomes : ....

Ans. (i) Heterozygous (ii) Yellow pod colour

(iii) Autosomes

14. Answer the following questions briefly

(i) What is a dihybrid ratio?

(ii) State Mendel's law of dominance. [2015]

(iii) State Mendel's law of segregation. [2014]

(iv) What are autosomes?

(v) Write the genotype of haemophilic son and carrier daughter.

(vi) A haemophilic man marries a normal homozygous woman. What is the probability that their daughter will be haemophilic?

Ans. (i) The ratio of each phenotype or appearance of the seeds in the F_2-generation obtained in a dihybrid cross is called dihybrid ratio, i.e. 9 : 3 : 3 : 1.

(ii) Law of dominance (first law) states that when two alternative forms of a trait or character are present in an organism, only one factor expresses itself in F_1-progeny. This factor is called dominant factor, while the other factor which remains hidden is called recessive factor.

(iii) This is the second law of inheritance. It states that during gamete formation, the alleles for each gene segregate from each other so that each gamete carries only one allele for each gene.

(iv) Autosomes are chromosomes that are not allosome, i.e. not sex chromosomes. There are similar number of chromosomes in both males and females (22 pairs).

(v) X^hY–Haemophilic son
X^hX–Carrier daughter

(vi) The possibility of a female becoming a haemophilic in the given condition is zero because for the daughter to be haemophilic the mother has to be atleast carrier and father should be haemophilic but here only father is haemophilic.

2 Marks Questions

15. In a certain species of animals, black fur (B) is dominant over brown fur (b).
Predict a genotype and phenotype of the offspring when both parents are Bb or have heterozygous black fur. **[2014]**

Ans.

Parents: (Black fur) Bb × (Brown fur) Bb

Gametes: (B) (b) × (B) (b)

♀ \ ♂	B	b
B	BB (Pure black)	Bb (Hybrid black)
b	Bb (Hybrid black)	bb (Pure brown)

F_1-generation

Phenotypes 3 : 1
Black Brown

Genotypes 1 : 2 : 1
Pure black Hybrid black Pure brown

16. A pure breeding red flower variety of pea plant (RR) is crossed with a pure breeding white flower variety of pea plant (rr). Draw a Punnett square to find out the phenotypic and genotypic ratios of the progeny belonging to the F_2-generation. **[2023]**

Ans. A pure breeding red flower variety of pea plant (RR) is crossed with a pure breeding white flower variety of pea plant (rr).

F_1 generation

♀ \ ♂	R	R
r	Rr	Rr
r	Rr	Rr

F_2-generation

♀ \ ♂	R	r
R	RR	Rr
r	Rr	rr

Phenotypic ratio is 3:1
Genotypic ratio is 1:2:1

17. Name the two sex-linked diseases in humans. **[2009]**

Ans. Colour blindness and haemophilia are the two sex-linked diseases in humans.

18. State Mendel's 'law of segregation'. **[2023]**

Ans. Refer to text on page no. 21.

3 Marks Questions

19. List any three features of garden pea with their dominant and recessive traits.

Ans.

Characters	Dominant	Recessive
Stem height	Tall	Short/Dwarf
Colour of seed	Yellow	Green
Shape of seed	Round	Wrinkled

20. State three reasons why pea plant was selected by Mendel for conducting his experiments.

Ans. The three reasons why Mendel chose pea plant for his experiment were

(i) Pea plants are bisexual and hence, can be both self-pollinated and cross-pollinated.

(ii) Varieties with contrasting traits were available in pure forms.

(iii) Several generations could be studied within a short period of time in pea plants, since it has a short lifespan.

21. Briefly explain the sex-linked inheritance taking colour bilndness as an example.

Ans. Sex-linked inheritance is the appearance of a trait which is due to the presence of an allele exclusively located on X-chromosome or Y-chromosome.
This can be classified into two types, i.e. X-linked inheritance and Y-linked inheritance.
Colourblindness is a sex-linked recessive disorder that leads to the failure in discrimination between red and green colour. Since, the gene for colourblindness is present on the X-chromosome, the disease is more commonly observed in males as they have only one X-Chromosome (X^cY).

Section-II [5 Marks]

Structured Questions

1. Given below is a schematic diagram showing Mendel's experiment on sweet pea plants having axial flowers with round seeds (AARR) and terminal flowers with wrinkled seeds (aarr). Study the same and answer the questions that follow

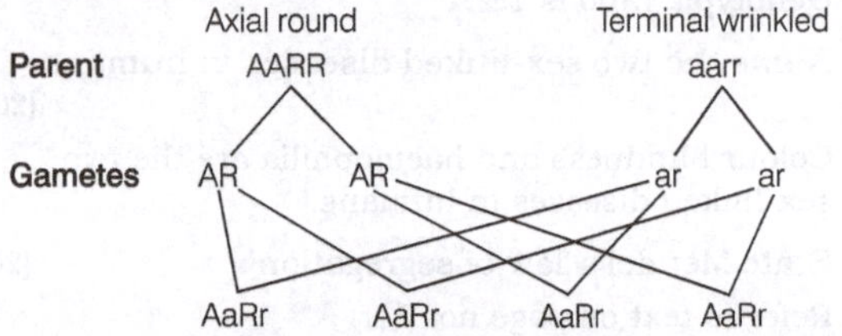

(i) Give the phenotype of F_1 progeny.

(ii) Give the phenotypes of F_2 progeny produced by the self-pollination of F_1 progeny.

(iii) Give the phenotypic ratio of F_2 progeny.

(iv) Name and explain the law introduced by Mendel on the basis of the above observation. [2013]

(v) Which law is also called the law of purity of gametes?

Ans. (i) Phenotype of F_1 progeny is axial flowers with round seeds.

(ii) On selfing F_1-generation

AaRr × AaRr

♀ \ ♂	AR	Ar	aR	ar
AR	AARR	AARr	AaRR	AaRr
Ar	AARr	AArr	AaRr	Aarr
aR	AaRR	AaRr	aaRR	aaRr
ar	AaRr	Aarr	aaRr	aarr

Phenotype of F_2 progeny are axial round (9), axial wrinkled (3), terminal round (3) and terminal wrinkled (1).

(iii) Phenotypic ratio of F_2 progeny is 9:3:3:1.

(iv) Mendel introduced the law of independent assortment on the basis of above observation. This law states that when two pairs of characters are considered, the distribution of alleles of one character into the gametes is independent of the distribution of the alleles of other character.

(v) Law of segregation is also known as the law of purity of gametes.

2. In Mendel's experiments, tall pea plants (T) are dominant over dwarf pea plants (t). [2019]

(i) What is the phenotype and genotype of the F_1-generation if a homozygous tall plant is crossed with a homozygous dwarf plant?

(ii) Draw a Punnett square board to show the gametes and offspring when both the parents are heterozygous for tallness.

(iii) What is the phenotypic ratio and genotypic ratio of the above cross in (ii)?

(iv) Define hybrid.

(v) What is a dihybrid cross?

Ans. (i) **Phenotype** All tall plants were produced. **Genotype** Tt (tall plants).

(ii) When both the parents are hetrozygous then

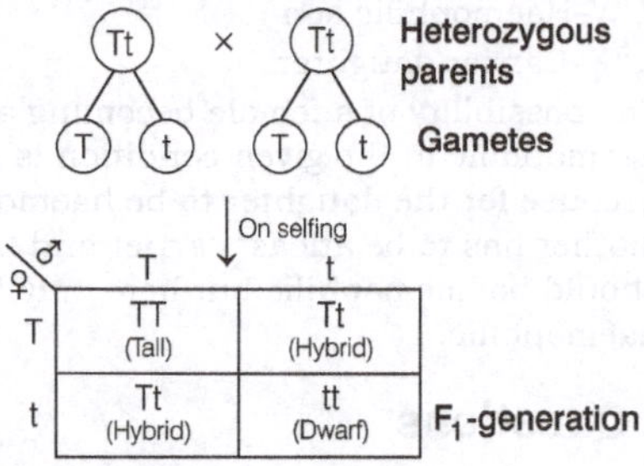

(iii) **Phenotypic ratio** 3 : 1 (Tall : Dwarf)
Genotypic ratio 1 : 2 : 1 (TT : Tt : tt)

(iv) Hybrid in genetics, is an offspring obtained from a cross between two genetically different parents.

(v) **Dihybrid cross** The type of cross performed by considering two pairs of contrasting characters at a time is called a dihybrid cross.

3. A homozygous tall plant (T) bearing red coloured (R) flowers is crossed with a homozygous dwarf (t) plant bearing white (r) flowers.

(i) Give the genotype and phenotype of the plants of F_1-generation.

(ii) Mention the possible combinations of the gametes that can be obtained from the F_1-hybrid plant.

(iii) State the Mendel's law based on such a cross.

(iv) Mention the phenotypes of the offsprings obtained in F_2-generation.

(v) What is the phenotypic ratio obtained in F_2-generation? [2016]

Ans. (i)

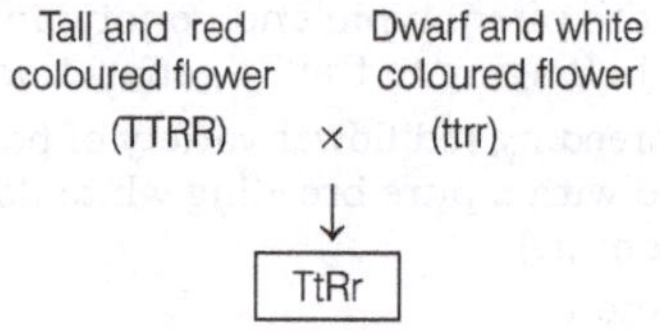

Genotype TtRr; **Phenotype** Tall and red coloured flower

(ii) The possible combinations of the gametes that can be obtained from the F_1 hybrid plant are

(TR), (tR), (Tr), (tr)

(iii) **Law of independent assortment** (third law) is based on the observation obtained from dihybrid crosses.
According to this law, when two pairs of contrasting characters are combined in a hybrid,

segregation of the members of one pair of character into the gamete is independent of the members of the another pair of character at the time of gamete formation.

(iv) The following phenotypes are obtained in F_2-generation.

(a) Tall and red flower

(b) Dwarf and red flower

(c) Tall and white flower

(d) Dwarf and white flower

(v) The phenotypic ratio obtained in F_2-generation is 9:3:3:1

4. In a homozygous pea plant, axial flowers (A) are dominant over terminal flowers (a).

(i) What is the phenotype and genotype of the F_1-generation if a plant bearing pure axial flowers is crossed with a plant bearing pure terminal flowers?

(ii) Draw a Punnett square board to show the gametes and offspring when both the parent plants are heterozygous for axial flowers.

(iii) What is the phenotypic ratio and genotypic ratio of the above cross shown in (ii)?

(iv) State the Mendel's law associated with this cross.

(v) Name two genetic disorders commonly seen in human males. [2017]

Ans. (i) If a plant bearing pure axial flowers (AA) is crossed with a plant bearing pure terminal flowers (aa), the phenotype of flowers of F_1-generation will be axial flowers while the genotype will be Aa.

(ii) The Punnett square representing the given cross is as follows

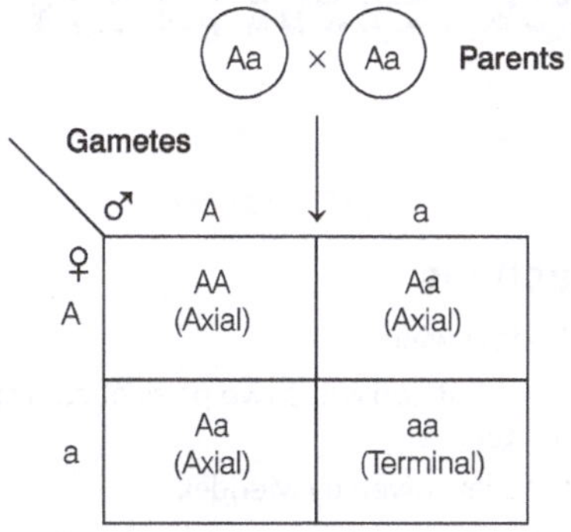

(iii) **Phenotypic ratio** 3(Axial) : 1 (Terminal)
Genotypic ratio 1(AA) : 2(Aa) : 1(aa)

(iv) Law of dominance is associated with this cross. It states that when two alternative forms of traits or characters are present in an organisim, only one factor expresses itself in F_1 progeny and the other remains suppressed.

(v) Colour blindness and haemophilia are the two genetic disorders commonly seen in human males.

Chapter Assessment

Section-I

1 Mark Questions

1. Name the following.
   (i) A cross that considers two pairs of contrasting characters.
   (ii) Second law given by Mendel.
   (iii) A sex-linked recessive disorder that results in failure of discrimination between red and green colour.

2. Correct and rewrite the following statements by changing the underlined words.
   (i) <u>Allele</u> is a unit of inheritance.
   (ii) <u>Polydactyly</u> is an inability to straighten the little finger.

3. Give suitable biological reason for the following.
   Rare cases of haemophiliac males occur but no haemophiliac female is yet found.

4. Match the following columns.

	Column I		Column II
A.	Homozygous	1.	It is the condition in which both the alleles are different
B.	Heterozygous	2.	It is the condition in which both the alleles are identical
C.	Phenotype	3.	It is the genetic makeup of an organism
D.	Genotype	4.	The characters which are visible from outside

5. Choose the correct answer from the four options given below.

(i) Mendel crossed pure breeding varieties, first by taking only one feature at a time. It was termed as
(a) monohybrid cross
(b) dihybrid cross
(c) test cross
(d) back cross

(ii) The Mendel's law which explains the dihybrid ratio is
(a) law of purity of gametes
(b) law of dominance
(c) law of segregation
(d) law of independent assortment

(iii) X-linked genes can never pass from
(a) father to daughter
(b) mother to son
(c) mother to daughter
(d) father to son

(iv) In general, the possibility of a female becoming haemophilic is
(a) most (b) 50% (c) rare (d) 25%

6. Fill in the blanks by using suitable words.
   (i) The fundamental physical and functional unit of heredity is known as ....
   (ii) An organism with two copies of the same allele is .... for that trait.
   (iii) .... is the ratio of dihybrid cross.
   (iv) In humans, ... type of sex chromosomes are present.
   (v) The family pedigree of Queen Victoria shows the inheritance of ....

7. State the main function of the following.
   (i) Genes
   (ii) Dominant allele

8. Mention one difference between each of the following pairs on the basis of what is given in the bracket.
   (i) Autosomes and Allosomes (no. of chromosomes)
   (ii) Polydactyly and Albinism (nature of trait)

9. Give suitable biological/technical terms for the following.
   (i) An inherited character with a detectable variant.
   (ii) Total absence of skin pigment.

10. Briefly explain the following terms.
    (i) Genetics
    (ii) Gene locus
    (iii) Sex-linked inheritance

11. Answer the following questions briefly.
    (i) What is meant by the term variation?
    (ii) Which type of gene fails to express itself in the presence of a contrasting allele?
    (iii) State the dominant and the recessive traits for the position of flower in pea plant.

2 Marks Questions

12. A pea plant with pure yellow (YY) round (RR) seeds was crossed with a plant having pure green (yy) wrinkled (rr) seeds. Explain the results obtained in F_2-generation with the help of a cross.

13. What is meant by linkage? State its significance in heredity.

3 Marks Questions

14. Explain briefly 'Mendel's Principles of Inheritance'.

15. Write a short note on sex-determination in human beings.

16. A colourblind child is born to a normal couple. Work out a cross to show how it is possible. Mention the sex of this child.

Section-II [5 Marks]

Structured Questions

17. A homozygous tall plant (T) bearing yellow seeds (Y) flowers is crossed with a homozygous dwarf plant (t) bearing green seeds (y)
    (i) Give the genotypes and phenotypes of the F_1-generation.
    (ii) Give the possible combinations of the gametes that can be obtained from the F_1-hybrid.
    (iii) Give the phenotypic dihybrid ratio of the offspring of the F_2-generation when two plants of the F_1-generation above are crossed.
    (iv) Would the results obtained be same if both the plants were homozygous dominant for tallness and of red colour?
    (v) Name the type of cross being worked upon.

18. Given below is a schematic diagram showing Mendel's experiment on sweet pea plants with yellow round seeds (YYRR) and green wrinkled seeds (yyrr). Answer the questions that follow

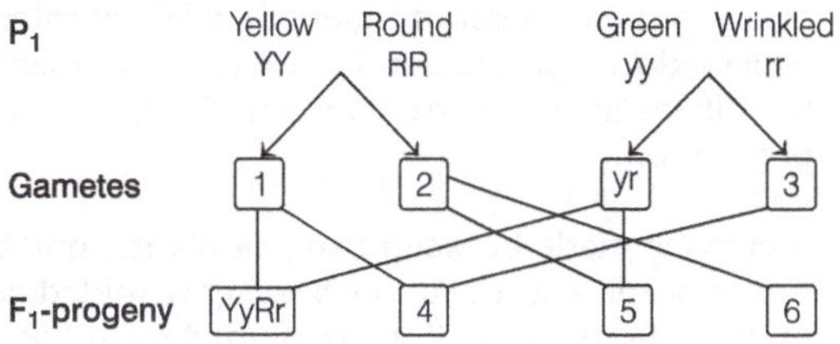

    (i) Complete the diagram by filling in the blanks numbered 1-6.
    (ii) Give the phenotype of progeny.
    (iii) Name the phenotypes produced in F_2 progeny by self-pollination of F_1 progeny.
    (iv) Name the law deduced by Mendel on the basis of above observations.
    (v) Which phenomenon is an exception to the law deduced by the above cross?

For explanations scan the given QR Code

Olympiad Section*

Brain Teasing Questions asked in Previous Olympiads

1 Alleles are variant forms of a gene that are located at the same position or genetic locus, on a chromosome. An allele frequency is calculated by dividing the number of times the allele of interest is observed in a population by the total number of all the alleles at that particular genetic locus in the population.

A cross is made between two pea plants, one bearing round seeds and the other bearing wrinkled seeds. All pea plants in the F_1 progeny had round seeds. When the F_1 progeny were self-pollinated and the F_2 progeny analysed, it was observed that 300 plants had round seeds while 100 plants had wrinkled seeds. What is the frequency of the dominant allele that is responsible for seed shape in the F_2 progeny? **[INJSO 2020]**

(a) 25% (b) 50%
(c) 75% (d) 100%

2 Black fur in mice (B) is dominant to brown fur (b). Long tails (T) are dominant to short tails (t). What fraction of the progeny of crosses (BbTt × BBtt) will be expected to have black fur and short tails? **[IJSO 2019, Doha, Qatar]**

(a) 1/16 (b) 3/16
(c) 3/8 (d) 1/2

3 A plant (parental) bearing red flowers is self-pollinated and two kinds of progeny are obtained: plants with red flowers and plants with white flowers in a ratio 3:1. Based on this observation, which one of the following statements regarding genes controlling the flower colour is correct. **[INJSO 2015]**

(a) The parental plant had one kind of allele for the flower colour
(b) Two genes control flower colour
(c) The parental plant had two different alleles for the flower colour
(d) All progeny plants with red flower colour have the same genotype as that of the parent

4 Haemophilia and colourblindness are the disorders caused by X-chromosome linked recessive gene. A woman has one X-chromosome, having gene for haemophilia and colourblindness. The other X- chromosome has wild allele for both the characters. She marries a man having phenotype normal for both the traits. Which of the following statements is most likely for the progeny? **[INJSO 2012]**

(a) All daughters haemophilic and colourblind
(b) 50% haemophilic sons and 50% colourblind sons
(c) 50% haemophilic colourblind sons and 50% normal sons
(d) 25% haemophilic daughters and 75% colourblind sons

5 A pure dwarf *Pisum sativum* (pea) plant was treated with Gibberellic Acid (GA_3). It then becomes tall. If this plant is crossed with a pure tall plant, what will be the phenotype in the next generation? **[INJSO 2011]**

(a) 100% tall
(b) 50% tall and 50% dwarf
(c) 75% tall and 25% dwarf
(d) 100% dwarf

6 Consider the following human disorders. **[NSEB 2010]**

(i) Haemophilia
(ii) Down's syndrome
(iii) Cystic fibrosis
(iv) Colour blindness
(v) Night blindness

Which of these disorders exhibit Mendelian pattern of inheritance?

(a) II, III and IV
(b) I, II and III
(c) I, III and V
(d) I, III and IV

Answers

1. (b) **2.** (d) **3.** (c) **4.** (c) **5.** (a) **6.** (d)

**These questions may or may not be asked in the examination, have been given just for additional practice required for olympiads, scholarship exams etc. For detailed explanations refer Page No. 247.*

CHAPTER 03

Absorption by Roots

Chapter Inside

• Roots • Processes Involved in Absorption • Absorption of Water and Minerals in Plants • Experiments Related to Absorption and Conduction of Water

Water acts as an excellent solvent and is required by plants for all their cellular activities. It is the major source of protoplasm. Without the constant supply of water and nutrients, the plants cannot carry on any of its physiological activities. The absorption of water and minerals from the soil takes place *via* roots of plants which is further conducted to all parts of the plant body through xylem. This constitutes the circulatory system of plants. It is necessary for their survival, growth and development.

In this chapter, we will explore the term root and thereafter its functions to show how water and minerals are carried by them from the soil.

Roots

The roots are branched parts at the lower end of a plant. They fix the plant in the soil (anchorage). They also help the plants to absorb mineral and water from the soil. The major absorption of water occurs from the root hair.

The structure of a typical root shows different zones as shown in the figure

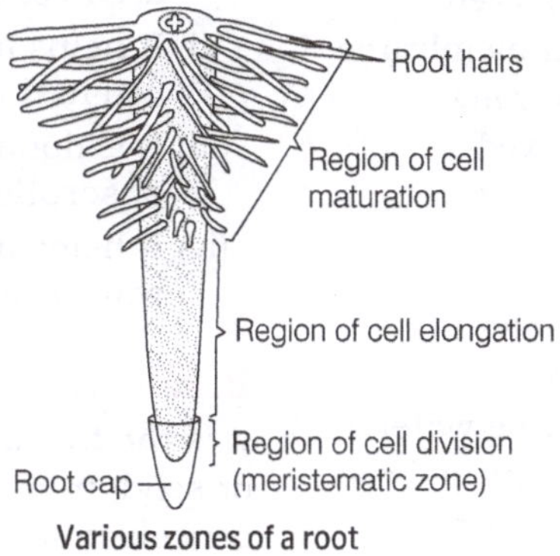

Various zones of a root

Characteristics of Roots for Absorbing Water

Following characteristics of roots are helpful in absorbing water

(i) Large Surface Area

The plants have extensive root system which grows rapidly in soil. Surface area of roots is enormous because of the presence of root hairs. If the root hairs of plant are laid from one end to another, a significant length in kilometers is covered. For example, in 4-month old rye plant, the total length of the root system is estimated to be 620 km with a daily increase of 5 km. This increases the area for the absorption of water.

(ii) Thin Walls

Root hairs present at the tip of root are thin-walled extensions of the outer walls of the epidermal cells of roots. Root hairs have vacuoles filled with cell sap (a liquid material). They are also surrounded by two layers, i.e. cell wall and cell membrane.

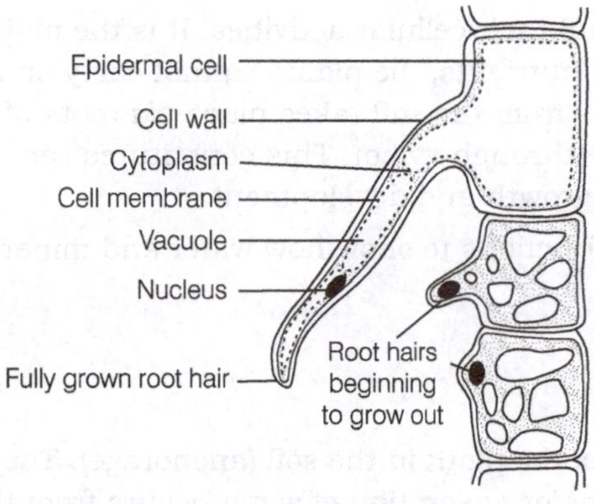

Root hair showing various parts

The cell wall is thin and freely permeable, i.e. permits free movement of water and dissolved substances to and from the cell. The cell membrane is very thin but semipermeable, i.e. it permits passage of water but with selected dissolved molecules.

(iii) Highly Concentrated Cell Sap

Root hair vacuoles, have some salts dissolved in them therefore, root hair cells have high concentrated cell sap than the surrounding water. This character is an important requirement to draw in water from outside by a process called osmosis, that is why, water diffuses from outside into the root cells.

Check Your LEARNING...

1 In which zone of a root, the root hairs are present?
2 Name the three characteristics of roots for absorbing water.
3 Which structure helps to increase the surface area of roots?
4 Name the organelle in roots, which is filled with highly concentrated cell sap.

Processes Involved in Absorption

The entire process of absorption of water and mineral salt is the result of some important processes such as imbibition, diffusion, osmosis, plasmolysis, etc.

1. Imbibition

It is a special phenomenon by which water or any other liquid is adsorbed by the solid particles of a substance, i.e. the living or dead plant cells by surface attraction.

The solid particles which imbibe water or any other liquid are called **imbibants**, while the liquid which is imbibed is called **imbibate**.

The **hydrophilic** or **water loving substances** have the tendency to imbibe water or moisture which causes them to swell up, e.g. swelling up of dry seeds, swelling and jamming of wooden doors, etc., on exposure to moist air/water.

Imbibition Pressure

The pressure developed by imbibant, when submerged in pure imbibing liquid is called imbibition pressure.

Significance of Imbibition

Imbibition plays following major roles

(i) It helps the seed to germinate by breaking the seed coats.

(ii) It helps in the movement of water from cell to cell in the plant body.

(iii) It is dominant in the initial stage of water absorption by roots.

(iv) It helps in ascent of sap (upward movement of water) *via* root hairs.

2. Diffusion

It is the free movement of molecules (be it gas, liquid or solid) from the region of their higher concentration to the region of their lower concentration without the expenditure of energy. It is a slow process and is independent of living system.

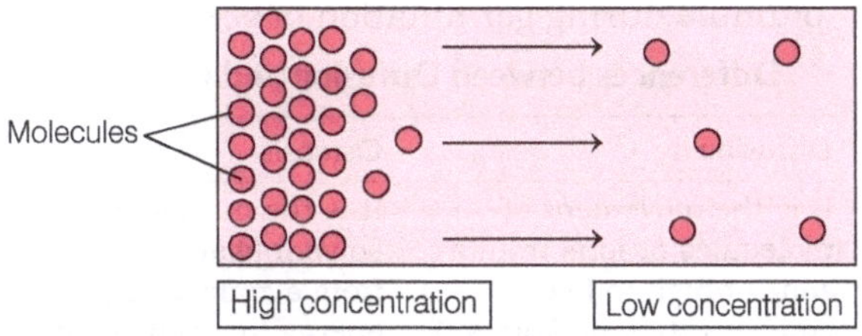

Diffusion of molecule

Diffusion Pressure

The diffusing particles in a medium exert a pressure which is directly proportional to their concentration. This pressure is known as **diffusion pressure**. Higher the concentration of diffusing particles, greater will be their diffusion pressure.

Significance of Diffusion

(i) It is a means of transport of gases in plants.
(ii) Transpiration of water from stomata occurs by diffusion.
(iii) It distributes ions and molecules into the protoplasm.

Differences between Imbibition and Diffusion

Imbibition	Diffusion
In this, the adsorption of solvent or water takes place by a solid substance.	It is the movement of molecules from the region of their high concentration to a region of low concentration.
The molecules of water or any other liquid are adsorbed at the surface of hydrophilic colloids (e.g. cellulose, starch, proteins, polypeptides, etc).	The diffusing particles/molecules get distributed uniformly throughout the available space.
The imbibant swells up but the swelling is less than volume of imbibate.	No overall change in volume is seen.

3. Osmosis

Discovery of osmosis was done by **Pfeffer**. It is defined as the movement of water molecules from the region of their higher concentration to a region of lower concentration through a semipermeable membrane.

Osmosis takes place spontaneously in response to a driving force. It is a passive process, i.e. does not require any input of energy.

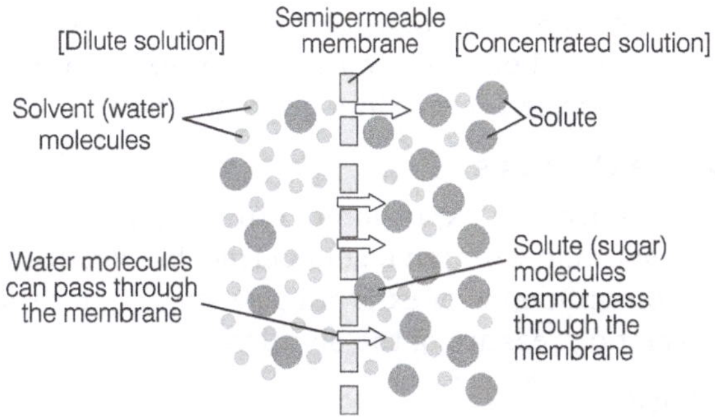

Schematic representation of osmosis and the nature of semipermeable membrane

Osmosis can be of following two types, depending upon the concentration of solute inside the cell and the surrounding medium.

(i) **Exosmosis** It is the **outward movement** of water molecules through the semipermeable membrane when the medium surrounding the cell is more concentrated (hypertonic). In this condition, cell shrinks and becomes **flaccid**.

(ii) **Endosmosis** It is the **inward movement** of water molecules through the semipermeable membrane when the medium surrounding the cell is less concentrated (hypotonic) or diluted than the medium inside the cell. In this condition, cell swells up and becomes **turgid**.

Types of Membranes

Depending upon the permeability the membranes are classified into four types

(i) **Impermeable membrane** It does not permit the passage of either a solvent or a solute molecules, e.g. cutinised or suberised cell walls.
(ii) **Permeable membrane** It allows the passage of both the solute and solvent molecules across it, e.g. cellulosic cell wall, lignified cell walls.
(iii) **Semipermeable membrane** It allows free movement of solvent but only few selected solute molecules can pass through it, e.g. membranes of parchment paper and copper ferrocyanide, etc.
(iv) **Differentially permeable membrane** It allows useful substances to diffuse in and harmful substances to diffuse out, e.g. all biological membranes.

Osmotic Pressure

For a solution it is the minimum pressure which must be applied to the solution in order to prevent the passage of solvent into the solution through a semipermeable membrane. It is measured by using an instrument called **osmometer**.

The osmotic pressure of a solution largely depends upon the ratio between the number of solute and solvent particles present in a given solution.

Reverse Osmosis

It is the process of expulsion of pure water from a solution through a semipermeable membrane under the influence of external pressure higher than the osmotic pressure of the solution.

Tonicity

It is the relative concentration of the solutions which determines the direction of the diffusion or osmosis. Based on the tonicity, solutions are divided into three main types

(i) **Hypotonic solution** For any two solutions with different concentrations, it is the solution having lower solute concentration or more solvent concentration. Hypotonic solutions have the tendency of exosmosis, i.e. they are the solvent providers.

(ii) **Isotonic solution** For any two solutions when the relative concentration of water molecules and the solute on either sides is equal. In this case, osmosis does not takes place.

(iii) **Hypertonic solution** For any two solutions, it is the solution having higher solute concentration or low solvent concentration. In this case, endosmosis takes place, i.e. water or solvent moves towards the solution.

Applications of Tonicity

Knowledge of tonicity helps in identifying the probable osmosis type in a cell as described below

(i) **If a cell is in contact with a hypotonic solution** then in the cell endosmosis takes place and cell becomes turgid.

(ii) **If a cell is in contact with an isotonic solution** then osmosis does not takes place and size of cell remains the same.

(iii) **If a cell is in contact with a hypertonic solution** then exosmosis takes place and cell shrinkes.

Significance of Osmosis

Osmosis is helpful in many ways as given below

(i) It helps in the maintenance of cell turgidity.

(ii) It plays a vital role in stomatal movement during transpiration.

(iii) It helps in the movement of liquids across biological membranes.

(iv) Absorption of water from soil by root hairs is due to osmosis.

(v) It regulates the opening and closing of stomata.

(vi) It plays a key role in growth of radicle and plumule during germination of seeds.

Differences between Diffusion and Osmosis

Diffusion	Osmosis
It is the movement of molecules or ions from a zone of high to low concentration or from a zone of lower free energy, until they are evenly spread in the medium.	It is the movement of solvent (water) molecules from a zone of higher free energy to a zone of lower free energy through a semipermeable membrane.
It can occur in any type of medium, i.e. solid, liquid or gaseous.	It occurs only in liquid medium.
Semipermeable membrane is not involved.	Semipermeable membrane is involved.

Check Your LEARNING...

1 Which process is the means of transport of gases in plants?
2 Which membrane allows the movement of both solvent and solute across it?
3 Give an example of a semipermeable membrane.
4 How is osmotic pressure measured?
5 What is an isotonic solution?
6 Mention one significance of osmosis.

4. Turgidity

When water moves into a plant cell, the vacuole gets bigger, pushing the cell membrane against cell wall. This increases the pressure within the cell making it **firm** or **turgid**. The pressure exerted by the cell wall stops too much water to enter into the cell and prevents cell lysis (bursting of cell membrane).

Two kinds of pressures are generated by a turgid cell, namely turgor pressure and wall pressure.

(i) **Turgor Pressure** (TP) It is the pressure exerted by the protoplasm against the cell wall in the cell.

(ii) **Wall Pressure** (WP) It is the back pressure exerted by the cell wall against the protoplasm of a fully turgid cell.

Normally, wall pressure is equal and opposite to turgor pressure.

Significance of Turgidity

(i) It provides rigidity to soft tissues like leaves in a plant and maintains proper shape.

(ii) It helps the roots to push through the hard grounds.

(iii) The opening and closing of stomata is regulated by turgidity.

(iv) It develops root pressure in root cells.

(v) Turgor movements results in rapid drooping of leaves in *Mimosa* plant.

5. Flaccidity

It is the condition in which a cell looses water from its cytoplasm due to exosmosis. Such a cell is known as **flaccid cell**, e.g. wilting property of leaves when plant is exposed to the Sun. It is basically a reverse process of turgidity.

Relation between Turgor Pressure, Wall Pressure and Osmotic Pressure

When a cell is in a turgid state, it is said to be in equilibrium, as no more water enters or gets out of the cell.

Turgor pressure balances the wall pressure and osmotic pressure, as there is no absorption of water even when concentration of solutes inside cell may be greater than the outside.

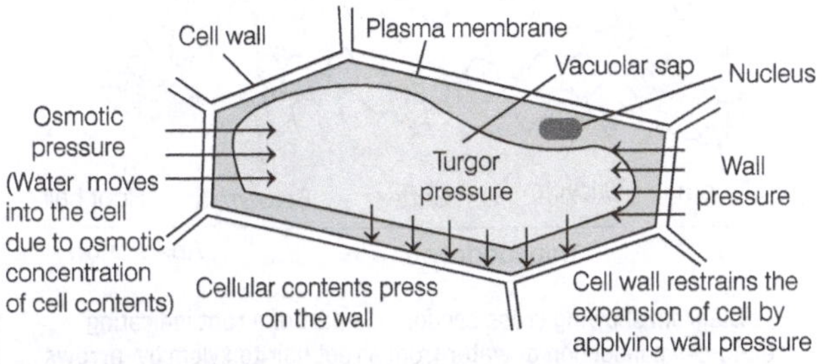

Relationship between the osmotic, turgor and wall pressure

6. Plasmolysis

It occurs when water moves out of the cell, when it is placed in a hypertonic solution, due to exosmosis. Due to plasmolysis, plant cell loses its original appearance, i.e. protoplasm shrinks and plasma membrane is pulled away from the cell wall. This makes cell look flaccid in appearance.

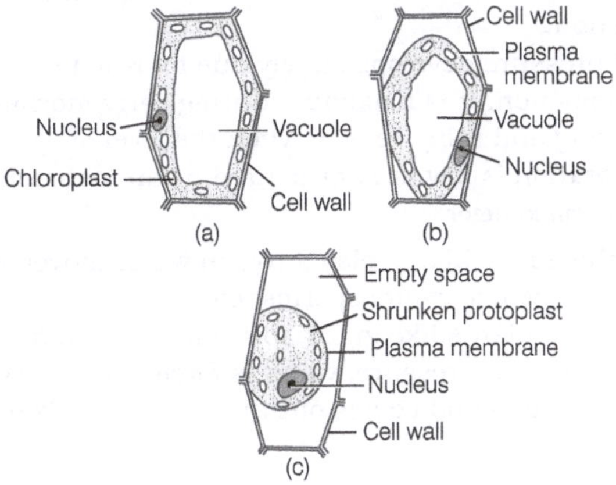

Diagrammatic representation of plasmolysis (a) Fully turgid cell (b) Partially plasmolysed cell (c) Plasmolysed cell

Significance of Plasmolysis

(i) It is used in killing bacteria that grow on or contaminate food items, such as meat, jams, pickles, etc., by adding large amount of salt or sugar in it. In such conditions, the bacteria die due to the loss of water (plasmolysis) from their cell body.

(ii) It can also be used to kill weeds which are grown in play grounds, gardens, etc. This is achieved by sprinkling large amount of salt at their base.

7. Deplasmolysis

It is exactly the reverse of plasmolysis in which the protoplasm of the cell returns to its original position when favourable conditions are provided, e.g. when the cell is placed in pure water or hypotonic solution. This again makes the cell normal (turgid) and it attains the original shape and size.

For example, if a plant cell is placed in salt solution, it becomes plasmolysed but if the same cell is placed in tap water, its original state will reappear, i.e. it will become deplasmolysed.

Differences between Plasmolysis and Deplasmolysis

Plasmolysis	Deplasmolysis
It occurs when tissue cell is placed in hypertonic solution.	It occurs when tissue cell is placed in hypotonic solution.
It is a result of exosmosis.	It is a result of endosmosis.
It is not reversible after a long period of time.	It is reversible even after a long period of time.

Check Your LEARNING...

1. How are wall pressure and turgor pressure related ?
2. What is the relationship among turgor, wall and osmotic pressure?
3. Give the biological reason of adding extra salt in pickles and sugar in jams.
4. How can we deplasmolyse the cell?
5. Which processes of osmosis is involved in case of plasmolysis and deplasmolysis?

Absorption of Water and Minerals in Plants

In plants, a complex movement of materials takes place in different directions. The water taken up by the roots, the absorbed minerals and the food manufactured by leaves, all need to be distributed to various parts of a plant. The short distance transportation is carried out by the processes like diffusion and osmosis as discussed earlier in this chapter.

However, for long distance transport, special vascular tissues are present in plants. These are

(i) **Xylem** This is mainly responsible for the transport of water and minerals from roots to aerial parts of the plant.

(ii) **Phloem** This is mainly responsible for the transport of organic and inorganic substances such as food, etc., from leaves to other parts of the plant.

Types of Absorption

Absorption of water or minerals by roots takes place by the following two processes

(i) **Passive absorption or Passive transport** It is the mechanism of movement of substances (ions and molecules) into root cells simply by diffusion, i.e. without the expenditure of energy from the region of their higher concentration to the region of their lower concentration.

(ii) **Active absorption or Active transport** It is the mechanism of transport of molecules (ions) against the concentration gradient, i.e. from the region of lower concentration to the higher concentration with the help of energy in the form of ATP.

Direction of molecules in active transport is just opposite to that of diffusion. Nutrient molecules such as potassium, zinc, nitrates, sulphates, etc., do not pass through the cell membrane because of their higher concentration inside the root cells. Thus, these molecules are forcibly carried inside the cell, against their concentration gradient.

Differences between Active and Passive Absorptions

Active absorption	Passive absorption
It takes place from the region of lower to higher concentration.	It takes place from the region of higher to lower concentration.
Expenditure of energy in the form of ATP is required.	Energy is not required.
It requires carriers for transport of ions across the cell membrane.	It does not require carriers for the transport of ions.

Ascent of Sap (Water Movement up a Plant)

It is the upward movement of water along with minerals from roots to upper parts of the plant (such as leaves and other growing points) by the stems. It occurs through the tracheary elements of xylem.

Path followed by water during transport is given below

Root hair → Cortex cells → Endodermis → Passage cells → Xylem vessels

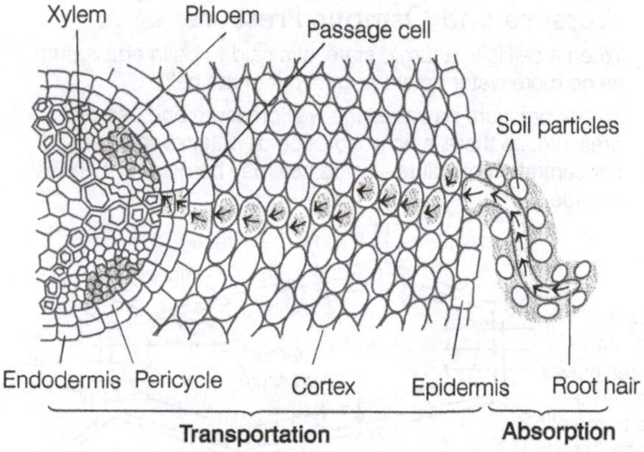

Diagram showing cross-section of a part of a root indicating cell-to-cell conduction of water from a root hair to xylem by arrows

Forces Responsible for Ascent of Sap

The upward movement of water is brought about by the virtue of three main forces.

These are as follows

1. Root Pressure

It is the pressure that develops in the xylem of roots mainly in cortical cells due to inflow of water. It pushes the water and minerals in the upward direction.

Root pressure develops largely due to osmotic phenomenon. It is maximum during early morning of spring and rainy season when the level of evaporation is low. It is measured by an instrument called **manometer**.

But this force fails to play a role in water movement in tall trees like gymnosperms, etc.

In certain plants like grass, tomato, etc., due to excessive root pressure, water is forced all the way through stem and comes out through the ends of leaf veins as tiny drops along the margins. This loss of excessive water is called **guttation**.

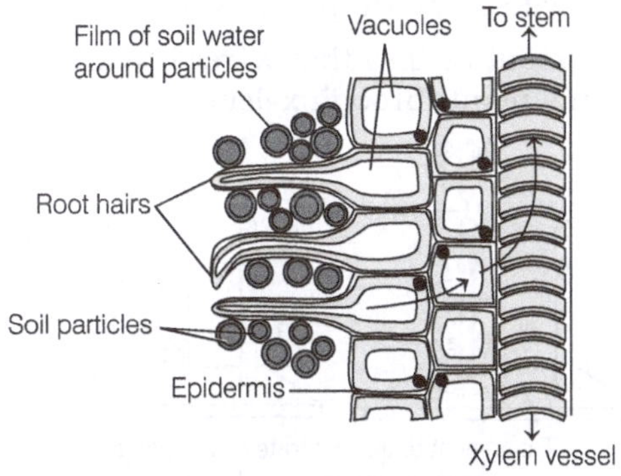

Root pressure builds up due to osmosis and turgidity of root cells, and up into the xylem vessels

2. Capillary Action

It is one of the forces contributing to ascent of sap. In this tracheids and vessels act as narrow tubes. This causes the water from a lower level to rise and fill up the vacuum created by the loss of water due to transpiration from the leaves.

Narrower the diameter of a tube, greater will be the height of water rising in it exerting a force called **capillary force**.

3. Transpirational Pull

This force is developed due to transpiration. In this, the water is lost from the leaf cells (mesophyll) to the intercellular space and develops a strong negative water potential. This negative pressure exerts an upward pull over the water column. Thus, this pull is called transpirational pull. This pull occurs due to involvement of two forces

(i) **Cohesive** The tendency of water molecules to stick together by strong force of attraction called **cohesive force**.

(ii) **Adhesive** The tendency of water molecules to stick to the walls of xylem vessels due to adhesive properties of water to cell wall called **adhesive force**.

Both cohesive and adhesive forces ensure that the water column is not broken.

Descent of Sap

The downward movement of sap is relatively simple. The manufactured food in leaves gets dissolved in water and flows down due to the force of gravity.

Experiments Related to Absorption and Conduction of Water

Experiment 1

Experiment to demonstrate the absorption of water by plant roots.

Procedure Take two test tubes *A* and *B* and fill both of them with water. In the first tube *A*, insert a freshly plucked plant (like balsam) with intact roots dipped in water. Add a few drops of oil to reduce water loss by evaporation.

Prepare a similar setup with test tube *B* without the plant. This acts as a control setup.

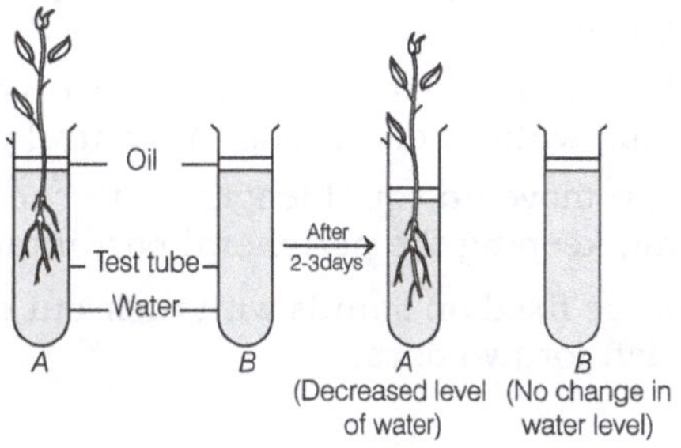

Demonstration of water by plant roots

Mark the level of water in both the tubes.

Leave the setup for a day or two and observe.

Observations The level of water in the test tube *A* decreases while no change is observed in test tube *B*. This indicates that the water is lost in test tube *A* and was absorbed by the roots.

Experiment 2

To show that xylem tissues conduct water in a plant.

Procedure Take a young medium-sized balsam plant. Wash it and place it in a beaker containing an eosin dye solution (pink) in water. It is to be noted that the roots should be completely submerged in the solution.

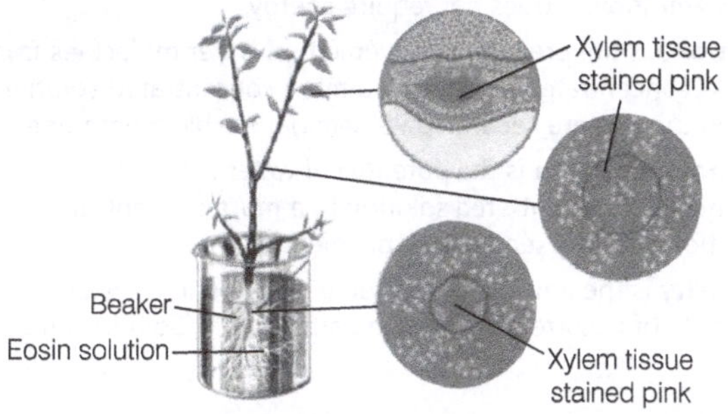

Experiment to show that water is conducted upwards through xylem

The setup is allowed to stand for about 3-4 hrs. After the period of 3-4 hrs, take the plant out of the solution and wash it in tap water. Cut and make a Transverse Section (TS) of the stem, leaves or roots. Examine them under a microscope.

You will observe that the xylem vessels are distinctly visible as they have taken the stain indicating that the solution moved through the xylem.

Experiment 3

To demonstrate the conduction of water through xylem by ringing experiment.

Procedure Take two balsam plants and cut them under water in order to prevent bubbles from entering in roots. Keep the cut ends of the plants dipped in water.

In setup *A*, remove about 3 cm long outer ring of stem (phloem) without disturbing the central part.

In setup *B*, remove an equal length of the central part (xylem), keeping the peripheral part intact.

The shoots are fixed on stands with their cut ends in water and left for two days.

Observation The leaves in setup *A* remain turgid and stand out almost normally while in setup *B*, leaves get wilted and drop downwards.

The experiment verifies that water is conducted upward in a plant through xylem.

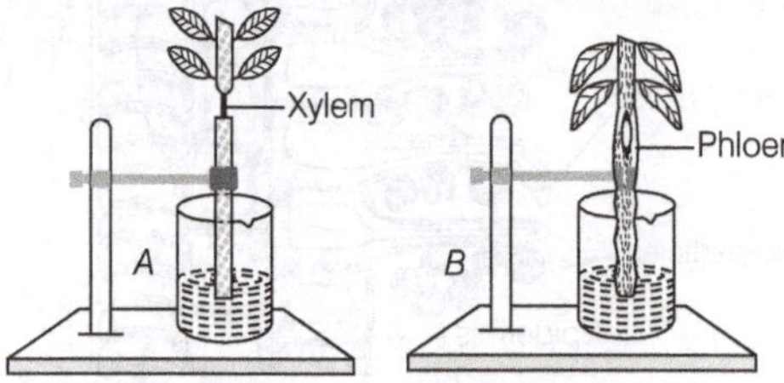

Experiment to demonstrate conduction of water upwards through xylem

Check Your LEARNING...

1 How does long distance transport of water and minerals in plants take place?
2 Name the three main forces responsible for ascent of sap.
3 Which force fails to play a role in water movement in tall trees?
4 What is the colour of eosin dye solution?
5 Which process in plants is demonstrated using ringing experiment?

QUiCK Revision

- **Absorption of water and minerals** in plants takes place with the help of xylem. It is necessary for survival, growth and development of plant.
- **Water** is the most important component required by plant for all its activities such as transportation, transpiration, photosynthesis, mechanical support, etc.
- **Mineral nutrients** are required by plants for growth and cellular activities.
- **Roots** form the major organ for absorption of water from soil and **root hairs** play a distinct role in absorption.
- **Imbibition** is a process of adsorption of water by solid particles of a substance without forming a solution.
- **Diffusion** is a process of movement of molecules from a region of their higher concentration to a region of their lower concentration. It does not require energy.
- **Osmosis** is the process of movement of water molecules from a less concentrated solution to a more concentrated solution when the two are separated *via* semipermeable membrane.
- **Osmotic pressure** is the potential of water molecules to move from a less concentrated solution to a more concentrated solution across a semipermeable membrane.
- **Tonicity** is the amount of tension developed in a system on account of occurrence of solute particles in it. Solutions may be isotonic, hypertonic or hypotonic when the tonicity of two solutions is compared.
- **Turgidity** is the condition of a cell in which it cannot accommodate more water.
- **Turgor pressure** The pressure exerted by the protoplasm against the cell wall is called turgor pressure or pressure potential.
- **Plasmolysis** is the shrinkage of protoplast and its movement away from the cell wall due to exosmosis. It occurs when a cell is placed in hypertonic solution. Reversal of plasmolysis is **deplasmolysis.**
- **Water absorption** in plants occurs mainly by two mechanisms, i.e. active absorption and passive absorption.
  - **Passive absorption** is the movement of substances into root cells by simple diffusion without using energy.
  - **Active absorption** is the uptake of substances against the concentration gradient by using energy stored in ATP molecules.
- **Ascent of sap** is the long distance transport of water *via* xylem tissue. It is due to many forces such as root pressure, cohesion and adhesion, transpiration pull and capillarity.
- **Root pressure** is the positive hydrostatic pressure developed in the roots due to excess of water absorption.

Chapter Practice

Section-I

1 Mark Questions

1. Name the following.
   (i) A major component of all the cells, i.e. a universal medium in which all substances can be dissolved.
   (ii) A mineral required for the synthesis of chlorophyll in plants.
   (iii) Name the phenomenon by which living or dead plant cells absorb water by surface attraction. **[2012]**
   (iv) Name the process by which root hairs absorb water from the soil. **[2017]**
   (v) The outward movement of water molecules causing the cell to become flaccid.
   (vi) The process which causes raisins to swell, when kept in water.
   (vii) A solution which causes water to move into the cell making it swell up.
   (viii) Back pressure exerted by the cell wall against the protoplasm.
   (ix) Process of uptake of mineral ions against the concentration gradient using energy from the cell. **[2016, 15]**
   (x) The force that forms continuous water column in xylem.

Ans. (i) Water (ii) Magnesium (Mg^{2+})
(iii) Imbibition (iv) Osmosis
(v) Exosmosis (vi) Endosmosis
(vii) Hypotonic (viii) Wall pressure
(ix) Active transport (x) Cohesion

2. Correct and rewrite the following statements by changing the underlined words.
   (i) The first process by which water gets into the seed coat during germination is <u>osmosis</u>.
   (ii) Free movement of solutes in and out of the cell takes place across the <u>cell membrane</u>. **[2017]**
   (iii) The plasma membrane present in plant cell is <u>impermeable</u> to solutes.
   (iv) Osmosis is <u>active</u> transport of molecules in cells.
   (v) The cell sap of root hair is <u>hypotonic</u>. **[2018]**
   (vi) <u>Xylem</u> transports starch from the leaves to all parts of the plant body. **[2018]**
   (vii) The upward movement of water through xylem is called <u>guttation</u>.

Ans. (i) The first process by which water gets into the seed coat during germination is imbibition.
(ii) Free movement of solutes in and out of the cell takes place across the cell wall.
(iii) The plasma membrane present in plant cell is semipermeable to solutes.
(iv) Osmosis is passive transport of molecules in cells.
(v) The cell sap of root hair is hypertonic.
(vi) Phloem transports starch from the leaves to all parts of the plant body.
(vii) The upward movement of water through xylem is called ascent of sap.

3. Give biological reasons for the following.
   (i) The wooden frames of doors get jammed during the monsoon season. **[2013]**
   (ii) A closed can of dried seeds bursts open if water somehow enters the can.
   (iii) A normal osmotic concentration of blood is maintained in our body.
   (iv) Potato cubes when placed in water become firm and increase in size. **[2011]**
   (v) Plants growing in fertilised soil are often found to wilt if the soil is not adequately watered. **[2018]**
   (vi) The fishes living in freshwater cannot survive in sea water.
   (vii) Microorganisms like bacteria and fungi do not grow in pickles, jams and squashes, etc.
   (viii) Root hairs become flaccid and droop when excess fertilisers are added to the moist soil around them. **[2019]**

Ans. (i) Wooden doors swell up in rainy season due to imbibition.
(ii) The dried seeds absorb the water by imbibition and swell up. The swelling creates pressure and exerts it on the walls. This can cause the seeds to burst open the closed can.
(iii) Osmotic concentration is maintained in order to prevent dehydration of cells which lead to their shrinkage.
(iv) Endosmosis takes place when potato cubes are placed in water that acts as a hypotonic medium. The cells of potato become turgid and potato cubes become firm. Thus, they increase in size.
(v) If the soil is fertilised and not well-watered, the concentration of the soil solution becomes high and water begins to move from the root hair cells to soil due to exosmosis. If this process continues for a long time, plasmolysis takes place and it leads to wilting of plants.

(vi) As compared to freshwater, the sea water is saline and is hypertonic for freshwater fishes. It causes plasmolysis of cells in the fishes due to which they die.

(vii) Pickles, jams, squashes, etc., are preserved with hypertonic solution of sugar or salt which causes plasmolysis of microbial cells.

(viii) When fertilisers are added to the moist soil around root hairs, it will form hypertonic solution, resulting the protoplasm to shrink. Hence, the root hairs become limp or flaccid.

4. (i) Match the following columns.

Column I	Column II
A. Xylem	1. Semipermeable
B. Phloem	2. Permeable
C. Cell membrane	3. Downward flow of sap
D. Root pressure	4. Upward flow of water
E. Cell wall	5. Manometer

(ii) Match the following columns.

Column I	Column II
A. Plasmolysis	1. Active transport
B. Absorption of ions from soil against concentration gradient	2. Exerted by cell sap on cell wall
C. Turgor pressure	3. Hypertonic medium
D. Phloem	4. Adsorption of water by living or dead cells of plants
E. Imbibition	5. Translocation of food

Ans. (i) A–4, B–3, C–1, D–5, E–2
(ii) A–3, B–1, C–2, D–5, E–4

5. Choose the correct answer from the four options given below.

(i) A component common in both the processes, i.e. absorption of water and transportation of minerals in plants is
(a) air (b) water
(c) soil (d) light

Ans. (b)

(ii) Root hairs are surrounded by two layers, among these, which one is selectively permeable to certain specific substances only ?
(a) cell wall
(b) cell membrane
(c) cytoplasm
(d) None of these

Ans. (b)

(iii) Marine fish when placed in tap water bursts because of [2017]
(a) endosmosis (b) exomosis
(c) diffusion (d) plasmolysis

Ans. (a)

(iv) A cell is placed in a solution and shrinkage of this cell is observed in the medium. The solution is
(a) hypertonic (b) isotonic
(c) hypotonic (d) None of these

Ans. (a)

(v) A plant *Mimosa pudica* shows folding of its leaves within 2-3 sec when touched. This happens due to the presence of
(a) flaccid movements (b) turgor movements
(c) plasmolysis (d) osmosis

Ans. (b)

(vi) A plant cell may burst when [2016]
(a) turgor pressure equalises wall pressure
(b) turgor pressure exceeds wall pressure
(c) wall pressure exceeds turgor pressure
(d) None of the above

Ans. (b)

(vii) The pressure developed in the roots due to continuous inward movement of water by cell to cell osmosis [Semester I 2021]
(a) Root pressure (b) Wall pressure
(c) Turgor pressure (d) Air pressure

Ans. (c)

(viii) When a cell is placed in a .... solution, it becomes plasmolysed. [Semester I 2021]
(a) distilled water (b) hypertonic
(c) isotonic (d) hypotonic

Ans. (b)

(ix) Deplasmolysis occurs when a plasmolysed cell is placed in [2023]
(a) concentrated salt solution
(b) tap water
(c) concentrated sugar solution
(d) hypertonic salt solution

Ans. (b)

(x) Water absorption by roots occurs when
(a) solute concentration is high in cell sap
(b) solute concentration in soil is high
(c) there is no light
(d) the plant is respiring rapidly

Ans. (a)

(xi) For absorption of water and minerals, the effective process is
(a) diffusion (b) osmosis
(c) ionic exchange (d) All of these

Ans. (d)

(xii) What role does the xylem tissue play in plants? [Semester I 2021]
(a) Conducts water and minerals in leaves
(b) Does not conduct water and minerals in stems
(c) Conducts food and nutrients to roots
(d) Conducts food nutrients to all parts of the plant

Ans. (a)

(xiii) A shoot from a balsam plant is kept in a beaker containing eosin solution (pink). The pink colour will be distinctly seen in the [Semester I 2021]

(a) xylem (b) phloem
(c) epidermis (d) cortex

Ans. (a)

(xiv) The root pressure is inhibited by

(a) decreased aeration
(b) fluctuating temperature
(c) increased evaporation
(d) All of the above

Ans. (d)

6. Fill in the blanks by using suitable words.

(i) Root hair is an extension of ....
(ii) Water potential of a cell is lowered by the addition of ....
(iii) When plants absorb water from the soil, the water potential of root cell is .... than the soil.
(iv) .... is the phenomenon of contraction of the cytoplasm from the cell wall. [2011]
(v) The concentration of the cell sap .... as plasmolysis takes place.
(vi) The condition opposite to turgid is ....
(vii) Metabolic energy of the cell is utilised in .... absorption of water.
(viii) .... does not require an energy input to operate.
(ix) Root pressure can be measured by ....

Ans. (i) epidermal cell (ii) solutes
(iii) lower (iv) Plasmolysis
(v) increases (vi) flaccid
(vii) active (viii) Passive transport
(ix) manometer

7. The following paragraph is related to absorption of water from the soil. Copy and complete the following paragraph by selecting the correct word from those given in the box. You may use the term only once.

exosmosis, hypertonic, osmosis, isotonic, hypotonic, cortical, endosmosis

Water enters the root hair from the soil by the process of .... This is because the solution in the soil is ......, whereas the cell sap in the root hair cell is .... The water then passess through the ...... cells by cell to cell ...... and reaches the xylem of the root. [2014]

Ans. Water enters the root hair from the soil by the process of **endosmosis**. This is because the solution in the soil is **hypotonic**, whereas the cell sap in the root hair cell is **hypertonic**. The water then passes through the **cortical** cells by cell to cell **osmosis** and reaches the xylem of the root.

8. Choose the odd one out from the following terms given below and name the category to which other three belong.

(i) Soil water, Root hair, Cell of cortex, Epidermis, Xylem
(ii) Hypertonic solution, Endosmosis, Turgid cell, Deplasmolysis.

Ans. (i) **Odd term** is soil water.
Rest others are parts of roots.
(ii) **Odd term** is hypertonic solution.
Rest three are related to increased protoplast volume.

9. Given below are two sets of six terms. In each case, rewrite the terms in correct order of logical sequence.

(i) Cell wall, Nuclear membrane, Nucleoplasm, Cytoplasm, Nucleolus, Cell membrane
(ii) Xylem, Soil water, Cortical cells, Root hair[2023]

Ans. (i) Cell wall → Cell membrane → Cytoplasm → Nuclear membrane → Nucleoplasm → Nucleolus
(ii) Soil water → Root hair → Cortical cells → Xylem

10. Expand the following biological abbreviations.

(i) OP (ii) WP

Ans. (i) Osmotic Pressure (ii) Wall Pressure

11. State the exact location of the following.

(i) Root cap
(ii) Phloem

Ans. (i) Root cap is found at the meristemetic zone, i.e. region of cell division of a root.
(ii) Phloem is located on the outer side of the vascular bundle.

12. Given below are certain structures. Fill in the blanks with their suitable functions.

(i) Root hairs ....
(ii) Turgidity ....
(iii) Active absorption ....
(iv) Xylem .... [2015]
(v) Phloem ....

Ans. (i) Water absorption
(ii) Strengthens soft parts of plants
(iii) Mineral absorption
(iv) Upward water transport in plants
(v) Translocation of food molecules

13. Mention one diffference between each of the following pairs on the basis of what is given in the bracket.

(i) Diffusion and Osmosis (definition) [2015]
(ii) Endosmosis and Exosmosis (movement of water)
(iii) Hypertonic solution and Hypotonic solution (osmotic pressure)

(iv) Osmotic pressure and Turgor pressure (function)

(v) Turgor pressure and Wall pressure (definition) [2014]

(vi) Flaccid condition and Turgid condition (type of medium)

(vii) Active transport and Diffusion (significance in plants) [2017]

Ans. (i) Difference between diffusion and osmosis is as follows

Diffusion	Osmosis
Movement of molecules of substance from the region of higher concentration to lower one when two are in direct contact.	Movement of water (solvent) from the region of higher concentration to lower one through semipermeable membrane.

(ii) Differences between endosmosis and exosmosis is as follows

Endosmosis	Exosmosis
Water moves into the cell.	Water moves out of the cell.

(iii) Difference between hypertonic solution and hypotonic solution is as follows

Hypertonic solution	Hypotonic solution
Its osmotic pressure is more.	Its osmotic pressure is less.

(iv) Difference between osmotic pressure and turgor pressure is as follows

Osmotic pressure	Turgor pressure
It helps in the absorption of water.	It helps in keeping the plant erect.

(v) Difference between turgor pressure and wall pressure is as follows

Turgor pressure	Wall pressure
Pressure exerted by the protoplasm against the cell wall.	Back pressure exerted by the cell wall on the protoplasm.

(vi) Difference between flaccid condition and turgid condition is as follows

Flaccid condition	Turgid condition
It is a condition when cell is placed in a hypertonic solution.	It happens when a cell is placed in hypotonic solution.

(vii) Difference between active transport and diffusion is as follows

Active transport	Diffusion
Uptake of mineral ions into root cells occurs through active transport.	Exchange of gases between the plant and its outside environment occurs through diffusion.

14. Give biological/technical terms for the following.

(i) A process that helps in ascent of sap *via* root hairs.

(ii) Movement of molecules of a substance from their higher concentration to lower concentration when they are in direct contact. [2018]

(iii) A membrane which allows the passage of molecules selectively. [2012]

(iv) A solution in which the relative concentration of water molecules and solute on either sides of cell membrane is the same. [2013]

Ans. (i) Imbibition

(ii) Diffusion

(iii) Selectively permeable membrane

(iv) Isotonic solution

15. Briefly explain the following terms.

(i) Imbibants

(ii) Osmosis [2012]

(iii) Tonicity

(iv) Turgor pressure [2015]

(v) Flaccid cell

(vi) Root pressure

Ans. (i) The solid particles which imbibe water are called imbibants.

(ii) The diffusion of water (solvent) from its region of higher concentration to its region of lower concentration through a semipermeable membrane is called osmosis.

(iii) The ability of a solution surrounding a cell to cause that cell to gain or lose water is called tonicity.

(iv) The pressure exerted by cell contents on a plant cell wall is called turgor pressure.

(v) When a cell looses water from its cytoplasm due to exosmosis then that cell is called flaccid cell.

(vi) The pressure that develops in the xylem due to inflow of water is called root pressure. It pushes water and minerals in the upward direction.

16. Answer the following questions briefly.

(i) What role does root pressure play in water movement in plants?

(ii) Which two forces are involved in transpiration pull theory?

(iii) Is there a need of long distance transport system in plants?

(iv) How does most of the water move within the roots?

(v) Keep some freshly cut flowers in a solution of food colour. Wait for some time for the dye to rise in the flower, when the stem of the flower is held up in light, coloured strand can be seen inside. Can this experiment demonstrate which tissue is conducting water up the stem?

Ans. (i) Root pressure is responsible for pushing up water to small height in the stem. It re-establishes the continuous chain of water molecules in the xylem, which often break under the enormous tensions created by transpiration.

(ii) The two forces are

(a) **Cohesion** The attraction among water molecules.

(b) **Adhesion** The attraction between water molecules and walls of xylem.

(iii) Yes, the long distance transport system is needed in plants as substances have to moved across very long distances like to flowers, roots, leaves, etc., for which diffusion and osmosis are not sufficient.

(iv) Most of the water moves by transpiration pull, cohesion and adhesion property of water molecules within the root.

(v) Yes, it shows that xylem tissues conduct water in the stem.

2 Marks Questions

17. Write any two functions of roots.

Ans. Two functions of roots are

(i) They fix the plant in the soil (anchorage).

(ii) They help the plants to absorb water and minerals from the soil.

18. List any two importance of diffusion in plants.

Ans. Two importance of diffusion in plants are as follows

(i) Gaseous exchange with the atmosphere through stomata.

(ii) Some ions are absorbed by the simple diffusion during passive salt intake.

19. State any two functions of turgor pressure.

Ans. Two functions of turgor pressure are as follows

(i) It helps in movement in plants.

(ii) It also aids in cell enlargement.

20. What is active transport? **[2023]**

Ans. Active transport is defined as a process that involves the movement of molecules from a region of lower concentration to a region of higher concentration against a gradient with the help of energy in the form of ATP.

3 Marks Questions

21. Roots possess certain characteristics that help them absorb maximum water. Write about three of them.

Ans. Roots are able to absorb maximum water due to the following characteristics

(i) **Large surface area** This is due to the presence of root hairs, which increase the area for water absorption.

(ii) **Thin walls of root hairs** Thin and selectively permeable cell membrane of root hair allow passage of water and selected dissolved molecules.

(iii) **Highly concentrated cell sap** In root hair vacuole, some salts are dissolved in it thus, making cell sap highly concentrated. It allows for endosmosis.

22. Write any three significances of the phenomenon turgidity.

Ans. Three significances of turgidity are

(i) It provides rigidity to soft tissues like leaves and maintains proper shape.

(ii) The phenomenon regulates the opening and closing of stomata.

(iii) It helps the roots to push through the hard grounds.

23. Will the ascent of sap be possible without the cohesion and adhesion of water molecules? Explain.

Ans. The cohesion and adhesion of water molecules alone creates pressure of about 350 atm, which is responsible for conducting water to great height in tall trees without breaking the water column. On the other hand, all forces such as imbibition pressure and root pressure have been found to create pressure of only 50 atm. So, ascent of sap is not possible without cohesion and adhesion of water molecules.

Section-II **[5 Marks]**

Structured Questions

1. The diagram given below represents a layer of epidermal cells showing a fully grown root hair. Study the diagram and answer the questions that follow. **[2011]**

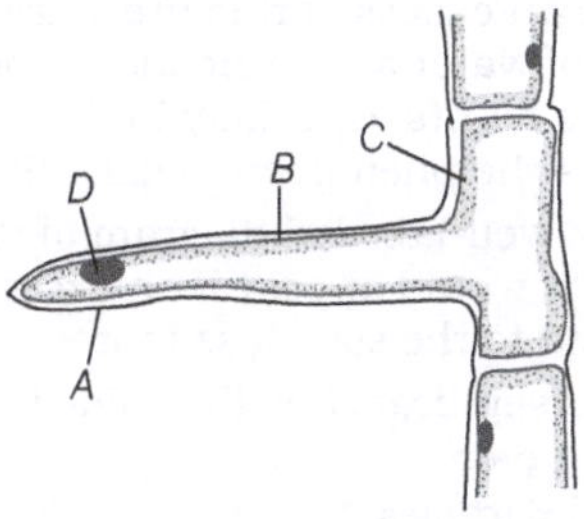

(i) Name the parts labelled as *A*, *B*, *C* and *D*.

(ii) The root hair cell is in a turgid state. Name and explain the process that caused this state.

(iii) Mention one distinct difference between the parts labelled as *A* and *B*.

(iv) Define root hairs.

(v) Write any two characteristics possessed by root in order to draw water from soil.

Ans. (i) The parts *A*, *B*, *C* and *D* can be labelled as

A – Cell wall of root hair

B – Cell membrane of root hair

C – Cytoplasm

D – Nucleus

(ii) The soil medium is hypotonic, thus endosmosis would have occurred, due to which the root hair cell absorbed water and became turgid.

(iii) *A* (cell wall) is freely permeable, whereas *B* (cell membrane) is semipermeable.

(iv) Root hairs are thin-walled extensions of outer wall of epidermal cells of roots present at the tip of root.

(v) Following characteristics are possessed by roots in order to draw water from soil

(a) Plants have extensive root system which grows rapidly in soil.

(b) Root hairs provide large surface area which increase the area for absorption of water.

2. The figure given below is diagrammatic representation of a part of the cross-section of the root hair zone. Study the same and then answer the questions that follow. **[2016]**

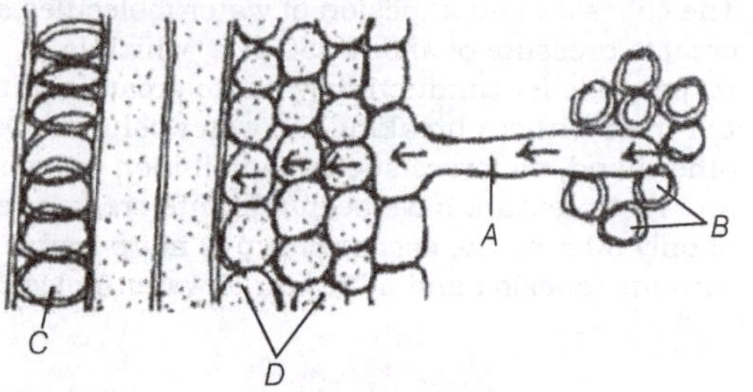

(i) Name the parts indicated by the guidelines *A-D*.

(ii) Which is the process that enables the passage of water from the soil into the root hair?

(iii) Name the pressure that is responsible for the movement of water in the direction indicated by the arrows. Define it.

(iv) Due to an excess of this pressure sometimes drops of water are found along the leaf margins of some plants especially in the early morning. What is the phenomenon called?

(v) Draw a well-labelled diagram of the root hair cell as it would appear if an excess of fertiliser is added to the soil close to it.

Ans. (i) The parts indicated by the guidelines *A-D* are

A – Root hair

B – Soil particles

C – Xylem

D – Cortex

(ii) Endosmosis is the process that enables the passage of water from the soil into the root hair.

(iii) Osmotic pressure is responsible for the movement of water in the direction indicated by the arrows. It is the potential of water molecules to move from a less concentrated solution to a more concentrated solution across a semipermeable membrane.

(iv) Due to an excess of this pressure sometimes drops of water are found along the leaf margins of some plants especially in the early morning. The phenomenon is called guttation.

(v) Due to addition of excess of fertiliser, the root hair will appear shrunken.

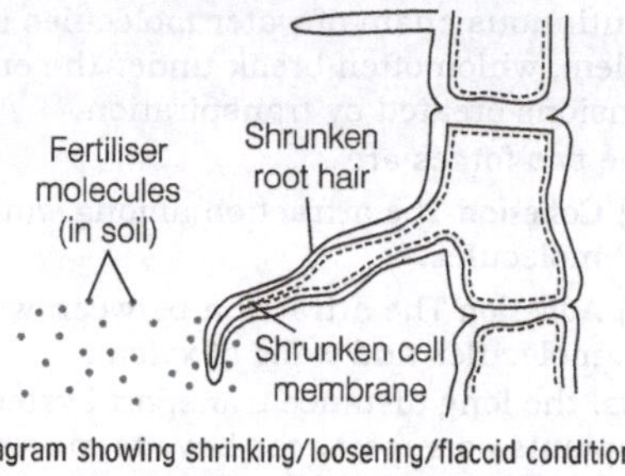

Diagram showing shrinking/loosening/flaccid condition

3. Roots help in the absorption of water. A root hair contains cell sap which has higher concentration of salts as compared to the outside soil water.

(i) How do root hairs increase the absorption of water by plants?

(ii) Write any one condition which leads to guttation in plants.

(iii) Root pressure cannot account for the translocation of water. Why?

(iv) Mention two conditions which allow the root pressure to occur.

(v) What is transpiration pull?

Ans. (i) Root hairs increase the surface area of roots which help in making contact with large volume of water.

(ii) One condition which leads to guttation in plants, i.e. increased root pressure.

(iii) Root pressure cannot account for translocation of water because it fails to play role in movement of water in tall plants like gymnosperms.

(iv) Two conditions which allow the root pressure to occur are

(a) High humidity (b) Low transpiration

(v) Transpiration pull is the force of pulling, produced inside the xylem tissue which helps in the upward movement of water.

4. Observe the figure given below and answer the following questions.

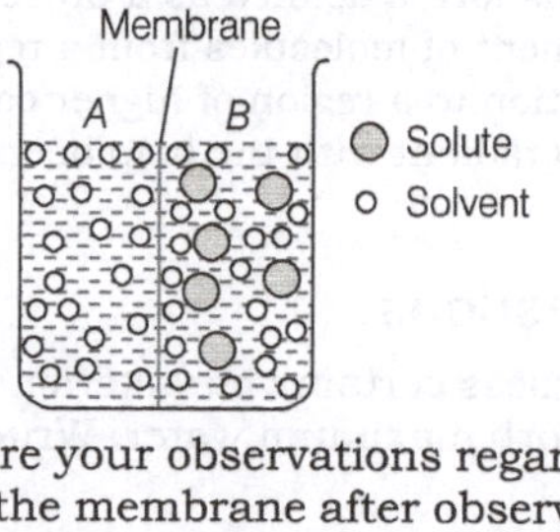

(i) What are your observations regarding the pore size of the membrane after observing the distribution of solute and solvent across the membrane.

(ii) What will be the direction of solvent movement?

(iii) List any two conditions that affect this process.

(iv) In which direction, will the net movement of solvent molecules be?

(v) Name the phenomenon that concludes the above result.

Ans. (i) Since, no solute particle is observed in *A*, the pore size of membrane is large enough only to allow solvent particles but not the solute particles.
(ii) Solvent molecules can move in both the direction across the membrane.
(iii) Temperature and tonicity of the solution affect this process.
(iv) The net movement of solvent molecules will be from its higher concentration to its lower concentration.
(v) Osmosis concludes the above result.

5. Given below is the diagram of an apparatus setup to study a very important physiological process.

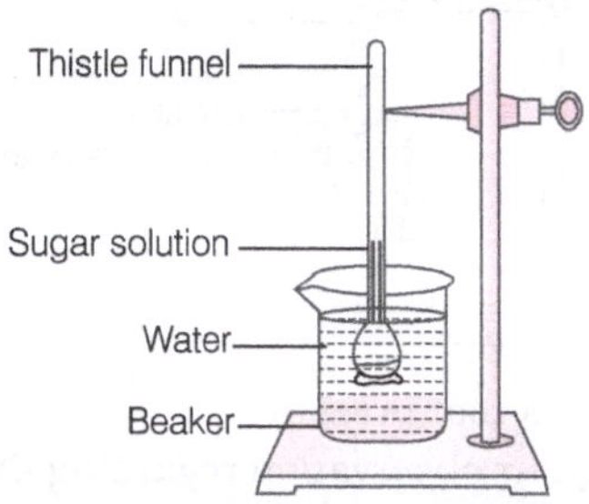

(i) Name the process being studied.
(ii) Explain the process.
(iii) What change would you observe in the thistle funnel containing sugar solution after about 10 minutes?
(iv) Is sugar solution hypertonic or hypotonic?
(v) Name the part of the plant cell which is represented by the sugar solution.

Ans. (i) The process being studied is osmosis.
(ii) Osmosis is a process of diffusion of water molecules from the region of higher concentration to that of lower concentration through semipermeable membrane.
(iii) After about 10 minutes, the sugar solution in the thistle funnel will rise up.
(iv) Sugar solution is hypertonic in nature as it is more concentrated than water.
(v) Cell sap of the root hair is the part of the plant cell which is represented by the sugar solution.

6. A candidate in order to study the process of osmosis has taken 3 potato cubes and put them in 3 different beakers containing 3 different solutions. After 24 hours, in the first beaker the potato cube increased in size, in the second beaker, the potato cube decreased in size and in the third beaker, there was no change in the size of the potato cube. The following diagrams show the result of the same experiment.

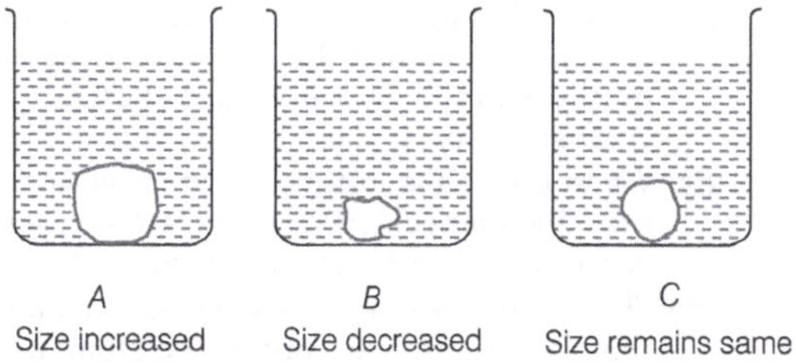

(i) Give the technical terms of the solutions used in beakers *A*, *B* and *C*.
(ii) In beaker *C*, the size of the potato cube remains the same. Explain the reason in brief.
(iii) Write the specific feature of the cell sap of root hairs which helps in absorption of water.
(iv) What is osmosis?
(v) How do a cell wall and a cell membrane differ in their permeability? **[2014]**

Ans. (i) The technical terms of the solution used in beakers *A*, *B* and *C* are
A – Hypotonic solution
B – Hypertonic solution
C – Isotonic solution
(ii) In beaker *C*, the concentration of water and solute is same in solution as that in the potato cube. Due to which no osmosis occurs and the size of potato cube remains same.
(iii) The concentration of cell sap is higher in the root hairs as compared to soil water. Thus, endosmosis takes place, facilitating absorption of water.
(iv) Refer to text on page no. 35.
(v) Cell wall is freely permeable, while cell membrane is semipermeable.

7. Turgor pressure balances both wall pressure and osmotic pressure as there is no absorption of water even when concentration of solute inside the cell may be greater than outside.
(i) Define turgidity.
(ii) What are the two pressures exerted by turgid cell?
(iii) Write the significant difference between the two pressures generated by turgid cell.
(iv) When the cell is in turgid state it is said to be in equilibrium. Why?
(v) How is turgor pressure helpful in regulating opening and closing of stomata?

Ans. (i) Turgidity is the state of a cell in which the cell wall is rigid and stretched by an increase in the volume of vacuole due to absorption of water.
(ii) The two pressures exerted by turgid cell are
(a) Turgor pressure
(b) Wall pressure

(iii) Turgor pressure is the pressure exerted by the protoplasm against the cell wall, while wall pressure is the back pressure exerted by cell wall against the protoplast.

(iv) When the cell is in turgid state it is said to be in equilibrium because at this state neither the water is absorbed nor it gets out of the cell.

(v) The turgor pressure caused due to osmotic flow of water in guard cells control the stomatal opening and closing. When turgor pressure becomes high, stomata opens and it closes when turgor pressure is reduced.

8. The diagram given below represents a plant cell after being placed in a strong sugar solution. Study the diagram and answer the questions that follow

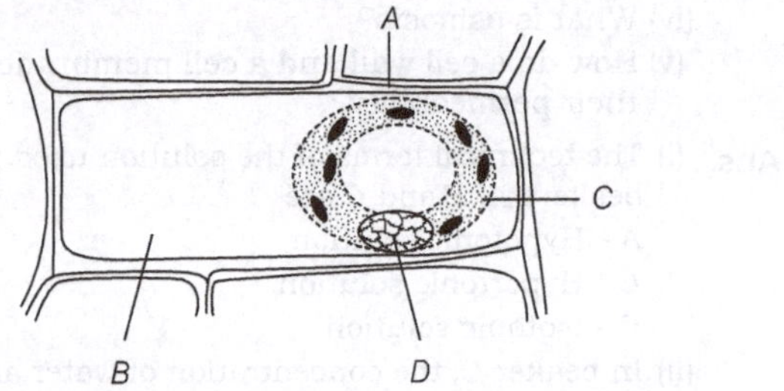

(i) What is the state of the cell shown in the diagram?

(ii) Name the structure that acts as a selectively permeable membrane.

(iii) Label the parts labelled as *A-D* in the diagram.

(iv) How can the above cell be brought back to its original condition? Mention the scientific term for the recovery of the cell.

(v) State any two features of the above plant cell which is not present in animal cell. **[2017]**

Ans. (i) The cell shown in the figure is plasmolysed (flaccid state).

(ii) Plasma membrane acts as a selectively permeable membrane.

(iii) The parts labelled as *A-D* are

A – Cell wall B – Hypertonic solution

C – Plasma membrane *D* – Nucleus

(iv) The cell can be returned back to its original condition, if it is placed in a hypotonic medium or pure water for some time.

Scientific term for the recovery of the cell is deplasmolysis.

(v) The two features of the given plant cell which are not present in animal cells are

- Cell wall
- Chloroplast

9. Observe the figure demonstrating root pressure given below and answer the following questions.

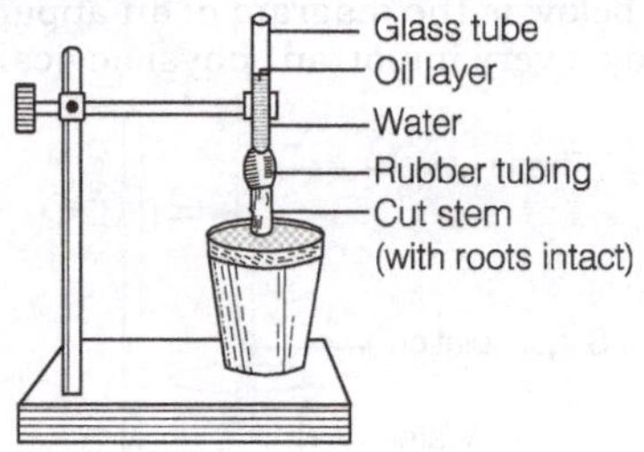

(i) What is root pressure?

(ii) List your observation regarding the water level after some time.

(iii) Oil layer has been added over the water. Why?

(iv) How does root pressure help the stem in the given setup?

(v) During which time of the day, root pressure is maximum?

Ans. (i) Refer to text on page no. 38.

(ii) The water level increases after some time.

(iii) Oil prevents the evaporation of water from the tube by inhibiting the contact between tube and its surrounding.

(iv) The root pressure forces the water to move upward in the stem.

(v) During early morning of spring and rainy season, root pressure is maximum.

Chapter Assessment

Section-I

1 Mark Questions

1. Name the following.
   (i) The structure through which thin, delicate root hairs extend.
   (ii) Absorption of water by the roots occurs by this means.
   (iii) The vascular tissue which helps in active mineral transport.
   (iv) In tall trees, the ascent of sap occurs through this process.
   (v) Force between water molecule.
2. Correct and rewrite the statements by changing the underlined words.
   (i) The process by which molecules distribute themselves evenly with in the space they occupy is termed as <u>imbibition</u>.
   (ii) The space between the cell wall and plasma membrane in plasmolysed cell is filled with <u>isotonic solution</u>.
3. Give biological reasons for the following.
   (i) We gargle with saline water in case of sore throat.
   (ii) Transplanting of seedling to a flower bed in the evening is better than doing so in the morning.
4. (i) Match the following colums.

	Column I		Column II
A.	Diffusion	1.	Energy
B.	Active absorption	2.	Mixing of molecules
C.	Root pressure	3.	Exosmosis
D.	Hypertonic solution	4.	Unicellular
E.	Root hair	5.	Cortical cells

(ii) Match the following columns.

	Column I		Column II
A.	Xylem	1.	Conduction of food molecules
B.	Transpiration pull	2.	Water absorption
C.	Root pressure	3.	Ascent of sap
D.	Phloem	4.	Cohesion-adhesion forces

5. Choose the correct answer from the four options given below.

(i) The force developed due to osmosis is
(a) turgor pressure (b) flaccidity
(c) osmotic pressure (d) imbibition pressure

(ii) Movement of molecules from the region of their higher concentration to the lower concentration region without the involvement of a semipermeable membrane is
(a) active transport (b) diffusion
(c) osmosis (d) None of these

(iii) Transport of food molecules from the source to all the parts is a/an
(a) active transport
(b) passive transport
(c) imbibing process
(d) None of the above

(iv) In which type of mineral absorption theory, is ATP required?
(a) Active mineral absorption
(b) Passive mineral absorption
(c) Both (a) and (b)
(d) None of the above

(v) A shoot from a balsam plant is kept in eosin solution (pink in colour) for 3-4 hours. The pink colour is most likely to be observed in
(a) cortex (b) epidermal cells
(c) phloem tissue (d) xylem tissue

6. (i) Fill in the blanks by using suitable words.
   (a) .... serves as the medium for transport of inorganic salts and food molecules throughout the plant.
   (b) Absorption of water by the plant cells through surface attraction is called ....
   (c) A plasmolysed cell becomes turgid when placed in solution that is ....
   (d) Osmometer measures .... pressure.

(ii) Complete the following statements by choosing the correct alternative out of those given in brackets.
   (a) Approximately 98% of the water is absorbed by plants through ...... (passive absorption/active absorption/plasmolysis).
   (b) The force exerted by the .... is essential for conduction of water specially in herbaceous plants (transpirational pull/root hairs).
   (c) The loss of xylem in a plant will lead a plant to loose its .... (flaccidity/turgidity/osmotic capability).

7. Choose the odd one out from the following terms given below and name the category to which other three belong.

   Endosmosis, Plasmolysis, Temporary and Permanent wilting

8. Given below is the set of five terms. Rewrite the terms in correct order of logical sequence.
   Cortical cell, Root hair, Xylem, Water, Vein
9. Expand TP.
10. State the exact location of xylem.
11. State the main function of the following.
   (i) Capillary action (ii) Manometer
12. Mention one difference between of the following pairs on the basis of what is given in the bracket.
   (i) Imbibition and Diffusion (definition)
   (ii) Osmosis and Plasmolysis (definition)
   (iii) Transport of water or minerals and Food molecules (mode of transport)
13. Give biological/technical terms for the following.
   (i) A condition of leaves that occurs due to the loss of turgidity.
   (ii) The pressure built up by roots due to continuous absorption of water which pushes the sap up through the stem.

2 Marks Question

14. How are water and minerals absorbed in plants? What are the two types of absorption taking place in plants?

3 Marks Question

15. How do you classify solutions based on tonicity?

Section-II [5 Marks]

Structured Questions

16. Observe the figure given below and answer the following questions.

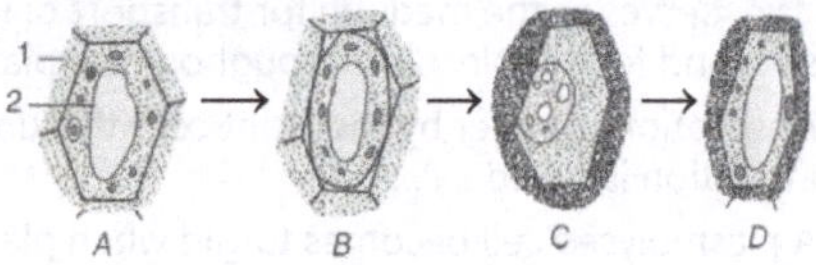

   (i) State the nature of solution marked (1).
   (ii) What process has been depicted in figures *C*-*D*?
   (iii) What will be present in the space marked as (2)?
   (iv) In which figures, turgor pressure will be zero?
   (v) In which figures, wall pressure will be positive?
17. Observe the diagram given below and answer the following questions.

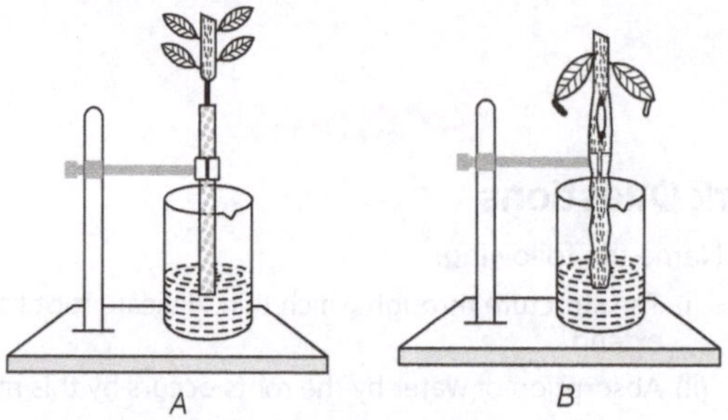

   (i) Identify the aim of the experiment.
   (ii) Some parts of the stem in both the shoots have been removed. Name the conducting tissue in shoot *A* and in shoot *B* that have been removed.
   (iii) What will you observe at the end of this experiment?
   (iv) Write about xylem tissue in brief.
   (v) In plants, which is accompanied by diffusion and transpiration pull?
18. A complete ring of a bark is removed from a tree. The tree continued to live but after about one month the part above the removed ring got swelled up and below the ring shrinked up.
   (i) Why does the bark above the ring swell up?
   (ii) Why the bark below the ring shrinks up?
   (iii) Name the tissue which shows bidirectional conduction of material?
   (iv) Name the tissue which transports substance using passive transport.
   (v) Name the pressure that helps in the movement of water up in the xylem of root.

For explanations scan the given QR Code

Olympiad Section*

Brain Teasing Questions asked in Previous Olympiads

1 In an experiment, plant and animal cells were placed in different solutions (*A, B, C* and *D*) as shown below. The outcome of placing them in these solutions is also indicated in the figure.

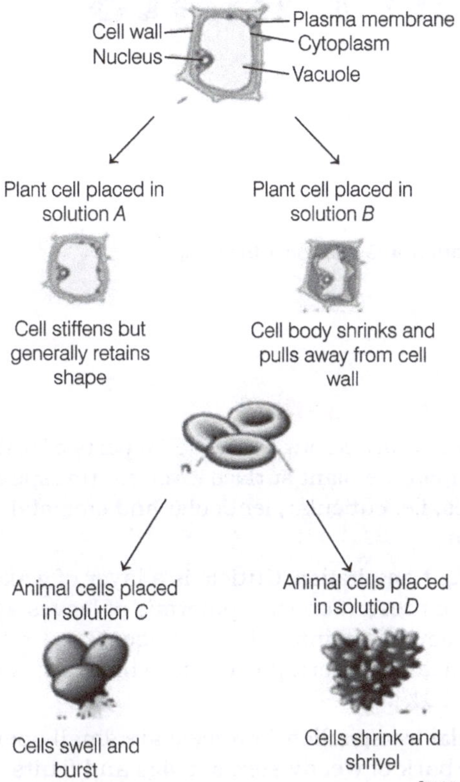

[INJSO 2016]

Identify the nature of the solutions *A, B, C* and *D*.

(a) *A* and *C* are hypotonic, *B* and *D* are hypertonic
(b) *A* and *C* are hypertonic, *B* and *D* are hypotonic
(c) *A* and *D* are hypotonic, *B* and *C* are hypertonic
(d) *A* and *D* are hypertonic, *B* and *C* are hypotonic

2 Students were studying cellular processes such as osmosis and plasmolysis. To make them understand the concept better, the teacher asked them to study the effect of a given solution on a specific plant cell. They placed the plant material in a given solution and studied the pattern of movement of water for about two hours duration. It was observed that there was no net movement of water during this period from the cell into the solution or *vice-versa*. Which of the following condition must be true in the given situation? **[INJSO 2015]**

(a) Turgor pressure is more than the wall pressure
(b) Turgor pressure is equal to the wall pressure
(c) Turgor pressure is less than the wall pressure
(d) Turgor pressure is zero and wall pressure has a negative value

3 Consider a beaker with a partition made up of sieved glass plate such that the beaker now contains two spaces, A and B. The beaker contains distilled water to which sugar was added in space A. **[INJSO 2013]**

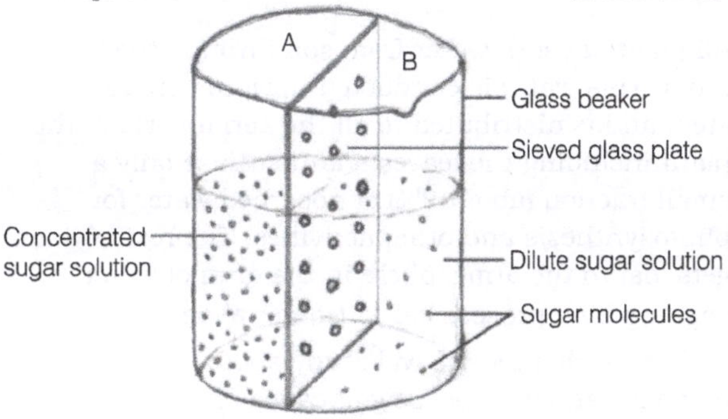

As you can see in the image, some molecules of sugar have moved to the region B.
Which of the following is the correct term for describing this process?

(a) Osmosis
(b) Diffusion
(c) Plasmolysis
(d) Imbibition

4 Anna is studying salt uptake (absorption) by the roots in a plant. Which of the following features does not play a role in the salt uptake in plants? **[INJSO 2013]**

(a) pH of the soil
(b) Temperature
(c) Light conditions
(d) Soil bacteria

Answers

1. (a) **2.** (b) **3.** (b) **4.** (d)

**These questions may or may not be asked in the examination, have been given just for additional practice required for olympiads, scholarship exams etc. For detailed explanations refer Page No. 247.*

CHAPTER

04

Transpiration in Plants

Chapter Inside

• Transpiration • Experiments Related to Transpiration • Guttation • Bleeding

All plants absorb water from soil through their roots. This water is conducted upward through stem and is distributed to all the aerial parts of the plant including the leaves. Plants utilise only a small fraction (about 2%) of absorbed water for photosynthesis and other activities. The rest of it gets lost to the atmosphere in the form of water vapours by a process called **transpiration**.

So in this chapter, we will study about demonstrations, types, significance and adaptations in plants and factors affecting transpiration.

Transpiration

The process of loss of water in the form of vapour from the exposed or aerial parts of a plant (such as leaves, etc.) is called transpiration. It is a vital process for both plants and environment and consequently to humans.

The loss of water through transpiration creates a suction force which helps in the upward movement of water from roots through xylem, i.e. **ascent of sap** (as discussed in earlier chapter).

Types of Transpiration

Transpiration is carried out by the aerial parts of plants. Depending upon the plant surface involved, transpiration is of three types, i.e. cuticular, lenticular and stomatal transpiration.

1. **Cuticular transpiration** Cuticle is a layer of wax-like covering present on the epidermis of leaves and herbaceous stems. It provides a relatively impermeable covering through which less water is lost (3-10%).
2. **Lenticular transpiration** Lenticels are small openings on the bark of woody stems, twigs and fruits. These allow diffusion of gases for both respiration and photosynthesis. Loss of water vapour through lenticels is called lenticular transpiration (about 0.1%).
3. **Stomatal transpiration** The loss of water vapour, which occurs through stomata is called stomatal transpiration. It accounts for 80-90% of the total water vapour loss from the plants.

Note
- Bark transpiration is a minor mode of transpiration which occurs very slowly from the otherwise impermeable corky covering of the older stem.
- After leaf fall in autumn, lenticels are the only site of water loss in deciduous trees.

Structure of Stomata

Stomata (sing. stoma) are the minute pores found in the epidermal layer of leaves and green stems. Each stoma is surrounded by the two **guard cells** which are of two different shapes, i.e. kidney-shaped (in dicot leaves) and dumb-bell-shaped (in monocot leaves).

Stomata are called as **turgor operated valves**. Generally, stomata are open during the daytime and closed at night. But in succulents like cacti, stomata close during day and open at night.

The number, structure, distribution, opening and closing of stomata influence the rate of transpiration.

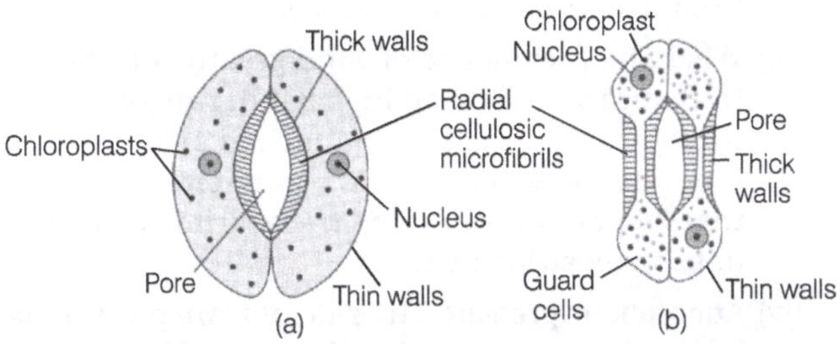

Open stomata : (a) Dicotyledonous (kidney-shaped)
(b) Monocotyledonous (dumb-bell-shaped)

The number of stomata may range from 1,000-10,000 per cm^2 as they vary from plant to plant.
For example, in **isobilateral leaves** (mostly in monocots), same number of stomata are found on the upper and the lower surfaces, whereas in **dorsiventral leaves** (mainly found in dicot plants), the number of stomata are very few on upper surface in comparison to those found on lower surface.
Stomata are absent in the leaves of submerged hydrophytes (*Hydrilla* and *Vallisneria*).

Mechanism of Stomatal Transpiration

A large number of spongy mesophyll cells are present in the leaves between the upper and lower epidermis and have their surfaces exposed to the intercellular spaces. These communicate with the outer atmosphere through stomata and give-off some water in the atmosphere, in the form of water vapours.

The osmotic diffusion of water from xylem vessels (in leaves) maintains the turgidity of mesophyll cells. The water continuously evaporates from these cells, thus saturating the air inside the intercellular spaces.

The water from these intercellular spaces gets diffused into the other connecting intercellular spaces and finally reaches to the sub-stomatal space, from where it escapes out through the stomata. Since outer atmosphere is unsaturated as compared to internal air.

This complete movement of water vapour from the cell surface to the outer atmosphere occurs by the process of diffusion. The molecules of water in the form of vapours move from the region of their higher concentration to their lower concentration.

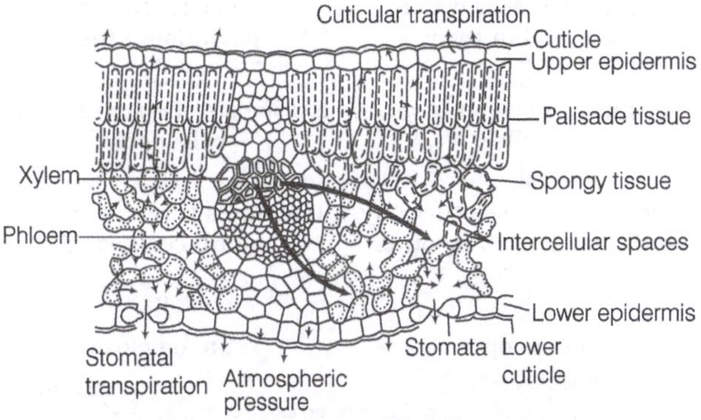

Vertical section of leaf indicating diffusion of water vapour through stomata

Regulation of Transpiration
(Mechanism of Opening and Closing of Stomata)

The process of transpiration in plants is regulated by the opening and closing of stomata. Transpiration occurs as long as the stomata are open and it stops when they are closed.
The opening and closing of stomata depend upon the **turgid** or **flaccid** state of guard cells or the amount of water and solutes present in the guard cells. The inner walls of guard cells are thick and elastic in nature.
The opening and closing of stomata can be understood by the following theory

Potassium Ion Exchange Theory

According to the potassium ion exchange theory, the guard cells become turgid when K^+ gradient is setup in the cells (during daytime). This causes the stomatal pores to open up and transpiration occurs.
At night, reverse happens, i.e. the K^+ ions leak out, turning the guard cells flaccid thus, closing the stomatal pores.

The process of opening and closing of stomata is outlined below

Opening of stomata	Closing of stomata
During day/light	During night/dark
⇓	⇓
Accumulation of K^+ ions by the guard cells	Loss of K^+ ions by the guard cells
⇓	⇓
Increased solute concentration of guard cells	Decreased solute concentration in them
⇓	⇓
This decreases water potential in them	This increases water potential in them
⇓	⇓
Endosmosis of water in guard cells	Exosmosis of water in guard cells occur
⇓	⇓
Leads to increased turgidity and thus stretching outer wall	Decreases turgidity making guard cell flaccid
⇓	⇓
Stoma open	Stoma close

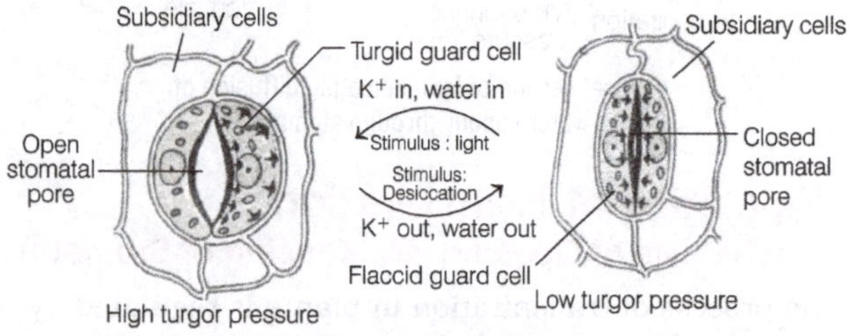

Representation of active K^+ transport mechanism of opening and closing of stomata

Factors Affecting the Rate of Transpiration

The rate of transpiration can be affected by both internal and external factors

Internal Factors

(i) **Leaf area** The larger the total leaf area of a plant, more is the rate of transpiration.

(ii) **Leaf structure** The plants growing in dry conditions or arid areas show certain anatomical modifications to reduce the rate of transpiration, e.g. leaves in some plants are reduced to spine to minimise the rate of transpiration.

(iii) **Water content of leaves** If the water content of leaves decreases due to insufficient absorption of water by roots, then the leaves wilt to reduce transpiration.

(iv) **Succulence** Succulent leaves and stem contain latex in their tissues which holds water and reduces rate of transpiration.

External Factors

(i) **Light intensity and temperature** It increases the transpiration by raising the temperature of leaves. A rise in temperature of the leaf increases vapourisation of water in the internal atmosphere of leaf causing rapid water loss by transpiration. The water loss gets doubled with every 10°C rise in temperature.

(ii) **Humidity of air** Humidity is the amount of water vapour in the air. Low and high humidity of air affect the transpiration. High humidity reduces the rate of transpiration and a lesser humid environment increases it.

(iii) **Wind** The prevalence of wind greatly affects transpiration. During high wind, rate of transpiration is greatly enhanced as it removes the water vapours transpired, thereby, not allowing the transpiring surface to become saturated.

(iv) **Atmospheric pressure** The rate of transpiration is inversely proportional to the atmospheric pressure. Lowering of atmospheric pressure increases the rate of transpiration.

(v) **Carbon dioxide (CO_2) concentration** Increase in carbon dioxide level in outside atmosphere over 0.03% (normal) results in stomatal closure and causes decrease in transpiration.

Transpiration and Photosynthesis: A Compromise

The process of photosynthesis requires an adequate amount of water for its activity. Transpiration reduces the supply of available water for photosynthesis. As a result, the guard cells shut the stomata and become flaccid, i.e. closed, thereby reducing the supply of carbon dioxide (CO_2) for photosynthesis.

Check Your LEARNING...

1 During transpiration in which form the water is lost?
2 State different types of transpiration.
3 Name a plant in which stomata are absent.
4 When the guard cells are flaccid, what will happen to the stomata?
5 Succulence of stems and leaves affects transpiration. How?

Adaptations in Plants to Reduce Excessive Transpiration

Many plants that grow in unfavourable conditions, i.e. dry, humid climate have evolved a number of permanent adaptations in order to reduce the rate of transpiration.

Some of them are given below

(i) **Sunken stomata** In dry environment, the stomata of leaves are deep seated in the leaf to reduce transpiration, e.g. *Nerium*.

(ii) **Thick cuticle on leaves** In banyan and most evergreen trees, a thick waxy cuticle develops over the epidermis to reduce loss of water by transpiration.

(iii) **Narrow leaves** In some plants, leaves become narrower by rolling or folding to reduce exposed surface area for transpiration, e.g. lavender.

(iv) **Fewer stomata** In some plants, the number of stomata may be reduced to reduce the rate of transpiration.

(v) **Loss of leaves** In some plants, there is complete loss of leaves during the dry season, e.g. tropical deciduous tree and in some, complete change of leaves to spines, e.g. cacti.

(vi) Some plants (succulent plants) of the family–Crassulaceae reduce water loss by opening their stomata only at night, when the air is cooler and more humid. Carbon dioxide obtained at night is stored and is used next day during photosynthesis when the stomata remain closed.

(vii) **Epidermal hairs** Leaf surface may be covered by thick coating of epidermal hairs to reduce transpiration, e.g. *Cucurbita*.

Significance of Transpiration

The significance of transpiration can be understood with the help of below mentioned advantages and disadvantages

Advantages of Transpiration

Transpiration acts as a significant phenomenon for the plants. Some major advantages of transpiration are given below

(i) **Cooling effect** Transpiration reduces temperature of the plant leaf giving a cooling effect to the plant.

(ii) **Suction force** Transpiration creates a suction force (transpiration pull) along with other factors which are responsible for rise of water in tall plants.

(iii) **Distribution of water and mineral salts** Transpiraton helps in the distribution of water and mineral salts to various plant organs as it tends to draw water from various organs to leaves.

(iv) **Maintenance of turgidity** Transpiration maintains the shape and structure of the plant parts by keeping the cells turgid.

(v) **Contribution in precipitation** It contributes to atmospheric humidity and thus is a major contributor to precipitation.

(vi) **Osmosis** Transpiration helps in osmosis. Water is absorbed by roots *via* osmosis and leaves the plant *via* transpiration.

(vii) Transpiration helps in exchange of gases in the plants.

Disadvantages of Transpiration

If excess amount of transpiration occurs, it may lead to

(i) **Wilting** When transpiration exceeds absorption through roots, leaf cells become flaccid causing wilting of plants.

(ii) **Stunted growth** Excessive transpiration causes stunted growth of the plant.

(iii) **Abscission** During water scarcity, transpiration results in the closing of stomata following the production of abscisic acid. It causes premature leaf fall or delayed flowering and fruit production.

(iv) **Energy expenditure** Transpiration requires energy hence, it is a gross energy expenditure.

As the process of transpiration has both advantages and disadvantages significantly, hence many scientists consider this process as a "Necessary Evil".

Antitranspirants

These are the chemical substances which reduce the rate of transpiration. These are used in dry farming.

Some of these are as follows

- Phenyl Mercuric Acetate (PMA) closes the stomata for more than two weeks partially.
- Aspirin (Salicylic acid)
- Abscisic Acid (ABA)
- Oxi-ethylene
- Silicon oil
- CO_2
- Low viscous wax

Check Your LEARNING...

1 In which kind of the plants, the sunken stomata are present?
2 In which plant family opening of stomata occurs only at night?
3 Mention any one significance of transpiration.
4 Excessive transpiration causes abscission. Give reason.
5 Name three substances which act as antitranspirants.

Experiments Related to Transpiration

To demonstrate transpiration in plants, several experiments can be performed.

These experiments are discussed below

Experiment 1 (a)

Experiment to demonstrate loss in weight due to transpiration.

Procedure Take a test tube and fill it with water.

Insert a cut twig in it and carefully pour a layer of oil over the water.

This oily layer prevents water loss through evaporation from the water surface.

Place the test tube in a small beaker and weigh them together. Then remove the tube and keep it straight in a test tube stand for few hours.

Weigh the tube again by placing it in same beaker.

After some time, it can be observed that the water level in the test tube goes down. This shows the phenomenon of water loss through transpiration.

Since, there are no roots to actively absorb water, so if there is a difference in weights, it indicates loss of water by the shoot due to transpiration.

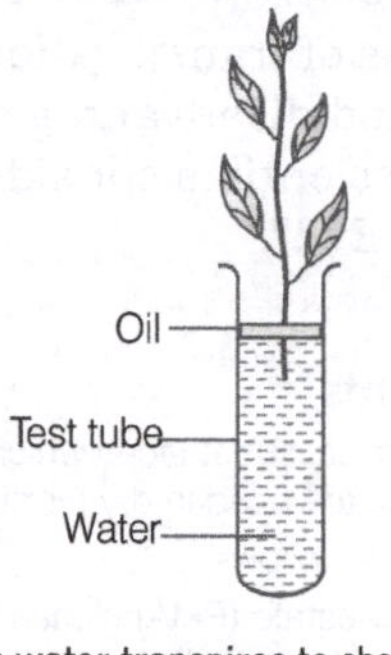

A shoot inserted in water transpires to show loss in weight

Experiment 1 (b)

To study loss in weight of a potted plant by transpiration.

Procedure A small light weight potted plant can be weighed before and after the end of specified time period.

The pot and the soil surface should be completely covered, preventing water loss from surfaces other than the plant as shown in figure.

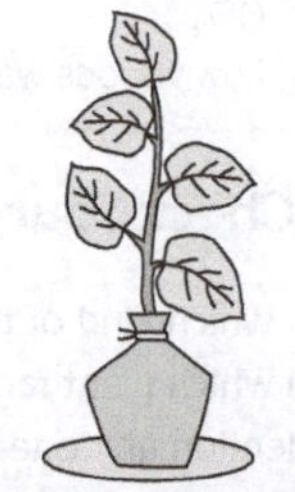
A potted plant with covered soil surface and pot

The loss in weight of plant during the specified time period occurs due to water loss by transpiration.

An improvement in the weighing method can be made by using a glass bottle with a graduated side tube, filled with water and a tube fitted into it (shown in figure).

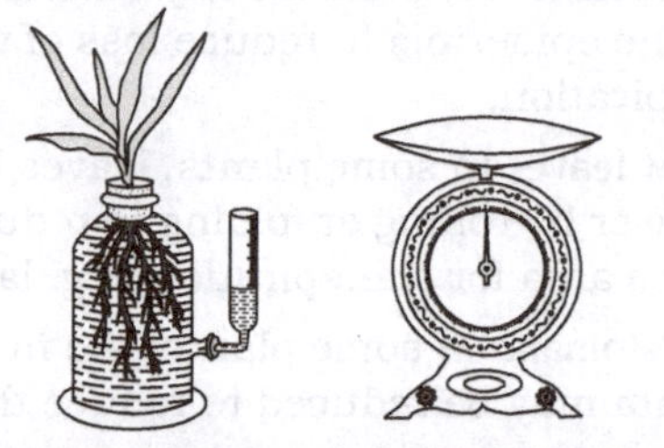
An experimental setup indicating loss of water by volume as well as by weight

So, when the water level in the side tube falls, it will demonstrate the loss of water through transpiration from the leaves.

This would indicate the volume of water loss that can be compared with the loss in weight with the help of a weighing machine or by converting cc into grams (1 cc water weighs 1g).

Experiment 2 (a)

Bell Jar Experiment To demonstrate transpiration in plants.

Procedure For this experiment, arrange three setups as follows

Setup A Take a small, well-watered potted plant, preferably one with broad leaves. Enclose the pot completely within a polythene bag and tie the mouth of the bag tightly around the base of the stem. This is done to prevent the escape of water vapour from the pot. Now, cover the entire plant under a bell jar.

Setup B Arrange another similar plant and cover it with a bell jar exactly in the same manner as the first one. Keep a piece of **dry cobalt chloride paper** by the side of the plant inside the bell jar. The paper may be pinned to a wooden stick or to a strip of cork sheet.

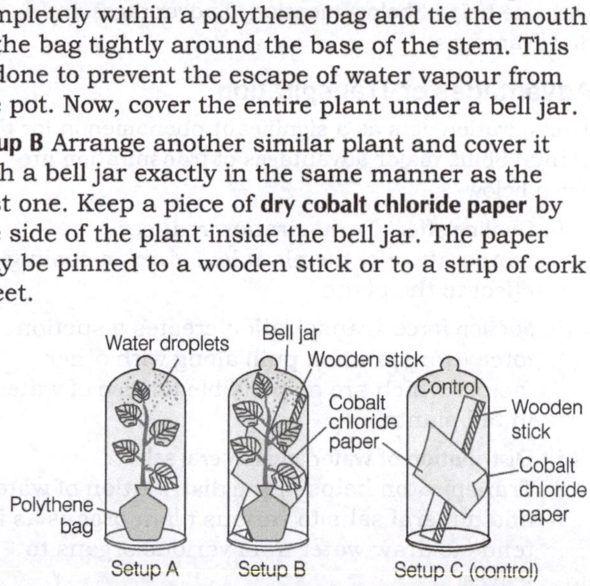

An experiment to demonstrate transpiration in plants

Setup C Take a bell jar without a plant. Pin only a similar piece of dry cobalt chloride paper to wooden stick or strip of cork sheet. This paper is the control for the experiment.

Now, keep all three bell jars together in the sunlight for approximately half an hour.

It is observed that

(i) The first bell jar (A) would show water vapour condensing on its inner walls.

(ii) The second bell jar (B) would also show a similar condensation and at the same time, the initially blue cobalt chloride paper in it would turn pink due to its exposure to moisture.

(iii) The blue colour of the cobalt chloride paper in the third bell jar (C) does not change at all. It is because there are no water drops on the jar's inner walls. It proves that there was no moisture in the air due to transpiration as there was no plant in it.

Experiment 2 (b)

To demonstrate unequal rate of transpiration in a dorsiventral leaf.

Procedure Take a healthy potted plant. Attach pieces of dry cobalt chloride paper on the two surfaces of a leaf held in position by two glass slides tied together by a rubber band or clip on either side.

Apply vaseline on either side of the glass slide in order to make it air tight. Keep the plant in sunlight for a few hours.

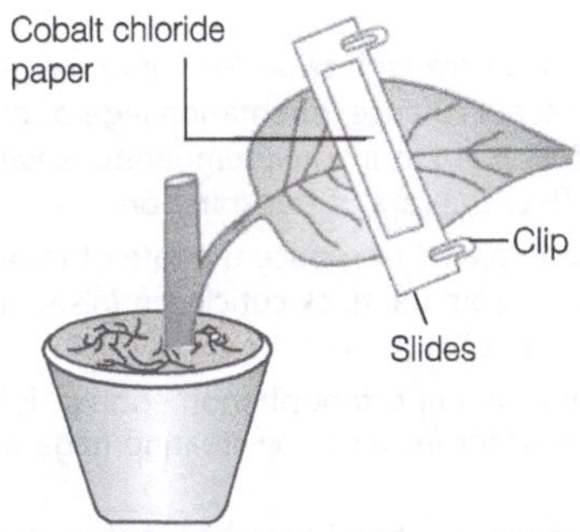

After some time, it is observed that the piece of cobalt chloride paper facing the upper surface of leaf does not turn pink or takes a longer time in turning pink as compared to the paper attached to the lower surface.

This proves that more transpiration takes place from the lower surface of the leaves due to a large number of stomata found on it.

Experiment 3

Measurement of rate of transpiration by Ganong's potometer

Potometer is an apparatus that measures the rate of water intake by a plant shoot which is almost equal to the water lost through transpiration. It does not measure transpiration directly, but measures the water uptake by the cut shoot.

To initiate the experiment, cut a twig of a suitable plant obliquely with a sharp knife and fix it immediately into the upper end of the apparatus.

Fill the entire apparatus with water (it is to be noted that there should be no air spaces in between).

Introduce an air bubble into the horizontally graduated capillary tube (dipped inside the beaker) by lifting the bent capillary tube above beaker for some time so that air is sucked in. By introducing the air bubble, the rate of water uptake can be easily calculated.

This can be done by noting the movement of an air bubble over a fixed distance on the scale of the capillary tube.

The reservoir in the apparatus helps to bring air bubble to its original position. This can be done by releasing some more water into the capillary tube by opening the stop-cock. Leave the apparatus undisturbed for some time.

After few hours, it is observed that the air bubble has started moving through the horizontal capillary tube of potometer. This can be easily detected by noting the readings given on the capillary tube scale.

This experiment shows that as the process of transpiration proceeds, a suction force is setup due to which the water is pulled from the beaker which makes the bubble to move along.

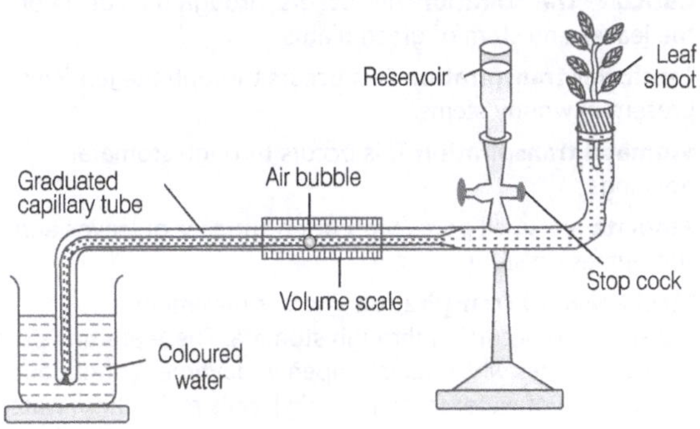

Ganong's potometer

Limitations of Using Potometer

There are some limitations of using a potometer.

These are

(i) Introducing the air bubble is not very easy.

(ii) The twig may not remain alive if the experiment takes a long time.

(iii) Any change in the outside temperature can affect the position of the air bubble in the capillary tube.

Guttation

It occurs during warm humid conditions, i.e. when the amount of root pressure is high and rate of transpiration is low. Many herbaceous plants tend to lose small quantities of water in the form of drops from the **hydathodes** (water glands, i.e. pores present along leaf margin) or water stomata. These tiny drops appear mainly along the margins or tips of the leaves especially during the early morning time. These drops are rich in mineral salts, organic acids, carbohydrates and nitrogenous compounds.

Thus, guttation is exudation of water in the form of droplets from the leaf margins. Guttation can be seen in garden nasturtium, grasses, tomatoes, potatoes and *Colocasia*.

Conditions for Guttation

(i) The presence of large amount of water in the plant.

(ii) Suitable temperature (at very low temperatures, practically no guttation takes place).

(iii) All conditions that inhibit transpiration favour guttation.

Bleeding

The exudation of sap from the injured parts of the plants is called bleeding. When a cut is made in the stem of a plant growing in well-watered soil, xylem sap starts oozing out.

It happens due to root pressure. It is very common in mulberry. In *Calotropis* and *Euphorbia*, oozing of milky latex is seen.

Check Your LEARNING...

1 Name an experiment for the demonstration of transpiration.
2 State the use of reservoir in the potometer.
3 Name one type of commonly used potometer.
4 Mention any one limitation of using potometer.
5 What do you understand by bleeding from plant?.

QUiCK Revision

- Transpiration is the loss of water in the form of water vapours from the aerial parts of the plant.
- **Rate of transpiration** It is the amount of water lost by plant in specified time unit per surface area. It can be measured by weighing method, potometer method, etc.
- Transpiration is of three types, i.e. **cuticular, lenticular** and **stomatal** transpirations.
- **Cuticular transpiration** This occurs through the cuticle of the leaves and stem of green plants.
- **Lenticular transpiration** This occurs through the lenticels present in woody stems.
- **Stomatal transpiration** This occurs through stomatal openings.
- **Stomata** are small pores present on surfaces of leaves and sometimes on stem.
- **Mechanism of transpiration** There is maximum transpiration occurring through stomata. These are tiny pores on leaf surfaces which remain open in daytime. Continuous evaporation of water from mesophyll cells make them water deficient. These cells draw water from neighbouring cells in order to makeup water deficiency.
- **Regulation of transpiration** The rate of transpiration is regulated by closing and opening of stomata. In the hot windy mid-day, plants reduce transpiration by keeping stomata closed.
- **Factors affecting transpiration** Both internal factors (leaf area, structure, succulence, orientation, age of plant) and external factors (light, humidity, temperature, wind, soil, water, etc) affect the rate of transpiration.
- **Adaptations** in plants to reduce the rate of transpiration include sunken stomata, thick cuticle, cutinised hairs and reduced number of stomata.
- Transpiration is an important phenomenon as it helps in the absorption of water from soil by creating negative suction pressure.
- **Antitranspirants** are chemicals which reduce the rate of transpiration when applied to plant surfaces, e.g. dimethyl silicon, wax emulsions.
- **Ganong's potometer** is used to measure the rate of transpiration. It is a specially designed apparatus in which movement of bubble in water-filled tube septum shows the amount of water transpired in a unit time.
- **Guttation** is a phenomenon taking place in some plants having tiny pores on the leaf tips and margins called **hydathodes**. Under high humidity and high water content in soil, these plants form water droplets at the edges of leaves.
- **Bleeding** is the exudation of sap from injured plant parts.

Chapter Practice

Section-I

1 Mark Questions

1. Name the following.
   (i) The openings on the barks of trees through which transpiration occurs. **[2023]**
   (ii) The dumb-bell-shaped structure on leaves which surround stoma.
   (iii) The plant in which stomata are absent.
   (iv) The apparatus used to compare the rate of transpiration in cut shoot.

Ans. (i) Lenticels (ii) Guard cells
(iii) *Hydrilla* (iv) Potometer

2. Correct and rewrite the following statements by changing the underlined words.
   (i) Transpiration takes place in all plants.
   (ii) Lenticular transpiration takes place during day time only.
   (ii) The cobalt chloride paper when exposed to moisture turns into black colour.
   (iv) More transpiration occurs from the upper surface of a leaf.

Ans. (i) Transpiration takes place only in plants with green leaves.
(ii) Lenticular transpiration takes place throughout day and night.
(iii) The cobalt chloride paper when exposed to moisture turns into pink colour.
(iv) More transpiration occurs from the lower surface of a leaf.

3. Give biological reasons for the following.
   (i) In some xerophytes, leaves are modified into spines.
   (ii) Balsam plants wilt during mid-day even if the soil is well-watered. **[2014]**
   (iii) Some desert plants have sunken stomata on their leaves.
   (iv) On a bright sunny day, the leaves of certain plants roll up.
   (v) Transpiration is a necessary evil.

Ans. (i) Xerophytes grow in dry conditions where water is less, therefore in order to reduce transpiration their leaves are modified into spines.
(ii) During mid-day, the rate of transpiration is more than the rate of absorption of water. The cells lose turgidity. So, plants show wilting of leaves.
(iii) Many plants, specially those which grow in a dry climate evolve a variety of permanent adaptations to curtail transpiration. Sunken stoma is one such adaptation in desert plants.
(iv) On a bright sunny day, the rate of transpiration is high. This leads to the excess loss of water from leaves which is not compensated by water absorption from the roots.
As a result, the guard cells and other cells of the leaf become flaccid and the leaves roll up.
(v) Transpiration controls the rate of water absorption. It also helps in the absorption of minerals and regulates the temperature.
At the same time, it has disadvantage that leads to water deficiency in plants and thus, impairs the processes of photosynthesis, growth, etc. It is therefore said that 'transpiration is a necessary evil'.

4. (i) Match the following columns.

Column I	Column II
A. Kidney-shaped	1. Leaves
B. Mesophyll cells	2. *Nerium*
C. Sunken stomata	3. Guard cell
D. Epidermal hair	4. Cucurbits

(ii) Match the following columns.

Column I	Column II
A. Transpiration	1. Loss of water as water vapour from the surface of water bodies
B. Evaporation	2. Hydathodes
C. Guttation	3. Green leaves
D. Stomata	4. Water lost in the form of vapour from aerial parts of the plant.

Ans. (i) A–3, B–1, C–2, D–4
(ii) A–4, B–1, C–2, D–3

5. Choose the correct answer from the four options given below.
   (i) Which of the following best defines transpiration? **[Semester I 2021]**
   (a) It is the loss of water in the form of droplets from the aerial parts of plant
   (b) It is the loss of water in the form of water vapour from the underground parts of the plant
   (c) It is the loss of water in the form of water vapour from the aerial parts of the plant
   (d) It is the loss of water in the form of water vapour from all parts of the plant

Ans. (c)

(ii) What is the function of cuticle on leaves? [Semester I 2021]
(a) Prevents photosynthesis
(b) Reduces transpiration
(c) Protects leaves from grazing animals
(d) Gives colour to leaves

Ans. (b)

(iii) Permanently open structures seen on the barks of old woody stems. [Semester I 2021]
(a) Stomata (b) Hydathodes
(c) Lenticels (d) Epidermal pores

Ans. (c)

(iv) In tall tree, maximum amount of water loss occurs through
(a) stomatal transpiration
(b) cuticular transpiration
(c) lenticular transpiration
(d) transpiration through bark

Ans. (c)

(v) Where are the guard cells found in a plant? [Semester I 2021]
(a) Around the root hairs (b) Around the lenticels
(c) Around the thylakoids (d) Around the stoma

Ans. (d)

(vi) During the mechanism of opening and closing of stomata, the important factor is
(a) the protein content of the cells
(b) the turgid and flaccid state of the guard cells
(c) the starch content of the cells
(d) the presence of chloroplast in the guard cells

Ans. (b)

(vii) Which one of the following will not directly affect transpiration?
(a) Temperature
(b) Light
(c) Wind speed
(d) Chlorophyll content of leaves

Ans. (d)

(viii) Which one of the following does not affect the rate of transpiration? [2019]
(a) Light (b) Humidity
(c) Wind (d) Age of the plant

Ans. (*) All the above factors affect the rate of transpiration.
However, age of plant is an internal factor affecting transpiration rate.

(ix) Rate of transpiration increases with an increase in
(a) CO_2 concentration (b) atmospheric humidity
(c) root shoot ratio (d) temperature

Ans. (d)

(x) With the decrease in atmospheric pressure, the rate of transpiration will
(a) increase (b) decrease rapidly
(c) decrease slowly (d) remain the same

Ans. (a)

(xi) In which condition of the day, amongst the following, the transpiration will be maximum?
(a) Hot, dry, windy (b) Hot and humid
(c) Humid and cool (d) Humid and windy

Ans. (a)

(xii) Which of the following conditions suits for the maximum transpiration pull?
(a) Open stomata, dry atmosphere and moist soil
(b) Open stomata, high humid atmosphere and well-irrigated soil
(c) Open stomata, high humid atmosphere and dry soil
(d) Close stomata, dry atmosphere and dry soil

Ans. (a)

(xiii) The chemical used in the demonstration of experiment on transpiration is
(a) potassium hydroxide
(b) sodium hydroxide
(c) cobalt chloride
(d) calcium chloride

Ans. (c)

(xiv) The paper used to demonstrate unequal transpiration in a dicot leaf is [2023]
(a) filter paper (b) litmus paper
(c) starch paper (d) cobalt chloride paper

Ans. (d)

(xv) Transpiration is useful to the plant because it [Semester I 2021]
(a) creates a suction force for absorption of water from the soil
(b) helps in photophosphorylation
(c) synthesises glucose
(d) splits water molecules

Ans. (a)

(xvi) Hydathodes are related to which of the following process? [Semester I 2021]
(a) Transpiration (b) Absorption of water
(c) Photosynthesis (d) Guttation

Ans. (d)

(xvii) The process of guttation takes place
(a) when the root pressure is high and the rate of transpiration is low
(b) when the root pressure is low and the rate of transpiration is high
(c) when the root pressure equals the rate of transpiration
(d) when the root pressure as well as rate of transpiration are high

Ans. (a)

(xviii) In which of the following conditions, plants lose water by guttation?
(a) Soil is wet and atmosphere is dry
(b) Soil is wet and atmosphere is humid
(c) Both soil and atmosphere are dry
(d) Rate of transpiration is high

Ans. (b)

6. Fill in the blanks by using suitable words.

(i) Plants become cool as a result of ....

(ii) Transpiration normally takes place in the presence of ....

(iii) 95% of the total transpiration takes place through ....

(iv) Stomata are of two different shapes, i.e. .... and ....

(v) Guard cells become .... when they gain water and become .... when they lose water.

(vi) Transpiration helps in creating .... force and in eliminating excess ....

(vii) Closing of ...... and shedding of leaves reduce .... .

(viii) .... is used to measure the rate of transpiration.

Ans. (i) transpiration (ii) sunlight

(iii) stomata

(iv) kidney-shaped, dumb-bell-shaped

(v) turgid, flaccid

(vi) suction, water

(vii) stomata, transpiration

(viii) Ganong's potometer

7. Choose the odd one out from the following terms given below and name the category to which other three belong.

(i) Transpiration, Photosynthesis, Phagocytosis, Guttation [2014]

(ii) CO_2, Silicon oil, Oxi-ethylene, Auxin

(iii) Light, Wind, Atmospheric pressure, Water content of leaves.

Ans. (i) **Odd term** is phagocytosis.
Rest three are terms related to plant physiology.

(ii) **Odd term** is auxin.
Rest three are antitranspirants (i.e. reduce the rate of transpiration).

(iii) **Odd term** is water content of leaves.
Rest three are the external factors which affect the rate of transpiration.

8. Given below are the sets of five terms each. Rewrite the terms in correct order of logical sequence.

(i) Thick wall, Guard cell, Epidermal cell, Chloroplast, Thin wall

(ii) Spongy tissue, Upper epidermis, Stoma, Palisade tissue, Sub-stomatal space [2013]

(iii) Stoma, Mesophyll cells, Xylem, Substomatal space, Intercellular space (loss of water due to transpiration). [2010]

(iv) Loss of ion, Exosmosis, Decrease solute concentration, Increase water potential, Guard cell flaccid

Ans. (i) Epidermal cell, Thin wall, Guard cell, Chloroplast, Thick wall

(ii) Upper epidermis, Palisade tissue, Spongy tissue, sub-stomatal space, Stoma

(iii) Xylem, Mesophyll cells, Intercellular space, sub-stomatal space, Stoma

(iv) Loss of ion, Decrease solute concentration, Increase water potential, Exosmosis, Guard cell flaccid

9. State the exact location of the following.

(i) Cuticle (ii) Lenticels

(iii) Hydathodes (iv) Guttation

Ans. (i) Cuticle is present on the epidermis of leaves.

(ii) Lenticels can be found on the bark of woody stem.

(iii) Hydathodes are present along leaf margin.

(iv) Guttation occurs through hydathodes which are located near the end of veins.

10. State the main function of the following.

(i) Lenticels (ii) Sunken stomata

(iii) Epidermal hair

Ans. (i) Lenticels are responsible for the exchange of respiratory gases.

(ii) Sunken stomata usually found in succulent xerophytes reduce transpiration.

(iii) Thick coat of epidermal hairs on leaf help in reducing transpiration.

11. Mention one difference between each of the following pairs on the basis of what is given in the bracket.

(i) Transpiration and Translocation (definition)

(ii) Leaf and Liver (form in which glucose is stored) [2018]

(iii) Stomata and Lenticels (location)

(iv) Stomatal transpiration and Cuticular transpiration (amount of water lost)

(v) Evaporation and Transpiration (factors controlling)

(vi) Transpiration and Perspiration (parts involved)

(vii) Guttation and Bleeding in plants (cause) [2011]

Ans. (i) Difference between transpiration and translocation is as follows

Transpiration	Translocation
It is the loss of water in the form of vapour.	It is the transportation of food materials within the plant body.

(ii) Difference between leaf and liver is as follows

Leaf	Liver
Glucose is stored in the form of starch.	Glucose is stored in the form of glycogen.

(iii) Difference between stomata and lenticels is as follows

Stomata	Lenticels
Minute opening present mainly on the surface of leaves.	These are found on the bark of woody stems.

(iv) Difference between stomatal transpiration and cuticular transpiration is as follows

Stomatal transpiration	Cuticular transpiration
Water loss is more.	Water loss is less.

(v) Difference between evaporation and transpiration is as follows

Evaporation	Transpiration
It is a physical change controlled by the temperature and humidity of the atmosphere.	It is a vital and partly a physical process controlled by both internal and external factors.

(vi) Difference between transpiration and perspiration is as follows

Transpiration	Perspiration
It takes place mainly through stomata.	It takes place through sweat pores.

(vii) Difference between guttation and bleeding is as follows

Guttation	Bleeding
It is exudation of water from leaves, occurring when the amount of root pressure is high and rate of transpiration is low.	It is the exudation of cell sap from the injured or cut part of a plant, due to increased root pressure.

12. Give biological/technical terms for the following.

(i) The wax-like layer on the epidermis of leaves which reduce the transpiration. [2018]

(ii) The permanently open structures seen on the bark of an old woody stem. [2013]

(iii) Chemical substance used to reduce rate of transpiration.

(iv) An apparatus that measures the rate of water uptake in a cut shoot due to transpiration. [2017]

(v) Exudation of sap from injured parts of a plant. [2008]

Ans. (i) Cuticle (ii) Lenticels
(iii) Antitranspirant (iv) Potometer
(v) Bleeding

13. Briefly explain the following terms.

(i) Transpiration [2023]
(ii) Dorsiventral leaves (iii) Endosmosis
(iv) Guttation (v) Wilting

Ans. (i) Transpiration is the process of loss of water from the exposed part of plant in the form of vapour.

(ii) A dorsiventral leaf is the one that has two surfaces differing from each other in appearance and structure.

(iii) The inward movement of water into cell is called endosmosis.

(iv) The exudation of water drops from the edges or tips of leaves through hydathodes is called guttation.

(v) Wilting is the loss of turgidity of leaves and other soft aerial parts causing drooping, folding and rolling of leaves. It occurs when rate of transpiration exceeds rate of absorption.

14. Answer the following questions briefly.

(i) How are guard cells adapted for transpiration?

(ii) Atmospheric humidity promotes transpiration from a green plant. Do you agree? [2008]

(iii) Explain how the rate of transpiration is affected on a windy day. [2009]

(iv) Along with water what other components are lost during guttation?

Ans. (i) The outer wall of guard cell is thin, while the inner wall is thick. The guard cells control the opening and closing of stomata by changing their turgidity.

(ii) No, high atmospheric humidity reduces the rate of outward diffusion of the internal water vapour across stomata, thereby reducing the rate of transpiration.

(iii) On a windy day, the water vapour released from the leaves by transpiration are removed faster and the leaf does not get saturated with water vapour. So, transpiration is more.

(iv) The other components lost during guttation along with water are mineral salts, organic acids, carbohydrates and nitrogenous compounds.

16. Choose between the two options to answer the question specified in the brackets for the following. Lenticels or stomata (Which one remains open always)? [2018]

Ans. Lenticels

2 Marks Questions

17. State any two adaptations in plants to reduce transpiration. [2023]

Ans. Adaptations in plants to reduce transpiration are as follows

- The leaves in the desert plants are modified into spines to decrease the surface area for transpiration.
- A waxy layer called cuticle on the surface of the leaves lowers the transpiration rate.

18. Illustrate the movement of water in leaves.

Ans. Transpiration from the leaves sets up a pressure gradient between the outside air and the air spaces of the leaf. The gradient is transmitted into the photosynthetic cells and on all water-filled xylem in the leaf vein. This facilitates movement of water from xylem to the guard cells of stomata.

19. Leaves of certain plants roll up on a hot sunny day. Explain by giving suitable reasons. [2023]

Ans. Leaves of some plants roll up on a bright sunny day to reduce the effective surface area for transpiration. The reduced surface area ultimately reduces the rate of transpiration.

20. Explain why transpirations pull is necessary.

Ans. Transpiration pull is necessary because it helps in the absorption and upward movement of water and minerals from roots to the leaves. It protects the plants from being damaged by bright sunlight.

3 Marks Questions

21. What is the role of transpiration in transportation? Explain with diagram.

Ans. The loss of water in transpiration creates a suction which pulls water from the xylem cells of roots. Thus, water reaches to the upper part of the plant by transpiration pull.

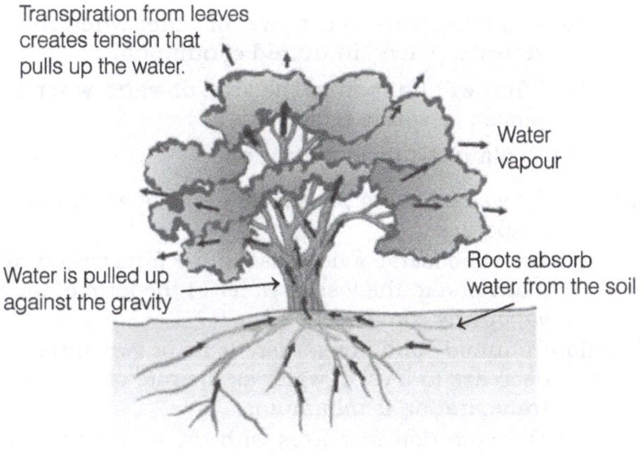

Water molecule and minerals

22. Write about any three internal factors, explaining how they affect rate of transpiration.

Ans. The rate of transpiration can be affected by internal factors such as

(i) **Leaf area** The rate of transpiration is high in plants having broad leaves as compared to those plants having narrow leaves.
Thus, greater the surface area, greater is the rate of transpiration.

(ii) **Succulence** The succulent leaves and stem have mucilage covering in their tissues. This reduces the rate of transpiration by holding water.

(iii) **Age of plant** The rate of transpiration is different at different age of plant. It is slow at the seedling stage, maximum at maturity and gradually decreases near senescence.

Section-II [5 Marks]

Structured Questions

1. Most of the water absorbed by the plants is lost by them in the form of vapours. Only small fraction is utilised by the plant.

(i) Why do plants absorb more water than they require?

(ii) Briefly explain how the rate of transpiration is affected by CO_2 concentration.

(iii) Write any two major advantages of transpiration.

(iv) Write any two morphological changes adapted by plants in order to reduce transpiration.

(v) What are anti-transpirants?

Ans. (i) Plants absorb more water than they require because the percentage of minerals is very low in water hence to continue the supply of minerals they absorb more water.

(ii) Increase in CO_2 level in atmosphere result in stomatal closure and cause decrease in transpiration.

(iii) Two advantages of transpiration are

(a) It reduces the temperature of the leaf giving a cooling effect to plant.

(b) It helps in the distribution of water and mineral salts to various plant organs.

(iv) Two morphological adaptations are

(a) Sunken stomata

(b) Epidermal hairs

(v) Anti-transpirants are physical or chemical agents which help in reducing the excessive loss of water through transpiration.

2. Stomata are tiny pores present on leaf surface and green stem. These generally open during daytime and play role in exchange of gases.

(i) What happens when the guard cells are full of water?

(ii) Draw the well-labelled diagram of stomata found in monocot leaves.

(iii) How does K ion concentration regulate the opening of stomata?

(iv) What happens when K^+ ion concentration decreases?

(v) Movement of water vapour from cell surface to the outer atmosphere involves which process?

Ans. (i) When the guard cells are full of water, they swell and become turgid. This causes guard cells to bend away from each other and result in opening of stomata.

(ii)

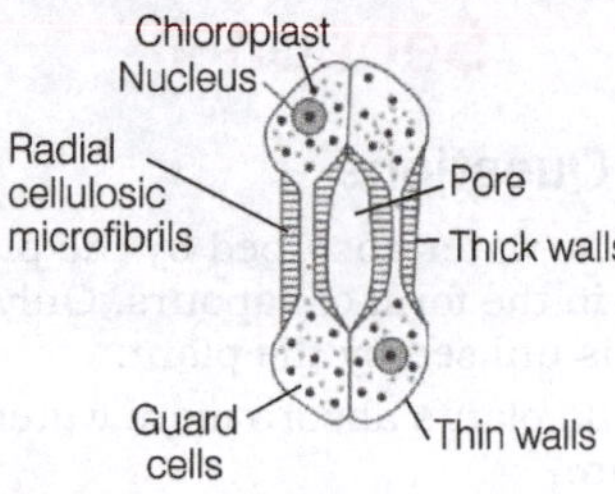

(iii) During daytime concentration of K^+ ions increases and the guard cells become turgid due to endosmosis. Hence result in opening of stomatal pores.

(iv) During night time, when concentration of K^+ ions decreases, the guard cells become flaccid and thus the stomatal pores close.

(v) Diffusion is the movement of water vapour from cell surface to the outer atmosphere.

3. The figure given below represents an experimental setup with a weighing machine to demonstrate a particular process in plants. The experimental setup was placed in bright sunlight. Study the diagram and answer the following questions. **[2014]**

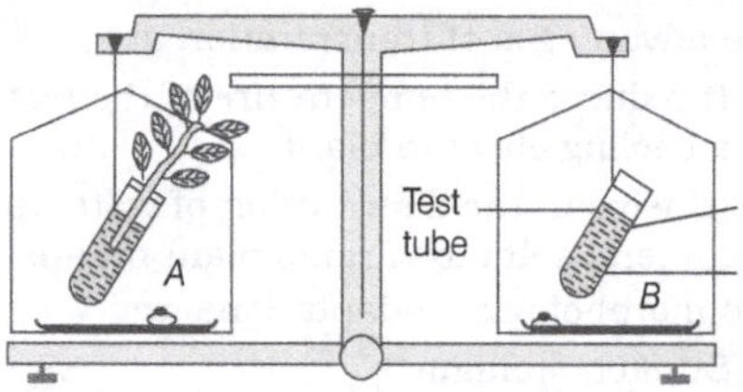

(i) Name the process intended for study.

(ii) Define the above mentioned process.

(iii) What was observed when the weight of the test tube (*A* and *B*) taken before and after the experiment? Give reasons to justify your observation in *A* and *B*.

(iv) What is the purpose of keeping the test tube *B* in the experimental setup?

(v) Mention two effects of above mentioned process in plant if it occurs in excess.

Ans. (i) The process intended for study is transpiration.

(ii) Transpiration is the process of loss of water in the form of vapour from the aerial parts of the plant.

(iii) It was observed after the experiment that the test tube *A* has risen up due to the loss of weight and in test tube *B*, the weight remains unchanged. This happens because in test tube *A* plant undergoes transpiration and loses water while in test tube *B*, no transpiration occurs because there was no plant in the test tube. Also direct evaporation was prevented from the surface so, weight remains unchanged.

(iv) Test tube *B* was kept in the experimental setup as a control.

(v) Stunted growth and wilting are the two effects of the process occur in excess.

4. The diagram below represents a process in plants. The setup was placed in bright sunlight. Answer the following questions. **[2018]**

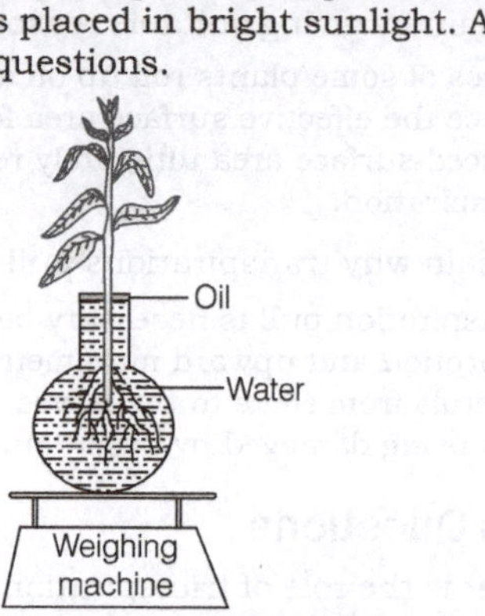

(i) Why was oil added to the water?

(ii) When placed in bright sunlight for four hours, what do you observe with regard to the initial and final weight of the plant? Give a suitable reason for your answer.

(iii) What happens to the level of water when this setup is placed in humid conditions?

(iv) What will happen to the level of water when it is placed in windy conditions?

(v) Explain the term 'guttation'.

Ans. (i) Oil was added to prevent any loss of water due to evaporation.

(ii) We will observe a decrease in the final weight of plant due to the loss of water in the form of water vapour by transpiration.

(iii) In humid conditions, there is no or very little decrease in level of water as the rate of transpiration is minimum.

(iv) Transpiration increases with the velocity of wind. Thus, water level will decrease in windy conditions.

(v) Guttation is the process of loss of water in the form of water droplets through hydathodes present along leaf margin. It occurs when the amount of root pressure is high and rate of transpiration is low.

5. An apparatus shown below was setup to investigate a physiological process in plants. The setup was kept in sunlight for two hours. Droplets of water were then seen inside the bell jar. Answer the questions that follow. **[2015]**

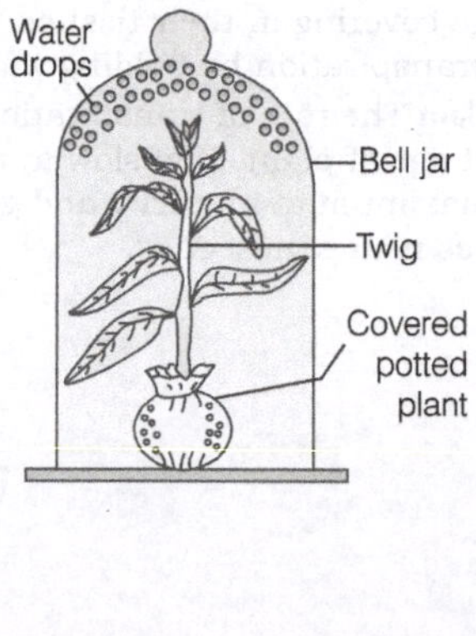

(i) Name the process being studied.
(ii) Explain the process named in (i) above.
(iii) Why was the pot covered with a plastic sheet?
(iv) Suggest a suitable control for this experiment.
(v) How is the above mentioned process useful for plant?

Ans. (i) The process being studied through this experiment is transpiration.
(ii) Refer to text on page no. 52. 'Transpiration'.
(iii) Pot was covered with a plastic sheet so as to prevent the escape of water vapour from the pot.
(iv) Control for the experiment can be the empty plastic sheet with its mouth tied (without any plant in it) kept in the sunlight. This will not show any drops of water on the bell jar.
(v) This process helps in transport of minerals and also provides cooling effect to plant.

6. Given below is an apparatus which was setup to investigate a physiological process in plants. The setup was placed in bright sunlight. Answer the questions that follow.

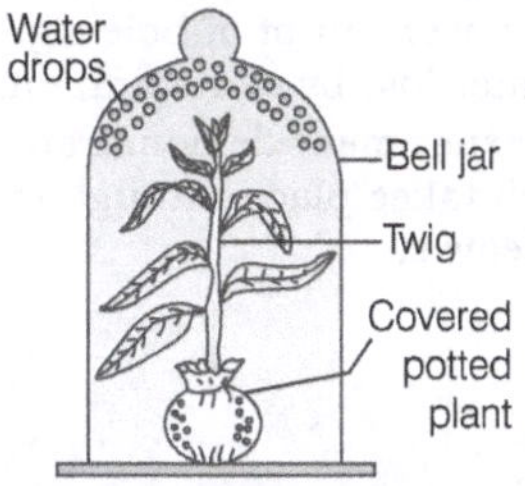

(i) Name and define the process being studied.
(ii) Why was it necessary to enclose the pot in a rubber sheet?
(iii) Mention two external factors which can accelerate the above process.
(iv) List two adaptations in plants to reduce the above process.
(v) Draw a neat and labelled diagram of a stomatal apparatus.

Ans. (i) The process being studied is transpiration. It is the process of loss of water in the form of vapour from the exposed or aerial parts of a plant (such as leaves, etc.).
(ii) It was necessary to enclose the pot in a rubber sheet to prevent the escape water vapours from the pot.
(iii) The two external factors which can accelerate transpiration are
(a) Temperature (b) Humidity
(iv) Adaptations to reduce the transpiration are
(a) The presence of sunken stomata.
(b) The presence of thick cuticle on leaves.
(v)

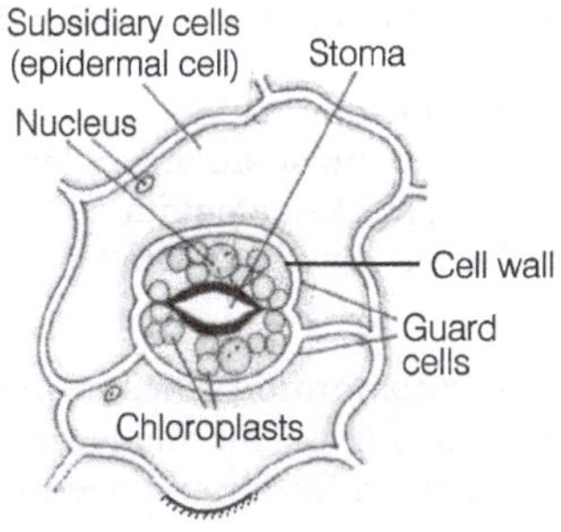

Stomatal apparatus

7. Given below is the diagram of an experimental setup to study the process of transpiration. Cobalt chloride papers are fixed on the upper as well as lower surface of the leaf. Answer the questions that follow. **[Semester I 2021]**

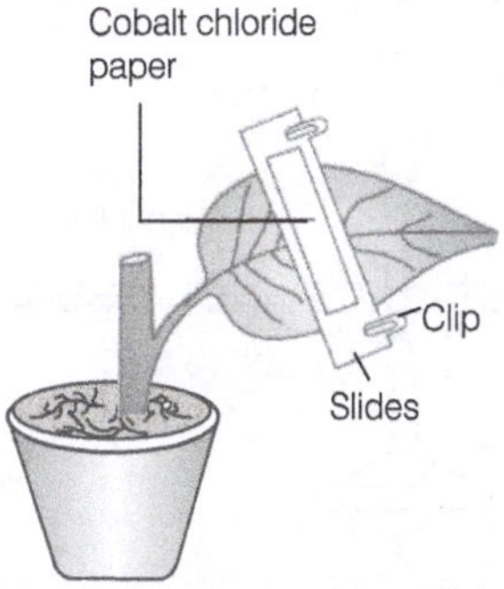

(i) Which is the aim of the experiment?
(a) To prove that more transpiration occurs from the lower surface of a dicot leaf
(b) To prove that more transpiration occurs from the upper surface of dicot leaf
(c) To prove that transpiration is equal on both sides of the leaf
(d) To prove that transpiration does not take place in a dicot leaf

Ans. (a)

(ii) What is the colour of dry cobalt chloride paper?
(a) Pink (b) Blue
(c) Brown (d) White

Ans. (b)

(iii) After about an hour, what change if any, would you expect to find in the cobalt chloride paper placed on the upper and lower surface of the leaf.
(a) Upper surface-Pink, Lower surface-Blue
(b) Upper surface-White, Lower surface-Blue
(c) Upper surface-Less pink, Lower surface-More pink
(d) Upper surface-More pink, Lower surface-Less pink

Ans. (c)

(iv) Two adaptations in plants to reduce the transpiration are
(a) narrow leaves, thin cuticle
(b) fewer stomata, broad lamina of leaves
(c) thin cuticle, sunken stoamta
(d) narrow leaves, fewer stomata

Ans. (d)

(v) The rate of transpiration is less when there is
(a) high humidity in the air and low temperature
(b) less humidity in the air and decrease in atmospheric pressure
(c) bright sunlight and high temperature
(d) more wind and low intensity of sunlight

Ans. (a)

8. The diagram of an apparatus given below demonstrates a particular process in plants. Study the same and answer the questions that follows. **[2016]**

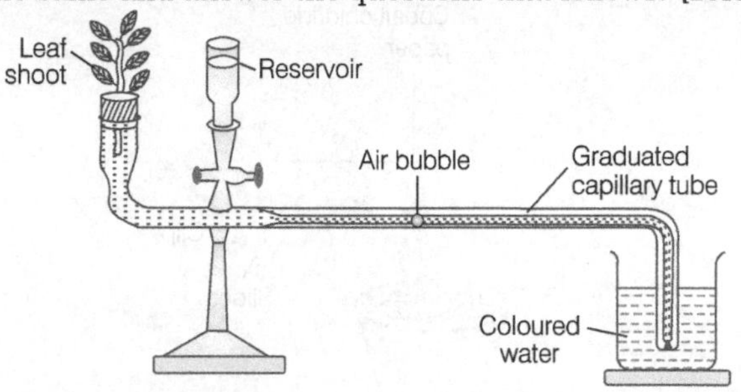

(i) Name the apparatus.
(ii) Which phenomenon is demonstrated by this apparatus?
(iii) Explain the phenomemon mentioned in (ii) above.
(iv) State two limitations of using this apparatus.
(v) What is the importance of the air bubble in this experiment?
(vi) Name the structure in a plant through which the above process takes place.

Ans. (i) The given apparatus is Ganong's potometer.
(ii) Transpiration is demonstrated by this apparatus.
(iii) Transpiration is the loss of water as vapours from aerial parts of the plant into the atmosphere.
(iv) Two limitations of Ganong's potometer are
(a) Introduction of air bubble is not easy.
(b) The twig may die if the experiment takes long time.
(v) The movement of bubble signifies the amount of water lost by transpiration.
(vi) The experiment demonstrates transpiration which takes place through stomata present on the leaves.

Chapter Assessment

Section-I

1 Mark Questions

1. Name the following.
   (i) The cell which controls opening and closing of stomata.
   (ii) The chemical used to test the rate of transpiration on either side of leaf.
   (iii) The metallic cation involved in opening and closing of stomata.
2. Correct and rewrite the statements by changing the underlined words.
   (i) Major part of transpiration occurs from cuticle and very little from lenticels.
   (ii) In bleeding, the exudate is mainly water and mineral.
3. Give biological reasons for the following.
   (i) Some plants show wilting in their leaves during mid-day even when the soil is well-watered.
   (ii) Despite growing in moist condition, loss of water through leaf margin is observed in banana plant.
   (iii) In succulents like cacti, stomata are closed during day.
4. (i) Match the following columns.

	Column I		Column II
A.	Exudation of sap from the injured parts of plant	1.	Bleeding
B.	Helps in loss of water vapours due to transpiration	2.	Guard cells
C.	Control the opening and closing of stomata	3.	Lenticels
D.	Protects the surface and reduces water loss	4.	Stomata
E.	Help in gaseous exchange	5.	Cuticle

   (ii) Match the following columns.

	Column I		Column II
A.	Transpiration	1.	Cactus
B.	Movement of water	2.	Stomata
C.	Guttation	3.	Maize plant
D.	Low rate of transpiration	4.	Xylem
E.	High rate of transpiration	5.	Hydathodes

5. Choose the correct answer from the four options given below.
   (i) Which of the following is not involved in the process of transpiration?
   (a) Roots (b) Leaves
   (c) Bark (d) Lenticels
   (ii) After leaf falls in the autumn, which of the following is the only site of water loss in deciduous trees?
   (a) Cuticle
   (b) Lenticel
   (c) Stomata
   (d) Bark
   (iii) In which of the following plants, leaf surface may be covered by thick coating of epidermal hair to reduce transpiration?
   (a) Cucurbits (b) Banyan
   (c) *Nerium* (d) Lavender
6. Fill in the blanks by using suitable words.
   (i) Openings found more on the under surface of the dorsiventral leaf are ....
   (ii) The leaves of the .... plants have thick cuticles.
   (iii) In *Nerium*, stomata are ....
   (iv) Transpiration .... with wind speed.
   (v) .... is an antitranspirant.
7. Given below are five terms each. Rewrite the terms in the correct order as to be in logical sequence of opening of stomata.
   Increased solute concentration, Endosmosis of water, Increased turgidity, Accumulation of   ions, Decreased water potential
8. State the exact location of the following.
   (i) Transpiration
   (ii) Mesophyll cell
   (iii) Stoma
9. State the main function of the following.
   (i) Guard cells
   (ii) Suction force
   (iii) Diffusion
10. Mention one difference between each of the following pairs on the basis of what is given in the bracket.
   (i) Transpiration and Guttation (effect)
   (ii) Evaporation and Guttation (define)

11. Give the biological/technical term for the following.
   (i) Loss of water as droplets through leaves of an intact plant.
   (ii) A chemical substance which closes stomata for more than two weeks.

12. Briefly explain the following terms.
   (i) Isobilateral leaves (ii) Turgor operated valves

13. Answer the following questions briefly.
   (i) Mention any two adaptations found in plants to reduce transpiration.
   (ii) Does leaf area affect the rate of transpiration?

2 Marks Questions

14. On a rainy day, there is no transpiration. Explain.

15. If 50% of the leaves are removed from a plant, what will be effect on transpiration and why?

3 Marks Questions

16. 'The movement of water is through transpiration pull'. Discuss if this statement is 100% true. Give explanation for your answer.

17. Well-watered plants transpire more during sunny and windy days than in cool and calm mornings. Comment.

Section-II [5 Marks]

Structured Questions

18. Observe the diagram and answer the following questions.

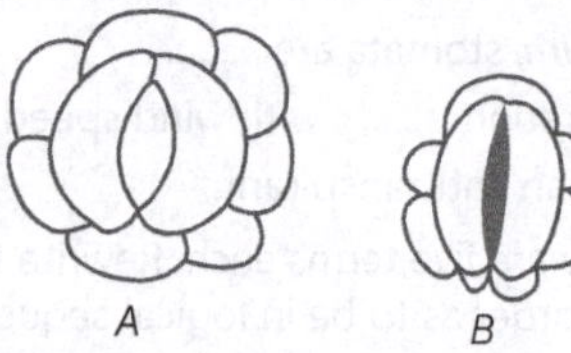

   (i) In which type of plants, i.e. in monocots or dicots, these types of guard cells found?
   (ii) Which of these shows a higher water content (*A*) or (*B*)?
   (iii) State the conditions of the guard cells in (*A*) and (*B*).
   (iv) What is the effect of K^+ion in both the conditions.
   (v) Which condition of stomata is seen in the plant of family–Crassulaceae during daytime?

19. The given diagram represents an experiment to demonstrate a certain phenomenon in a green plant.

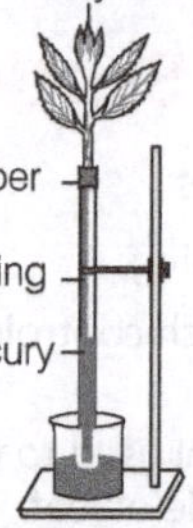

   (i) Has the level of mercury in the glass tubing risen or fallen?
   (ii) Name the life process of the plant which has caused the change in the level of mercury.
   (iii) What is the difference between stomata and lenticels?
   (iv) State any three advantages of this process to the plant.
   (v) Which conducting tissue of the plant does the glass-tubing represent-xylem or phloem?

20. Water is necessary for plants but only a small amount of water taken up by the roots is used for growth and metabolism. The remaining is lost by transpiration and guttation.
   (i) The most valid and recent explanation for stomatal movement is ....
   (ii) Write any two factors which affect stomata opening.
   (iii) Which factor is the most important in the regulation of transpiration?
   (iv) A cut twig having fresh flower and bud is kept in minute amount of water containing salt. It remains fresh for longer period what can be the reason.
   (v) What is the rate of transpiration in plants growing in hills?

For explanations scan the given QR Code

Olympiad Section*

Brain Teasing Questions asked in Previous Olympiads

1 Match the processes (A–D) listed in Column I with the correct descriptions given in Column II and choose the correct answer. **[INBO 2021]**

	Column I		Column II
A.	Osmosis	1.	Diffusional space outside plasma membrane
B.	Guttation	2.	Diffusional space within plasma membrane
C.	Apoplast	3.	Movement of water across membrane
D.	Symplast	4.	Fluid exudate

(a) A-3, B-4, C-1, D-2 (b) A-4, B-3, C-2, D-1
(c) A-3, B-2, C-1, D-4 (d) A-3, B-4, C-2, D-1

2 Observe the experimental setup shown here carefully and answer the following question. **[INBO 2019]**

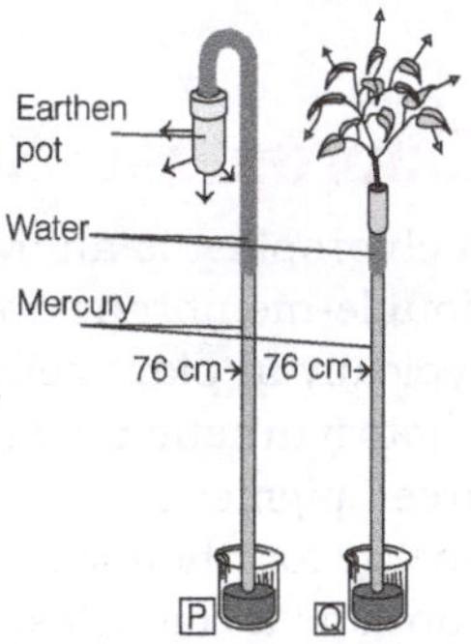

Which of the following hypothesis is the experimental setup designed to test ?

(a) The amount of water required by a plant increases with increase in the rate of evaporation of water through transpiration
(b) The process of transpiration can generate enough pressure to pull water up the column
(c) The increase in the atmospheric pressure increases the rate of transpiration in plants
(d) The process of water transport though stem requires an unbroken column of liquid

3 Guttation (picture below) in small plants happens at night and is due to osmosis. Which of the following statements describes how the process of guttation occurs? **[IJSO 2018, University of Botswana]**

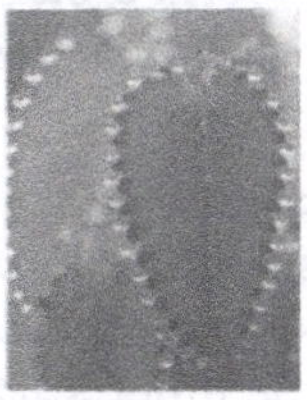

(a) Positive pressure generated in the roots pushes water out of the xylem in the leaves
(b) Water accumulates in the leaves because evaporation happens slower than transpiration
(c) Water is pulled up in large quantities to leaves because of an increase in solute concentrations in the leaves
(d) Water from dew gathers on the surface of plant leaves

4 In an experiment involving treatments to demonstrate transpiration, six experimental setups were as follows

I. Woody plant with only leaves coated with vaseline jelly.
II. Woody plant with only stem coated with vaseline jelly.
III. Woody plant without any coating of vaseline jelly.
IV. Herbaceous plant with only stem coated with vaseline jelly.
V. Herbaceous plant with only leaf coated with vaseline jelly.
VI. Herbaceous plant without any coating of vaseline jelly. **[INJSO 2017]**

Cobalt chloride ($CoCl_2$) paper (changes from blue to pink when wet) was attached to the leaves and stem. The plants were well-watered and kept under adequate sunlight. The following were proposed

	Colour change of $CoCl_2$ paper on	
Plants	**Leaves**	**Stem**
I	Blue	Blue
II	Pink	Pink
III	Pink	Blue
IV	Blue	Blue
V	Blue	Pink
VI	Pink	Blue

Which of the above is/are correct?

(a) I, II and V
(b) Only II
(c) III, IV and VI
(d) Only V

Answers

1. (a) **2.** (b) **3.** (a) **4.** (d)

**These questions may or may not be asked in the examination, have been given just for additional practice required for olympiads, scholarship exams etc. For detailed explanations refer Page No. 247.*

CHAPTER

05

Photosynthesis

Chapter Inside

- Chloroplast : Site of Photosynthesis • Stomata • Raw Materials for Photosynthesis
- Mechanism of Photosynthesis • Adaptations of Leaves for Photosynthesis • Factors Affecting Photosynthesis
- Importance of Photosynthesis • Carbon Cycle • Experiments Based on Photosynthesis

Food is the foremost requirement of all living beings on Earth as it provides chemical energy to carryout various metabolic activities.

Plants (autotrophs) are capable of synthesising food or organic material through photosynthesis, whereas animals (heterotrophs) derive food from plants directly or indirectly. **Photosynthesis** is a physiological process in which living plant cells that contain chlorophyll, synthesise food in the form of glucose and starch, from CO_2 and water, using light energy.

Overall reaction of photosynthesis can be summarised as follows

$$\underset{\text{Carbon dioxide}}{6CO_2} + \underset{\text{Water}}{12H_2O} \xrightarrow[\text{Chlorophyll}]{\text{Sunlight}} \underset{\text{Sugar}}{C_6H_{12}O_6} + \underset{\text{Water}}{6H_2O} + \underset{\text{Oxygen}}{6O_2} \uparrow \text{(Byproduct)}$$

In plants and algae, photosynthesis takes place in organelles called **chloroplast**. A typical plant cell contains 10-100 chloroplasts.

Chloroplast : Site of Photosynthesis

A chloroplast is an oval, minute and double-membrane bound cell organelle found typically in plant cells. It contains an complete photosynthetic machinery within it. It contains a green pigment called **chlorophyll**, which absorbs light energy for photosynthesis. Internally, chloroplast contains a colourless, proteinaceous ground substance known as **stroma** and a membrane system containing a number of disc-like sacs known as **thylakoids**.

At some places, the thylakoids arrange themselves to form a stack of coin-like structure, visible as a cylindrical dense granular bodies called **grana** (green in colour).

Each stack of thylakoid sacs is connected by a structure known as **stroma lamellae**, which helps in keeping the sacs at a distance from each other. On the inner surface of the lamella membrane, small spherical structures called **quantasomes** are present.

These are the structural and functional units of chloroplast.

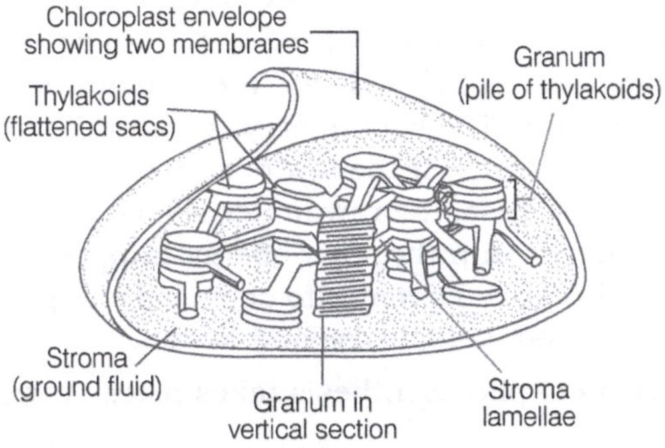

A diagram showing internal structure of chloroplast as revealed by electron microscope

The chloroplasts mainly occur in chlorenchymatous cells, particularly in mesophyll of leaves. They are also found in the guard cells of the stomata and in the outer layers of the green stems.

Stomata

These are tiny openings present in large numbers on the lower epidermis of the leaf. They are responsible for the **gaseous exchange** in the process of photosynthesis, respiration and transpiration. Stomata open during the daytime in the presence of light to allow CO_2 to diffuse into it. On the other hand, they get closed when plants are not photosynthesising, i.e. in the absence of light. The opening and closing of stomata depends on the turgidity of the guard cells. They have a thick and rigid **inner** wall facing the opening and a thin elastic **outer** wall on the opposite side. Their cytoplasm contains chloroplasts.

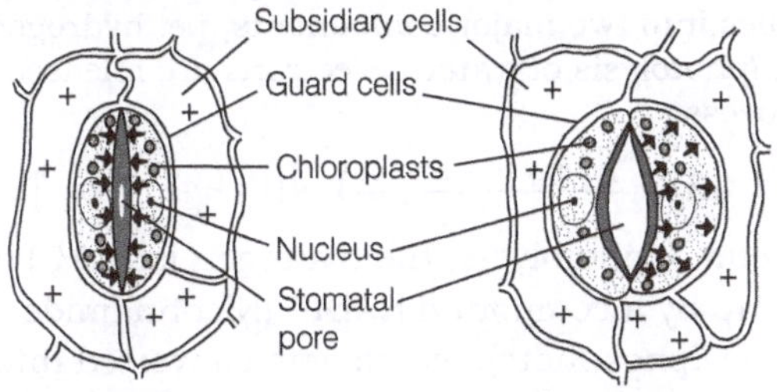

Opening and Closing of Stomata

The opening and closing of stomata is based on the concentration of certain substances like glucose and potassium (K^+) ions. Based on this fact, there are two theories that govern the opening and closing of stomata.

(i) Sugar concentration theory (old)

(ii) Potassium ion (K^+) exchange theory (recent)

According to potassium ion (K^+) theory, the opening of stomata is due to the entry of K^+ ions in the guard cells. This is aided by the ATP produced by the plant during the daytime (when it photosynthesises) and leads to opening of stomata.

The stomatal closure, on the other hand, occurs during the night time when no photosynthesis takes place. The K^+ ions leak out of the guard cells making the stomata lose its turgidity and thus resulting in closure of stomatal pore. A detailed description of this theory is given in the previous chapter.

Raw Materials for Photosynthesis

Before studying the mechanism of photosynthesis, let's take a brief look on the essential materials required for the process of photosynthesis. These basically involves

A. Photopigments

B. Chemical (Raw) materials

C. Light or solar energy

The photopigments required for photosynthesis majorly include chlorophyll and carotenoids.

Chlorophyll

It is the most important pigment in plants. It facilitates photosynthesis and gives green colour to the plants. The molecule of chlorophyll consists of a porphyrin ring with Mg^{2+} ions at its centre and a long hydrocarbon chain attached to the porphyrin ring.

There are nine different types of chlorophyll pigments found in plants like **chlorophyll-*a*, chlorophyll-*b***, etc., out of which chlorophyll-*a* is the most widely occurring. Chlorophyll absorbs blue, violet and red wavelengths of light more intensely, while green wavelength is weakly absorbed.

The green light is reflected away from the chlorophyll (chloroplast) so it appears green. Chlorophyll is highly sensitive to light especially sunlight. Too much exposure of light can destroy it (solarisation). However, the formation of chlorophyll also depends on the exposure of plants to light.

Carotenoids

These are a large group of hydrocarbon pigments found in plants. **Xanthophylls** are yellow coloured pigments and **carotene** is an orange pigment. These pigments are not visible due to dominance of green colour of chlorophyll but can be observed in leaves before they fall. Carotenoids protect the chlorophyll from photo-oxidation. They also absorb and transfer the light energy to chlorophyll centre.

The raw materials required for photosynthesis are CO_2 and water

Carbon Dioxide

Plants absorb CO_2 from the atmosphere and use it as a substrate. CO_2 enters the leaf by diffusion, down the concentration from atmosphere, through the stomata.

It gets converted to glucose at the end of reaction.

Water

Plants absorb water from the soil with the help of roots. It is said that the oxygen produced in the end of reaction comes from water.

Light Energy

Energy from the Sun is necessary for photosynthesis to take place. It activates photosystems present in photopigment.

Photosystems

The light harvesting complexes in plants are the photosystems. These are made up of hundreds of pigment molecules bounded by proteins. The photosystem contains a reaction centre, where the actual photosynthetic reaction occurs.

Photosystems are of two types, I and II,

PS-I It absorbs solar energy at 700 nm and supplies the electron to $NADP^+$.

PS-II It absorbs solar energy at 680 nm and supplies the excited electrons to the cytochrome centre.

Check Your LEARNING...

1. Name the cell organelle that traps light energy for making food for the plants.
2. What are quantasomes?
3. State the location of chlorophyll molecule in the chloroplast?
4. What is the role of water in the mechanism of photosynthesis?
5. Why is light energy necessary for photosynthesis?

Mechanism of Photosynthesis

Photosynthetic process begins when the sunlight falls on the **mesophyll cells** of the leaf. Both palisade and spongy mesophyll cells are the principal centre for this activity. The light energy is trapped by the chlorophyll present on the layers of mesophyll cells. During the process, the raw materials, i.e. CO_2 and water, together with the solar energy trapped by the chlorophyll, get converted into chemical energy in the form of food, i.e. glucose and starch.

The process of photosynthesis takes place in two phases

1. Light reaction (photochemical phase)
2. Dark reaction (biosynthetic phase)

1. Light Reaction (Photochemical Phase)

This is a **light dependent phase,** where a quick succession of chemical reactions initiated by light occurs, that is why it is also called **photochemical phase**. The light of visible wavelengths, i.e. 400-700 nm are absorbed by chlorophyll molecules present in the **thylakoids of the chloroplast.**

This phase is completed in two main sub-stages as follows

Photolysis of Water

It is splitting of water into H^+ and O_2 in the presence of light. This process occurs in the grana of chloroplast and it gets completed into two steps

Step 1 Activation of chlorophyll The chlorophyll molecule gets activated by absorbing photons of the light energy.

Step 2 Splitting of water The absorbed energy by the activation of chlorophyll is used in splitting of water molecules into two major components, i.e. hydrogen and O_2 (photolysis of water). Electrons are released in this process.

$$2H_2O \xrightarrow{\text{Energy of 4 photons}} 4H^+ + 4e^- + O_2 \uparrow$$

At the end of photolysis, the hydrogen ions (H^+) are picked up by a compound **NADP**$^+$ (Nicotinamide Adenine Diphosphate), which gets converted into **NADPH** (Nicotinamide Adenine Dinucleotide Phosphate Hydrogen).

$$NADP^+ + e^- + H^+ \xrightarrow{\text{Enzyme}} NADPH$$

The oxygen component of water is released in the form of O_2 (molecular oxygen).

$$2O \longrightarrow O_2 \uparrow$$

Photophosphorylation

It is the process in which **ADP** (Adenosine Diphosphate) is converted into **ATP** (Adenosine Triphosphate) by the addition of one phosphate (Pi) group, i.e. inorganic phosphate. It involves the utilisation of the energy from the photons of sunlight. So simply, it is addition of a phosphate group 2 ADP in the presence of sunlight.

$$\text{ADP} + \text{Pi} \xrightarrow{\text{sunlight/photons}} \text{ATP}$$

To summarise, light reaction involves conversion of light energy to chemical energy in the form of ATP and NADPH molecules.

2. Dark Reaction (Biosynthetic Phase/Calvin Cycle)

The phase in which synthesis of organic substances takes place is called biosynthetic phase. The term 'dark reaction' does not mean that the reaction is occurring only at night. It is light independent which means that presence or absence of light does not hinder these reactions.

That is why, these are also called **'light independent reactions'**. This reaction takes place in the **stroma** or **matrix** of the chloroplast. The dark reaction and light reaction take place simultaneously with the time gap of less than one thousand of a second.

During dark reaction, fixation and reduction of CO_2 occur. It results in the formation of carbohydrates by the utilisation of ATP and NADPH (produced as the result of light reaction). RuBP (Ribulose Bisphosphate) acts as a primary acceptor of atmospheric CO_2 in the beginning of this phase and at the end of the cycle, glucose is synthesised and RuBP is regenerated. This process occurs through Calvin cycle.

Calvin Cycle (C_3 Pathway)

In dark reaction, the reduction of CO_2 occurs in the stroma of chloroplasts by a series of sequential reactions known as Calvin cycle (named after its discoverer **Melvin Calvin**).

Calvin cycle although does not require light, but it occurs during the day, when a green plant is producing high levels of ATP and NADPH. The three major steps of Calvin or C_3 cycle are summarised below

(i) **Carboxylation** It is the most crucial step of the Calvin cycle in which utilisation of CO_2 takes place for the carboxylation of RuBP. This reaction is catalysed by the enzyme **RuBP carboxylase**, which finally results in the formation of 2 molecules of 3PGA (3-Phosphoglyceric Acid).

$$CO_2 + \text{RuBP} + H_2O \xrightarrow[\text{Mg}^{2+}]{\text{RuBisCO}} 2\ (\text{3PGA})$$

(ii) **Reduction** After the carboxylation reaction, reduction of PGA takes place through a series of reactions leading to the formation of glucose.

(iii) **Regeneration** This step requires one ATP molecule for phosphorylation. Hence, for every CO_2 molecule that enters the Calvin cycle, 3 molecules of ATP and 2 molecules of NADPH are required.

The overall reaction of this phase is

$$6\text{RuBP} + 6CO_2 + 18\text{ATP} + 12\text{NADPH} + 12e^- \longrightarrow$$
$$6\text{RuBP} + C_6H_{12}O_6 + 18\text{ADP} + 18\text{Pi} + 12\text{NADP}^+ + 6H_2O$$

The hydrogen ions combine with CO_2 to form glucose, which later gets stored in the form of starch by the process of **polymerisation** (where several molecules of glucose are formed from one molecule of starch).

Note Dark reaction does not require direct sunlight, but it depends on the products of the light reaction.

End Products of Photosynthesis

At the end of a photosynthetic reaction, the products formed are

(i) **Glucose** The simple carbohydrates formed during photosynthesis can be utilised in/for respiration, food storage and growth, e.g. the glucose is either immediately utilised by the cells or stored as sucrose, starch or cellulose and used in the synthesis of complex molecules like proteins, fats, etc.

(ii) **Oxygen** Some fraction of oxygen is used in respiratory process by plants (photorespiration) and rest diffuses out into the atmosphere through stomata.

(iii) **Water** It is reused by plants for photosynthetic process.

Check Your LEARNING...

1 Name the two main steps involved in the mechanism of photosynthesis.
2 What do ATP and ADP mean? What are the roles of these molecules in the energy metabolism of a cell?
3 Why is the nickname 'dark reaction' not entirely correct for the chemical stage of photosynthesis?
4 Why is Calvin cycle called C_3 cycle?
5 Explain the process of carboxylation in dark reaction.
6 Name the products produced during photosynthesis.

Adaptations of Leaves for Photosynthesis

Leaves of some plants are adapted in various ways to perform the process of photosynthesis.

These are as follows

(i) Presence of more stomata to allow rapid exchange of gases like CO_2 and O_2.
(ii) Arrangement of more number of chloroplasts on the upper surface of leaves, so as to capture maximum amount of light.
(iii) Large and expanded surface area of leaves for absorbing maximum light.
(iv) Presence of transparent cuticle and upper epidermis to allow light to enter freely and move easily and to reduce evaporation.
(v) Thinness of leaves, which reduce the distance between cells, so as to facilitate the rapid transport of raw materials like H_2O, CO_2, etc.
(vi) Arrangement of leaves at right angle to the sunlight, so as to trap the maximum solar radiation.
(vii) Extensive vein system in leaves aids in rapid transport to and from the mesophyll cells.

Factors Affecting Photosynthesis

Rate of photosynthesis is affected by the several internal and external factors. These are given below

External Factors

External factors that affect the rate of photosynthesis are

(i) **Intensity of light** Rate of photosynthesis increases with the increase in the intensity of light (upto a certain limit) and *vice-versa.*
(ii) **Quality of light** Rate of photosynthesis is higher in red and blue light than in any other light.
(iii) **CO_2 concentration** Rate of photosynthesis increases with rise in CO_2 concentration, but upto a certain limit. It acts as a **limiting factor** in photosynthesis.
(iv) **Temperature** Rate of photosynthesis also increases with the rise in temperature, but upto a limit, thereafter, it decreases. The optimum temperature for photosynthesis is about 35°C. Above 40°C, the related enzymes get destroyed and thus, photosynthesis does not occur.
(v) **Water content** Rate of photosynthesis decreases with the scarcity of water due to less absorption through soil or excessive loss through transpiration. A decrease in water content of leaves reduces the rate of photosynthesis due to the closure of stomata.

Internal Factors

Internal factors that affect the rate of photosynthesis are

(i) **Chlorophyll content in leaves** Less amount of pigment affects the occurrence of photosynthesis as sufficient light cannot be trapped.
(ii) **Structure of leaf** We have already discussed the adaptations of leaf to carryout photosynthesis. If the parameters are not met, the photosynthetic rate is suffered.
(iii) Internal concentration of CO_2 in leaf tissue.
(iv) Age of leaf
(v) **Protoplasm** Dehydration of protoplasm for some reasons, reduces the photosynthetic rate in plants.
(vi) **Accumulation of end products** The progress of photosynthesis in the green cells is maintained as long as the concentration of the products formed (sugar and starch) is minimum. Their accumulation slows down the process of photosynthesis.

Importance of Photosynthesis

Photosynthesis is important for supporting life on Earth in the following ways

(i) It provides food to all organisms through food chain.
(ii) Photosynthesis gives off oxygen, which acts as a life supporting gas.
As a result of photosynthesis, some amount of oxygen produced is used by the plant itself for

the process of respiration. But the major amount of O_2 is diffused out into the atmosphere through stomata. Thus, this oxygen which gets diffused out, is not a waste material because it acts as a life supporting gas for other living organisms including humans on Earth.

(iii) It helps in maintaining balanced level of O_2 and CO_2 in the atmosphere.

(iv) The fossil fuels like coal, petroleum and natural gas are formed by the decomposition of photosynthetic organisms.

Carbon Cycle

It is a series of chemical reactions, involving removal of carbon from the air, its usage by living organisms in the form of food and is finally returned to the atmosphere. The steps involved in carbon cycle are as follows

(i) Photosynthetic plants use carbon in the form of CO_2 from the atmosphere to produce carbohydrates like sugar and starch.

(ii) Carbon is circulated through the food chain and passes on to animals including humans.

(iii) During respiration in plants and animals, carbohydrates are oxidised to release energy and CO_2. The former is consumed in body whereas the latter is given out into atmosphere.

(iv) After the death of plants and animals, decomposers (bacteria and fungi) carryout the decay or breakdown of organic matter in dead bodies. During this process, CO_2 is released into the atmosphere.

(v) Other processes which release CO_2 back into the atmosphere are combustion of fuels like wood, coal, petroleum, etc., heating limestones in lime kilns and volcanic eruptions.

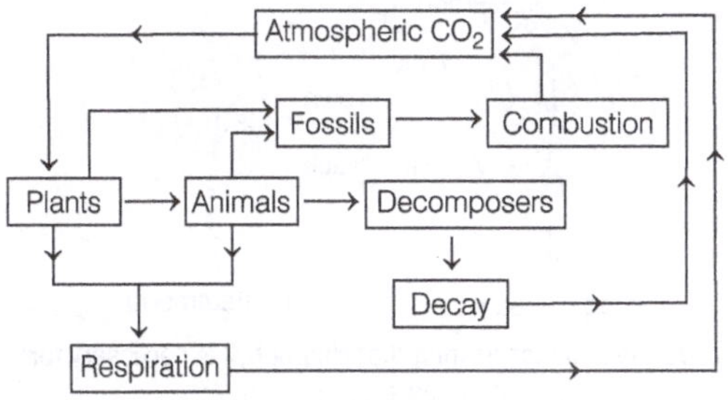

Green plants perform photosynthesis by utilising CO_2 and H_2O in the presence of sunlight and chlorophyll. In this process, CO_2 is transformed into simple carbohydrate (sugar) and O_2 is liberated as byproduct.

Carbohydrates (sugar) are further broken into simpler molecules, i.e. glucose, fructose, etc. These glucose molecules provide energy for the synthesis of other biologically important molecules or are converted into other substances.

Check Your LEARNING...

1 Enlist any two adaptations of leaves for photosynthesis.
2 What is the optimum temperature for photosynthesis?
3 Name two internal factors which affect the rate of photosynthesis.
4 How fossil fuels are formed?
5 What is carbon cycle?

Experiments Based on Photosynthesis

Number of experiments have been performed to prove that various raw materials are required for photosynthesis, i.e. light, CO_2, water and chlorophyll. Optimum conditions are essential for the process of photosynthesis to take place.

Before discussing the experiments, it is important to know about the **process of destarching** (i.e. removal of starch) and its importance in plants. Destarching is carried out in following manner.

To destarch the leaves, they are kept in a dark room (with no exposure of natural or artificial light) for 1 or 2 days. By doing this, all starch from the storage organs of the leaves will be removed.

Experiment 1

To test the leaf for the presence of starch.

Procedure Pluck the leaf and boil it in water for a minute, so that all the cells are killed.

Remove the leaf from water and boil it in alcohol or methylated spirit to remove its chlorophyll. This will make leaf little hard and brittle.

Now, place the leaf again in hot water to soften it. Spread the leaf in petri dish and pour iodine solution on it dropwise with the help of dropper.

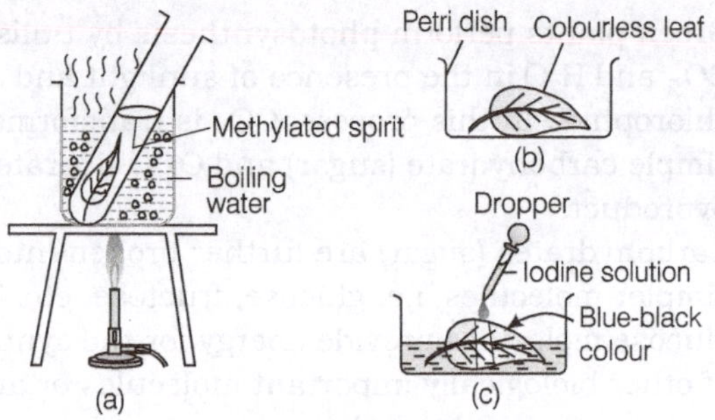

Experimental setup for starch test

The leaf shows a blue-black colour, which indicates the presence of starch in leaf. A leaf that lacks starch shows brown colouration.

Experiment 2

To show that sunlight is necessary for photosynthesis.

Procedure Take a potted plant and destarch it for 48 hours. Cover one of the leaf with black paper (with a star design being cut).
Keep the pot under the sunlight. Remove it after 1 hour and test the covered leaf for the presence of starch, by pouring iodine solution on it.

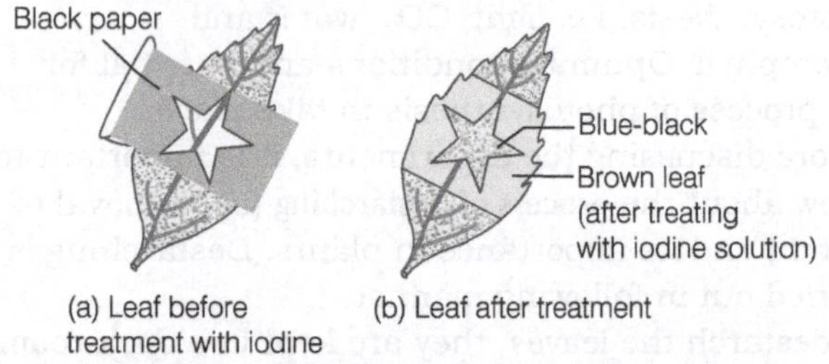

Experiment demonstrating that sunlight is necessary for photosynthesis

It will be observed that uncovered leaves and the part of the leaf, which was able to get light through the cut design will turn blue-black colour.

This indicates the presence of starch, while the portion which was covered with black paper will turn into brown colour (showing the absence of starch). This experiment thus, proves that the light is an essential requirement for the process of photosynthesis to take place.

Experiment 3

To show that CO_2 is necessary for photosynthesis.

Procedure Take destarched potted plant.

Take wide mouthed corked bottle and put strong KOH solution or soda lime in it. KOH solution absorbs all CO_2 present in a bottle. Insert about half of the leaf inside the bottle through the split cork as shown in the figure.

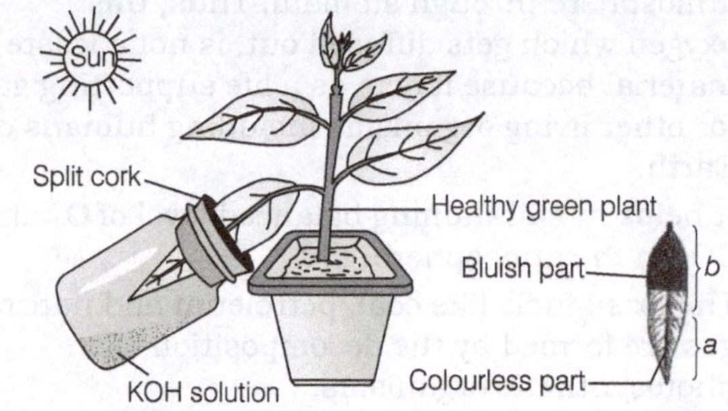

Experiment to prove that carbon dioxide is necessary for photosynthesis

Place the whole apparatus in light and test the leaf for starch after 8 hours.

Portion of the leaf inside the bottle and within cork gives negative test for starch because CO_2 is not present in the bottle. The exposed part of the leaf showed blue black colouration. It proves that CO_2 is necessary for photosynthesis.

Experiment 4

To show that chlorophyll is necessary for photosynthesis.

Procedure Take a potted plant with variegated leaves (having different colour zones, i.e. green and non-green areas), e.g. *Croton*, *Coleus*, etc.

First, destarch the leaves by keeping them in the dark room for about 2-3 days. Then restarch them by keeping the plant in the Sun.

After few hours of keeping the plant under sun, pluck one leaf. Draw the outline on a paper, marking the green and non-green areas on the outline.

Now, testing the leaf for starch, it is observed that only the areas of leaf which were green (contain chlorophyll), will turn into blue-black colour, thus showing the presence of starch, while the non-green areas will not.

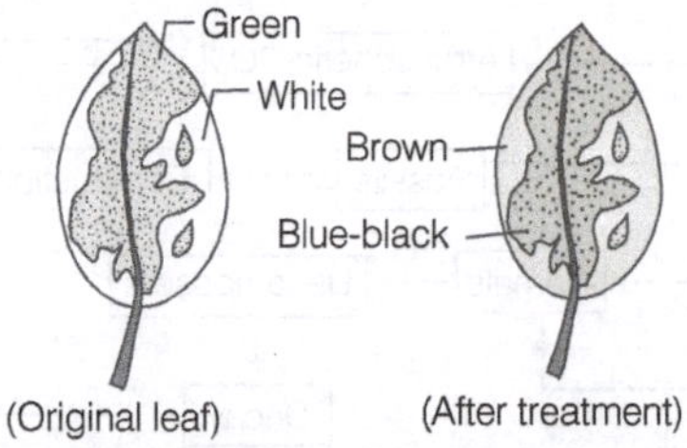

Coleus leaf demonstrating that chlorophyll is necessary for photosynthesis (by starch test)

This experiment proves that photosynthesis can occur only in the presence of chlorophyll, which is present in the green areas of the leaf.

Experiment 5

To show that oxygen is released during photosynthesis.

Procedure Fill a beaker with pond water and keep the water plant (e.g. *Hydrilla*) into the beaker.

Cover the plant by a short-stemmed funnel (it is to be noted that funnel should not touch the base of the beaker).

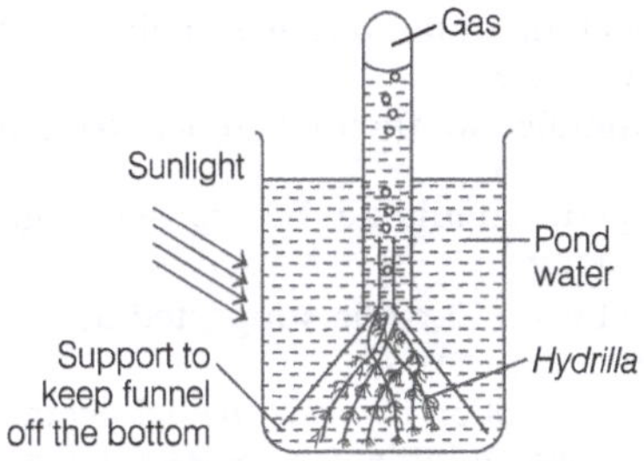

Experiment to show that oxygen is given out during photosynthesis

Now take a test tube full of water and invert it over the stem of the funnel. Allow the setup to stand in the sunlight for few hours. After few hours, you will observe the presence of bubbles in the inverted test tube, which get collected in the form of gas in the test tube.

The gas formed is oxygen. The presence of oxygen is confirmed by bringing a glowing splinter near the tube that bursts into flame on getting oxygen availability. This demonstrates that O_2 is liberated as a byproduct in photosynthesis.

Check Your LEARNING...

1 How are the leaves of a plant destarched?
2 Why do we perform iodine test?
3 What is the role of KOH in experiment 3?
4 Which plant leaf is taken in chlorophyll testing (exp.4) and why?
5 How will you prove that oxygen is released during photosynthesis?

QUiCK Revision

- **Photosynthesis** is the biggest biological reaction occurring on Earth. By this process, the green plants manufacture food (carbohydrate) with the help of chlorophyll using carbon dioxide and water in the presence of sunlight.
- **Chloroplast** is an important cell organelle found only in plants which act as a site of photosynthesis. The chlorophyll pigment is found in the membrane of thylakoids of chloroplast which harvest solar energy to be used in the process.
- The mechanism of photosynthesis occurs in two steps, i.e. light reaction and dark reaction.
- **Light reaction** occurs in the presence of light. It has two steps
  - (i) **Photolysis of water** occurs in the presence of light and Mn^{2+} ions to produce oxygen and electrons.
  - (iii) **Photophosphorylation** means formation of ATP from ADP and inorganic phosphates. During light reaction, NADPH and ATP are produced which are called **reducing power** to be used in dark reaction.
- **Dark reaction** is light independent reaction which occurs in the stroma of the chloroplast. During this, CO_2 is reduced to produce glucose molecule through series of biochemical reactions called **Calvin cycle**.
- **Glucose** is the end product of photosynthesis which forms sucrose. It gets translocated in different parts of the plant to be used as source of energy. Excess sucrose and glucose get polymerised from starch.
- **Leaves** of plants get modified to perform photosynthesis. These adaptations are increased number of stomata to facilitate CO_2 availability, arrangement of more chloroplast on the light falling surfaces of leaves, larger surface area of leaves, etc.
- There are **certain factors** which affect the rate of photosynthesis. The **external factors** include intensity, quality and duration of light, CO_2 concentration, temperature, water availability. The **internal factors** affecting photosynthesis are chlorophyll content, CO_2 concentration in leaf tissue, age of leaf, accumulation of end products and conditions of protoplasm.
- **Carbon cycle** is a series of chemical reactions, involving removal of carbon from the air, its usage by living organisms in the form of food and its final return to the atmosphere.

Chapter Practice

Section-I

1 Mark Questions

1. Name the following.
   (i) The cell organelle responsible for photosynthesis. [2009]
   (ii) The structural and functional unit of chloroplast.
   (iii) The colour in which the rate of photosynthesis is minimum.
   (iv) The site of light reaction in the cells of a leaf.
   (v) The primary acceptor of atmospheric CO_2 in dark reaction.
   (vi) The photosynthetically active wavelength.
   (vii) Carbohydrates in plants are stored in this form.
   (viii) Any two plants that do not perform photosynthesis.
   (ix) Aquatic plant used in the lab to demonstrate O_2 liberation during photosynthesis. [2014]

Ans. (i) Chloroplast (ii) Quantasomes
(iii) Green (iv) Grana
(v) RuBP (vi) 400-700 nm
(vii) Glucose (viii) *Cuscuta* and mushroom
(ix) *Hydrilla*

2. Correct and rewrite the following statements by changing the underlined words.
   (i) The immediate product of photosynthesis is <u>sucrose</u>.
   (ii) Light dependent reaction occurs in the <u>stroma</u> of chloroplast.
   (iii) During photosynthesis, oxygen is liberated from <u>carbon dioxide</u>.
   (iv) <u>Benedict solution</u> is used to test the presence of starch in leaf.
   (v) The solvent used to dissolve the chlorophyll pigments while testing a leaf for starch is <u>soda lime</u>. [2017]

Ans. (i) The immediate product of photosynthesis is glucose.
(ii) Light dependent reaction occurs in the grana of chloroplast.
(iii) During photosynthesis, oxygen is liberated from water.
(iv) Iodine solution is used to test the presence of starch in leaf.
(v) The solvent used to dissolve the chlorophyll pigments while testing a leaf for starch is alcohol or methylated spirit.

3. Give biological reasons for the following.
   (i) Light reaction is called the photochemical phase.
   (ii) Dark reaction is called the biosynthetic phase.
   (iii) Sleeping under a tree at night is not advisable. [2010]
   (iv) Animals owe their existence to chlorophyll. [2008]
   (v) A plant should not be exposed to green light for long.
   (vi) All life on Earth is supported by photosynthesis. [2019]

Ans. (i) Light reaction involves the light coming from Sun, which initiates a series of chemical reactions in the thylakoids of chloroplast. So, it is known as photochemical phase.
(ii) In dark reaction, stepwise synthesis of glucose occurs using certain enzymes. It is a light independent reaction. So, it is known as biosynthetic phase.
(iii) Sleeping under a tree at night is not advisable because plants respire at night due to which the atmosphere surrounding the tree is rich in CO_2, which is harmful for us.
(iv) Animals owe their existence to chlorophyll, because plants with chlorophyll produce food, which in turn is used by all living organisms for their existence.
(v) If the plant get long exposure to green light, it may get starved and die because green light cannot be absorbed by plants properly and photosynthesis is inhibited in this light.
(vi) Photosynthesis is important for supporting life on Earth as it provides food to all organisms through food chain and gives off oxygen, which acts as a life supporting gas.

4. (i) Match the following columns.

Column I	Column II
A. KOH solution	1. Leaves with green and non-green areas.
B. Variegated leaves	2. To test liberation of O_2 during photosynthesis.
C. *Hydrilla*	3. Presence of starch gives blue-black colour.
D. Iodine	4. Absorbs the CO_2 released during photosynthesis.

(ii) Match the following columns.

	Column I		Column II
A.	Oxygen and water	1.	Stimulated by light
B.	Glucose (sugar)	2.	Machinery
C.	Chloroplast	3.	Raw materials
D.	CO_2 and water	4.	Byproducts
E.	Grana	5.	End product

Ans. (i) A–4, B–1, C–2, D–3
(ii) A–4, B–5, C–2, D–3, E–1

5. Choose the correct answer from the four options given below.

(i) The site of photosynthesis process in plants is
(a) ribosomes (b) chloroplasts
(c) pyrenoids (d) nucleus

Ans. (b)

(ii) Stroma is the ground substance in
(a) ribosomes (b) cytoplasm
(c) chloroplast (d) vacuoles

Ans. (c)

(iii) The main photosynthetic pigment is
(a) chlorophyll-*a* (b) carotene
(c) chlorophyll-*b* (d) xanthophyll

Ans. (a)

(iv) Green plants absorb solar energy and convert simple inorganic raw materials like carbon dioxide (CO_2) and water (H_2O) into food. This process is known as photosynthesis. Which of the following reactions illustrates the above process of photosynthesis?

(a) $CO_2 + O_2 \xrightarrow[\text{Chlorophyll}]{H_2O,\ \text{sunlinght}} C_6H_{12}O_6 + \text{Energy}$

(b) $CO_2 + H_2O \xrightarrow[\text{Chlorophyll}]{\text{Sunlight}} \underset{\text{Sugar}}{C_6H_{12}O_6} + O_2 + H_2O$

(c) $C_6H_{12}O_6 + O_2 \xrightarrow[\text{Chlorophyll}]{\text{Sunlight}} CO_2 + H_2O$

(d) None of the above

Ans. (b)

(v) The individual flattened stacks of membranous structures inside the chromoplasts are known as [2016]
(a) grana (b) stroma
(c) thylakoids (d) cristae

Ans. (c)

(vi) NADP is expanded as [Semester I 2021]
(a) Nicotinamide Adenosine Dinucleotide Phosphate
(b) Nicotinamide Adenine Dinucleotide Phosphate
(c) Nicotinamide Adenine Dinucleolus Phosphate
(d) Nicotinamide Adenosine Dinucleolus Phosphate

Ans. (b)

(vii) The site of light reaction in the cells of a green leaf is [2023]
(a) nucleus
(b) grana of chloroplast
(c) cytoplasm
(d) stroma of chloroplast

Ans. (b)

(viii) Grana of chloroplast is not the [Semester I 2021]
(a) site of light independent phase
(b) site of light dependent phase
(c) site of photolysis
(d) site of photon absorption

Ans. (a)

(ix) The process of conversion of ADP to ATP during photosynthesis is [Semester I 2021]
(a) polymerisation (b) photophosphorylation
(c) photorespiration (d) photolysis

Ans. (b)

(x) Given below are the adaptations found in leaves to favour the occurrence of photosynthesis process. Select a statement which is incorrect.
(a) Presence of numerous stomata
(b) Large surface area of leaves
(c) Increased chloroplasts on upper surface
(d) The thinness of leaves

Ans. (c)

(xi) A destarched plant is one whose
(a) leaves are free from chlorophyll
(b) aerial parts are free from starch
(c) leaves are free from starch
(d) plant is free from starch

Ans. (c)

(xii) A plant is kept in a dark cupboard for about 48 hours before conducting any experiment on photosynthesis to [2013]
(a) remove chlorophyll from the leaves
(b) remove starch from the plant
(c) ensure that no photosynthesis occurs
(d) ensure that the leaves are free from starch

Ans. (b)

(xiii) Arrange the given steps of the experiment showing that light is necessary for photosynthesis in a sequence.
I. Treat with iodine.
II. Fasten the leaf with two strips of black paper.
III. Place the plant in sunlight for 8 hours.
IV. Destarch the plant.
Choose the correct option.
(a) I, II, III and IV (b) III, IV, I and II
(c) II, III, IV and I (d) IV, II, III and I

Ans. (d)

6. Fill in blanks by using suitable words.
   (i) The carbon dioxide from atmosphere enters the leaf through ....
   (ii) In the process of photosynthesis, ... energy is converted into .... energy.
   (iii) $\ldots\ldots + 12H_2O \xrightarrow[\text{Sunlight}]{\text{Chlorophyll}} \ldots\ldots + 6\,H_2O + \ldots\ldots$.

Ans. (i) stomata
(ii) light, chemical
(iii) $6CO_2$, $C_6H_{12}O_6$, $6O_2$

7. Insert the word, given in the box to complete the blanks in the paragraph given below. A word can be used only once.

Photosynthesis, Stroma, Grana, Lamellae, Thylakoids, Chlorophyll, Photolysis

A chloroplast is oval in shape and is bounded by two membranes. ......(i).... is the ground substance present in chloroplast. A number of disc-like covered sacs called ....(ii)..... are present arranged like stalk of coins forming a cylindrical dark green granular bodies called ...(iii)...... . These bodies are connected by .....(iv)..... .

Ans. (i) Stroma (ii) thylakoids (iii) grana (iv) lamellae

8. Complete the following paragraph by filling in the blanks (i-v) with appropriate words/terms/ phrases.

To test the leaf for starch, the leaf is boiled in water to (i).......... . It is next boiled in methylated spirit to (ii) ....

The leaf is placed in warm water to soften it. It is then placed in a dish and (iii) .... solution is added. The region which contains starch turns (iv)....... and the region which does not contain starch turns (v) ..... . [2018, 11]

Ans. To test the leaf for starch, the leaf is boiled in water to (i) **kill** the cells. It is next boiled in methylated spirit to (ii) **remove chlorophyll.**
The leaf is placed in warm water to soften it. It is then placed in a dish and (iii) **iodine** solution is added. The region which contains starch turns (iv) **blue-black** and the region which does not contain starch turns (v) **brown.**

9. Choose the odd one out from the following terms given below and name the category to which other three belong.
   (i) Stroma, Thylakoid, Grana, Guard cell
   (ii) Guard cell, Epidermal cell, Fret, Stomatal pore

Ans. (i) **Odd term** is guard cell.
Rest three are structural components of chloroplast.
(ii) **Odd term** is fret.
Rest three are structural components of stomata.

10. Given below are sets of five terms each. Rewrite the terms in correct order of a logical sequence beginning with the term that is underlined.
   (i) Photolysis, <u>Chlorophyll activation</u>, O_2 production, Photophosphorylation, NADPH production
   (ii) H_2O, O_2, Grana, H^+ and OH^-, <u>Photons</u>

Ans. (i) Chlorophyll activation, Photolysis, O_2 production, photophosphorylation, NADPH production
(ii) Photons, Grana, H_2O, O_2, H^+ and OH^-

11. Expand the following biological abbreviations.
   (i) ADP (ii) RuBP

Ans. (i) Adenosine Diphosphate
(ii) Ribulose Bisphosphate

12. State the exact location of the following.
   (i) Chloroplast [2013]
   (ii) Stroma
   (iii) Thylakoid [2019]
   (iv) Dark reaction

Ans. (i) Chloroplasts are mainly found in the mesophyll cells located between the upper and lower epidermis of the leaves.
(ii) Stroma is the fluid matrix within the chloroplast.
(iii) A membrane system containing a number of disc-like sacs known as thylakoids is located in chloroplast.
(iv) Dark reaction occurs in the stroma of chloroplast.

13. State the main function of the following.
   (i) Chlorophyll
   (ii) Thylakoids [2012]
   (iii) Guard cells [2016]
   (iv) KOH

Ans. (i) Chlorophyll absorbs photons of sunlight and helps in the splitting of water molecules into hydrogen ions and hydroxyl ions.
(ii) The function of thylakoid is to trap the light energy and to transform this energy into chemical energy form, i.e. ATP and NADPH to be used in dark reactions.
(iii) Guard cells regulate the opening and closing of stomata.
(iv) KOH is used to absorb CO_2 in experimental setup.

14. Mention one difference between each of the following pairs on the basis of what is given in the bracket.
   (i) Stoma and Stroma (structure)
   (ii) Stroma and Grana (function)
   (iii) NADP and ATP (expand the abbreviations) [2017]
   (iv) Photolysis and Photophosphorylation (definition) [2016]
   (v) ATP and AIDS (expand the abbreviations) [2018]

Ans. (i) Difference between stoma and stroma is as follows

Stoma	Stroma
It is the opening of the stomata *via* which transpired water and respiratory gases pass.	It is the part/region in the chloroplast (matrix), where dark reaction of the photosynthesis takes place.

(ii) Difference between stroma and grana is as follows

Stroma	Grana
It is the site of dark reaction.	It is the site of light reaction.

(iii) Difference between NADP and ATP is as follows

NADP	ATP
Nicotinamide Adenine Dinucleotide Phosphate	Adenosine Triphosphate

(iv) Difference between photolysis and photophosphorylation is as follows

Photolysis	Photophosphorylation
It is a process of splitting of water molecule into $2H^+ + 4e^-$ $+ 1/2\,O_2$ in the presence of sunlight by activated photosynthetic pigments.	It is a process of formation of ATP from ADP and inorganic phosphate by the utilisation of energy released by electrons emitted during photolysis of water.

(v) Difference between ATP and AIDS is as follows

ATP	AIDS
Adenosine Tri Phosphate.	Acquired Immuno Deficieny Syndrome.

15. Give biological/technical terms for the following.
(i) A leaf in which stomata are equally distributed on both of its surfaces.
(ii) Destruction of photosynthesising pigments in very strong light.
(iii) The process of splitting of water molecule into H^+ and O_2.
(iv) Temperature at which rate of photosynthesis is maximum.

Ans. (i) Isobilateral leaf (ii) Solarisation
(iii) Photolysis (iv) Optimum temperature

16. Briefly explain the following terms.
(i) Photophosphorylation (ii) Grana
(iii) Destarching

Ans. (i) Formation of ATP from ADP and phosphate by the utilisation of energy is termed as photophosphorylation.
(ii) Structure formed by the stacking of thylakoids in chloroplast is called grana.
(iii) Destarching is the process of removal of starch from the leaves of the plants usually before going for experimentations.

17. Answer the following questions briefly.
(i) What do the plants release as a side product of the important process of photosynthesis?
(ii) Does moonlight support photosynthesis? Find out.
(iii) How does the chlorophyll molecule get activated during light reaction?
(iv) Which two processes lead to gaseous exchange *via* stomata?
(v) How is destarching of leaves carried out?

Ans. (i) Plants release oxygen as a side product during the important process of photosynthesis.
(ii) The intensity of moonlight is several thousand times less than that of direct sunlight. It is insufficient for the light dependent phase of photosynthesis. So, it does not support photosynthesis.
(iii) The chlorophyll molecule gets activated by absorbing photons of light energy.
(iv) Photsynthesis and transpiration lead to gaseous exchange *via* stomata.
(v) To destarch the leaves, the plant is kept in dark room (with no exposure to natural or artificial light) for one or two days.

2 Marks Questions

18. Respiration is said to be the reversal of photosynthesis. Comment.

Ans. Respiration is a catabolic process while photosynthesis is an anabolic process. During respiration, O_2 is taken and CO_2 is given out while during photosynthesis, CO_2 is taken and O_2 is given out.

19. You want to study the effect of the absence of chlorophyll in leaves on photosynthesis.
(i) What will be the aim of your experiment?
(ii) Name the plant you will select for this experiment.

Ans. (i) To show that chlorophyll is necessary for photosynthesis.
(ii) Plant with variegated leaves like *Coleus*.

20. It is said that the work being carried out is divided in the chloroplast. Can you justify this division of labour in the chloroplasts?

Ans. Division of labour appears clearly in the chloroplast, i.e. the membrane system is responsible for the synthesis of ATP and NADH. The dark reactions, i.e. reduction of CO_2 into carbohydrates and formation of sugar occurs in the stroma of chloroplasts, where enzymes are present.

21. Name the end products of light reaction of photosynthesis. Mention the fate of each of them.

Ans. ATP, NADPH and oxygen are the products of light reaction. ATP and NADPH are used in the reduction step of biosynthetic phase of photosynthesis. Oxygen is liberated into the atmosphere.

22. (i) Write the summary of dark reaction by an equation.
(ii) How do the raw materials reach the plant cell?

Ans. (i) $6CO_2 + 12NADPH + 18ATP \longrightarrow$
$C_6H_{12}O_6 + 12NADP^+ + 18ADP + 18Pi + 6H_2O$
(ii) Water enters the leaf through midrib and veins from stem and roots. CO_2 enters through stomata from the atmosphere.

23. Mention any two adaptations of plants for photosynthesis.

Ans. Two adaptations of plants for photosynthesis are
(i) Large surface area of the leaves.
(ii) Presence of more chloroplasts towards the upper surface.

24. Explain the significance of photosynthesis for animals.

Ans. The food in the form of starch is stored by plants in different parts of the plant like fruits, grains and leaves, etc. As heterotrophs, all the animals depend on these plant products directly or indirectly. Hence, the photosynthesis in plants is very important for the sustenance of life on Earth.

3 Marks Questions

25. Explain the structure of chloroplast.

Ans. **Structure of chloroplast** A chloroplast is oval in shape. It is bounded by two membranes. The ground substance present in chloroplast is stroma. There are disc-like closed sacs present, that are called thylakoids. Many thylakoids are placed one above the other like a stack of coins that are called as granum. Extending throughout the stroma, a system of membranes is present that is called as lamellae. These are joined to the thylakoids and help in separating grana.

26. How are the different pigments involved in the process of photosynthesis?

Ans. Various pigments are involved in photosynthesis like chlorophyll-*a* which acts as a chief pigment in photosynthesis and other pigments like chlorophyll-*b*, xanthophyll and carotenoids absorb light and transfer energy to chlorophyll-*a*. Pigments other than chlorophyll-*a* are called accessory pigments, which enable a wider range of wavelength of incoming light to be utilised for photosynthesis.

27. Suppose there were plants that had a high concentration of chlorophyll-*b* but lacked chlorophyll-*a*, would they carryout photosynthesis? Also mention why do plants have chlorophyll-*b* and other accessory pigments.

Ans. The plant having high concentration of chlorophyll-*b* but lacking chlorophyll-*a* will not carryout photosynthesis. Chlorophyll-*a* is the major pigment responsible for trapping light. Other thylakoid pigments like chlorophyll-*b*, xanthophylls and carotenoids, which are called accessory pigments, also absorb light and transfer the energy to chlorophyll-*a*. Indeed, they not only enable a wider range of wavelength of incoming light to be utilised for photosynthesis, but also, protect chlorophyll-*a* from photooxidation.

28. What conditions enable RuBisCO to function as an oxygenase? Explain the ensuring process.

Ans. Carboxylation is the most crucial step of the Calvin cycle, where CO_2 is utilised for the carboxylation of RuBisCO. This reaction is catalysed by the enzyme RuBP carboxylase which results in the formation of 2 molecules of 3PGA. Since, this enzyme also has an oxygenation activity, it would be more correct to call it RuBP carboxylase-oxygenase or RuBisCO.

Section-II [3/5 Marks]

Structured Questions

1. The given diagram is a diagrammatic representation of the internal structure of an organelle, found in a plant cell. Study the same and then answer the questions that follows.

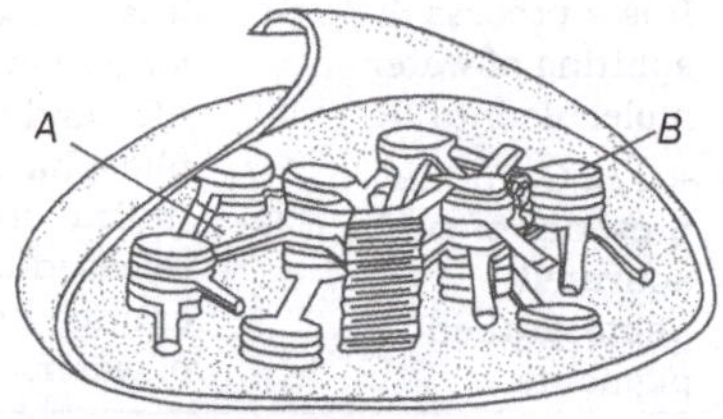

(i) Identify the organelle.
(ii) Name the physiological process occurring in this organelle.
(iii) Mention one way, in which this process is beneficial to man.
(iv) Name the phases of the process occurring in the parts labelled as '*A*' and '*B*'.
(v) A chemical substance $NADP^+$ plays an active part in one of the phases. Give the expanded form of $NADP^+$ and state its role in the above process.
(vi) Represent the physiological process mentioned in (ii) above in the form of a chemical equation. [2008]

Ans. (i) The organelle shown in the diagram is chloroplast.
(ii) The process of photosynthesis occurs in the chloroplast.
(iii) Photosynthesis gives food and the life saving gas, i.e. oxygen.
(iv) Phases of the process occur in parts labelled are
Part *A*–Dark reaction
Part *B*–Light reaction.
(v) Nicotinamide Adenine Dinucleotide Phosphate ($NADP^+$). It picks up hydrogen ion $[H^+]$ during the photolysis of water in light reaction.
(vi) $6CO_2 + 12H_2O \xrightarrow[\text{Chlorophyll}]{\text{Sunlight}} C_6H_{12}O_6 + 6H_2O + 6O_2 \uparrow$

2. The following figure shows the effect of light on the rate of photosynthesis. Based on the graph, answer the questions that follow.

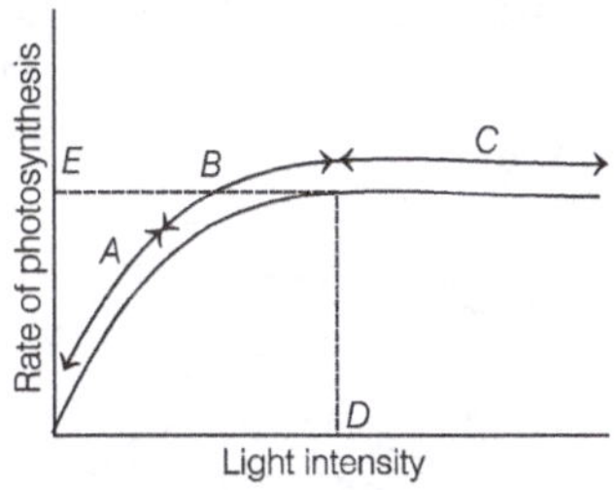

(i) At which point/s (*A*, *B* or *C*) in the curve, light acts as a limiting factor?
(ii) What does region A depicts?
(iii) What do *C* and *D* represent on the curve?
(iv) Which factor other than light will act as a limiting factor for the process?
(v) Why does photosynthesis not occur beyond a certain temperature?

Ans. (i) At points *B* and *C* of the curve, the rate did not increase with an increase in its concentration, because light becomes a limiting factor under these conditions.
(ii) Region A depicts photosynthesis under optimal light conditions.
(iii) Points *C* represent the region where rate of photosynthesis remains constant even after increasing incident light.
Point *D* shows optimum point at which maximum photosynthesis is recorded.
(iv) CO_2 concentration and temperature act as limiting factor for the process.
(v) Photosynthesis does not occur beyond a certain temperature (~40°C) as higher temperatures destory the enzymes that participate in the process.

3. The given diagrams represent the relationship between a mouse and a physiological process that occurs in green plants. Study the diagrams and answer the questions that follow.

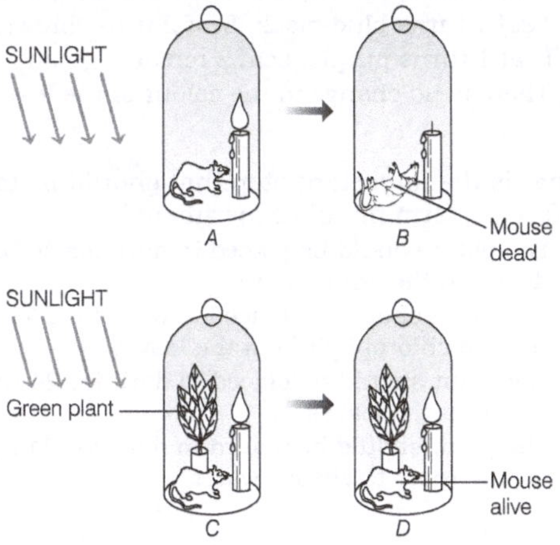

(i) Name the physiological process occurring in the green plant that has kept the mouse alive.
(ii) Explain the physiological process mentioned above.
(iii) Why did the mouse die in bell jar *B*?
(iv) What is the significance of the process as stated in (i) for life on Earth?
(v) Represent the above mentioned physiological process in the form of a chemical equation. **[2017]**

Ans. (i) Photosynthesis, occurring in the green plant, has kept the mouse alive.
(ii) Photosynthesis is the process by which plants that possess chlorophyll use energy from sunlight to produce sugar in the presence of CO_2 and water with the help of chlorophyll. Oxygen is released in the process.
(iii) The oxygen present in the bell jar *B* was utilised in the burning of candle. Therefore in the absence of O_2, mouse died.
(iv) Photosynthesis is important for supporting life on Earth in the following ways
- It provides food to all organisms through food chain.
- It gives off O_2 which acts as a life supporting gas.
- It helps in maintaining the balanced level of O_2 and CO_2 in the atmosphere.

(v) $$\underset{\text{Carbon dioxide}}{6CO_2} + \underset{\text{Water}}{12H_2O} \xrightarrow[\text{Chlorophyll}]{\text{Sunlight}} \underset{\text{Glucose}}{C_6H_{12}O_6} + \underset{\text{Water}}{6H_2O} + \underset{\text{Oxygen}}{6O_2}\uparrow \text{(Byproduct)}$$

4. The following diagram demonstrates a physiological process taking place in green plants. The whole setup was placed in bright sunlight for several hours. Study the diagram and answer the questions that follow.

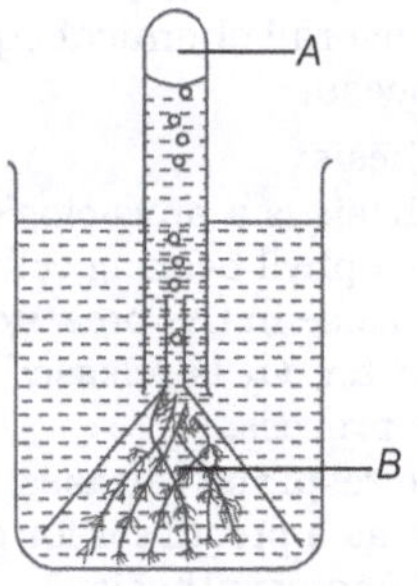

(i) What aspect of the physiological process is being examined?
(ii) Explain the physiological process mentioned in (i) above.
(iii) Label the parts *A* and *B* in the diagram.
(iv) Write a well-balanced chemical equation for the physiological process explained in (ii) above.
(v) What would happen to the rate of bubbling of the gas if a pinch of sodium bicarbonate is added to the water in the beaker? Explain your answer. **[2016]**

Ans. (i) Release of O_2 in photosynthesis.

(ii) Photosynthesis is the manufacturing of sugar (glucose) and oxygen by green plants in the presence of sunlight with the help of chlorophyll, H_2O and CO_2.

(iii) The parts *A* and *B* are labelled as
A–Oxygen in test tube.
B–Green plant, *Hydrilla*

(iv) $6CO_2 + 12H_2O \xrightarrow[\text{Sunlight}]{\text{Chlorophyll}} C_6H_{12}O_6 + 6H_2O + 6O_2$

(v) Addition of $NaHCO_3$ will increase the rate of photosynthesis because of increase in CO_2 available in water.

5. The diagram below shows two test tubes *A* and *B*. Test tube *A* contains a green water plant. Test tube *B* contains both a green water plant and a snail. Both test tubes are kept in sunlight. Answer the questions that follows.

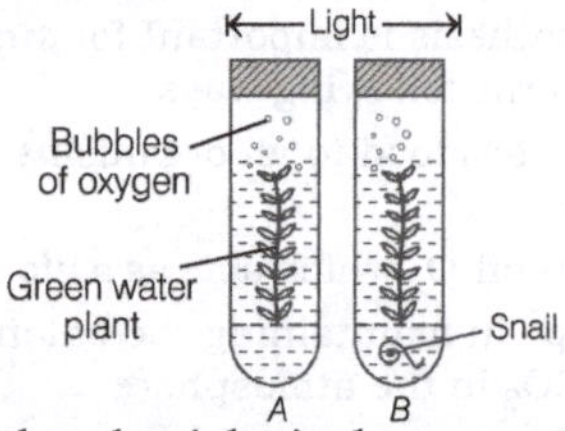

(i) Name the physiological process that releases the bubbles of oxygen.

(ii) Explain the physiological process as mentioned above in (i).

(iii) What is the purpose of keeping a snail in test tube *B*?

(iv) Why does test tube *B* have more bubbles of oxygen?

(v) Give an example of a water plant that can be used in the above experiment.

(vi) Write the overall chemical equation for the above process. **[2015]**

Ans. (i) Photosynthesis

(ii) Photosynthesis is a physiological process by which chlorophyll bearing cells of the plant prepare glucose in the presence of sunlight using CO_2 and water. O_2 is released as byproduct during the process.

(iii) Snail while respiring releases carbon dioxide which acts as a precursor for green plant for the process of photosynthesis.

(iv) Test tube *B* have more bubbles of oxygen because the snail which is respiring, releases carbon dioxide which is used by the green plant for the process of photosynthesis and thus due to high rate of photosynthesis, the formation of oxygen will be more.

(v) *Hydrilla* is an example of a water plant that can be used in the above experiment.

(vi) $6CO_2 + 12H_2O \xrightarrow[\text{Chlorophyll}]{\text{Sunlight}} C_6H_{12}O_6 + 6H_2O + 6O_2 \uparrow$

6. The diagram given below represents an experiment to demonstrate a particular aspect of photosynthesis. The letter 'A' indicates a certain condition inside the flask. Answer the quesitons that follow. **[Semester I 2021]**

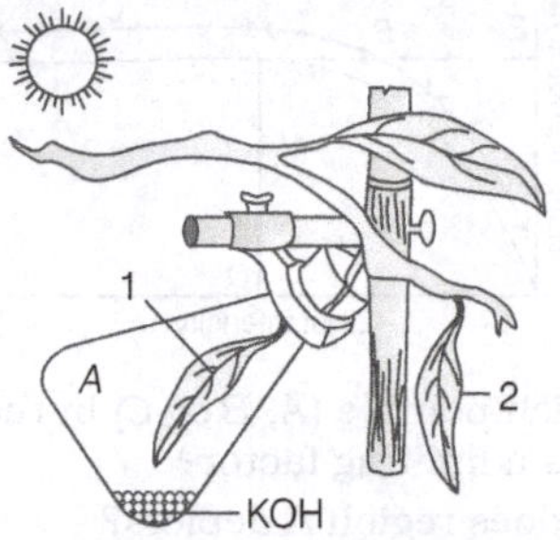

(i) What is the aim of the experiment?
(a) To show that oxygen is released during photosynthesis
(b) To show that photosynthesis occurs in the presence of KOH
(c) To show that chlorophyll is necessary for photosynthesis
(d) To show that carbon dioxide is necessary for photosynthesis

Ans. (d)

(ii) What is the special condition inside the flask?
(a) Air inside the flask is free of oxygen
(b) Air inside the flask is free of carbon dioxide
(c) Air inside the flask is free of nitrogen
(d) KOH purifies the air inside the flask

Ans. (b)

(iii) An alternative chemical that can be used instead of KOH is
(a) sodium hydroxide
(b) sodium chloride
(c) potassium chloride
(d) potassium permanganate

Ans. (a)

(iv) In what manner, do the leaves 1 and 2 differ at the end of the starch test?
(a) Leaf 1 turns brown, Leaf 2 turns blue-black
(b) Leaf 1 turns blue-black, Leaf 2 turns brown
(c) Leaf 1 turns purple, Leaf 2 remains green
(d) There is no change in the colour of the leaves

Ans. (a)

(v) What is the important step that should be taken before performing this experiment?
(a) The plant should be placed in dark for 24 hrs. to destarch the entire plant
(b) The plant should be placed in dark for 24 hrs. to remove chlorophyll from the leaves
(c) The plant should be placed in dark for 24 hrs. to destarch the leaves
(d) The plant should be placed in dark for 24 hrs. for the roots to absorb water

Ans. (c)

7. A potted plant was taken in order to prove a factor necessary for photosynthesis. The potted plant was kept in the dark for 24 hrs. One of the leaves was covered with black paper in the centre. The potted plant was then placed in sunlight for a few hours.
   (i) What aspect of photosynthesis was being tested?
   (ii) Why was the plant placed in the dark before beginning the experiment?
   (iii) During the starch test, why was the leaf
   (a) boiled in water?
   (b) boiled in methylated spirit ?
   (iv) Write a balanced chemical equation to represent the process of photosynthesis.
   (v) Draw a neat diagram of a chloroplast and label its parts. **[2014]**

Ans. (i) The aspect that is studied is that sunlight is necessary for photosynthesis.
(ii) Plant is placed in the dark before beginning the experiment to make the leaves free from starch.
(iii) (a) Leaf was boiled in water to kill the cells.
(b) Leaf was boiled in methylated spirit to remove the chlorophyll.
(iv) Refer to Ans. 5 (vi).
(v) Refer to Fig. on page no. 71.

8. A potted plant with variegated leaves was kept in dark for 24 hours and then placed in bright sunlight. Answer the following questions. **[2023]**

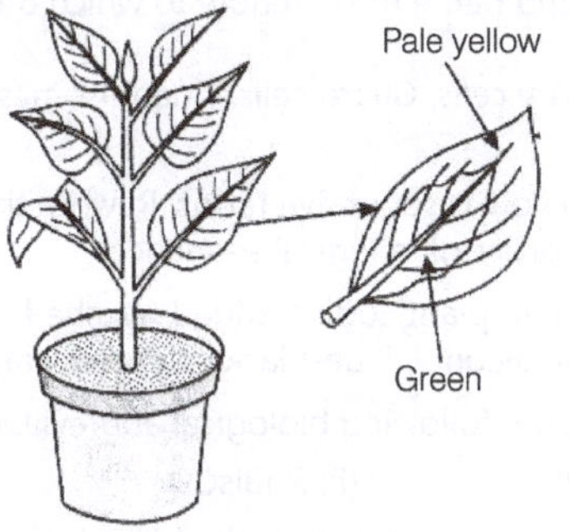

   (i) Which aspect of photosynthesis is being tested in the above diagram?
   (ii) Why was the plant kept in the dark for 24 hours?
   (iii) After the starch test what will be the colour of the yellow and green parts of the leaf? Give reasons to support your answer.

Ans. (i) Sunlight is the important aspect of photosynthesis which is tested here in this experiment.
(ii) The plant was kept in dark to eliminate the starch in the leaves.
(iii) After the starch test the green parts of the leaf will become blue black while the yellow parts lacking chlorophyll will show negative starch test.

9. The diagram given below represents an experiment to prove the importance of a factor in photosynthesis. Answer the questions that follow. **[2019]**

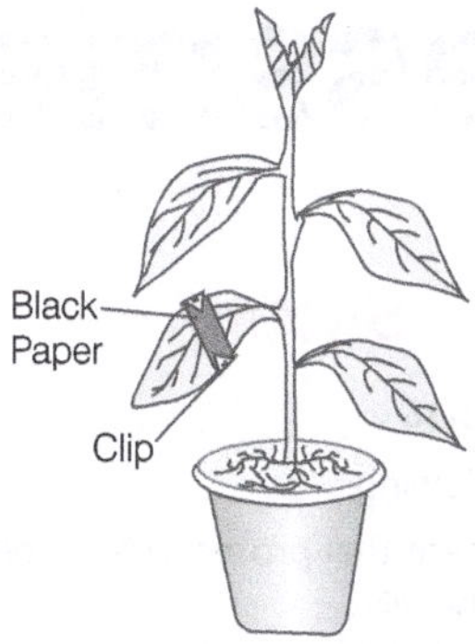

   (i) Name the factor studied in this experiment.
   (ii) What will you observe in the experimental leaf after the starch test ?
   (iii) Explain the process of photosynthesis.
   (iv) Give a balanced chemical equation to represent the process of photosynthesis.

   Or Write the overall chemical equation for photosynthesis. **[2023]**

   (v) Draw a neat, labelled diagram of an experimental setup to show that oxygen is released during photosynthesis.

Ans. (i) Sunlight
(ii) Uncovered leaf which was able to get light will turn into blue-black colour which indicates the presence of starch, while the portion which was covered with black paper will turn into brown colour showing the absence of starch.
(iii) The process of photosyntesis begins when the sunlight falls on the mesophyll cells of the leaf. The light energy is trapped by the chlorophyll present in the layers of mesophyll cells. During the process, the raw materials, i.e. CO_2 and water together with the solar energy trapped by the chlorophyll gets converted into chemical energy in the form of food, i.e. glucose and starch.
(iv) $6CO_2 + 12H_2O \xrightarrow[\text{Chlorophyll}]{\text{Sunlight}}$

$$C_6H_{12}O_6 + 6H_2O + 6O_2 \text{ (Byproduct)}$$

(v)

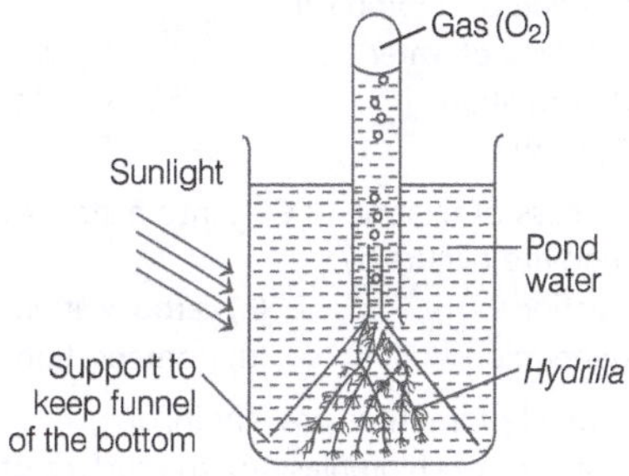

Experiment to show that oxygen is given out during photosynthesis

Chapter Assessment

Section-I

1 Mark Questions

1. Name the following.
   (i) The pigment that protects chlorophyll from photooxidation.
   (ii) The type of chlorophyll known as universal photosynthetic pigment. [2008]
   (iii) The plant (any one) used to test the presence of chlorophyll in plants.
2. Correct and rewrite the following statements by changing the underlined words.
   (i) <u>Chlorophyll-*b*</u> is the most abundant pigment in plants.
   (ii) Increased K^+ ion concentration in guard cells make them <u>hypotonic</u>.
3. Give biological reasons for the following.
   All food chains begin with green plants. [2018]
4. Match the following columns.

	Column I		Column II
A.	PS-I	1.	Orange coloured pigment
B.	PS-II	2.	Absorbs light energy of 700 nm
C.	Xanthophyll	3.	Absorbs light energy of 680 nm
D.	Carotene	4.	Yellow coloured pigment

5. Choose the correct answer from the four options given below.
   (i) The function of light energy used in photosynthesis is to
   (a) split CO_2 (b) activate chlorophyll
   (c) reduce CO_2 (d) None of these
   (ii) The first reaction of photosynthesis is
   (a) excitation of chlorophyll
   (b) photolysis of water
   (c) ATP formation
   (d) CO_2 fixation
   (iii) The process of fixation of CO_2 into a stable organic intermediate occurs by
   (a) reduction (b) carboxylation
   (c) regeneration (d) isomerisation
   (iv) Chlorophyll pigment is present in/on
   (a) the stroma of chloroplast (b) the surface of chloroplast
   (c) the grana of chloroplast (d) the lamellar membrane
   (v) Among the following given options, which one should not act as a limiting factor for photosynthesis?
   (a) Chlorophyll (b) CO_2
   (c) Light (d) Oxygen
   (vi) The covered portion of the leaf in the experiment to demonstrate necessity of light during photosynthesis, is observed to remain yellow because it
   (a) did not receive sunlight (b) contained starch
   (c) was destarched (d) Both (a) and (c)
6. Fill in the blanks by using suitable words.
   (i) .... is the secondary pigment present in leaf.
   (ii) Instead of using KOH, ... can also be used to detect the presence of CO_2 during photosynthesis.
   (iii) The site of light reaction in the cells of a leaf is ....
   (iv) The CO_2 present in the atmosphere enters the stomata by ....
   (v) To decolourise a leaf, it should be left for ....
7. Choose the odd one out from the following terms given below and name the category to which other three belong.
   Subsidiary cells, Guard cells, Quantasomes, Stomatal pore
8. Given below is set of five terms. Rewrite the terms in correct order of a logical sequence.
   Destarched plant, Iodine added, Washed in water, A leaf boiled in alcohol, Blue-black coloured leaf
9. Expand the following biological abbreviations.
   (i) ATP (ii) RuBisCO
10. State the exact location of the following.
    (i) Photolysis of water
    (ii) Fixation of CO_2
11. State the main function of the following.
    (i) Chloroplast (ii) RUBP
    (iii) Glucose (as a product of photosynthesis)
12. Mention one difference between each of the following pair on the basis of what is given in the bracket.
    Photosynthesis and Respiration (time of occurrence)
13. Give the biological/technical terms for the following.
    (i) Organisms unable to prepare their own food.
    (ii) A plant with no green leaves lack this pigment.
    (iii) The process of conversion of ADP to ATP during the first phase of photosynthesis.

14. Briefly explain the following term stomata.
15. Mention any one adaptation found in plants which favour the process of photosynthesis.

2 Marks Question

16 Mention the name of the enzyme that catalyses the carboxylation as well as oxygenation reaction. In which cell organelle is this enzyme found?

3 Marks Question

17. Cyclic photophosphorylation results in the production of ATPs and not NADPH. Give reasons.

Section-II [5 Marks]

Structured Questions

18. The figure given below represents an experimental setup to study a physiological process in plants.

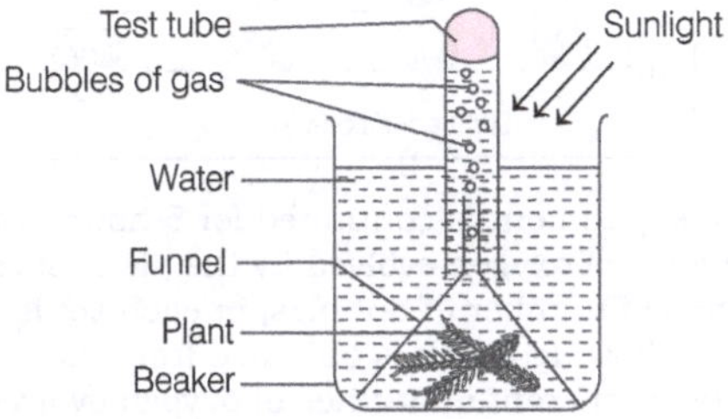

(i) Name the physiological process being studied.
(ii) Name the plants that are being used in experiment.
(iii) How is the inference of experiment being drawn?
(iv) What precautions must be taken in experiment?
(v) Name any two plants with variegated leaves.

19. A potted plant with variegated leaves was taken in order to prove a factor necessary for photosynthesis. The potted plant was kept in the dark for 24 hours and then placed in bright sunlight for a few hours.

Observe the diagrams and answer the questions that follow.

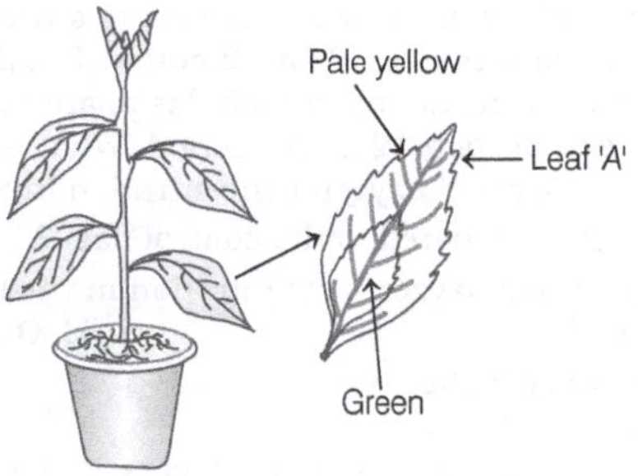

(i) Why is a variegated leaf taken for the experiment?
(ii) Which mineral ion is essential for the process of photosynthesis?
(iii) Why was the plant kept in the dark before beginning the experiment?
(iv) What will be the result of the starch test performed on leaf 'A' shown in the diagram? Give an example of a plant with variegated leaves.
(v) Draw a neat labelled diagram of a chloroplast.

For explanations scan the given QR Code

Olympiad Section*

Brain Teasing Questions asked in Previous Olympiads

1 A flask containing photosynthetic green algae and a control flask containing no algae are both placed under a light source, which are set to switch ON for 12 hours and then OFF for 12 hours. The dissolved oxygen concentrations in both flasks are monitored at the end of each 12 hours period. What will be the relative dissolved oxygen concentration in the flask with algae compared to the control flask?

The dissolved oxygen concentration in the flask with algae will **[IJSO 2019, Qatar]**

(a) always be higher
(b) always be lower
(c) be higher in the light, but the same in the dark
(d) be higher in the light, but lower in the dark

2 Which of the following statements is/are true for maize (*Zee mays*)? **[INJSO 2012]**

I. CO_2 is fixed only once in the process of photosynthesis.
II. CO_2 is fixed twice in the process of photosynthesis.
III. It undergoes the process of photorespiration.
IV. CO_2 can be fixed even in very low concentrations during photosynthesis.

Codes

(a) I and III (b) Only II (c) I and IV (d) II and IV

3 ATP is known as the energy currency of a cell. ATP is synthesised from ADP and Pi. The reaction is catalysed by an enzyme called as ATP synthase. When the enzyme and substrate (ADP) are distant inside the cell, the reaction cannot take place spontaneously. Which of the following statements best explains the cause for the ATP synthase and ADP to interact? **[INJSO, 2012]**

(a) Electronegativity of ADP attracts ATP synthase
(b) ADP will be actively pumped to ATP synthase
(c) Random movements will bring ADP to ATP synthase
(d) ADP and ATP synthase always remain bound to oxysomes

4 *Hydrilla* sp., an aquatic plant is immersed in water in a beaker. A funnel is kept inverted on it. A test tube filled with water is inverted on the nozzle of the funnel.

Four such sets are prepared and each of them is exposed to different wavelengths of light, which were as follows **[INJSO 2013]**

Set I: Yellow light
Set II: Blue light
Set III: Red light
Set IV: Green light

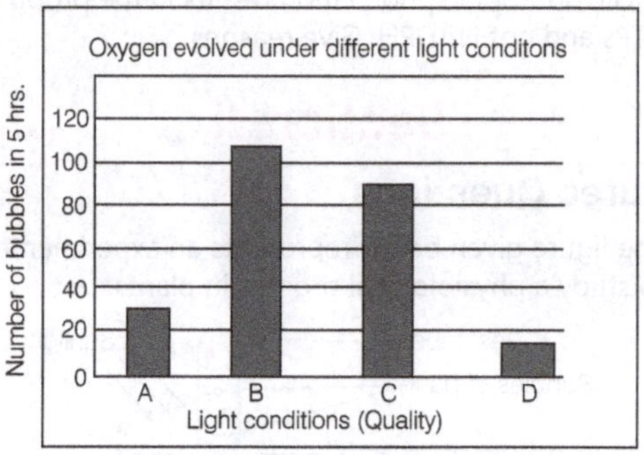

The experiment is continued for 5 hours and the amount of oxygen evolved by the plant (measured in terms of number of bubbles) in each set is measured. The following graph is obtained from the data which details different quantities of oxygen evolved when exposed to different quality of light A, B, C and D. Which of the following combinations match correctly with the data represented in the graph?

(a) A-Red, B-Green, C-Blue and D-Yellow
(b) A-Green, B-Yellow, C-Red and D-Blue
(c) A-Blue, B-Red, C-Yellow and D-Green
(d) A-Yellow, B-Red, C-Blue and D-Green

5 Assimilation of CO_2 by photosynthesis in cacti growing in arid regions occurs in two stages. In stage 1, CO_2 uptake and fixation occurs at night and CO_2 is stored in the form of malate in vacuoles. In stage 2, during the day, the malate moves to the chloroplast where it is decarboxylated and the released CO_2 is refixed by RuBP carboxylase. The main reason for this is **[IJSO 2013, India]**

(a) Cacti require light for RuBP carboxylase activity
(b) Cacti close their stomata during the day, so availability of CO_2 for RuBP carboxylase activity is low during the day
(c) Cacti can fix CO_2 only at an acidic pH that is provided by malate
(d) Cacti have chloroplasts that are impermeable to CO_2 but are permeable to malate

Answers

1. (d) **2.** (d) **3.** (c) **4.** (d) **5.** (b)

**These questions may or may not be asked in the examination, have been given just for additional practice required for olympiads, scholarship exams etc. For detailed explanations refer Page No. 247.*

CHAPTER

06

Chemical Coordination in Plants

Chapter Inside

- Plant Hormones • Plant Movements

All living organisms (plants or animals) respond and react to changes that occur in their environment by showing certain movements of their body parts. These responses to external stimuli are produced by various organs in a systematic and controlled manner which is known as **coordination**.

For control and coordination, animals have both the nervous system and hormones. However, the plants respond to stimuli and coordinate *via*. hormones only. In this chapter, we will study about plant hormones and movement in plants.

Plant Hormones

Cells cannot continuously create and transmit electrical impulses. Thus, most multicellular organisms use another means of communication between different cells called the **chemical coordination**. The chemicals used in such communication are known as **hormones**.

The term **'hormone'** was first used by **William Bayliss** and **Ernest Starling** in 1902. The term **phytohormone** (for plants) was coined for distinguishing the plant hormones from the animal hormones.

The hormones work as messengers (also in animals) to control and coordinate plant movements. They are produced at one location and transported across the plant body for functioning. Plants respond to production of these hormones by growth.

However in certain cases, hormones also negatively affect the plant growth. In this section, we will study about major plant hormones, their discovery and their physiological functions in plants.

Auxins

It was the first plant growth regulator to be discovered. Auxins are produced in the actively growing regions of plants, i.e. shoot (stem) and root apices. From here, they migrate to other sites as and when required. In plants, the first auxin was isolated from coleoptile tips of oat seedlings by **F.W. Went**.

Auxins are of following two types

(i) **Natural Auxins**
- IAA (Indole Acetic Acid)
- IBA (Indole Butyric Acid)

(ii) **Synthetic Auxins**
- 2, 4 D (2, 4 Dichlorophenoxy acetic acid)
- NAA (Naphthalene Acetic Acid)

Physiological Effects of Auxin

The physiological effects of auxin in plants are as follows

(i) **Root initiation** Auxin inhibits the elongation of primary root. But, it can stimulate the initiation of lateral and adventitious roots. Auxins are used to induce formation of roots on stem cutting. NAA and IBA are often used for rooting.

(ii) **Flowering** NAA and 2,4-D are often employed for inducing flowering in litchi and pineapple. However, it delays fall of leaves.

(iii) **Parthenocarpy** Auxins can induce the formation of fruits without involving fertilisation, e.g. banana, tomatoes, etc. These fruits are called **parthenocarpic fruits**.

(iv) **Cell elongation** It stimulates the elongation of cell in the shoot and promotes cell enlargement.

(v) **Apical dominance** It is a phenomenon in which apical buds inhibit the growth of lateral buds. Apical buds accomplish this by producing auxins. It inhibits the growth of lateral buds.

(vi) **Cell division** Auxin initiates and promotes cell division in vascular cambium, e.g. NAA.

Gibberellins

These were first discovered in Japan from a fungus *Gibberella fujikuroi*. This fungus causes **foolish seedling disease of rice** (Bakanae disease).

Almost 100 types of gibberellins have been reported till now. These are denoted as GA_1, GA_2, GA_3 and so on. $GA_3(C_{19}H_{22}O_6)$ is the first discovered and most studied gibberellin. This hormone is mainly distributed in meristematic regions like stem apex, root apex, buds, seeds, etc.

Physiological Effects of Gibberellins

The physiological effects of gibberellins are as follows

(i) **Fruit growth** Gibberellins promote growth of fruits. It increases length of bunches of grapes.

(ii) **Malting** Gibberellins (GA_3) are used in breweries. It increases malt production in barley grains.

(iii) **Delayed ripening and senescence** Gibberellins cause delay in ripening of citrus fruits.

(iv) **Rapid maturity** Gibberellins cause quicker growth in conifers. Thus, they are used to obtain economically important seeds. Similarly, **bolting** (elongation of flowering stem before harvesting of crop) is induced by artificial treatment with gibberellin.

(v) **Breaking seed dormancy** Gibberellin causes mobilisation of food. Due to this, seed and bud dormancy is broken.

(vi) **Elongation of dwarfs** Gibberellins enhance the longitudinal growth of internodes in dwarf plants.

(vii) **Parthenocarpy** Gibberellins are considered more efficient than auxins to produce parthenocarpic fruits.

(viii) **Stem and leaf growth** Gibberellins can stimulate stem elongation, e.g. in sugarcane, it elongates stem size.

(ix) **Seed germination** Gibberellins promote seed germination. They stimulate the synthesis of hydrolytic enzymes like amylases, proteases, etc.

Cytokinin

It was discovered by **Skoog** (1950) and **Miller** (1955). Cytokinins are widely distributed in plants. They are mainly produced in root tips and from there they are transported through xylem cells.

Physiological Effects of Cytokinins

The physiological effects of cytokinins are as follows

(i) **Flowering** Cytokinin induces flowering in plants like in *Lemna* and *Wolffia*. It is also responsible for breaking dormancy.

(ii) **Promotes cell division and organ formation** Cytokinins are essential for cell division. High auxin to cytokinin ratio favours root development. High cytokinin to auxin ratio favours shoot development.

(iii) **Promotes lateral bud development in dicots** Cytokinins counter act apical dominance. They promote lateral bud formation even in the presence of apical buds.

(iv) **Development of chloroplast** Cytokinins promote chloroplast formation. They also increase the rate of chlorophyll formation.

Ethylene

It is the only gaseous plant hormone. It causes fruit ripening. All parts of seed plants produce ethylene. Maximum synthesis of ethylene occurs during the ripening of fruits and tissues undergoing senescence. It is widely utilised in agriculture practices.

Physiological Effects of Ethylene

The physiological effects of ethylene are as follows

(i) **Fruit ripening** Ethylene stimulates ripening of fruits such as tomatoes, lemons, oranges, etc. It also increases the rate of respiration. It causes dehiscence of dry fruits.

(ii) **Abscission** (falling) **and senescence** (ageing) It enhances abscission and senescence of leaves, fruits and flowers.

(iii) **Breaking dormancy** Ethylene is responsible for breaking dormancy of different plant organs, but not of lateral buds.

(iv) **Root and root hair initiation** Ethylene in low concentration promotes growth of roots. It can initiate root hair formation also.

(v) **Flowering** Ethylene usually inhibits flowering. But in some plants (e.g. pineapple and mango), it induces flowering.

Abscisic Acid (ABA)

It is the only growth retarding hormone. It is found in fruits, seeds and in the chloroplast of leaves. ABA is produced when a plant is exposed to stress hence, is also known as **stress hormone**. The common stresses include lack of water, saline soils, cold temperature and frost.
ABA is also known as the **growth inhibitor** as it inhibits the growth of plant by slowing down plant metabolism.

Physiological Effects of ABA

The physiological effects of ABA are as follows

(i) **Induces stomatal closure** ABA causes stomata to close during stress conditions.

(ii) **Bud dormancy** ABA induces axillary buds to become dormant during winters.

(iii) **Abscission** It causes abscission in leaves, flowers and fruits.

(iv) **Geotropism in roots** Application of ABA on root results in geotropism.

(v) ABA is applied to green oranges. It is done to turn them yellow.

(vi) ABA in most cases acts opposite to gibberellins.

Check Your LEARNING...

1 Which hormone is present in actively growing regions like shoot and root apices?
2 Name the hormone capable of inducing parthenocarpy.
3 Which hormone induces flowering?
4 Name the only gaseous plant hormone
5 Stomatal closing is induced by which hormone?
6 Identify the hormone(s) which inhibit(s) growth in plants. Auxin, abscisic acid, gibberellin and cytokinin.

Plant Movements

These are changes in the position of plants or their parts which occur in response to some stimulus. This **Stimulus** may be defined as any change in the external environment. The movement of plants is broadly classified into two main types

(i) **Movement independent of growth** This type of movement does not involve growth of the plant, e.g. the 'sensitive' or 'touch-me-not' (chhui-mui) plant (*Mimosa pudica*) shows peculiar response to touch. The leaves of this plant begin to fold up and droop in response to touch.

(ii) **Movement dependent on growth** This type of movement involves the growth of the plant, e.g. when a seed germinates, the root goes down and the stem comes up into the air always.
Usually these kind of movements include tropic movements.

Immediate Response to Stimulus

Sensitive plants give immediate response to the stimulus. Movement of part of plant occurs at a point different from the point of touch.
So, plant must communicate the information that a touch has occurred. This is done in the following manner

(i) Plants use electrical-chemical means to convey the information from cell to cell.

(ii) Plant cells change their shape by changing the amount of water in them, resulting in either swelling or shrinking of cell.

Tropic Movements

When the stimulus has a particular direction and the movement of plant occurs in the direction of the stimulus (either towards the stimulus or in the opposite direction), the movement is called as **tropic movement**.

Types of Tropic Movements

The types of tropic movements are based on environmental triggers like light, gravity of Earth, water and certain chemicals.

(i) **Phototropic movement** (stimulus– light) The movement of the plant part in response to light is called **phototropic movement** and the phenomenon involved is called **phototropism**. As the shoot grows towards light, it is known as **positive phototropism** and growth of root away from the light is called **negative phototropism**, e.g. if a plant gets unilateral light, its shoot will bend in the same direction.

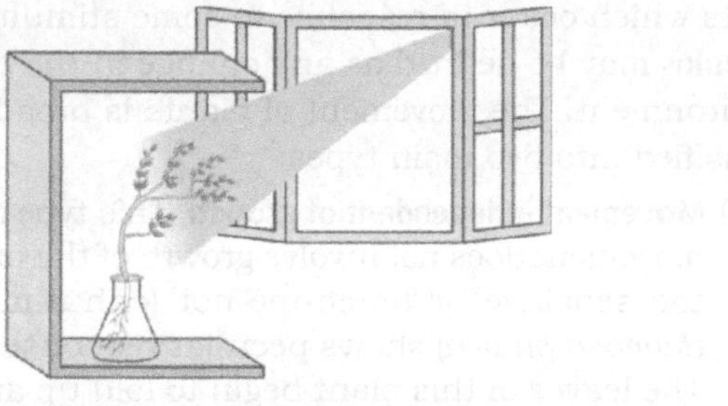

Response of the plant to the direction of light

(ii) **Geotropic movement** (stimulus–gravity) The movement of plant part in response to gravity is called **geotropic movement** and the phenomenon involved is called **geotropism**. When the tip of the stem grows away from the Earth's gravitational force, it is known as **negative geotropism** and when the root tips grow towards gravity, it is known as **positive geotropism**.

Roots always move towards centre of gravity (downward). For example, when bean or gram seed is sown in moist soil, after a few days, the stem grows away from the force of gravity and the root grows towards the force of gravity.

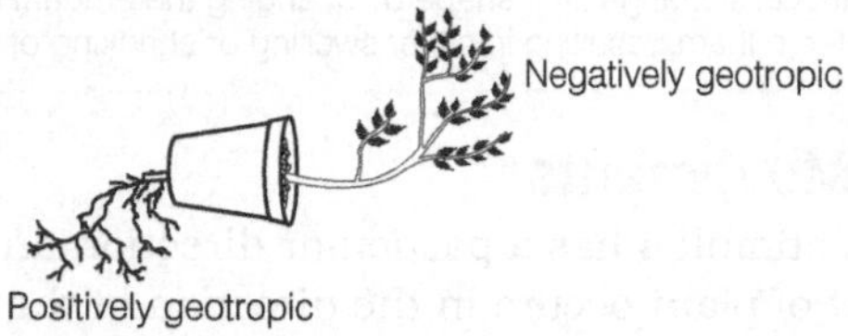

Response of the plant to the direction of gravity

Geotropism can be demonstrated in laboratory with the help of an instrument called **Clinostat**.

(iii) **Hydrotropic movement** (stimulus– water) It is the growth of the plant in response to water. The phenomenon involved in this is called **hydrotropism**. When the plant grows towards the source of water (moisture), the movement is **positive hydrotropism** (e.g. root). This ensures the availability of water to roots. When the plant grows away from the source of water (moisture), it is known as **negative hydrotropism** (e.g. shoot).

For example, during seed germination, the roots grow towards the moist soil (downwards) where water is abundantly present. While shoot grow away from the moist soil.

(iv) **Thigmotropic movement** (stimulus–touch) In thigmotropism, the growth or movement of plants occurs in response to touch.

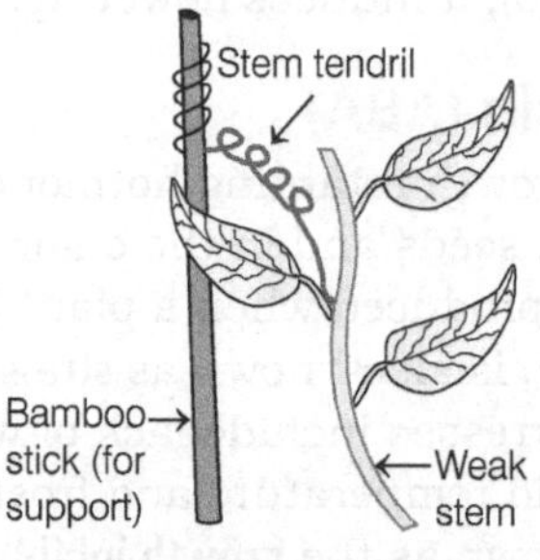

Thigmotropism in plant

For example, the tendrils of plants like sweet pea, grapes, *Cuscuta* are sensitive to touch. When these tendrils come in contact with any support, the part of tendril in contact with the object does not grow as rapidly as other parts of the plant. The tendrils then start to circle around the object and cling to the available support.

(v) **Chemotropic movement** (stimulus-chemical) It is the growth of the plant in response to a chemical stimulus and the phenomenon involved is called **chemotropism**, e.g. growth of pollen tube towards ovules induced by a sugary substances as stimulus during fertilisation. Another example is the movement of fungi growing towards the areas richer in food, and the movement of tentacles in *Drosera* towards the source of nutrients.

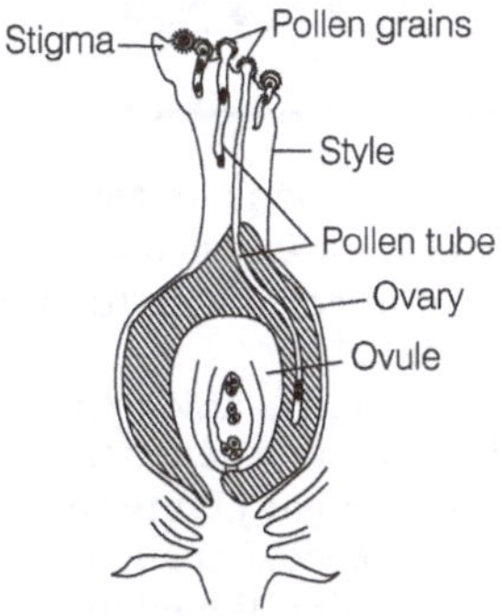

Chemotropism in plant tube

Check Your LEARNING...

1 The roots of a plant show what kind of tropism in response to light?

2 Identify the movement in the tip of stems when it grows away from the Earth's gravitational force.

3 Negative hydrotropism is shown by which part of a plant?

4 Identify the movement which is common in plants like pea, pumpkin and cucumber?

5 Which kind of movement is visible in following cases?

(i) Movement of pollen tube.

(ii) Movement of tentacles in *Drosera*.

QUiCK Revision

- In plants, **control and coordination** is carried out by chemical substances called **hormones** (phytohormones).
- **Plant hormones** are the chemical substances naturally produced in plants for regulation of growth and development, responses, etc.
- **Growth promoters** are chemical substances that perform growth promoting activities like cell enlargement, cell division, seed formation, flowering and fruiting, etc.
- **Auxins** are indole derivatives. They help in cell elongation and division, parthenocarpy, etc.
- **Gibberellins** help in stems and flower growth, breaking dormancy, etc.
- **Cytokinins** promote cell division, development of shoots and delay ageing of leaves.
- **Ethylene** is the only gaseous, fruit ripening hormone.
- **Growth inhibitors** that perform growth inhibiting activities like dormancy and abscission.
- **Abscisic acid** inhibits growth, promotes senescence, induces stomatal closure, etc.
- **Plant movements** occur in response to a stimuli, can be of two types, i.e. tropic or nastic.
- **Tropic movements** The movement of plant occurs in the direction of stimulus, e.g. phototropism, geotropism, hydrotropism, chemotropism and thigmotropism.
  - **Phototropism** is growth movement of plant in response to light.
  - **Geotropism** is growth movement of plants in response to the force exerted by the Earth (gravity).
  - **Hydrotropism** is the movement of plant parts towards the source of water.
  - **Thigmotropism** is the movement of plant parts in response to touch.
  - **Chemotropism** is the movement of plant parts in response to chemical substances.

Chapter Practice

Section-I

1 Mark Questions

1. Name the following.
   (i) A hormone which delays fall of leaves.
   (ii) Hormone responsible for elongation of cells in shoot.
   (iii) Hormone responsible for growth of stem.
   (iv) A hormone which prevents ageing of plant parts.
   (v) Hormone responsible for promotion of cell division.
   (vi) A gaseous plant hormone which promotes ripening of fruits. [2023]
   (vii) The one plant growth hormone, which retards growth during extremely dry season.
   (viii) Two types of tropic movements.

Ans. (i) Auxin (ii) Auxin
(iii) Gibberellin (iv) Cytokinin
(v) Cytokinin (vi) Ethylene
(vii) Abscisic acid
(viii) Two types of tropic movements are
(a) Geotropism (b) Chemotropism

2. Name the plant growth regulators which can be used when you are asked to
   (i) induce rooting in a twig
   (ii) delay leaf senescence
   (iii) induce growth in axillary buds
   (iv) quickly ripen a fruit

Ans. (i) Auxins (like IAA) (ii) Gibberellin
(iii) Cytokinin (iv) Ethylene

3. Correct and rewrite the following statements by changing the underlined words.
   (i) Auxins like <u>NAA</u> are isolated from plants.
   (ii) <u>Auxins</u> stimulate stem elongation.
   (iii) Hormone discovered by <u>Skoog and Miller</u>, inhibits the growth of lateral bud.
   (iv) Maximum synthesis of <u>cytokinins</u> occurs in tissues undergoing senescence.
   (v) The phenomenon involved in the growth of pollen tube towards ovule is <u>thigmotropic</u> movement.

Ans. (i) Auxins like IAA are isolated naturally from plants.
(ii) Gibberellins stimulate stem elongation.
(iii) Hormone discovered by F.W. Went, inhibits the growth of lateral bud.
(iv) Maximum synthesis of ethylene occurs in tissues undergoing senescence.
(v) The phenomenon involved in the growth of pollen tube towards ovule is chemotropic movement.

4. Give biological reasons for the following.
   (i) In pineapple, auxin is used.
   (ii) Rice plant infected with fungus *fujikuroi* grow foolishly tall.
   (iii) Gibberellic acid is able to induce reversal of dwarfism in many genetically dwarf plants.
   (iv) Spraying of sugar plants with gibberellins increases the yield of sugar.
   (v) Cut leaves when dipped in cytokinins stay green for longer period.

Ans. (i) Auxin is used in pineapple to promote flowering.
(ii) Rice plant infected with fungus grows foolishly tall because the fungus *Gibberella fujikuroi* produces GA in plants causing abnormal growth of stem, in rice plant.
(iii) In genetically dwarf plants, the level of GA is low but introducing GA externally, can cause rapid elongation growth in such plants.
(iv) Spraying gibberellins increase the length of internodes and increased internodes will produce more sugar.
(v) Cut leaves when dipped in cytokinins stay green for longer period because cytokinin retards ageing of plant organs by promoting protein synthesis and mobilisation of nutrient resources.

5. (i) Match the following columns.

	Column I		Column II
A.	IAA	1.	Elongation of dwarfs
B.	Cytokinin	2.	Flowering in pineapple
C.	Gibberellic acid	3.	Cell division
D.	Ethylene	4.	Cell wall elongation

(ii) Match the following columns.

	Column I		Column II
A.	Light	1.	Thigmotropism
B.	Touch	2.	Phototropism
C.	Gravity	3.	Hydrotropism
D.	Sugar	4.	Geotropism
		5.	Chemotropism

Ans. (i) A–4, B–3, C–1, D–2
(ii) A–2, B–1, C–4, D–5

6. Fill in the blanks by using suitable words.
   (i) ..... help in breaking the seed and bud dormancy.
   (ii) High .... ratio promotes shoot development.
   (iii) Stomatal closure is induced by .... hormone.
   (iv) The stem and the leaves of a plant are .... phototropic .
   (v) A root of plant grows downward, this is called ....

Ans. (i) Gibberellins (ii) cytokinin to auxin
(iii) ABA (iv) positively
(v) positive geotropism

7. Choose the correct answer from the four options given below.

(i) Auxin inhibits the growth of
(a) apical buds
(b) lateral axillary buds
(c) root on stem cuttings
(d) parthenocarpic development of fruits

Ans. (b)

(ii) Which one of the following plant hormones is responsible for phototropism in plants?
(a) Cytokinin (b) Gibberellins
(c) Ethylene (d) Auxin

Ans. (d)

(iii) The plant hormone used to speed up the malting process in brewing industry is
(a) GA_3 (b) ethylene (c) auxin (d) cytokinin

Ans. (a)

(iv) Which of the following is a plant hormone?
(a) Adrenaline (b) Cytokinin
(c) Glucagon (d) Oxytocin

Ans. (b)

(v) A plant hormone responsible for inducing morphogenesis during plant tissue culture is
(a) ethylene (b) gibberellin
(c) cytokinin (d) abscisic acid

Ans. (c)

(vi) High auxin to cytokinin ratio favours the
(a) root development
(b) shoot development
(c) formation of undifferentiated cells
(d) None of the above

Ans. (a)

(vii) Plant hormones, which promote growth are
(a) gibberellins and ethylene
(b) auxin and ethylene
(c) auxin, cytokinin and gibberellins
(d) cytokinin and abscisic acid

Ans. (c)

(viii) The plant hormone triggering the fall of mature leaves and fruits from plants is
(a) auxin (b) gibberellin
(c) abscisic acid (d) kinetin

Ans. (c)

(ix) The stress hormone is
(a) auxin (b) cytokinin
(c) ethylene (d) abscisic acid

Ans. (d)

(x) Both ethylene and ABA are responsible for
(a) promoting abscission of leaves and fruits
(b) inducing dormancy of seeds
(c) stimulation of apical dominance
(d) ripening of fruits

Ans. (a)

(xi) Which of the following is not an example of tropism?
(a) Growth of pollen tube towards sugary substance
(b) Folding up of the leaves of *Mimosa pudica* when touched
(c) Twining of tendrils around a support in response to touch
(d) None of the above

Ans. (b)

(xii) A plant's response to light is known as
(a) geotropism (b) hydrotropism
(c) photonasty (d) phototropism

Ans. (d)

(xiii) The roots of a plant are
(a) positively phototropic but negatively geotropic
(b) positively geotropic but negatively phototropic
(c) negatively hydrotropic but positively phototropic
(d) positively phototropic but negatively geotropic

Ans. (b)

(xiv) When roots of a plant always move towards water, even if it means going against the pull of gravity. This indicates
(a) geotropism (b) negative geotropism
(c) hydrotropism (d) positive geotropism

Ans. (c)

(xv) The climbing parts of plants like tendrils grow towards any support which they come in contact with and wind around them for support. This is an example of
(a) thigmotropism (b) nastic movements
(c) geotropism (d) chemotropism

Ans. (a)

8. Choose the odd one out from the following terms given below and name the category to which the other three belong.

(i) NAA, 2, 4-D, ABA, IAA
(ii) Bakanae disease, Fruit ripening, Rapid maturity, Parthenocarpy
(iii) Chlorophyll formation, Flowering, Break dormancy, Induce organ formation
(iv) Bud dormancy, Senescence, Fruit ripening, Gaseous hormone

Ans. (i) **Odd term** is ABA.
Others are either natural or synthetic auxin.
(ii) **Odd term** is fruit ripening.
Other physiological effects belong to gibberellins.
(iii) **Odd term** is break dormancy.
Other physiological effects belong to cytokinin.
(iv) **Odd term** is bud dormancy.
Other physiological effects belong to ethylene.

9. Expand the following biological abbreviations.
(i) PGR (ii) IAA (iii) GA (iv) ABA

Ans. (i) Plant Growth Regulator
(ii) Indole Acetic Acid
(iii) Gibberellic Acid
(iv) Abscisic Acid

10. State the exact location of the following hormones in plants.
(i) Auxin (ii) Gibberellin
(iii) Ethylene (iv) Abscisic acid

Ans. (i) Auxin is found on the tip of root and shoot of plant.
(ii) Gibberellin is found in seeds, young leaves and roots.
(iii) Ethylene is mainly found in fruits.
(iv) Abscisic acid is found in the chloroplast of leaves.

11. State the main function of the following.
(i) Phytohormones (ii) Cytokinin
(iii) Ethylene (iv) ABA

Ans. (i) Phytohormones are involved in flowering, ripening of fruits, seed germination, etc.
(ii) Cytokinin promotes cell division.
(iii) Ethylene stimulates ripening of fruits.
(iv) Abscisic acid induces seed and bud dormancy.

12. Mention one difference between each of the following pairs on the basis of what is given in the bracket.
(i) Auxins and Gibberellins (seed dormancy)
(ii) Auxin and Abscisic acid (growth)
(iii) Thigmotropic movement and Chemotropic movement (stimulus)
(iv) *Cuscuta* and *Drosera* (type of tropic movement)

Ans. (i) Difference between auxins and gibberellins is as follows

Auxins	Gibberellins
They play no role in seed dormancy.	They suppress seed dormancy.

(ii) Difference between auxin and abscisic acid is as follows

Auxin	Abscisic acid
It promotes growth in plants.	It inhibits growth in plants.

(iii) Difference between thigmotropic movement and chemotropic movement is as follows

Thigmotropic movement	Chemotropic movement
Thigmotropic growth occurs in response to the touch.	Chemotropic growth occurs in response to a chemical stimulus.

(iv) Difference between *Cuscuta* and *Drosera* is as follows

Cuscuta	*Drosera*
This shows thigmotropic movement.	This shows chemotropic movement.

13. Give the biological/technical terms for the following.
(i) The period of decreased functional capacity between reproductive maturity and death of an organism.
(ii) A device to measure the length of a plant.
(iii) The movement of roots in response to presence of water/moisture nearby.
(iv) The movement of plant parts towards a chemical substance.

Ans. (i) Senescence (ii) Auxanometer
(iii) Hydrotropism (iv) Chemotropism

14. Briefly explain the following terms.
(i) Apical dominance
(ii) Bolting
(iii) Abscission
(iv) Geotropism

Ans. (i) Apical dominance is a phenomenon in which the apical bud grows due to the presence of higher concentration of auxin at the tip of shoot and suppress the growth of lateral buds.
(ii) Bolting is the elongation of internodes just prior to flowering.
(iii) Abscission is the separation of leaves, flowers and fruits from the plant body.
(iv) Geotropism is the movement of plant part in response to the force of gravity.

15. Answer the following questions briefly.
(i) A young green plant receives sunlight from one direction only. What will happen to its shoot and roots?
(ii) Mention why gibberellin is named so?
(iii) In what way, tropic movements are different from other types of movements?
(iv) Why are roots known as positively geotropic?
(v) What do we call the movement of shoot towards light?

Ans. (i) The shoot of the plant will bend towards the light, whereas roots will bend away from the light.
(ii) Gibberellin was named after the fungus, which is the source of it, i.e. *Gibberella fujikuroi.*
(iii) The tropic movements are directional with respect to the stimulus they received.
(iv) The roots always grow towards the Earth due to gravity that is why they are positively geotropic.
(v) The movement of shoot towards light is called positive phototropism.

2 Marks Questions

16. How control and coordination is carried out in plants?

Ans. In plants, control and coordination is brought about by means of chemical substances called phytohormones. In addition to them, environmental factors like water, temperature and light control growth and development.

17. How are IBA and 2, 4-D useful in agriculture?

Ans. IBA and 2, 4-D are used to induce formation of roots on cuttings of many ornamental, horticultural and forest trees. 2, 4-D can also be used as a weedicide.

18. Mention any two functions of plant hormone gibberellins.

Ans. Two functions of plant hormone gibberellin are

(i) Elongation of dwarf plants.

(ii) They help in overcoming natural dormancy of buds, seeds, etc., and help them to grow.

19. In an experiment, the callus produced from internode's segments did not proliferate until a substance was added to it. Identify this substance and its role in the experiment.

Ans. Callus is an undifferentiated mass of cells. It proliferates only when nutrient medium containing auxin was supplemented with cytokinin hormone because it stimulates growth of plant tissues.

20. Which of the following movements are tropic, identify along with names?

(i) Opening of flower

(ii) Roots moving downwards

(iii) Shoots moving towards light

(iv) Twirling of a tendril

Ans. Tropic movements are

(i) Opening of a flower is not a tropic movement.

(ii) Roots moving downwards – Geotropism

(iii) Shoots moving towards light – Phototropism

(iv) Twirling of a tendril – Thigmotropism

21. By giving an example, explain how does a plant respond to an external stimuli.

Ans. Take a healthy potted plant. Keep this plant inside a dark room by the side of an open window. After a few days, it is observed that the plant bends towards the open window (that is, towards light). This shows that the plant respond to an external stimuli, i.e. light in above example.

22. What is meant by positive and negative phototropism?

Ans. **Positive phototropism** When the plant shows the growth movement by bending towards the light source, it is positive phototropism.

Negative phototropism When the plant or its parts (like roots) respond to light by growing away from it is negative phototropism.

3 Marks Questions

23. Write a short note on discovery, physiological functions and agricultural/horticultural applications of auxins.

Ans. Auxin is a powerful growth stimulant.

(i) **Discovery** It was first isolated from human urine. Auxins are generally produced by the growing apices of the stems and roots of plants.

(ii) **Physiological functions** They help to initiate rooting in stem cuttings (an application widely used for plant propagation). Auxins promote flowering in pineapples. They also help to prevent fruit and leaf drop at early stages, but promote the abscission of older mature leaves and fruits.

(iii) **Agricultural/horticultural applications** Auxins also induce parthenocarpy, e.g. in tomatoes.
They are widely used as weedicides, e.g. 2, 4-D which are used to kill dicotyledonous weeds. They also control xylem differentiation and help in cell division.

24. How are gibberellins useful in agriculture to improve productivity? Give any three points in support of your answer.

Ans. Gibberellins are useful in agriculture in the following ways

(i) Application of gibberellins increases the length of the stem and increases the yield of sugar in sugarcane.

(ii) Gibberellins promote seed germination.

(iii) They can cause fruits like apple to elongate and improve in shape.

25. (i) Which plant hormone is present in greater concentration in the areas of rapid cell division?

(ii) Give one example of a plant growth promoter and a plant growth inhibitor.

Ans. (i) Cytokinin is present in greater concentration in the areas of rapid cell division.

(ii) An example of a plant growth promoter is gibberellins and an example of a plant growth inhibition is abscisic acid.

26. 'The role of ethylene is both positive and negative'. Justify the statement.

Ans. The role of ethylene is both positive and negative. Ethylene is a simple gaseous PGR. It is synthesised in large amount by tissues undergoing senescence and ripening. It also promotes senescence and abscission of plant organs especially in leaves and flowers. This is its negative effect. As a positive effect, ethylene breaks seed and bud dormancy, initiates germination in peanut seeds, sprouting of potato tubers. It promotes internode/petiole elongation in deep water rice plants. It helps leaves/inner parts of the shoot to remain above water.

Section-II [3/5 Marks]

Structured Questions

1. Study the diagram given below and answer the questions that follow. [2023]

(i) Name the phenomenon depicted by the shoot in the above diagram.
(ii) Which plant hormone plays an important role in the above movement?
(iii) Complete and rewrite the given statement by filling in the correct terms:
Shoots show positive .... whereas, roots show positive ....

Ans. (i) The phenomenon depicted by the shoot in the above diagram is phototropism.
(ii) Auxin plays an important role in phototropism.
(iii) Shoots show positive **phototropism** whereas, roots show positive **geotropism**.

2. The diagram given below is an instrument which is used to eliminate the effect of gravity. Answer the following questions that follows.

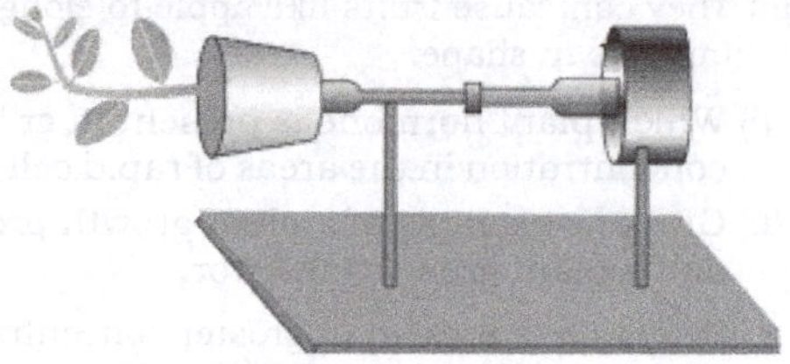

(i) Name the instrument.
(ii) What is the use of this instrument in this experiment?
(iii) Why does the plant grow straight?
(iv) What will happen if the rotation of the instrument is stopped?
(v) Can plants grow with no gravity?

Ans. (i) The given instrument is Clinostat.
(ii) This instrument neutralises the effect of gravity by rotating.
(iii) The plant grows straight due to equal distribution of auxin that causes equal growth on all sides and no curvature takes place.
(iv) If the rotation of Clinostat is stopped for a considerable period of time then the tip of the stem is observed to grow curve and grow upwards.
(v) Yes, in case of absence of gravity, plants may use other environmental factors like light, to grow.

3. Given below is an experimental setup to demonstrate a particular tropic movement in germinating seeds. Study the diagram and answer the questions that follow. **[2019]**

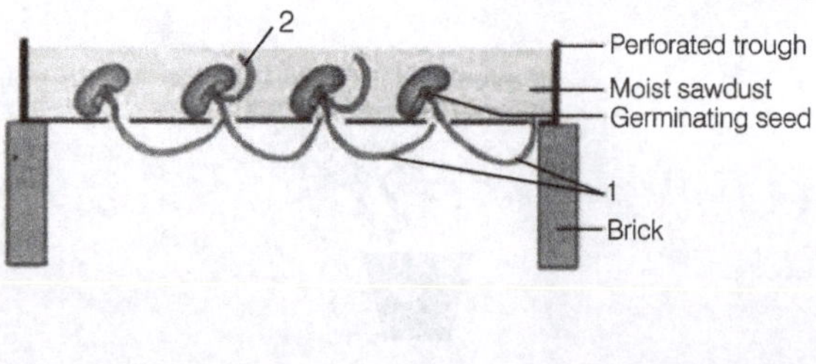

(i) Label the parts 1 and 2.
(ii) Name the tropic movement shown by part 1.
(iii) Part 1 is affected by two stimuli. Name them. Which one of the two is stronger?
(iv) What is thigmotropism? Give one example.
(v) What is meant by 'positive' and 'negative' tropic movements in plants?

Ans. (i) The parts 1 and 2 are labelled as
1-Radicle, 2-Plumule
(ii) The tropic movement shown by part 1 is hydrotropism.
(iii) Part 1 is affected by two stimuli, i.e. gravity and water. Water is stronger.
(iv) Growth movement of plants in response to touch stimulus, known as thigmotropism, e.g. sweet pea.
(v) Movement of the parts of plant towards the source of stimulus is positive movement while the movement of the part of plant away from the source of stimulus is negative tropic movement.

4. Tropism is a plant movement that is determined by the stimulus. When the stimulus is received by the plant, specific part of the plant shows response in the form of growth movement.
(i) Through an experimental setup, demonstrate how hydrotropism occurs in plant.
(ii) Which hormone helps in growing the shoot and root in specific direction?
(iii) Give examples of plants which show thigmotropic movements.
(iv) Other than in pollen tube, where one can find chemotropic movement in plants?
(v) Which part of plant shows negative geotropism?

Ans. (i) The growth of plant parts towards or away from water is called hydrotropism.
It is shown in the diagram given below

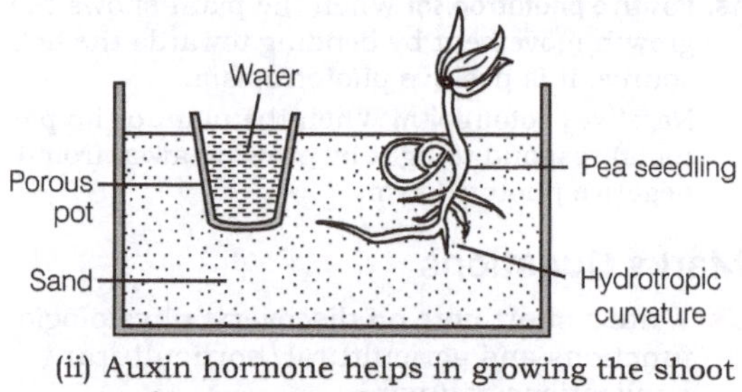

(ii) Auxin hormone helps in growing the shoot and root in specific direction.
(iii) Sweat pea, grapes, *Cuscuta*, etc., show thigmotropic movements.
(iv) Converison of flower to fruits.
(v) Stem shows negative geotropism.

Chapter Assessment

Section-I

1 Mark Questions

1. Name the following.
   (i) Only hormone that is gaseous in nature.
   (ii) The hormone which is responsible for phototropism.
   (iii) Plant hormone capable of breaking apical dominance.
   (iv) Plant hormone which is used for killing weeds (dicots).
   (v) Hormone that induces flowering in long day plants.
2. Correct and rewrite the following statements by changing the underlined words.
   (i) Ascorbic acid is a naturally occurring plant hormone.
   (ii) The bending of plant stem towards light is caused by cytokinin hormone.
3. Give biological reasons for the following.
   (i) The electrical-chemical signals are not considered an efficient means of communication in plants.
   (ii) Roots are called as positively hydrotropic.
4. Match the following columns.

	Column I		Column II
A.	Auxin	1.	Apical dominance
B.	Cytokinin	2.	Shoot development
C.	Gibberellin	3.	Dormancy
D.	Abscisic acid	4.	Parthenocarpy

5. Choose the correct answer from the four options given below.
   (i) Application of *A* may induce parthenocarpy. Here, *A* can be
   (a) auxin (b) cytokinin
   (c) gibberellin (d) Both (a) and (c)
   (ii) A plant's response to light is known as
   (a) geotropism (b) hydrotropism
   (c) phototropism (d) photonasty
   (iii) The movement of a plant part in response to the force of attraction exerted by the Earth is
   (a) hydrotropism (b) geotropism
   (c) chemotropism (d) phototropism
6. Fill in the blanks by using suitable words.
   (i) The plant hormone is a/an .... substance.
   (ii) A phytohormone not associated with plant growth is ....
   (iii) .... is present in greater concentration in young fruits and seeds.
   (iv) Gibberellins are widely used in .... and ....
7. Complete the table given below by filling the blanks present.

Plant hormones	Sites of synthesis	Functions
Auxins	*A*	Promote cell elongation.
Gibberellin	Apical buds and roots.	*B*
C	In green fruits and seeds at the beginning of wintering season.	*D*

8. Expand the following biological abbreviations.
   (i) NAA
   (ii) 2, 4-D
9. State the main function of auxin.
10. Give biological/technical terms for the following.
    (i) The phenomenon of development of seedless fruit without fertilisation.
    (ii) The movement of plant that occurs in the direction of stimulus.
11. Mention one difference between each of the following pairs on the basis of what is given in the bracket.
    (i) Gibberellins and Cytokinin (function)
    (ii) Ethylene and Abscisic acid (function)
12. Briefly explain the following terms.
    (i) Clinostat
    (ii) Hydrotropic movement
13. Answer the following questions briefly.
    (i) What are the chemical substances that perform control and coordination in plants called?
    (ii) Write an example of plant hormone that promotes growth.
    (iii) How does abscisic acid work against growth promoting hormones?
    (iv) How is geotropism necessary for plant?

2 Marks Questions

14. What conditions can induce the phenomenon of bolting naturally and how can it be induced artificially?
15. What would be expected to happen if,
    (i) GA_3 is applied to rice seedlings?
    (ii) Dividing cells stop differentiating?
    (iii) A rotten fruit gets mixed with unripe fruits?
    (iv) The callus is only supplied with auxin?
16. How the given hormones are antagonist to each other?
    (i) Auxin and cytokinins
    (ii) Cytokinin and abscisic acid
17. 'Plants also perform chemical coordination'. Elaborate.

3 Marks Questions

18. What is 'phototropism'? How does it occur in plants?
19. Why do tendrils coil around hard rough objects they come in contact with?
20. Which one of the plant growth regulators would you use if you are asked to
    (i) induce rooting in a twig?
    (ii) quickly ripen a mango?
    (iii) delay leaf senescence?
    (iv) induce growth in axillary buds?
    (v) bolt a rosette plant?
    (vi) induce immediate stomatal closure of leaves?
21. Mention the factors which prove that phytohormones act together but opposite to each other.

Section-II [5 Marks]

Structured Questions

22. The diagram shows an experiment on a type of tropic movement in plant.

    (i) What is the aim of the experiment?
    (ii) What is *A* and *B*?
    (iii) What is the observation of this experiment?
    (iv) Why is the movement of *A* and *B* in different directions?
    (v) Why is the movement of *A* observed in upward direction?
23. Plant growth regulators are variously described as plant growth substance. These are the small, simple organic molecules of diverse chemical composition produced naturally in higher plants that control the growth and other physiological functions.
    (i) Who discovered auxin and from where?
    (ii) Name the scientist who first coined the term hormone.
    (iii) How many types of gibberellins have been reported till date?
    (iv) Which hormone can be used to induce geotropism in roots of plants?
    (v) Which two plants are exception to the property of ethylene to inhibit flowering?

For explanations scan the given QR Code

Olympiad Section*

Brain Teasing Questions asked in Previous Olympiads

1 Plants show phototropism, wherein shoots respond by bending towards light. The plant hormone auxin is responsible for this phototropic effect. An experiment was carried out where the tip of growing seedling was cut and placed horizontally with its cut end in equal contact with two gelatin blocks as shown in the figure (P) below. Auxin diffuses into the gelatin blocks. After some time, the gelatin blocks were placed on seedling stump as shown in the figure (R). The complete experiment was carried out in dark condition. **[INJSO 2016]**

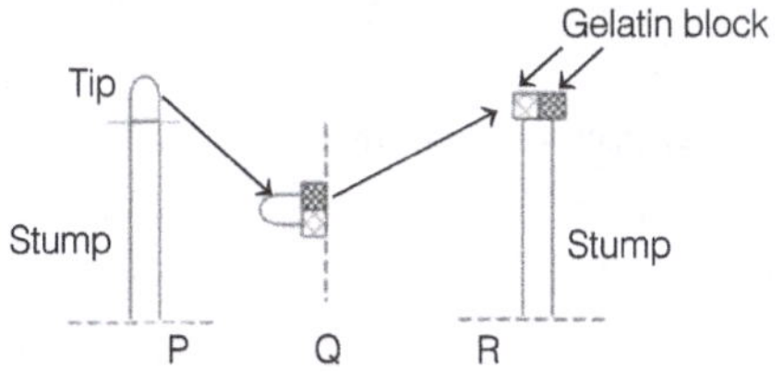

Which one of the following represents the correct result after a few days?

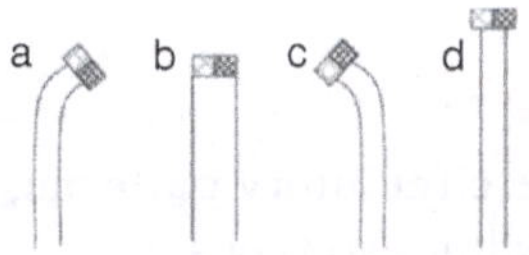

2 Charles Darwin observed that seedlings grow towards light. He called this response 'phototropism.' In an experiment, two light sources are used to illuminate each seedling. Each source is indicated by a yellow circle in the diagrams below. The larger yellow circle represents a light source with twice the illumination than the light source represented by the smaller yellow circle. **[IJSO 2013, India]**

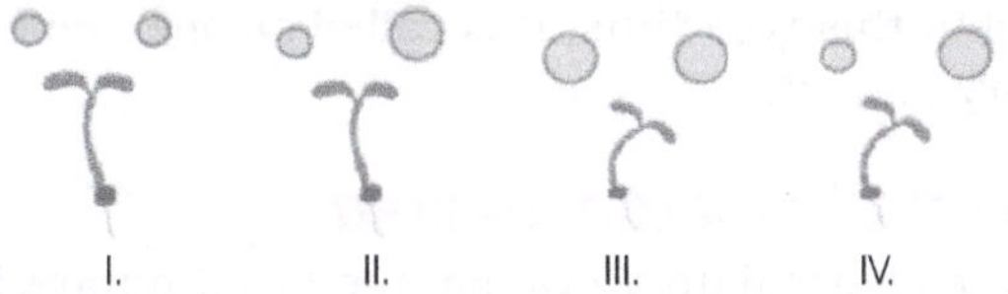

Which of the above responses would be observed?

(a) Only IV (b) Only II

(c) I and III (d) I and IV

3 Thermal imaging is a technique used to detect mutant varieties of plants that over produce Abscisic Acid (ABA). Such plants are warmer than the surrounding plants. This can be explained as **[INBO 2009]**

(a) an elevated level of ABA increases the rate of metabolism thereby producing more heat

(b) overproduction of ABA is mostly observed in C_4 plants which require high optimum temperatures for photosynthesis

(c) increased levels of ABA in cell sap will increase the rate of transpiration causing drying of the plant. This in turn will cause such a plant to be warmer than the surrounding plants

(d) increased ABA will not allow the stomata to open completely and thereby reduce evaporative cooling of the plant

4 Charles Darwin and his son, Francis experimented with phototropism of grass seedlings by placing a metal foil blindfold over different parts of the seedling's coleoptile.

A simplified version of their results is shown below. Which of the following statements best explains their results?

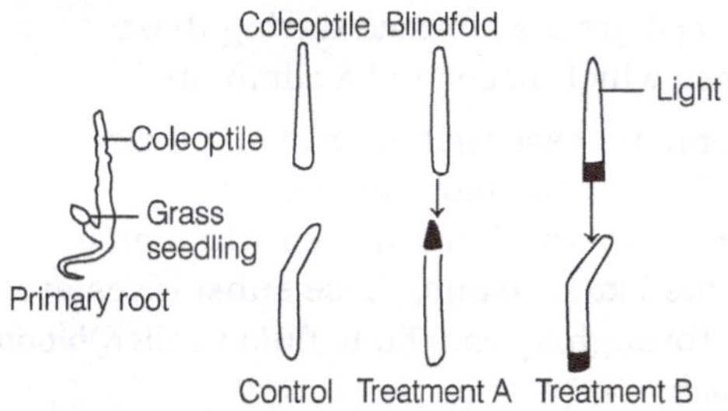

(a) The light signal is perceived a few millimetres below the tip and these cells cause the coleoptile to grow toward the light

(b) Both the seedling root and coleoptile perceive and respond to light in the same manner

(c) A chemical messenger must travel from the base of the coleoptile to the tip

(d) The light signal is perceived at the tip of the coleoptile, but the growth response occurs a few millimetres below the tip

Answers

1. (a) **2.** (d) **3.** (d) **4.** (d)

**These questions may or may not be asked in the examination, have been given just for additional practice required for olympiads, scholarship exams etc. For detailed explanations refer Page No. 247.*

CHAPTER

07

Circulatory System

Chapter Inside

• Circulatory System • Human Circulatory System • Lymphatic System

All living cells require nutrients, oxygen and other essential materials for their growth and survival. These substances take part in various metabolic processes of the cell. Various toxic substances are also formed during these processes which needs to be eliminated.

It is therefore, essential to have an efficient mechanism for the movement of these substances to and from the cells. In higher organisms like humans, these substances are carried through special body fluids called **blood** and **lymph**.

The flow of these fluids inside the body is known as **circulation** and the organs involved in this process together constitute the **circulatory system**. Thus, circulatory system is defined as a vast network of organs and vessels that is responsible for the flow of blood, nutrients, hormones, oxygen and other gases to and from the cells.

Circulatory System

Depending upon the circulatory patterns, the circulatory systems are of following two types

(i) Open Circulatory System

In this type of circulatory system, blood pumped by the heart is passed through a vessel into the spaces or body cavities known as **sinuses**, e.g. arthropods, molluscs, protochordates, etc. Capillary system (i.e. interconnecting vessels between arteries and veins) is not found in this type thus, it is called as open type of circulatory system.

(ii) Closed Circulatory System

In this type of circulatory system, the blood pumped by the heart is always circulated inside the vessels (i.e. it is never present in large spaces or sinuses). Evolutionarily, this pattern is considered to be the most advanced as it supplies blood to the deepest tissues of the body. It is found in annelids and chordates (including humans).

Human Circulatory System

The circulatory system in humans is divided into two parts

1. Blood circulatory system
2. Lymphatic system

Blood Circulatory System

It includes blood, heart and blood vessels.

Blood

It is a fluid connective tissue, found circulating inside the body. The blood is bright red in colour, when taken from an artery (contains oxygenated blood) and its colour is dark red when taken from a vein (contains deoxygenated blood). Its pH is 7.3-7.5, i.e. slightly alkaline in nature. The amount of blood present in an average adult human is 4-6 litres.

Composition of Blood

The blood is composed of following two main components

1. Plasma

It is the liquid portion of the blood without corpuscles which is slightly yellow in colour (straw coloured). It constitutes about 50-60% of the total blood. Plasma mainly consists of water (90-92%), proteins (7-8%), inorganic salts like sodium chloride and sodium bicarbonate (1%) and other substances such as glucose, urea, hormones, etc., in trace amount.

Plasma Proteins

Proteins provide viscosity to the plasma. Major proteins found in plasma are fibrinogen, serum globulins and serum albumins.

Functions of Plasma

Various functions performed by plasma are as follows

(i) Helps in the transport and uniform distribution of heat all over the body.
(ii) Provides body immunity.
(iii) Maintenance of blood pH.
(iv) Helps in the prevention of blood loss.
(v) Fibrinogen helps in blood clotting, globulin helps in defence mechanism and albumin maintains the osmotic balance.

Note Serum is the left out liquid part when the fibrinogen proteins are removed from the plasma as a clot.

2. Blood Corpuscles (Formed Elements)

These elements of the blood constitute about 45% of the blood. These include erythrocytes (RBCs), leucocytes (WBCs) and thrombocytes (platelets).

(i) **Erythrocytes** (RBCs) They are the most abundant type of cells found in the blood. Mammalian RBCs are biconcave disc-like structures. Sometimes, due to an abnormality (mutation), RBCs become fragile and sickle-shaped. This condition is called **sickle-cell anaemia.**

Erythrocytes are extremely small in size (about 7 μm). Due to this, they can move easily through the capillaries in the body.
Humans have 4-6 million/mm^3 RBCs in blood. Mature RBCs in mammals are enucleated, i.e. they **lack nucleus** which makes them biconcave, thus increasing their surface area to volume ratio for carrying more oxygen.

RBCs of mammals also **lack endoplasmic reticulum** and **mitochondria.** It means that these cells have increased flexibility for their movement and cannot use oxygen for themselves (cellular respiration occurs in mitochondria).
Thus, all the oxygen absorbed from the lungs is transported to other tissues. RBCs are red in colour due to the presence of a red coloured pigment called **haemoglobin,** which acts as an oxygen carrier molecule. It is formed of an iron part called **haem** and a protein, **globin.**

The average lifespan of a mature RBC is only 120 days, after which it gets destroyed in the spleen **(graveyard of RBCs)** and liver.

A person living at high altitude has high number of RBC count. It is because of the low concentration (pressure) of O_2 at high altitudes and less O_2 binding capacity of the haemoglobin. Abnormal increase in the RBC number is called **polycythaemia** and their abnormal decrease is called **erythropenia.**

Function The major function of RBCs is to transport respiratory gases to the tissues. Oxygen is transported as oxyhaemoglobin whereas CO_2 is carried in the form of carbaminohaemoglobin.

Note
- The process of RBCs formation is called **haemopoiesis** or **erythropoiesis.** RBCs are produced in the bone marrow of long bones like ribs, sternum, ileum, etc (**cradle of RBCs**).
- Camel and Llama (camelidae) are exceptional among mammals in having oval RBCs with nucleus.
- Haemoglobin has strong affinity for carbon monoxide and together they form a stable compound, carboxyhaemoglobin, thus, causing carbon monoxide poisoning.

(ii) **Leucocytes** (WBCs) These are the most active and motile constituents of blood. They differ from RBCs as they are nucleated (have nucleus) and lack the coloured pigment haemoglobin. WBCs are irregular or amoeboid in shape and are generally short-lived, i.e. only 12-14 days. WBCs are produced in red bone marrow, lymph nodes and sometimes in liver and spleen.

Leucocytes also show the property of **diapedesis**, i.e. oozing out, as they have the ability to move out of capillaries into the tissues with the help of pseudopodia.

They comprise 5000-9000 mm^3 of human blood.

Increase in the number of WBCs results in a disease called **leukaemia**. Decrease in the number of WBCs causes a disease called **leucopenia**.

Leucocytes are of following two major types

(a) **Granulocytes** They have regularly lobed nucleus and are **granulated**, as they contain numerous granules in their cytoplasm. They are further divided as **neutrophil, basophil** and **eosinophil** on the basis of the dyes with which they are stained.

(b) **Agranulocytes** They are not granulated, i.e. cytoplasm is not granular. These are divided into **lymphocytes** and **monocytes**.

Different Types of White Blood Cells (leucocytes) After Staining

Two major categories of WBCs	Cell types	Distinguishing features	Functions
Granular	Neutrophils (62%)	Nucleus with 3-4 lobes. Granules stain with neutral dyes.	Engulf bacteria. (phagocytosis)
	Eosinophils (2.3%)	Nucleus with 2 lobes. Granules stain dark red with eosin (acid dye).	Engulf bacteria. Secrete antitoxins, associated with allergy reactions
	Basophils (0.4%)	Nucleus large indistinctly lobed. Granules stain with basic dyes, i.e. methylene blue.	Release chemicals (such as histamine) during inflammation which dilate blood vessels.
Agranular	Lymphocytes (30%)	Smallest type of WBCs. It has single large nucleus.	Produce antibodies.
	Monocytes (5.3%)	Largest WBCs, kidney-shaped nucleus. Transform into macrophages at the site of infection.	Ingest germs.

Function The major function of leucocytes is to provide defence mechanism for body. They have the ability of **phagocytosis** or **engulfing the foreign particles**, e.g. neutrophils. Some WBCs help in reducing inflammation caused by injury or trauma (e.g. monocytes, neutrophils). WBCs also produce antibodies that provide immunity and help in killing foreign particles, e.g. lymphocytes. **Pus** is composed of dead WBC and tissue cells which are destroyed by bacteria.

(iii) **Thrombocytes** (Blood platelets) These are cell fragments produced from **megakaryocytes** (i.e. the special cells found in the bone marrow). They are minute, oval or round, enucleated structures found floating in the blood. They are 20000-400000/mm^3 in blood. Their lifespan is about 3-5 days after which they get destroyed in the spleen alongwith RBCs.

Function Their main function is to help in clotting or coagulation of blood.

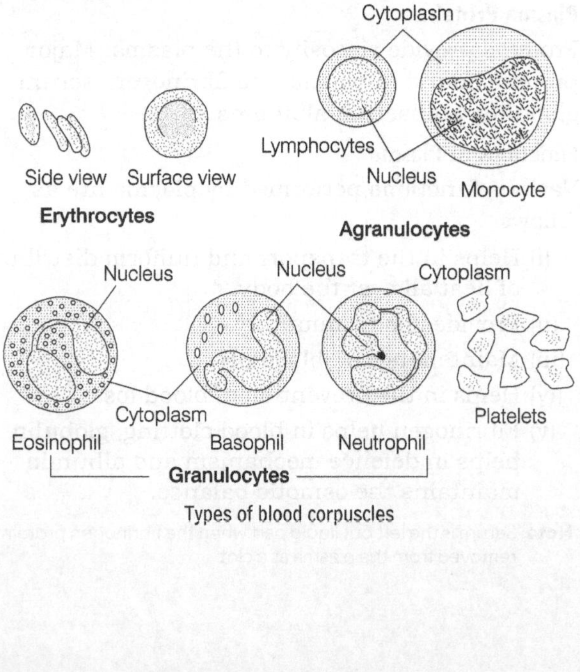

Types of blood corpuscles

Functions of Blood

Blood performs the following important functions

(i) Helps in the transportation of respiratory gases (O_2, CO_2, etc).
(ii) Helps in healing the wounds.
(iii) Maintains body pH, water and ionic balance.
(iv) Fights against infections by forming body immunity.
(v) Helps in transportation of hormones from endocrine glands to target organs.
(vi) Coagulation of blood.
(vii) Helps in transportation of body wastes from different body parts to kidneys.
(viii) Maintains normal body temperature.

Check Your LEARNING...

1 Which type of circulatory system is found in humans?
2 Name the constituents of plasma.
3 Which organ is called graveyard of RBCs?
4 Name the disease caused due to an abnormal decrease in RBCs count.
5 Name one animal which have oval RBCs.
6 How lymphocytes provide immunity to the body?

Blood Groups

Although blood of every human being appears similar but it differs in certain aspects. The plasma membrane of RBCs contains certain glycoproteinaceous molecules known as **antigens**. These are the chemicals that can induce immune response. They differ in different individuals thus, providing them a characteristic blood group.

Two common types of blood grouping systems found in human beings are as follows

1. ABO System

It was reported by **Karl Landsteiner** in 1900 and is based on the presence or absence of antigen A or antigen B on the surface of RBCs. Similarly, the plasma of different individuals contains two natural antibodies or agglutinins. These are the proteins produced in response to antigens.
Person with blood group A have antigen A on the surface of their RBCs and have antibodies against antigen B in their plasma, while in person having blood group B, the case is *vice-versa* to blood group A.

Person with blood group AB have both antigen A and B on the surface of RBCs and no antibodies for either of the antigens in their plasma. Persons with blood group O do not contain any antigen but they have antibodies against both the antigens A and B.

Blood Transfusion

It is a mechanism of injecting blood into the body of the patients (undergoing operation or any other injury) from a healthy person. The person who gives blood is known as **donor**, while a person receiving blood from a healthy person is known as **recipient**.
A person with blood group 'O' is known as **universal donor** (as it lacks antigen) and can donate blood to the person with any blood group, i.e. A, B, AB or O, while a person with blood group 'AB' is known as **universal recipient** as it has both antigens but no antibody.
In blood transfusion, the corpuscle factor or antigen of the donor should be compatible with the plasma factor or antibody of the recipient, otherwise the corpuscles of donated blood become agglutinated and block the blood vessels which may prove fatal.

It can be well-explained through the table given below.

Blood Groups and Donor Compatibility

Blood groups	Antigens on RBCs	Antibodies in plasma	Donor's group	Recipient group
A	A	Anti-B	A, O	A, AB
B	B	Anti-A	B, O	B, AB
AB	A, B	Nil	AB, A, B, O	AB
O	Nil	Anti-A, B	O	A, B, AB, O

2. Rhesus (Rh) System

It is another type of blood group system found in human beings. The blood of most people contains a unique factor known as **Rh factor** (it was named after it was first discovered in **Rhesus monkey**).
Rh factor is based on the presence of an antigen on the surface of RBCs. Thus, the person having Rh antigen on their RBCs are called **Rh positive** (Rh^+), while person who does not have Rh antigen on their RBCs are called **Rh negative** (Rh^-).

Rh Incompatibility

During pregnancy, it is seen that when father's blood is Rh^+ and mother's blood is Rh^-, Rh^+ being a dominant character expresses in the foetus and

causes a serious problem. The first Rh^+ child of Rh^- mother do not suffer, from any problem but the blood of foetus stimulates the formation of anti-Rh^+ (antibodies) in the mother's blood.
In the subsequent pregnancies, the anti-Rh (antibodies) in the mother's blood destroy the foetal Rh^+ RBCs and results in **Haemolytic Disease of the Newborn** (HDN) or **erythroblastosis foetalis** or **rhesus baby syndrome.**
During blood transfusion, the first transfusion between Rh^+ and Rh^- blood causes no harm because Rh^- person develops anti-Rh (antibodies) in his blood. But, in the second transfusion of Rh^+ blood to Rh^- blood, the anti-Rh (antibodies) in the later's blood destroy the RBCs of the donor.

Blood Coagulation

It is a mechanism of formation of a clot when an injury or trauma occurs. It has been seen that when a blood vessel is cut during an injury, blood does not continue to flow for a longer time, instead it stops flowing after some time.

If somebody fails to exhibit this property of clotting that person would continue to bleed when gets injured as he/she may lack one or the other factor that normally controls clotting of blood. This can even lead to the death of that person.
Blood clotting is a complex process which involves a series of steps to get completed.
It occurs in following three steps

(i) When the blood flows out through the wound, the injured cells and blood platelets (thrombocytes) release an enzyme called **thromboplastin** (also called **thrombokinase** or **factor** X).
Thromboplastin helps in the formation of an enzyme prothrombinase (which inactivates heparin) that converts the inactive plasma protein, **prothrombin** into its active form **thrombin**.

(ii) Thrombin acts as a **proteolytic enzyme** to convert **fibrinogen** molecule (produced from the liver in the presence of vitamin-K) to form insoluble **fibrin monomer**. This reaction requires **thrombokinase** or **prothrombokinase**, an enzyme complex, which is formed by a series of linked enzymatic reactions (cascade process). It involves various factors present in the plasma, in their inactive state.

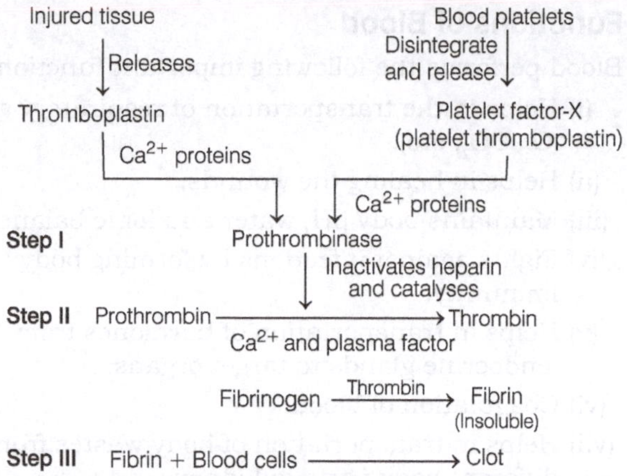

(iii) These fibrin monomers polymerise to long, sticky fibres called **fibrins**, in which dead and damaged elements of blood are trapped. This finally leads to the formation of a **clot** or **coagulum**. It is a dark reddish-brown **scum** formed over the surface of injury. Within 2-5 minutes after clot formation, a yellow fluid called **serum** oozes out.
The formation of a blood clot (thrombi) inside a blood vessel, obstructing the flow of blood through the circulatory system is called **thrombosis**. Even when a blood vessel is not injured, blood clots may form in the body under certain conditions.
Thrombosis in coronary artery may result in heart attack. A clot that breaks and begins to travel around the body is known as an **embolus**.

Anticoagulants

Normally, inside an intact blood vessel, the blood does not coagulate because of the presence of an active anticoagulant, i.e. **heparin** or **antiprothrombin**. Apart from this, procoagulants are also present in the blood, but in their inactive forms. Hirudin found in leeches is also an anticoagulant. Sodium oxalate and sodium citrate are used as anticoagulants in labs, blood banks, etc.

Note
- Blood blister is a type of blister that forms when subdermal tissues and blood vessels are damaged by skin trauma, such as forcible pinching.
- Defibrinated blood is the blood from which fibrin has been removed.
- Insufficient vitamin-K in body leads to inefficient blood clotting.

Check Your LEARNING...

1 Who reported ABO blood grouping system for the first time?
2 Give one difference between the blood groups 'O' and 'AB'.
3 Which blood group is called universal donor?
4 What is thrombosis?
5 Give the technical term for the clot that breaks and travels around the body.
6 Name an anticoagulant used in blood banks for storing blood.

The Heart

Heart is the main pumping organ found in the thoracic cavity of human beings, i.e. between the two lungs and above the diaphragm.
It is made up of cardiac muscles having unique features like automatic contraction and these muscles do not get fatigued the whole life.

External Structure

It is about the size of our close fist and is protected by a double membranous covering known as **pericardium**. The space between the two pericardial membranes is filled with **pericardial fluid**, which protects the heart from any mechanical injury and shocks. It also helps in reducing friction during heartbeat.

Human heart is comprised of four main chambers, i.e. two relatively small upper chambers called **auricles** (sing. atria) and two larger lower chambers called **ventricles.** The right atrium is slightly larger than the left atrium.

Internal Structure

Internally, the chambers of heart, i.e. two auricles (atria) and two ventricles are separated by different septa and valves. The chambers of heart are discussed below

1. **Auricles or Atria** These are the upper, two thin-walled and smaller chambers. They serve to receive the blood, therefore these are called **receiving chambers** (right atrium and left atrium). Both the right and left atria are separated by a thin, muscular wall known as **interatrial septum**.
   (i) **Right atrium** This right chamber receives only **impure** (deoxygenated) blood. It receives impure blood from various parts of the body, through two major veins, i.e. superior and inferior vena cava. It also receives blood from the walls of the heart itself (through a coronary sinus).
   (ii) **Left atrium** This chamber is meant to receive only **pure** (oxygenated) blood. It receives blood from lungs through four **pulmonary veins** (i.e. two from each lung).

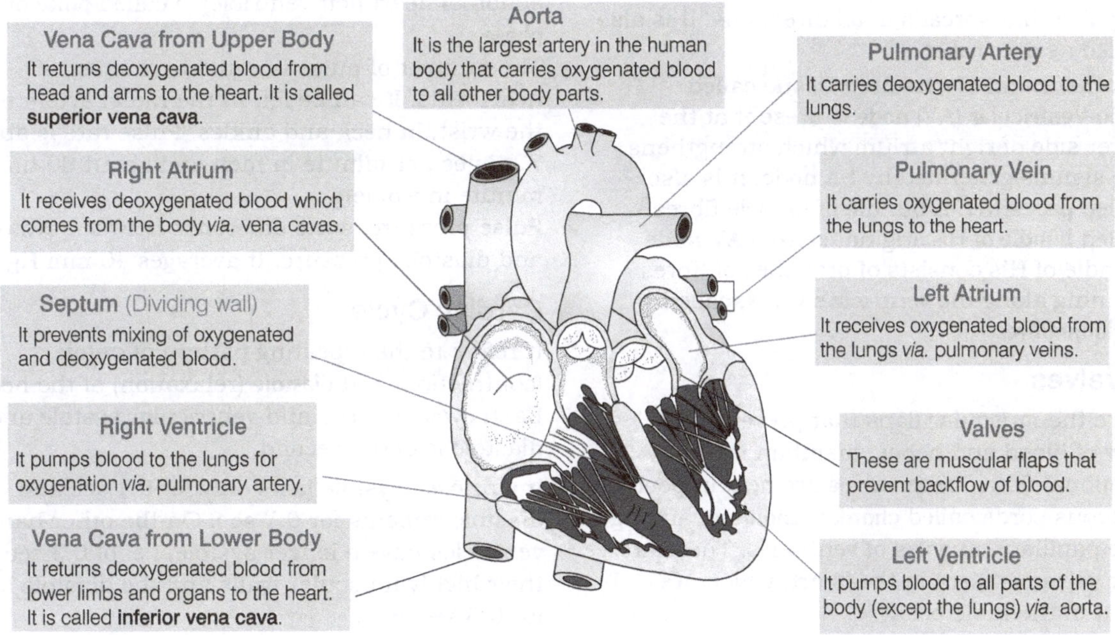

Human heart with different vessels and their functions

2. **Ventricles** These are two lower thick-walled chambers of the heart that pumps the blood away from the heart. They function as **pumping chambers**. Both right and left ventricles are separated by the **interventricular septum**.

   The atrium and the ventricle of the same side are also separated by another septum, a thick fibrous tissue called **Atrio-Ventricular** (i.e. AV) **septum.**

   (i) **Right ventricle** It receives impure blood from right atrium and pumps blood into the **pulmonary artery** (two in number), which further takes this blood to the lungs for purification (oxygenation).

   (ii) **Left ventricle** It receives pure (oxygenated) blood from left atrium and pumps its into the aorta (largest artery in the pathway), which in turn takes this blood to whole body organs.

   From the base of aorta, two coronary arteries arise which supply blood to heart muscles. At the corner of right auricle near the opening of vena cava, a band of muscles is present. It is known as **Sino-Atrial** (SA) **node.** It generates impulse that spreads in all directions. It is also called as **pacemaker.**

   Another band of muscular tissue called **Atrio-Ventricular** (AV) **node** is present at the lower side of right atrium which strengthens the signals generated by SA node. It is also called **pacesetter.** A bundle of muscle fibres called **bundle of His** originates from AV node. Bundle of His consists of branches of fibres running along the ventricle's walls, called **Purkinje fibres.**

Heart Valves

These are the muscular flaps that prevent the backflow of blood and hence, maintain its unidirectional flow. These valves are held in position by tendinous cords called **chordae tendineae**, arising from the papillary muscles of ventricles. There are different valves present in the heart, which are described in the table below

Valves of Human Heart

Heart valves	Locations	Actions
Tricuspid valve (Right atrio-ventricular valve)	Between right atrium and right ventricle.	During ventricular contraction, it prevents blood to move from right ventricle into right atrium.
Pulmonary semilunar valve	At the entrance of pulmonary artery.	During ventricular relaxation, it prevents blood to move from pulmonary trunk into right ventricle.
Mitral (bicuspid or left atrio-ventricular valve)	Between left atrium and left ventricle	During ventricular contraction, it prevents blood to move from left ventricle into left atrium.
Aortic semilunar valve	At the entrance of aorta	During ventricular relaxation, it prevents blood to move from aorta into left ventricle.

Functioning of Human Heart : Heartbeat and Pulse

The heart regularly and rhythmically contracts and relaxes at short intervals throughout life without pause and fatigue. This inherent activity of heart is called its **heartbeat.** Each heartbeat has two phases, i.e. **contraction phase** or **systole** and **relaxation phase** or **diastole.**

The rate of throbbing felt in arteries due to pumping action of heart (left ventricle) is called **pulse** or **atrial phase.**

The number of pulse is equal to number of heartbeats. It can be felt in the radial artery near the wrist, in neck and ankles. Pulse rate is about 72 times per minute in men and about 80 times per minute in women.

Pulse pressure is the difference between systolic and diastolic pressure. It averages 40 mm Hg.

Cardiac Cycle

It refers to the repeating pattern of **systole** (contraction) and **diastole** (relaxation) of the heart. Each cycle of atrial and ventricular systole and diastole is of 0.8 second.

In auricles, systole lasts only for 0.1 sec and diastole remains for 0.7 sec. On the other hand, ventricles have a longer systole, i.e. of 0.3 sec due to their highly muscular walls and the diastole lasts for 0.5 sec only.

The successive events of the cardiac cycle are briefly described below

(i) **In atrial systole**, the atria contract due to the wave of contraction, stimulated by the SA node. The blood is forced into the ventricles as the bicuspid and tricuspid valves are open. It takes 0.1 second.

(ii) **Ventricular systole** Both ventricles contract, forcing blood through the pulmonary artery to the lungs and through the aorta to the rest of the body. It takes 0.3 seconds.

(iii) **Atrial diastole** The atria relax, although the ventricles are still contracted. Blood enters the atria from the large veins called **vena cava** coming from the body. This takes 0.3 seconds.

(iv) **Ventricular diastole** The ventricular relax and become ready to fill with blood from the atria as the next cycle begins. This takes about 0.5 seconds.

Heart Sounds

Heart produces two sounds in short succession followed by a small gap. The first sound called **Lubb** is produced due to the sharp closure of tricuspid and mitral valves at the start of ventricular systole. The second sound called **Dupp** is produced due to the closure of aortic semilunar valve and pulmonary semilunar valve at the beginning of ventricular diastole, which prevents the backflow of blood into ventricles.

'Lubb' and 'Dupp' are the sounds heard through a stethoscope.

Cardiac Output

It is the volume of blood ejected from the left or right ventricle per minute.

It is calculated by the formula,

Cardiac output

= Stroke Volume (SV) × Heart Rate (HR)

= 70 mL × 75 per min = 5250 mL per min

The stroke volume depends mainly on venous return, i.e. the amount of blood delivered to the heart by the veins.

The Heart rate is heart beats perminute.

Blood Pressure

The pressure exerted by the flow of blood on the elastic wall of arteries is called **blood pressure**. It is greater during systole than during the diastole. In a normal person, the systolic pressure is 120 mm Hg and diastolic pressure is 80 mm Hg. Blood pressure changes with age and health of the person. A rise in blood pressure above 140/90mm Hg is known as **hypertension** or **high blood pressure**. It is measured by **sphygmomanometer** (invented by **Samuel Ritter von Basch** in 1881).

Check Your LEARNING...

1 Name the type of muscles present in heart.
2 Which is the largest artery in the human body?
3 What is the function of inferior vena cava?
4 What is the function of Mitral valve in human heart?
5 What is the duration of ventricular diastole?
6 How much blood is pumped as a stroke volume?
7 What is sphygmomanometer?

Blood Vessels

These are the branched tubes which extend from heart to all parts of the body. There are three main types of blood vessels which carry blood towards and away from the heart as follows

(i) **Artery** It is a blood vessel whose function is to carry blood away from the heart and towards any other organ. The blood flows in spurts in arteries. An artery is comprised of thick walls and narrow central lumen (core). Arteriole is the smallest final branch of artery which further breaks up into the capillaries.

(ii) **Vein** It is a type of blood vessel which carries blood away from the organs and towards the heart. The flow of blood in veins is found to be uniform. It is comprised of thinner walls and a larger central lumen than arteries. Veins are formed by the merging of finer branches called venules. Veins contain a thin pocket type valve towards the heart which help them to prevent backflow of blood.

(iii) **Capillary** It is a narrow tube-like blood vessel, comprised of a single layer of endothelial cells. Capillaries have the ability of contracting (vasoconstriction) and dilating (vasodilation) with the decrease and increase in the blood supply to various body parts.

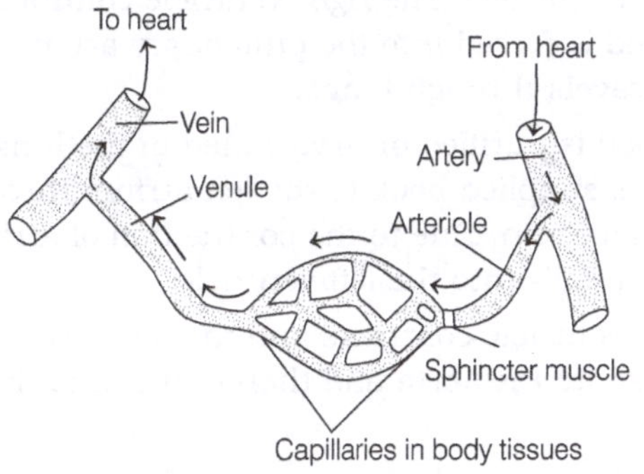

A diagrammatic relationship of artery, capillaries and vein

These are summarised in the table given below

Comparison between Arteries, Veins and Capillaries

Arteries	Veins	Capillaries
Carries blood from the heart.	Take blood to the heart.	Carries blood from arteries to veins.
Blood flows under high pressure.	Blood flows under low pressrue.	Pressure rises then gradually falls down, as blood flows from arteries to veins.
Blood flows in pulses.	No pulse.	Pulse gradually disappears.
Thick muscular walls (upto 2mm).	Thinner walls with connective layer.	Walls are one cell thick, i.e. single-celled.
Small lumen	Large lumen	Leaky and red blood cells travel in single file.
No semilunar valves	Semilunar valves	No semilunar valves.
Carry oxygenated blood (except pulmonary artery).	Carry deoxygenated blood (except pulmonary vein).	Blood slowly loses its oxygen.

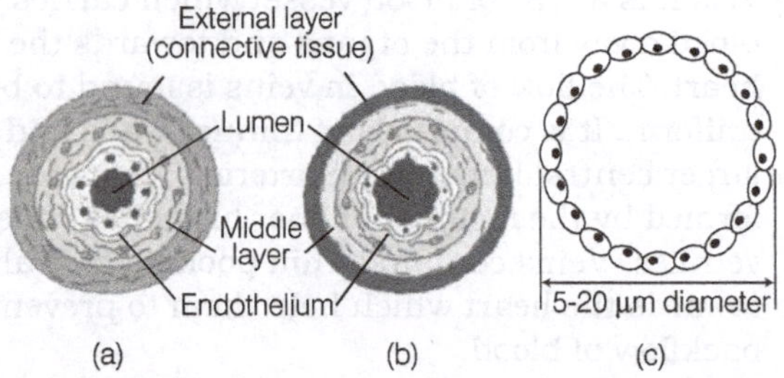

Structural difference between (a) artery, (b) vein, (c) capillary

Pattern of Blood Circulation in Humans

In humans, the impure blood from the body parts is brought to the right atrium and then, it passes into the right ventricle. The right ventricle contracts and the blood is forced into the pulmonary artery. This blood travels through lungs.

The blood is purified or oxygenated in the lungs and then it is supplied back to the left atrium through pulmonary vein. Due to the contraction of atrium, the blood falls into the left ventricle.

The left ventricle contracts and the blood goes rushing into the aorta and then to the other body parts.

Within the human body, the blood flows in the following manner

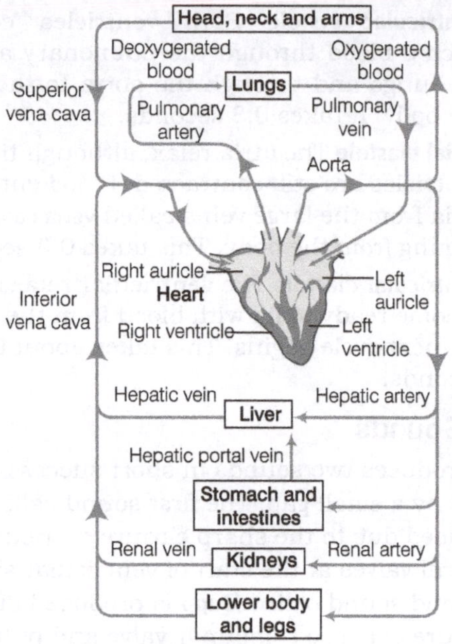

Double Circulation

Blood in human beings flows twice in the heart before it completes one round. It is comprised of one short pathway, i.e. pulmonary circulation and another long pathway, i.e. systemic circulation.

Due to this reason, the blood flow in humans is known as double circulation. This type of circulation is divided into two phases as follows

(i) **Pulmonary circulation** The movement of blood from heart to the lungs and back to the heart constitutes the pulmonary circulation. Movement of blood in pulmonary circulation occurs in the following ways

The deoxygenated blood from the body enters into the right atrium.

⇩

As the right atrium contracts, the blood passes into the corresponding dilated lower chamber known as the right ventricle.

⇩

Right ventricle thus, pumps blood to the lungs for oxygenation *via.* pulmonary artery.

⇩

Oxygenated blood then comes back to the left auricle of heart through four pulmonary veins, i.e. two from each lung.

(ii) **Systemic circulation** The circulation of blood from heart to different parts of the body except lungs and back to the heart constitutes the systemic circulation. Movement of blood in systemic circulation occurs in the following ways

As the left atrium of the heart expands, the oxygenated blood from lungs enters into it.

↓

The left atrium then contracts and pass the blood to the corresponding expanded left ventricle.

↓

The blood is finally pumped to the whole body *via.* aorta as the muscular left ventricle contracts.

The double circulation in human body can be understood by following flowchart

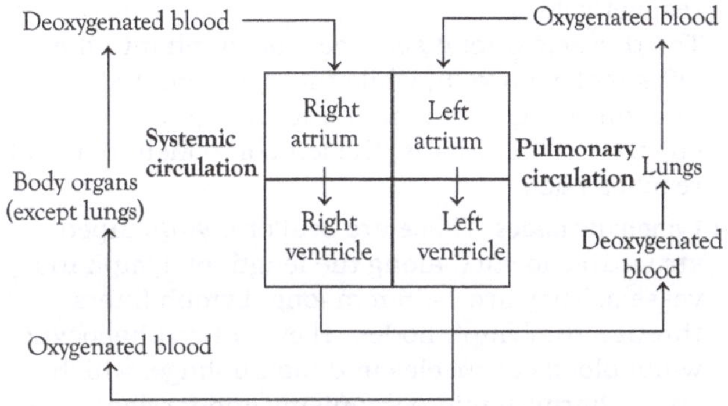

Flowchart showing double circulation

Significance of Double Circulation

Double circulation ensures the complete separation of oxygenated and deoxygenated blood while it enters the heart. In this type of circulation, the blood flows fast with high pressure which provides a higher metabolic rate. It is found in higher, reptiles, birds and mammals.

Portal System

The vein that collects blood from one body part by one set of capillaries and sends blood to another body part by another set of capillaries, instead of sending it to heart is called **portal vein.**

Portal vein together with the capillaries which supply blood to specific parts, makes a portal system. Vertebrates have three portal systems, i.e. renal, hypophyseal and hepatic.

(i) **Renal portal system** It is mainly present in amphibians and fishes, reduced to some extent in reptiles and birds. It is absent in mammals. It transports blood from posterior region of the body to kidneys by renal portal veins. Kidney removes waste products from the blood before it reaches heart. In mammals, blood from the posterior region directly reaches the heart.

(ii) **Hypophyseal system** It is a small portal system with in the pituitary body. It helps the hormones from hypothalamus to reach the anterior pituitary lobe.

(iii) **Hepatic portal system** The veins from the stomach and intestine instead of carrying blood directly to posterior vena cava, first enter the liver as a combined **hepatic portal vein**, which further breaks up into small capillaries and forms a hepatic vein that joins to the posterior vena cava. Thus, the portal vein begins and ends in capillaries.

Function Hepatic portal system acts as a store to regulate the quantity of nutrients flowing in the blood, i.e. it helps in storing excess of nutrients in liver and allows the required amount of nutrients like heparin, fibrinogen, prothrombin and vitamin-A to flow in the blood.

Also, if certain poisons are absorbed through food, the detoxification of food occurs in the liver.

Tissue Fluid (Extracellular Fluid)

As the blood passes through the capillaries of the arterial system into the tissues, some water along with many water soluble substances comes out in the spaces between the cells of tissues.

But a very small amount of proteins come out from the capillary with the plasma, leaving the larger proteins and most of the formed elements in the blood vessel. The fluid, thus released out is called **interstitial fluid** (tissue fluid) or **Extracellular Fluid** (ECF).

Distant cells of the body which are not in contact with capillaries, use or absorb O_2 and other substances from this fluid and in turn, give off CO_2 and other wastes back to it. This tissue fluid enters into the lymphatic vessels.

Check Your LEARNING...

1 Give the difference between arteries, veins and capillaries on the basis of the type of blood they carry.

2 Name the two major circulations of blood in the human body.

3 Define portal vein.

4 Which portal system is absent or lacking in mammals?

5 What is ECF?

Lymphatic System

This system of human comprises of lymph, lymphatic capillaries, lymphatic vessels, lymphatic ducts and lymphatic nodes. Let us explore them one by one.

(i) **Lymph** Tissue fluid after entering the lymph vessels is known as lymph. It only flows in lymphatic vessels and lymph organs. Both blood and lymph are called as the **fluid connective tissues.**

Composition of lymph It is a colourless fluid containing plasma and WBCs (specialised lymphocytes). The overall composition of lymph is similar to blood with the exception of absence of RBCs, platelets and some plasma proteins and in having less calcium and phosphorus than blood.

Functions of Lymph

Lymph performs the following important functions

(a) It acts as an important carrier of nutrients, hormones, etc.

(b) Absorption of fat occurs through lymph in the **lacteals** present in the intestinal villi.

(c) It helps in the **renewal of ECF**.

(d) Maturation of lymphocytes, i.e. B-cells and T-cells, occurs with the help of lymph nodes, releasing them into the lymph.

(e) It helps in keeping tissue cells moist.

Differences between Blood and Lymph

Blood	Lymph
It is red in colour due to the presence of haemoglobin in red blood cells.	It is colourless as red blood cells are absent.
It consists of plasma, RBCs, WBCs and platelets.	It consists of plasma and WBCs.
Glucose concentration is low.	Glucose concentration is higher than blood.
Clotting of blood is a fast process.	Clotting of lymph is comparatively slow.
It transports materials from one organ to other.	It transports materials from tissue cells into the blood.
Flow of blood is fast.	Lymph flows very slowly.
Its plasma has more contents of proteins, calcium and phosphorus.	Its plasma has less content of protein, calcium and phosphorus.
It moves away from the heart and towards the heart.	It moves in one direction, i.e. from tissues to subclavians.

(ii) **Lymphatic capillaries** They lie close to the blood capillaries, but differ from them to the extent that they end blindly. The lymphatic capillaries of intestinal regions, which absorb the digested fats are called **lacteals.**

(iii) **Lymphatic vessels** The lymphatic capillaries unite to form larger lymphatic vessels. They are composed of an outer coat of fibrous tissue, middle coat of muscular tissue and an inner lining of endothelial cells. The lymphatic vessels have numerous valves.

(iv) **Lymphatic ducts** Lymph vessels of left and right side of the body combines to form a thoracic duct or left lymphatic duct and right lymphatic duct, respectively.
The thoracic duct discharges its lymph into the left subclavian vein, while the right lymphatic duct discharges its lymph into the right subclavian vein. Thus, the left component of blood reaches back.

(v) **Lymphatic nodes** These are oval or bean-shaped structures located along the length of lymphatic vessels. They are 1-25 mm long. Lymph filters through the lymph nodes. They contain phagocytic white blood corpuscles and macrophage, which engulf harmful microorganisms and foreign particles from the lymph.

(vi) **Lymphatic Organs and Glands**

- The **tonsils** on the sides of the neck are lymph glands.
- The **spleen** is a large lymphatic organ. It is reddish-brown in colour. Spleen is found in the abdomen behind the stomach and above the left kidney. It acts as a blood reservoir, produces lymphocytes and destroys worn out red blood cells.
- Other lymphoid organs of human body are thymus gland, and payer's patches.

Check Your LEARNING...

1 Why does the lymph contain much less proteins than the plasma?
2 What is the main function of lymph?
3 Which fluid helps to moist tissue cell?
4 Write one main difference between blood and lymph.

QUiCK Revision

- The circulatory system is formed with blood as a carrier that circulates throughout the body.
- **Circulatory system** facilitates circulation of substances *via*. body fluids. **Open circulatory system** (invertebrates) allows direct contact between blood and tissue cells. In **closed circulatory system**, there is no direct contact between blood and tissue cells. Also, blood flows through closed vessels, e.g. annelids, some molluscs and mammals, etc.
- **Body fluids** are the medium of transport in the body. These can be intracellular and extracellular. Blood, lymph and CSF are extracellular fluids.
- **Blood** is a specialised connective tissue containing fluid matrix, plasma and formed elements (i.e. RBC, WBC and platelets). On the basis of surface antigen on RBC's, **blood group system** are classified as ABO and Rh. Rh incompatibility leads to erythroblastosis foetalis and transfusion reactions. **Coagulation** is a blood function facilitated by platelets and several clotting factors.
- **Human heart** is present between the lungs in thoracic cavity, i.e. mediastinum slightly tilted to left. It is covered with pericardium. Heart wall is made up of three layers, i.e. epicardium, myocardium and endocardium. Human heart has two auricles separated by interatrial septum; two ventricles separated by interventricular septum. Auricles and ventricles are separated by an auriculoventricular septum.
- **Heart valves** are tricuspid (between right atrium and ventricle), pulmonary, Mitral (between left atrium and ventricle), aortic, Eustachian and Thebasian valve.
- **Blood vessels** are vessels carrying blood to and from the heart and body organs. These are seen as arteries (heart to body), veins (body to heart) and capillaries (between arteries and veins) in human body.
- **Heartbeat** is the regular and rhythmic contraction of the heart. Human heartbeats about 75 times/minute. It occurs in two phases, i.e. **systole** (contraction) and **diastole** (relaxation).
- **Cardiac cycle** is the repeating pattern of the systole and diastole of the heart. Each cycle is of 0.8 second.
- **Heart sounds** are produced by beating of heart. **Lubb** (first sound) is produced when atrioventricular valves close. **Dupp** (second sound) is produced by closure of semilunar valves.
- **Cardiac output** is the volume of blood ejected from left or right ventricle into aorta per minute. It is stroke volume × heart rate. Cardiac output is not constant, it varies with physical activities performed.
- **Blood pressure** is the pressure exerted by blood flow on arterial walls. Normal range is 120 mm Hg (systolic) and 80 mm Hg (diastolic). It can be measured by **sphygmomanometer**. Another pressure called **pulse pressure** is the difference between systolic and diastolic pressure (40 mm Hg).
- **Double circulation** constitutes two pathways *viz*. **pulmonary** and **systemic circulation.**
- **Portal systems** are vascular arrangements where blood from capillaries of one organ is transported to capillaries of another organ. It can be hepatic (between parts of alimentary canal and liver), renal and hypophysial.
- **Human lymphatic system** contains lymph capillaries, vessels, lymphatic ducts and nodes. Tonsils, thymus gland, Peyer's patches and spleens are other lymphoid organs which secrete lymph.
- **Lymph** is a colourless or yellowish extracellular fluid. It is an important component of our body's defence system.

Chapter Practice

Section-I

1 Mark Questions

1. Name the following.
   (i) The iron containing respiratory pigment in erythrocytes.
   (ii) The straw coloured fluid part of the blood.
   (iii) The compound formed when haemoglobin combines with carbon dioxide in blood. [2019]
   (iv) The mineral element essential for the clotting of blood. [2012, 11]
   (v) The protective covering of the heart. [2014]
   (vi) Blood vessels carrying blood to the left atrium.
   (vii) The phase of cardiac cycle in which the auricles contract. [2012]
   (viii) The instrument used to measure heartbeat.
   (ix) The blood vessel which supplies blood to the liver. [2018]
   (x) The vein which drains the blood from the intestine to liver. [2016]

Ans. (i) Haemoglobin
(ii) Plasma
(iii) Carbaminohaemoglobin
(iv) Calcium
(v) Pericardium
(vi) Pulmonary vein
(vii) Auricular systole
(viii) Stethoscope
(ix) Hepatic artery
(x) Hepatic portal vein

2. Correct and rewrite the following statements by changing the underlined words.
   (i) The process of RBC formation is called <u>diapedesis</u>.
   (ii) Oxygenated blood from the lungs pour into <u>right auricle</u>.
   (iii) The pulse-beat per minute of normal human adult is <u>82</u>.
   (iv) The blood vessel which supply blood to kidney is <u>renal vein</u>.

Ans. (i) The process of RBC formation is called erythropoiesis.
(ii) Oxygenated blood from the lungs pour into left auricle.
(iii) The pulse-beat per minute of normal human adult is 72.
(iv) The blood vessel which supply blood to kidney is renal artery.

3. Give biological reasons for the following.
   (i) A matured mammalian erythrocyte lacks nucleus and mitochondria. [2016, 11]
   (ii) A mature mammalian erythrocyte lacks nucleus and mitochondria but is efficient in its functioning. [Semester II 2022, 2006]
   (iii) The wall of the ventricles is thicker than the auricles. [2013]
   (iv) Blood flows in arteries with spurts and high pressure. [2016]
   (v) The arteries are deep seated in the body.
   (vi) Blood flowing away from the stomach and intestines is put into circulation *via.* the liver and not directly to heart.

Ans. (i) Lack of nucleus and mitochondria helps in providing more surface area for maximum absorption and transport of oxygen.
(ii) A mature RBCs/Erythrocyte is biconcave, disc-like structure that lack nucleus and mitochondria but is efficient in functioning because lack of nucleus and mitochondria provide large surface area to volume ratio for maximum absorption and transport of oxygen.
(iii) Ventricles have thicker walls than auricles because they are meant to pump blood with high pressure so that it reaches to larger distances.
(iv) The blood is pumped from heart with high pressure to the various distant parts of the body by arteries so, it flows with spurts and high pressure.
(v) The arteries possess thick and muscular elastic walls. They do not have valves in their inner linings. The blood flows with jerks and under great pressure through them. So, these are deep seated in the body.
(vi) The veins starting from the stomach and the intestines do not directly convey the blood to the posterior vena cava. Instead, they first enter the liver as a combined hepatic portal vein.
This vein breaks up into capillaries in contrast to the general characteristics of a vein and a new vein is formed by their reunion which joins the posterior vena cava. Due to this, extra nutrients in the blood are absorbed and stored into liver, while only the required amount is sent to different parts of body.

4. (i) Match the following columns.

Column I	Column II
A. Basophils	1. Phagocytes
B. Neutrophils	2. Secrete histamine and heparin
C. Eosinophils	3. Allergic reaction
D. Lymphocytes	4. Immunity

(ii) Match the following columns.

	Column I		Column II
A.	SA node	1.	0.8 seconds
B.	Muscle fibres located in the heart	2.	Pacemaker
C.	Cardiac cycle	3.	Cardiac muscle
D.	Heart muscle	4.	Purkinje fibres

(iii) Match the following columns.

Column I	Column II
A. Superior vena cava	1. Carries oxygenated blood
B. Inferior vena cava	2. Carries deoxygenated blood
C. Pulmonary artery	3. Brings deoxygenated blood from lower part of the body to the right atrium.
D. Pulmonary vein	4. Brings deoxygenated blood from upper part of the body to the right atrium.

(iv) Match the following columns.

	Column I		Column II
A.	RBC	1.	Aortic valve
B.	Heart	2.	Pacemaker
C.	An entrance to aorta	3.	Enucleated
D.	SA node	4.	Myogenic

Ans. (i) A–2, B–1, C–3, D–4 (ii) A–2, B–4, C–1, D–3
(iii) A–4, B–3, C–2, D–1 (iv) A–3, B–4, C–1, D–2

5. Choose the correct answer from the four options given below.

(i) The lifespan of an RBC is **[2023]**
(a) 120 days (b) 220 days
(c) 20 days (d) 2 weeks

Ans. (a)

(ii) Human blood consists of
(a) fluid matrix (b) plasma
(c) formed elements (d) All of these

Ans. (d)

(iii) The mineral elements in haemoglobin **[Semester II 2022]**
(a) manganese (b) iron
(c) sodium (d) calcium

Ans. (b)

(iv) The agranulocytes responsible for immune response of the body are
(a) basophils (b) neutrophils
(c) eosinophils (d) lymphocytes

Ans. (d)

(v) Which of the following cells do not exhibit phagocytic activity?
(a) Monocytes (b) Neutrophil
(c) Basophil (d) Macrophage

Ans. (c)

(vi) Pericardium covers the **[Semester II 2022]**
(a) heart (b) brain
(c) spinal cord (d) eyeball

Ans. (a)

(vii) When the right atrium contracts, blood flows from the right atrium into the
(a) aorta (b) left atrium
(c) pulmonary artery (d) right ventricle

Ans. (d)

(viii) The heart sound 'Dup' is produced when **[2023]**
(a) semilunar valves open
(b) atrioventricular valves close
(c) semilunar valves close
(d) atrioventricular valves open

Ans. (c)

(ix) While recording the pulse rate, where exactly does a doctor press on our wrist? **[2019]**
(a) Nerve (b) Vein (c) Artery (d) Capillary

Ans. (c)

(x) The blood vessel that carries oxygenated blood is **[Semester II 2022]**
(a) pulmonary (b) pulmonary vein
(c) renal vein (d) hepatic vein

Ans. (b)

(xi) Which of the following chambers of heart first receives blood from the systemic circulation?
(a) Right auricle (b) Right ventricle
(c) Left auricle (d) Left ventricle

Ans. (a)

(xii) Systemic circulation is

(a) Left ventricle $\xrightarrow[\text{blood}]{\text{Deoxygenated}}$ Tissues $\xrightarrow[\text{blood}]{\text{Oxygenated}}$ Right ventricle

(b) Right ventricle $\xrightarrow[\text{blood}]{\text{Oxygenated}}$ Tissues $\xrightarrow[\text{blood}]{\text{Deoxygenated}}$ Right auricle

(c) Left ventricle $\xrightarrow[\text{blood}]{\text{Deoxygenated}}$ Tissues $\xrightarrow[\text{blood}]{\text{Oxygenated}}$ Right auricle

(d) Left ventricle $\xrightarrow[\text{blood}]{\text{Oxygenated}}$ Tissues $\xrightarrow[\text{blood}]{\text{Deoxygenated}}$ Right auricle

Ans. (d)

(xiii) Oxygenated blood to liver is supplied by **[2023]**
(a) hepatic artery
(b) hepatic vein
(c) inferior vena cava
(d) hepatic portal vein

Ans. (a)

(xiv) The chief function of lymph nodes in mammals is to
(a) produce WBCs (b) produce hormones
(c) destroy old RBCs (d) destroy pathogen

Ans. (d)

6. Fill in the blanks by using suitable words.
   (i) .... is the blood plasma from which fibrinogen has been removed.
   (ii) The red blood corpuscles are .... and .... shaped cells without ....
   (iii) The iron pigment, ... gives red colour to the blood.
   (iv) Oxygen combines with haemoglobin present in RBC and forms .... **[2015]**
   (v) RBCs are produced in ....
   (vi) .... and monocytes are phagocytic cells.
   (vii) Thromboplastin is required for .... in the body.
   (viii) .... ions play a significant role in clotting.
   (ix) Cells get oxygen and nutrients from .... fluid.
   (x) The membranous covering of the heart is ....
   (xi) The blood vessel leaving the left ventricle of the mammalian heart is the ....
   (xii) The chamber of heart which pumps blood into aorta is ....
   (xiii) Ventricles have .... walls as compared with those of auricles.
   (xiv) Ventricles give rise to two large blood vessels called .... and ....
   (xv) The pacemaker is present near the opening of the .... and the atrioventricular node found near the ...... septum above the tricuspid valve.
   (xvi) The blood vessel which transports blood from heart to organs is called ....
   (xvii) Arteries are .... walled and the veins are .... walled blood vessels.
   (xviii) The blood vessel that begins and ends in capillaries is .... **[2011]**
   (xix) The sequence of one systole followed by one diastole is termed as the ....

Ans. (i) Serum (ii) biconcave, disc, nucleus
(iii) haemoglobin (iv) oxyhaemoglobin
(v) bone marrow (vi) Neutrophils
(vii) blood clotting (viii) Calcium
(ix) tissue (x) pericardium
(xi) aorta (xii) left ventricle
(xiii) thick muscular (xiv) pulmonary artery, aorta
(xv) superior vena cava, interauricular
(xvi) artery (xvii) thick, thin
(xviii) portal vein (xix) cardiac cycle

7. Choose the odd one out from the following terms given below and name the category to which other three belong.
   (i) Basophils, Neutrophils, Monocytes, Eosinophils.
   (ii) Lumen, Muscular tissue, Connective tissue, Pericardium **[2018]**
   (iii) Mitral valve, Sino-atrial node, Aorta, Pulmonary vein
   (iv) Aorta, Pulmonary vein, Vena cava, AV node

Ans. (i) **Odd term** is monocytes.
The remaining three are granulocytes.
(ii) **Odd term** is pericardium.
Rest others are components of blood vessels.
(iii) **Odd term** is Sino-Atrial (SA) node.
Others structures found in the left side of the heart.
(iv) **Odd term** is AV node.
Rest others are types of blood vessels.

8. Given below are sets of terms each. Rewrite the terms in correct order of a logical sequence.
   (i) Fibrin, Platelets, Thromboplastin, Fibrinogen, Thrombin **[2017]**
   (ii) Purkinje fibres, AV node, SA node, Bundle of His
   (iii) Intestine, Liver, Intestinal artery, Hepatic vein, Hepatic portal vein **[2013]**

Ans. (i) Platelets → Thromboplastin → Thrombin→ Fibrinogen → Fibrin
(ii) SA node → AV node → Bundle of His → Purkinje fibres
(iii) Intestinal artery → Intestine → Hepatic portal vein → Liver → Hepatic vein

9. Expand the following biological abbreviations.
   (i) RBCs (ii) Rh-factor
   (iii) HDN (iv) AV node

Ans. (i) Red Blood corpuscles
(ii) Rhesus factor
(iii) Haemolytic Disease of Newborn
(iv) Atrio-Ventricular node

10. State the exact location of the following.
   (i) Tricuspid valve **[2014]**
   (ii) Semilunar valve **[Semester 2022, 18, 13]**
   (iii) Mitral valve

Ans. (i) Tricuspid valve is found between the right auricle and right ventricle.
(ii) Pulmonary semilunar valve is located at the base of the pulmonary trunk.
(iii) Mitral valve is found between the left auricle and left ventricle.

11. State the main function of the following.
   (i) Lymphocyte **[Semester II 2022, 16]**
   (ii) Thrombocyte **[Semester II 2022, 11]**
   (iii) Fibrinogen
   (iv) Globulin
   (v) Neutrophils **[Semester II 2022]**
   (vi) Coronary artery **[2019, 11]**

Ans. (i) Lymphocytes keep away infection by producing antibodies against foreign particles.
(ii) Thrombocytes help in blood clotting.
(iii) Fibrinogens are inactive components of blood plasma. Under the action of enzyme, thrombin, they form a clot or coagulum (a network of threads called fibrin) in which dead and damaged elements of blood are trapped.

(iv) Globulins are primarily involved in immunity, i.e. defence mechanism of the body.
(v) Neutrophils are phagocytic cells which destroy foreign organisms entering the body.
(vi) Coronary artery supplies oxygenated blood to the walls of heart.

12. Mention one difference between each of the following pairs on the basis of what is given in the bracket.
(i) Erythrocytes and Leucocytes (function) [2011]
(ii) Lymphocytes and Neutrophils (structure of the nucleus).
(iii) Plasma and Serum (composition)
(iv) Bicuspid valve and Tricuspid valve (function) [2013]
(v) Beginning of the ventricular systole and the End of ventricular diastole (type of heart sound) [2011, 06]
(vi) Lubb and Dupp (name of the valves whose closure produce the sound). [2016]

Ans. (i) Difference between erythrocytes and leucocytes is as follows

Erythrocytes	Leucocytes
They transport respiratory gases.	They produce antibodies and protect the body from disease causing germs.

(ii) Difference between lymphocytes and neutrophils is as follows

Lymphocytes	Neutrophils
Nucleus is large with a dent-like depression.	3- 4 lobed nucleus is present.

(iii) Difference between plasma and serum is as follows

Plasma	Serum
Fibrinogen is present.	Fibrinogen is absent.

(iv) Difference between bicuspid valve and tricuspid valve is as follows

Bicuspid valve	Tricuspid valve
It guards the opening and backflow when blood rushes from left auricle into left ventricle.	It guards the opening and backflow when blood rushes from right atrium into right ventricle.

(v) Difference between beginning of ventricular systole and end of ventricular diastole is as follows

Beginning of ventricular systole	End of ventricular diastole
During this event, first heart sound Lubb is produced.	During this event, second heart sound Dupp is produced.

(vi) Differencee between Lubb and Dupp is as follows

Lubb	Dupp
Mitral and tricuspid valve.	Aortic and pulmonary valve.

13. Give biological/technical terms for the following.
(i) The fluid portion of blood. [2014]
(ii) Cellular components of blood containing haemoglobin. [2017]
(iii) WBCs squeeze through the walls of the capillaries into the surrounding tissue. [2018, 12]
(iv) The process by which white blood cells engulf harmful microbes. [2008]
(v) The relaxation phase of the heart. [2018]

Ans. (i) Plasma (ii) Erythrocyte
(iii) Diapedesis (iv) Phagocytosis
(v) Diastole

14. Briefly explain the following terms.
(i) Formed elements
(ii) Diapedesis [2014, 06]
(iii) Cardiac output
(iv) Venule

Ans. (i) Cells and other cellular structures present in the blood are called formed elements.
(ii) Diapedesis is the process by which white blood cells squeeze out through the walls of capillaries to reach at the site of infection.
(iii) Volume of blood pumped by heart per minute is known as cardiac output.
(iv) A venule is a very small blood vessel in the microcirculation that allows deoxygenated blood to return from the capillary beds to the larger blood vessels called veins.

15. Answer the following questions briefly.
(i) Blood is called river of life. Comment.
(ii) Circulatory system can also be called as a 'transport system'. Do you agree? Comment.
(iii) Sino-atrial node is called the pacemaker of our heart. Why?
(iv) Why are valves present in heart and veins?
(v) What are the two types of blood circulation in humans? [Semester II 2022]

Ans. (i) Blood is called so, because blood plasma helps in transportation of materials like nutrients, gaseous wastes, hormones, etc., within the body, which is very essential for the survival of life.
(ii) Circulatory system helps in the transport of , , hormones, metabolic wastes, etc. So, it can also be called as a transport system.
(iii) Sino-atrial node of heart is responsible for initiating and maintaining the rhythmic activity, therefore it is known as the pacemaker of the heart.

(iv) Valves are present in heart and veins to ensure that blood does not flow backward in their respective source chambers.

(v) The two type of blood circulation in human heart are
- **Pulmonary circulation** It is a short loop from the heart to the lungs and back again.
- **Systemic circulation** It carries blood from the heart to all the other parts of the body and back again.

2 Marks Questions

16. Why do we consider blood as a connective tissue?

Ans. Blood is a mobile connective tissue derived from mesoderm, which consists of fibre-free fluid matrix, plasma and other cells. It is called so, as it regluarly circulates in the body and takes part in the transport of materials.

17. Draw a diagram of the different blood cells as seen in a smear of human blood. **[2014]**

Ans.

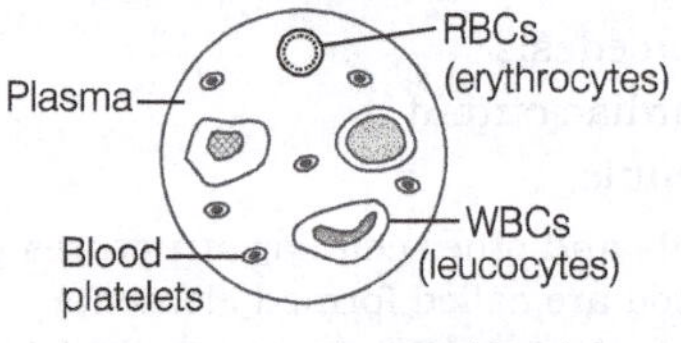

Smear of human blood

18. Mention any two functions of blood. **[2023]**

Ans. Functions of blood are
- Transportation of oxygen from the lungs to the tissues.
- Transportation of digested food from the small intestine to the tissues and cells around the body.

19. What is the importance of plasma proteins?

Ans. Fibrinogen, globulins and albumins are the major plasma proteins. Fibrinogens are needed for clotting or coagulation of blood. Globulins are primarily involved in defence mechanism of the body and the albumins help in osmotic balance.

20. What is the significance of time gap in the passage of impulse from sino-atrial node to the ventricle?

Ans. The time gap in the passage of impulse from sino-atrial node to the ventricles allows ventricles to relax. Fall in the ventricular pressure results in the closing of semilunar valves which prevent the backflow of blood into the ventricles.

21. Give the exact location of pulmonary semilunar valve. When does it close? **[Semester II 2022]**

Ans. The pulmonary semilunar valve is located at the entrance of pulmonary artery. They close at the begining of ventricular distole in order to prevents blood to move from pulmonary trunk into right ventricle.

22. Choose between the two options to answer the questions specified in the brackets for the following.

(i) Blood in the renal artery or renal vein (Which one has more urea?). **[2018]**

(ii) Blood in the pulmonary artery or pulmonary vein (Which one contains less oxyhaemoglobin?). **[2018]**

Ans. (i) Renal artery (ii) Pulmonary artery

23. From where to where do the following blood vessels carry blood? **[2013]**

(i) Hepatic vein (ii) Hepatic portal vein

Ans. (i) Hepatic vein carries blood from liver to posterior vena cava.

(ii) Hepatic portal vein carries blood from intestine to liver.

24. Mention the phases of blood pressure. When are they seen?

Ans. Phases of blood pressure are

(i) Systolic blood pressure is seen during the contraction of left ventricle.

(ii) Diastolic blood pressure is seen during the relaxation of left ventricle.

3 Marks Questions

25. Why is closed circulatory system more efficient than the open system?

Ans. The closed circulatory system considerably enhances the speed, precision and efficiency of circulation. The blood flows far more rapidly and takes less time to circulate through the closed system and return to the heart. This quickens the supply and removal of materials to and from the tissues by the blood.

26. Mention the following.

(i) Average lifespan of RBCs.

(ii) The two major categories of WBCs.

(iii) Blood cells involved in leukaemia.

Ans. (i) 120 days (approximately).

(ii) Granulocytes and agranulocytes.

(iii) WBCs.

27. Blood does not clot in blood vessels. What do you think? Give reasons in support of your answer.

Ans. It is not possible for the blood to clot in blood vessels due to the following reasons

(i) Anticoagulants like heparin are present in the blood naturally.

(ii) The endothelium of the blood vessels is intact.

(iii) The coagulating factors remain inactive in the blood.

28. One of the ABO blood groups is sometimes called the universal donor. Which group do you think it is and why?

Ans. Individuals with blood group O are called universal donors. These individuals do not have either A or B antigens on the surface of their RBCs, but their blood serum contains antibodies against both A and B antigens.

Therefore, blood group O individuals can receive blood only from a group O individual, but they can donate blood to individuals of any ABO blood group (i.e. A, B, O or AB).

29. Name any three substances transported by blood.

Ans. Three substances transported by blood are

(i) Oxygen from the lungs to the tissues.

(ii) Carbon dioxide from the tissues to the lungs.

(iii) Body wastes from different body parts to the kidneys.

30. What is the significance of hepatic portal system in the circulatory system?

Ans. Significances of hepatic portal system in circulatory system are

(i) The liver absorbs excess of fats and glucose so as to use them at the time of starvation, when blood passess through the hepatic portal system.

(ii) Harmful nitrogenous waste like ammonia is converted into urea, which is later removed by kidney.

(iii) Liver produces proteins which are transported through blood circulation, e.g. fibrinogen for blood clotting.

Section-II [3/5 Marks]

Structured Questions

1. Study the following diagram carefully and then answer the questions that follows.

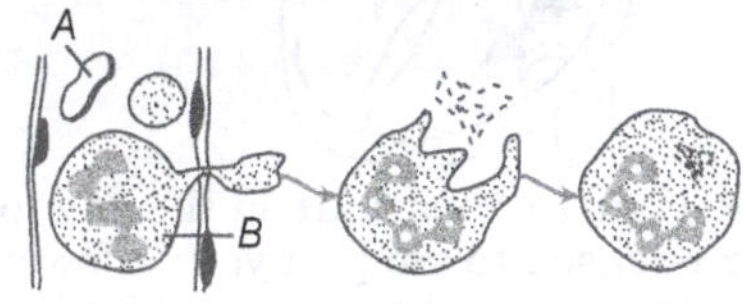

(a) (b) (c)

(i) Name the cell labelled as *A*.

(ii) Identify the phenomenon occurring in (a).

(iii) Mention two structural differences between *A* and *B*.

(iv) Name the process occurring in and also state the importance of this process in the human body. **[2011]**

Ans. (i) Cell labelled as *A* in the diagram is a red blood corpuscle.

(ii) The phenomenon occurring in part (a) is **diapedesis.**

(iii) Structural differences between *A* (RBCs) and *B* (WBCs) are

RBCs	WBCs
Biconcave in shape.	Amoeboid in shape.
Nucleus absent.	Nucleus present.

(iv) The process occurring in (b) and (c) in phagocytosis.

During this phenomenon, the WBC engulfs the disease causing germs that enter the body and thus, defends our body from these organisms.

2. Given below is a diagram of a human blood smear. Study the diagram and answer the questions that follows.

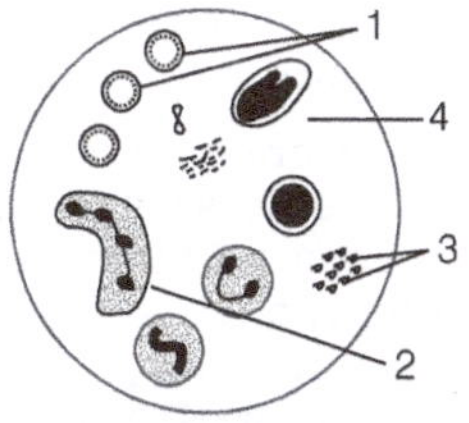

(i) Name the components numbered as '1'to'4'.

(ii) Mention two structural differences between the parts '1' and '2'.

(iii) Name the soluble protein found in part '4', which forms insoluble threads during clotting of blood.

(iv) What is the average lifespan of the component numbered '1'?

(v) Component numbered '1' do not have certain organelles but are very efficient in their function. Explain. **[2018]**

Ans. The components numbered as 1 to 4 are

(i) (1) RBCs, (2) WBC, (3) Platelets, (4) Plasma

(ii) Refer to Ans. 1(iii).

(iii) Plasma (4) contains a soluble protein fibrinogen. During blood clotting, soluble fibrinogen converts into fibrin (insoluble form) in the presence of enzyme thrombinase and Ca^{2+} ion.

(iv) The average lifespan of RBC (1) is 120 days.

(v) Mature RBCs are enucleated, i.e. they lack nucleus and endoplasmic reticulum which makes them more flexible thus, increasing their surface area to volume ratio for carrying more oxygen. They lack mitochondria which mean that red cells cannot use oxygen by themselves. Instead all the oxygen absorbed from the lungs is transported to all other tissues.

3. Human heart is a complex muscular organ which is composed of different chambers and associated with various blood vessels.
Besides these, pacemaker and pacesetter regulate the functioning of heart.

(i) Name any one chamber and one blood vessel asociated with heart.

(ii) Blockage of which blood vessel could interrupt the blood supply to corresponding part of heart?

(iii) Which vessel carry deoxygenated blood from lower portion of body to heart?

(iv) Mention any one difference between vena cava and aorta.

(v) Where does the pacemaker found in human heart?

Ans. (i) Left atrium; Dorsal aorta

(ii) If the coronary artery gets a clot, the corresponding part of the heart does not get blood supply. It may cause heart attack.

(iii) Inferior vena cava carries deoxygenated blood.

(iv) Vena cava has thin muscular walls while aorta has thick muscular walls.

(v) Pacemaker, i.e. SA node is found at the upper corner of right auricle.

4. Given below is a diagrammatic representation of a certain part of the process of circulation of blood in man. Study the same and then answer the questions that follows.

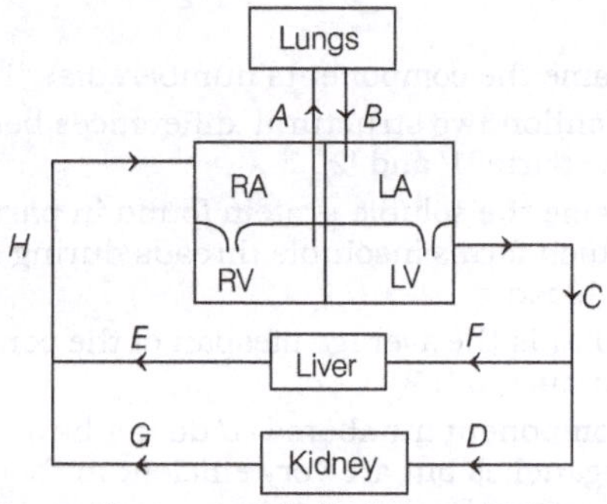

(i) Name the parts labelled as *A*, *B*, *D* and *F*.

(ii) Give the number and name of vessel which contains the maximum amount of urea a few hours after a protein rich meal.

(iii) Mention two structural differences between blood vessels '*C*' and '*H*'. **[2015]**

Ans. (i) The parts labelled as *A*, *B*, *D* and *F* are *A* –Pulmonary artery, *B* –Pulmonary vein, *D* –Renal artery, *F* –Hepatic artery

(ii) Blood vessel *E*, named as hepatic vein will contain the maximum amount of urea a few hours after the protein rich meal.

(iii) Two structural differences between blood vessels *C* and *H* are

Blood vessel *C* (Aorta)	**Blood vessel** *H* (Vena cava)
Lumen is small.	Lumen is large.
Valves are absent.	Valves are present.

5. The diagram given below represents the human heart in one phase of its functions. Study the diagram carefully and answer the questions that follows. **[2015]**

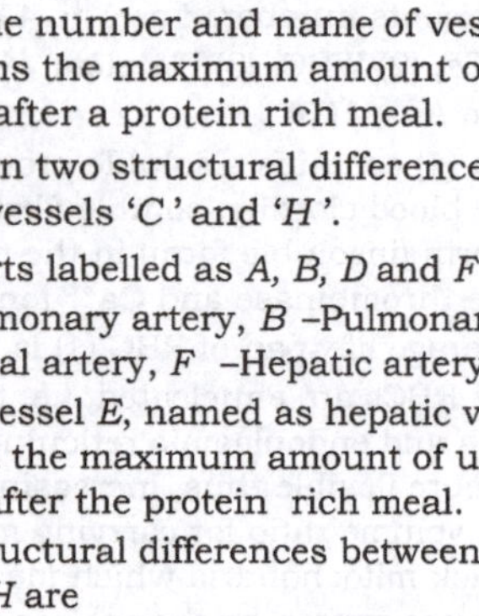

(i) Name the phase.

(ii) Which part of the heart is contracting in this phase? Give a reason to support your answer.

(iii) Name the parts numbered as 1 to 4.

(iv) Which type of blood flows through 2?

(v) State the function of the part numbered as 5.

(vi) Name the membrane that covers the heart.

Ans. (i) The phase is ventricular systole.

(ii) Ventricular muscles are contracting because both bicuspid and tricuspid valves are closed whereas both pulmonary semilunar and aortic semilunar valves are open to pump blood out of the two ventricles.

(iii) The parts numbered as 1 to 4 are 1-Pulmonary artery, 2-Aorta, 3-Bicuspid valve, 4-Aortic semilunar valves

(iv) Oxygenated blood flows through aorta (2).

(v) Part (5), pulmonary semilunar valves allow deoxygenated blood to flow from right ventricle to lungs and prevents its back flow.

(vi) The membrane that covers the heart is pericardium.

6. The given diagram represents a section of the human heart. Answer the questions that follows. **[2017]**

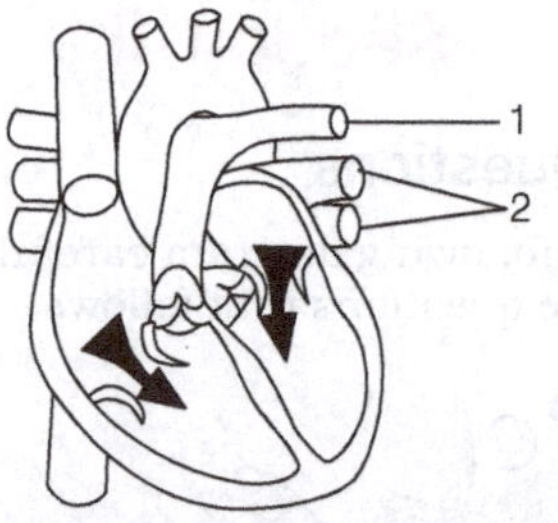

(i) Which parts of heart are in the diastolic phase? Give a reason to support your answer.

(ii) Label the parts numbered as 1 and 2 in the diagram. What type of blood flows through them?

(iii) What causes the heart sounds 'Lubb' and 'Dupp'?

(iv) Name the blood vessels that supply oxygenated blood to the heart muscles.

(v) Draw neat labelled diagrams of a cross-section of an artery and a vein.

Ans. (i) In the given figure, ventricles are in diastolic phase. The tricuspid and bicuspid valves are open. It occurs only when pressure in the ventricles falls. As a result blood flows from the atria into the ventricles.

(ii) The parts numbered as 1 and 2 are

1–Pulmonary artery, it carries deoxygenated blood to the lungs for purification.

2–Pulmonary veins, they bring oxygenated blood to the left atrium.

(iii) 'Lubb' sound is produced when tricuspid and mitral valves get closed, while 'Dupp' sound is produced when pulmonary and aortic semilunar valves get closed.

(iv) Blood vessel that supplies oxygenated blood to the walls of the heart is 'coronary artery'.

(v)

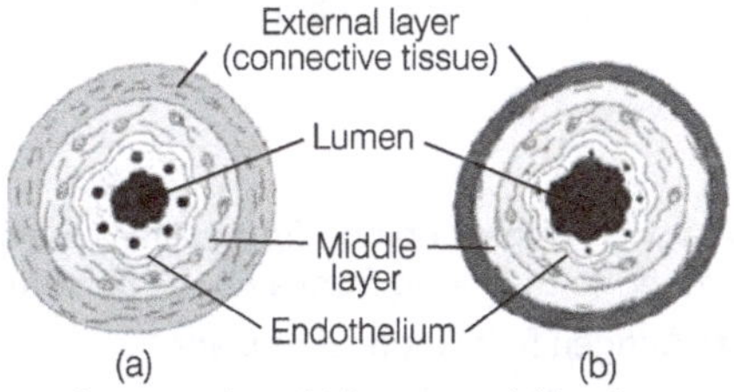

Cross-section of (a) artery and (b) vein

7. The diagram given below represents the human heart in one phase of its functional activities. Study the same and answer the questions that follows.

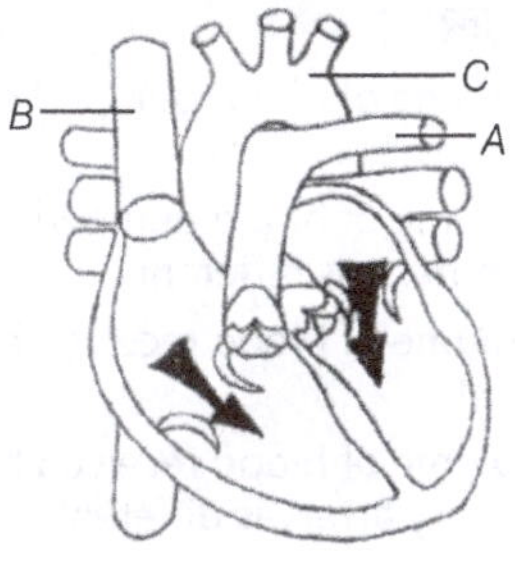

(i) Name the phase.

(ii) Label the parts as *A*, *B* and *C*.

(iii) Which part of the heart is contracting in this phase? Give a reason to support your answer.

(iv) Draw well-labelled diagrams of part *A* and *B* to show the structural differences between them. **[2013]**

Ans. (i) The phase is atrial systole and ventricular diastole.

(ii) The parts *A*, *B* and *C* in the given figure are labelled as *A*– Pulmonary artery, *B*– Superior vena cava, *C*– Aorta

(iii) Upper chambers, i.e. both the atria are contracting in this phase because blood is flowing downwards towards the ventricles.

(iv) Refer to fig. in Ans. 6 (v) (artery and vein).

8. The diagram given below shows the cross-section of two kinds of blood vessels. **[2012]**

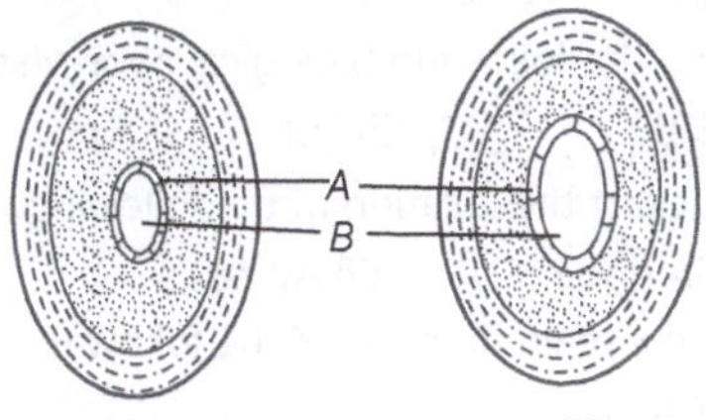

(a) (b)

(i) Identify the blood vessels (a) and (b). In each case, give a reason to support your answer.

(ii) Name the parts labelled as *A* and *B*.

(iii) When are the sound 'Lubb' and 'Dupp' produced during a heartbeat?

(iv) Name the blood vessel that

(a) begins and ends in capillaries.

(b) supplies blood to the walls of the heart.

Ans. (i) Blood vessel labelled as (a) is artery because it has narrow lumen and thick muscular wall and (b) is vein because it has wide lumen and thin muscular wall.

(ii) The parts labelled as *A* and *B* in the diagram are endothelium and lumen, respectively.

(iii) Refer to Ans 6 (iii).

(iv) (a) Blood vessel that begins and ends in capillaries is hepatic portal vein.

(b) Blood vessel that supplies blood to the walls of the heart is 'coronary artery'.

9. The diagram below depicts the human heart in one of its phases. Answer the questions that follow **[2023]**

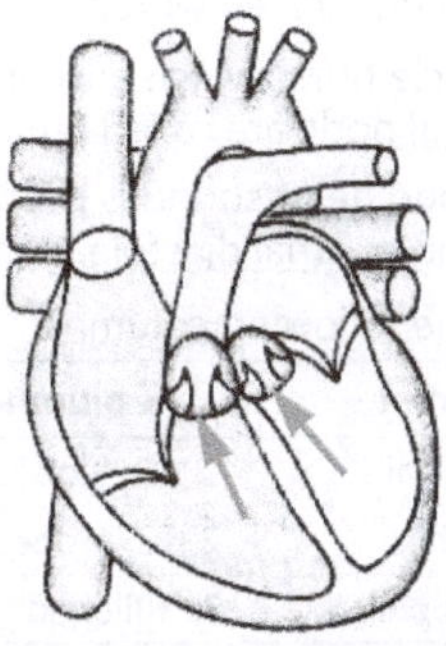

(i) Which part of the heart is in the contraction phase?

(ii) Give a suitable reason to justify your answer in (a).

(iii) Distinguish between systole and diastole.

Ans. (i) Here in this diagram ventricles are the contracting part of the heart.

(ii) The blood is moving into the respective arteries (Pulmonary artery and dorsal aorta) because the ventricles are contracting.

(iii) Differences between systole and diastole are as follows

Systole	Diastole
It happens when the heart muscle contracts and the blood moves to the aorta and pulmonary artery.	It happens when the heart muscle relaxes between two contractions and the heart is filled with blood.
Systole reduces the volume of the heart as all the blood gets pumped out.	Diastole increases the heart volume and makes it normal as the blood comes back in.

Chapter Assessment

Section-I

1 Mark Questions

1. Name the following.
   (i) The part inside the heart that initiates heartbeat.
   (ii) The structure that holds the heart valves in position.
   (iii) The blood corpuscles by which the human body is protected from invading bacteria.
2. Correct and rewrite the following statements by changing the underlined words.
   (i) The muscle fibres which arise from <u>Sino-atrial node</u> are called bundle of His.
   (ii) The second heart sound is produced at the beginning of <u>atrial diastole</u>.
3. (i) Match the following columns.

Column I	Column II
A. Eosinophils	1. 3-4 lobed
B. Basophils	2. 2-3 lobed
C. Neutrophils	3. Bilobed

   (ii) Match the following columns.

Column I	Column II
A. Lymphatic system	1. Carries oxygenated blood
B. Pulmonary vein	2. Immune response
C. Thrombocytes	3. To drain back the tissue fluid to the circulatory system
D. Lymphocytes	4. Coagulation of blood

4. Choose the correct answer from the four options given below.
   (i) Mark the pair of substances among the following which are essential for coagulation of blood.
   (a) Heparin and calcium ions
   (b) Calcium ions and platelet factors
   (c) Oxalates and citrates
   (d) Platelet factors and heparin
   (ii) Which of the following statements is incorrect?
   (a) An individual having 'O' blood group has anti 'A' and anti 'B' antibodies in his blood plasma
   (b) An individual having 'B' blood group cannot donate blood to a person of 'A' blood group
   (c) Blood group is designated on the basis of the presence of antibodies in the blood plasma
   (d) An individual having AB blood group is universal recipient
   (iii) What will happen if blood from a Rh–ve person is exposed to the blood from a Rh+ve person?
   (a) Antigen formation takes place
   (b) – ve and +ve Rh antigen cancel out each other
   (c) Nothing will happen
   (d) Antibody will form
   (iv) Which among the following is observed during each cardiac cycle?
   (a) The volume of blood pumped out by the right and left ventricles is same
   (b) The volume of blood pumped out by the right and left ventricles is different
   (c) The volume of blood received by each atrium is different
   (d) The volume of blood received by the aorta and pulmonary artery is different
5. Fill in the blanks by using suitable words.
   (i) Blood is slightly .... in nature.
   (ii) Monocytes have .... shaped nucleus.
   (iii) The plasma membrane of RBCs contains certain glycoproteinaceous molecules known as ....
   (iv) There are .... types of blood group, as per the Rh system.
   (v) In people with blood group O, the antigens .... and .... are not present.
   (vi) The blood pressure is low in .... circulatory system.
   (vii) The aorta arises from .... ventricle.
6. Choose the odd one out from the following terms given below and name the category to which other three belong.
   RBCs, ATP, WBCs, Platelets
7. Expand the following biological abbreviations.
   (i) SAN (ii) ECF
8. State exact the location of the following.
   (i) SA node (ii) AV node
9. State the main function of the following.
   (i) WBCs
   (ii) Vena cava
10. Mention one difference in each of the following pairs on the basis of what is given in the bracket.
    (i) SAN and AVN (function)
    (ii) Arteriole and Capillary (structure)

11. Give biological/technical terms for the following.

(i) The fluid that transports fatty acids and glycerol.

(ii) The fine blood vessels in the tissues through which exchange of materials occurs.

2 Marks Questions

12. Mention the value of systolic BP and diastolic BP of a normal human adult.

13. Observe the relationship between the first two words and give the suitable word/words for the fourth place.

(i) Lubb : Atrio-ventricular valves : : Dupp :

(ii) Coronary artery : Heart : : Hepatic artery :

3 Marks Questions

14. Name three structures which are present in all eukaryotic cells, but absent in RBCs.

15. The composition of lymph is similar to blood with some exceptions. State few of them.

16. Define the following terms

(i) Leukaemia (ii) Polycythaemia

(iii) Hypertension

Section-II [5 Marks]

Structured Questions

17. Given below is a simple diagram of the circulation of blood in a mammal showing the main blood vessels, the heart, lungs and body tissues. The blood vessel labelled *F* contains deoxygenated blood and the valve leading to it has three semilunar pockets.

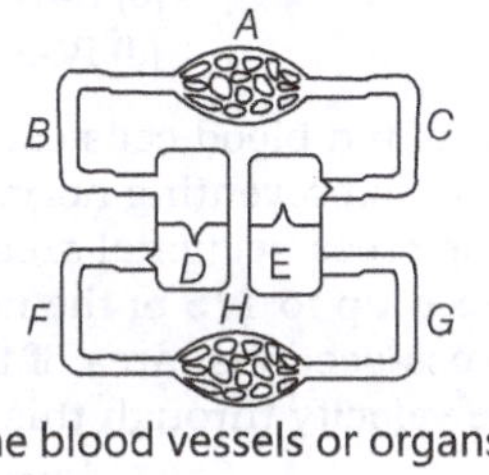

(i) Name the blood vessels or organs labelled as *A* and *H*.

(ii) Give one difference between *B* and *C*.

(iii) Which labelled part represents the pumping organ of body?

(iv) Identify the type of blood found in *F* and *G*.

(v) What do you mean by 'double circulation' of blood in mammals?

18. The diagram below represents a certain category of blood vessels showing the role of a special structure in their walls.

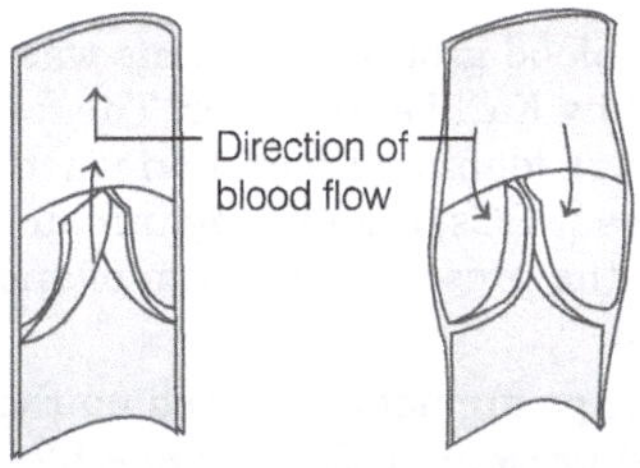

(i) Name the kind of blood vessels shown.

(ii) Name the structure shown inside the blood vessels.

(iii) Describe the role of these structures.

(iv) Mention one structural feature of vessel shown in diagram.

(v) What type of blood flows through these vessels?

19. Given below is a schematic representation of the circulatory system in man. Study the same and answer the questions that follows.

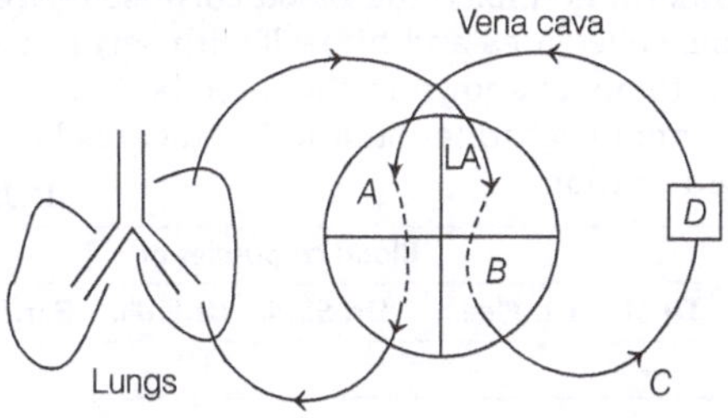

(i) Label the parts *A* to *D* indicated in the diagram.

(ii) Give one difference between the parts *A* and *B* based on

(a) their structure

(b) the nature of blood flowing through them.

(iii) What is the specific name for the type of blood circulation that takes place between the heart and the lungs?

(iv) Name the valve found at the beginning of the part labelled as *C*. **[2006]**

For explanations scan the given QR Code

Olympiad Section*

Brain Teasing Questions asked in Previous Olympiads

1 The ABO blood group in humans was first identified by Karl Landsteiner. The four blood groups were identified based on whether blood corpuscles (RBCs) clump (agglutinate) or do not clump in the presence of serum of another individual.

Blood groups are defined based on the molecules (antigens) present on RBCs, i.e. A blood group has A antigen, B blood group has B antigen, AB blood group has both A and B antigen, while O blood group have neither A or B antigen. The serum contains antibodies.

However, a normal person will not have antibodies for the antigen present on his own RBC. Agglutination occurs during transfusion if serum contains the antibody against the antigen present on the RBC. In the experiment by Landsteiner (Landst.), he mixed the blood corpuscles from five of his colleagues and himself with serum collected from them as shown in the table below. A '+' sign indicated agglutination and '–'indicates lack of agglutination. **[INJSO 2016]**

Serum	Blood corpuscles of					
	Dr.St.	**Dr. Pleen.**	**Dr. Strul.**	**Dr.Erdh.**	**Zar.**	**Landst.**
Dr. St	–	+	+	+	+	–
Dr. Pleen.	–	–	+	+	–	–
Dr. Strul.	–	+	–	–	+	–
Dr.Erdh.	–	+	–	–	+	–
Zar	–	–	+	+	–	–
Landst.	–	+	+	+	+	–

Deduce the blood group of Landsteiner (Landst.)

(a) A (b) B

(c) O (d) AB

2 Alka was walking through a forest. A leech caught one of her legs. It sucked blood and got detached from Alka's leg when it was full with blood. Find which of the following observations of the table in Column 'A' will be true in this case.

Further, from the options given below (a, b, c, d) find the correct option which matches the suitable explanation (in Column 'B') to your selected answer (in Column 'A').

	Column A		Column B
I.	Bleeding from Alka's leg will stop immediately.	1.	Leech produces only anticoagulant when it attaches human body.
II.	Bleeding from Alka's leg will stop immediately but she will feel acute pain immediately after the leech detaches from her leg.	2.	Leech produces anticoagulant as well as anti-inflammatory substance (histamine like) when it attaches to human body.
III.	Alka will continue to bleed for sometime with acute pain in her leg after the leech detaches from her leg.	3.	Leech plugs the blood vessel when it detaches from human body.
IV.	Alka will continue to bleed for sometime without any pain after the leech detaches from her leg.	4.	Leech plugs the blood vessel and removes anti-inflammatory substance when it detaches from the human body.

(a) I-3 (b) II-4 **[INJSO 2015]**

(c) III-1 (d) IV-2

3 Precipitation of red blood cells causes blockages in the blood vessels preventing normal tissue nutrition. The cross-sectional area of an arteriole can be reduced up to 1/5 of the normal value. When the cross-sectional area of the arteriole is reduced, the velocity through this reduced section will be **[IJSO 2014, Argentina]**

(a) higher than in the surrounding area where the cross-sectional arteriole area is greater

(b) equal to the velocity in the surrounding area where the cross-sectional arteriole area is greater

(c) lower than in the surrounding area where the cross-sectional arteriole area is greater

(d) Unchanged

Answers

1. (c) **2.** (d) **3.** (a)

**These questions may or may not be asked in the examination, have been given just for additional practice required for olympiads, scholarship exams etc. For detailed explanations refer Page No. 247.*

CHAPTER

08

Excretory System

Chapter Inside

• Excretion : Products and System • Human Excretory System
• Mechanism of Urine formation • Urine • Micturition

Various metabolic reactions which occur inside the body, whether **anabolic** (constructive, i.e. formation of complex molecules from simple ones) or **catabolic** (destructive, i.e. breakdown of complex molecules into simpler forms), release energy and form some substances that are not required by the body. These substances are called **waste products** and they need to be removed from the body at the earliest possible time, as they can be toxic to the body.

In this chapter, we will discuss how these waste products are formed and thereafter, the entire process of removal of these products (excretion) will be studied.

Excretion : Products and System

The process of removal of harmful metabolic waste products from the body is called **excretion**. It is an important process in all living beings. It also maintains the osmotic concentration of all the body fluids, i.e. **osmoregulation within the body**.

Excretory Products in Animals

Different animals excrete different nitrogenous compounds. Based on the excretory products produced by an organism, they are classified into three categories as follows

(i) **Ammonotelic** The organisms excreting ammonia as waste product are called ammonotelic and the process is called **ammonotelism,** e.g. aquatic amphibians, fishes, etc.
Ammonia is the most toxic form of nitrogenous waste thus, it requires the large amount of water for its elimination.

(ii) **Ureotelic** The organisms excreting urea as waste product are called ureotelic and the process is called **ureotelism**, e.g. mammals, amphibians (frog), etc. Urea is highly poisonous. If allowed to accumulate in the blood to a certain level, it causes death.

(iii) **Uricotelic** The organisms excreting uric acid in semi-solid form as waste product are called uricotelic and excretion process is called **uricotelism**, e.g. birds, reptiles, etc.

Excretory Organs in Higher Animals

The organs which are related with the process of formation, storage along with expulsion of excretory materials from the body are called excretory organs. In human beings, the process of excretion is brought about by the following organs

(i) **Kidney** It is the primary excretory organ for the excretion of liquid waste products in the form of urine.

(ii) **Skin** It bears several sweat glands under it. These glands secrete sweat which carries small amount of nitrogenous wastes, salts and excess water along with it. Sweating is mainly concerned with the process of thermoregulation, i.e. maintaining temperature of the body.

(iii) **Lungs** These are meant to excrete carbon dioxide (a waste product), which is formed during expiration (breathing out).

(iv) **Liver** It removes excess urea (formed by deamination of amino acids), bile pigments like bilirubin and other toxins. It also breakdown bad cholesterol, alcohol, nicotine and drugs thus it is known as a **detoxifying gland.**

Defaecation is not Excretion

Passing out or removal of faeces, i.e. defaecation is not considered as an excretory process. It is defined as the removal of undigested or indigestible food from the alimentary canal *via* anus.

Excretion is the removal of metabolic waste products formed due to various biochemical reactions and since faecal matter is not formed by metabolism, its removal is not considered as excretion.

Important Metabolic Wastes Excreted from the Body

Chemicals	Sources	Organs of excretion
Ammonia	Deamination (removal of amine group) of amino acids in liver	Kidneys
Bile pigments	Haemoglobin breakdown in liver	Liver (into small intestine)
Carbon dioxide	Breakdown of glucose in cells	Lungs
Inorganic ions	Food and water	Kidneys and salivary glands
Urea	Derived from ammonia	Kidneys and skin
Uric acid	Nucleotide breakdown in liver	Kidneys
Urochrome	Haemoglobin breakdown in liver	Kidneys
Water	Food and water; breakdown of glucose	Kidneys, skin and lungs

Check Your LEARNING...

1. Why is it important to remove nitrogenous waste from the body?
2. What mode of excretion is found in fishes and frog?
3. Name an organism which excretes uric acid.
4. The process of thermoregulation is concerned with which part of body?
5. How is defaecation different from excretion?
6. Water is excreted through which part of body?

Human Excretory System

Excretory system in humans consists of a pair of kidneys, a pair of ureters, urinary bladder and urethra.

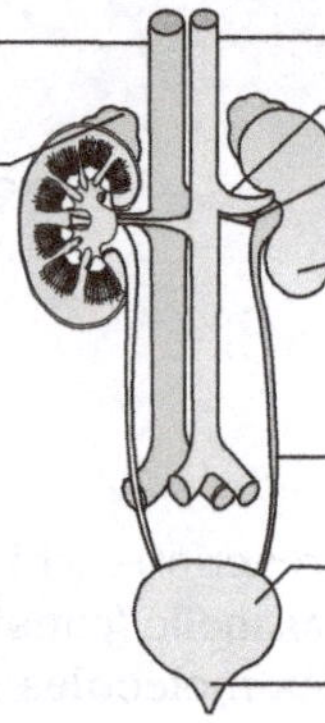

Excretory system in human

Kidneys

These are two bean-shaped structures, located on either side of the backbone in the abdominal cavity below the diaphragm and protected by the last two ribs. Right kidney is slightly lower than left kidney because liver takes much space at right side and pushes it down.

External Structure of Kidney

Each kidney is about 10 cm long, 6 cm wide and 3.5 cm thick. The outer surface of kidney is convex and the inner surface is concave.

At the inner concave surface, a notch-type structure called **hilum** is present, through which the supply of blood occurs, i.e. renal artery and renal vein pass in and out of the kidneys along with ureter.

The kidney is bounded externally by a thin sheet of white fibrous tissue called **renal capsule.**

Internal Structure of Kidney

Internally, each kidney is made up of two main regions, i.e. **outer cortex** and **inner medulla.** Each kidney is composed of enormous number of microscopic tubules called **nephrons** or **renal tubules** or **uriniferous tubules**, which are the functional units of the kidney. The cortex is the outer darker region which is dotted in appearance. The nephrons are highly coiled in this region.

The medulla is composed of finely stripped substance which are arranged in several conical projections called **renal** or **medullary pyramids**. Apex of each renal pyramid are called **papilla** which projects inwards, towards the pelvis.

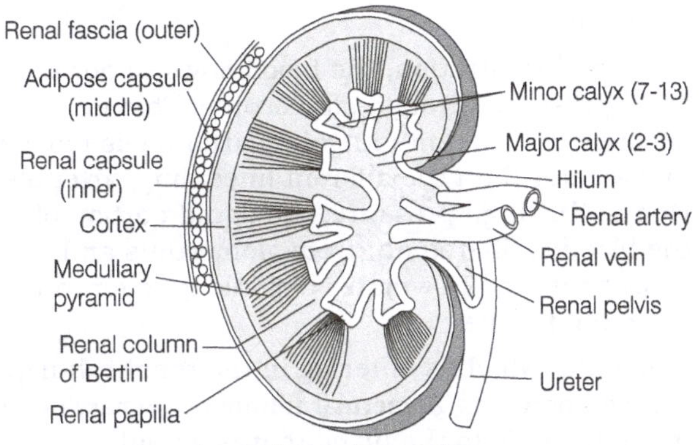

Longitudinal section of a kidney

Nephron

It is a highly coiled, tube-like structure. There are about 1 millions nephrons in both kidneys and each single tubule is about 4-5 cm long. It filters the blood in order to regulate chemical concentrations of water and soluble substances like sodium salts and thereby, produce urine. Each nephron consists of two parts, the **Malpighian body** or **renal corpuscle** and **renal tubules.**

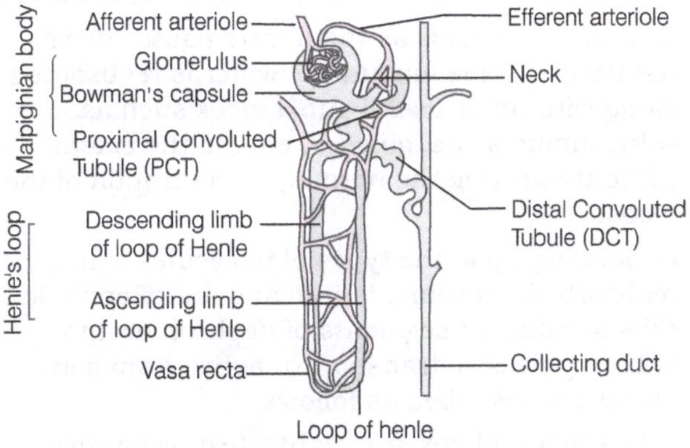

A diagrammatic representation of a nephron

(i) **Malpighian body** It lies in the cortex of the kidney. It is differentiated into two parts, i.e. Bowman's capsule and glomerulus.
Bowman's capsule is a single-celled, thin-walled, cup-like structure and **glomerulus** is a tuft of capillaries formed by afferent arteriole (a fine branch of renal artery).
Malpighian body filters out large solutes from the blood and delivers small solutes into the renal tubule for their modification.

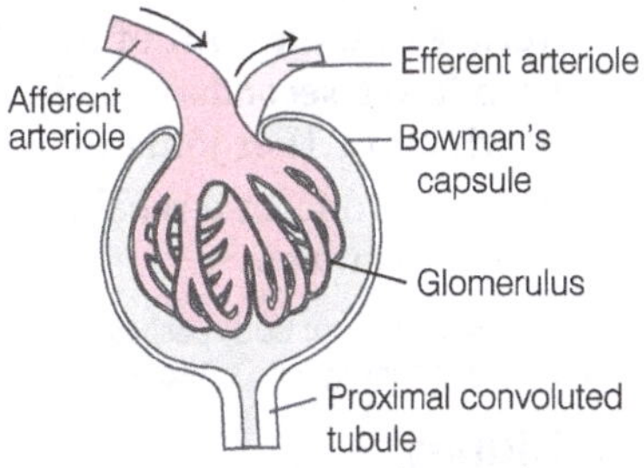

Malpighian body (renal corpuscle)

(ii) **Renal tubules** The Bowman's capsule leads into a coiled part of nephron called renal tubule. After passing through the renal tubules, the filtrate continues to the collecting duct system. The long and thin renal tubules are divided into three distinct regions as follows

(a) **Proximal Convoluted Tubule** (PCT) It is the starting point of the convoluted region which makes few coils and is found behind the neck of Malpighian body. PCT along with Bowman's capsule lies in the cortex region of the kidney.

(b) **Henle's loop** It is a U-shaped (hairpin-shaped) non-convoluted part of renal tubule that runs in the medulla region of kidney. It has a descending loop that ends into the medulla and an ascending loop that extends back from medulla into the cortex.

(c) **Distal Convoluted Tubule** (DCT) It is the end part of renal tubule lying in the cortex region of the kidney. It further opens up into a **collecting duct** which receives the waste products and then pour it into the pelvis of kidney as urine.

Blood Vessels of Renal Tubules

(i) A pair of renal arteries branch off from dorsal aorta and enter into the kidneys. Blood in these arteries contain high concentration of oxygen and nutrients.

(ii) Renal artery further gives rise to arterioles, which enter the Bowman's capsule and supplies blood to the glomerulus. These are known as **afferent arterioles**.

(iii) The afferent arteriole breaks into many capillaries, forming a knot-like mass called **glomerulus**, which fits closely inside the Bowman's capsule.

(iv) The capillaries forming the glomerulus reunite together and emerge out from the Bowman's capsule, forming an **efferent arteriole**, carrying blood away from the glomerulus.

(v) Efferent arteriole emerges out of the glomerulus and breaks up into a **secondary capillary network** (vasa recta), which further joins to form venules.

(vi) These venules join to form a **renal vein** that opens into the posterior vena cava.

Note The entire blood present in our body passes through the kidneys about 350-400 times per day with a rate of 1-2 liters per minute.

Functions of Kidney

(i) It helps in regulating water and electrolyte balance.

(ii) It helps in excreting metabolic waste products.

(iii) It helps in regulating pH of the blood.

(iv) It helps in the regulation of arterial pressure.

Ureters

These are the paired tubular structures arising from the **pelvis** of each kidney. The upper half of the ureter is located in the abdomen and lower half is located in the pelvic area. The tube has thick walls comprised of a fibrous, a muscular and mucus coat, which are able to contract. The urine produced in the kidneys constantly flows through these ureters and gets collected into the urinary bladder.

The valves present in the ureters prevent the backflow of urine during the contraction of bladder.

Urinary Bladder

It is a thin-walled, pear-shaped sac which is meant to store the urine temporarily. Urine enters the bladder *via* ureters and exits via urethra. It is located in the lower abdominal area of body near the pelvic bones.

Urethra

It is a membranous tube through which urine emptied from bladder is conducted out of the body. The **urethral sphincters** (circular muscle) keep the urethra closed and open it only at the time of urination. Its main function is to excrete waste products out of the body.

Check Your LEARNING...

1 What is the position of kidney in our body?

2 What are the two components of nephron that together form renal corpuscle?

3 Blood enters and leaves the glomerulus through different arterioles. Is it true? If yes, give their names.

4 Name the knot-like mass of blood capillary inside the Bowman's capsule.

5 Name the reservoir of urine in the body.

Mechanism of Urine Formation

Urine is an excretory product which is formed in the nephrons of the kidney. The process of formation of urine is called **uropoiesis.**

It is a three step process as described below

1. Glomerular Filtration or Ultrafiltration

It is the very first step in the process of formation of urine. It involves the filtration of blood in the glomerulus.

During ultrafiltration, the blood flows under a great pressure through glomerulus. This is because the efferent (outgoing) arteriole is narrow in diameter than the afferent (incoming) arteriole. Due to this high pressure, the liquid portion of the blood is filtered out from glomerulus and passes into the Bowman's capsule to enter into the renal tubule.

This fluid (which is entering in the renal tubule) is now known as **glomerular filtrate** or **primary urine**. It is hypotonic to the urine that is actually excreted out. The amount of the filtrate formed by the kidneys per minute is called **Glomerular Filtration Rate** (GFR).

Note About 160 litres of glomerular filtrate is produced in 24 hours.

2. Selective Reabsorption

During the second step of urine formation, glomerular filtrate in the form of dilute solution enters the renal tubule and various materials present in the filtrate are reabsorbed. As much as 99% of the materials in the filtrate are reabsorbed.

During the process as the filtrate passes down the tubule, some amount of water is reabsorbed along with other useful substances such as salts, amino acids, glucose, etc., to the extent without affecting the normal concentration of the blood.

Depending upon the types of molecules being reabsorbed, movements into and out of epithelial cells in different segments of nephron occurs either by passive transport or active transport. These are described as follows

(i) **Water** and **urea** are reabsorbed by passive transport (i.e. water is reabsorbed by osmosis and urea by simple diffusion).

(ii) **Glucose** and **amino acids** are reabsorbed by active transport.

(iii) The **reabsorption of Na^+** occurs both by passive and active transport.

Note Reabsorption of water by kidney tubules increases due to the effect of antidiuretic hormone or vasopressin.

3. Tubular Secretion

It is the last step in the formation of urine. The substances such as K^+, Na^+, H^+ and certain chemicals, which are not removed by filtration, are removed by this process. These are passed into the distal convoluted tubule during the process by the activity of cells of tubular walls, i.e. reabsorption and secretion.

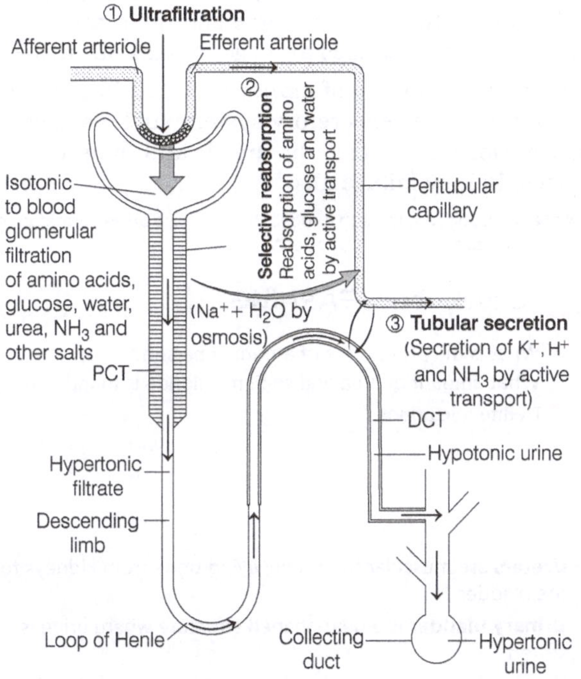

Diagram showing three main processes of urine formation

This step helps in the maintenance of ionic and acid-base balance of body fluids.

Summary of Urine Formation

Steps	Occurrence	Molecules
Glomerular filtration	Blood pressure pushes small molecules from the glomerular capsule.	Water, glucose, amino acids, salt, urea, uric acid and creatinine.
Tubular reabsorption	Diffusion and active transport bring back molecules to blood at the Proximal Convoluted Tubule (PCT).	Water, glucose, amino acids and salts.
Tubular secretion	Active transport moves molecules from blood to the Distal Convoluted Tubule (DCT).	Uric acid, creatinine, hydrogen ions, ammonia and drugs liter penicillin.
Reabsorption of water	Along the complete length of the nephron and notably at loop of Henle and collecting duct, water returns by osmosis and salt by active reabsorption.	Salt and water.
Excretion	Removal of metabolic waste in the form of urine.	Water, salts, urea, uric acid, ammonium and creatinine.

Check Your LEARNING...

1. What role does blood pressure play during glomerular filtration?
2. What is the main transformation present in glomerular filtrate compared to blood?
3. List the molecules that are filtered out during tubular secretions.
4. In which step of urine formation does excess of water, urea, glucose and amino acids are reabsorbed?

Urine

The filtrate left behind after the completion of all steps written above is known as urine. It is expelled out from the urethra present in the penis in males and directly to exterior in females. The expulsion is done under the impulse of nervous system.

This process of expelling out of urine is known as **urination** or **micturition.**

Urine is a transparent, light yellow fluid having pH of around 6 (slightly acidic in nature). Protein diet makes the urine acidic while vegetable diet makes it alkaline.

The colour of urine is yellow due to the presence of **urochrome**, a pigment formed by the breakdown of haemoglobin of worn out RBCs.

Normal urine in fresh form is faintly aromatic. It gives ammonical odours on standing due to conversion of urea into ammonia by bacteria.

The approximate volume of urine produced per day is 1 to 1.5 litres. Its specific gravity is about 1.003 to 1.035.

Composition of Urine

Normally, urine constitutes about 95% water and 5% solid wastes (including organic and inorganic substances).

Constituents of urine (in gm/ L of urine) are listed in the table given below

Composition of Urine

Organic (g/L)	**Inorganic** (g/L)
Urea-2.3	NaCl-9.0
Uric acid-0.7	KCl-2.5
Creatinine-1.5	Ammonia-0.6
Others-2.6	Others-2.5

Note Besides the normal constituents the urine may pass out certain abnormal constituent, i.e. blood cells (haematuria), glucose (glycosuria), albumin (albuminuria), bile pigments.

Micturition

The process of release of urine is called **micturition** and the neural mechanism causing it, is called the **micturition reflex**. Let us study how the process of micturition takes place.

Urine is produced and drained continuously by the nephron into the renal pelvis. From here, it is carried down to the ureters and then into the urinary bladder.

The bladder serves to store the urine temporarily till a voluntary signal is given by the **Central Nervous System** (CNS). As soon as the urine is collected, the muscular walls of the bladder distend to accommodate it.

The stretch receptors on the walls of the bladder set up reflexes, i.e. send signals to the CNS by stimulating the sensory nerve ending in the bladder, which causes an urge to pass out urine.

Any malfunctioning of kidney can lead to several disorders of the execretory system such as **gout**, **kidney stone** (renal calculi), **uremia** and in severe cases, kidney failure also.

Note Diuretics are the substances that increase urine formation or diuresis, e.g. tea, alcohol, etc.

Check Your LEARNING...

1 What is the pH of urine of a normal person?
2 What amount of urea and sodium chloride is found in urine?
3 Define micturition.

QUiCK Revision

- **Excretion** is the process of removal of waste material from the body.
- **Osmoregulation** is the process of maintaining osmotic and ionic concentration of body fluid.
- **Types of excretory products** depend on the habitat, feeding habits and metabolism of an organism. It can be ammonia (ammonotelism), urea (ureotelism) and uric acid (uricotelism).
- **Human excretory system** consists of two kidneys, two ureters, a urinary bladder and a urethra.
- **Human kidneys** are mesodermal in origin, with retroperitoneal arrangement (present outside coelomic cavity). Externally, they are reddish-brown, bean- shaped. Right kidney is smaller and placed lower as compared to left one.
- Internally, human kidneys contain three protective layers, i.e. **renal capsule**, **adipose capsule** and **renal fascia**. Kidney is divided into two zones, i.e. an **outer cortex** and an **inner medulla**.
- **Nephrons** are the structural and functional unit of kidneys. They consist of renal corpuscle or Malpighian body and renal tubules.
    - **Renal corpuscles** consist of **Bowman's capsule**, i.e. a cup-shaped structure containing network of thin capillaries called **glomerulus**.
    - **Renal tubules** are associated with process of reabsorption and secretion. They are formed of four parts, i.e. **proximal convoluted tubule**, **Henle's loop** (descending, ascending and a main loop), **DCT** and **collecting duct**.
- **Ureters** are muscular tubes conveying urine from kidneys to the bladder.
- **Urinary bladder** is a pear-shaped structure where urine is stored.
- **Urethra** is present in mammals only, it is a canal extending from bladder to outside *via* external urethral orifice.
- **Urine formation** is called **uropoiesis** and it occurs in three steps. These are ultrafiltration, selective reabsorption and tubular secretion.
    - **Ultrafiltration** occurs when blood containing water and solutes, enters the afferent arteriole in glomerulus. Glomerulus Filtration Rate (GFR) is the amount of filtrate formed by kidneys per minute (180 L/day).
    - **Selective reabsorption** is the absorption of almost 99% of filtrate in renal tubules. 65% of filtrate reabsorbed in PCT (Na^+, K^+, glucose, amino acids, etc.). Reabsorption is minimum in Henle's loop, absorption of Na^+ occurs in DCT and in collecting duct, water reabsorption occurs.
    - **Tubular secretion** is the phenomenon of secretion of metabolic wastes by tubular cells into the filtrate. It is an active process which occurs in PCT, DCT and collecting duct. It helps in the maintenance of ionic and acid-base balance of body fluid.
- **Urine** is pale yellow (due to urochrome pigment), slightly acidic (pH-6), normally transparent and faintly aromatic.
- **Micturition** is the release of urine from bladder. It occurs due to the contraction and relaxation of urinary bladder and urethral sphincter. The signal for micturition originates from a stretched bladder.

Chapter Practice

Section-I

1 Mark Questions

1. Name the following.
   (i) The organisms excreting urea as their excretory product.
   (ii) The functional units of kidney.
   (iii) The organ which produces urea. **[2017, 12]**
   (iv) An organic waste produced in man.
   (v) The structure formed by Bowman's capsule and glomerulus together.
   (vi) The branch of renal artery entering the Bowman's capsule.
   (vii) The pH of the normal urine.

Ans. (i) Ureotelic (ii) Nephron
(iii) Liver (iv) Urea
(v) Malpighian body (vi) Afferent arteriole
(vii) 6

2. Correct and rewrite the following statements by changing the underlined words.
   (i) The kidney is composed of number of neurons. **[2019]**
   (ii) The glomerulus helps in reabsorption.
   (iii) Urethra carries urine from kidney to the urinary bladder.
   (iv) Normal pale yellow colour of the urine is due to the presence of the pigment melanin. **[2018]**

Ans. (i) The kidney is composed of number of nephrons.
(ii) The glomerulus helps in ultrafiltration.
(iii) Ureter carries urine from kidney to the urinary bladder.
(iv) Normal pale yellow colour of the urine is due to the presence of the pigment urochrome.

3. Give biological reasons for the following.
   (i) Certain useful products like glucose, salt, etc., are filtered by ultrafiltration but not excreted.
   (ii) Reabsorption is called as selective reabsorption.
   (iii) It is necessary to maintain a normal osmotic concentration of the blood.

Ans. (i) Glucose, salt, etc., get reabsorbed in the proximal part of renal tubules, hence are not excreted.
(ii) Only certain selected materials such as glucose, some salts, etc., are reabsorbed in the renal tubule. Thus, it is called selective reabsorption.
(iii) To keep the body cells in a steady state, it is essential to maintain the osmotic concentration of blood.

4. (i) Match the following columns.

Column I	Column II
A. Liver	1. Blood supply to glomerulus
B. Skin	2. Knot-like tuft of blood capillaries in Bowman's capsule
C. Kidney	3. Deamination of amino acids
D. Glomerulus	4. Sweat glands
	5. Bean-shaped excretory organ

(ii) Match the following columns.

Column I	Column II
A. Proximal convoluted tubule	1. Formation of concentrated urine
B. Distal convoluted tubule	2. Filtration of blood
C. Henle's loop	3. Reabsorption of 70-80% of electrolytes
D. Micturition	4. Ionic balance
E. Renal corpuscle	5. Process of release of urine from the body

Ans. (i) A–3, B–4, C–5, D–2
(ii) A–3, B–4, C–1, D–5, E–2

5. Choose the correct answer from the four options given below.
   (i) Excretion process involves the
   (a) removal of nitrogenous waste
   (b) removal of byproducts of anabolism and catabolism
   (c) removal of bile pigments
   (d) All of the above

Ans. (d)

(ii) 'Aquatic animals excrete ammonia'. Which one of the following statements does not support this statement?
(a) Ammonia requires huge quantity of water to dissolve
(b) Ammonia is released from the body in gaseous state
(c) Ammonia is highly toxic and needs to be eliminated when formed
(d) Ammonia gets converted into less toxic form called urea and uric acid

Ans. (b)

(iii) The main nitrogenous waste formed in the human body **[Semester II 2022]**
(a) uric acid (b) urea
(c) ammonia (d) creatinine

Ans. (b)

(iv) The formation of urine in our excretory system is known as
(a) haemopoiesis (b) uropoiesis
(c) leucopoiesis (d) None of these

Ans. (b)

(v) Which substance is present in a lower concentration in the renal artery than in the renal vein?
(a) Amino acids (b) Carbon dioxide
(c) Glucose (d) Urea

Ans. (b)

(vi) The nephrons discharge their urine at the **[2016]**
(a) urinary bladder (b) urethra
(c) renal pelvis (d) renal pyramid

Ans. (c)

(vii) The proximal convoluted tubule of a nephron is present in
(a) medulla (b) cortex
(c) ureter (d) None of these

Ans. (b)

(viii) The structure that stores urine temporarily is **[Semester II 2022]**
(a) ureter (b) urethra
(c) urinary bladder (d) kidneys

Ans. (c)

(ix) Maximum amount of water from the glomerular filtrate is reabsorbed in
(a) PCT
(b) DCT
(c) ascending limb of Henle's loop
(d) descending limb of Henle's loop

Ans. (a)

(x) Ultrafiltrate generated by the glomerulus contain all the constituents of the blood plasma except
(a) protein (b) RBC
(c) WBC (d) All of these

Ans. (b)

(xi) The pale yellow colour of normal human urine is due to the pigment **[2023]**
(a) melanin
(b) anthocyanin
(c) urochrome
(d) haemoglobin

Ans. (c)

6. Fill in the blanks by using suitable words.

(i) The process of removal of waste products formed by metabolic activities is called ....
(ii) The outer part of a kidney is .... and the inner part is ....
(iii) Nephrons consist of two portions, ... where plasma is filtered and .... into which filtered fluid is passed.
(iv) The renal artery carries blood which supplies high concentration of .... and ...... for tissue respiration in the kidney cells.
(v) Water along with other useful substances like salts, amino acids, glucose, etc., are reabsorbed in ....
(vi) The process of uropoiesis that helps in maintenance of ionic and acid-base balance is ....
(vii) The process of release of urine is ....

Ans. (i) excretion (ii) cortex, medulla
(iii) renal corpuscle, renal tubule
(iv) oxygen, nutrients (v) renal tubule
(vi) tubular secretion (vii) micturition

7. Choose the odd one out from the following terms given below and name the category to which other three belong. **[2017]**

(i) Bile, Urea, Uric acid, Ammonia
(ii) Birds, Snakes, Mammals, Lizards
(iii) Kidney, Liver, Skin, Lungs, Pancreas
(iv) Urethra, Uterus, Urinary bladder, Ureter **[2014]**

Ans. (i) **Odd term** is bile.
Rest three are the type of excretory material in different organisms.

(ii) **Odd term** is mammals.
Rest four animals are uricotelic, they produce uric acid as their excretory product.

(iii) **Odd term** is pancreas.
Rest four organs help in the removal of wastes from the body.

(iv) **Odd term** is uterus.
Rest three are the part of excretory system.

8. Given below are the sets of five terms. Rewrite the terms in correct order of a logical sequence.

(i) Kidney, Urethra, Urinary bladder, Sphincter, Ureter
(ii) Renal vein, Renal artery, Afferent arteriole, Efferent arteriole, Glomerulus (pathway of blood through glomerulus) **[2012]**
(iii) Glomerulus, Loop of Henle, Distal convoluted tubule, Proximal convoluted tubule, Collecting duct
(iv) Filtration, Tubular secretion, Reabsorption of water, Tubular reabsorption, Excretion
(v) Renal fascia, Cortex, Renal column of Bertini, Renal capsule, Renal pelvis (outer to inner)

Ans. (i) Kidney, Ureter, Urinary bladder, Sphincter, Urethra
(ii) Renal artery, Afferent arteriole, Glomerulus, Efferent arteriole, Renal vein
(iii) Glomerulus, Proximal convoluted tubule, Loop of Henle, Distal convoluted tubule, Collecting duct
(iv) Filtration, Tubular reabsorption, Tubular secretion, Reabsorption of water, Excretion
(v) Renal fascia, Renal capsule, Cortex, Renal column of Bertini, Renal pelvis

9. Expand the following biological abbreviations.
(i) PCT (ii) DCT
(iii) GFR (iv) CNS

Ans. (i) Proximal Convoluted Tubule
(ii) Distal Convoluted Tubule
(iii) Glomerular Filtration Rate
(iv) Central Nervous System

10. State the exact location of the following.
(i) Kidneys
(ii) Malpighian body
(iii) Proximal convoluted tubule [2016]
(iv) Loop of Henle [2015]
(v) Ureters

Ans. (i) Kidneys are located below the diaphragm on the left and right sides, protected by the last two ribs.
(ii) Malpighian body lies in the cortex region of the kidney.
(iii) PCT along with Bowman's capsule lies in the cortex region of kidney.
(iv) Henle's loop is a U-shaped or hairpin-shaped region of renal tubule that runs in the medulla region of kidney.
(v) The upper half of the ureter is located in the abdomen and lower half of the ureter is located in the pelvic area.

11. State the main function of following.
(i) Sweat glands
(ii) Renal pelvis
(iii) Glomerulus
(iv) Loop of Henle
(v) Bladder sphincter

Ans. (i) Sweat glands eliminate extra water and salts through sweating, i.e. perspiration.
(ii) Renal pelvis is the proximal part of ureter that breaks into 2-3 branches towards kidney to form major calyx. It acts as a funnel that collects urine flowing into ureter.
(iii) Glomerulus is the part of nephron where filtration of blood occurs.
(iv) Loop of Henle absorbs the water and solutes from the glomerular filtrate.
(v) Bladder sphincter regulates the opening and closing of bladder for urination.

12. Mention one difference between each of the following pairs on the basis of what is given in the bracket. [2017]
(i) Renal cortex and Renal medulla (parts of the nephrons present)
(ii) Afferent and Efferent arterioles (function)
(iii) Bowman's capsule and Malpighian capsule (parts included) [2013]
(iv) Ureter and Urethra (function)

Ans. (i) Difference between renal cortex and renal medulla is as follows

Renal cortex	Renal medulla
Malpighian body, Proximal Convoluted Tubule (PCT) and Distal Convoluted Tubule (DCT) are found in renal cortex.	Henle's loop is found in renal medulla.

(ii) Difference between afferent and efferent arterioles is as follows

Afferent arteriole	Efferent arteriole
It transports blood to the glomerulus.	It transports blood away from the glomerulus.

(iii) Difference between Bowman's capsule and Malpighian capsule is as follows

Bowman's capsule	Malpighian capsule
It is a cup-shaped structure that indicates the beginning of nephron.	It is comprised of glomerulus and Bowman's capsule.

(iv) Differences between ureter and urethra is as follows

Ureter	Urethra
It transports urine from the kidney to urinary bladder.	It transports urine from urinary bladder to the exterior or outside of our body.

13. Give biological/technical terms for the following.
(i) The process of maintaining water and salt balance in the blood. [2018]
(ii) The hormone increasing reabsorption of water by kidney tubules. [2015]

Ans. (i) Osmoregulation
(ii) Antidiuretic hormone (vasopressin)

14. Briefly explain the following terms.
(i) Ammonotelism (ii) Osmoregulation
(iii) Efferent arteriole (iv) Cortex
(v) Medulla

Ans. (i) The phenomenon of removal of ammonia as excretory product is called ammonotelism.
(ii) The process of regulating water content and ion concentration in the body of an organism is called osmoregulation.
(iii) The branch of blood vessel that drains blood out from glomerulus is called efferent arteriole.
(iv) The outer region of kidney having dotted appearance is called cortex.
(v) The inner striated part of kidney is called medulla.

15. Answer the following questions briefly.
(i) Why should we drink a lot of water on the regular basis?
(ii) Urochrome is the pigment present in urine. How and where does this pigment is formed?
(iii) How does CNS receive the signals when there is an urge to pass urine?
(iv) What is the medical term used for the stone in kidney?

Ans. (i) We should drink a lot of water on the regular basis for the normal regulation of kidney functions.
(ii) Urochrome is formed by the breakdown of haemoglobin in liver.
(iii) Stretch receptors present in the walls of urinary bladder send signal to CNS by setting up reflexes.
(iv) Renal calculi is the medical term used for the stone in kidney.

2 Marks Questions

16. The excretion process is different from osmoregulation. How?

Ans. Excretion is the process of removal of toxic wastes from the body, whereas osmoregulation is the process of maintenance of sufficient amount of water and the ionic balance of body fluids in the body.

17. In what way, kidney is a homeostat organ?

Ans. Homeostasis means maintenance of a constant internal environment by an organism. Kidney helps to maintain a steady or constant state of internal atmosphere by excreting waste products and reabsorbing useful substances like water and salts of sodium and potassium. It also maintains the water content of blood constant.

18. Renal cortex has a dotted appearance and renal medulla has a striped appearance. Explain. **[2023]**

Ans. The nephron has two parts- a cup shaped body called Malpighian corpuscle or renal corpuscle and a tubular part called renal tubule. The cortex has a dotted appearance because of the presence of these Malpighian corpuscles. The striated appearance of the medulla is due to the renal tubule.

19. Mention the three major steps involved in the production of urine. **[Semester II 2022]**

Ans. The three major steps involve in the process of urine formation (uropoiesis) are
(a) Glomerular filtration
(b) Selective reabsorption
(c) Tubular secretion
These processes ensure the removal of waste and excess water from the body.

20. The composition of glomerular filtrate and urine is not the same. Comment.

Ans. The composition of glomerular filtrate and urine is not the same.
As the glomerular filtrate contains a large amount of water and other dissolved substances such as urea, uric acid, creatinine, amino acid, glucose, sodium, potassium, vitamins, etc., whereas urine on the other hand is a transparent, light yellow fluid, which is formed after reabsorption and secretion from the filtrate. It constitutes about 95% water and 5% of other organic (urea, nitrogen, creatine, etc.) and inorganic substances (Cl^-, Ca^{2+}, Fe^{2+}, etc.).

21. Where does the selective reabsorption of glomerular filtrate take place?

Ans. The selective reabsorption of glomerular filtrate takes place in Proximal Convoluted Tubule (PCT) and Distal Convoluted Tubule (DCT).
In PCT, all essential elements, nutrients, 70-80% of electrolytes and water are absorbed. Whereas, Distal Convoluted Tubule (DCT) is involved in conditional reabsorption of Na and water.

3 Marks Questions

22. Draw a labelled diagram of the longitudinal section of the kidney and briefly describe it.
Or Draw a neat diagram of a longitudinal section of a human kidney and lebel renal cortex and renal medulla on the diagram. **[Semester II 2022]**

Ans. The longitudinal section of kidney is given in diagram below

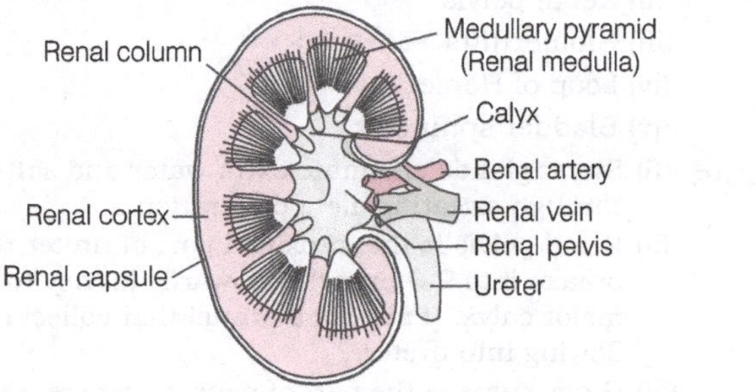

Longitudinal section of a kidney

The outer layer of the kidney is a tough capsule. Inside the kidney, there are two zones, i.e. medulla and cortex. Medulla is divided into few conical masses called medullary pyramids.
The cortex extends in between the medullary pyramids as renal columns called columns of Bertini.

23. (i) Draw a neat diagram of a single Malpighian capsule (body) and label the following parts. Glomerulus, Bowman's capsule, afferent arteriole and efferent arteriole.
Or Draw a neat, labelled diagram of Malpighian capsule. **[2023]**
(ii) Name and define the process that occurs in the glomerulus. **[2015]**

Ans. (i)

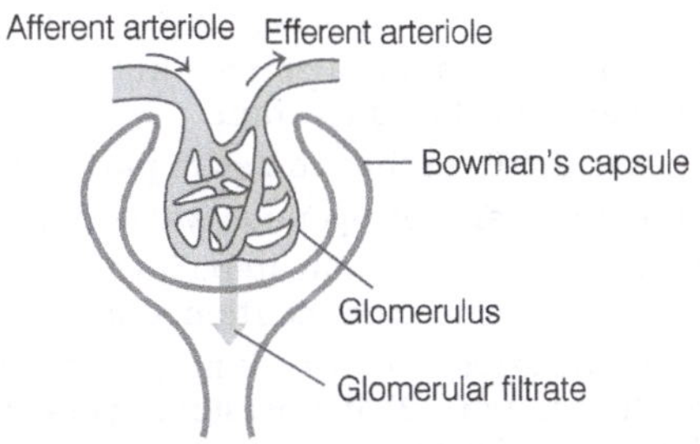

Malpighian capsule

(ii) Ultrafiltration is the process that occurs in the glomerulus. It is defined as the filtration of blood that takes place under high pressure.

24. Where do ultrafiltration, reabsorption and secretion occur in a nephron?

Ans. (i) Ultrafiltration occurs in Bowman's capsule.

(ii) Reabsorption occurs in PCT, loop of Henle, DCT and collecting duct.

(iii) Secretion occurs in PCT, loop of Henle and DCT.

Section-II [5 Marks]

Structured Questions

1. The diagram given below represents an organ system in the human body. Study the same and answer the questions that follow. **[2019]**

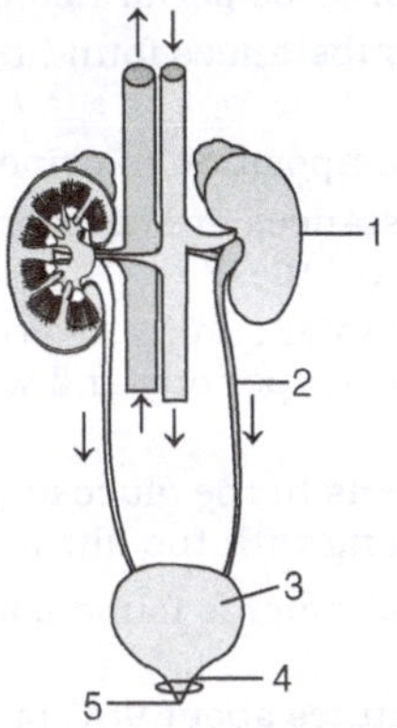

(i) Identify the system.

(ii) Label the parts marked as 2 and 4. Mention the function of part 5.

(iii) Name the structural and functional units of the part marked as 1.

(iv) What is the fluid that accumulates in part 3 ? Which is the main nitrogenous waste present in it?

(v) Draw a neat, labelled diagram showing the longitudinal section of part 1.

Ans. (i) Excretory system in human.

(ii) The parts marked as 2 and 4 are as ureter and sphincter muscles, respectively.
Part 5 is urethra. It acts as a passage through which urine and semen (in males) are excreted out of the body.

(iii) Nephron is known as the structural and functional unit of kidney (part 1).

(iv) Urinary bladder (part 3) contains the urine until it is released out. Urea is the main nitrogenous waste present in urine.

(v) The longitudinal section of part 1 is kidney.

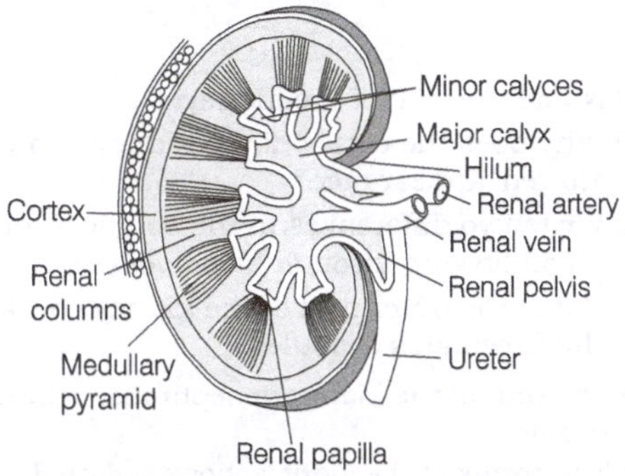

Longitudinal section of a kidney

2. In humans, the excretory system consists of one pair of kidney, a pair of ureters, a urinary bladder and a urethra. Each kidney has over a million tubular structures called nephrons.

(i) Which organ in human body maintains water balance in body?

(ii) Why is right kidney slightly lower in position compared to the left kidney?

(iii) Human beings have two bean-shaped kidney. Write about the structure of kidney.

(iv) Name two blood vessels, which enter and leave the kidney.

(v) Name the structure in which the glomerulus enclosed.

Ans. (i) Kidney maintains water balance in body.

(ii) Right kidney is slightly lower in position compared to the left kidney to adjust liver in the right side of the abdominal cavity.

(iii) The kidneys are bean-shaped structures about 10 cm long, 6 cm wide and 3.5 cm thick. The outer structure of kidney is convex while the inner surface is concave.

(iv) Renal artery enters the kidney carrying oxygenated blood with urea, uric acid and creatine, while renal veins leave the kidneys and carry deoxygenated blood without urea and uric acid.

(v) Bowman's capsule

3. Given below is a simple diagram of the human kidney cut open longitudinally. Answer the following questions.

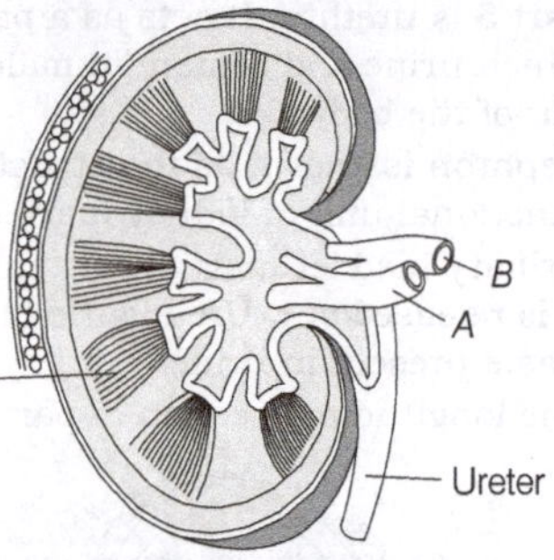

(i) Name the unit of the kidney.
(ii) Why does the cortex of the kidney show a 'dotted' appearance?
(iii) Write two differences in the composition of the blood flowing through blood vessels *A* and *B*.
(iv) Name the outer part of the kidney containing the Bowman's capsules.

Ans. (i) The unit of the kidney is nephrons/uriniferous tubules.
(ii) The cortex of the kidney shows a dotted appearance because of the presence of convoluted parts of the tubules, i.e. PCT and DCT.
(iii) Differences in the composition of the blood flowing through blood vesssels *A* and *B* are as follows

Renal vein (*A*)	Renal artery (*B*)
It contains less urea.	It contains more urea.
It contains less oxygen.	It contains more oxygen.
It contains more carbon dioxide.	In contains less carbon dioxide.

(iv) Cortex is the outer part of the kidney containing the Bowman's capsule.

4. The diagram given below is that of a structure present in a human kidney. Study the same and answer the questions that follow.

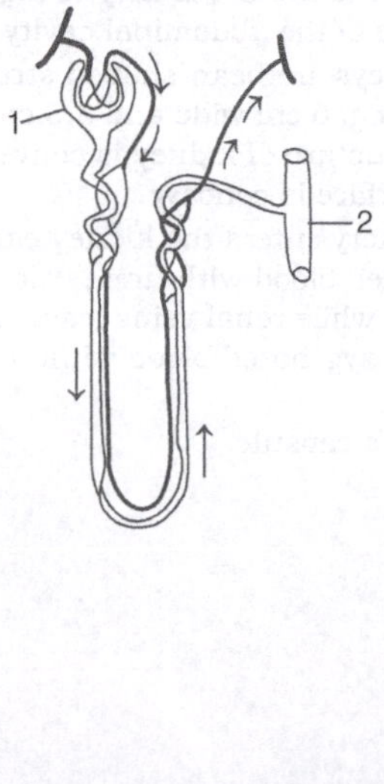

(i) Name the structure represented in the diagram.
(ii) What is the liquid entering part '1' called? Name two substances present in this liquid that are reabsorbed in the tubule.
(iii) What is the fluid that comes to part '2' called? Name the main nitrogenous waste in it.
(iv) Mention the three main steps involved in the formation of the fluid mentioned in (iii) above.
(v) Name the substance which may be present in the fluid in part '2', if a person suffers from diabetes mellitus. **[2018]**

Ans. (i) The structure represented in the diagram is nephron.
(ii) The liquid entering part 1 is called glomerular filtrate.
Glucose, amino acids, salts, etc., are present in glomerular filtrate and these get reabsorbed as filtrate passes down the tubule.
(iii) The fluid that comes to part 2 is called urine. Urea is the main nitrogenous waste (2.6 g/L) present in urine.
(iv) Three main steps of urine (part 2) formation are
(a) Ultrafiltration (glomerular filtration)
(b) Selective reabsorption
(c) Tubular secretion
(v) Glucose

5. Urine formation involves three main processes, i.e. filtration, reabsorption and secretion. Filtration is a non-selective process performed by the glomerulus.
(i) Name two substances found both in urine and sweat.
(ii) Write the composition of urine in human.
(iii) Which substances are reabsorbed in distal convoluted tubules?
(iv) What is the total quality of glomerulus filtrate produced by us per day and what does it contain?
(v) What happens to the glucose which enters the nephron along with the filtrate?

Ans. (i) Uric acid and water is found both in urine and sweat.
(ii) Urine constitutes about 95% of water and 5% of solid waste (inorganic and organic). Organic substances include urea, uric acid, creatinine, etc., while inorganic substances include NaCl, KCl, ammonia, etc.
(iii) Water and sodium are reabsorbed in distal convoluted tubules.
(iv) About 160 litres of glomerular filtrate is produced per day. It contains Na^+, K^+, Ca^{+2}, Cl^-, hormones, urea, salts in ionic stage, uric acids, glucose, water, amino acids, vitamins.
(v) The glucose which enters the nephron along with the filtrate is reabsorbed by blood capillaries surrounding the nephron.

Chapter Assessment

Section-I

1 Mark Questions

1. Name the following.
   (i) A thin sheet of fibrous tissue which surrounds kidney.
   (ii) The depression present on the concave surface of the kidney.
   (iii) The apex of each medullary pyramids.
   (iv) The component whose breakdown lead to the formation of urochrome.

2. Correct and rewrite the following statements by changing the underlined words.
   (i) Birds are <u>ureotelic</u> animals.
   (ii) Urine contains <u>3.6 gm/L</u> of urea.

3. Give biological reasons for the following.
   (i) Glucose is not found in the urine of a healthy person.
   (ii) There is frequent urination in winter than in summer.
   (iii) Person suffering from very low blood pressure pass no urine.

4. Match the following columns.

Column I (Functions)		Column II (Parts of excretory system)
A.	Ultrafiltration	1. Henle's loop
B.	Concentration of urine	2. Ureter
C.	Transport of urine	3. Urinary bladder
D.	Storage of urine	4. Malpighian corpuscle
		5. Proximal convoluted tubule

5. Choose the correct answer from the four options given below.

(i) The following substances are the excretory products in animals. Choose the most toxic form among them.
   (a) Urea
   (b) Uric acid
   (c) Ammonia
   (d) Carbon dioxide

(ii) A detoxifying gland present in our body which performs excretory functions is
   (a) thyroid (b) liver
   (c) hypothalamus (d) lungs

(iii) A large quantity of one of the following is removed from our body by lungs.
   (a) Only CO_2 (b) Only O_2
   (c) Both (a) and (b) (d) ammonia

(iv) Micturition reflex is a neural mechanism to
   (a) release sweat
   (b) formation of urine
   (c) release urine
   (d) release inorganic substance to the urine

(v) Identify the incorrect statement.
   (a) The outer layer of the kidney is called renal pelvis
   (b) Kidney is divided into outer cortex and inner medulla
   (c) Medulla is divided into medullary pyramids
   (d) The cortex extends in between the medullary pyramids, which is called as columns of Bertini

6. Fill in the blanks by using suitable words.
   (i) The sum total of all the chemical reactions that occur in a cell is known as ....
   (ii) The first step in urine formation is the ....
   (iii) The excretory system removes the waste products generated from several .... reactions occurring in our body.
   (iv) ...... and ...... are reabsorbed by passive transport.

7. Given below is the set of five terms and rewrite the terms in correct order of a logical sequence.

   Renal capsule, Cortex, Major calyx, Minor calyx, Medullary pyramid

8. State the exact location of the following.
   (i) Bowman's capsule
   (ii) Collecting duct

9. State the main function of the following.
   (i) Lungs
   (ii) Skin

10. Mention one difference between each of the following pair on the basis of what is given in the bracket.
   (i) Excretion and Defaecation (definition)
   (ii) PCT and DCT in a nephron (location)

11. Give biological/technical terms for the following.
   (i) Condition in which blood cells are found in urine.
   (ii) Phenomenon of removal of uric acid or excretory product.

12. Briefly explain the following terms.
(i) Selective reabsorption
(ii) Tubular secretion

13. Answer the following questions briefly.
(i) Which vessel of peritubular capillaries runs parallel to the loop of Henle ?
(ii) Write the name of two components of nephrons which together form renal corpuscle.
(iii) Which two substances are actively transported in glomerulus filters?
(iv) What is the pH of urine?

2 Marks Questions

14. Why it is said that kidneys help in the process of osmoregulation?

15. Organisms are classified on the basis of nitrogenous waste excreted by them. Explain.

16. What cause the liquid part of blood to filter out from glomerulus into the renal tubules?

3 Marks Questions

17. (i) Why nephrons are called as the 'filtering unit of kidney'?
(ii) How is urine produced?

18. Why is the removal of faeces from the alimentary canal not considered as excretion?

Section-II [5 Marks]

Structured Questions

19. Observe the diagram given below and answer the following questions.

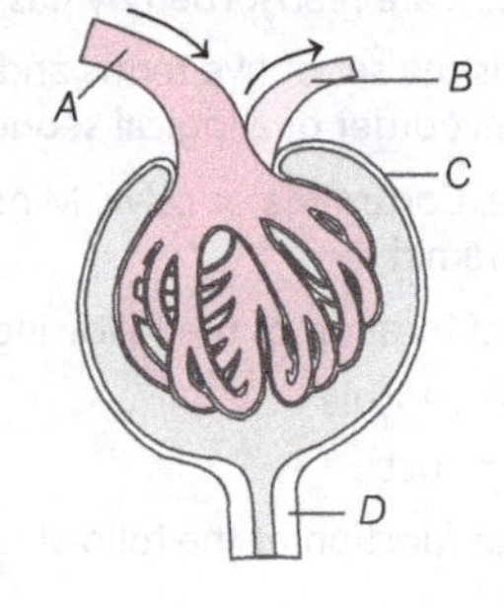

(i) In which part, ultrafiltration takes place? Identify this part.
(ii) Highest concentration of urea will be observed in which part? Name it.
(iii) Reabsorption of water occurs in which part? Name the part.
(iv) The figure given above is fundamental unit of which organ?
(v) Which types of tissues are found in glomerular region?

20. Study the diagram below and then answer the questions that follow.

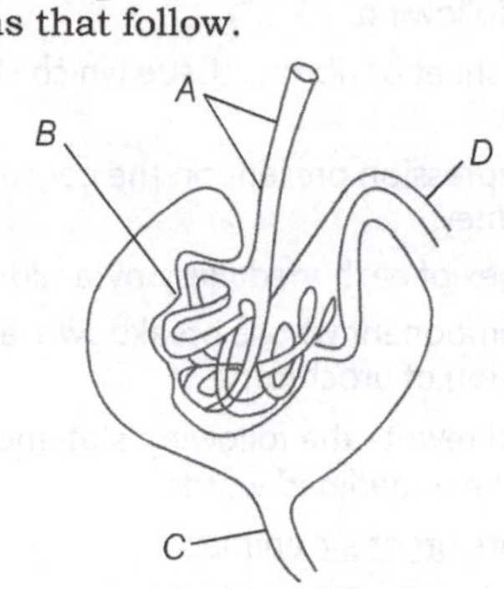

(i) Name the region in the kidney where the given structure is present.
(ii) Name the parts labelled as *A*, *B*, *C* and *D*.
(iii) Out of *A* and *D*, which has wider diameter?
(iv) What is the technical term given to the process occurring in *B* and *C*? Briefly.
(v) Why the urine is thicker in summers?

21. In humans, urine is the excretory product formed in the nephrons of the kidney. This process of formation of urine is called uropoiesis.
(i) What is the ratio of the concentrated filtrate to that of the initial filtrate?
(ii) Why does the standing urine give foul ammonic smell?
(iii) By which process, K^+, Na^+ and H^+ are removed?
(iv) Absorption of water, glucose, amino acids and salts involve which means of transport?
(v) Through which means of transport reabsorption of Na^+ takes place?

For explanations scan the given QR Code

Olympiad Section*

Brain Teasing Questions asked in Previous Olympiads

1 The figure below represents two types of nephrons (labelled as *A* and *B*) observed in mammals. **[IJSO 2021, Dubai]**

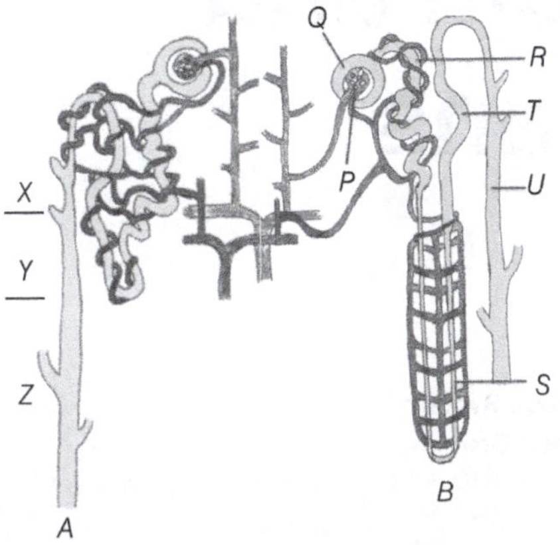

A- Type *A* nephron; *B*- Type *B* nephron; *P*- Glomerulus; *Q*- Bowman's capsule; *R*- Proximal convoluted tubule; *S*- Loop of Henle; *T*- Distal convoluted tubule; *U*- Collecting duct; *X*- Cortex; Y-Outer medulla; *Z*- Inner medulla

Which of the following statements regarding the nephrons is correct?

(a) In comparison to type *A* nephron, the urine produced by a type *B* nephron is likely to be more concentrated
(b) Type *B* nephron is likely to absorb more potassium ions as compared to type *A* nephron
(c) In comparison to type *B* nephron, in type *A* nephron, reabsorption of NaCl leads to subsequent osmosis of water from loop of Henle into the blood
(d) In comparison to type *B* nephron, type *A* nephron is likely to remove poisonous substances from the blood more efficiently

2 In a pilot study, the daily water loss of a group of subjects is monitored under different conditions. Three processes are monitored: diffusion (not sweating) of water through skin, lung ventilation, and urine production. The table shows the results in a random order. **[IJSO 2017, Netherlands]**

	Average daily loss of water in mL/day		
	Mild exercise at 20 °C	Mild exercise at 30 °C	Strenuous exercise at 20 °C
Process I	350	250	650
Process II	50	50	50
Process III	1400	1300	600

Which processes correspond to lung ventilation and urine production?

	Lung ventilation	Urine production
(a)	Process I	Process II
(b)	Process I	Process III
(c)	Process II	Process III
(d)	Process III	Process I

3 Different structures in animals allow maintenance of salt and water balance and excretion of metabolic waste. The functions of a species excretory organs and the composition of its excretions, both depend on the environment they inhabit. In the following table, Column I represents different taxa belonging to the animal kingdom. Column II shows some excretory structures. Select the right option which indicates the correlation between the number in Column I and the letter in Column II. **[IJSO 2015, Republic of Korea]**

	Column I		Column II
1.	Mammalia (Vertebrata)	A.	No excretory organs
2.	Gastropoda (Mollusca)	B.	Kidneys
3.	Hexapoda (Arthropoda)	C.	Malpighian tubules
4.	Asteroidea (Echinodermata)	D.	Nephridia

(a) 1-A, 2-B, 3-C, 4-D
(b) 1-B, 2-D, 3-C, 4-A
(c) 1-B, 2-A, 3-D, 4-C
(d) 1-C, 2-B, 3-D, 4-A

Answers

1. (a) **2.** (b) **3.** (b)

**These questions may or may not be asked in the examination, have been given just for additional practice required for olympiads, scholarship exams etc. For detailed explanations refer Page No. 247.*

CHAPTER 09

Nervous System and Sense Organs

Chapter Inside

- Nervous System
- Divisions of Nervous System
- Different Actions in the Body
- Sense Organs

An essential feature of living beings is their ability to detect changes in their environment. They also exhibit responses to external stimuli. This becomes possible only due to the presence of well-organised network of **neural system**.

It provides point to point connections for quick coordination for receiving and responding to stimuli. The nervous system in human beings is the most advanced in terms of evolution. The detailed structural and functional components of nervous system are discussed in this chapter.

Nervous System

The nervous system is the fastest system of communication within the body. It enables us to think, remember, react and to figure out the things around us. The nervous system performs the functions like control and coordination of all parts of the body, stores experiences as memory and maintains the internal environment of the body.

Neurons

The neural system consists of highly specialised cells called **neurons**. These are considered as the longest cell of the body. Neurons are the structural and functional unit of the nervous system. Human neural system has about 100 billion neurons. Fully formed neurons never divide and once a neuron is dead, it cannot be replaced.

Structure of Neuron

Structurally, a neuron is composed of three major parts

1. Cell Body (Cyton/Perikaryon/Soma)

Like a typical cell, it consists of cytoplasm, nucleus and cell membrane. The cytoplasm has typical cell organelles like mitochondria, Golgi apparatus, etc., with certain **granular bodies, neurofibrils, neurotubules** and **Nissl's granules**. Neurofibrils help in the transmission of impulses (a wave of disturbance or irritability). Nissl's granules contain RNA and proteins. Centrosomes are absent in cell body because neurons donot have the ability to divide.

2. Dendrites (Dendrons)

These are shorter, tapering and much branched cytoplasmic processes that project out of the cell body. They also contain Nissl's granules and are one to several in number. They conduct nerve impulses towards the cell body.

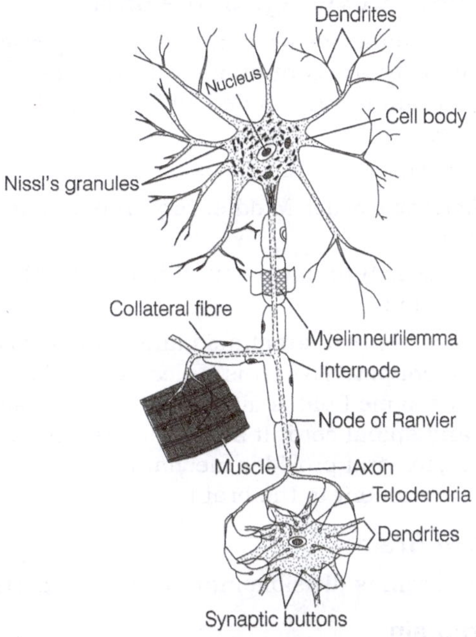

Structure of a neuron

3. Axon

It is a single, very long fibre-like process of uniform thickness. The axon contains neurofibrils and neurotubules but does not have Nissl's granules, cell organelles and granular bodies. In most neurons, axon is surrounded by a **myelin sheath**. This myelin sheath provides insulation to the axon. It is covered by the outermost thin sheath called **neurolemma**. The gaps between the two adjacent myelin sheaths are called **nodes of Ranvier**. Some axons may have side branches called **collaterals**. The axon ends (distal end) in a group of branches known as the **telodendria**. Formation of bunch of telodendria at the tip of neuron is called **terminal arborisation**. The Telodeudria of the axon meet the dendrites of another neuron to form a **synapse**.

Each branch terminates as a bulb-like structure called synaptic knobs, which possess mitochondria and secretory vesicles (containing chemicals called neurotransmitters). The axons transmit nerve impulses away from the cell body through a synapse.

Note Dendrites and axon are collectively called neurites. These are formally called the processes of neurons.

Types of Neuron

Neurons are of following three main types

(i) **Sensory neuron** It transmits information from the body to the central nervous system, i.e. brain and spinal cord.

(ii) **Motor neuron** It transmits information from the central nervous system to effectors such as muscles and glands.

(iii) **Relay** (association or connecting) **neuron** It serves as a link between the sensory and motor neurons. It is mainly found in brain and spinal cord.

Nerves

These are thread-like white structures which emerge out from the brain and spinal cord and branch out to usually all parts of the body. The aggregate of nerve cells is called **ganglion**. It is formed of a bundle of nerve fibres (axons of separate neurons) being enclosed in a tube-like sheath. Nerves are of following three main types

(i) **Sensory nerve** It consists of only sensory fibres.

(ii) **Motor nerve** It consists of only motor fibres.

(iii) **Mixed nerve** It consists of both sensory and motor fibres.

Transmission of Nerve Impulse

An impulse is a self propagated electrical current that travels from one end to another of a neuron for the passage of a message. All the information from the environment is detected by the **receptors** (sense organs) in the body. The neurons of the receptors transfer this information to the **Central Nervous System** (CNS) for the appropriate response through **sensory neurons** or sensory nerves. The information is processed in CNS and then information for appropriate response is send to effector organs through **motor neurons** or **motor nerves**.

At micro level the conduction of nerve impulse occur due to the movement of Na^+ and K^+ ions. The resting stage of a nerve fibre called polarised state which becomes depolarised due to sudden incoming of Na^+ ions. This states is immediately required by the expulsion of K^+. The maintenance of polarised state is done with the help of a sodium-potassium pump. ATP is used in the working of this pump.

The complete pathway followed by the nerve impulse in the body is given below

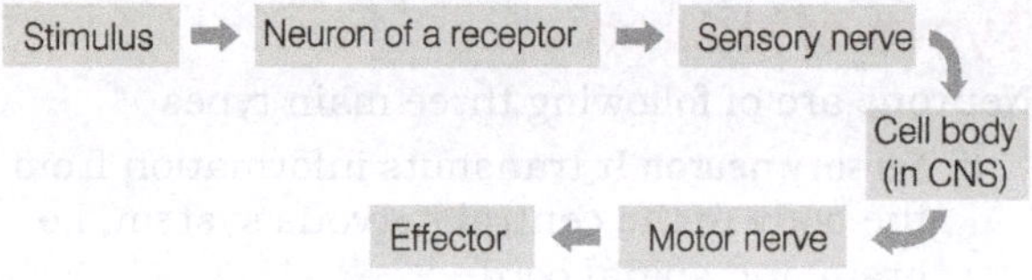

Pathway for nerve impulse

Synapse

It is the point of contact between the nerve endings of one neuron (axon) and the dendrites of another neuron, separated by a fine gap. This gap is called **synaptic cleft**.

When the impulse reaches the terminal end of an axon, **neurotransmitters** (the chemicals such as acetylcholine) are released into the synaptic cleft.

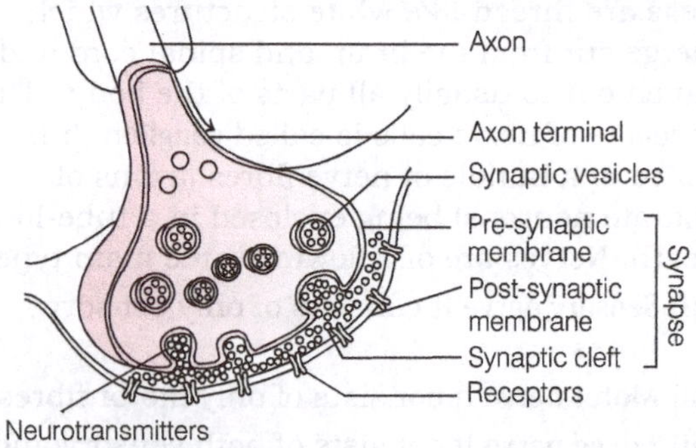

Axon terminal and synapse

These neurotransmitters set a nerve impulse in the dendrites and travel across the receptors present on the membrane of the next nerve ending.

Check Your LEARNING...

1 Give two functions of nervous system.
2 Which part of the neuron does not contain Nissl's granules?
3 Where neurolemma is found?
4 What are the synaptic knobs?
5 What does the aggregate of nerve cells called?
6 What are neurotransmitters?

Divisions of Nervous System

Nervous system is divided into two main divisions, i.e. Central Nervous System (CNS) and Peripheral Nervous System (PNS).

Central Nervous System (CNS)

It is the integrating and commanding centre of the nervous system. CNS is mainly comprised of two parts, i.e. brain and spinal cord.

1. Brain

The brain is the central information processing organ of our body and acts as the 'command and control system'of all body activities. It is the anterior most part of the central neural system, which is located in the cranium (cranial cavity) of the skull. It weighs about 1.4 kg and is made up of approximately 86 billion neurons.

Protective Coverings of the Brain

Inside the skull, the brain is protected by **meninges**. The meninges are continuous with the spinal cord. Human brain is surrounded by following 3 meninges

(i) **Duramater** Tough fibrous outermost covering.

(ii) **Arachnoid mater** Middle, very thin and delicate layer.

(iii) **Piamater** Innermost very thin and highly vascular.

The space between arachnoid and piamater is filled with **cerebrospinal fluid**. It is a clear and colourless fluid. The same fluid is also found in the spaces of brain and spinal cord. It acts as a cushion for the brain cortex and provides mechanical protection and nourishment to the brain.

Parts of Brain

Human brain is divisible into three main parts

(i) Forebrain

It is the largest part of the brain and is divided into olfactory lobe, cerebrum and diencephalon. All of these are discussed below

(a) **Olfactory lobes** These are paired lobes and functionally related with the sense of smell.

(b) **Cerebrum** It is the largest, most complex and most developed part of the human brain. Hence, it is considered as the **seat of intelligence**. It is divided into two main parts (halves) known as **cerebral hemispheres**. Each cerebral hemisphere is hollow from interior and has two regions, i.e. **outer cortex** and **inner medulla**.

The outer (cortex) portion is greyish in colour, containing all the cell bodies of the neuron. It is also known as **grey matter**. This grey matter mainly consists of cell bodies of non-myelinated neurons.

The large grooves formed by the layers of grey matter are called **gyri** and the small folds in it are called **sulci**.

The inner (medulla) portion is composed of **white matter**, which is mainly consist of cell bodies of myelinated neurons.

The two cerebral hemispheres are interconnected by a sheet of fibres known as **corpus callosum**. It is meant to transfer the information from one cerebral hemisphere to the another corpus callosum is found only in mammals.

Cerebrum enables us to think, invent, plan, memorise, reason, logic, etc. It mainly controls all the voluntary actions. It also contains subconscious mind where past experiences are stored.

(c) **Diencephalon** It consists of two major parts, **thalamus** (a major coordinating centre for sensory and motor signalling) and **hypothalamus** (mainly controls body temperature, urge for eating, drinking, anger, pleasure and actions of pituitary gland).

(ii) Midbrain

It is located in between the thalamus/hypothalamus (of forebrain) and pons (of hindbrain). It is the small tubular part (about 2cm long) of brain, which helps to relay information for vision and hearing.

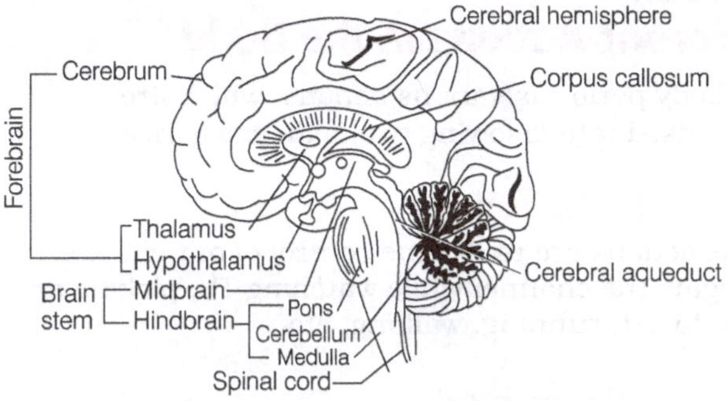

Diagram showing sagittal section of the human brain

(iii) Hindbrain

It further consists of following three main parts

(a) **Cerebellum** It is situated at the base, under the cerebrum of forebrain. It is also known as the **little brain**. It is composed of outer cortex and inner medulla consisting of grey and white matter, respectively. It has no convolutions but has numerous furrows. The main function of cerebellum is to coordinate the muscular activity and maintains the balance of the body.

(b) **Pons** It is located below the cerebellum and is responsible for carrying impulses from cerebellum to cerebrum. It also helps in the regulation of breathing movements.

(c) **Medulla oblongata** It is the lowermost portion of the hindbrain situated at the base of the skull. It continues behind as the spinal cord.
Its main function is to control the activities of internal organs like respiration, gastric secretions, beating of heart, peristaltic movements, etc.

The medulla oblongata, the pons and the midbrain form **brain stem** which connects forebrain to spinal cord.

Note
- Any damage to the medulla oblongata may lead to death of a person. The projecting process of the vertebra axis in the neck pierces the medulla under heavy shock, as a result of which involuntary actions such as breathing and heartbeats are stopped.
- **Electroencephalogram** (EEG) is an instrument which records the waves of brain.

2. Spinal Cord

It forms the posterior part of the CNS, running mid-dorsally in the neural canal of the vertebral column. In an adult, the spinal cord is about 42-45 cm long. Its diameter varies at different stages of growth. The spinal cord is formed of two types of nervous tissue, i.e. grey matter and white matter. The inner grey matter is surrounded by white matter. Simply, their arrangement is opposite to the one seen in brain.

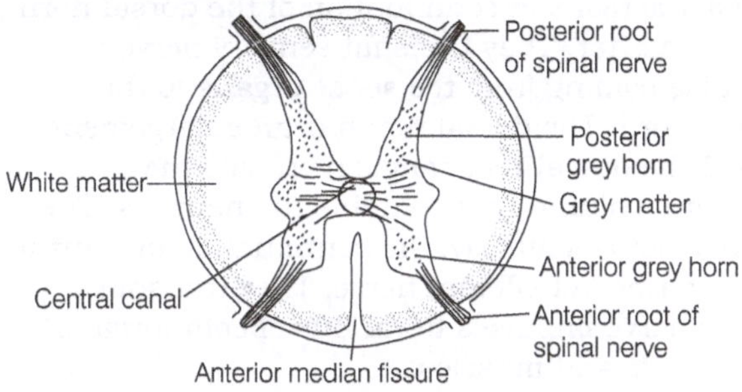

TS of spinal cord

The spinal nerve tracts are divisible into two parts *viz.* **ascending** (conducting sensory impulses towards brain) and **descending** (conducting motor impulses from brain) tracts. Spinal cord conducts impulses to and from the brain and controls most of the reflex activities. It also provides a mean of communication between spinal nerves and the brain.

Check Your LEARNING...

1. Which part is responsible for the protection of brain?
2. Name the fluid present in a space between arachnoid and piameter.
3. Name an instrument which records the waves of brain.
4. How does the spinal cord differ from the brain, in terms of arrangement of grey matter and white matter?

Peripheral Nervous System (PNS)

This system of brain mainly consists of all the nerves, which transmit impulses to and from the central nervous system.

It is sub-divided into two main divisions as follows

1. Somatic Nervous System (SNS)

It contains nerves that relay information in the form of impulses from CNS to the skeletal muscles. On the basis of their origin, nerves of SNS are further categorised as **cranial nerves** (arise from brain) and **spinal nerves** (arise from spinal cord). Cranial nerves are either **sensory** (e.g. olfactory, auditory), **motor** (e.g. innervating eye muscles) or **mixed** (e.g face, tongue) nerves. On the other hand, every spinal nerve is mixed nerve, having both sensory and motor fibres.

There are **12 pairs of cranial nerves** and **31 pairs of spinal nerves** in humans. Spinal nerves are classified into five groups, i.e. **cervical** (8 pairs in the neck), **thoracic** (12 pairs in thorax), **lumbar** (5 pairs in abdomen), **sacral** (5 pairs in hip region) and **coccygeal** (1pair in tail region).

Each spinal nerve is formed by the union of the two roots (dorsal and ventral) arising from the spinal cord.

The **dorsal root** is a continuation of the dorsal horn of grey matter. They transmit sensory nerve impulse coming from the sense organs to the spinal cord. The dorsal root has an enlargement called the dorsal root ganglion outside the vertebral column that contains the neurons. The **ventral root** is similarly, the continuation of ventral horn, formed of efferent nerve. They transmit motor nerve impulses to various effector organs like glands and muscles.

2. Autonomous Nervous System (ANS)

It consists of **sympathetic** and **parasympathetic** nervous systems and controls the involuntary actions of the internal organs. Nerves of sympathetic system arise from the spinal cord between the neck and the waist regions. The parasympathetic system is located at two places, one anteriorly in the head and neck and the other posteriorly in the sacral region. The sympathetic nervous system prepares the body for violent action against abnormal conditions.

Parasympathetic system is more concerned with re-establishing normal conditions after the violent act is over.

Functions of sympathetic nervous system	Functions of parasympathetic nervous system
Vasoconstriction in general and vasodilation of brain, heart, lungs and skeletal muscles.	Vasodilation of coronary vessels.
Dilates pupil.	Constricts pupil.
Increases lacrimal gland secretion.	Inhibits lacrimal gland secretion.
Inhibits salivary glands and digestive glands.	Stimulates secretion.
Accelerates heartbeat.	Retards heartbeat.
Dilates trachea, bronchi and lungs.	Contract trachea, bronchi and lungs.
Inhibits gut peristalsis.	Stimulates gut peristalsis.
Contracts anal sphincter.	Relaxes anal sphincter.
Relaxes urinary bladder.	Contracts urinary bladder.
Increases adrenal secretion.	Inhibits adrenal secretion.
Blood sugar increases (glucagon).	Blood sugar inhibits (insulin).
Semen ejaculation increases.	Increases external genitalia excitement and sex drive.
Increases sweat secretion.	Inhibits sweat secretion.
Contracts arrector pili.	Relaxes arrector pili.

Different Actions in the Body

Our body performs various actions, which are categorised into following two main categories

Voluntary Actions

These actions are under the control of our will, i.e. changing the channel while watching TV, picking an apple to eat, running, walking, etc.

Involuntary Actions

These actions are not under the control of our will and are performed instantaneously. These actions are therefore, called **reflexes,** e.g. flushing of tears, when some particles fall into an eye, withdrawal of hand after touching hot thing, shivering in cold, etc.

Differences between Involuntary and Voluntary Actions

Involuntary actions (Reflexes)	Voluntary actions
Mainly self-protective due to environment.	Fulfilment of a desired goal.
Initiated by some stimulus like touch, pain, pressure, heat, light, etc.	Initiated by a willing thought.

Involuntary actions (Reflexes)	**Voluntary actions**
Involve muscles and glands.	Involve only muscle.
Commands originate mostly in the spinal cord and autonomic nervous system and a few in the brain as well.	Commands originate in the brain.

Reflex Action and Reflex Arc

The entire process of response to a peripheral nervous stimulation that occurs involuntarily, i.e. without conscious effort or thought and requires the involvement of a part of the central nervous system is called a **reflex action**. The nervous pathway taken by nerve impulses in a reflex action is called **reflex arc**.

Mechanism of Reflex Action

(i) The reflex pathway comprises at least one afferent (receptor) neuron and one efferent (effector) neuron arranged in a series.

(ii) The afferent neuron receives signal from a sensory organ and transmits the impulse *via.* a dorsal nerve root into the CNS (at the level of spinal cord).

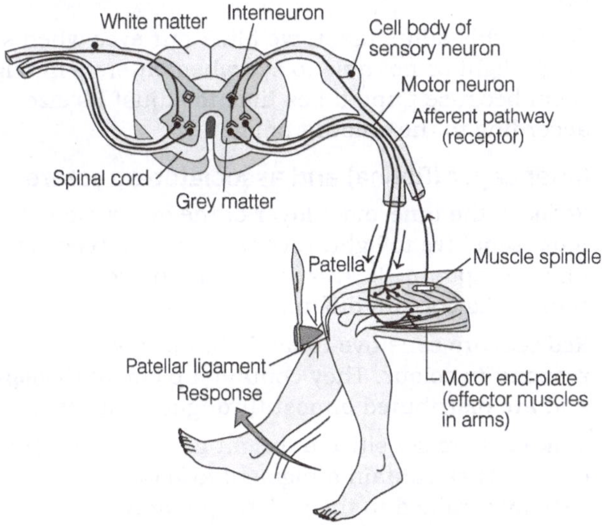

Diagrammatic representation of a reflex action

(iii) The efferent neuron then carries signals from CNS to the effector. The stimulus and response thus, form a reflex arc, e.g. knee jerk reflex as shown above in the figure. This general pathway is depicted below

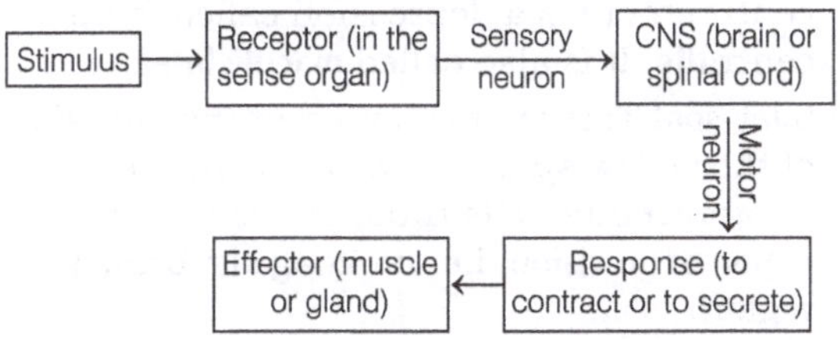

Types of Reflexes

Reflexes are categorised as follows

(i) **Natural** (unconditioned) **reflexes** These are the inborn reflexes and are inherited from parents, e.g. blinking of eyes, breastfeeding, swallowing, coughing, salivation, sneezing, withdrawal of hand on touching hot things, etc.

(ii) **Conditioned** (acquired) **reflexes** These reflexes are acquired after birth or adopted during the course of the lifetime, e.g. playing a musical instrument, applying brakes to vehicles, giving hand to a signal, using keys of the keyboard while working, tying shoe laces, wild animals trained in circus to perform acts, standing up when teacher enters the class, etc.

Differences between Unconditioned and Conditioned Reflexes

Unconditioned reflex (Inherited)	**Conditioned reflex** (Acquired)
Inborn, requiring no previous experience.	Developed by experience or learning.
Directly related to the stimulus.	Brought about by a condition totally different from the direct initial stimulus.
Similar in all humans (similar among all individuals of any one species).	Differs in different individuals, subjected to learning and experience.

Check Your LEARNING...

1. Name the different connections of spinal nerve.
2. Which part of nervous system helps in dilation of pupil?
3. Mention the types of reflexes involved in a reflex arc.
4. Give an example of acquired reflex.

Sense Organs

The sense organs enable us to detect all types of changes that occur in the environment. These organs send appropriate signals to the CNS, where all the inputs are processed and analysed.

The most complex sensory receptor consists of numerous **sense cells, sensory neurons** and **associated accessory structures**, e.g. eye (sensory organ for vision), the **ear** (sensory organ for hearing) and skin (touch, temperature).

Eye

In human beings, the pair of eyes are the organ of sight and vision. The eyes are located in the protective, deep bony cavities of the skull known as **eye sockets** or **orbits** on the front side of the head.

Main structural components of eye are as follows

(i) **Eyebrows** These are the arched eminences of skin, above the eyes, which bear hairs. They prevent rainwater or dust, etc., from entering into the eyes.

(ii) **Eyelids** These are the upper and lower movable part of the eyes which prevent the entry of dust particles into the eyes.

(iii) **Tear glands** (Lacrimal glands) They are located at the upper sideward portion of the orbit. Six to twelve ducts of the gland pour the secretion over the front surface. The tears help in keeping front surface of the eye lubricated and clean by washing away the dust particles. It contains an enzyme called **lysozyme**, having antiseptic property which helps in killing germs (like bacteria).Tears also communicate with emotions, e.g. you cry when you are sad, feel alone or extremely happy.

Structure of Eye : Eyeball

Human eyeball is nearly spherical in structure. It consists of three concentric layers, i.e. sclera, choroid and retina.

Outer (Sclerotic) Layer and associated structure

It is made up of tough fibrous tissue and is white in colour. It contains dense connective tissue, which maintains the shape of the eyeball.

The front white portion of the eye is the sclerotic layer, which further bulges out in the front and becomes transparent.

This transparent portion covers the coloured part of the eye and is known as **cornea**. Cornea lacks blood vessels thus, it can be easily removed and replaced in case of eye donations.

The entire surface of sclera is covered by a thin membrane called **conjunctiva**. When this membrane gets infected by a virus, it turns red and this is called **conjunctivitis**.

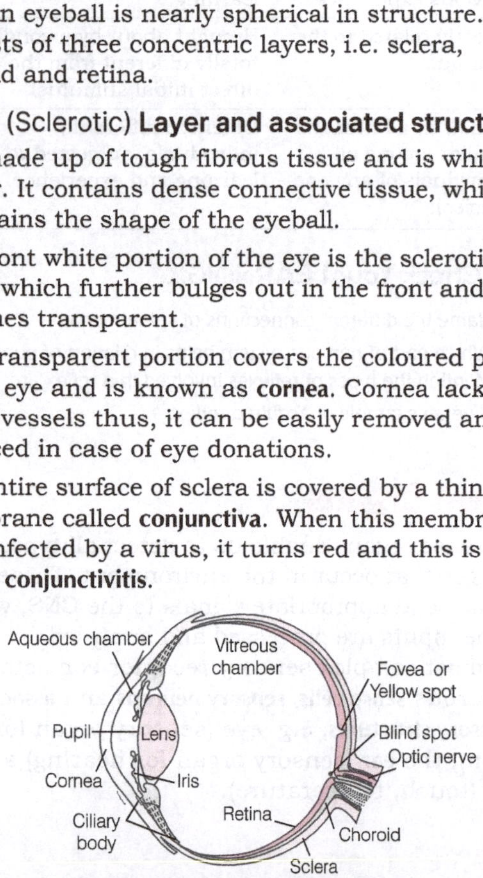

Diagram showing different parts of an eye

Middle (Choroid) Layer and associated structure

This layer is richly supplied with blood vessels in order to provide nourishment to the eyes. It is located beneath the sclera. It is thin over the posterior part of the eye, but becomes thick over the anterior part of eye to form **ciliary body**. It also contains a dark coloured pigment called **melanin**. It helps in preventing light rays from reflecting and scattering inside the eye.

The **eyeball** contains a transparent, biconvex crystalline structure called **lens**. Smooth muscles of ciliary body hold the lens in position by suspensory ligament and also help in altering the shape of the lens.

Iris is the extension of the choroid layer, which forms a pigmented circle of muscular layer attached to the ciliary body in front of the lens. Pigment of iris is responsible for the colour of the eye, i.e. either blue, black or brown.

Pupil is an aperture surrounded by the iris. The movement of muscle fibres of iris controls the size of pupil and regulates the amount of light entering the eye.

Due to this adjustment, we blink our eyes when see bright light or not able to see when enters a dimlight room because pupil takes time to adjust its size according to the amount of light.

Inner Layer (Retina) and associated structure

Retina is the innermost layer of the eye, which is most sensitive to light. It consists of two types of photoreceptor cells known as **rods** and **cones**. Both of these cells contain different photopigments.

Rod cells are sensitive to dimlight but does not respond to colour. They contain a pigment **rhodopsin** and are distributed almost throughout the retina.

Cone cells are sensitive to bright light and respond to colour. They contain a pigment **iodopsin** and are usually confined to the yellow spot only.

Retina contains 2 specialised spots over it. These are

(i) **Yellow spot** The distribution of rods and cones is not uniform inside the retina. Yellow spot is the area containing the maximum number of photoreceptor cells (mainly cones), therefore it is known as the **region of brightest vision**. At its centre, there is a depression called fovea centralis. It is also called **macula lutea.**

(ii) **Blind spot** This spot is found at the lateral side of the yellow spot. It does not contain any photoreceptor cells thus, this is known as the **region of no vision**, i.e. no image is formed in this region.

Spaces or Chambers of the Eye

The eye contains two chambers, i.e.

(i) **Aqueous chamber** The space between the cornea and lens is called the **aqueous** or **front chamber**. It contains a thin watery fluid called **aqueous humour**.

It helps in keeping the lens moist and prevents it from physical shock. It helps to refract light from the eye.

(ii) **Vitreous chamber** The space between the lens and retina is called the vitreous chamber. It is filled with a transparent gel-like substance called the **vitreous humour**. It helps to protect the retina. It also helps in maintaining the shape of the eyeball.

Mechanism of Vision

The vision in human eyes is binocular or stereoscopic vision, i.e. both the eyes can be focussed on a common object simultaneously. **Stereoscopic or Binocular vision** is formed by the overlapping of images (from both eyes) in the brain to give a three-dimensional effect. Besides humans, it is acquired by monkeys and apes. In the process an image is formed on the retina by successive refractions at the cornea, the aqueous humour, lens and vitreous humour.

The light-sensitive cells in the retina get activated upon illumination and generate electrical signals. These signals are sent to the brain via. the optic nerves. The brain interprets these signals and finally processes the information so that we can perceive objects. For a person of perfect vision, the range of clear vision is around 25 cm. The image formed on retina is inverted and real.

Light and Dark Adaptation

When a person enters a dark room from a brightly lighted area, the rhodopsin pigment of the rods gets regenerated which was earlier broken down due to bright light. It dilates the pupil and allows more light to enter the eye. This is called **dark adaptation.**

When a person moves from a dark room into a brightly lighted area, he experiences a dazzling effect for a short period of time. This is because the rhodopsin pigments gets bleached and their occurs contriction of pupil to reduce the light entering the eyes. This is called **light adaptation.**

Accommodation of Eye

The ability of eye to change its focus so as to see an object clearly is known as accommodation of eye. It is achieved by changing the curvature of lens by ciliary muscles. To see the distant objects, lens become flat and thin. To see the nearby objects, lens become rounded.

Common Defects of the Eye

The defects due to which the person cannot see the object distinctly and comfortably, are called **defects of vision**. The main defects of vision are discussed below

Myopia (Short Sightedness)

It is the defect in which a person cannot see distant objects clearly but can see nearby objects clearly. In this case, image forms in front of retina and not on the retina.

Causes This defect arises due to the decrease in focal length of the lens either by excessive curvature of eye lens or elongation of the eyeball (lens is too curved). As a result, the image is formed before retina.

Correction This defect can be corrected by using concave lens of appropriate power (negative power lens).

A concave lens of suitable power will bring the image back on the retina, thus, the defect is corrected.

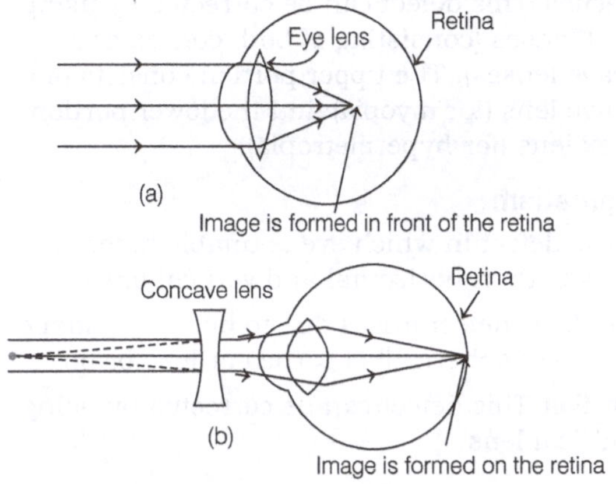

(a) Myopic eye, (b) Correction for myopic eye

Hypermetropia (Long Sightedness)

It is the defect in which a person cannot see nearby objects clearly but can see distant objects clearly. In this, image forms beyond the retina. It is also called hypermetropia or **hyperopia**.

Causes This defect arises due to following reasons

(i) Focal length of eye lens becomes large because lens is too flat.

(ii) Eyeball becomes too short so that the image is formed behind retina.

Correction Hypermetropia can be corrected by using convex lens of appropriate power (positive power lens). Hence, a convex lens of suitable power will bring the image back on retina, thus the defect is corrected.

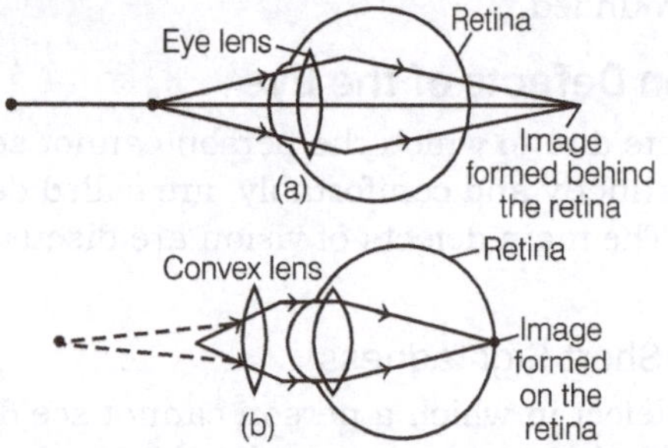

(a) Hypermetropic eye, (b) Correction for hypermetropic eye

Presbyopia (Old Age Long Sightedness)

This condition is found more commonly in old age people. In this defect, one cannot read comfortably and clearly. For most people, the near point gradually precedes away. Sometimes, a person may suffer from both myopia and presbyopia.

Causes This defect arises due to following reasons
(i) Weakness of ciliary muscles.
(ii) Hardening of eye lens.

Correction This defect can be corrected by using bifocal lenses (consisting of both convex and concave lenses). The upper portion consists of a concave lens (for myopia) and the lower portion of convex lens (for hypermetropia).

Astigmatism

It is the defect in which eye is unable to focus objects both in horizontal and vertical lines clearly.

Causes This defect arises due to imperfect shape (not perfect spherical) of cornea or lens or both.

Correction This defect can be corrected by using cylindrical lens.

Cataract

It is the condition in which crystalline lens of eye becomes milky and cloudy due to the growth of membrane over it. It generally occurs among people at an old age. This causes partial or complete loss of vision. It is possible to restore vision in this condition through the **cataract surgery**.

Check Your LEARNING...

1 What is the function of eyebrows?
2 Which muscle controls the movement of eye lens?
3 Why our eyes are of different colours?
4 Name the organisms possessing stereoscopic vision.
5 Mention the cause of presbyopia.

The Ear

Human ear is concerned with two functions, sensory functions such as hearing and maintenance of body balance. This organ receives sound waves during hearing. The ear analyses these sound waves for examining the pitch, intensity, quality and direction of these waves.

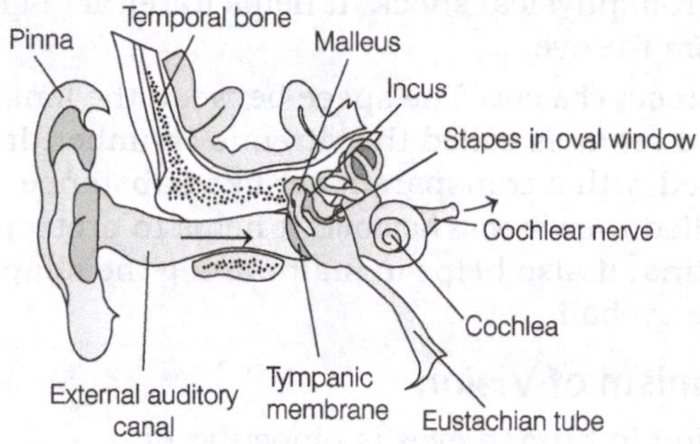

Diagramatic view of human ear

Structure of Ear

Each ear is divided into three main divisions as follows

Outer (External) Ear

This portion of ear mainly consists of **pinna** and **auditory canal** leading to the eardrum. It helps in the collection of soundwaves from environment. Outer ear also contains **ceruminous glands** which secrete ear wax or cerumen.

Middle Ear

This portion of the ear contains three ossicles or bones called **malleus** (hammer), **incus** (anvil) and **stapes** (stirrup), which are attached to each other in chain-like fashion. One end of hammer is attached to the eardrum (tympanic membrane) and the other free end is attached to the oval window of inner ear.
It opens into the **Eustachian tube**, which connects with the pharynx and maintains the pressure on each sides of the eardrum. An infection in throat may also lead to ear infections due to this connection.

Inner (Internal) Ear

This portion of ear consists of a labyrinth, i.e. fluid-filled chambers within the temporal bone of the skull. The fluid within the chambers of membranous labyrinth is called **endolymph**. The membranous labyrinth is divided into two main parts

(i) **Cochlea** It is a coiled portion of the labyrinth and has around two and half turns. Its inner winding cavity is divided into three parallel canals separated by membranes. Out of these, the middle canal contains areas, which have auditory sense cells called **organ of Corti** (for hearing).

An extracellular fluid called **'perilymph'** is found within the cochlea containing hair cells. The impulses from the cochlea of the ear are transmitted to the brain through **auditory nerve**.

(ii) **Semicircular canals** These are the set of three semicircular, interconnected tubes located inside each ear. Each canal widens to form **ampulla**. The ampulla contains sense cells (cristae), which provide dynamic equilibrium to body. Each canal is filled with the fluid called **endolymph** and contains motion sensor cells within the fluid.

A short branch joins the base of semicircular canals to cochlea. It has two parts *viz.* **utriculus** and **sacculus**. Together, these two parts constitute the **vestibule**. It contains sensory cells which provide static balance to the body .

Mechanism of the Hearing

Pinna (of outer ear) collects the sound waves from the surroundings. These waves pass through the **ear canal** (auditory canal) and fall on the **eardrum** (tympanum) or **tympanic membrane.**

The eardrum starts vibrating back and forth rapidly. These vibrations are amplified several times by the three bones in the middle ear and then these are passed to the liquid (endolymph) in the cochlea. Due to this, the liquid in the cochlea begins to vibrate and the pressure variations are turned into electrical signals by the cochlea. These electrical signals are carried by auditory nerve to the brain and the brain interprets them as sound and we get the sensation of hearing.

Role of Ear in Maintaining Balance of Body

When we move our head in different directions, the fluid inside the semicircular canal is also shaken, which is pushed against the sensory hair cells. This sends the nerve impulse through the nerve fibres to the brain (through the auditory nerve). The sensory cells in semicircular canal are concerned with the **dynamic equilibrium**, i.e. when body is in motion. The similar sensory cells are located in two parts of semicircular canal, i.e. **utriculus** and **sacculus**. These are concerned with the **static equilibrium** of the body, i.e. balance with respect to gravity.

Check Your LEARNING...

1. Name the three ossicles found in middle ear.
2. Name the fluid found in the chambers within temporal bone of the skull.
3. Give the location of perilymph in inner ear.
4. State the function of pinna.
5. Which part of inner ear converts the pressure variations into electrical signals?

QUiCK Revision

- **Nervous system** provides an organised network of point to point connections for quick neural coordination and fastest means of communication.
- The nervous system in all animals is composed of structural and functional units called **neurons** which can detect, receive and transmit different types of stimuli.
- **Human neural system** is divided into Central Nervous System (CNS) and Peripheral Nervous System (PNS).
- **Central Nervous System** (CNS) includes brain and spinal cord.
- **Human brain** is protected by cranium or skull and meninges. The meninges have three layers, i.e. **duramater**, **arachnoid** and **piamater**.
- **Cerebrum** is the largest part of human brain. It is the seat of memory, thought, reason, logic, etc.
- **Thalamus** is a part of diencephalon of the forebrain. It is a relay centre to cerebrum for pain and pressure.
- **Hypothalamus** is located below the thalamus. It controls the body temperature and controls the pituitary gland.
- **Cerebellum** is the part of brain which controls coordination of muscular movements.
- **Medulla oblongata** controls the involuntary activities like heartbeat, breathing, etc.
- **Spinal cord** is concerned with reflex action. In spinal cord, the grey matter lies inside and white matter is outside.
- **Peripheral Nervous System** (PNS) consists of nerves which transmit impulse to and from the CNS system. It is further divided into SNS and ANS.
- **Somatic Nervous System** (SNS) consists of 12 pairs of cranial nerves and 31 pairs of spinal nerves.
- **Autonomic Nervous System** (ANS) consists of sympathetic and parasympathetic nerve cords.
- **Reflex action** includes nerve bodies associated with CNS and its involuntary response to PNS. The pathway during reflex action is called **reflex arc**. These are of two kinds, (i) natural or unconditioned reflexes, (ii) conditioned reflexes.
- **Natural reflexes** are inborn, e.g. knee jerk.
- **Conditioned reflexes** are complicated and depend on experiences, e.g. applying brakes on seeing an obstacle.
- **Sensory organs** are the receptors which detect changes in the environment with the help of sensory receptors.
- **Human eyes** are the organ of sight which work on the principle of photographic camera. Eyebrows, eyelids and lacrimal glands are accessory organs associated with eye for its proper functioning.
- **Disorders** related to eye are myopia, hypermetropia, cataract, presbyopia and astigmatism.
- **Human ears** are a pair of statoacoustic organs meant for both balancing and hearing. Each ear is divided into external, middle and inner ear.

Chapter Practice

Section-I

1 Mark Questions

1. Name the following.
   (i) The cell body of a nerve cell. [2013]
   (ii) The three membranous coverings of the human brain. [Semester II 2022]
   (iii) The part of brain associated with memory. [2014]
   (iv) The part of brain that carries impulse from one hemisphere of the cerebellum to the other. [2016]
   (v) The layer of the eyeball that forms the transparent cornea. [2018]
   (vi) The covering that maintains the shape of the eyeball.
   (vii) The layer of the eyeball that provides nourishment to eye. [2019]
   (viii) The pigmented layer present beneath the sclera.
   (ix) The nerve that transmit impulses to the brain from eye. [Semester II 2022]
   (x) The kind of lens required to correct myopia. [2017]
   (xi) The ear ossicle, which is attached to the tympanum. [2014]
   (xii) The nerve that transmit impulse to the brain from ear. [Semester II 2022]

Ans. (i) Cyton
(ii) Pia mater, arachnoid and dura mater
(iii) Cerebrum (iv) Pons varolii
(v) Sclera (vi) Sclera (outermost layer)
(vii) Choroid layer (viii) Choroid
(ix) Optic nerve (x) Concave lens
(xi) Malleus or Hammer (xii) Auditory nerve

2. Correct and rewrite the following statements by changing the underlined words.
   (i) The outermost layer of meninges is piamater. [2016]
   (ii) Gyri and sulci are the folds of cerebellum.
   (iii) Maintaining balance of body and coordinating muscular activities is carried out by the cerebrum. [2019]
   (iv) Dendrites are the efferent processes of neuron.
   (v) The outermost layer of eye is choroid.
   (vi) The part of eye which can be donated from a clinically dead person is retina. [2019]
   (vii) Deafness is caused due to the rupturing of the pinna.

Ans. (i) The outermost layer of meninges is duramater.
(ii) Gyri and sulci are the folds of cerebrum. Cerebellum only contains gyri
(iii) Maintaining balance of body and coordinating muscular activities is carried out by the cerebellum.
(iv) Dendrites are the afferent processes of neuron.
(v) The outermost layer of eye is sclera.
(vi) The part of eye which can be donated from a clinically dead person is cornea.
(vii) Deafness is caused due to the rupturing of the eardrum (tympanic membrane).

3. Give biological reasons for the following.
   (i) A person after consuming alcohol walks clumsily. [2014]
   Or An alcoholic person walks unsteadily when drunk. [2014, 10]
   (ii) Injury to medulla oblongata leads to death. [2016, 07]
   (iii) The hand automatically shows the direction to turn a cycle without thinking. [2013]
   (iv) A person from bright sunlight outside enters a poorly light room and feels blinded for a short while.
   (v) We cannot distinguish colours in moonlight. [2014]
   (vi) We should not put sharp objects into our ears. [2018]
   (vii) Throat infections can lead to ear infections. [2013, 08]

Ans. (i) An alcoholic or drunk person walks clumsily because of the effect of alcohol on cerebellum. This is because cerebellum is mainly responsible for the coordination of muscular activities and maintaining the balance of body.
(ii) Medulla oblongata has pneumotaxis centre which controls breathing rate, heartrate, etc. Thus, any injury to this part of brain becomes fatal.
(iii) While riding a cycle, the hands automatically show the directions to turn a cycle without thinking this happens due to conditioned reflex which is adopted during the course of lifetime.
(iv) (a) Regeneration of the visual purple or rhodopsin (the pigment of the rods), which was earlier broken down due to bright light.
(b) Dilation of the pupil permitting more light to enter the eyes.
(v) Moonlight is dimlight during which cone cells of our eye do not function well therefore, the colour is not well perceived. Rod cells are mainly active in moonlight.
(vi) We should not put sharp objects into our ears as they can damage our eardrum (tympanic membrane) and can lead to deafness.
(vii) Eustachian tube connects with the pharynx. Thus, infection in throat may also lead to ear infections.

4. (i) Match the following columns.

Column I	Column II
A. Nerve impulse	1. Chemicals involved in the transmission of impulses at synapses.
B. Synaptic cleft	2. Gap between the pre-synaptic and post-synaptic neurons.
C. Neurotransmitters	3. An electrical wave-like response of a neuron to a stimulation.

(ii) Match the following columns.

Column I	Column II
A. Neurotransmitter	1. Myelinated fibre
B. Insulating sheath	2. Acetylcholine
C. Nodes of Ranvier	3. Myelinated sheath
D. Neurofibrils	4. Cyton

(iii) Match the following columns.

Column I	Column II
A. Diencephalon	1. Forebrain
B. Cerebrum	2. Spinal cord
C. Cerebellum	3. Hypothalamus
D. Central canal	4. Hindbrain

(iv) Match the following columns.

Column I	Column II
A. Cranial nerves	1. Voluntary action
B. Autonomous nervous system	2. Involuntary action
C. Watching TV	3. Somatic nervous system
D. Dilation of pupil (of eye)	4. Sympathetic nervous system

(v) Match the following columns.

Column I	Column II
A. External layer of eyeball	1. Choroid
B. Inner layer of eyeball	2. Orbits
C. Middle layer of eyeball	3. Sclera
D. Socket of the skull	4. Retina

Ans. (i) A–3, B–2, C–1 (ii) A–2, B–3, C–1, D–4
(iii) A–3, B–1, C–4, D–2 (iv) A–3, B–4, C–1, D–2
(v) A–3, B–4, C–1, D–2

5. Choose the correct answer from the four options given below.

(i) Which of the following is the functional unit of the nervous system?
(a) Neuron (b) Perikaryon
(c) Axon (d) Cyton

Ans. (a)

(ii) A structure of neuron comprises of
(a) cell body, synaptic knob, ganglia
(b) synaptic vesicles, ganglia, dendrites
(c) cell body, dendrites, ganglia
(d) cell body, dendrites, axon

Ans. (d)

(iii) Axons can be
(a) non-myelinated (b) myelinated
(c) Either (a) or (b) (d) None of these

Ans. (c)

(iv) A synapse is found between
(a) dendrite and dendrite
(b) axon terminal and axon terminal
(c) dendrite and axon terminal
(d) All of the above

Ans. (c)

(v) Chemicals which are released at the synaptic junction are called
(a) hormones (b) neurotransmitters
(c) cerebrospinal fluid (d) lymph

Ans. (b)

(vi) A mixed nerve
(a) contains both sensory and motor fibres
(b) carries sensations from two or more different sense organs
(c) has a common root but branches into two nerves to different organs
(d) has two or more roots from different parts of brain

Ans. (a)

(vii) Which of the following can be considered as the function of nervous system?
(a) Irritability
(b) Receive stimuli
(c) Conduction of enzymes
(d) To prepare the body against reactions

Ans. (a)

(viii) Which of the following is true about neurilemma?
(a) The cell membrane around the nerve cell
(b) A layer of fatty substance around axon
(c) A layer of specialised neuroglia around myelin sheath of nerve fibres
(d) The connective tissue around a nerve tract

Ans. (c)

(ix) Which of the following is mainly associated with the maintenance of the posture? **[2015]**
(a) Cerebrum (b) Cerebellum (c) Thalamus (d) Pons

Ans. (b)

(x) Which of the following pairs of brain part is not correctly matched with its function?
(a) Cerebellum – Balance of body
(b) Cerebrum – Memory
(c) Pons – Consciousness
(d) Medulla oblongata – Controls activities of internal organs

Ans. (c)

(xi) The number of cranial nerves in humas are [Semester II 2022]
(a) 12 (b) 31 pairs
(c) 31 (d) 12 pairs

Ans. (d)

(xii) The ventral root ganglion of the spinal cord contains cell bodies of the [2013]
(a) motor neuron (b) sensory neuron
(c) intermediate neuron (d) association neuron

Ans. (a)

(xiii) The number of spinal nerves in a human being are [2018]
(a) 31 pairs (b) 10 pairs
(c) 21 pairs (d) 30 pairs

Ans. (a)

(xiv) Stimulation of the nerves of the sympathetic nervous system [2023]
(a) accelerates heartbeat (b) constricts pupil of eyes
(c) increases peristalsis (d) retards heartbeat

Ans. (a)

(xv) Which of the following is not a natural reflex action? [2014]
(a) Knee-jerk
(b) Blinking of eyes due to strong light
(c) Salivation at the sight of food
(d) Sneezing when any irritant enters the nose

Ans. (c)

(xvi) A reflex arc in man is best described as movement of stimuli from [2012]
(a) receptor cell, sensory neuron, relaying neuron, effector muscles
(b) receptor cell, efferent nerve, relaying neuron, muscles of the body
(c) receptor cell, spinal cord, motor neuron, relaying neuron
(d) receptor cell, synapse, motor neuron, relaying neuron

Ans. (a)

(xvii) The circular opening in the centre of iris [Semester II 2022]
(a) lense (b) cornea
(c) sclera (d) pupil

Ans. (d)

(xviii) Aqueous humour is present between the [2018]
(a) lens and retina (b) iris and lens
(c) cornea and iris (d) cornea and lens

Ans. (d)

(xix) Vitreous humour is present between [2023]
(a) cornea and iris (b) lens and retina
(c) iris and lens (d) cornea and lens

Ans. (a)

(xx) Organ of corti is present inside the
(a) cochlea (b) semicircular canals
(c) sacculus (d) utriculus

Ans. (a)

6. Fill in the blanks by using suitable words.
(i) Nervous system controls and ...... the working of all parts of the body.
(ii) The axon transmits .... away from the cell body to a synapse.
(iii) The terminal portions of the axons have swollen bulb-like structure called ....
(iv) Certain chemicals called ...... are stored in synaptic knob.
(v) A bundle of axons enclosed in a tubular sheath is called ....
(vi) Dendrites and axon are collectively called ....
(vii) There are ...... meninges in the brain.
(viii) Grey matter is mainly composed of ....
(ix) ...... is the tough, fibrous outermost covering of brain.
(x) The fluid-filled between the meninges is called ....
(xi) There are 31 pairs of spinal nerves, emerging out of the ....
(xii) ...... movements are under our conscious control.
(xiii) .... movements are not under our conscious control.
(xiv) The three layers of the eye are ......, ... and ....
(xv) .... is the thin, transparent membrane covering the eye.
(xvi) The place of best vision in the retina of eye is .... .
(xvii) Place of no vision in the retina of the eye is ....
(xviii) .... is the capacity of the eye to focus at different distances.
(xix) .... vision is the condition in which both the eyes participate in viewing an object.
(xx) Astigmatism is corrected by using .... or .... lenses.
(xxi) Cochlea is filled with ....
(xxii) Tympanic chamber is filled with ....
(xxiii) The middle ear is separated from the external ear by the ....
(xxiv) Area in middle ear having auditory sense cells is ....
(xxv) .... is also known as external ear.
(xxvi) The three small bones in the middle ear are called ....

Ans. (i) coordinates (ii) impulses
(iii) synaptic knob (iv) neurotransmitters
(v) nerve (vi) neurites
(vii) three (viii) cytons
(ix) Duramater (x) cerebrospinal fluid
(xi) spinal cord (xii) Voluntary
(xiii) Involuntary (xiv) sclera, choroid, retina
(xv) Conjunctiva (xvi) yellow spot

(xvii) blind spot (xviii) Power of accommodation
(xix) Binocular (xx) spherical, cylindrical
(xxi) endolymph (xxii) perilymph
(xxiii) tympanic membrane
(xxiv) organ of Corti (xxv) Pinna
(xxvi) ear ossicles

7. Choose the odd one out from the following terms given below and name the category to which other three belong.
(i) Dendrites, Medullary sheath, Axon, Spinal cord [2018]
(ii) Cyton, Photon, Axon, Dendron [2019, 14]
(iii) Cerebrum, Cerebellum, Thalamus, Hypothalamus [2012]
(iv) Aqueous humour, Vitreous humour, Iris, Central canal [2017]
(v) Haemoglobin, Glucagon, Iodopsin, Rhodopsin [2014]
(vi) Malleus, Cochlea, Stapes, Incus [2023]
(vii) Semicircular canals, Cochlea, Tympanum, Utriculus [2013]

Ans. (i) **Odd term** is spinal cord.
Rest others are the parts of a nerve cell.
(ii) **Odd term** is photon.
Rest all are the parts of a neuron.
(iii) **Odd term** is cerebellum.
All others are the parts of forebrain.
(iv) **Odd term** is central canal (present in spinal cord).
Rest three structures are present in eye.
(v) **Odd term** is glucagon.
Rest all others are pigments found in the body.
(vi) **Odd term** is cochlea.
Rest three are bones present in human ear.
(vii) **Odd term** is tympanum.
Rest three are the different parts of internal ear.

8. Given below are the sets of terms each. Rewrite the terms in correct order of a logical sequence.
(i) Spinal cord, Motor neuron, Receptor, Effector, Sensory neuron [2013]
(ii) Receptor, Response, Effector, Spinal Cord [2023]
(iii) Oval window, Tympanum, Cochlea, Auditory canal, Ear ossicles (correct path through which a vibration of sound is transferred in the human ear) [2012, 06]
(iv) Cochlea, Malleus, Pinna, Stapes, Incus [2017]
(v) Fovea, Lens, Cornea, Conjunctiva [2023]

Ans. (i) Receptor, Sensory neuron, Spinal cord, Motor neuron, Effector
(ii) Receptor, Spinal cord, Effector, Response
(iii) Auditory canal, Tympanum, Ear ossicles, Oval window, Cochlea
(iv) Pinna, Malleus, Incus, Stapes, Cochlea
(Route of sound waves in hearing process)
(v) Conjunctiva, Cornea, Lens, Fovea

9. State the exact location of the following.
(i) Myelin sheath
(ii) Corpus callosum [2019, 13]
(iii) Ciliary body [2016]
(iv) Lacrimal gland
(v) Yellow spot [2014]
(vi) Organ of Corti [2011]
(vii) Incus [2019, 13]
(viii) Malleus [2018]
(ix) Dura mater [2023]
(x) Eustachian tube

Ans. (i) Myelin sheath surrounds the axon of neurons.
(ii) Corpus callosum is found between the two lobes of cerebrum called cerebral hemispheres.
(iii) Ciliary body is found in the anterior part of eye.
(iv) Lacrimal glands or tear glands are located at the upper sideward portion of the orbits (eye sockets).
(v) Yellow spot is located exactly behind the lens on the retina of the eye.
(vi) Organ of Corti is found in the endolymph, present in the middle canal of cochlea.
(vii) Incus is present in the middle ear between malleus and stapes.
(viii) Malleus is an ear ossicle (bone) present in the middle ear. Its one end is attached to eardrum.
(ix) Dura mater are located directly under your skull and vertebral column.
(x) Eustachian tube is found in the middle ear.

10. State the main function of the following.
(i) Cerebrospinal fluid [2014]
(ii) Neurotransmitter [2013]
(iii) Myelin sheath
(iv) Relay neuron
(v) Medulla oblongata [2019, 11]
(vi) Iris of the eye [2013]
(vii) Vitreous humour
(viii) Suspensory ligament of eye [2014]
(ix) Eustachian tube [2016, 14]
(x) Semicircular cannal [2010]

Ans. (i) Cerebrospinal fluid provides mechanical protection and nourishment to brain.
(ii) Neurotransmitters help in the conduction of nerve impulse at synapse.
(iii) Myelin sheath provides an insulation around the axon for increasing the speed of impulses.
(iv) Relay or connecting neuron serves as a link between the sensory and motor neurons. It is mainly found in brain and spinal cord.
(v) Medulla oblongata controls the involuntary activities of the brain.
(vi) Iris of the eye regulates the amount of light entering the eye.
(vii) Vitreous humour is the jelly-like substance which gives round-shape to the eyeball.
(viii) Suspensory ligament of the eyes helps in holding the lens in position.

(ix) Eustachian tube connects middle ear with pharynx and helps to maintain equal air pressure on either sides of the eardrum or tympanum.

(x) Semicircular canal helps in balances the body.

11. Mention one difference between each of the following pairs on the basis of what is given in the bracket.

(i) Cerebrum and Spinal cord (arrangement of nerve cell) **[2016]**

(ii) Thalamus and Hypothalamus (function)

(iii) Sensory neuron and Motor neuron (function)

(iv) Reflex action and Voluntary action (mode of action)

(v) Sympathetic system and Parasympathetic system (function)

(vi) Simple and Conditioned reflexes (origin)

(vii) Auditory nerve and Optic nerve (function)

(viii) Spinal nerves and Cranial nerves (number of nerves) **(2014)**

(ix) Rod cells and Cone cells (pigment)

(x) Aquoeous and Vitreous humours (location) **[2016]**

(xi) Near vision and Distant vision (shape of the eye lens) **[2014]**

(xii) Myopia and Hypermetropia (condition of eyeball)

Ans. (i) Difference between cerebrum and spinal cord is as follows

Cerebrum	Spinal cord
Outer part contains non-myelinated cell bodies giving a greyish appearance and inner part contains myelinated cell bodies giving white appearance.	Outer part contains myelinated cell bodies giving white appearance and inner part contains non-myelinated cell bodies giving greyish appearance.

(ii) Difference between thalamus and hypothalamus is as follows

Thalamus	Hypothalamus
It controls emotional and memory functions.	It regulates sexual behaviour, expression of emotional reactions and motivation.

(iii) Difference between sensory and motor neurons is as follows

Sensory neurons	Motor neurons
They transmit information from the organs to the main nervous system, i.e. brain and spinal cord.	They transmit information from the main nervous system to the various organs.

(iv) Difference between reflex action and voluntary action is as follows

Reflex action	Voluntary action
It is quick and happens in response to a sudden stimulus.	It is usually slow and happens in a pre-planned manner.

(v) Difference between sympathetic and parasympathetic nervous system is as follows

Sympathetic nervous system	Parasympathetic nervous system
It prepares the body for an abnormal situation.	It prepares the body for the normal functioning after abnormal situation.

(vi) Difference between simple and conditioned reflexes is as follows

Simple reflex	Conditioned reflex
These reflexes are inborn and are inherited from parents.	These reflexes are acquired after bith or adopted during the course of the lifetime.

(vii) Difference between auditory nerve and optic nerve is as follows

Auditory nerve	Optic nerve
It carries impulses from the ear to the brain.	It carries impulses from the eye to the brain.

(viii) Difference between spinal nerves and cranial nerves is as follows

Spinal nerves	Cranial nerves
These are 31 in pairs.	These are 12 in pairs.

(ix) Difference between rod cells and cone cells is as follows

Rod cells	Cone cells
They contain rhodopsin.	They contain iodopsin.

(x) Difference between aqueous humour and vitreous humour is as follows

Aqueous humour	Vitreous humour
It is present between the lens and cornea of the eye.	It is present between the lens and the retina of the eye.

(xi) Difference between near vision and distant vision is as follows

Near vision	Distant vision
Lens become more concave/too curved.	Lens become less convex/too flat.

(xii) Difference between myopia and hypermetropia is as follows

Myopia	Hypermetropia
Elongation of eyeball, as a result the image is formed before retina.	Eyeball becomes too short as a result the image is formed behind retina.

12. Given below are groups of terms. In each group, the first pair indicates the relationship between the two terms. Rewrite and complete the second pair on a similar basis.

(i) Eye : Optic nerve : : Ear : .... **[2017]**

(ii) Hearing : Organ of Corti :: Balancing : .... **[2015]**

Ans. (i) Auditory nerves (ii) Vestibule

13. Expand the following biological abbreviations.
(i) CNS (ii) SNS

Ans. (i) Central Nervous System
(ii) Somatic Nervous System

14. Give biological/technical terms for the following.
(i) The protective covering of brain and spinal cord. [2012]
(ii) A thin membrane covering the entire front part of the eye. [2014, 06]
(iii) The structure that carries visual stimuli from retina to the brain. [2012]
(iv) Eye lens losing flexibility resulting in a kind of long sightedness in elderly people. [2018, 12]
(v) The three tiny bones present in the middle ear. [Semester II 2022]

Ans. (i) Meninges (ii) Cornea
(iii) Optic nerve (iv) Presbyopia
(v) Ossicles

15. Explain the following terms.
(i) Synapse [2012]
(ii) Cranium
(iii) CSF
(iv) Reflex action [2023]
(v) Power of accommodation [2016, 12, 10, 07]
(vi) Cochlea
(vii) Organ of Corti

Ans. (i) Synapse is the point of contact between the axon endings of one neuron with the dendrites of the other neuron. The impulse is transmitted from one neuron to the other through the synapse.
(ii) Cranium is a box-like bony structure that protects the brain by covering it.
(iii) The space between the arachnoid and piamater is filled with CSF (Cerebrospinal Fluid).
This fluid protects the brain from mechanical injuries by absorbing the shocks.
(iv) A reflex action is a spontaneous, automatic and involuntary response to a stimulus.
(v) The adjustment of the eye to enable it to focus at various distances is called power of accommodation.
(vi) The membranous labyrinth of inner ear is filled with a fluid called endolymph. The coiled portion of the labyrinth is called cochlea.
(vii) Organ of Corti is a structure located on the basilar membrane of inner ear, which contains hair cells that act as auditory receptors.

16. Answer the following questions briefly.
(i) Where does the largest number of neurons are found in human body?
(ii) In what way, sulci are different from gyri?
(iii) Explain how the human eye adapts itself to bright light and dimlight.
(iv) Which part of the human ear gives 'dynamic balance' and 'static balance' to the body?

Ans. (i) The largest number of neurons are found in the brain, i.e. about 80-90 billion neurons.
(ii) The cortex of the cerebrum is covered by a number of small, deep and shallow folds called sulci, whereas, the convolutions of the brain, i.e. larger grooves (folds) that cover the cortex of the cerebrum is called gyri.
(iii) Pupil is an aperture surrounded by the iris. The movement of muscle fibres of iris controls the size of pupil and regulates the amount of light entering the eye. Due to this adjustment, we blink our eyes when see bright light or not able to see when enters a dimlight room because pupil takes time to adjust its size according to the amount of light.
(iv) **Dynamic balance** Sensory cells in semicirular canal are concerned with dynamic balance.
Static balance Utriculus and sacculus.

2 Marks Questions

17. Draw a neat diagram of neuron and label any two parts.

Ans. Refer to page 141.

18. Write a short note on synapse.

Ans. Synapse is the point of contact between the nerve endings of one neuron (axon) and the dendrites of another neuron separated by a fine gap. This gap is called synaptic cleft. When the impulse reaches the terminal end of an axon, neurotransmitters (the chemicals such as acetylcholine) are released.

19. Explain what does nervous system consist of.

Ans. The nervous system consists of
(i) **Central Nervous System** (CNS) It comprises brain and spinal cord.
(ii) **Peripheral Nervous System** (PNS) It comprises cranial and spinal nerves.
(iii) **Autonomic Nervous System** (ANS) It comprises parasympathetic and sympathetic nerves.

20. The diagram given below is that of a human brain. Answer the questions that follow [Semester II 2022]

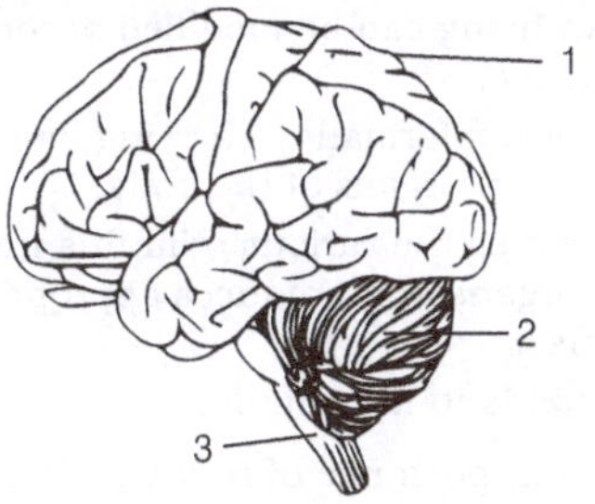

(i) Label the parts numbered 2 and 3.
(ii) State any one function of the part numbered 1.

Ans. (i) The labelled part 2 and 3 represents cerebellum and medulla.
(ii) The part labelled as 1 is cerebrum and one of its function is to control all the voluntary actions.

21. What are the two functions of cerebellum? [2023]

Ans. Functions of cerebellum are as follows
- It maintains the balance of the body.
- It also coordinates various muscular activities of the body.

22. Explain the mechanism of focusing the image of a distant object in our eye when we raise our head after reading a book.

Ans. While reading a book (near by vision), the lens of our eye is more convex or rounded but when we focus our eye on a distant object, the ciliary muscles are relaxed.

The lens becomes concave or flattened. This accommodation power of eye enables us to have a clear vision of objects at varying distances.

23. How do we perceive colours?

Ans. The daylight (photopic) vision and colour vision are the functions of cones. In the human eye, there are three types of cones, which possess their own characteristic photopigments. They respond to red, green and blue lights. The sensations of different colours are produced by various combinations of these cones and their photopigments.

When these cones are stimulated equally, a sensation of white light is produced.

24. Choose between the two options to answer the questions specified in the brackets for the following.

(i) Sclerotic layer or choroid layer (Which one forms the iris?) [2018]

(ii) Perilymph or endolymph (Which one surrounds the organ of Corti?) [2018]

Ans. (i) Choroid

(ii) Endolymph

3 Marks Questions

25. Mention the functions of the human brain.

Ans. The human brain performs the following functions

(i) It coordinates activities of the body.

(ii) It stores information, so that behaviour of human being can be modified according to past experience.

(iii) It receives information carrying impulses from all the sensory organs of the body.

(iv) It correlates the various stimulus from different sense organs and produces appropriate response.

(v) It responds to the impulses.

26. Give three importance of reflex action.

Ans. Reflex action is important because

(i) It enables the organism for an immediate response to a harmful stimulus.

(ii) It reduces the overloading in brain.

(iii) It increases the chances of survival of an organism.

27. Identify the reflexes given below in humans. Write against each, the kind of reflex it is (natural or conditional).

(i) Watering of mouth on seeing a favourite dish.

(ii) Knee-jerk

(iii) Closing of eyelids, if a strong beam of light is flashed across.

(iv) Tying of shoe laces while talking.

Ans. (i) Watering of mouth on seeing a favourite dish–Conditional

(ii) Knee-jerk– Natural

(iii) Closing of eyelids, if a strong beam of light is flashed across–Natural.

(iv) Tying of shoe laces while talking–Conditional

28. During a street fight between two individuals, mention the effects on the following organs by the autonomous nervous system, in the table given below (one has been done for you as an example.) [2011]

Organs	Sympathetic nervous system	Parasympathetic nervous system
Lungs	Dilates bronchi and bronchioles	Constricts bronchi and bronchioles
Heart		
Pupil of the eye		
Salivary gland		

Ans. Refer to table on page no. 144.

29. How are rods different from cones?

Ans. **Rod cells** are the cells which are sensitive to dimlight but do not respond to colour. They contain a pigment **rhodopsin** and are distributed almost throughout the retina. On the other hand, **cone cells** are sensitive to bright light and respond to colour. They contain a pigment **iodopsin** and are usually confined to the yellow spot only.

30. Explain the mechanism of generation of light-induced impulse in the retina.

Ans. Light induces dissociation of the retinal from opsin resulting in changes in the structure of the opsin. This causes change in membrane permeability. As a result, potential differences are generated in the photoreceptor cells.

This produces a signal that generates action potentials in the ganglion cells through the bipolar cells. These action potentials (impulses) are transmitted by the optic nerves to the visual cortex area of the brain, where the nerve impulses are analysed and the image formed on the retina is recognised.

31. Draw a diagram of the human eye as seen in a vertical section and label the part which suits the following functions/description.

(i) The layer which prevents reflection of light.

(ii) The structure that alters the focal length of the lens.

(iii) The region of distinct vision.

(iv) The part which transmits the impulse to the brain.

(v) Outermost transparent layer of the eye.

(vi) Fluid in the anterior part of the eye. [2008]

Ans.

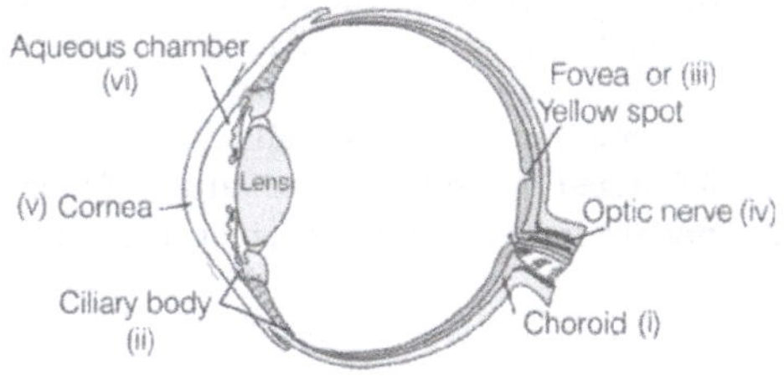

32. Study the diagram given below and answer the questions that follow [Semester II 2022]

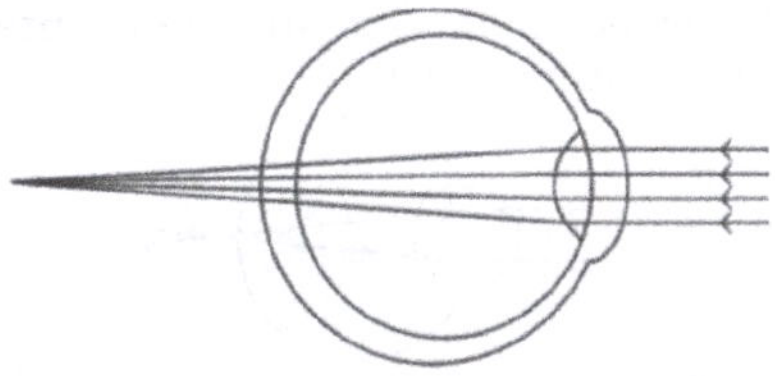

(i) Identify the defect of the eye by mentioning the technical term.

(ii) Mention one reason for this defect.

(iii) Name the type of lens used to correct this defect.

Ans. (i) Hyper metropia

(ii) One of the reason for this defect is that the eyball becomes too short due to which the image is formed behind retina.

(iii) Convex lens

Section-II [5 Marks]

Structured Questions

1. The given diagram is an external view of the human brain. Study the same and answer the questions that follows. [2017]

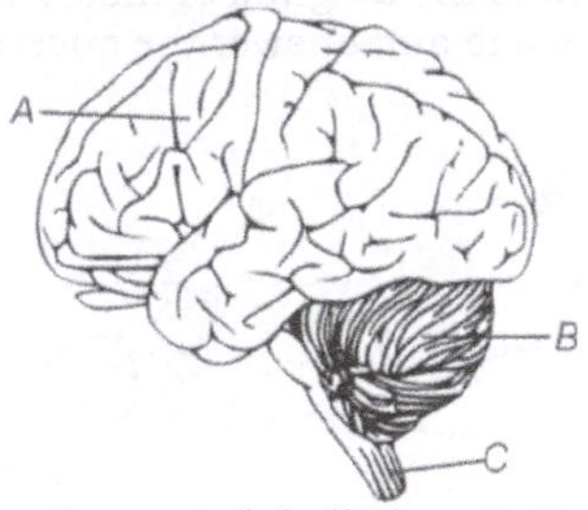

(i) Name the parts labelled as *A*, *B* and *C* in the diagram.

(ii) State the main functions of the parts labelled as *A* and *B*.

(iii) What are the structural and functional units of the brain? How are the parts of these units arranged in *A* and *C*?

(iv) Mention the collective term for the membranes covering the brain.

(v) What is the function of cerebrospinal fluid?

Ans. (i) The parts labelled as *A*, *B* and *C* are *A*–Cerebrum, *B*–Cerebellum and *C*–Spinal cord.

(ii) The main functions of the parts labelled as *A* and *B* are as follows

A (Cerebrum) – Site of controlling memory, reasoning, thinking, perception, emotions and speech.

B (Cerebellum) – Maintains posture, equilibrium and muscular coordination.

(iii) The structural and functional unit of brain is called neuron.

In cerebrum (*A*) the outer portion is greyish in colour containing all the cell bodies of non myelinated the neuron. It is called grey matter, while the inner portion is composed of white matter which mainly consists of cell bodies of myelinated neurons.

Spinal cord (*C*) also contains grey and white matter, but in opposite arrangement as that of brain (grey matter – inner side and white matter –outer side).

(iv) The collective term used for the membranes covering the brain is meninges.

(v) Cerebrospinal fluid provides mechanical protection and nourishment to brain.

2. The following diagram represents the human brain as seen in an external view. Study the same and then answer the questions that follows.

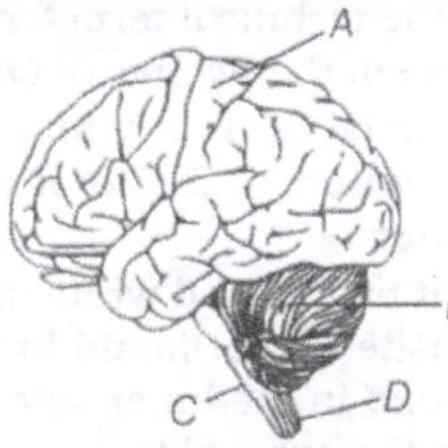

(i) Name the parts labelled as *A*, *B*, *C* and *D*.

(ii) Mention the difference in the arrangement of the nerve cells in the parts labelled as *A* and *D*.

(iii) What is the main function of the parts labelled as *C* and *D*?

(iv) Name the sheet of nerve fibres that connect the two halves of the part labelled as *A*.

Ans. The parts labelled as *A* to *D* are

(i) *A*– Cerebrum, *B*– Cerebellum

C–Medulla oblongata, *D*– Spinal cord

(ii) In part *A* (cerebrum), grey matter found outside and white matter is inside.

In part *D* (spinal cord), white matter is outside and grey matter is inside.

(iii) The main functions of the parts labelled as *C* and *D* are as follows
C–Medulla oblongata, it controls all involuntary movements of internal organs, e.g. breathing movements of lungs and beating of heart.
D–Spinal cord, it relays messages from brain to different parts of body.

(iv) Corpus callosum is the bundle of nerve fibres that connect the two halves of the parts labelled as *A* (cerebral hemispheres).

3. The diagram given below shows the internal structure of a spinal cord depicting a phenomenon. Study the diagram and answer the questions that follows.

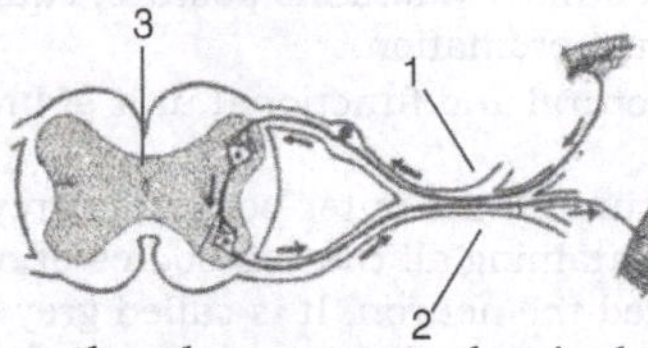

(i) Name the phenomenon that is depicted in the diagram. Define the phenomenon.
(ii) Give the technical term for the points of contact between the two nerve cells.
(iii) Name the parts numbered as 1, 2 and 3.
(iv) How does the arrangement of neurons in the spinal cord differ from that of the brain?
(v) Mention two ways by which the spinal cord is protected in our body. **[2018]**

Ans. (i) The given figure shows the phenomenon of reflex action. It is an involuntary or instantaneous reaction in response to a stimulus, e.g. coughing, blinking of eyes, sneezing, etc.
(ii) Synapse is the technical term for the points of contact between the two nerve cells.
(iii) The parts numbered as 1, 2 and 3 are as
1– Sensory neuron, 2– Motor neuron
3– Grey matter
(iv) Arrangement of grey and white matter in spinal cord is opposite to that found in brain. Grey matter is found in the inner side and the white matter is on the outer side.
(v) The spinal cord is well-protected by three membranous coverings known as meninges and cerebrospinal fluid.

4. Given below is a diagrammatic depicting a defect of the human eye, study same and then answer the questions that follows.

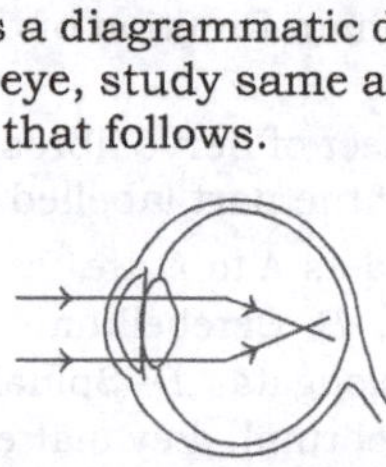

(i) Name the defect shown in the diagram.
(ii) What are the two possible reasons that cause this defect?
(iii) Name the type of lens used to correct this defect.
(iv) With the help of a diagram show how the defect shown above is rectified using a suitatble lens. **[2016]**

Ans. (i) The defect shown in the diagram is myopia (short sightedness) as the image form before the retina.
(ii) Two possible reasons are
(a) Elongation of the eyeball
(b) Caused by excessive curvature of lens.
(iii) Concave lens is used to correct this defect.
(iv)

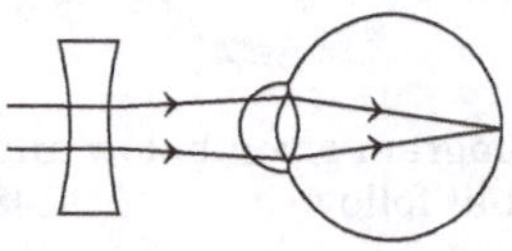

5. Given below is a diagrammatic representation of a defect of the human eye.

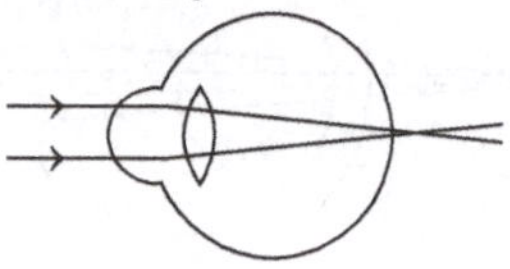

(i) Identify the defect.
(ii) Mention two possible reasons for the above defect.
(iii) State how the defect can be rectified.
(iv) Name the part of the eye responsible for maintaining the shape of the eyeball. **[2007]**

Ans. (i) The defect is hypermetropia because the image is formed behind the retina.
(ii) This defect arises due to the following reasons
(a) Focal length of eye lens becomes large.
(b) Eyeball becomes too short so that the image is formed behind the retina.
(iii) This defect can be corrected by using convex lens of appropriate power. A convex lens of suitable power will bring the image back on retina.
(iv) Sclera layer is the part of eye responsible for maintaining the shape of eyeball.

6. Given below is the diagram of the human ear. Study the same and answer the questions that follows.

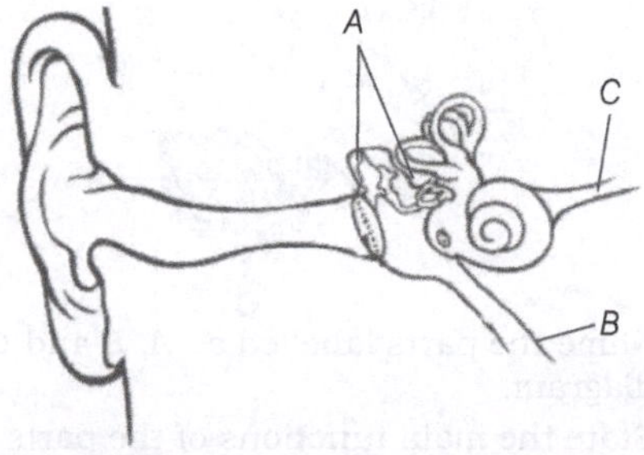

(i) Give the biological term for the part labelled as '*A*' and state its function.

(ii) Name the part labelled as '*B*' and state its function.

(iii) Name the part labelled as '*C*' and state its function.

(iv) Give the function of ear wax. [2007]

Ans. (i) Part '*A*' is ear ossicles, which help in transmitting the sound waves from external to the internal ear.

(ii) Part '*B*' is called as Eustachian tube, which acts as ventilator to equalise pressure of air on both the sides of tympanic membrane that forms the outer boundary of middle ear.

(iii) Part '*C*' is auditory nerve (vestibular and cochlear nerve), which carries hearing impulses to the brain.

(iv) Ear wax helps to lubricate the tympanum for proper functioning.

7. The diagram given below represents the structure found in the inner ear. Study the same and then answer the questions that follows.

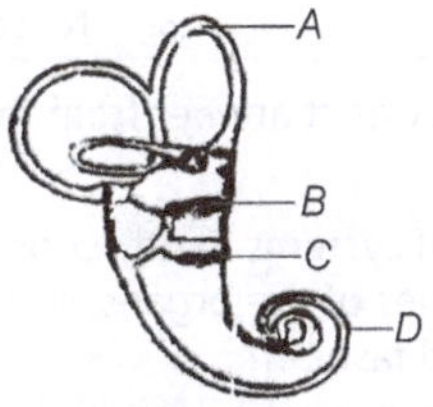

(i) Name the parts labelled as *A*, *B*, *C* and *D*.

(ii) Name the part of the ear responsible for transmitting impulses to the brain.

(iii) Which of the above labelled part is responsible for dynamic equilibrium?

(iv) Name the audio receptor cells, which pick up vibrations.

(v) Name the fluid present in the inner ear.

Ans. (i) The parts labelled as *A* to *D* are

A – Semicircular canals

B – Utriculus

C– Sacculus

D – Cochlea

(ii) Auditory nerve is the part of ear responsible for transmitting impulses to the brain.

(iii) The labelled part *A*, i.e. semicircular canal is responsible for dynamic equilibrium.

(iv) Organ of Corti are the audio receptor cells, which pick up vibrations.

(v) Endolymph fluid present in the inner ear.

8. Human eye is a specialised receptor which helps an individual in seeing an object through a complex coordination of various structures like lens, cornea, aqueous and vitreous humours, retina, etc.

(i) What is meant by power of accommodation of the eye?

(ii) What is the shape of the lens during (a) near vision, (b) distant vision?

(iii) Name the two structures in the eye responsible for bringing about the change in the shape of the lens.

(iv) Name the cells of the retina and their respective pigments which get activated (a) in dark, (b) in light. [2011]

Ans. (i) To see an object clearly, its image should be sharp and focus in each eye. The process of focusing the eye to see objects at different distances is called accommodation. This is mainly brought about by a change in the curvature of the elastic lens making it thinner or thicker.

(ii) The shape of lens is as follows

(a) During near vision, lens is more concave or rounded.

(b) During distant vision, lens is thin and flat.

(iii) Ciliary muscles and suspensory ligaments are the two structures in the eye responsible for bringing about the change in the shape of lens.

(iv) (a) In the dark, rod cells get activated and their pigment is rhodopsin.

(b) In the light, cone cells get activated and their pigment is iodopsin.

9. In humans, ears serve the purpose of hearing as well as in balancing the body. Anatomically, ear is divided in three parts, *viz.* outer ear, middle ear containing ear ossicles and inner ear.

(i) Give the technical term for the structure found in the inner ear.

(ii) Name the three small bones present in the middle ear. What is the biological term for them collectively?

(iii) Name the part of the ear associated with (a) static balance, (b) hearing, (c) dynamic balance.

(iv) Name the nerve which transmits messages from the ear to the brain. [2011]

Ans. (i) Membranous labyrinth

(ii) Hammer, anvil and stirrup are the three small bones present in the middle ear.
Ear ossicles is the biological term used for these bones collectively.

(iii) Different parts associated with following are

(a) For static balance–Utriculus and sacculus

(b) For hearing–Cochlea

(c) For dynamic balance–Semicircular canals

(iv) Refer to Ans. 7(ii).

Chapter Assessment

Section-I

1 Mark Questions

1. Name the following.
   (i) The cytoplasmic process of the cell body of a neuron.
   (ii) The long extension from the cell body of a motor neuron.
   (iii) Wave of electrical disturbance that sweeps over the nerve cell.
   (iv) The lower part of the brain, which contains reflex centre like cardiac centre, respiratory and vasomotor centre.
   (v) A condition in which the lens turns opaque.
2. Choose the odd one out from the following terms given below and name the category to which other three belong.
   Rods, Cones, Rhodopsin, Cataract
3. Give biological reason for the following.
   We see clearly at the central region of the retina.
4. (i) Match the following columns.

Column I	Column II
A. Transmission of impulses towards the cell body	1. Dendrites
B. Interpret impulses	2. Axon
C. Transmission of impulses away from the cell body	3. Cell body
D. Insulation around axon	4. Myelin sheath

   (ii) Match the following columns.

Column I	Column II
A. Cerebrum	1. Controls vision and hearing
B. Cerebellum	2. Regulates breathing movements
C. Pons	3. Seat of intelligence
D. Midbrain	4. Maintains body posture

   (iii) Match the following columns.

Column I	Column II
A. The blind spot	1. Colour of the eye
B. Ciliary muscle	2. Shape of the lens
C. The yellow spot	3. Free of rod cells
D. Iris	4. Vitreous humour
	5. Centre of the retina
	6. No sensory cells

5. Choose the correct answer from the four options given below.
   (i) Which pair of systems jointly coordinates and integrates all the activities of the organs, so that they function in a synchronised fashion?
   (a) Neural and respiratory system
   (b) Neural and digestive system
   (c) Neural and endocrine system
   (d) Neural and circulatory system
   (ii) Synaptic knob possesses
   (a) granular vesicles (b) Nissl's vesicles
   (c) synaptic vesicles (d) None of these
   (iii) Synaptic vesicles contain chemicals called
   (a) synaptic fluid (b) neurotransmitters
   (c) vesicular fluid (d) All of these
   (iv) In autonomic nervous system, nerves arise from
   (a) neck region of the spinal cord
   (b) coccygeal region of the spinal cord
   (c) Between (a) and (b)
   (d) brain
   (v) The minimum distance for clear vision is
   (a) 10 cm (b) 20 cm
   (c) 25 cm (d) 35 cm
   (vi) Lens implantation is required in
   (a) myopia (b) hyperopia
   (c) cataract (d) astigmatism
   (vii) The aperture in the eye through which light enters is the
   (a) pupil (b) conjunctiva
   (c) ciliary muscles (d) choroid

6. Fill in the blanks by using suitable words.
   (i) Fibres of the tract of pons form .... matter.
   (ii) The nervous system of human being is derived from the embryonic ....
   (iii) .... is known as the integrating and command centre of the nervous system.
   (iv) .... is located below the cerebellum.
   (v) ...... of our ear is shaped like a snail.
7. Rearrange the following incorrect sequence pertaining to what is given within brackets at the end.
   (i) Cerebellum, Medulla oblongata, Pons, Cerebrum, Midbrain (sequence of parts of human brain)
   (ii) Pupil, Yellow spot, Lens, Aqueous humour (correct path of entry of light into the eye from an object).
8. State the main function of hypothalamus.
9. State the exact location of yellow spot.
10. Explain the following terms.
    (i) Stereoscopic vision
    (ii) Cataract

2 Marks Questions

11. Discuss the significance of tears.
12. Mention the characteristics of the image that falls on the retina of the eye.

3 Marks Questions

13. Categorise the following under the headings, stimulus and response.
    (i) Seeing a green light turning into red at a road crossing, before applying the brakes.
    (ii) Pain in the eye if something falls into it.
    (iii) Withdrawal of hand on touching a hot plate.
14. What do you understand by association of neuron or interneuron?
15. When you watch a movie from a very short distance from the screen in a cinema hall, you do not enjoy. Why?
16. State the changes that occur in the following structures when the eye accommodates for near vision.
    (i) Ciliary muscle
    (ii) Suspensory ligament
    (iii) Lens
17. Given below is the diagram of a neuron. Identify *A* to *E* and name them correctly.

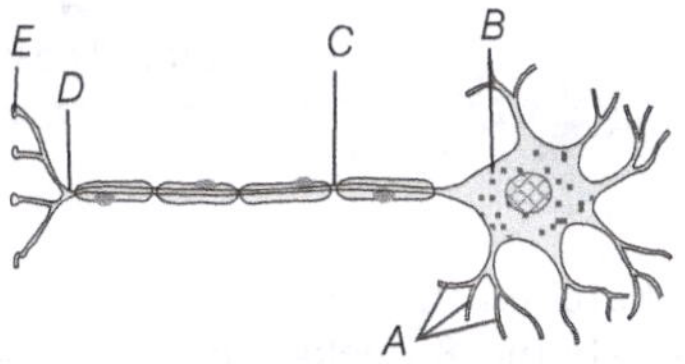

Section-II [5 Marks]

Structured Questions

18. Study the diagram shown below and answer the following questions that follows.

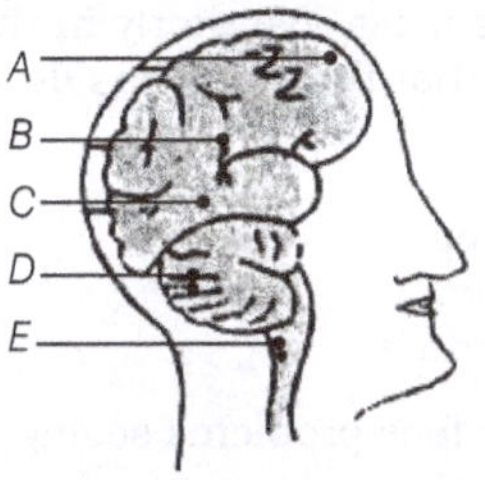

    (i) What would result due to
       (a) damage to part *C*?
       (b) damage to part *D*?
    (ii) Name the brain membranes.
    (iii) Why is the brain surface highly convoluted with ridges and grooves?
19. The given figure shows the structure of a mammalian eye.

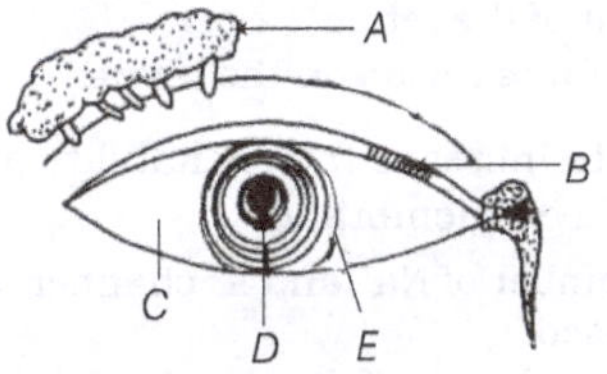

    (i) Label the parts *A-E*.
    (ii) State the function of part *A*.
    (iii) What type of tissue is found in part *C* ?
    (iv) How functions of *D* and *E* are interconnected?
    (v) What is the term used for the ability of human beings in having both eyes facing forward?

For explanations scan the given QR Code

Olympiad Section*

Brain Teasing Questions asked in Previous Olympiads

1 A newly hatched chick grows to fully adult male or female in about 18 weeks' time. During this time, different body parts show characteristic growth pattern. In an experiment, a pair of goggles were fixed on the eyes of a chick immediately after hatching such that only red wavelength of light passes through them. When the goggles are removed at the end of 7 days, the chick develops a peculiar eye defect. Given that longer wavelengths of light focus most posteriorly in the eye, the most likely defect that the chick has developed is [INJSO 2019]

(a) myopia
(b) hypermetropia
(c) astigmatism
(d) colour blindness

2 Some people face problems seeing distant objects clearly. They, however, have no problem seeing nearby objects. A person wears a spectacle with concave lenses to see distant objects. He is able to see nearby object clearly without using lenses. When this person is reading without using the spectacles the image will be formed .... [INJSO 2018]

(a) on the blind spot
(b) behind the retina
(c) in front of the retina
(d) in the fovea region on the retina

3 In order to increase the excitability of a patch of neuronal cell membrane [INBO 2014]

(a) the number of Na^+ and K^+ channels should be increased
(b) the capacitance of the membrane should be increased
(c) the thickness of the membrane should be reduced
(d) the content of charged lipids in the membrane should be increased

4 Lips are more sensitive to temperature or touch than forearm skin. This is because of the [INBO 2014]

(a) higher frequency of action potentials
(b) greater height of the action potential
(c) faster transmission of the action potential
(d) large number of neurons stimulated in the CNS

5 Which of the following statement(s) is/are correct statement(s) with respect to motor neurons? [INJSO 2013]

I. They are multipolar.
II. They are unipolar.
III. They carry messages from CNS (Central Nervous System) to muscle fibres or glands.
IV. They carry messages from sensory receptors to CNS.

Codes

(a) Only I
(b) Only II
(c) Only I and III
(d) Only I and IV

6 Anil, an 8th grade student, was asked to draw a figure explaining how the mammalian eye collects and focuses light, converting it into electrical signals. Which of the following flowcharts correctly represents the process? [INJSO 2011]

(a) Light → Cornea → Aqueous humour → Pupil → Lens → Vitreous humour → Retina → Action potentials in neurons → Optic nerve → Brain
(b) Light → Sclera → Vitreous humour → Pupil → Lens → Aqueous humour → Retina → Action potentials in neurons → Optic nerve → Brain
(c) Light → Sclera → Cornea → Aqueous humour → Pupil → Lens → Vitreous humour → Retina → Action potentials in neurons → Optic nerve → Brain
(d) Light → Cornea → Aqueous humour → Iris → Lens → Vitreous humour → Retina → Action potentials in neurons → Optic nerve → Brain

7 Human beings, as they grow old, may have problems with their eyes. One of them involves the cornea and can develop due to the decreased traansparency of this eye layer. This problem can successfully be solved through transplantation operation.
Which of the following statements makes this operation more likely to be successful comparing to other transplantation operations? [IJSO 2009, Baku, Azerbaijan]

(a) Cornea is an eye layer situated in the frontal part of the eye
(b) Cornea is not in direct contact with light-sensitive cells
(c) With age the role of cornea in an eye is minimised
(d) There are no blood vessels in the cornea

Answers

1. (a) **2.** (d) **3.** (a) **4.** (d) **5.** (c) **6.** (a) **7.** (d)

**These questions may or may not be asked in the examination, have been given just for additional practice required for olympiads, scholarship exams etc. For detailed explanations refer Page No. 247.*

CHAPTER 10

Endocrine System

Chapter Inside

- Endocrine Glands and Hormones • Human Endocrine System • Regulation of Hormones : Feedback Mechanism • Comparative Study of Nervous System and Endocrine System

Chemical coordination is one of the important aspect in human body as it helps to regulate the complex reaction timely and in appropriate sequence. The chemicals involved in these reactions are secreted by specialised glandular structures into the bloodstream called **endocrine glands**. Collectively, these chemicals (hormones) and the glands constitute the endocrine (*endo*–inside, *crine* – separate) system.

The science associated with the study of structure, mechanism of action, functions, diagnosis and treatment of disorders caused by the endocrine glands is known as **Endocrinology**.

Thomas Addison is the **Father of Endocrinology**.

Endocrine Glands and Hormones

The endocrine glands are called **ductless glands**, i.e. lack ducts. They pour their secretions directly into the surrounding blood which further transports them to the site of action or distantly located target organ. Their secretions are called **hormones** or **internal secretions.**

Hormones

These are **non-nutrient chemicals**, which are produced in trace amounts and act as **intercellular messengers**. These are responsible for regulating the biological processes in the body. The organised endocrine glands also secrete a number of new molecules in addition to the hormones.

Vertebrates have large number of chemicals acting as hormones that provide coordination, while invertebrates possess very simple endocrine system with few hormones.

Note The first hormone **secretin** was discovered by **William M Bayliss** and **Ernest H Starling** in 1902.

General Characteristics of Hormones

(i) Hormones are chemical regulators that are produced and poured directly into the bloodstream. They are carried throughout the body by the circulatory system.

(ii) The sites of their production and actions are different. They are low molecular weight molecules produced in very small quantity and are biologically active. They diffuse readily through the cell membranes.

(iii) They regulate the physiological processes by chemical means. After performing their function, the hormones are eventually carried to the liver by blood where they are either destroyed or converted to inactive substance by liver cells and excreted by kidneys. Thus, these are not stored in the body.

(iv) The excess (hypersecretion) or deficient (hyposecretion) secretion of hormones leads to serious health consequences as they help to cope up with the emergency conditions such as trauma, dehydration, etc.

(v) Hormones produce more or less similar effect in different species.

Chemical Nature of Hormones

Hormones are organic compounds of diverse nature. Chemically, hormones can be **proteinaceous** (FSH, LH, TSH, etc.), **peptides** (ACTH, oxytocin, vasopressin, etc.), **steroids** (sex hormones) or **amino acid derivatives** (thyroxine, epinephrine, etc).

Besides endocrine glands, human body contains **exocrine glands** secretions of which reach to target organs through the ducts. The major differences between endocrine and exocrine glands are tabulated below

Differences between Endocrine and Exocrine Glands

Endocrine glands	Exocrine glands
They do not have ducts.	They have ducts.
They secrete hormones.	They secrete enzymes, milk, saliva, etc.
The target sites of the endocrine glands are present away from the gland.	The target sites of the gland are located close to the gland.
They release products directly into the bloodstream.	They release products to an internal organ or the external surface through a duct.
e.g. Thyroid gland pituitary gland.	e.g. Lacrimal gland (secretes tears), salivary glands.

Human Endocrine System

It consists of the following endocrine glands

1. Pituitary gland
2. Thyroid gland
3. Pancreas (only endocrine part)
4. Adrenal glands

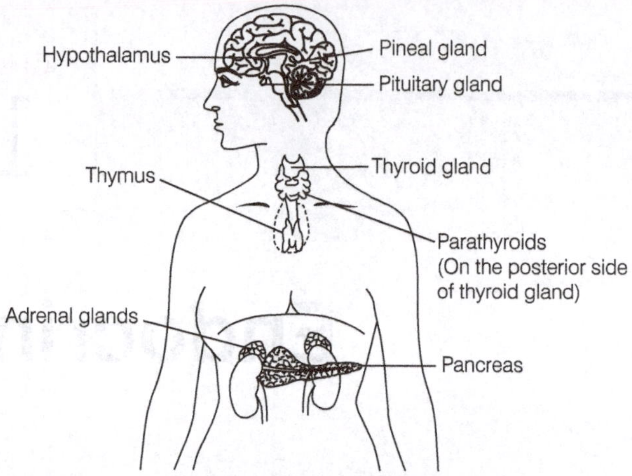

Human endocrine system

In humans, the complete endocrine system works under the influence of **hypothalamus**, which is located below the thalamus of forebrain.

The structure and functions of major endocrine glands are discussed below

Pituitary Gland (Hypophysis)

It is the smallest endocrine gland, but serves very important role in the human endocrine system. It directly or indirectly controls almost all other endocrine glands of the body. Thus, it is also known as **master gland**.

Origin

It originates from the ectoderm of the embryonic germ layers.

Location and Structure

It is **reddish-grey** in colour and is roughly oval in shape. It is about a size of a pea seed. The pituitary gland is located in a small bony cavity of the brain called **sella turcica**.

Anatomically, this gland is formed of two major portions, i.e.

(i) **Adenohypophysis** (ii) **Neurohypophysis**

The adenohypophysis includes the **anterior** and **intermediate lobe** of pituitary, while neurohypophysis is the **posterior lobe** of this gland.

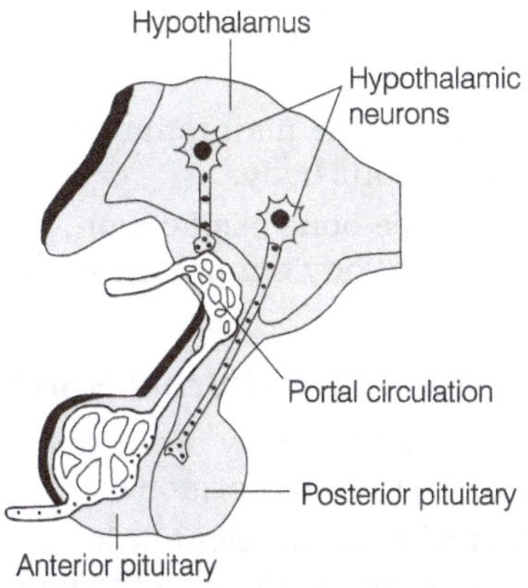

Diagrammatic representation of pituitary and its relationship with hypothalamus

Hormones of Anterior Pituitary

The anterior pituitary regulates several physiological processes including stress, growth, reproduction and lactation. The anterior pituitary is also known as **pars distalis**. The hormones secreted by this region are called **tropic hormones**. These types of hormones stimulate other endocrine glands to produce their specific hormones.

These hormones are given below with their functions

(i) **Growth Hormone** (GH) It stimulates the somatotropic cells of anterior lobe of pituitary gland to release its growth hormone called **somatotropin**. It stimulates body growth, protein, fat and carbohydrate metabolism.
Oversecretion of this hormone during childhood causes **gigantism** (excessive growth of bones), whereas in adulthood, it causes **acromegaly** (excessive growth of bones in the face and in the hands and feet). Its low secretion results in stunted growth, i.e. **pituitary dwarfism**.

(ii) **Prolactin** (PRL) The prolactin releasing hormone regulates the growth of mammary glands and stimulates the production of milk in them.

(iii) **Thyroid Stimulating Hormone** (TSH) It stimulates the synthesis and secretion of thyroid hormones from the thyroid gland.

(iv) **Adrenocorticotropic Hormone** (ACTH) This hormone stimulates the synthesis and secretion of steroid hormones called **glucocorticoids** from the adrenal cortex.

(v) **Gonadotropin Hormone** It secretes **Luteinizing Hormone** (LH) and **Follicle Stimulating Hormone** (FSH).

- **Luteinizing Hormone** (LH) In males, it stimulates the synthesis and secretion of hormones called **androgens** from testis. In females, it induces ovulation of fully mature follicles (**Graafian follicles**)
It is also involved in the maintenance of corpus luteum and associated secretion of progesterone.
- **Follicle Stimulating Hormone** (FSH) In males, the FSH and androgens together regulate spermatogenesis. In females, this hormone stimulates the growth and development of ovarian follicles.

Hormones of Intermediate Pituitary

The intermediate pituitary lobe is also known as **pars intermedia**. This portion of adenohypophysis secretes only one hormone, i.e. **Melanocyte Stimulating Hormone** (MSH). MSH acts on melanocytes (melanin containing cells) and regulates the pigmentation of the skin.

Hormones of Posterior Pituitary

The posterior lobe of pituitary releases two main hormones, which are synthesised and secreted by hypothalamus. These are

(i) **Oxytocin** It acts on the smooth muscles of pregnant mother and stimulates a vigorous contraction of uterus at the time of childbirth. It also plays role in ejection of milk from the mammary glands in females. Hence, it is also known as the **birth hormone**.

(ii) **Vasopressin/ADH** This hormone acts mainly at the kidney, stimulating the reabsorption of water and electrolytes by the distal tubules, thereby reducing the loss of water through urine (diuresis).
Deficiency of Antidiuretic Hormone (ADH) causes a type of diabetes known as **diabetes insipidus** in which person suffers from loss of water due to frequent urination resulting in excessive thirst and dehydration.

Check Your LEARNING...

1. Who is rewarded as Father of Endocrinology?
2. Name two proteinaceous hormones.
3. Name two exocrine glands.
4. Which gland is known as 'master gland'?
5. Write the functions of Follicle Stimulating Hormone (FSH).
6. Melanocyte stimulating hormone acts on which part of the body?
7. Which hormone is called 'birth hormone'?

Thyroid Gland

The thyroid gland is known to be the largest endocrine gland.

Origin

It is endodermal in origin, i.e. originates from the endoderm of the embryo. The thyroid gland is bilobed and highly vascular organ.

Location and Structure

It surrounds the front of the neck just below the larynx and is composed of two lobes. Each of its lobe is located on either sides of the trachea in the neck, interconnected with each other through, a thin flap of connective tissue called **isthmus**.

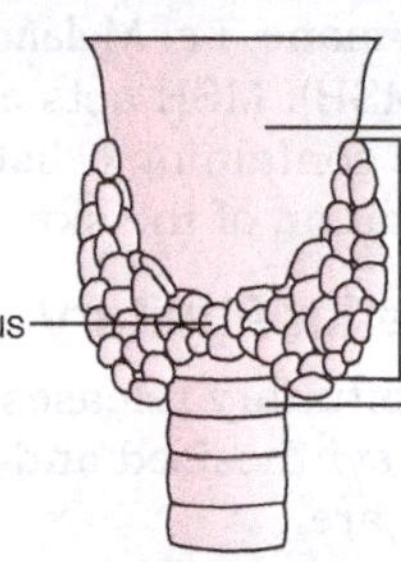

Diagrammatic view of the position of thyroid gland (ventral side)

It is composed of follicles (round in shape) held together by loose connective tissue called **stromal tissues**. Each thyroid follicle is composed of follicular cells, each of which enclose a cavity.

Hormones

The hormones secreted by the thyroid gland are

(i) **Tetraiodothyronine or thyroxine** (T_4) and **triiodothyronine** (T_3) Both these hormones are released from follicular cells of thyroid gland. They are the iodinated forms of amino acid (tyrosine). T_3 and T_4 hormones have similar effects, thus these are collectively known as **Thyroid Hormone** (TH).

(ii) **Calcitonin** (CT) or **Thyrocalcitonin** This hormone is proteinaceous in nature. It controls calcium and phosphorus balance in the blood plasma.

Functions of Thyroid Hormones

Thyroid hormones serve several functions in the body, such as

(a) These hormones regulate and maintain the **Basal Metabolic Rate** (BMR), i.e. both T_3 and T_4 hormones increase the overall metabolic rate of the body.

(b) They support the process of formation of red blood cells and also help in controlling the metabolism of carbohydrates, proteins and fats.

(c) They influence the maintenance of water and electrolyte in our body.

(d) They influence bone ossification, mental development, body temperature and overall growth.

Disorders Caused by Thyroid Hormones

Following abnormalities may occur due to hypo or hypersecretion of thyroid hormones

I. **Hypothyroidism** Insufficient or low secretion of thyroxine hormone may lead to following three conditions

(i) **Simple goitre** It occurs due to insufficient amount of iodine in food. Due to this disorder, the thyroid gland gets enlarged. Swollen neck is one of its symptoms.

This condition is common in the people living in hilly regions where iodine is deficient in soil and hence in the food grown there.

(ii) **Cretinism** It is seen in children. Hypothyroidism in women at the time of pregnancy mainly affects the physical and mental growth of children, due to which he/she has retarted growth (dwarfism) and mental development.

(iii) **Myxoedema** It occurs due to improper functioning of thyroid gland in adults. Symptoms include puffy appearance due to deposition of fat under skin.

II. **Hyperthyroidism** It is the condition during which rate of synthesis and secretion of thyroid hormone is increased to abnormally higher levels. It may occur due to cancer of the thyroid gland or due to development of nodules of the thyroid gland. It adversely affects the body physiology of an organism.

Exophthalmic goitre It occurs due to the excessive secretion of thyroxine secretion. It is characterised by protruted eyeballs, increased metabolism, shortness of breath and restlessness.

Check Your LEARNING...

1 State the origin and location of thyroid gland.
2 What are stromal tissues?
3 State one main function of thyrocalcitonin hormone.
4 Which hormone is responsible for regulating the normal basal metabolism?
5 On the basis of change in thyroxine levels, how can you differentiate between cretinism and exophtalmic goitre?

Pancreas

It is a composite gland that acts as both exocrine and endocrine gland. Such glands are also called **heterocrine gland.**

Origin

It originates from the endoderm of the embryonic germ layers.

Location

It lies below the stomach, in the loop of duodenum.

Structure

It is elongated yellowish gland that consists of large number of acini and ducts. Besides these, pancreas consists of 1-2 millions of small group of specialised cells, called **Islets of Langerhans** (after the name of their discoverer **Paul Langerhans** in 1869) which are scattered in entire gland. In normal human pancreas, these cells represent only 1-2% of the pancreatic tissue.

Each islet (*islet*–little islands) consists of following cells

(i) α-**cells** (about 25%) secrete a peptide hormone called **glucagon.**

(ii) β-**cells** (about 60%) They secrete another peptide hormone called **insulin.**

(iii) δ-**cells** They secrete **somatostatin** which inhibits the secretion of insulin and glucagon.

Hormones

Glucagon and **insulin** have antagonistic effect on blood glucose level. This could be understood from the functioning given below

(i) **Glucagon** It is a peptide hormone secreted by α-cells.

Functions of Glucagon

(a) It acts mainly on liver cells (hepatocytes) and stimulates glycogenolysis (breakdown of glycogen) which results in an increased blood sugar known as **hyperglycaemia.**

(b) Apart from this, glucagon also stimulates the process of gluconeogenesis (synthesis of glucose molecules from fat and protein) which also contributes to hyperglycaemia. Glucagon is known as **hyperglycaemic hormone** because it reduces the cellular glucose uptake and utilisation.

(ii) **Insulin** It is a peptide hormone seereted by β-cells. It mainly acts on **hepatocytes** and **adipocytes** (cells of adipose tissue) and helps in increasing the cellular glucose uptake and utilisation. As a result, the movement of glucose takes place rapidly from blood to liver cells and cells of adipose tissues thereby, decreasing the blood glucose level (**hypoglycaemia**).

Functions of Insulin

(a) This peptide hormone plays a major role in regulation of glucose level in the blood. It stimulates the conversion of glucose to glycogen (glycogenesis) in the target cells.

(b) Decreases gluconeogenesis.

(c) Decreases glycogenolysis

(d) Also reduces the catabolism of proteins and fats.

(e) Increases synthesis of fat in the adipose tissue from fatty acids.

Abnormalities of Insulin Hormone

Low secretion of insulin hormone in humans is responsible for causing **diabetes mellitus** or **hyperglycaemia.**

Symptoms include

(i) The person starts losing glucose (sugar) in urine (glycosuria) and has high level of glucose in the blood.

(ii) A diabetic person loses weight and feels more thirsty due to the loss of water by frequent urination.

Oversecretion of insulin results in lowering of sugar level in the blood known as **hypoglycaemia** due to which a person may enter a state of coma or even death may occur.

In a diabetic patient, overdose of insulin results in **insulin shock** due to hypoglycaemia. Patient can be recovered by giving sugar promptly.

Check Your LEARNING...

1 Why is pancreas referred to as heterocrine gland?
2 What are Islets of Langerhans?
3 What is meant by hyperglycaemia ?
4 How hypoglycaemia is caused in human?
5 Why diabetic patient feels so thirsty?

Adrenal Glands (Suprarenals)

Location

Our body has a pair of adrenal glands, each located at the anterior part or top of each kidney.

Structure

Adrenal glands are conical, yellowish bodies composed of two types of tissues, i.e. peripheral adrenal cortex and central adrenal medulla.

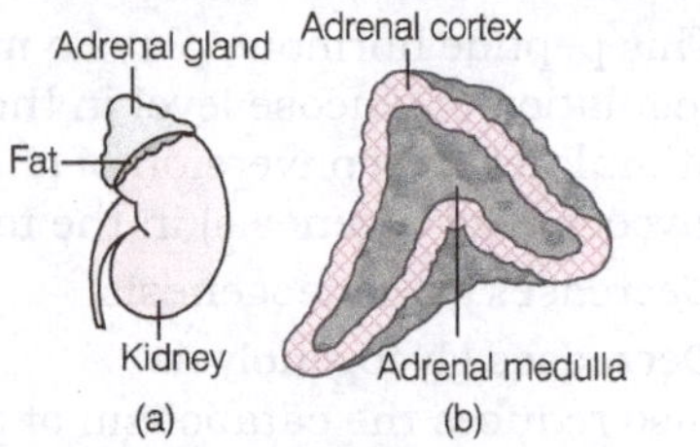

Diagrammatic representation of adrenal gland
(a) Adrenal gland above kidney
(b) section showing two parts of adrenal gland

Adrenal Cortex

It is an external, firm and pale-yellowish tissue derived from the mesoderm of embryo. It is formed of three concentric layers, i.e. an inner, a middle and an outer layer. Hormones secreted by these three layers of adrenal cortex are collectively known as **corticoids.**

Three groups of steroid hormones are secreted by adrenal cortex such as

(i) **Glucocorticoids** Cortisol is the main glucocorticoid found in our body.

Functions

- Cortisol regulates the metabolism of carbohydrates, fats and proteins in the body.
- It stimulates the liver for the synthesis of carbohydrates from non-carbohydrate sources (like amino acids and glycerol). This process is known as **gluconeogenesis**. Thus, it increases blood glucose concentration.
- It is involved in the maintenance of cardiovascular system and in proper functioning of kidney by regulating salt and water balance in body.
- Cortisol produces anti-inflammatory reactions and functions in the suppression of immune response. It stimulates the production of RBCs and helps the body to adapt to stresses like heat, cold, etc.

(ii) **Mineralocorticoids** Aldosterone is the major mineralocorticoid found in our body.
It mainly acts on renal tubules, stimulating the reabsorption of Na^+ and water. It also stimulates the excretion of K^+ and phosphate ions from the body.

Functions

Its main functions are to regulate the balance of electrolytes, body fluid volume, osmotic pressure and blood pressure of the body.

(iii) **Sexocorticoids** (Androgens) Adrenal cortex produces a small quantity of androgenic steroids, i.e. sex hormone (androgens), both in males and females. These hormones are secreted as **DHEA** (Dihydroxy Epiandrosterone), which acts as a precursor of both testosterone and oestrogen.

Functions

- They play a major role in the growth of axial, pubic and facial hair during puberty.
- Development of acne in a young girl is due to the overproduction of these hormones.
- They play an important role in the development of embryo (foetus).

Abnormalities of Hormones from Adrenal Cortex

- **Hyposecretion of hormones** from adrenal cortex causes **Addison's disease.** Symptoms include loss of skin pigment, loss of weight, low blood sugar, sensitivity to cold and susceptibility to infections, etc.
- **Hypersecretion of cortisol** from adrenal cortex causes **Cushing's syndrome.** Symptoms include high blood sugar (hyperglycaemia), obesity, weakening of bones (osteoporosis), retention of salt and water in tissues, etc.
- **Hypersecretion of sexocorticoids** causes **adrenal virilism** in females. The female develops male secondary sexual characters such as appearance of beard, moustaches, etc.
- **Hypersecretion of aldosterone** causes **Conn's syndrome** or **aldosteronism.** It results in high Na^+, low K^+, high blood pressure, muscular weakness, etc.

Adrenal Medulla

The adrenal medulla lies in the centre of the adrenal gland. It is an internal, soft, dark reddish-brown tissue derived from the ectoderm.

The adrenal medulla secretes two hormones, i.e.

(i) **Adrenaline** (epinephrine)

(ii) **Nor-adrenaline** (nor-epinephrine)

Activation of Adrenaline and Nor-adrenaline

Both hormones belong to the category of compounds known as **catecholamines** and are secreted in response to any kind of stress, danger and during emergency situations like increased respiratory rate, heartbeat, etc.

The nerve endings of the autonomic nervous system at the time of stress or danger stimulates the adrenal medulla to release both these hormones. These are also known as **emergency hormones** or **hormones of fight, flight** or **fright.**

Functions of Adrenaline and Nor-adrenaline

Effects of adrenaline and nor-adrenaline hormones on various body organs and processes are given below

Human system	Adrenaline	Nor-adrenaline
Heart rate	Increases	Decreases
Cardiac output	Increases	Slightly increases
Blood pressure	Raised in general	No change
Skin vessels	Dilates some, constrict other	Constricts all
CNS	Increases mental anxiety	No effect
Oxgen consumption	Increases	No effect
Blood sugar	Increases	Slightly increases

Note Adrenal gland is known as **gland of 4S** because it controls sugar metabolism, salt concentration, stress or strain and sexual activities.

Regulation of Hormones : Feedback Mechanism

It is the mechanism of maintaining the normal balanced state between the rise and fall of hormones, i.e. to slow down the process, if excess amount of hormone is secreted and to speed up the process, if very low amount of hormone is released. The mechanism is usually negative feedback, although a few positive feedback mechanisms are also known.

Negative Feedback Control

It is a closed loop in which synthesis of hormone stops or lowers, when its blood level rises above the normal. For example, if the level of glucose rises in the blood, it is detected by β-cells of the pancreas and it produces more insulin. This promotes absorption of glucose by the cells and its level is brought back to normal. The result is inhibition of insulin.

Positive Feedback Control

In this feedback, the production of hormone is further stimulated by its action, e.g. uterine contractions during childbirth stimulate the release of oxytocin into the mother's blood. This further intensifies uterine contractions, thus causing more oxytocin release. Production and release of oxytocin stop after the birth of the baby.

Feedback Control by Thyroid Stimulating Hormone

Thyroid stimulating hormone stimulates the synthesis and secretion of thyroid hormones from thyroid gland. The hypothalamus is stimulated by some external stimulus produced to thyroid releasing hormone. This stimulates anterior pituitary to secrete a specific hormone, i.e. Thyroid Stimulating Hormone (TSH).

TSH inturn stimulates thyroid gland to produce the hormone thyroxine.

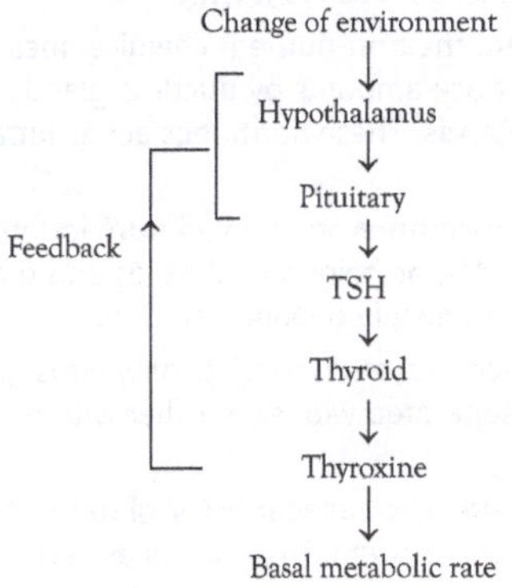

Feedback control by TSH

If the level of thyroxine in blood is high, it exerts a negative feedback effect on hypothalamus and anterior pituitary. If the level of thyroxine is less than normal, it stimulates hypothalamus to produce more Thyroid Stimulating Hormone-Releasing Factors or TSH-RF (positive feedback).

But, if thyroxine is present in more amount, the hypothalamus secretes less TSH-RF (negative feedback).

Comparative Study of Nervous System and Endocrine System

We already know that both the endocrine and nervous system work in coordination with each other. However, significant differences exist between their activation, mechanism and responses.

Some of these differences are given in the table below

Features	Nervous system	Endocrine system
Signal	Electrical signals as nerve impulses. Chemical transfer of information by synapses.	Chemical signals only.
Signal speed	Rapid.	Comparatively slower.
Effects generated	Localised but short- lived.	General effects can be short spanned or long lasting.
Potential for modifications	The responses can be improved from previous experiences.	No learning from previous responses.

Check Your LEARNING...

1 State the location of adrenal glands.
2 What are corticoids? Which part of adernal gland produces them?
3 What is gluconeogenesis?
4 Expand DHEA.
5 State the symptoms of Addison's disease.
6 Which hormone is involved in the dilation of pupil?
7 Which mechanism usually results in inhibition of the secretion of a hormone in case it is present in excess?

QUiCK Revision

- **Endocrine system** is needed to regulate the cellular functions continuously as the nerve fibres do not innervate all cells of the body, which is done with the help of special chemical messengers called **hormones.**
- **Hormones** are the non-nutrient chemical messengers produced in trace amounts by ductless glands called **endocrine glands**. These hormones act as intracellular messengers.
- **Chemically hormones** are derived from iodothyronines, amines, peptides, proteins and steroids and the chemical nature of the molecule depends on them.
- Human endocrine system consists of various glands present in our body separated with each other with no anatomical links.
- **Pituitary gland** also called **master gland** is the regulating unit of hormonal system. The hormones secreted by **anterior pituitary** are growth hormone, gonadotropic hormones, prolactin, adrenocorticotropic hormone and thyroid stimulating hormone. **Intermediate pituitary** secretes melanocyte stimulating hormone. **Posterior pituitary** releases the hormones ADH and oxytocin (synthesised by hypothalamus) in the time of need.
- **Thyroid gland** is the largest endocrine gland made up of two lobes connected to each other by isthmus. It is composed of follicles and stromal tissues which is made up cuboidal epithelium. The hormones synthesised by these follicles are thyroxine (T_4), triiodothyronine (T_3) and calcitonin.
- **Pancreas** is a heterocrine gland. Its endocrine part consists of cells called **Islets of Langerhans** which is further composed of α, β and δ-cells, they secrete glucagon, insulin and somatostatin, respectively. Glucagon and insulin have antagonistic effect on blood glucose level.
- **Adrenal glands** are composed by adrenal cortex and adrenal medulla. **Adrenal cortex** is responsible for the secretion of 20 steroid hormones called **corticoids**, which are mineralocorticoids, glucocorticoids and sexocorticoids. On the other hand, **adrenal medulla** produces **adrenaline** (epinephrine) and **nor-adrenaline** (nor-epinephrine). **Catecholamines** from adrenal medulla are responsible for the 3F, i.e. 'fight', 'flight' and 'fright' during stressful condition. They are lipolytic, proteolytic and also promote glycogenolysis.
- Feedback mechanism present in our body helps in maintaining a stable state by accelerating or inhibiting a process. The two feedback mechanisms are positive and negative. Out of these, negative feedback mechanism is much seen.

Chapter Practice

Section-I

1 Mark Questions

1. Name the following.
   (i) The gland that is also called hypophysis.
   (ii) The pituitary hormone which stimulates the contraction of uterus during childbirth. [2017]
   (iii) The hormones secreted by islets of Langerhans. [2014]
   (iv) The hormone that releases glucose into the blood.
   (v) The hormone that controls Na^+ and K^+ metabolism in the body.
   (vi) The hormone secreted by outermost layer of adrenal cortex.

Ans. (i) Pituitary gland (ii) Oxytocin hormone
(iii) Insulin and glucagon (iv) Glucagon
(v) Aldosterone (vi) Mineralocorticoids

2. Correct and rewrite the following statements by changing the underlined words.
   (i) Thyroid gland is both exocrine and endocrine in function.
   (ii) Hormones like GH, FSH, ICSH, etc., are secreted by pineal gland.
   (iii) Aldosterone is a glucocorticoid.
   (iv) Pancreas is known as the gland of 4S.

Ans. (i) Pancreas is both exocrine and endocrine in function.
(ii) Hormones like GH, FSH, ICSH, etc., are secreted by anterior pituitary gland.
(iii) Aldosterone is a mineralocorticoid.
(iv) Adrenal gland is known as the gland of 4S.

3. Give biological reasons for the following.
   (i) Hormonal responses are slower than reflex actions.
   (ii) Simply goitre is usually seen in people living in the hilly regions. [Semester II 2022]
   (iii) Adrenal glands are also called glands of emergency.
   (iv) Some women have facial hair-like beard and moustache. [2017]

Ans. (i) Hormonal responses are slower than reflex actions because hormones which initiate and control the responses are chemicals transported by blood. On the contrary in reflex actions, the impulses are electrical in nature and are transmitted by specialised cells called neurons that make up nerve tissue.
(ii) Goitre is usually seen in people living in hilly areas because of insufficient iodine in their diet. They drink water from river and streams fed by melting show which is iodine deficient. Even-their diet has little iodine.
(iii) Adrenal glands are called glands of emergency because hormones of adrenal medulla increase the metabolism to prepare the animal to face immediate physical and emotional stress and emergency situations.
(iv) Some women have facial hair-like beard and moustache due to the hypersecretion of sexocorticoids from adrenal gland.

4. (i) Match the following columns. [2023]

	Column I	Column II
A.	Hyposecretion of thyroxine in adults	1. Diabetes insipidus
B.	Hyposecretion of insulin	2. Myxoedema
C.	Hypersecretion of growth hormone in childhood	3. Dwarfism
D.	Hyposecretion of ADH	4. Gigantism
E.	Hypersecretion of thyroxine	5. Diabetes mellitus
		6. Exophthalmic goitre
		7. Cretinism

(ii) Match the following columns.

	Column I	Column II
A.	Cretinism	1. Hypersecretion of adrenal cortex
B.	Diabetes insipidus	2. Hyposecretion of thyroxine
C.	Exophthalmic goitre	3. Hyposecretion of growth hormone
D.	Adrenal virilism	4. Hyposecretion of vasopressin
E.	Dwarfism	5. Hyposecretion of adrenal cortex
		6. Hypersecretion of growth hormone
		7. Hypersecretion of thyoxine

[2018]

Ans. (i) A–2,7, B–5, C–4, D–1, E–6 (ii) A–2, B–4, C–7, D–1, E–3

5. Choose the correct answer from the four options given below.
   (i) Father of Endocrinology is
   (a) Huxley (b) Thomas Addison
   (c) Abel (d) Kimball and Murlin

Ans. (b)

(ii) Which of the following glands is known as master gland?
(a) Adrenal glands (b) Kidneys
(c) Pituitary (d) Pancreas

Ans. (c)

(iii) Gigantism and dwarfism are the diseases related to
(a) prolactin hormone of mammary gland
(b) growth hormone of adenohypophysis
(c) Luteinizing hormone of pituitary gland
(d) thyroid stimulating hormone of thyroid gland

Ans. (b)

(iv) Gigantism and acromegaly are due to [Semester II 2022, 16]
(a) hyposecretion of thyroxine
(b) hyposecretion of growth hormone
(c) hypersecretion of thyroxine
(d) hypersecretion of growth hormone

Ans. (d)

(v) Cretinism, mental retardation, low intelligence quotient, abnormal skin, deaf-mutism, etc., are the results of
(a) hyperthyroidism (b) goitre
(c) hypothyroidism (d) Both (b) and (c)

Ans. (c)

(vi) Identify the correct statement.
(a) Hyperthyroidism adversely affects the body physiology
(b) Hypothyroidism causes cretinism
(c) Hypothyroidism causes goitre
(d) All of the above

Ans. (d)

(vii) Cretinism and myxoedema are due to [2014]
(a) hypersecretion of thyroxine
(b) hypersecretion of growth hormone
(c) hyposecretion of thyroxine
(d) hyposecretion of growth hormone

Ans. (c)

(viii) A gland which secretes both hormone and enzyme is [2013]
(a) pituitary (b) pancreas (c) thyroid (d) adrenal

Ans. (b)

(ix) Islets of langerhans are located in [Semester II 2022]
(a) liver (b) pituitary gland
(c) spleen (d) pancreas

Ans. (d)

(x) Alpha cells of pancreas secrete [2023]
(a) glycogen (b) glucose
(c) glucagon (d) insulin

Ans. (c)

(xi) The child frightened by the loud noise, runs quickly to his mother. Which substance helps in this response?
(a) Adrenaline (b) Insulin
(c) Amylase (d) Protease

Ans. (a)

(xii) To maintain the constant steady state of our body, hormonal secretion is regulated by
(a) positive feedback (b) negative feedback
(c) Both (a) and (b) (d) Neither (a) nor (b)

Ans. (c)

6. Complete the following table by filling in blank spaces (i) to (vi).

Glands	Substances produced	One important function
Islets of Langerhans	(i)	(ii) ....
(iii)	Adrenaline	(iv) ....
(v)	LH	(vi) ....

Ans.

Glands	Substances produced	One important function
Islets of Langerhans	Insulin (i)	Decreases sugar level in the body (ii)
Adrenal (iii)	Adrenaline	Increases heartbeat (iv)
Pituitary (v)	LH	Stimulates the production of progesterone (vi)

7. Fill in the blanks by using suitable words.
(i) Nervous system and ...... are very closely associated.
(ii) The glands with ducts are known as ....
(iii) ...... gland stimulates secretion of different hormones and is also responsible for growth.

Ans. (i) endocrine system (ii) exocrine glands
(iii) Pituitary

8. Complete the following paragraph by filling in the blanks (i) to (v) with appropriate words.

The amount of urine output is under the regulation of a hormone called (i) .... secreted by the (ii) .... lobe of the pituitary gland. If secretion of this hormone is reduced, there is an increased production of urine. This disorder is called (iii) .... Sometimes excess glucose is passed with urine due to hyposecretion of another hormone called (iv) .... leading to the cause of disease called (v) .... [2016]

Ans. (i) ADH (ii) posterior
(iii) diabetes insipidus (iv) insulin
(v) glycosuria

9. Choose the odd one out from the following terms given below and name the category to which other three belong. [2017]
(i) ACTH, TSH, ADH, FSH
(ii) Cortisone, Somatotropin, Adrenocorticotropic hormone, Vasopressin [2016]
(iii) Oxytocin, Insulin, Prolactin, Progesterone [2014]
(iv) Adrenal gland, Thyroid gland, Pituitary gland, Liver [2012]
(v) Addison's disease, Cushing's syndrome Acromegaly, Leukemia [2019]
(vi) Insulin, Adrenaline, Pepsin, Thyroxine [2019]

Ans. (i) **Odd term** is ADH.
Rest three are the hormones of anterior pituitary gland.
(ii) **Odd term** is cortisone.
Rest hormones are secreted by pituitary gland.
(iii) **Odd term** is insulin.
Rest other hormones are involved in pregnancy and lactation.
(iv) **Odd term** is liver.
Rest three are endocrine glands.
(v) **Odd term** is leukemia.
Rest diseases/syndromes are caused due to hyposecretion or hypersecretion of hormones.
(vi) **Odd term** is pepsin.
Rest are amino acid derived hormones.

10. Given below are the sets of five terms each. Rewrite the terms in correct order of a logical sequence.
(i) Posterior pituitary, Hypothalamic neurons, Portal circulation, Target organs, Hypothalamus
(ii) TSH, External stimulus, Anterior pituitary, Hypothalamus, Thyroxine

Ans. (i) Hypothalamus, Hypothalamic neurons, Portal circulation, Posterior pituitary, Target organs
(ii) External stimulus, Hypothalamus, Anterior pituitary, TSH, Thyroxine

11. Expand the following biological abbreviations. **[2019, 14]**
(i) TSH (ii) GH (iii) BMR (iv) ADH
(v) ACTH **[Semester II 2022]**

Ans. (i) Thyroid Stimulating Hormone
(ii) Growth Hormone
(iii) Basal Metabolic Rate
(iv) Anti-Diuretic Hormone
(v) Adrenocorticotropic Hormone

12. State the exact location of the following. **[2016, 12]**
(i) Thyroid gland **[2023]**
(ii) Adrenal gland (iii) Pancreas
(iv) Islets of Langerhans **[2023]**

Ans. (i) Thyroid gland is located in the front of neck region, just below the larynx.
(ii) Adrenal glands are situated above each kidney, as a cap-like structure.
(iii) Pancreas is found below the stomach, in the loop of duodenum.
(iv) Islets of Langerhans - These are endocrine cells found in the pancreas that secrete hormones.

13. State the main function of the following.
(i) Growth hormone (ii) Oxytocin

Ans. (i) Growth hormone stimulates body growth, protein, fat and carbohydrate metabolism.
(ii) Oxytocin acts on smooth muscles and stimulates vigorous contraction of uterus during childbirth.

14. Mention one difference between each of the following pairs on the basis of what is given in the bracket.
(i) Simple goitre and Exophthalmic goitre (cause of the disorder) **[2017]**
(ii) Diabetes mellitus and Diabetes insipidus (cause) **[2012]**
(iii) Acromegaly and Myxoedema (symptom)

Ans. (i) Difference between simple goitre and exophthalmic goitre is as follows

Simple goitre	Exophthalmic goitre
It is caused by the deficiency of iodine.	It is caused by the overactivity of thyroid gland.

(ii) Difference between diabetes insipidus and diabetes mellitus is as follows

Diabetes insipidus	Diabetes mellitus
It is caused due to low secretion of ADH.	It is caused due to low secretion of insulin.

(iii) Difference between acromegaly and myxoedema is as follows

Acromegaly	Myxoedema
It is characterised by long bones of hand and legs which gives a person gorilla-like appearance.	It is characterised by puffy appearance due to accumulation of fat in subcutaneous tissue.

15. Give biological/technical terms for the following.
(i) Group of hormones which influence other endocrine glands to produce hormones. **[2014, 12]**
Or Hormones which regulate the secretion of other endocrine glands. **[2018]**
(ii) A condition which results in abnormally long bones, long lower jaw bone due to the hypersecretion of a pituitary hormone.
(iii) The hormone responsible for water exchange in the renal tubules.
(iv) The endocrine cells present in pancreatic gland.

Ans. (i) Tropic hormones
(ii) Acromegaly
(iii) ADH/Vasopressin
(iv) Islets of Langerhans- α, β and δ-cells

16. Briefly explain the following terms.
(i) Corticoids **[2014, 10]**
(ii) Tropic hormones **[2017]**
(iii) Diabetes insipidus **[2013]**

Ans. (i) Hormones secreted by all three layers of adrenal cortex are collectively known as corticoids.
(ii) Tropic hormones are the hormones which stimulate other endocrine glands to produce their specific hormones.
(iii) Diabetes insipidus is the condition which occurs due to low secretion of vasopressin or antidiuretic

hormone from the posterior lobe of pituitary gland. The disease is characterised by excretion of large amounts of urine and subsequent dehydration and thirst.

17. Answer the questions briefly.
(i) Mention any two characteristics of hormones.
(ii) 'Hormones are soluble in water as well in lipids'. Justify the statement.
(iii) Enlist the symptoms shown by a person having problem of thyroxine oversecretion.
(iv) What does insulin shock mean?
(v) What is the effect of adrenaline on the arterioles of digestive system and what is its biological advantage?

Ans. (i) Two characteristics of hormones are as follows
(a) Hormones act on target organs or cells, away from their source.
(b) Hormones are produced in very small quantity but are biologically very active.
(ii) Chemically, hormones are of diverse nature. Proteinaceous hormones like FSH and amine hormones like adrenaline are water soluble. In contrast, steroid hormones like testosterone are derived from cholesterol and these are lipid soluble.
(iii) The symptoms shown by a person having problem of thyroxine oversecretion are
(a) increased metabolic rate and heartbeat
(b) protruded eyes and restless ness
(iv) If an overdose of insulin is given to a diabetic patient, the patient may become unconscious due to hypoglycaemia. It is known as insulin shock.
(v) Adrenaline constricts the arterioles of digestive system. It reduces the blood supply to digestive system and allows more blood to reach the muscles in emergency situation.

2 Marks Questions

18. Describe what happens to hormones after they have brought about their effects on their target organs.

Ans. After they have performed their function, hormones are eventually carried to the liver by blood where they are either destroyed or converted to inactive substances by the liver cells and are excreted by the kidneys.

19. When does the secretion of adrenocorticotropin take place in the body? What is the purpose of its secretion?

Ans. Adrenocorticotropin is secreted when Adrenocorticotropin Releasing Hormone (ACRH) stimulates the corticotroph cells of anterior lobe of pituitary gland.
It is released because its stimulation is responsible for the synthesis and secretion of glucocorticoids and mineralocorticoids from the adrenal cortex of adrenal gland.

20. Which hormones are secreted by the posterior pituitary gland? What function does each serve? Where are these hormones actually produced?

Ans. Oxytocin and vasopressin are secreted by the posterior pituitary gland.
Oxytocin acts on smooth muscles of pregnant mother and stimulates vigorous contraction of uterus during the childbirth. On the other hand, vasopressin/ADH acts mainly on the kidney and stimulates the reabsorption of water and electrolytes by distal tubules.
Both these hormones are actually synthesised by hypothalamus.

21. What is adrenal virilism? What cause this condition? **[Semester II 2022]**

Ans. Adrenal virilism is a disorder arises due to hyposecretion of sex corticoids by the adrenal cortex. It is mainly observed in females. The female suffering from this syndrome develop certain male characteristics such as beard, moustaches, and deep male voice, etc. male suffering from this syndrome may become infertile due to suppressed gonadal function.

3 Marks Questions

22. Which hormonal hyposecretion is responsible for the following?
(i) Diabetes mellitus (ii) Goitre
(iii) Cretinism

Ans. (i) Diabetes mellitus is due to the hyposecretion of insulin.
(ii) Goitre is due to the hyposecretion of thyroxine (T_4).
(iii) Cretinism is due to the hyposecretion of thyroxine hormone.

23. Complete the following table by filling in the marked blanks with an appropriate terms/answers. **[2017]**

Glands	Hormones produced	Functions
Thyroid	*A*	*B*
C	*D*	Dilates pupil of eye
E	Insulin	*F*
G	ADH	*H*
I	*J*	Conversion of glycogen to glucose

Ans.

Glands	Hormones produced	Functions
Thyroid	Thyroxine (*A*)	It regulates the basal metabolism of the body (*B*)
Adrenal medulla (*C*)	Adrenaline (*D*)	Dilates pupil of eye
Beta cells of pancreas (*E*)	Insulin	Lower the sugar level in the blood (*F*)

Posterior pituitary gland (*G*)	ADH	Increases reabsorption of water from kidney (*H*)
Alpha cells of pancreas (*I*)	glucagon (*J*)	Conversion of glycogen to glucose

24. Mention the name of diseases based on the symptoms given below.
    (i) Excessive growth of bones in face, hands and feet.
    (ii) Loss of skin pigment, weight loss, low blood sugar.
    (iii) Appearance of male secondary sexual characters in females.

Ans. (i) Acromegaly (ii) Addison's disease
(iii) Adrenal virilism

Section-II [5 Marks]

Structured Questions

1. Given below is the outline of the human body showing the important glands. [2016]

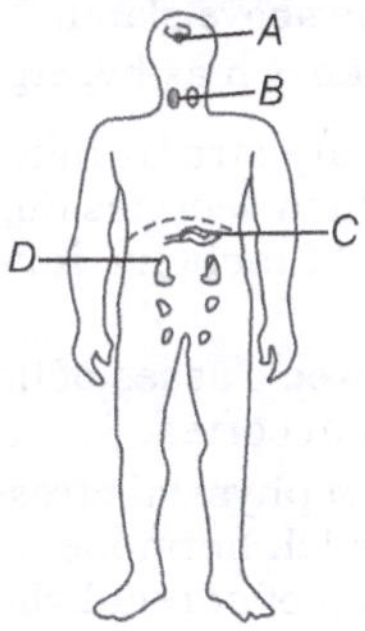

(i) Name the glands labelled as *A-D*.
(ii) Name the hormone secreted by part *B*. Give one important function of this hormone.
(iii) Name the endocrine part of the gland labelled as *C*.
(iv) Why is the part labelled as *A* called the master gland? Which part of the forebrain controls the gland labelled as *A*?
(v) Name the gland that secretes the 'emergency hormone'.

Ans. (i) The gland parts *A–D* are labelled as
A–Pituitary *B*–Thyroid
C–Pancreas *D*–Adrenal
(ii) Thyroid gland (*B*) produces thyroxine which controls the basal metabolic rate of the body.
(iii) The part '*C*' represents the islets of Langerhans (i.e. the endocrine part of the pancreas) which secretes two hormones, namely insulin and glucagon.
(iv) Pituitary gland (*A*) controls the secretions of other endocrine glands of the body. Its secretions are controlled by hypothalamus.
(v) Adrenal gland produces adrenaline, i.e. the emergency hormone.

2. Observe the diagram given below and answer the questions that follow.

(i) The figure depicts a condition caused by hyposecretion of a hormone. Identify this condition.
(ii) Suggest the underlying cause for this condition.
(iii) Name any two diseases resulting due to same cause.
(iv) What would a person suffer from, if there was hypersecretion of thyroid gland?
(v) Name the disease caused by improper thyroid functioning, resulting in puffy eyes.

Ans. (i) This given condition is goitre.
(ii) Enlargement of thyroid gland due to iodine deficiency.
(iii) Cretinism and myxoedema are two diseases resulting due to same cause.
(iv) The person will suffer from exophthalmic goitre.
(v) Myxoedema caused by improper thyroid, functioning, resulting in puffy eyes.

3. The given diagram represents the location and structure of an endocrine gland. Study the same and answer the questions that follow. [2017]

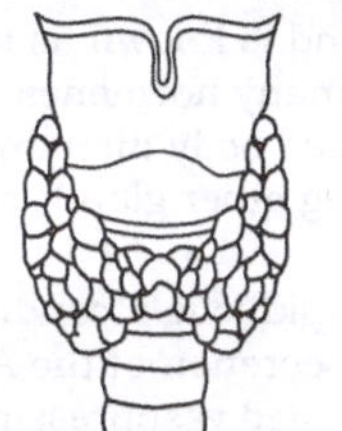

(i) Name the endocrine gland shown in the diagram.
(ii) Name the secretion of the gland which regulates basal metabolism.
(iii) Name the mineral element required for the synthesis of the above mentioned hormone.
(iv) Name the disease caused due to undersecretion of the above mentioned hormone in children.
(v) Name the disease caused due to hypersecretion of the above mentioned hormone.

Ans. (i) The given diagram is of thyroid gland.
(ii) Thyroxine hormone, secreted by the thyroid gland is responsible for the regulation of normal basal metabolism of the body.
(iii) Thyroxine requires iodine in order to be synthesised.

(iv) Undersecretion of thyroxine hormone causes cretinism in children.
(v) Hypersecretion of thyroxine hormone can cause exophthalmic goitre.

4. The diagram given below represents an endocrine gland in the human body. Study the diagram and answer the questions that follow. [2019]

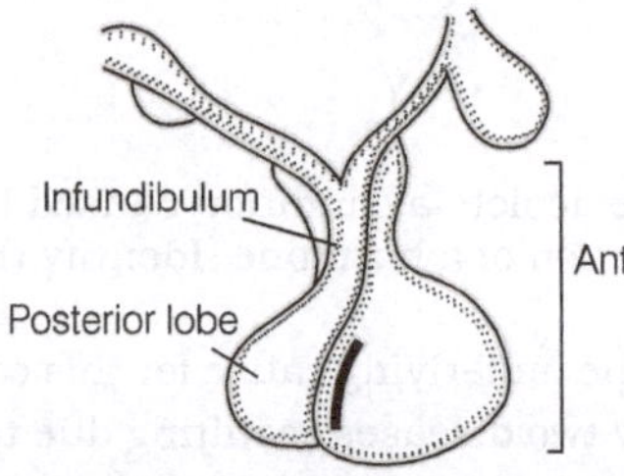

(i) Identify the endocrine gland. Where is it located?
(ii) Why is the above gland referred to as the 'master gland'?
(iii) Name the hormone which in hyposecretion causes diabetes insipidus. How does this disorder differ from diabetes mellitus ?
(iv) Explain the term 'hormone'. What is the role of tropic hormones in the human body?
(v) Which lobe of the above gland secretes
(a) oxytocin
(b) ACTH
(c) growth hormone?

Ans. (i) This endocrine gland is pituitary gland. It is located below the hypothalamus in a small bony cavity of the brain called sella turcica.
(ii) Pituitary gland is known as master gland because it produces many hormones that travel throughout the body directing certain processes or stimulating other glands to produce other hormones.
(iii) Diabetes insipidus is a condition that results from insufficient secretion of the Antidiuretic Hormone (ADH) also called vasopressin. It is characterised by the excessive thirst and excretion of large amounts of severely dilute urine. Diabetes mellitus is a group of metabolic disorders characterised by the excessive levels of the sugar (glucose) in the blood.
(iv) Hormones are chemical regulators that are produced and poured directly into the bloodstream. Their site of production and actions are different.
Tropic hormones regulate the secretion of other endocrine glands
(v) (a) **Oxytocin** It is released into the blood from the posterior lobe of the pituitary gland.
(b) **ACTH** Anterior pituitary lobe releases Adrenocorticotropic Hormone to stimulate cortisol production in the adrenal glands.
(c) **Growth hormone** Anterior lobe of pituitary gland secretes growth hormone.

5. A sample of urine was diagnosed to contain high content of glucose and ketone bodies.
(i) Which endocrine gland and hormone is related to this condition?
(ii) Name the cells on which this hormone acts.
(iii) What is the condition called and how can it be rectified?
(iv) Name the specialised cells present in the above gland.
(v) Which hormone is known as hyperglycaemic hormone?

Ans. (i) Pancreas gland and insulin hormone are related to this condition.
(ii) Insulin hormone mainly acts on hepatocytes (liver cells) and adipocytes (cells of adipose tissue) and enhances cellular glucose uptake and utilisation.
(iii) Prolonged hyperglycaemia leads to a complex disorder called diabetes mellitus. It is associated with the loss of glucose through urine and formation of harmful compounds known as ketone bodies. Diabetic patients are successfully treated with insulin therapy.
(iv) Islets of Langerhans are the specialised cells present in the above gland.
(v) Glucagon is known as hyperglycaemic hormone.

6. Adrenal glands are structurally formed of cortex and medulla which secretes different hormones. Due to its varied functions, it is also known as 'gland of 4S'.
(i) Name the three classes of hormones secreted by the adrenal cortex.
(ii) At the time of physical stress like fall in blood pressure, which hormone is secreted, from which portion of adrenal gland?
(iii) Why is adrenal gland called gland of 4S?
(iv) How does Cushing's syndrome differ from Conn's syndrome?
(v) Mention any two symptoms of undersecretion of aldosterone.

Ans. (i) Three classes of hormones are mineralocorticoids, glucocorticoids and sexocorticoids which are secreted by the adrenal cortex.
(ii) Under given condition, adrenaline will be secreted from the adrenal medulla.
(iii) Adrenal gland controls four functions, which start with 'S'. These are sugar metabolism, salt concentration regulation, stress and strain controlled by epinephrine and sexual activities controlled by sexocorticoids. Thus, it is called gland of 4S.
(iv) Cushing's syndrome is caused due to the oversecretion of glucocorticoids or cortisol. In contrast, Conn's syndrome is caused due to the oversecretion of mineralocorticoids or aldosterone.
(v) Undersecretion of aldosterone causes Addison's disease which is characterised by
- low blood sugar
- loss of skin pigmentation

Chapter Assessment

Section-I

1 Mark Questions

1. Name the hormone responsible for the following functions.
   (i) Increase in heartbeat.
   (ii) Regulates basal metabolism.
   (iii) Regulates the functioning of the male and female reproductive organs.
   (iv) Increased reabsorption of water in kidneys.
2. Correct and rewrite the following statements by changing the underlined words.
   (i) Hormones are <u>extracellular</u> chemical messengers which regulate various biological processes.
   (ii) <u>ACTH</u> and <u>oxytocin</u> are derived from protein.
   (iii) <u>Prolactin</u> is called the birth hormone.
3. Give biological reasons for the following.
   (i) People living in the hilly areas often have swollen necks.
   (ii) 'Glucagon is hyperglycaemic hormone'.
4. Match the following columns.

Column I	Column II
A. T_4	1. Hypothalamus
B. FSH	2. Thyroid
C. GnRH	3. Secretion of androgens
D. LH	4. Spermatogenesis

5. Choose the correct answer from the four options given below.
   (i) Given below are four statements about hormones. Identify the statement which is not related with the hormones.
   (a) The targets are located away from the source glands
   (b) They are secreted directly into the blood
   (c) Like catalysts they can be reused
   (d) Their production is in minute quantities
   (ii) Thyroid secretion is primarily regulated by
   (a) body temperature
   (b) iodine content of the body
   (c) glucagon
   (d) thyroid stimulating hormone
6. Fill in the blanks with the correct alternative from those given in the brackets.
   (i) Cortex and medulla are two regions of ...... gland. (thyroid/adrenal)
   (ii) Cretinism is caused due to ...... of thyroxine. (undersecretion/oversecretion)
   (iii) Glucagon is secreted by .... (α-cells/β-cells)
7. Choose the odd one out from the following terms given below and name the category to which other three belong.
   ADH, TSH, NADP, ACTH
8. Expand the following biological abbreviations.
   (i) FSH (ii) PRL
9. State the exact location of the following.
   (i) Islets of Langerhans
   (ii) Pituitary gland
10. State the main function of the following.
   (i) LH (ii) TSH
11. Mention one difference between each of the following pair on the basis of what is given in the bracket.
   Endocrine gland and Exocrine gland (secretion)
12. Explain the following terms.
   (i) Dwarfism (ii) Gluconeogenesis
13. Answer the following questions briefly.
   (i) What is meant by the term endocrinology?
   (ii) Where are tropic hormones synthesised and stored?

2 Marks Questions

14. Why is chemical and hormonal coordination necessary?
15. Name the disease in which there is a reduced renal absorption of water with a consequent elimination of a large volume of very dilute urine. What is its cause?

3 Marks Question

16. (i) Which endocrine gland and its part is involved in the secretion of insulin?
   (ii) When does a doctor prefer insulin injections for a patient and what is the role of insulin in controlling level of glucose in blood?

Section-II [5 Marks]

Structured Questions

17. Study the diagram given below and then answer the questions that follows.

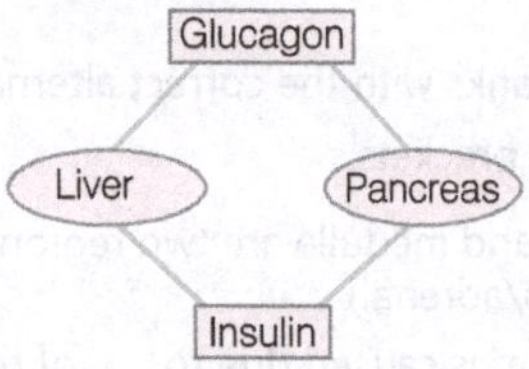

(i) Name the cells of the pancreas that produce
(a) glucagon (b) insulin

(ii) State the main function of
(a) glucagon (b) insulin

(iii) Why is pancreas referred to as an 'exo-endocrine gland'?

(iv) Why is insulin not given orally but is injected into the body?

(v) What is the technical term for the cells of the pancreas that produce endocrine hormones?

18. Hormones travel *via.* bloodstream to organs or tissues. Several hormones regulate many of the body functions, including growth, development metabolism, etc.,

(i) Which gland is called emergency gland of the body? Why?

(ii) Name the structure that controls the master gland.

(iii) Name a hormone that is proteinaceous in chemical nature.

(iv) Which hormone is produced by the pituitary gland in both males and females but functional only in females?

(v) What is the source of FSH?

For explanations scan the given QR Code

Olympiad Section*

Brain Teasing Questions asked in Previous Olympiads

1 Daily changes in the concentration of which hormone are represented by the graph?

↓ = Arrow indicating the time of food consumption [INJSO 2012]

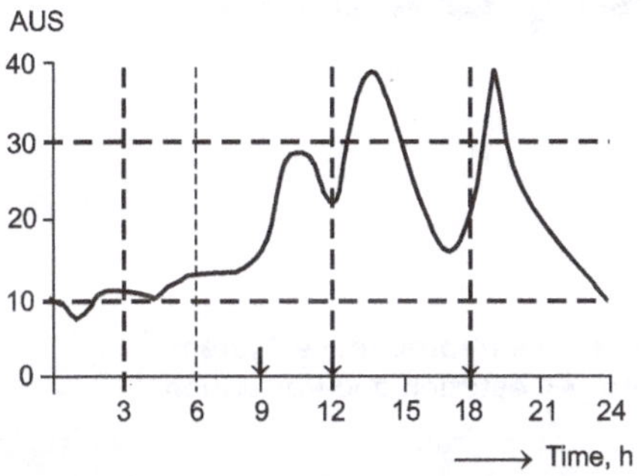

(a) Thyroxine (b) Glucagon
(c) Insulin (d) Cortisol

2 Individuals with diabetes are prescribed a low glycemic index diet. The reason for this is that [INBO 2021]

(a) their dietary carbohydrate requirement is lower than that of non-diabetic individuals
(b) they cannot assimilate complex carbohydrates such as starch
(c) they need to have slow but sustained release of glucose in their blood
(d) they can tolerate lower, but not higher than normal blood sugar levels

3 When treated with proteases, the extract of which of the endocrine glands would lose its hormonal influence? [INBO 2014]

(a) Ovary (b) Pineal gland
(c) Pituitary gland (d) Adrenal cortex

4 A baby born to a diabetic mother sometimes shows signs of hypoglycaemia for some period just after birth. This is due to [INBO 2011]

(a) continued maternal insulin activity
(b) utilisation of sugar from baby's blood for its activities after birth
(c) increased fetal insulin level to counter excess sugar from mother
(d) reduced production of maternal insulin as a result of diabetes

5 The following flowchart represents the feedback loops that regulate secretion of thyroid hormones (T_3 and T_4). Such secretion essentially regulates the basic metabolism rate in mammals. The '+' and '–' signs represent positive and negative regulation, respectively.

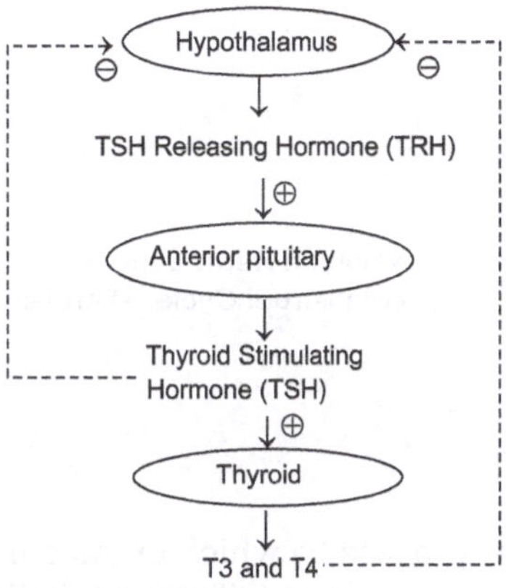

Three disease conditions are being studied where (x) the anterior pituitary fails to produce TSH, (y) the thyroid fails to produce T_3 and T_4 and (z) the hypothalamus fails to secrete TRH. In the table below, match the hormone levels in Column A with the disease conditions in Column B.

	Column A		Column B
(i)	Low TRH, low TSH and low T_3, T_4	(x)	Anterior pituitary fails to produce TSH
(ii)	High TRH, high TSH and low T_3, T_4	(y)	Thyroid fails to produce T_3 and T_4
(iii)	High TRH, low TSH and low T_3, T_4	(z)	Hypothalamus fails to secrete TRH

Which of the following is the correct match for the above? [IJSO 2013, India]

(a) (i)–(x) ; (ii)–(y) ; (iii)–(z)
(b) (i)–(z) ; (ii)–(y) ; (iii)–(x)
(c) (i)–(y) ; (ii)–(x) ; (iii)–(z)
(d) (i)–(z) ; (ii)–(x) ; (iii)–(y)

Answers

1. (c) **2.** (c) **3.** (c) **4.** (c) **5.** (b)

*These questions may or may not be asked in the examination, have been given just for additional practice required for olympiads, scholarship exams etc. For detailed explanations refer Page No. 247.

CHAPTER

11

Reproductive System

Chapter Inside

• Human Reproduction • Male Reproductive System • Female Reproductive System • Menstrual Cycle • Fertilisation • Implantation • Placenta • Gestation and Parturition

The biological process by which organisms produce their young ones (offspring) similar to themselves is called **reproduction**. It helps to maintain the continuity of life on Earth because no organism lives forever. Reproduction therefore, helps in the increase of population of the species. It also help in the transfer of characteristics of parents to their offspring. Reproduction can be of the following two major types

(i) **Asexual reproduction** This type of reproduction produces individuals without the fusion of gametes. It occurs in unicellular and lower organisms, e.g. *Hydra* reproduces by small buds, bacteria reproduce by fission, etc. It also occurs in many plants which reproduce by vegetative reproduction.

(ii) **Sexual reproduction** This type of reproduction involves the fusion of gametes, i.e. sex cells (single-celled or haploid) of male and female to produce a new cell called **zygote** (double-celled or diploid). It multiplies mitotically to give rise to multicellular organisms like animals and higher plants.

Human Reproduction

Humans are sexually reproducing **viviparous** (i.e. give birth to young ones) organisms. They show prominent **sexual dimorphism** due to which male and female differ from each other by a number of primary and secondary sex characters. **Primary sex characters** are those which are present since birth, e.g. external genitalia in males and females. Whereas, **secondary sexual characters** differ characteristically in males and females. These characters help to identify and attract sex partners. Organs producing gametes are called **reproductive organs**.

These are divided into following two main parts

(i) **Primary sex organs** These include the gonads of both males (testes) and females (ovaries), which are responsible for producing gametes, i.e. sperms (in males) and eggs (in females).

(ii) **Secondary or Accessory sex organs** These include all the structures that do not produce gametes but help in the process of reproduction. These structures have distinct roles from fertilisation to growth, development and birth of the baby, e.g. penis, uterus, etc.

Puberty

The onset of reproductive life is called puberty. It is the time when reproductive organs start maturing to become fully functional and start producing male and female gametes. After puberty, **secondary sexual characters** start becoming visible. In males, puberty starts at the age of 11-16 years and changes like broadening of chest and shoulders, growth of moustaches and beard, enlargement and erection of penis and broadening of pectoral girdle occurs in them. These changes are produced under the influence of testosterone, produced by testis.

In females, puberty starts at the age of 10-14 years and changes like enlargement of breasts, growth of auxiliary and pubic hairs, start of menstrual cycle and broadening of pelvic girdle occurs in them. The hormone which predominantly affects these changes is oestrogen, released by ovary.

Male Reproductive System

It is located in the pelvic region. The structures present in this system are either paired or unpaired.

It consists of the following organs

Primary Sex Organs

Testis are the primary sex organs in men. Their description is given ahead

Testis

These are the **male gonads**, i.e. the site where the **male gametes** or **sperms** are produced. A pair of testis is situated outside the abdominal cavity within the thin-wallled sac **scrotum.**

In the embryonic stages, testis remain within abdomen, but shortly before birth, they descend into the scrotum through inguinal canal.
Each testis is divided into 200-300 compartments called **testicular lobules.** Each lobule contains 1-3 highly convoluted seminiferous tubules, blood vessels and nerves embedded in loose connective tissue containing interstitial cells.

Scrotum

It is a pouch-like structure of pigmented skin arising from the lower abdominal wall and hanging between the legs. Scrotum keeps the temperature of testis about 2-2.5°C lower than the internal body temperature, which is essential for the production and survival of sperms. The process of production of sperms is called spermatogenesis. Scrotum regulates the temperature of testis by the movements of its wall. The scrotum wall loosen during hot temperature, so that testis move away from the body. During cold temperature, the scrotum wall contracts so as to bring the testis close to the body.

Seminiferous Tubule

It is the structural and functional unit of testis in which sperms are produced (spermatogenesis). Each seminiferous tubule is lined on its inside by two types of highly specialised cells as given below

(i) **Sertoli cells** (nurse cells)

(ii) **Male germ cells** (spermatogonia)

Sertoli cells are tall, pyramidal cells which provide nutrition to the developing germ cells. Male germ cells multiply to produce sperm cells.
The region outside the seminiferous tubules called **interstitial spaces** contain small blood vessels and masses of cells called **interstitial cells** or **Leydig cells.** These cells synthesise and secrete the testicular hormones called **androgens** or **testosterone.** Leydig cells are endocrine in function and thus, regulate and maintain male sex characteristics.

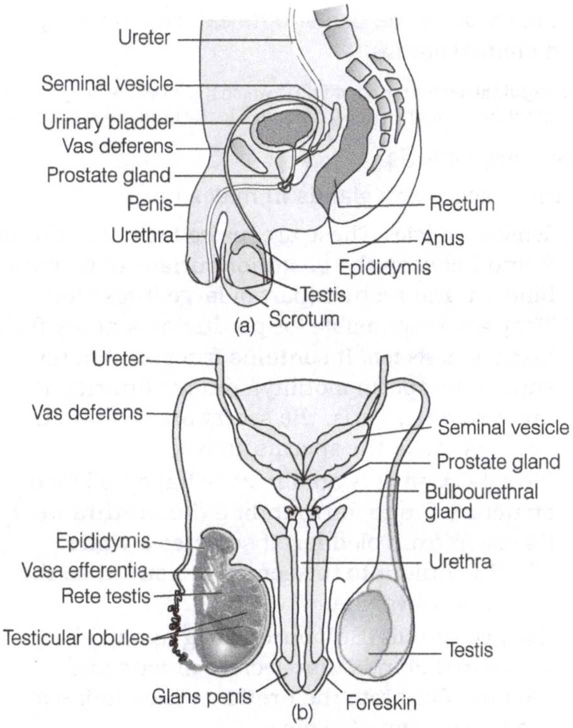

The male reproductive system : (a) Sectional view of male pelvis, (b) Anterior view of male pelvis

Secondary Sex Organs

They consist of the following structures.

Accessory Duct System

These ducts store and transport the sperms from the testis to the outside through urethra. The male sex accessory ducts include **tubuli recti, rete testis, vasa efferentia** (intratesticular ducts), **epididymis, vas deferens** and **urethra** (extratesticular ducts).

The sperms after being produced in seminiferous tubules, pass into network of tubes called **tubuli recti.** From these tubes, sperms pass to 12 to 14 efferent ducts and then to epididymis.

Epididymis is a long tube, which is greatly coiled and tightly packed to form an elongated flattened body. It is located along the posterior surface of each testis.

Sperms undergo physiological maturation, acquiring motility and fertilising capacity (i.e. **capacitation**) in epididymis. After that, they pass down to the tail of epididymis, where they stay for a very short period before entering the two **vas deferens** or **sperm ducts.**

The vas deferens ascends to the abdomen, pass through inguinal canal and loops over urinary bladder. It receives a duct from seminal vesicle to form **ejaculatory duct**. The duct passes through the prostate gland and opens into the **urethra.**

The urethra originates from the urinary bladder and extends through the penis to its external opening called **urethral meatus.**

Note **Inguinal hernia** is a condition in which the intestine bulges into scrotum through inguinal canal, due to the pressure in abdomen.

Accessory Glands

The three accessory glands in males are

(i) **Seminal vesicles** These are paired tubular glands found between the posterior surface of urinary bladder and rectum (part of large intestine). They are responsible for producing a milky fluid known as **semen.** It contains fructose (energy source for sperm motility), mucus (lubricant) and proteins. Thus, the secretion of seminal vesicles make the sperms active.

(ii) **Prostate gland** It is an almond-shaped bilobed structure found surrounding the urethra near its origin from bladder. It secretes a white alkaline fluid into the semen to neutralise the acidic pH of vagina.

(iii) **Cowper's glands** (Bulbourethral glands) These are paired glands that secrete mucus and alkaline fluid into the urethra which helps in the lubrication of penis.

External Genitalia (Penis)

It is the external copulatory organ in males located in front of scrotum. It is highly vascular structure containing erectile tissues and vascular spaces. During sexual stimulation, its vascular spaces get filled by blood thus, making it rigid and erect. It serves as a passage for both semen and urine to move out from the body.

The process of expulsion of semen from the urethra is called **ejaculation.**

Semen

The secretions of accessory sex glands and mucus are added to the sperms to form **seminal fluid** or **semen or seminal plasma.** These secretions provide medium for the transmission of sperms, give nourishment and activate sperms to keep them viable and motile. In a single ejaculation, about 2-3 mL of semen is released which contains 2-4 million sperms.

Sperm

A mature sperm cell or spermatozoa is a microscopic, tadpole-shaped structure of about 2-5 μm in diameter and 60 μm long. It comprises of three main parts.

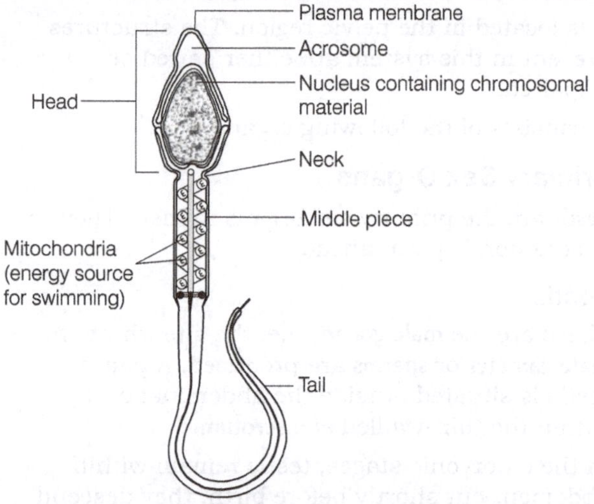

Structure of sperm

(i) **Head** It is an oval-shaped flat structure. It is composed of a large nucleus, which contains genetic material (22 +X or 22 +Y chromosomes) and a small cap-like structure known as **acrosome.** This acrosome secretes hydrolytic enzyme hyaluronidase which facilitates the entry of sperm into the egg by dissolving the wall of egg cell.

(ii) **Neck** It consists of funnel-shaped basal body and a pair of centrioles lying at the right angle to each other.

(iii) **Middle piece** It is cylindrical in shape and is known as powerhouse of the sperm cell because it possesses mitochondria that provide energy (in the form of ATP) to the sperm to swim in the female reproductive tract.

(iv) **Tail** It is a long, slender structure, which acts as the locomotory organ of the sperm due to its lashing movements for propulations.

Pathway of Sperm Transport in Male

Seminiferous tubules (sperms) → Network of tubules → Efferent duct → Epididymis → Vas deferens or Sperm duct → Urethra

Check Your LEARNING...

1 Name the male reproductive cells of mammals.
2 Name the sac in which testes are present in man.
3 What is ejaculation?
4 What makes sperm viable and motile?
5 Give one function of semen.

Female Reproductive System

The reproductive system of females comprises of the following reproductive organs

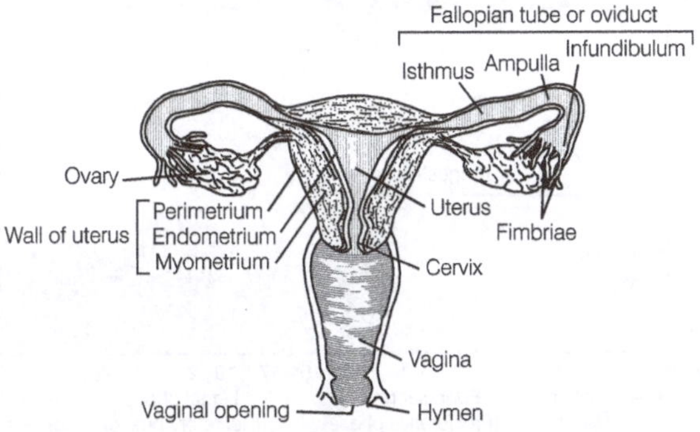

Female reproductive system

Primary Sex Organs

Ovaries are the primary sex organs in females. These are two small oval-shaped bodies, responsible for producing female gametes, i.e. **ova** (egg cells). These are located near kidneys and remain attached to the lower cavity of abdomen through mesovarium of ovarian ligaments.

Oogenesis is the process of production of mature ovum from the ova producing cells in each ovary every alternate month. A mature egg is contained in a cellular sac-like structure known as **follicle** (secrete oestrogen). It gets enlarged in size and becomes **Graafian follicle. Ovulation** is the process in which Graafian follicle ruptures to release the egg cell from the ovary. The egg cell is collected by the **fimbrae** of Fallopian tube and moved into it.

The remaining part of Graafian follicle (after release of egg) persists for a short time, after which it gets converted into **corpus luteum**. It is a yellow mass of endocrine tissue responsible for secreting hormone **progesterone**, which prepares uterus for pregnancy. In the absence of pregnancy, corpus luteum degenerates.

Secondary Sex Organs

These are as follows

Accessory Ducts

The following parts constitute the accessory ducts

(i) **Oviducts** (Fallopian tubes) These are two small tubes, around 10-12 cm long, located on either sides of the uterus near the kidney. The cilia of fimbriae of oviducts funnel are responsible for picking up and pushing the released egg into the oviduct. After receiving the ovum these oviducts provide appropriate conditions for its fertilisation with sperm and then transports it to the uterus by the consequent muscular contractions or peristalsis.

(ii) **Uterus** It is a hollow pear-shaped organ located in the pelvic cavity between the urinary bladder and rectum. It is also known as **womb** because it is the place where development of embryo takes place. The lower part of uterus called **cervix** is very narrow. The sperms enter into the uterus through this part.

(iii) **Vagina** It is the muscular tube-like structure meant to receive male penis during copulation and it also acts as a passage for the baby during childbirth. The opening of vagina is normally covered by a membrane called **hymen** or **virgin knot**. It usually gets ruptured due to strenuous physical excercise, urinary tract infections, sexual intercourse, etc.

Accessory Glands

(i) A pair of vestibular or **Bartholin's gland** occurs one on each side of the vaginal orifice, which moisten the vagina. They are small rounded bodies. These glands correspond to the Cowper's gland of the male and secrete a clear viscous fluid during sexual excitement. This fluid serves as a lubricant during copulation and parturition.

(ii) Two **mammary** or **milk producing glands** (breast) are present in each normal female. These are responsible for the secretion of milk.

External Genitalia (Vulva)

These are the external genital organs of females. These include mons pubis, labia majora, labia minora and clitoris. The most anterior structure of vulva is the **mons pubis**. It is covered with skin and pubic hairs. The two longitudinal folds of skin are called **labia majora** (labia means 'lips'), which forms the boundary of vulva. It is equivalent to male scrotum. Labia majora covers two additional folds of skin called **labia minora**. Both protect the vaginal and urethral opening.

In the uppermost angle of vulva, in front of the urethral opening, a small erectile structure called **clitoris** is present. It is highly sensitive because of the presence of numerous nerve endings and it is equivalent to male penis.

Menstrual Cycle

It is the series of changes occurring in the wall of uterus (endometrium) of human females that prepares the uterus to receive a fertilised egg (i.e. for pregnancy). The first menstruation begins at puberty, i.e. at an age of around 12-13 years and is known as **menarche**. It continues till the age of 40-45 years and then stops **(menopause)**.

The complete period from menarche to menopause is known as the **reproductive period in females**. This period is marked by a characteristic event repeated every month in the form of menstrual flow. It continues from the day of the onset of the flow to the next onset, i.e. after around 27-28 days and may have variations. It gets temporarily stop during pregnancy.

The complete period of menstrual cycle is divided into following four main phases

(i) **Menstrual phase** This is the first phase that lasts for around 3-5 days. Periodic discharge of blood is seen during this phase due to the shedding of the uterine wall, endometrium.

(ii) **Follicular phase** It is the formation of a new egg in follicle under the influence of follicle stimulating hormone. It lasts for around 5-12 days. This is the period in which secondary follicle changes into Graafian follicle (as the follicle grows) and again reactivates the wall of uterus (to become thickened and supplied with lot of blood vessels) due to the production of **oestrogen** by ovary in large amount.

(iii) **Ovulatory phase** In this period, the rupture of Graafian follicle, i.e. ovulation occurs. The released egg travels down the oviduct. It occurs on about 13-14th day of the menstrual cycle. During this phase, the pituitary hormone called Luteinizing hormone (LH) attains its peak.

(iv) **Luteal phase** It continues for around 10 days. During this phase, uterus lining gets thickened to receive fertilised egg and the remaining part of the Graafian follicle transforms into the yellow body called **corpus luteum**, an endocrine gland/tissue that produces **progesterone** hormone.

(a) In the absence of fertilisation, corpus luteum degenerates and causes shedding of the uterus lining again on the 28th day.

(b) If the egg gets fertilised, it gets attached to the uterus (implantation). The menstrual flow does not occur because the level of progesterone (hormone secreted by corpus luteum) increases, which keeps the uterus in a state suitable for implantation.

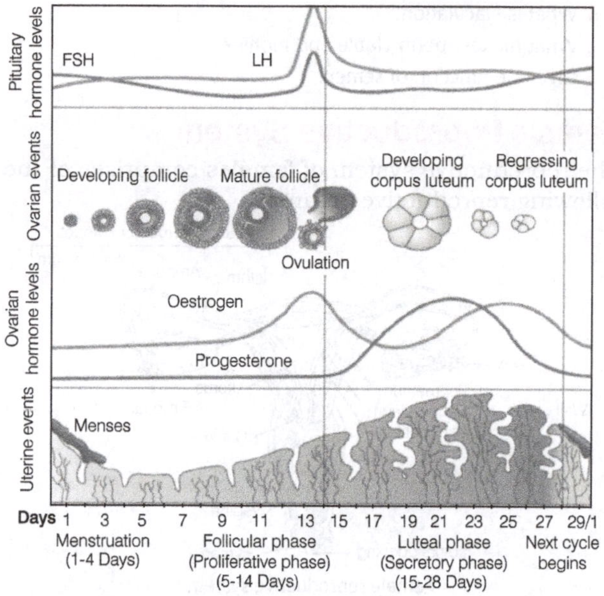

Uterine changes in relation to follicular changes during menstrual cycle

Ovum (Egg)

It is microscopic structure about 100-130 μm in diameter, non-motile gamete having the genetic material (22 +X) in the nucleus. The ovum possesses three coverings, inner plasma membrane, i.e. **oolemma** or **vitelline membrane,** middle **zona pellucida** and outer cellular **corona radiata**. The cytoplasm of ovum is called **ooplasm**. Human ovum is **alecithal** (i.e. yolk is absent) and contains a large haploid nucleus called **germinal vesicle** or **pronucleus**.

The Pathway of Egg Transport in Female

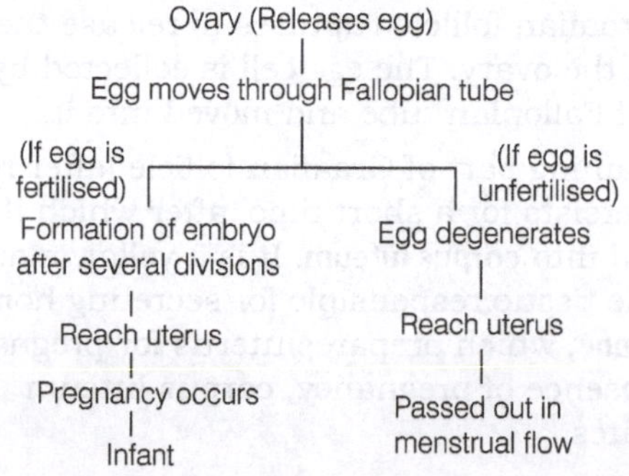

Check Your LEARNING...

1. Name the structure of human reproductive system in which ova are formed.
2. Name the hormone released by corpus luteum.
3. Why uterus is also known as womb?
4. State the function of Bartholin's glands in human female reproductive system.
5. Name the four phases of menstrual cycle.
6. Give one function of progesterone.

Fertilisation

It is the process of fusion of male gamete (sperm) and the female gamete (ovum) in order to produce a zygote. Process of fertilisation in human is internal, i.e. takes place in the Fallopian tube.

The discharge of semen by male through penis into the vagina (near the cervix of the uterus) of the female during coitus is called **insemination**. Out of millions of sperms released, only few are able to reach the upper parts of the oviducts, rest of them die on their way and get absorbed. The most active and motile sperms enter the uterus and reach the Fallopian tube, where they penetrate the ovum (egg). In doing so, the tail is left outside and only the head part that contains nucleus enters the egg.

After the entry of sperm into the ovum, the (haploid) nucleus of egg and sperm fuse together. As a result, a zygote is formed which is a diploid cell containing 23 pairs of chromosomes.

The most favourable time for conception is 12-14 days after the onset of menstruation or soon after ovulation.

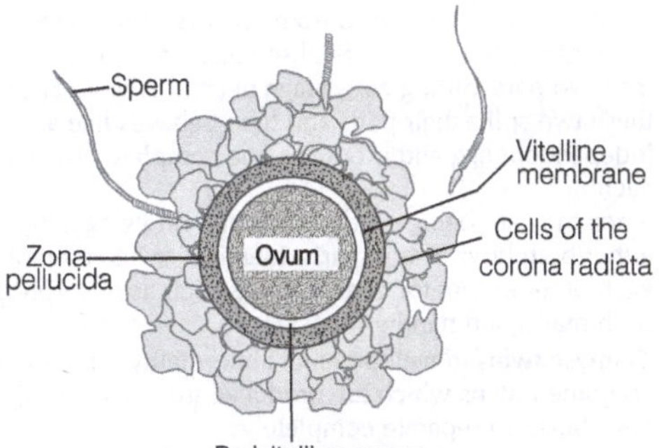

Ovum surrounded by few sperms

Implantation

It is the attachment of developing embryo within the uterus about 5-7 days after ovulation. The mitotic division starts as the zygote moves through the oviduct towards the uterus, forming 2, 4, 8, 16 daughter cells called **blastomeres**. This process is called **cleavage**. The embryo with 8-16 blastomeres formed at the end of fourth day is called **morula**. The morula continues to divide and transforms into fluid-filled embryo called **blastocyst**.

The blastomeres in the blastocyst are arranged into an outer layer called **trophoblast**, which is nutritive in function and the inner group of cells attached to trophoblast called the **inner cell mass**.

The trophoblast layer then gets attached to the endometrium. The inner cell mass differentiates into the **embryo**. The trophoblast cells produce enzymes that allow the blastocyst to digest the uterine endometrium producing a pit in which the developing embryo settles.

The endometrium grows over it to cover the blastocyst. This process that results in fixing of blastocyst to endometrium, is called implantation and it leads to **pregnancy**. The pregnancy is the state of carrying the unborn young one inside the human body.

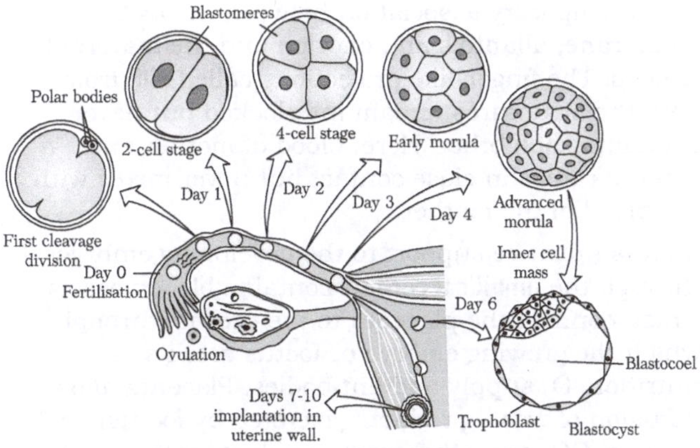

Foetal development during the first and second weeks

The embryo continues to develop in the uterus and by the end of five weeks of pregnancy, its heart and circulatory system gets functional. From seven weeks of gestation and onwards, the embryo is called **foetus**, as it looks like a baby.

Foetal Membranes

These are also called **extraembryonic membranes** because they are not a part of the body of the embryo. These membranes play some role in supporting the life of pre-embryo, the embryo and the foetus. These membranes are formed from the trophoblast. These include

(i) **Amnion** It is a thin membrane that covers the embryo. It later expands to become fluid-filled (it is also called **amniotic fluid**) amniotic sac that fully encloses the embryo. It provides an aqueous environment in which the embryo is protected from shocks and keep even pressure all around the embryo. It also restricts some foetal movements and prevents sticking of foetus to the amnion.

(ii) **Allantois** It is a tiny sausage-shaped pouch, which arises from the gut of the embryo near the yolk sac. It supplies the blood vessels to the placenta and is involved in nutrition and excretion.

(iii) **Chorion** It completely encloses the developing embryo and extraembryonic tissues. The chorion facilitates the transfer of nutrients, gases and wastes between the embryo and the mother's body.

(iv) **Yolk sac** It is a membrane that surrounds the yolk. It is the first extraembryonic membrane to make appearance in mammal, but gets reabsorbed before the embryo is formed.

Placenta

It is a temporary association between the foetal membrane, allantois and chorion and the maternal tissues. The finger-like projections called **villi** from both the structures remain interlocked but never open into each other. Here, blood of mother and embryo comes in close contact but never mixes with the blood of the mother.

It gives nutritive support to the developing embryo through the **umbilical cord.** It contains blood vessels which connect the placenta to the uterus, through which the growing embryo or foetus gets its nutrition, O_2 supply and antibodies. Placenta allows diffusion of waste products (excreted by foetus) such as urea, CO_2 and other waste products into mother's body for elimination.

However, it prevents the passage of germs from mother to foetus but certain viruses like HIV, alcohol, nicotine, etc., can pass through it. Placenta also acts as an endocrine gland. It produces hormones like oestrogen and progesterone.

These hormones help to maintain the pregnancy. Presence of progesterone and HCG (Human chorionic gonandotropin) in urine confirms pregnancy.

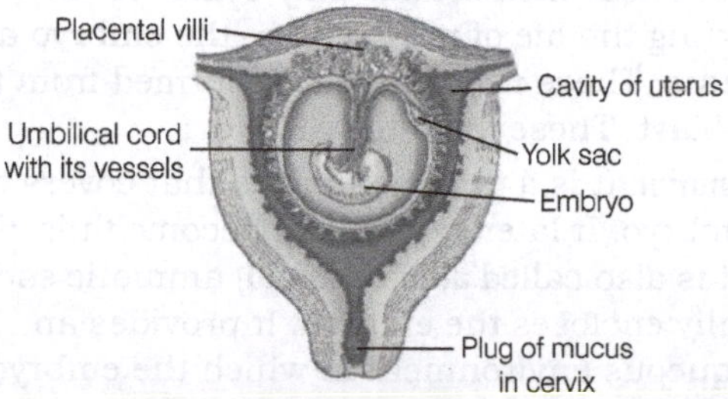

The human foetus within the uterus

Note Placenta provides a blood barrier between the mother and foetus blood. If it would have been absent, the high blood pressure of mother's blood would damage the delicate tissues of foetus.

Gestation

It is the time period during which the embryo remains in the uterus (after the last day of menstruation to the day of childbirth). The gestation period is of about 9 months or 280 days in human females.

Parturition (Childbirth)

It is the act of delivering of a baby which occurs due to the vigorous contractions of the uterus at the end of pregnancy.

The baby is pushed out from uterus (head first). Within few minutes, the blood vessels in umbilical cord shrink after which it is tied and cut. The placenta is then shed and expelled out of uterus as after birth.

Oxytocin hormone is responsible for these contractions in human female resulting into the childbirth.

Twins

These are the offsprings produced by same pregnancy. Twins can be of three types as discussed below

(i) **Fraternal twins** (produced from two eggs) These twins are produced when two eggs are released from ovaries at a time and both may get fertilised to produce two individuals. These twins may be either both boys or both girls or can be one boy and one girl. Fraternal twins are either **diovular** (produced from two ova) or **dizygotic** (produced from two zygotes or fertilised eggs).

(ii) **Identical twins** (produced from one egg) These are produced when a single fertilised egg, get split and separate into two parts during early stage of cell division. Each of these two splits their parts and then behaves like an independent egg and produces one complete individual each.
Since they are being produced from a single egg, they are either both boys or both girls. Identical twins resemble each other except for certain things such as fingerprints, birth marks and handwritings.

(iii) **Siamese twins** (developmental abnormality) These are conjoined twins which are produced from a single egg who have failed to separate completely.

Check Your LEARNING...

1 Define insemination.
2 What number of blastomeres are contained in morula?
3 Which layer of blastocyst is nutritive in function?
4 Give one function of chorion.
5 What is the gestation period in human female?

QUiCK Revision

- **Reproduction** is the process to produce new organisms of the same species.
- Reproduction is of two types, i.e. **asexual** and **sexual**. Asexual reproduction means to reproduce without the production of gametes. Sexual reproduction involves the fusion of gametes.
- Organs to produce gametes are **gonads**. Humans are unisexual organisms, i.e. have different male and female sexes and each sex has reproductive organs (gonads) and accessory structures.
- **Human male reproductive system** includes a pair of testis, seminal vesicle, prostate gland, Cowper's gland and penis.
- **Human female reproductive system** includes ovary, oviducts, uterus, cervix, accessory glands (Bartholin's gland and mammary glands), vagina and external genitalia.
- **Menstrual cycle** in females refers to the cyclic changes occurring in the wall of the uterus which prepares it for pregnancy. It is divided into four main phases, (i) Menstrual phase, (ii) Follicular phase, (iii) Ovulatory phase and (iv) Luteal phase.
- **Fertilisation** is a process of fusion of male and female gametes which occur at Fallopian tube after discharge of semen during the sexual act.
- **Implantation** It is the phenomenon of attachment and development of embryo inside the uterus.
- **Embryonic membranes** are amnion, allantois, chorion and yolk sac.
- **Placenta** is an intimate connection between all foetal membranes and the maternal tissue.
- **Parturition** is an act of expulsion of developed foetus from mother's uterus after completion of gestation period (280 days in humans).
- **Twins** are offsprings produced by a single pregnancy.
- **Fraternal twins** are produced from two separate eggs fertilised by sperms. Childern produced are not identical.
- **Identical twins** are produced when single egg gets fertilised and divides into two cells. These cells act as single separate zygote cells. These could be either both boys or girls and are identical.

Chapter Practice

Section-I

1 Mark Questions

1. Name the following.
   (i) Thin-walled sac of skin that covers the testis. [2014]
   (ii) The cells of the testis that produce male hormones. [2011]
   (iii) The accessory gland in human males whose secretion activates the sperms. [2017]
   (iv) The hormone secreted by Graafian follicle.
   (v) The layer of cells forming the outer wall of the blastocyst.
   (vi) The structure formed by the villi of the embryo and the uterus of the mother. [2015]
   (vii) The structure which connects the placenta and the foetus. [2019]
   (viii) Period of complete intrauterine development of the foetus. [2017]
   (ix) The permanent stoppage of menstruation in human females around the age of 45 years. [2023]

Ans. (i) Scrotum
(ii) Interstitial cells (Leydig cells)
(iii) Seminal vesicle
(iv) Oestrogen
(v) Trophoblast/Trophoectoderm
(vi) Placenta
(vii) Umbilical cord
(viii) Gestation
(ix) Menopause

2. Correct and rewrite the following statements by changing the underlined words.
   (i) Androgens are produced by <u>Sertoli cells</u>.
   (ii) <u>Vagina</u> is equivalent to the male penis.
   (iii) The Graffian follicle, after ovulation turns into a hormone producing tissue called <u>corpus callosum</u>.
   (iv) <u>Gestation</u> is the process of fixing of zygote to uterine wall.
   (v) The protective sac which develops around the developing embryo is called <u>pericardium</u>. [2019]

Ans. (i) Androgens are produced by Leydig cells.
(ii) Clitoris is equivalent to the male penis.
(iii) The Graffian follicle, after ovulation turns into a hormone producing tissue called corpus luteum.
(iv) Implantation is the process of fixing of zygote to uterine wall.
(v) The protective sac which develops around the developing embryo is called amnion.

3. Give biological reasons for the following.
   (i) When ovum gets fertilised, menstrual cycle stops temporarily in a woman.
   (ii) A woman cannot conceive after menopause.
   (iii) Chances of pregnancy to occur are the most favourable around 14-15th day of the menstrual cycle.
   (iv) The placenta is an important structure for the development of a foetus. [2018]
   (v) The umbilical cord is the lifeline of the foetus.

Ans. (i) When an ovum gets fertilised, the progesterone hormone level increases which prevent the development of another follicle and stops menstrual cycle.
(ii) After menopause, no ovulation occurs, i.e. no egg is available for fertilisation. So, a woman cannot conceive.
(iii) On about 14-15th day of the menstrual cycle, the follicle ruptures (ovulation) and the released egg travels down the oviduct. Therefore, chances of pregnancy to occur are the most favourable around this period of the menstrual cycle.
(iv) Placenta is a disc-shaped organ formed inside the female body which remains attached to the uterine wall. It gives nutritive support to the developing embryo through a cord known as umbilical cord. It contains blood vessels which connect the placenta to the uterus through which a growing embryo or foetus gets its nutrition and O_2 supply.
(v) The umbilical cord is a tough structure that serves as the blood vascular connection between the foetus and uterine wall. The maternal blood carries nutrients, oxygen, hormones and water to the placenta, where they are absorbed and passed on to the embryo through the blood vessels of the umbilical cord.
Therefore, it is the lifeline of the foetus.

4. (i) Match the following columns.

	Column I		Column II
A.	Expulsion of semen	1.	Spermatogenesis
B.	Prostate gland	2.	Milk
C.	Mammary gland	3.	Ejaculation
D.	Production of sperms	4.	Alkaline fluid

(ii) Match the following columns.

	Column I		Column II
A.	Acrosome	1.	Attachment of embryo in the uterus
B.	Gestation	2.	Time during which the embryo remains in the uterus
C.	Parturition	3.	Sperm's head
D.	Implantation	4.	Childbirth

(iii) Match the following columns.

	Column I (Structures)		Column II (Functions)
A.	Corpus luteum	1.	Increases the force of uterine contraction
B.	Seminiferous tubules	2.	Secretion of progesterone
C.	Oxytocin	3.	Serves as the connection between foetus and uterine wall
D.	Endometrium	4.	Nutrition of foetus
E.	Umbilical cord	5.	Produces male gametes in large number

Ans. (i) A–3, B–4, C–2, D–1
(ii) A–3, B–2, C–4, D–1
(iii) A–2, B–5, C–1, D–4, E–3

5. Choose the correct answer from the four options given below.

(i) Testis produce the hormone
(a) oestrogen (b) oxytocin
(c) progesterone (d) testosterone

Ans. (d)

(ii) A single highly coiled tube where sperms are stored, get concentrated and mature is known as **[2015]**
(a) epididymis (b) vas efferentia
(c) vas deferens (d) seminiferous tubule

Ans. (a)

(iii) Seminal plasma, the fluid part of semen is not contributed by
(a) seminal vesicle (b) prostate
(c) urethra (d) Bulbourethral gland

Ans. (c)

(iv) The middle piece of sperm provides
(a) nucleus (b) energy (c) locomotion (d) food

Ans. (b)

(v) Which one of the following is the correct route during the transport of sperm in male (human)?
(a) Vas deferens → Epididymis → Urethra
(b) Epididymis → Vas deferens → Urethra
(c) Epididymis → Urethra → Vas deferens
(d) Urethra → Epididymis → Vas deferens

Ans. (b)

(vi) Which of the following is not a part of the female reproductive system in human beings? **[2017]**
(a) Uterus
(b) Ovary
(c) Ureter
(d) Fallopian tube

Ans. (c)

(vii) Finger-like projections of the oviduct funnel are called
(a) cilia (b) fimbriae
(c) cervix (d) clitoris

Ans. (b)

(viii) The onset of menstruation in the female is termed as
(a) ovulation (b) menarche
(c) menopause (d) parthenogenesis

Ans. (b)

(ix) Ovulation occurs **[2017]**
(a) at the beginning of menstrual cycle
(b) in the mid of the menstrual cycle
(c) at the end of the menstrual cycle
(d) during any time of the menstrual cycle

Ans. (b)

(x) On which day of menstrual cycle, does ovulation take place? **[2019]**
(a) 5th day (b) 28th day
(c) 14th day (d) 1st day

Ans. (c)

(xi) Which of the following is not true for the process of ovulation in humans ?
(a) The egg is released from Graafian follicle
(b) The egg is fertilised in Fallopian tube
(c) The egg passes through fimbriated funnel of Fallopian tube
(d) The fertilised egg passes out of female's body

Ans. (d)

(xii) Fertilisation is the process of fusion of male gamete and the female gamete to produce a/an
(a) embryo (b) infant
(c) zygote (d) child

Ans. (c)

(xiii) The association between the foetus and mother is called
(a) embryonic membrane (b) placenta
(c) amnion (d) chorion

Ans. (b)

(xiv) The period of intrauterine development of the embryo is known as
(a) embryonic development
(b) gestation period
(c) parturition
(d) implantation

Ans. (b)

6. Fill in the blanks by using suitable words.
(i) Humans are ...... organisms.
(ii) The unit of testis is ....
(iii) The testosterone hormone is secreted by the ...... cells.
(iv) The male copulatory organ is ....
(v) The structure which helps to penetrate egg membrane of the ovum is ......
(vi) The follicle which contains the mature ovum is called ....
(vii) The part where fertilisation occurs in human female is ....
(viii) The process of releasing of egg from the ovary is called ....
(ix) The process of development of ovum in the ovary is called ....
(x) The shedding out of the endometrium along with blood is called ....
(xi) The umbilical cord connects ...... and ....
(xii) The embryo inside the uterus is protected from jerks or mechanical shocks by ....
(xiii) The period of complete development of the foetus till birth is termed ....
(xiv) The expulsion of the foetus from the body of the mother is called ....
(xv) A hormone secreted in a female to facilitate parturition is ....

Ans. (i) unisexual (ii) seminiferous tubule
(iii) interstitial (iv) penis
(v) acrosome (vi) Graafian follicle
(vii) oviduct/Fallopian tube (viii) ovulation
(ix) oogenesis (x) menstruation
(xi) foetus, placenta (xii) amniotic fluid
(xiii) gestation (xiv) parturition
(xv) oxytocin

7. Copy and complete the following by filling in the blanks (i) to (v) with appropriate words.

The human female gonads are ovaries. A maturing egg in the ovary is present in a sac of cells called .... (i). As the egg grows larger, the follicle enlarges and gets filled with a fluid and is now called the .... (ii) follicle. The process of releasing the egg from the ovary is called .... (iii). The ovum is picked up by the oviducal funnel and fertilisation takes place in the .... (iv). In about a week, the blastocyst gets fixed in the endometrium of the uterus and this process is called ....(v). **[2014]**

Ans. The human female gonads are ovaries. A maturing egg in the ovary is present in a sac of cells called (i) **ovarian follicle**. As the egg grows larger, the follicle enlarges and gets filled with a fluid and is now called the (ii) **Graafian follicle**.

The process of releasing the egg from the ovary is called (iii) **ovulation**. The ovum is picked up by the oviducal funnel and fertilisation takes place in the (iv) **oviduct**. In about a week, the blastocyst gets fixed in the endometrium of the uterus and this process is called (v) **implantation**.

8. Choose the odd one out from the following terms given below and name the category to which other three belong.
(i) Prostate gland, Cowper's gland, Seminal vesicle, Seminiferous tubules **[2018]**
(ii) Cowper's gland, Urethral gland, Lacrimal gland, Seminal vesicles, Prostate gland **[2014]**
(iii) Menstrual phase, Telophase, Follicular phase, Luteal phase **[2023]**
(iv) Ovary, Fallopian tube, Ureter, Uterus **[2016, 12]**

Ans. (i) **Odd term** is seminiferous tubules.
Rest three are accessory glands of male reproductive system.
(ii) **Odd term** is lacrimal gland.
Rest three are accessory glands of male reproductive system.
(iii) **Odd term** Telophase
Category Others are stages of menstrual cycle.
(iv) **Odd term** is ureter.
Other three belong to female reproductive system.

9. Given below are the sets of five terms. Rewrite the terms in correct order of a logical sequence.
(i) Testis, Urethra, Sperm duct, Epididymis **[2023]**
(ii) Vagina, Ovary, Uterus, Oviduct, Cervix (pathway of egg after ovulation) **[2010]**
(iii) Implantation, Fertilisation, Parturition, Ovulation, Gestation (stages leading to formation of foetus and birth) **[2012]**
(iv) Uterus, Parturition, Fertilisation, Gestation, Implantation **[2017]**

Ans. (i) Testis → Epididymis → Sperm duct → Urethra
(ii) Ovary → Oviduct → Uterus → Cervix → Vagina
(iii) Ovulation → Fertilisation → Implantation → Gestation → Parturition
(iv) Fertilisation → Uterus → Implantation → Gestation → Parturition (Mechanism of childbirth)

10. State the exact location of the following.
(i) Testis **[2019]**
(ii) Seminal vesicle **[2014]**
(iii) Prostate gland **[2017, 12]**
(iv) Amnion **[2011]**
(v) Amniotic fluid **[2023, 19]**

Ans. (i) Testis are found in a thin-walled sac called scrotum, located outside the abdomen in order to escape from high body temperature.
(ii) Seminal vesicle is found between the urinary bladder and rectum in males.
(iii) Prostate gland is found surrounding the urethra of human male.
(iv) Amnion is double membranous structure found around the embryo in the uterus.
(v) Amniotic fluid occupies the space between amnion and foetus in the embryo.

11. State the main function of the following.
(i) Sertoli cells
(ii) Interstitial cells
(iii) Leydig cells [2016]
(iv) Vas deferens
(v) Seminal vesicles [2019]
(vi) Prostate glands
(vii) Corpus luteum [2016]
(viii) Uterus
(ix) Vagina

Ans. (i) Sertoli cells provide nutrition to the developing sperms, i.e. germ cells.
(ii) Interstitial cells are found in seminiferous tubules. They secrete the male sex hormone, testosterone into the blood and maintain male sex characteristics.
(iii) Leydig cells produce testosterone (the male hormone).
(iv) Vas deferens stores and transports the sperms from the testis to the outside through urethra.
(v) Seminal vesicles produce a milky fluid called semen. It is rich in fructose, mucus and proteins. Thus, it (semen) makes sperms active.
(vi) Prostate gland secretes an alkaline fluid into the semen to neutralise the acidic pH of vagina.
(vii) Corpus luteum produces and secretes progesterone (the female hormone).
(viii) Uterus gives suitable environment for the implantation of embryo. It contains amniotic fluid which protects the embryo from shocks and jerks.
(ix) Vagina receives the semen from the male penis and serves as the birth canal during parturition.

12. Mention one difference between each of the following pairs on the basis of what is given in the bracket.
(i) Sexual and Asexual reproduction (general features)
(ii) Cowper's gland and Prostate gland (nature of secretion)
(iii) Sperm and Semen (general feature)
(iv) Sperm duct and Fallopian tube (function) [2016]
(v) Sperm and Ovum (motility)
(vi) Testosterone and Oestrogen (organ which secretes) [2018]
(vii) Corpus luteum and Corpus callosum (function) [2014]
(viii) Menarche and Menopause (time of occurrence)
(ix) Ovulation and Parturition (definition)

Ans. (i) Difference between sexual reproduction and asexual reproduction is as follows

Sexual reproduction	Asexual reproduction
Two individuals are involved.	One individual is involved.

(ii) Difference between Cowper's gland and prostate gland is as follows

Cowper's gland	Prostate gland
Produces a mucoid fluid which serves as lubricant.	It produces a white alkaline fluid which neutralises acidic nature of female reproductive tract.

(iii) Difference between sperm and semen is as follows

Sperm	Semen
It is formed inside the testis.	It is formed inside the seminal vesicles glands.

(iv) Difference between sperm duct and Fallopian tube is as follows

Sperm duct	Fallopian tube
It carries sperms from testis to seminal vesicle.	Union of male and female gametes takes place in this tube.

(v) Difference between sperm and ovum is as follows

Sperm	Ovum
It is motile in nature.	It is non-motile.

(vi) Difference between testosterone and oestrogen is as follows

Testosterone	Oestrogen
It is secreted by testis.	It is secreted by ovary.

(vii) Difference between corpus luteum and corpus callosum is as follows

Corpus luteum	Corpus callosum
It is the remain of Graafian follicle which secretes female sex hormone, e.g. progesterone.	It is the region that connects the left and right cerebral hemispheres of forebrain.

(viii) Difference between menarche and menopause is as follows

Menarche	Menopause
It occurs between 10-14 years of age.	It occurs between 40-45 years of age.

(ix) Difference between ovulation and parturition is as follows

Ovulation	Parturition
It is the release of ovum from the ruptured Graafian follicle.	It is the expulsion of the child from the mother's uterus.

13. Give biological/technical terms for the following.

(i) The canal through which the testis descend into the scrotum just before the birth of a male baby.

(ii) The onset of menstruation in a young girl. **[2018, 13]**

(iii) The phase in the menstrual cycle in which the remnant of follicle in the ovary turns to corpus luteum. **[2012]**

(iv) Complete stoppage of menstrual cycle in females. **[2016]**

(v) The fertilised egg **[2010]**

(vi) Fixing of developing zygote (blastocyst) on the uterine wall. **[2015]**

(vii) The fluid which surrounds the foetus. **[2018]**

Ans. (i) Inguinal canal (ii) Menarche
(iii) Luteal phase (iv) Menopause
(v) Zygote (vi) Implantation (vii) Amniotic fluid

14. Briefly explain the following terms.

(i) Inguinal canal (ii) Ejaculation
(iii) Ovulation (iv) Fertilisation
(v) Umbilical cord

Ans. (i) The inguinal canal is the passage, which allows the descend of testis from abdomen to scrotum along with their ducts, blood vessels, nerves, etc.

(ii) Release of semen in the vagina of female during sexual intercourse is known as ejaculation.

(iii) Ovulation is the release of ovum from Graafian follicle in the ovary.

(iv) Fertilisation is the union of sperm and ova to produce a zygote.

(v) A cord of blood vessel connecting the placenta to the foetus for its nourishment, respiration, excretion, etc., is known as umbilical cord.

15. Answer the following questions briefly.

(i) The path of sperm transport is given below. Provide the missing steps in blank boxes.

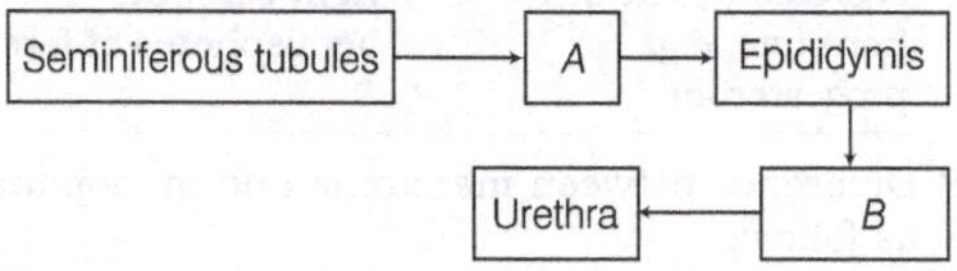

(ii) Is it true that the foetus inside the mother's uterus breathe? If yes, how?

(iii) What is the significance of amniotic fluid? **[2015]**

(iv) Twins may or may not be identical. Comment.

(v) Given below is a group of terms. In group, the first pair indicates the relationship between the two terms. Rewrite and complete the second pair on a similar basis. **[2017]**

Foetus : Amnion : : Heart :

Ans. (i) *A*–Efferent duct, *B*–Vasa deferentia

(ii) No, the foetus does not breathe inside the mother's uterus. It exchanges gases with the help of placenta.

(iii) Amniotic fluid is significant for the developing foetus in the mother's womb as it protects the foetus from jerks and serves as a medium to all its requirements.

(iv) Twins may not be identical as in the case of fraternal twins, which are produced from two eggs. Twins may be identical in case of identical twins, which are produced from a single egg.

(v) Pericardium (amnion is a covering that protects the foetus. Similarly, pericardium protects the heart).

2 Marks Questions

16. What is the significance of the human testes being located in scrotal sacs outside the abdomen? **[2023]**

Ans. The presence of testes outside the abdominal cavity in the scrotum keeps the temperature of testes 2-3 degrees Celsius below the temperature of the body which is important for the production of sperm.

17. Mention any two functions of the human foetal placenta. **[2023]**

Ans. Functions of foetal placenta are as follows

- The placenta provides nutrients and oxygen to the embryo while also eliminating carbon dioxide and waste materials produced by the embryo.
- The placenta produces hormones such as oestrogens, human Chorionic Gonadotropin (hCG), and progesterone.

18. Briefly explain the structural features of vulva.

Ans. Vulva constitutes the external genital organs of female. It has two openings *viz.* vagina and urethra which are guarded by labia minora and labia majora. In front of urethral opening, a highly sensitive erectile organ called clitoris is present.

3 Marks Questions

19. Describe the cellular structure of a seminiferous tubule.

Ans. A seminiferous tubule is lined on the inside by two types of highly specialised cell, i.e. male germ cells and large Sertoli cells. The male germ cells undergo spermatogenesis to produce sperms, while the Sertoli cells provide nutrition to the developing sperms.
The region outside the seminiferous tubules called interstitial spaces have blood vessels and Leydig cells. Leydig cells synthesise and secrete the male sex hormones called androgens (testosterone).

20. What are the events that take place in the ovary and uterus during follicular phase of the menstrual cycle?

Ans. Refer to text on page no. 184.

21. A human female experiences two major changes, menarche and menopause during her life. Mention the significance of both the events.

Ans. In human females, initiation of menstruation at puberty (between age 9-15 years) is called menarche. Menstrual cycle ceases after around 40-50 years of age that is termed as menopause.

Menarche signifies the maturation and ability of the female reproductive system to bear child. It marks the capability of the ovaries to produce mature oocyte (female gamete) that can now be fertilised by the sperm and the capability of uterus in supporting the foetal growth and development.

Menopause signifies the end of child bearing age. At this age, supply of healthy eggs is very low, the levels of the hormones secreted by the ovaries decline and the menstruation stops. The uterus no longer remains conductive for foetal growth.

Section-II [5 Marks]

Structured Questions

1. The organs of male reproductive system help in the production of sperms and their transference to outside. They constitute both primary and secondary sex organs.
   (i) Name any two accessory glands in males.
   (ii) What functions do seminal vesicle and sperm duct serve in males?
   (iii) What would be the consequence of impaired Leydig cells?
   (iv) Why are Sertoli cells called nutritive cells?

Ans. (i) In males, two accessory glands are seminal vesicle and prostate gland.
(ii) Secretion of seminal vesicle serves as a medium for the transportation of the sperms.
Sperm duct/Vas deferens carry the sperms to urethra.
(iii) Leydig cells or Interstitial cells produce testosterone (male sex hormone). If these cells get impaired, secondary sexual characters would not appear in males.
(iv) Sertoli cells are called nutritive cells as they act as nurse cells to provide nutrition to the developing sperms.

2. The diagram shown below is the longitudinal section of a testis of man. Study it carefully and answer the questions that follows. [2017]

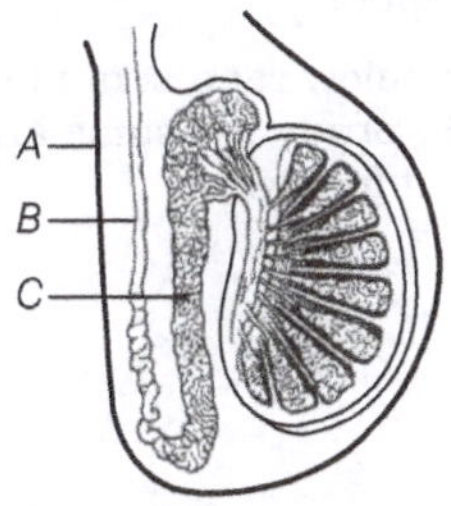

(i) Label the parts labelled as *A*-*C* in the diagram.
(ii) In which part of the testis are the sperms produced?
(iii) State the functions of the parts labelled as *A* and *C* in the diagram.
(iv) Name the cells that secrete testosterone.
(v) Draw a neat, labelled diagram of a sperm. [2023]

Ans. (i) The parts labelled as *A*–*C* are
A – Scrotum
B – Sperm duct (vas deferens)
C – Epididymis
(ii) Sperms are produced in seminiferous tubules.
(iii) The functions of the parts labelled as *A* and *C* are
A (Scrotum), it provides optimal temperature for developing sperms.
C (Epididymis), sperms are stored in epididymis, till they get matured and become motile.
(iv) Interstitial cells (Leydig's cells) secrete testosterone.
(v) The diagram of a sperm is given below as

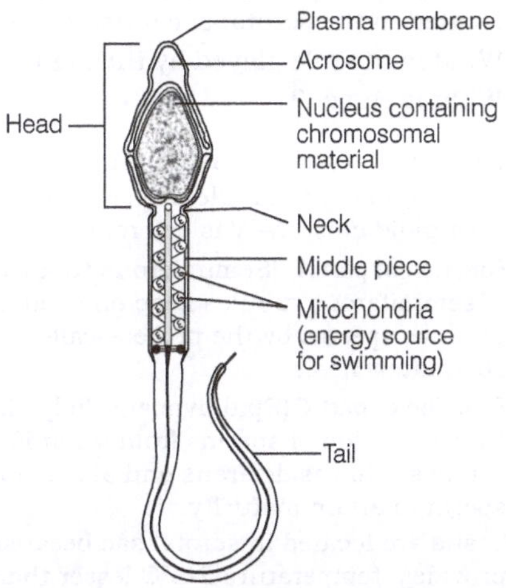

3. The diagram given below shows the male urinogenital system of a human being. Study the diagram and answer the questions that follows. [2015]

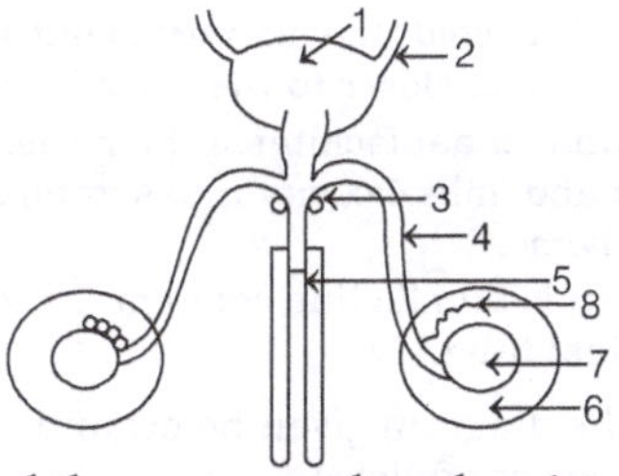

(i) Label the parts numbered as 1 to 8.
(ii) Name the corresponding structure of part (4) in female reproductive system.
(iii) What is the role of part 7?

Ans. (i) The parts numbered as 1 to 8 are

1 – Urinary bladder	2 – Ureter
3 – Prostate gland	4 – Vas deferens
5 – Urethra	6 – Scrotum
7 – Testis	8 – Epididymis

(ii) Fallopian tube
(iii) The testis forms the important part of male reproductive organ. It is responsible for the sperm formation and testosterone production.

4. Given below is a diagram of the lateral section of a testis of a man. Study the same and answer the questions that follows. [2013]

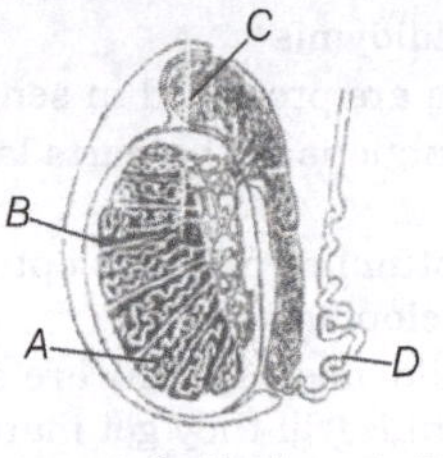

(i) Label the parts labelled as *A-D* of the diagram.
(ii) State the functions of the parts labelled as *A* and *C*.
(iii) What is the significance of the testis being located in the scrotal sac outside the abdomen?
(iv) What is the role played by the inguinal canal?
(v) What is semen? [2013]

Ans. (i) The parts labelled as *A* and *B* are
A – Seminiferous tubule, *B* –Testicular lobes,
C – Epididymis, *D* – Vas deferens

(ii) **Function of part *A*** (Seminiferous tubules) The cells of seminiferous tubules keep on dividing and produce sperms by the process called spermatogenesis.
Function of part *C* (Epididymis) It helps in transportation of sperms from seminiferous tubules into vas deferens and also helps the sperm to attain maturity.

(iii) Testis are located in scrotal sac because it provides temperature 2-3°C lesser than the normal body temperature, which is required for the maturation of sperms. So, when it is too hot the skin of scrotal sac gets loose and testis are taken away from the body and on the other hand when it is cold, the skin gets contracts and the testes come closer to the body for warmth.

(iv) Inguinal canal facilitates the movement of testis from abdominal cavity into scrotal sac or *vice-versa*.

(v) Semen is an alkaline combination of sperms and seminal fluid.

5. Study the diagram given below and answer the questions that follows.

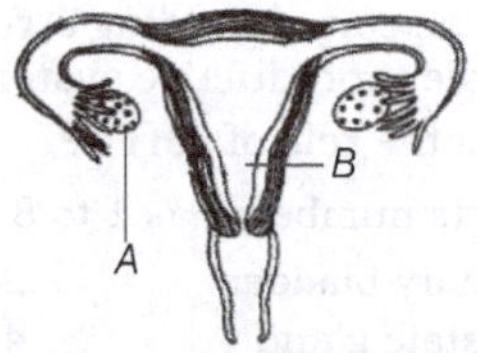

(i) Name the part labelled as *A*. Name any two hormones produced by the labelled as part *A*.
(ii) What happens to the part labelled as *B*.
(a) If fertilisation takes place.
(b) If fertilisation does not take place.
(iii) Where does fertilisation occur? [2012]

Ans. (i) Part *A* is labelled as ovary.
Two hormones produced by ovary are
(a) Oestrogen (b) Progesterone

(ii) (a) If fertilisation takes place, part *B* (uterus) gets prepared to receive the embryo. The endometrial lining gets thickened and highly vascularised.
(b) If fertilisation does not take place, the endometrial lining of uterus (part *B*) erodes out to cause bleeding. It is known as menstruation or menstrual flow.

(iii) Fertilisation occurs in the Fallopian tube/oviduct.

6. The diagram given below represents a system in the human body. Study the diagram and answer the following questions . [2019]

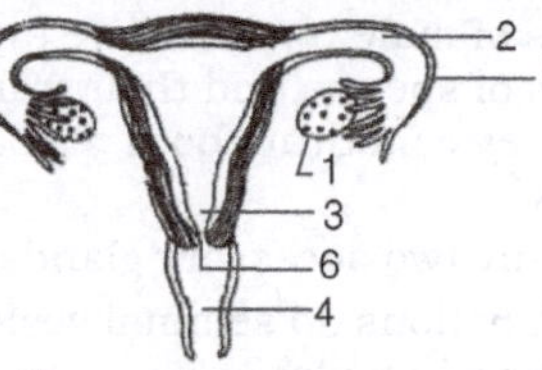

(i) Identify the system.
(ii) Label the parts numbered as 5 and 6.
(iii) Name the two hormones secreted by part 1.
(iv) Mention the number and the name of the part involved in fertilisation and implantation from the above diagram.
(v) Mention the surgical methods of contraception in human males and human females.

Ans. (i) Female reproductive system
(ii) The parts numbered as 5 and 6 are
Part 5- Funnel of oviduct
Part 6 - Cervix
(iii) The two hormones secreted by part 1 (ovary) are progesterone and oestrogen.
(iv) Fertilisation in Fallopian tube (Part 2).
Implantation occurs in uterus (Part 3).
(v) • Vasectomy is a surgical procedure for male contraception.
• Tubectomy is a surgical method for female contraception.

7. The diagram below represents two reproductive cells *A* and *B*. Study the same and then answer the questions that follows.

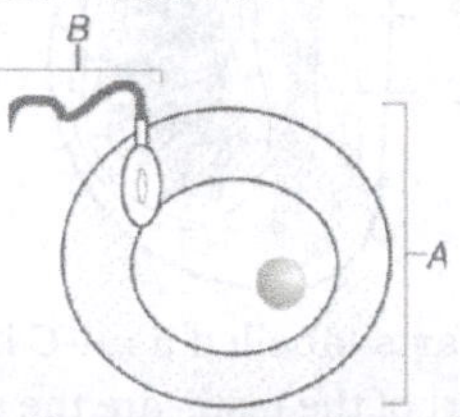

(i) Identify the reproductive cells *A* and *B*.
(ii) Name the specific part of the reproductive system where the above cells are produced.
(iii) Where in the female reproductive system, do these cells unite?

(iv) Name the main hormones secreted by the (*A*) ovary, (*B*) testis.

(v) Name an accessory gland found in the male reproductive system and state the function of its secretion. **[2011]**

Ans. (i) The reproductive cells are
A–Egg/Ovum *B*–Sperm

(ii) Ovum is produced in ovary, while sperm in testis.

(iii) These cells (sperm and ovum) unite in the oviduct (Fallopian tube), when fertilisation takes place.

(iv) Ovary (*A*) produces progesterone and oestrogen. Testis (*B*) produces testosterone.

(v) Seminal vesicle is an accessory gland. Its secretion provides a medium for the transportation of sperms.

8. The diagram given below is that of a developing human foetus. Study the diagram and then answer the questions that follows. **[2016]**

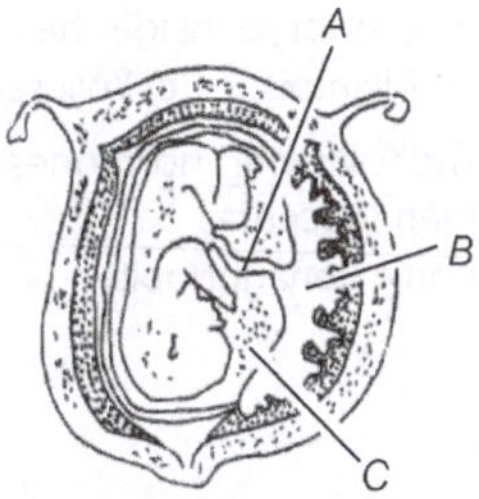

(i) Label the parts labelled as *A*- *C* in the diagram.

(ii) Mention any two functions of the part labelled as *B* in the diagram.

(iii) Explain the significance of the part labelled as *C* in the diagram.

(iv) Define the term gestation. What is the normal gestation period of the developing human embryo?

(v) Mention the sex chromosomes in a male and female embryo.

Ans. (i) The parts *A*–*C* are labelled as
A–Umbilical cord
B–Placenta
C–Amniotic fluid

(ii) Two functions of the part labelled as *B* (Placenta) are as follows

(a) Placenta supplies nutrition and oxygen to the developing foetus.

(b) It also produces endocrine hormone hCG needed for normal foetus growth.

(iii) Amniotic fluid (*C*) is a good shock absorber, so it protects the foetus.

(iv) Gestation is the time taken by fertilised egg to develop into fully formed baby. It approximately takes 40 weeks in human which is equal to 280 days or 9 months.

(v) The sex chromosome in a male–XY and in female– XX.

9. Given below are diagrams showing the different stages in the process of fertilisation of an egg in the human female reproductive tract.
Study the diagrams and answer the questions that follows.

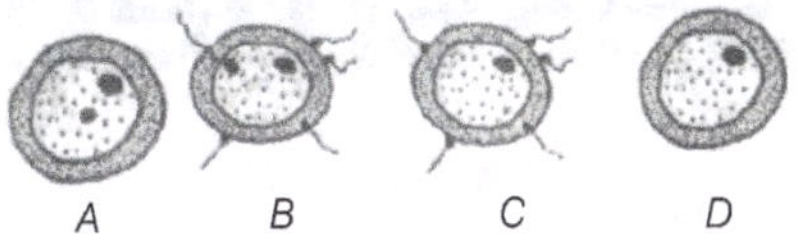

(i) Arrange the letters given above each diagram in a logical sequence to show the correct order in the process of fertilisation.

(ii) Where does fertilisation normally take place? What is 'implantation' that follows fertilisation?

(iii) Mention the chromosome number of the egg and zygote in humans.

(iv) Explain the term 'gestation'. How long does gestation last in humans?

(v) Draw a neat, labelled diagram of a mature human sperm. **[2018]**

Ans. (i) The correct order in the process of fertilisation is

$$D \rightarrow C \rightarrow B \rightarrow A$$

(ii) Process of fertilisation takes place in the Fallopian tubes of female reproductive organs.
After fertilisation, implantation takes place. It is the phenomenon of attachment of developing embryo within the uterus. It leads to the state of pregnancy.

(iii) Human egg contains 23 chromosomes (haploid), while zygote contains 46 chromosomes (diploid).

(iv) Refer to Q-8 (iv)

(v) Refer to Q- 2 (v)

10. Fertilisation in human restores the diploid condition in zygote. This diploid cell undergoes further divisions and transforms into a structure which develops into embryo, surrounded by extraembryonic membranes.

(i) How does the sperm penetrate through the zona pellucida in human ovum?

(ii) Name the embryonic membrane involved in the formation of placenta in humans.

(iii) What happens to the zygote after fertilisation?

(iv) Name the female sex hormones and structures which secrete them.

(v) How is the foetus protected?

Ans. (i) Sperm penetrates through zona pellucida with the help of secretions from acrosome.

(ii) Chorion and allantois are invloved in the formation of placenta in humans.

(iii) After fertilisation, the zygote divides to form multiple-celled embryo which is implanted in the uterus for further development.

(iv) Oestrogen is produced by ovarian follicle and placenta. Progesterone is produced by corpus luteum, ovary and placenta.

(v) The human foetus is protected by the amnion layer having amniotic fluid.

Chapter Assessment

Section-I

1 Mark Questions

1. Name the following.
   (i) The part of the human sperm where acrosome is found.
   (ii) The powerhouse of the sperm cell.
   (iii) The opening of vagina is often covered partially by a membrane.
   (iv) The layers formed during embryonic development.
2. Correct and rewrite the following statements by changing the underlined words.
   (i) <u>Secondary sexual characters</u> are present since birth.
   (ii) <u>Vagina</u> is also known as womb.
3. Give biological reason for the following.
   Most often only the embryo is formed at a time although there are two ovaries in women.
4. (i) Match the following columns.

Column I	Column II
A. Ovulation	1. Complete stoppage of menstrual cycle
B. Menopause	2. Formation of ovum
C. Oogenesis	3. Formation of sperm
D. Spermatogenesis	4. Release of ovum

(ii) Match the following columns.

Column I	Column II
A. Scrotal sac	1. Parturition
B. Prostate gland	2. Fertilisation
C. Epididymis	3. Maturation of spermatozoa
D. Oviduct	4. Alkaline fluid
E. Oxytocin	5. Temperature regulation

5. Choose the corect answer from the four options given below.

(i) The testis in humans are situated outside the abdominal cavity inside a pouch called scrotum. It serves the purpose of
   (a) escaping any possible compression by the visceral organs
   (b) providing more space for the growth of epididymis
   (c) providing a secondary sexual feature for exhibiting the male sex
   (d) maintaining the scrotal temperature lower than the internal body temperature

(ii) Sertoli cells are found in
   (a) heart (b) liver
   (c) germinal epithelium (d) seminiferous tubules

(iii) The tube that leads the ovary to the uterus is
   (a) uterus (b) Fallopian duct
   (c) umbilical cord (d) placenta

(iv) Rupture of the follicle and release of the ovum from the ovary is called
   (a) menstruation (b) ovulation
   (c) spermiation (d) fertilisation

(v) Which extraembryonic membrane in humans prevents desiccation of the embryo inside the uterus?
   (a) Chorion (b) Allantois (c) Yolk sac (d) Amnion

(vi) Which one of the following hormones is not a secretory product of human placenta?
   (a) Human chorionic gonadotropin
   (b) Prolactin
   (c) Oestrogen
   (d) Progesterone

(vii) The endometrium is the lining of
   (a) bladder (b) vagina (c) uterus (d) oviduct

6. Fill in the blanks by using suitable words.
   (i) Only one parent is required in case of ...... reproduction.
   (ii) ...... marks the beginning and attainment of sexual maturity.
   (iii) Facial hairs in males are examples of ...... characters.
   (iv) Seminiferous tubules produce ....
   (v) The secretion of ...... gland makes the semen alkaline.
   (vi) ...... is the state of carrying the unborn young one inside the body.
7. Choose the odd one out from the following terms given below and name the category to which other three belong.
   (i) Ovary, Fallopian tube, Bulbourethral glands, Uterus
   (ii) Puberty, Menopause, Menstruation, Menarche
8. Given below is a set of four terms. Rewrite the terms in correct order of a logical sequence.
   Luteal phase, Follicular phase, Menstrual phase, Ovulatory phase
9. State the exact location of the epididymis.
10. State the main function of the following.
    (i) Scrotum (ii) Ovary
    (iii) Oviduct (iv) Mammary gland

11. Mention one difference between each of the following pairs on the basis of what is given in the bracket.
    (i) Graafian follicle and Corpus luteum (definition)
    (ii) Implantation and Gestation (process)
    (iii) Identical and Fraternal twins (formation)
    (iv) Embryo and Foetus (time of formation)
    (v) Morula and Blastocyst (fate)
12. Give biological/technical terms for the following.
    (i) The structure in which testis are present in man.
    (ii) Packing tissues between coils of seminiferous tubules.
    (iii) The period of intrauterine development of embryo.
13. Briefly explain the following terms.
    (i) Reproductive period
    (ii) Corpus luteum
14. Answer the following questions briefly.
    (i) What is sexual reproduction?
    (ii) What are the four major parts of male reproductive system?
    (iii) What is understood by the term hymen?
    (iv) Write the names of any three extraembryonic membranes in human.

2 Marks Questions

15. In what ways, primary reproductive organs are different from secondary or accessory reproductive organs?
16. Write the sequence of the regions through which a mature sperm travels from the seminiferous tubules upto the urethral opening.
17. What is placenta? Explain its purpose in pregnancy.

3 Marks Questions

18. Write a short note on accessory glands in females.
19. Briefly explain the fate of an egg in female, if it remains unfertilised.
20. Millions of sperms are produced but only one sperm fertilises the egg. Is it true? Explain.

Section-II [5 Marks]

Structured Questions

21. The male reproductive system is mostly located outside of the body and plays a dual role as it is responsible for sexual function as well as urination. The entire male reproductive system is dependent on hormones.
    (i) What are seminiferous tubules?
    (ii) State the source of fructose that provides energy to sperm for its motility.
    (iii) Which hormone secreted by acrosome dissolves the egg wall facilitating the entry of sperm in the egg?
    (iv) Which part of the human sperm is called the powerhouse of the sperm cell? Why?
    (v) Where do sperms undergo physiological maturation?
22. Given below is a diagrammatic representation of the ventral sectional view of the female reproductive system. Answer the questions that follows.

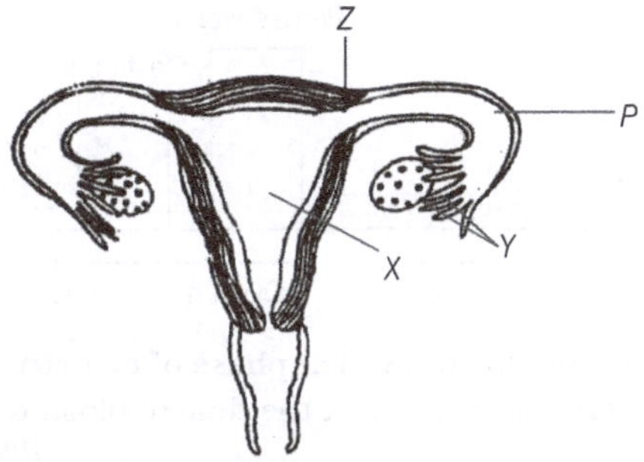

    (i) State the funciton of *Y*.
    (ii) What would happen if site *Z* of both sides is blocked?
    (iii) During which phase of menstrual cycle, the lining of *X* is thickened and shredded?
    (iv) Where does cleavage and implantation occur?
    (v) Name any two harmful substances that can cross placenta.
23. The given diagram is of a developing embryo in a mother's womb. Answer the questions that follows.

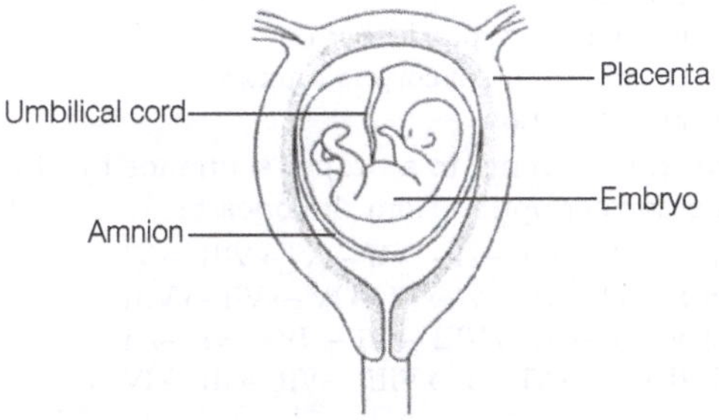

    (i) Write the functions of amnion.
    (ii) Which part in the given diagram helps in the respiration of foetus?
    (iii) When is an embryo called foetus?
    (iv) Presence of which hormone in urine confirms pregnancy?
    (v) What is 'after birth'?

For explanations scan the given QR Code

Olympiad Section*

Brain Teasing Questions asked in Previous Olympiads

1 The figure below gives the level of ovarian and gonadotropic hormone in a blood sample of a normal healthy female of 35 years.

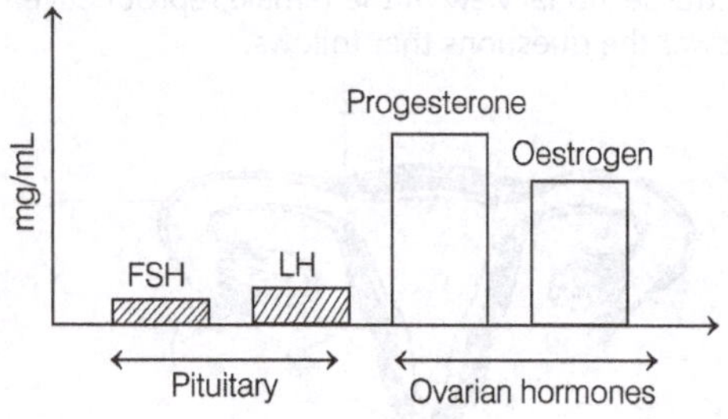

According to you, which phase of menstrual cycle was she undergoing at the time of blood test? **[INJSO 2011]**

(a) Menstrual phase
(b) Proliferative phase
(c) Ovulatory phase
(d) Luteal or Secretory phase

2 Some important events that occur during the menstrual cycle are given below.

I. Proliferation of endometrial wall
II. LH surge
III. Secretion of oestrogen
IV. Secretion of progesterone
V. Ovulation
VI. Growth of corpus luteum
VII. Degeneration of corpus luteum
VIII. Menstruation

Put these events in a proper sequence by choosing the correct option from the ones below.

(a) II → IV → III → I → VII → V → VIII → VI
(b) III → I → II → V → VI → IV → VII → VIII
(c) V → I → VI → VIII → III → IV → VII → II
(d) II → V → VI → I → VIII → VII → III → IV

3 The following greaph shows the levels of pituitary hormones during a menstrual cycle. What do *A* and *B* represent?

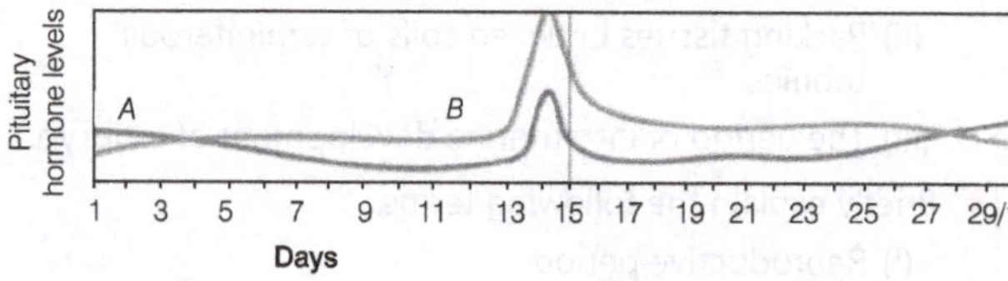

	A	*B*
(a)	LH	FSH
(b)	Oestrogen	Progesterone
(c)	FSH	LH
(d)	Progesterone	Oestrogen

4 In an experiment, sperms were removed from epididymis of a man. They were added in a dish containing appropriate media and oocyte. No fertilisation was seen. However, when sperms from epididymis were directly placed in uterus of an ovulated woman, she became pregnant. These observations suggest that

(a) the sperms need to travel some distance to attain fertillising ability
(b) the oocyte secretes some biochemicals or factors which give sperms the ability to fertilise
(c) the hormones in the female body help sperms to attain fertilising ability
(d) the contents of female reproductive tract interact with sperms and activate them for fertilisation

5 If an adult human female took a drug that inhibited the release of LH, which of the following would not occur?

(a) The menstrual cycle
(b) Release of an ovum from a mature follicle
(c) Secretion of FSH (Follicle Stimilating Hormone) from the pituitary
(d) Secretion of oestrogen by the follicle cells

Answers

1. (d) **2.** (b) **3.** (c) **4.** (d) **5.** (b)

*These questions may or may not be asked in the examination, have been given just for additional practice required for olympiads, scholarship exams etc. For detailed explanations refer Page No. 247.

CHAPTER

12

Population and Its Control

Chapter Inside

• Population • Population Explosion • Population in India • Population Control

Population

Population is a group of organisms of the same species occupying a particular space at a particular time. It can be defined as the summation of all living organisms of the same species or group in a geographical area, where they live and inbreed among themselves.

Presently the population throughout the world has seen an alarming increase. The rising human population has become most serious problem and put challenges for mankind by creating deficiency of the resources. In this chapter, we will study about population, its related aspects and thereafter, its effects on resources and how to control population size.

Terms Related to Population

(i) **Population density** It is the measurement of population per unit area or per unit volume at a given time. All the populations inhabiting the same area constitute a **biotic community**.

(ii) **Growth rate of population** It is defined as the difference between the birth rate and death rate in a given population at a given time. If the birth rate is higher than death rate, the population increases. But the birth rate is lower than death rate, the population declines.

(iii) **Population growth** It is the change in the population over a period of time. It is the collection of interbreeding organisms of a particular species. Technically, population growth refers to any species, but is always used for humans.

The population growth is affected by

(a) **Emigration** The number of people moving out of a particular region or country.

(b) **Immigration** The addition of new people to already existing population in a region from other areas or countries. Population growth can cause following problems

- Decrease in natural resources
- Decrease in per capita income
- Decrease in health condition

(iv) **Demography** It is the scientific statistical study of human population. There are five demographic factors in a population.These are **literacy**, **mortality**, **marriage, migration** and **social mobility**.

These factors, which work continuously to determine three phenomena of demography, i.e. size, composition and distribution.

(v) **Census** It is the procedure of systematically acquiring and recording information about the members of given population. It is an official counting or survey and study of human population after every 10 years.

Population Explosion

A rapid increase in the size of population over a relatively short period is called **population explosion.** The combination of a continuing high birth rate and low death rate is the major cause of population explosion. Population in the world is currently upgrowing at a rate of around 1.13% per year and 1.2% per year in India.

Terms Related to Population Explosion

Important terms related to the population explosion are given below

(i) **Birth rate** (Natality) It is defined as the total number of live births per 1,000 individuals of a population per year. It results in increased population size and population density.
The actual birth rate which is obtained under existing conditions is termed as **realised natality** or **fertility rate** and it is inversely related to environmental resistance.

(ii) **Death rate** (Mortality) It is defined as the total number of deaths per 1,000 individuals of a population per year. It results in decrease in population size and population density, but decrease in death rate results in increased population growth rate.
(a) **Infant mortality** It refers to the death of a child less than one year of age. It is measured as the number of deaths of children under one year of age per 1000 live births.
(b) **Maternal mortality** It refers to the death of either a pregnant woman or death of woman within 42 days of delivery, spontaneous abortion or termination, providing death is associated with pregnancy or its treatment.

(iii) **Vital index** It is the percentage ratio of natality and mortality in a unit population at a unit time.

Major Causes of Sharp Rise in Population Worldwide

Population increase is directly associated with the following factors

(i) **Increased birth rate** Increase in the number of people in reproducible age due to advanced medical help is the most common reason of extensive population growth.

(ii) **Large scale immunisation** The control of communicable and non-communicable diseases by the antibiotics or the prophylactic vaccinations has reduced the number of deaths. Improved medical attention and awareness also contribute to the rise in population.

(iii) **Education and awareness** The awareness about the reproduction related aspects, diseases and their prevention and hygiene has helped in the rise of population.

(iv) **Improved food and nutrition** Due to new agricultural practices, the food production has improved and new storage methods have reduced the food wastage. More food availability reduces the death of individuals due to starvation and improvement in nutritional quality keeps an individual healthy and free from diseases.

(v) **Role of government policies** Many steps have been implemented by government as in India to reduce the number of unnecessary deaths, which include clean public toilets, clean roads, proper drainage systems, regular checkups of all facilities, etc.

Note If no control on population growth rate is observed, the populations in the next 700 years would increase so much that only 1 sq. foot of Earth would be available per person.

Effects of Population Explosion

The rising human population causes following problems

1. Overexploitation of Resources

Any material either natural or artificial, used by humans for their growth, development and welfare is known as **resource**. The rising human population is creating pressure on the limited resources. As the result of this, resources are facing their overexploitation which is contributing to their price rise as well. The six main resources under pressure in context of rise in population are as follows

(i) **Food** An important necessity for all living beings is food. Many advance methods have been applied to increase the yield of good quality food, but they are not enough because the population increases in geometric progression, i.e. 1, 2, 4, 8...., whereas food production occurs in arithmetic progression, i.e. 1, 2, 3, 4, 5, 6..... . A level would therefore be reached where the entire world would suffer from food shortage.

(ii) **Water** The availability of clean, contamination free drinking water will become more scarce with the growing population.

(iii) **Forests** These are reservoirs of many valuable resources and also maintain the balance in the ecosystem. Vast areas of the forests have already been cleared for human settlements like housing, schools, hospitals, etc.

(iv) **Land** It is required for buildings, farming, roads, etc. The area of land is fixed on the Earth and will not increase as per our demand. Usable land is becoming less available with growing population.

(v) **Energy** It is required for cooking, industrial processes, transportation, etc. Energy is obtained from fossil fuels, which are non-renewable (these resources are lost forever once used completely). At present, coal and petroleum are two main energy sources. With population increase, these energy reserves are depleting fast.

(vi) **Minerals** These are utilised by many industries to produce different materials required by us. Increased population has raised the utilisation of minerals like iron, copper, aluminium, etc., at a faster rate.

2. Population Growth due to Urbanisation

Urbanisation is also an effect of population increase. With increase in population, people move from small rural area to urban area in search of work and opportunities. This shift of population from rural area to urban area is called **urbanisation**. This urbanisation put challenges on natural resources and lead to following consequences

- Due to increase in population in urban areas, agriculture land is used for residential and other purposes like schooling, hospital, etc.
- Due to urbanisation, there is an increase in demand of fuels, electricity, food, etc., which threatens the extinction of natural resources like coal, petroleum, etc.
- Urbanisation is also responsible for raising living standards of the people. This results in accumulation of more household goods, electric equipments, clothes, vehicles, etc.

Sustainable Development

To avoid the problems of depletion of natural resources, concept of sustainable development should be followed. It is the process of development to sustain natural systems and their yields, which can be maintained for a long time without any damage to the environment. The concept of sustainable development encourages growth that meet the current basic human needs, while preserving the resources for the needs of the future generations.

The sustainable development can be achieved by taking following measures

(i) Recycling and reusing natural resources.

(ii) Increase use of renewable resources such as solar energy, wind power, etc.

(iii) Sensible use of available natural resources.

Check Your LEARNING...

1 Name the five demographic factors in a population, which work continuously to determine three phenomena of demography.

2 What would happen if there is no control on population growth in coming 700 years?

3 What do you mean by urbanisation?

4 Mention two measures to achieve sustainable development.

Population in India

The population of India is rising at an alarming rate. At present, India is the second most populated country in the world. It has only 2.42% of the world's land, but supports more than 17.5% of world's population. Current Indian population is a little more than 1.21 billion.

Note The billionth child was born on May 11, 2000, at Safdarjung hospital, New Delhi.

Major Causes of Population Explosion in India

The factors responsible for the increase in population in India are as follows

(i) Illiteracy and lack of recreation due to which many people in rural areas do not know the functioning of reproductive system.

(ii) In India, people belief that children are the gift of God and a sign of prosperity. Therefore, people belonging to lower society make no effort to avoid pregnancy.

(iii) People believe that male child is usually of great help to the aged parents. So, they continue to give birth till they have a male child.

(iv) Due to low economic conditions, children are considered helping hands for their parents, which also affects their education and food availability.

(v) The high mortality rate in infants makes people think it is safer to produce more children.

(vi) Religious and social customs refrain some families to accept family planning norms.

Note July 11, every year is celebrated as World Population Day to create awareness among people about the growing population and how it affects our environment.

Consequences of Population Explosion in India

Overpopulation has lead to various serious problems. Some of these are given below

(i) **Shortage of food supply** If the population keeps on increasing and the production of food does not increase in a similar proportion, it leads to shortage of food.

(ii) **Unemployment** Overgrowing population is a main and the foremost reason for unemployment. As number of people increases, the need for job also increases. Therefore, more number of people remain unemployed as sufficient number of jobs are not available. Along with unemployment increase, a decrease in per capita income is also visible with population increase.

(iii) **Education** With increasing population, more people need to be educated. This creates difficulties for the Government in order to provide education to all.

(iv) **Poverty** Family tends to become poor, if there are more persons in it and the income is less. Therefore, poverty increases with the birth of each child in the family.

(v) **Decreased open spaces** Because all the members in family require adequate space for living, so more houses are constructed which results in decrease in open spaces.

(vi) **Pollution** The increased population leads to all kinds of pollution, i.e. land, air, soil and water.

(vii) **Overexploitation of resources** It is done to meet the requirements of growing population. This may also be seen in the form of unequal distribution of wealth. Thus, over exploitation along with unequal distribution of wealth is one of the major consequences of population explosion.

Overall large population (overpopulation) of a country is the result of having large families where the quality of life also goes down.

Disadvantages of Large Family

There are several disadvantages of large family, like

(i) Economic pressure on the parents with poor housing and clothing condition.

(ii) Health condition of the mother deteriorates due to frequent pregnancies.

(iii) Lesser attention of the parents towards various needs of the children.

(iv) Children suffer from malnutrition.

(v) Insufficient education to children.

Check Your LEARNING...

1 What percentage of India's population constitutes of the world's population?

2 How high mortality rate in infants, is a cause of population explosion in India?

3 When the World Population Day is celebrated?

4 Give one serious consequence of overpopulation.

5 State one disadvantage of large family.

Population Control

To overcome the consequences of overpopulation, it is mandatory to control the rate of population growth. Control measures in the form of awareness about family planning, contraceptions, etc., can be done.

Measures to Control Population Explosion

To prevent the adverse effect of overcrowding and population explosion, following measures must be taken.

(i) **Improved education facilities** It is necessary for each person of the society to be well-educated for understanding all the criteria and impacts of population explosion. Awareness and education motivates people to take steps in right direction.

(ii) **Sex education** Reproductive or sex education must be provided to the people at young age. The orthodox belief to have atleast one male child can be modified by education in small towns. Spacing between the children is also a good measure. The concept of small family, happy family should be implemented widespread.

(iii) **Marriageable age** In order to check the population growth, the age of marriage must be raised which will be a more effective means for the control of population. In India, the marriageable age for a boy is 21 and for a girl is 18.

(iv) **Family planning** It was introduced in 1951 in India. The department which plays a significant role in controlling population and is committed to provide advice and help about family planning is known as **Family Welfare Centre Department**.

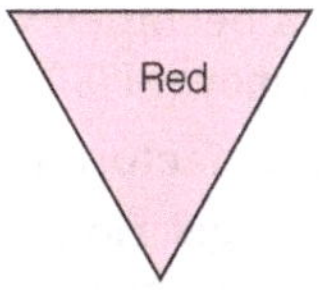

Sign of family welfare

The **inverted red triangle** is a popular sign in India for family welfare.

Contraception or Birth Control

The prevention or regulation of conception by preventive methods or devices that limit the number of offsprings is called contraception or birth control. These devices are called **contraceptives**.

An ideal contraceptive should be

(i) User-friendly
(ii) Easily available
(iii) Effective
(iv) Reversible with no or least side effects
(v) Should not interfere with the sexual drive/desire and/or the sexual act of the user.

Methods of Contraception

Contraception can be achieved by the following methods

1. Natural Contraception

These methods are based on the principle of avoiding chances of egg meeting the sperm. Some of them are as follows

(i) **Periodic abstinence** In this, the couples avoid coitus (intercourse) from day 10-17 of the menstrual cycle, because ovulation occurs mostly during this time (it is called the **fertile period**) to avoid conception.

(ii) **Coitus interruptus or Withdrawal method** In this method, the male partner withdraws his penis from the vagina just before ejaculation so as to avoid insemination.

(iii) **Lactational amenorrhea** It refers to the stoppage of menstruation during the period of lactation following parturition. Because ovulation does not occur in this period, the chances of conception are minimum or nil.

2. Barrier Methods

These methods prevent sperms and ovum from physically meeting in order to prevent fertilisation. These methods are available for both males and females.

These are as follows

(i) **Condoms** These are made up of thin rubber or latex sheath and are used to cover the penis in males and vagina and cervix in females (femidome). These are used just before coitus, so that ejaculated semen would not enter female reproductive tract.

(ii) **Cervical caps, diaphragms and vaults** These are also made up of rubber and are inserted into the female reproductive tract to cover the cervix during intercourse. They prevent conception by blocking entry of sperms through cervix. These are reusable.

(iii) **Spermicides** These are chemicals applied at the surface of vagina before intercourse. These contain spermicides (that kill spermatozoa) such as lactic acid, citric acid, boric acid, zinc sulphate and potassium permanganate. Spermicides are available in the form of creams, jellies and foams.

3. Intrauterine Devices (IUDs)

These devices contain either copper or progesterone and are inserted by doctors in the uterus through vagina. These are a form of long, reversible contraceptive method. IUDs prevent the implantation of blastocyst (embryo). They may be Lippe's loop and copper-T. Levonorgestrel (LNG) 20 is a hormonal IUD.

4. Oral Contraceptives

These are the preparations of hormones, either progestogens or progestogen-oestrogen combinations in the form of **pills** (tablets), used by the females. They alter or inhibit ovulation and fertilisation, e.g. Mala-D, Mala-N, Saheli (non-hormonal), etc.

5. Surgical (Sterilisation) Methods

These are the terminal methods used by male/female partner to prevent any more pregnancies. These are the permanent methods which block the transport of gametes and thereby, prevent conception.

It is called **vasectomy in men** and **tubectomy in women.**

(i) **Vasectomy** A small part of the vas deferens is cut or tied up through a small incision in the scrotum in males.

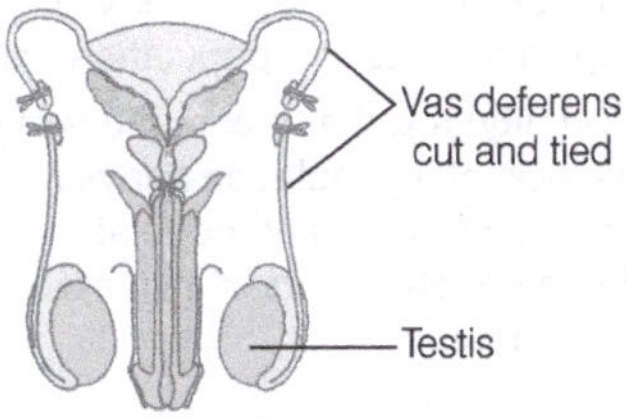

Vasectomy in male

(ii) **Tubectomy** A small part of the Fallopian tube is cut or tied up through a small incision in the abdomen or vagina in female.

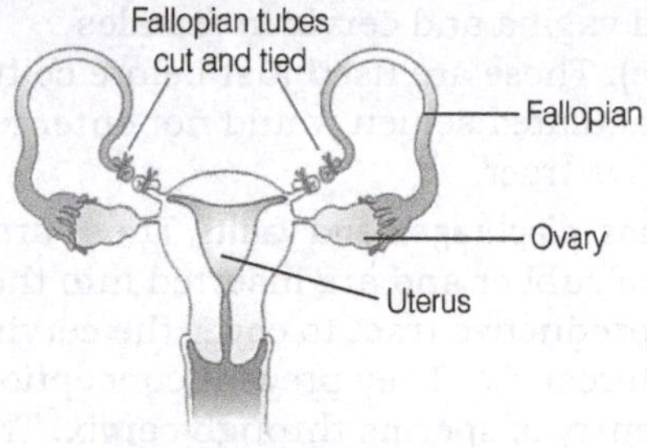

Tubectomy in female

Both these techniques are known to be highly effective and poorly reversible.

Medical Termination of Pregnancy (MTP)/ Induced Abortion

Intentional or voluntary termination (abortion) of pregnancy before full term or before the foetus becomes viable is called **Medical Termination of Pregnancy** (MTP).

Various factors that lead to MTPs are

(i) To get rid of unwanted pregnancies due to casual unprotected intercourse during which the contraceptive is not used.

(ii) In case, where continuation of pregnancy is harmful to either foetus, mother or even both.

Note MTP was legalised in 1971. MTP is considered relatively safe upto 12 weeks of pregnancy (during first trimester). It becomes more risky after the period of 12 weeks. It is a last resort available in the absence of other options.

Check Your LEARNING...

1 When was family planning introduced in India?
2 Lactational amenorrhea is reliable upto how much time?
3 Name one barrier contraceptive for males.
4 What do birth control pills contain?
5 Name a permanent method of contraception in female.
6 What is the main purpose of MTP.

QUiCK Revision

- **Population** is defined as summation of all living organisms of the same species or group in a geographical area where they live and inbreed among themselves.
- **Population density** It is the measurement of population per unit area or per unit volume at a given time.
- **Growth rate of population** It is defined as the difference between the birth rate and death rate in a given population at a given time.
- **Population growth** It is the change in the population over a period of time.
- **Demography** It is the statistical study of human population.
- **Census** It is the official counting of human population after every ten years.
- **Population explosion** It is a sudden increase in the population in a relatively small period of time. It occurs due to increased health facilities and better living conditions.
- **Birth rate** (Natality) It is the total number of live births per 1,000 individuals of a population per year. It results in increased population size and population density.
- **Death rate** (Mortality) It is the total number of deaths per 1,000 individuals of a population per year. It results in decrease in population size and population density, but decrease in death rate results in increased population growth rate.
- Measures to control population explosion are
  (i) Improved education facilities
  (ii) Sex education
  (iii) Check on marriageable age
  (iv) Family planning
- **Birth control** is an only solution of checking population growth. These methods are categorised as follows
  - **Natural methods** of birth control involve avoiding chances of meeting sperm and ovum. It can be done by periodic abstinence, coitus interruptus and lactational amenorrhea, etc.
  - **Barrier methods** are based on prevention of ovum and sperms coming closer. It is achieved by using condoms, diaphragms, cervical caps, vaults, spermicides, etc.
  - **Intrauterine Devices** (IUDs) are the devices introduced into the uterus in order to suppress the motility and fertilising ability by releasing ions such as Cu^{2+} which makes uterus unsuitable for implantation. These include Lippes loop, Cu-T, LNG-20, Progestasert, etc.
  - **Oral contraceptives** are hormonal preparations in the form of pills. These can alter or inhibit ovulation and implantation, e.g. Saheli, Mala-D, Mala-N, etc.
  - **Surgical or Sterilisation methods** are used in male/female to prevent pregnancy. They are available as tubectomy in females and vasectomy in males.
- **Medical Termination of Pregnancy** (MTP) It is the intentional termination of pregnancy before reaching full term.

Chapter Practice

Section-I

1 Mark Questions

1. Name the following.
   (i) Group of organisms living in a geographically localised area with capacity of interbreeding.
   (ii) The term used for the number of individuals inhabiting per unit area. [2016]
   (iii) A rapid increase in size of a population influenced by certain factors.
   (iv) The percentage ratio of natality and mortality in a unit population at a unit time.
   (v) A contraceptive device consisting of a small thimble-shaped cup that is placed over the uterus to prevent the entrance of spermatozoa.

Ans. (i) Population
(ii) Population density
(iii) Population explosion
(iv) Vital index
(v) Cervical cap

2. Correct and rewrite the following statements by changing the underlined words.
   (i) Immigration is the number of people moving out of a particular region.
   (ii) Realised natality is directly related to environmental resistance.
   (iii) Oral contraceptives are the preparations of copper ions.
   (iv) MTP is safe upto 25 weeks of pregnancy.

Ans. (i) Emigration is the number of people moving out of a particular region.
(ii) Realised natality is inversely related to environmental resistance.
(iii) Oral contraceptives are the preparations of hormones.
(iv) MTP is safe upto 12 weeks of pregnancy.

3. Give biological reasons for the following.
   (i) There is a need to check the present rate of urbanisation. [2017]
   (ii) Education is very important for population control. [2018]
   (iii) The need to limit the size of the family is more vital today than ever before.
   (iv) The birth rate in India is very high. [2019]

Ans. (i) There is a need to check the present rate of urbanisation to reduce the pressure on resources such as forest, fossil fuels, etc.
(ii) Education is important for population control because it allows the individual to understand the criteria and impacts of population explosion. It helps in making people aware about the benefits of small families and large families.
(iii) Due to growth in population every year, the country has to spend more on food, clothing and housing. A large population produces more waste causing pollution and disturbing the ecological balance. So, the need to limit the size of family is more vital today than ever before.
(iv) The birth rate in India is very high because of
- Illiteracy due to which many people in rural areas do not know the functioning of reproductive system and family planning.
- Traditional belief that children are the gift of God and a sign of prosperity.
- Desire for a male child in the family as people believe that male child is usually of great help to the aged parents.

4. (i) Match the following columns.

Column I	Column II
A. Increased growth rate	1. Recycling and reuse
B. Population explosion	2. Excess of population
C. Sustainable development	3. Birth rate exceeds death rate

(ii) Match the following columns.

Column I	Column II
A. IUD	1. Cover cervix
B. Vault	2. Available as jellies and foams
C. Spermicide	3. Copper-T

Ans. (i) A–3, B–2, C–1
(ii) A–3, B–1, C–2

5. Choose the correct answer from the four options given below
   (i) Birth rate is the number of lives birth
   (a) per 100 people per decade
   (b) per 1000 people per year
   (c) per 1000 people per decade
   (d) per 100 people per year

Ans. (b)

(ii) The statistical study of human population is called
(a) mortality
(b) demography
(c) natality
(d) equality

Ans. (b)

(iii) Identify a non-renewable natural resource that is overexploited due to increased population.
(a) Coal (b) Petroleum
(c) Both (a) and (b) (d) Wind

Ans. (c)

(iv) Ideal contraceptive should not be
(a) user-friendly (b) effective
(c) expensive (d) easily available

Ans. (c)

(v) Copper releasing IUDs are used for suppressing the
(a) activity of ova (b) activity of uterus
(c) motility of sperms (d) motility of ova

Ans. (c)

(vi) Surgical method of sterilisation in a woman involves cutting and tying of [2017]
(a) ureter (b) uterus
(c) urethra (d) oviduct

Ans. (d)

6. Fill in the blanks by using suitable words.
(i) The actual birth rate obtained under existing conditions is termed as .... and it is .... propotional to environmental resistance.
(ii) Population increases in .... ratio, while the food production occurs in .... ratio.
(iii) Population control can be achieved by ...... and ....
(iv) Family planning is denoted by .... inverted triangle.
(v) Pregnancy can be avoided by the use of ....
(vi) Periodic abstinence means to avoid coitus from .... day of menstrual cycle.

Ans. (i) realised natality, inversely
(ii) geometric, arithmetic
(iii) sex education, family planning
(iv) red-coloured
(v) contraceptives
(vi) 10-17th

7. State whether the following statements are true or false.
(i) Mortality is the number of deaths per thousand of the population per decade. [2007]
(ii) Vasectomy is the surgical method of sterilisation in men. [2005]
(iii) Tubectomy is the surgical method of sterilisation in men. [2017]

Ans. (i) False, mortality is the number of deaths per thousand of the population per year.
(ii) True
(iii) False, vasectomy is the surgical method of sterilisation in males whereas tubectomy is the surgical method of sterilisation in females.

8. Choose the odd one out from the following terms given below and name the category to which other three belong.
Copper-T, Foams, Condoms, Jellies

Ans. **Odd term** is condoms.
Rest three are spermicidal agents.

9. Expand the following biological abbreviations.
(i) MMR (ii) IUD (iii) MTP

Ans. (i) Maternal Mortality Rate
(ii) Intra-Uterine Device
(iii) Medical Termination of Pregnancy

10. State the main function of the following.
(i) Census (ii) Spermicidal foam
(iii) Vasectomy

Ans. (i) Census helps in estimating the current population size and growth trend.
(ii) Spermicidal foams help to kill the sperms in female reproductive tract.
(iii) Vasectomy helps in providing permanent contraception in males.

11. Mention one difference between each of the following pairs on the basis of what is given in the bracket.
(i) Demography and Population density (definition) [2017]
(ii) Natality and Mortality (definition) [2012]
(iii) Vasectomy and Tubectomy (part cut end tied) [2015, 13]

Ans. (i) Difference between demography and population density is as follows

Demography	Population density
The scientific statistical study of human population is called demography.	It is the measurement of population per unit area at a given time.

(ii) Difference between natality and mortality is as follows

Natality	Mortality
It refers to the number of births during a given period in the population that are added to initial density.	It refers to the number of deaths in the population during a given period.

(iii) Difference between vasectomy and tubectomy is as follows

Vasectomy	Tubectomy
It involves surgical cutting of a part of vas deferens and ligation of cut ends to prevent sperm transfer.	It involves surgical cutting of a part of Fallopian tube and ligation of the cut ends to prevent fertilisation.

12. Give biological/technical terms for the following.
(i) Statistical study of human population. [2014, 12]
(ii) The difference between the birth rate and the death rate. [2018]
(iii) Contraception achieved by avoiding insemination during intercourse.
(iv) Surgical method of contraception in females.

Ans. (i) Demography (ii) Growth rate
(iii) Coitus interruptus (iv) Tubectomy

13. Briefly explain the following terms.
(i) Growth rate of population [2017]
(ii) Natality [2015]
(iii) Explain the term 'population density'. [2023]

Ans. (i) Growth rate of population is defined as the difference between the birth rate and death rate of a population.
(ii) Natality is defined as the ratio of the number of births to the size of the population. It is also termed as birth rate.
(iii) Population density means the number of people living per unit area. It is normally written as per square km.

14. Answer the following questions briefly.
(i) Write any two major reasons for the population explosion in the world. [2013]
(ii) Write any two major reasons for the population explosion in India. [2023, 15, 14, 12]

Or

State two reasons for the increase of population in India.
(iii) What is the present rate of growth of population in India and world?
(iv) What are the age restrictions for marriage for boys and girls in India? [2009]
(v) Is the use of contraceptives justified?

Ans. (i) Two major reasons for the population explosion in the world are as follows
- Abundance of food
- Decreased death rate

(ii) Two major reasons for the population explosion in India are
- Illiteracy
- Religious and social beliefs

(iii) The present rate of growth of population of India is 1.2% per year and 1.13% per year in the world.
(iv) Age restriction for marriage for boys is 21 years and for girls, it is 18 years in India.
(v) Use of contraceptives is justified because they help in controlling the growth of population, avoid unwanted pregnancies. Some contraceptives like condoms also help in preventing STDs (Sexually Transmitted Diseaes).

2 Marks Questions

15. The present population growth rate in India is alarming. Suggest two ways to check it.

Ans. Ways to check population growth rate are
(i) By increasing marriageable age and by promoting use of birth control measures.
(ii) By educating people about the consequences of uncontrolled population growth.

16. Name any two resources which come under pressure due to rising population. [2023]

Ans. (a) Food (b) Land

17. Name the two surgical methods of population control. [2023]

Ans. Vasectomy and tubectomy.

18. Classify the following contraceptive measures into different methods of birth control.
(i) Saheli
(ii) Condoms
(iii) Diaphragm
(iv) Cervical caps

Ans. (i) Oral pills
(ii) Barrier method
(iii) Barrier method
(iv) Barrier method

3 Marks Questions

19. Write any six factors which have contributed to a rapid rise of human population in recent time in the world.

Ans. Six factors which have contributed to a rapid rise of human population in recent time in the world are as follows
(i) Better healthcare for all age groups.
(ii) Food shortage minimised due to green revolution.
(iii) Widespread immunisation against fatal diseases.
(iv) Reduced death rate due to better medical facilities.
(v) Proper nutrition specially to the growing children.
(vi) More children reaching the reproductive age.

20. List any three consequences of population explosion in India.

Ans. Population explosion/overpopulation in India has led to some serious problems which are as follows

(i) **Education** It is one of the consequence of overpopulation as government tend to face difficulties in providing education to all.

(ii) **Poverty** If there are more members in a family and the income is less, the family becomes naturally poor. It also results in social unrest.

(iii) **Unemployment** Overgrowing population is the foremost reason for unemployement. As number of people will increase, the need for job will also increase and if sufficient number of jobs are not available, more number of people will remain jobless.

21. How can the knowledge of reproduction process help people in limiting the size of their families? Give two concrete examples.

Ans. Knowledge of reproduction process can help people in limiting the size of their families. This can be illustrated by following examples

(i) By becoming aware, people will get rid of the belief that children are God's gift. This would help in changing their mindsets and they would then understand the importance of small family.

(ii) By understanding the reproduction process, a person can understand how different methods of contraception work. They would be able to adopt a suitable contraception method based on their requirement.

22. Is sex education necessary in schools? Why?

Ans. Yes, sex education is necessary in schools because

(i) Students should become part of such education, so that they overcome hesitation and gain confidence to discuss any problem or doubt with their teacher or parents.

(ii) Counselling and awareness regarding reproductive organs, safe and hygienic sexual practices will play an important role in making people reproductively healthy.

23. Describe three manners in which fertilisation of human ovum by a sperm can be prevented.

Ans. Fertilisation of human ovum by a sperm can be prevented by the following methods

(i) Condoms are the barriers made up of thin rubber or latex sheath. These are used to cover the penis in the male or vagina and cervix in females.

(ii) Diaphragm, cervical caps and vaults are the barriers made up of rubber that are introduced in the female reproductive tract to cover cervix.

(iii) Spermicidal creams, jellies and foams are introduced in vagina to kill the sperms.

Section-II [5 Marks]

Structured Questions

1. The diagram given below represents a surgical sterilisation method in males. Study the same and answer the questions that follow.

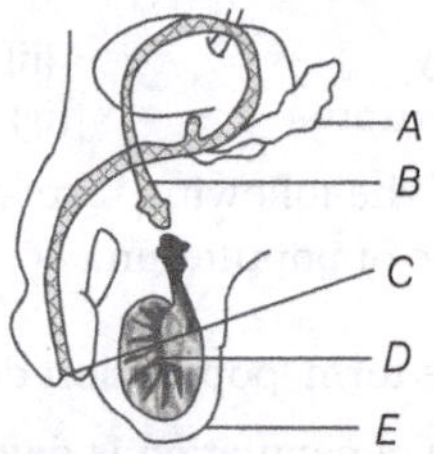

(i) Name the parts labelled as *A*, *B*, *C*, *D* and *E*.

(ii) Give the name of the surgical method represented in the diagram.

(iii) Which part is ligated or cut?

(iv) Suggest an alternative method of contraception that can be used by male.

(v) Name the chemical that kill the sperms and where it is used.

Ans. (i) The parts labelled as *A* to *E* are

A – Seminal vesicle
B – Sperm duct or vas deferens
C – Urethra
D – Testis
E – Scrotum

(ii) Vasectomy

(iii) Sperm duct or vas deferens (*B*) is the part that is ligated or cut.

(iv) Condom is an alternative method of contraception that can be used by male.

(v) Spermicides kill the sperms and these are placed in vagina in the form of cream, jelly, etc.

2. Observe the figure given below and answer the questions that follows.

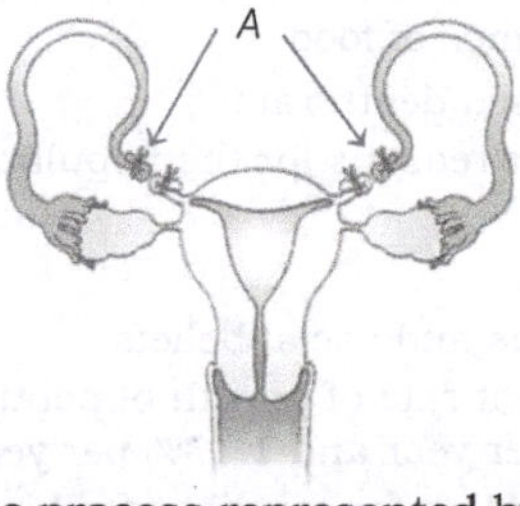

(i) Name the process represented by the figure.

(ii) List atleast one advantage of these processes.

(iii) What does '*A*' represent in diagram?

(iv) Name any two oral contraceptives used by females.

(v) Name the device which is placed in uterus to achieve contraception.

Ans. (i) The figure represents tubectomy.

(ii) Tubectomy helps to control population number.

(iii) A represents the ligated oviduct in females in order to prevent the fusion of egg with the sperms, thus avoiding pregnancy.

(iv) Two oral contraceptives used by females are Mala-D and Saheli.

(v) Intra-uterine devices like Cu-T are placed in uterus. They provide long-term contraception that can be reversed anytime.

3. Population explosion is a major issue for developing countries because it traps people in a web of poverty and illiteracy. In order to control overgrowing population, various methods of contraception are available now-a-days.

(i) Why are awareness campaigns related to population explosion necessary in India?

(ii) Give the names of any two natural methods of conception.

Also discuss the principle they are based on.

(iii) On what principle surgical methods of conception are based?

(iv) In last few years, which areas of improvement in India have helped in population explosion?

(v) Suggest few ways to check population growth.

Ans. (i) These campaigns help people to understand the problems faced by families and the nation due to increasing population. Also, the benefits of having small family are being told through these campaigns.

(ii) Lactational amenorrhea and periodic abstinence are natural methods of conception. These methods work on the principle of avoiding the chance of meeting between ovum and sperm.

(iii) The main principle behind surgical methods of contraception is that these prevent gamete transport through vas deferens or oviducts.

(iv) Some of the areas of improvement leading to population explosion are increased food production, better medical facilities, better education, etc.

(v) Few ways to check population growth are as follows

(a) By raising marriageable age of the females to 18 years and that of males to 21 years.

(b) By promoting use of birth control measures to motivate smaller families.

Chapter Assessment

Section-I

1 Mark Questions

1. Name the following.
   (i) The difference between birth rate and death rate.
   (ii) A movement of population from its area that reduces the number of particular species.
2. Correct and rewrite the following statements by changing the underlined words.
   (i) Infant <u>natality</u> is death of a child less than one year of age.
   (ii) Population increases by <u>arithmetic</u> progression.
3. Fill in the blanks by using suitable words.
   (i) .... is official counting of human population.
   (ii) An expected reason for population explosion is the increased number of individuals in .... age.
   (iii) Government of India legalised MTP in ....
4. Match the following columns.

	Column I		Column II
A.	Mala-D	1.	Chemical method
B.	LNG-20	2.	Oral contraceptive
C.	Spermicide	3.	IUDs
D.	Vasectomy	4.	Surgical method

5. Choose the correct answer from the four options given below.
   (i) Identify the factor directly responsible for rapid rise in the world population during 20th century.
   (a) Increased food production
   (b) Improved transportation
   (c) Education and awareness
   (d) Antibiotics and vaccinations
   (ii) A mother of a 1 year old daughter wanted to space her second child. What could be the method for this?
   (a) An IUDs (b) Tubectomy
   (c) Oral pills like Saheli (d) Both (a) and (c)
6. Expand the following biological abbreviations.
   (i) Cu-T (ii) LNG
7. Choose the odd one out from the following terms given below and name the category to which other three belong.
   Mala-D, Sheli, Mala-N, LNG-20
8. Mention one difference in each of the following pairs on the basis of what is given in the bracket.
   (i) Mala-D and Saheli (composition)
   (ii) Coitus interruptus and Periodic abstinence (method)
9. State the exact location of the following devices are used.
   (i) Femidome
   (ii) Cervical cap
10. Give biological reason for the following.
    Sterilisation techniques are generally fullproof methods of contraception with least side effects. Yet, this is the last option for the couples.
11. Explain the following terms.
    (i) Death rate or mortality
    (ii) Sustainable development
    (iii) Contraceptives
12. Answer the following questions briefly.
    (i) What is population explosion?
    (ii) What are the disadvantages of hormonal contraceptives?

2 Marks Questions

13. Mention two reasons for the high birth rate in India.
14. Explain spermicides. Also mention their use and mode of contraceptive action.

3 Marks Question

15. In what circumstances, MTP is recommended?

Section-II [5 Marks]

Structured Questions

16. Given below are hypothetical figures in regard to population (in crores) of two countries 'A' and 'B' during last four decades.

Countries	1971	1981	1991	2000
A	6.4	9	10.6	11
B	12.4	12.4	12	11.86

(i) Rate of growth of population of which country has increased tremendously?

(ii) In which country, negative population growth rate is observed?

(iii) What can be the reason for tremendous growth?

(iv) Write any two disadvantages of large families?

(v) What is the role of Family Wefare Centre Department?

17. 'Saheli' is an approved marketable contraceptive pill which was developed by CDRI, Lucknow. It is often seen in advertisements as a method of family planning.

(i) What is the principle behind using it as a method to control population growth?

(ii) How will you convince people who say it is religiously wrong to use them to avoid pregnancy?

(iii) Mention the advantages of using pills as contraceptives.

(iv) Give an example of one hormonal and one non-hormonal pill.

For explanations scan the given QR Code

Olympiad Section*

Brain Teasing Questions asked in Previous Olympiads

1 Malaria is a disease caused by *Plasmodium*. The *Plasmodium* spreads from an individual to the others by a mosquito vector. A vector species of *Plasmodium* carrying mosquito lives in a forest together with two different species of monkeys, X and Y. Species X is immune to *Plasmodium*, but species Y is not. That *Plasmodium* carrying mosquito is a food source for a particular bird in the forest. If all the birds were suddenly eliminated by hunters, which of the following statements would be an immediate observable consequence? **[IJSO 2016, Bali-Indonesia]**

(a) Increased mortality (death rate) in species X
(b) Increased mortality in species Y
(c) Increased mortality in the *Plasmodium*-carrying mosquitoes
(d) No increased mortality in both species X and Y

2 The graph comparing the effectiveness of different methods of contraception.

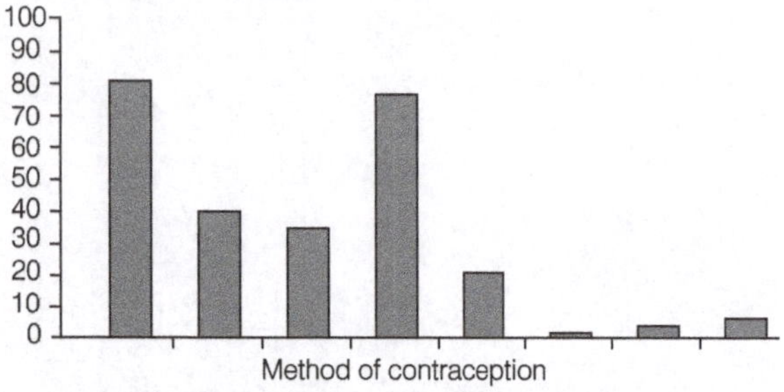

Which of the following statements is correct?

(a) The sterilisation and douche methods can be considered good methods of avoiding pregnancy
(b) The condom is completely effective in preventing pregnancy
(c) Ninety eight per cent of pregnancies can be prevented by using hormone pills
(d) The contraceptive success rate of the rhythm method, where sex is avoided during ovulation is about 35%

3 The given figure represents locations in human female reproductive system that are affected by different birth control measures. Identify them and select the correct option.

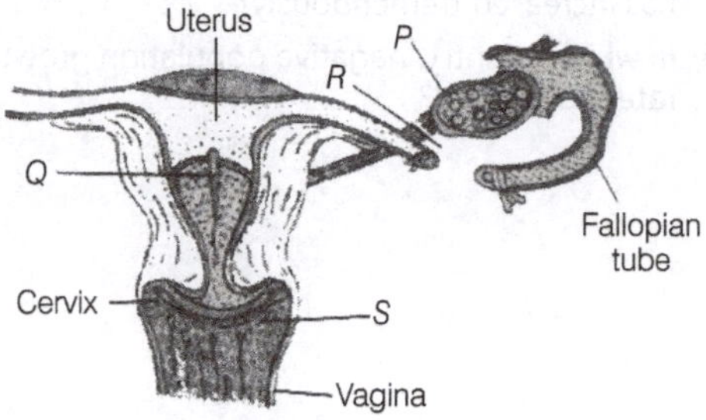

	P	*Q*	*R*	*S*
(a)	Copper-T	Birth control pills	Tubectomy	Condom
(b)	Birth control pills	Copper-T	Tubectomy	Diaphragm
(c)	Birth control pills	Diaphragm	Ovariectomy	Copper-T
(d)	Copper-T	Birth control pills	Ovariectomy	Diaphragm

4 Birth control methods may be hormonal, mechanical or surgical. Choose the correct option that contains example of these birth control methods.

	Hormonal	**Mechanical**	**Surgical**
(a)	Condom	Spermicide	Rhythm
(b)	Intrauterine Device (IUD)	Rhythm	Condom
(c)	Pill	IUD	Vasectomy
(d)	Vasectomy	Pill	Spermicide

Answers

1. (b) **2.** (c) **3.** (b) **4.** (c)

**These questions may or may not be asked in the examination, have been given just for additional practice required for olympiads, scholarship exams etc. For detailed explanations refer Page No. 247.*

CHAPTER

13

Human Evolution

Chapter Inside

Evolution is the sequence of gradual and slow changes from simple life forms to complex life forms, i.e. from primitive organisms that lived over millions of years ago to new organisms that exist today. Human beings are the most recent and highly evolved among these organisms. In this chapter, we will study various theories of evolution and evolution of human.

Theories of Evolution

A number of theories have been put forward to explain the pattern of evolution leading to the formation of new species. The important theories of evolution are described below

Lamarck's Theory of Evolution (Lamarckism)

Jean Baptiste de Lamarck proposed his idea of evolution in 1809 in his book *Philosophie Zoologique*. It is popularly known as **the inheritance of acquired characters.**

He proposed that the changes in structure or function of any organ acquired during the lifetime of an organism in response to changes in surrounding environment are inherited by its offspring. These acquired characters are keep on accumulating over a period of time and lead to the origin of new species.

Postulates of Lamarckism

Lamarckism is based on the following postulates

(i) **Tendency to increase in size** Organisms and their organs have natural tendency to continuously increase in size, generation after generation.

(ii) **Direct effects of the environment** Continuous changes in the environmental conditions directly influence the nature, habits, ways of living of an organism and their structural organisation.

(iii) **Use and disuse of organs** Changes in the environment create new needs in living organisms. To meet these new needs, certain organs are being used greatly and certain organs are lesser used or disused. The continuous use of an organ keeps it functional and makes them stronger and more efficient. Continuous disuse of an organ leads to gradual reduction in its size and finally it disappears.

(iv) **Inheritance of acquired characters** The characters acquired by an organism during its lifetime are inherited by the next generation. In every generation, some new characters are acquired and older characters keep on improving. After several generations, the species get modified into a new one.

Evidences of Lamarckism

There are following evidences of Lamarckism

(i) **Evolution of long neck and forelimbs of giraffe** Lamarck postulated that the ancestors of giraffe had short neck and forelimbs who used to graze on grass. Due to change in environment, these areas became arid. The vegetation was gradually replaced by tall trees. To obtain leaves for food, they had to stretch their neck and forelimbs.

Evolution of long neck in giraffe

Constant stretching led to the elongation of neck and forelimbs in giraffe. This change was transmitted to the next generation. In due course of time, it resulted in present day long neck and long forelimbs of giraffe.

(ii) **Vestigial organs** The organs which are present in reduced form and do not perform any function in the body are called vestigial organs. They correspond to the fully developed functional organs of related animals. They are believed to be the remnants of organs which were complete and functional in their ancestors, e.g. nipples (mammae) in male, splint bones in the hindlimb of horse, etc.

In human beings, there are about 90 vestigial organs. Some of these are as follows

(a) **Wisdom teeth** The third pair of molars are vestigial in humans. They erupt late in life and sometimes they even fail to erupt.

(b) **Vermiform appendix** The human appendix is the remnant structure which is found attached to the caecum. It is large and functional in herbivore animals. In them, it contains bacteria that produce cellulase enzyme for the digestion of cellulose. The presence of non-functional appendix in man indicates that the ancestors of man had a diet rich in cellulose. The changed food habits over time led to the reduction of this organs in present day man.

(c) **Muscles of pinna** External ear of human is called pinna. Many mammals move their pinna for collecting sound waves from the atmosphere. This part is non-functional in humans.

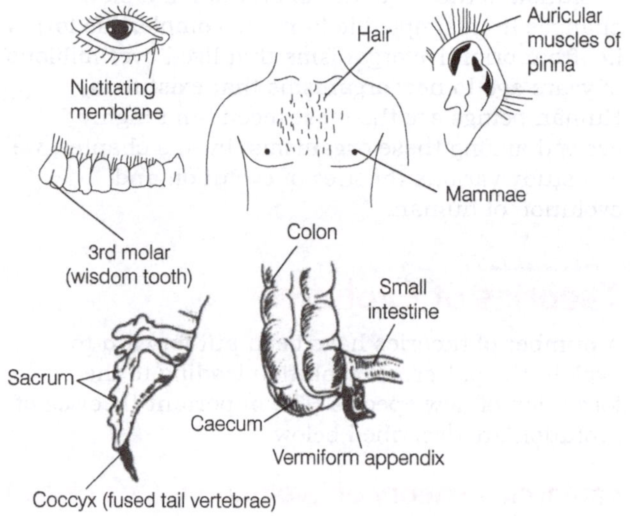

Some vestigial organs in human body

Criticism of Lamarckism

Lamarckism or theory of inheritance of acquired characters was discarded due to the following reasons

(i) Blind, deaf and lame parents do not produce abnormal (blind, deaf or lame) offsprings.

(ii) Wounds scars of parents do not appear in their offsprings.

(iii) Despite the use of iron shoes to keep their feet short by Chinese women, their young ones at birth have normal feet size.

(iv) **Weismann** removed the tail of mice continuously for 22 generations, but a tailless mice was not produced in any generation.

Darwin's Theory of Natural Selection (Darwinism)

Charles R Darwin (1809–1882) was a British naturalist. He postulated the 'theory of origin of species by natural selection' which is based on several facts, observations and deductions. It is popularly known as Darwinism.

Of the various theories, Darwinism is the most widely accepted theory because it provides a convincing explanation. During his voyage to Galapagos Islands by HMS Beagle ship, Darwin observed various types of plants and animals. In 1859, he published his observations and conclusions in a book *'Origin of Species'*. The credit of 'Natural Selection Theory' goes to **Charles Darwin** and **Alfred Russel Wallace.**

Postulates of Darwinism

Darwin's theory of organic evolution by natural selection is based on following principles

(i) **Overproduction** (Rapid multiplication) All organisms possess enormous fertility. They multiply in a geometric proportion with some organisms producing very large number of species. Despite of this high rate of reproduction of a species, its number remains constant under fairly stable environment.

Some Examples of Overproduction of Some Animals

Organisms	Eggs/Young ones (whole number)
Female salmon	2,80,00000 eggs/season
Oyster	60-80 million eggs/yr
Codfish	10 million eggs
Elephant	6 offsprings/entire life
Rabbit	24 offsprings/yr

(ii) **Struggle for existence** The limited resources present in an environment are the main cause of struggle for existence, which may occur at following three levels

(a) **Intraspecific struggle** It is the struggle among the individuals of same species for their common requirements like food, shelter, mate, breeding places, etc. Intraspecific struggle is very severe, e.g. young trees in a forest, cannibalism (eating individual of its own species), human wars, etc.

(b) **Interspecific struggle** It is the struggle between the individuals of different species for their similar requirements like food and space. For example, a frog feeds on insects and is prayed upon by snakes while kite feeds on both frogs as well as snakes.

(c) **Environmental struggle** It is the struggle of living forms against the environmental conditions like extreme heat, cold, drought, earthquakes, storms, disease, volcanic eruption, etc.

(iii) **Appearance of variations** All individuals are dissimilar in some of their characters except the identical twins. This dissimilarity is mainly due to the variations. These are the small or large differences among the individuals. Variations allow some individuals to better adjust with their environment.

(iv) **Natural selection or Survival of the fittest** The organisms which are provided with favourable variations would survive, while the unfit are finished. Originally, it was an idea of **Herbert Spencer** (1820-1903) who used the phrase 'survival of the fittest' first time, while **Darwin** named it natural selection. Survival of the fittest refers to the idea that the natural selection tends to favour those organisms that are most fit to survive in reproductive age, in a particular environment, to produce offsprings.

Note Origin of new species by gradual modification is called speciation.

Evidences Related to Darwinism and Natural Selection

It has the following evidences

(i) Rate of reproduction, limitation of resources, competition and struggle for existence can be seen in nature normally.

(ii) Abundance of variation is evidenced by the absence of two similar individuals except monozygotic twins, which also show some environmental variations.

(iii) Production of new varieties of plants and animals through artificial selection. These show evidences that the nature having vast resources can easily produce new species through the natural selection.

Industrial Melanism

Industrial melanism in peppered moth (*Biston betularia*) is an example of natural selection. In England 1850s before industrialisation, there were more white-winged moths on trees than dark-winged or melanic forms. The light-bodied moths were able to blend with the light coloured bark of trees of lichens and escaped from their enemies. But after industrialisation, i.e. in 1920, dark-winged moths became more than white-winged moths.

This is because during industrialisation, the tree trunks covered by white lichens became dark due to air pollution (dust and soot particles).

Due to this, white-winged moths could be easily seen and eaten by the predators as they failed in camouflaging (hide or disguise the presence of a person, animal or object). This shows that in a mixed population, those that can better adapt, survive and increase in population size.

(a) (b)

(a) Original population; 10% dark-coloured phenotypes
(b) Several generations later; 80% dark-coloured phenotypes

Note Branching of descent means different species descend from common ancestors and get adapted in different habitats, e.g. Darwinian finches.

Criticism of Darwin's Natural Selection Theory

Darwin's theory was widely accepted, but **Sir Richard Owen** and **Adam Sedgewick** criticised it due to following reasons

(i) Darwin emphasised on the **inheritance of small variations**, which are mainly non-heritable and useless for evolution.
(ii) He could not explain the presence of vestigial organs and effect of their use and disuse.
(iii) Darwinism failed to explain the arrival of the fittest.
(iv) Natural selection failed to explain the evolution of terrestrial animals from the aquatic organisms.
(v) Natural selection failed to explain some adaptations such as electric organs in fish, mimicry in Karama butterfly, etc.
(vi) Darwin was unaware about the knowledge of heredity.
(vii) Darwinism does not account for the degeneration of certain animal organs.

Check Your LEARNING...

1 In which book, Lamarck proposed the theory of evolution?
2 What are aquired characters according to Lamarck?
3 Name the vestigial organs present in human.
4 Name the ship by which Darwin travelled?
5 Who proposed the theory of natural selection?
6 Who used the phrase "Survival of fittest" first time?

Human Evolution

Human is the wisest creature on the Earth. Some people consider human beings as a supreme creation. Biologists explain human as just another animal based on its body structure and working. **Carolus Linnaeus** placed man among the monkeys and apes. **Charles Darwin** stated that man was one or more animal species whose origin and evolution could be traced just like that of any other species.

He published his idea about human ancestry in the book *'Descent of Man'* and *'Selection in Relation to Sex'*. He suggested that man, apes and monkeys have a common ancestor.

The unique qualities of human are language, advanced thoughts and culture evolved through the natural selection.

The course of human phylogeny like other mammals can be followed only from the fossil records.

Human beings belong to a single family (Hominidae), a single genus (*Homo*), a single species (*sapiens*) and a single sub-species (*sapiens*). It has four races (Mongoloid, Negroid, Caucasoid and Australoid).

Characteristics of Human

The modern man shows the following characteristic features, which were acquired during the course of evolution

(i) **Large brain and cranial cavity** Man has extra ordinary large brain and high intelligence. The volume of cranial cavity is more (1450 cc) in human than apes and monkeys.
(ii) **Upright posture** Upright posture is due to major changes in musculo-skeletal system. Consequently, legs became longer for balancing the body, abdominal region became short, thorax became broad and flat.

(iii) **Bipedal locomotion** Due to bipedal locomotion, forelimbs or hands got free to do other functions.

(iv) **Forelimbs** The forelimbs evolved into efficient grasping and manipulating devices for carrying things, making tools and hurling weapons.

(v) **Opposable thumb** (Dexterity) During evolutionary change in human, thumb (pollex) has been brought opposite to fingers thus, enabling the hand for better grasping power.

(vi) **Orthognathous face** In *Homo sapiens,* face is orthognathous with protruding canines of the lower jaw, whereas ape's face is prognathous, i.e. protruded out into a short muzzal.

(vii) **Binocular vision** Human beings possess binocular and stereoscopic vision, which enables the depth perception and distance estimation.

(viii) **Loss of body hairs** Body hairs are present in vestigial form.

History of Human Evolution

The study of living and fossil primates shows that the **primates** (including monkey and man) has descended from a common ancestor and separated from the main stock (of a homonisation) during Oligocene period. Fossil records are the best evidence which show intermediate forms between apes and man.

The evolutionary history of man can be divided into following three steps only for the convenience of study.

(i) Prior to ape man.

(ii) Ape man (including prehistoric man).

(iii) True man (including the living modern man).

The fossil records prior to ape man include

- ***Dryopithecus*** Common ancestor of man and apes. Their arms and legs were almost equal in length. They had semi-erect posture, large canines without brow ridges, 4 feet tall with cranial capacity 325-500 cc.
- ***Ramapithecus*** Earliest man-like primate or first hominoid. They walked erect, ate hard nuts and seeds like modern man and had jaws and teeth similar to humans.

The various fossil records of ape man are as follows.

Australopithecus (First Ape Man)

- Its height was 1.5 m and had both human and ape's characters.
- It was fully bipedal hominid, i.e. they walked nearly straight.
- It lived from 4–1.5 million years ago in caves during Pleistocene period.
- It had erect posture and omnivorous diet.
- Its cranial capacity (brain volume or size) was 500 –700 cc, i.e. equivalent to modern gorilla.
- Brow ridges projected over the eyes and lacked chin.
- It had protruding jaws (i.e. prognathous face) and modern man-like teeth.
- Distinct lumbar curve was present in vertebral column.

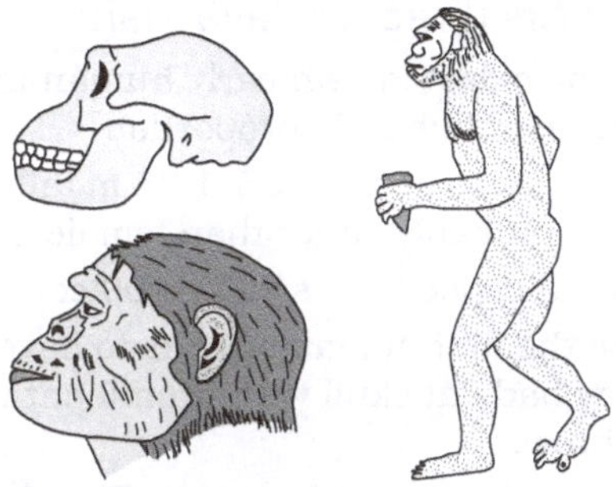

Australopithecus

- Its thighs and hips were adapted for erect standing, walking and running.
- Its arms were somewhat less mobile than ours and pelvis was broad.
- Its ankle bones were intermediate between human and ape.

Their body was covered with hairs

Homo habilis (Skillful man, Handyman or Tool maker)

- *Homo habilis* are called as the **first tool maker** because they had developed the most primitive stone tools.
- *Homo habilis* were about 1.2-1.5 m tall and they lived in Africa about two million years ago.
- Their cranial capacity was 700-800 cc. They have a large head and less protruding face. Their body was covered with hair. The chin was absent.
- *Homo habilis* were carnivorous and possessed small canines.
- They were lived in small community or groups in caves. They greatly cared for the young one.
- Perhaps they showed sexual division of labour and communicated with visual signals and simple audible sounds.

- They were more erect than *Australopithecus* and showed bipedal locomotion.

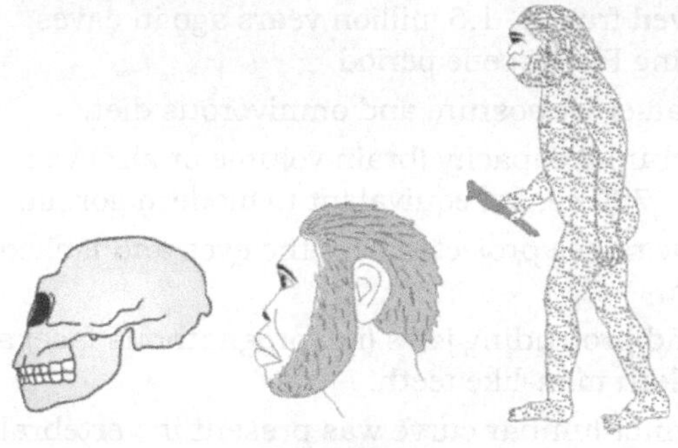

Homo habilis

Homo erectus (Erect or Java Man)

- They are the oldest known early human to have modern human like body proportion.
- *Homo erectus* was about 1.55–1.75 m tall, with males were probably larger than females.
- Their cranial capacity was 800-1100 cc.
- They were the first human species to have fleshy nose. They had flat skull with prominent ridges over the brow.
- They had short arm and long legs. The short arms depict that the tree climbing ability was lost completely in them. The long legs depict that they were better suited for long distance migrations.
- They were the first one to walk upright and stood erect thus, named so. These are also known as *Homo ergaster*.
- Their forehead was receding, jaws were still projecting and chin was absent. They had small canines and large molar teeth.
- They were the first hominid to live in hunter-gatherer society.
- Hair on the body were further reduced.

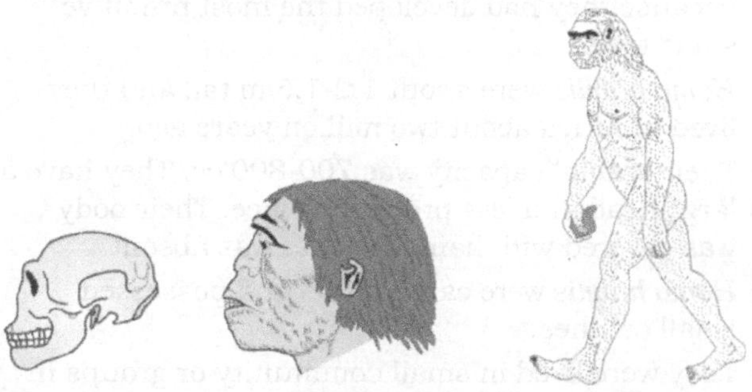

Homo erectus

Homo sapiens neanderthalensis (Neanderthal Man)

- Neanderthal man existed in the late Pleistocene period.
- They walked upright with bipedal movement.
- They had a height of about 160cm (5.5 feet).
- The face was slightly prognathous and had low brows, receding jaws, high domed heads presence of wisdom teeth and less hair on the body.
- The cranial capacity of neanderthal man was 1300-1600 cc, average 1450 cc.
- The jaw was deep with no chin and skull bones were thick.
- Culturally, these were more advanced than Java and Peking man.
- They used to kill the large animals by group attack and had knives to butcher them.
- Neanderthal man was omnivorous and cannibal, who used fire for cooking and warmth. They used animal skin as clothing to protect themselves and to adapt in cold environment.
- It is believed that Neanderthal man had the concept of life and death and followed rituals. It is also believed that they buried dead bodies.

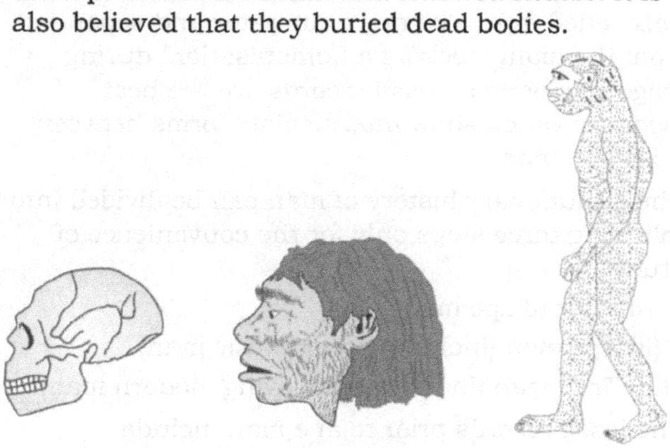

Neanderthal man

Homo sapiens fossilis (Cro-Magnon Man)

- Cro-Magnon lived during old stone age which is also known as **Palaeolithic age** (began more than 2 million years ago).
- Cro-Magnon man was almost similar to modern man with about 1.8 m height, orthognathous face, broad and arched forehead, strong jaws, elevated nose and well-developed chin as well as dentition.

- They lacked eyebrow ridges and their body was less hairy.
- Cranial capacity was about 1650 cc, i.e. much more than modern man (1450 cc).
- They were intelligent, hard worker, swift footed and cave dweller hunters.
- They could run fast with bipedal movement and lived in families.
- They used spears, bows and arrows as tools, which were made up of stones, bones or elephant tusks.
- They were omnivorous and wore skin clothes.
- Probably they succeeded from neanderthal man and distributed in Africa, Europe and Middle East.
- They made extraordinary paintings on the cave walls, which represent a reindeer, bison and wild bear.

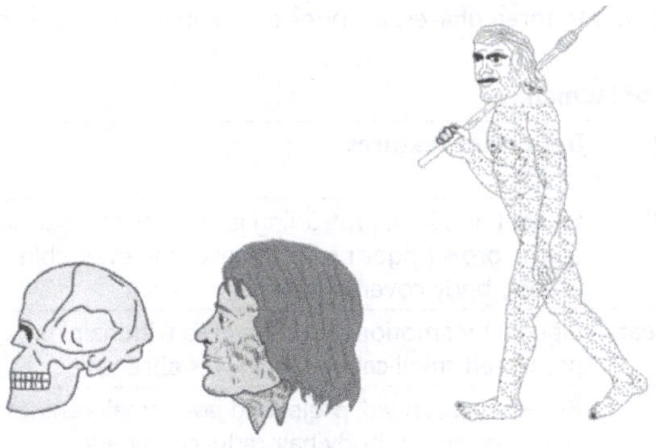
Cro-Magnon man

Homo sapiens sapiens (Living Modern Man)

- Its average cranial capacity is 1450 cc, which is lesser than Cro-Magnon.
- Its limbs are straight and arms are shorter than legs.
- It shows erect posture with upright head, complex cerebral hemispheres and cerebellum.
- It is distinguished from Cro-Magnon merely by slight raising of skull cap, reduction in volume of cranial cavity (1300-1600 cc), thinning of skull bones and formation of four curves in the vertebral column.
- Forehead is steep with reduced brow ridges and well-developed chin.
- Hair on limbs and body highly reduced.

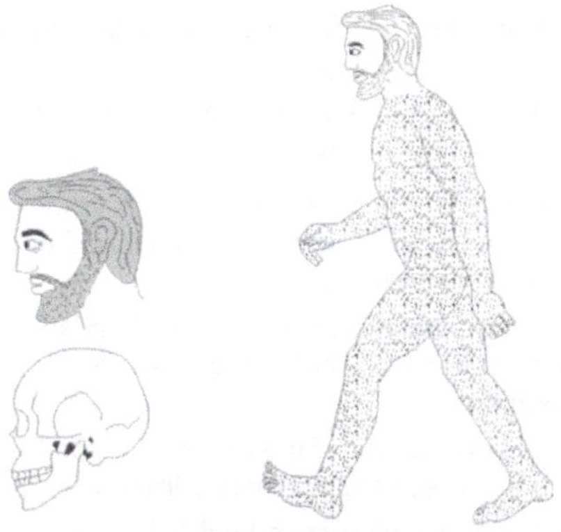
Modern man

Future Man (*Homo futuris*)

The organic evolution is a continuous process of nature, which is still continued at present and probably will remain in future too. It is believed that in future, human could be changed as a result of the factors like **gene mutation, gene recombination** and **natural selection.**

According to the forecasting of **HL Shapiro**, an American anthropologist, the future man (named *Homo futuris*) will possess following characteristics

(i) Height will be increased.

(ii) Body hair will reduce and skull may become dome-shaped.

(iii) Body and cranium will be more developed.

(iv) The fifth finger probably may reduce.

(v) The age or lifespan will increase.

Check Your LEARNING...

1. Which man is known as the tool maker?
2. Which hominid is also known as ***Homo ergaster***?
3. Write the two characteristics of erect man.
4. Among the human ancestors, who had the brain size of more than 1000 cc?
5. Cro-Magnon man was present in which age?
6. Mention the scientific name of modern man.

QUiCK Revision

- The term **'Evolution'** was first used by **Herbert Spencer** in 1852.
- **Lamarck** (1809) proposed a theory (Lamarckism) that states living things change by inheriting acquired characteristics, e.g. giraffes stretched their necks to reach food and their offspring inherited stretched necks.
- Lamarck's theory was the first to admit that species changed due to use and disuse of organs.
- **Charles Darwin** (1859) published the book *Origin of Species by Means of Natural Selection* or the preservation of favoured races in the struggle for life, which has been recognised as one of the most important books ever written. A very similar theory was also proposed by **Alfred Wallace**.
- Essentially, Darwin suggested that random variations take place in living things and that some external agent in the environment selects those individuals which are better able to survive (survival of the fittest). The method of selecting individuals is known as **natural selection**.
- Some evidences in favour of the theory of natural selection came from modifications seen in the beaks of finches on Galapagos Island. Also pedigree of some animals like horse, camel, etc., supports the theory of natural selection.
- Darwin was criticised by some scientists because his theory fails to explain arrival of the fittest over specialisation of organs, vestigial organs, somatic and germinal variations, etc.
- **Human** is the wisest creature on the Earth whose origin and evolution can be traced just like that of any other species. Few books written on evolution and theories of evolution are *Decent of Man* by **Charles Darwin**, *Mans Place in Nature* by **TH Huxley**.
- **History of human evolution** The evolutionary history of man can be divided into three phases, i.e. prior to ape man, ape man and true man.

Various Stages of Evolution of Human

Names	**Cranial Capacity** (cm^3)	**Food/Posture** (Height)	**Important features**
Australopithecus africans (first ape man)	500-700	Essentially ate fruits, fully erect, 1.5 m	Bipedal hominid, protruding jaws (modern man-like teeth), brow ridges projected over the eyes, chin absent, body covered with hair
Homo habilis (the first hominid tool maker)	700–800	Probably did not eat meat, fully erect (1.2-1.5 m)	Bipedal locomotion, body covered with hair possessed small canines, chin was absent.
Homo erectus (the erect man and Java man)	800–1100	Probably ate meat 150-180 cm tall	Receding forehead, projecting jaws, small canines, chin was absent, body hair reduced, bipedal locomotion, thick brow ridges.
Homo neanderthalensis (the neanderthal man, first civilised man)	1450	Omnivorous, 1.5-1.66 m tall	Bipedal movement, low brows, receding jaws, reduced body hair, chin absent.
Homo sapiens fossilis (the fossil modern man or Cro-Magnon man)	1650	Omnivorous, 1.8 m	Broact and arched forehead, strong jaws, well developed chin, body less hairy, eye brow ridges absent.
Homo sapiens sapiens (the living modern man)	1300–1600	Omnivorous, 1.5-1.8 m	Steep forehead with reduced braw ridges, well developed chin, reduced body hair.

Chapter Practice

Section-I

1 Mark Questions

1. Name the following.
   (i) The writer of the book *'Philosophie Zoologique'*.
   (ii) The part of digestive system, which is vestigial in humans.
   (iii) Name of the struggle among individuals of same species for common resources.
   (iv) The first ape man.

Ans. (i) Jean Baptiste de Lamarck
(ii) Vermiform appendix
(iii) Intraspecific struggle
(iv) *Australopithecus*

2. Correct and rewrite the following statements by changing the underlined words.
   (i) The theory of inheritance of acquired characters was proposed by Watson and Crick. [2019]
   (ii) The first molars are vestigial in humans.
   (iii) Industrial melanism is an example of interspecific struggle.
   (iv) *Australopithecus* is a common ancestor of man and apes.

Ans. (i) The theory of inheritance of acquired characters was proposed by Lamarck.
(ii) The third molars are vestigial in humans.
(iii) Industrial melanism is an example of natural selection.
(iv) *Dryopithecus* is a common ancestor of man and apes.

3. Give biological reasons for the following.
   (i) Vestigial organs give an idea about evolution.
   (ii) Natural selection operates when nature selects for fitness.
   (iii) The increased population of dark coloured moths coincided with the loss of lichens (on tree barks) during industrialisation period in England.

Ans. (i) Those organs, which no longer have a function in our body are known as vestigial organs. These organs have reduced structurally as well as functionally. It appears that these organs were once well-developed and functional in ancestors and later, due to their less use they become reduced. For examples, vermiform appendix in man is reduced and functionless while in herbivores, vermiform appendix along with caecum is used for digestion of cellulose. It gives an idea that human had herbivorous food habit and cellulose containing food items were major part of their diet.
(ii) Nature selects for fitness based on the characteristics which are inherited. So, there must be a genetic basis for getting selected and to evolve. In other words, there are some organisms which are better adapted to survive in an otherwise hostile environment. Adaptive ability is inherited and it has a genetic basis; hence, fitness is the end result of the ability to adapt and get selected by nature.
(iii) During post-industrialisation period, the tree trunks got dark because of industrial smoke and soot, so the dark coloured moths were able to hide without any risk of predation, survived and increased in population. White-winged moths did not survive due to increased predation.

4. (i) Match the following columns.

	Column I		Column II
A.	Inheritance of acquired character	1.	Darwin
B.	Origin of species	2.	HL Shapiro
C.	*Homo futuris*	3.	Lamarck

(ii) Match the following columns.

	Column I		Column II
A.	First ape man	1.	*Homo erectus*
B.	Java man	2.	*Homo sapiens fossilis*
C.	Cro-Magnon man	3.	*Homo futuris*
D.	Future man	4.	*Australopithecus*

Ans. (i) A–3, B–1, C–2 (ii) A–4, B–1, C–2, D–3

5. Choose the correct answer from the four options given below.
   (i) Lamarck's theory of evolution is also called as
   (a) theory of natural selection
   (b) inheritance of acquired characters
   (c) survival of the fittest
   (d) theory of special creation

Ans. (b)

   (ii) Lamarckism fails to explain which of the following phenomenon?
   (a) Absence of all the forelimbs amongst amphibians
   (b) Exceptionally long neck of giraffe
   (c) An intellectual person having a dull son
   (d) Loss of vision in cave dwelling mammals

Ans. (c)

(iii) Concept of inheritance of acquired characters was disapproved by the experiments of
(a) Oparin (b) Weismann
(c) Fox (d) Darwin

Ans. (b)

(iv) Darwin's theory of evolution fails to explain the
(a) role of environment
(b) origin and transmission of variations
(c) overproduction
(d) survival of the fittest

Ans. (b)

(v) Darwin proposed the theory of origin of species by
(a) hybridisation
(b) natural selection
(c) mutation
(d) acquired characters

Ans. (b)

(vi) The common ancestor to both man and ape is
(a) *Australopithecus* (b) *Dryopithecus*
(c) *Sinanthropus* (d) *Homo erectus*

Ans. (b)

(vii) In the evolution of man, *Homo erectus* is considered to be evolved from
(a) *Dryopithecus* (b) *Ramapithecus*
(c) *Homo habilis* (d) Cro-Magnon

Ans. (c)

(viii) The false statement about cro-Magnon man is
(a) his cranial cavity was less than *Homo sapiens*
(b) he walked erect and was swift
(c) he was intelligent and cultured
(d) he started metal work, painting and farming

Ans. (a)

(ix) Most of the cave paintings discovered are associated with
(a) Cro-Magnon man (b) *Homo erectus*
(c) Neanderthal man (d) *Dryopithecus*

Ans. (a)

(x) The major advantage of bipedal locomotion is that it
(a) increases speed
(b) reduces body weight
(c) releases the forelimbs for other better functions
(d) provides better body support

Ans. (c)

6. Fill in the blanks by using suitbale words.
(i) Weismann discarded the theory proposed by ....
(ii) Continuity of existence of the fittest was called .... by Darwin.
(iii) Traits selected for evolution by natural selection are beneficial to ....
(iv) The scientific name of Java man is ....
(v) *Homo sapiens* arose in ....

Ans. (i) Lamarck (ii) natural selection
(iii) species (iv) *Homo erectus*
(v) Africa

7. Choose the odd one out from the following terms given below and name the category to which other three belong.
(i) Wisdom tooth, Nictitating membrane, Vermiform appendix, Vertebral column
(ii) Overproduction, Natural selection, Struggle for existence, Vestigial organs

Ans. (i) **Odd term** is vertebral column.
Rest three represent vestigial organs that are non-functional in humans.
(ii) **Odd term** is vestigial organs.
Rest three are the postulates of Darwinism.

8. Given below are the sets of five terms. Rewrite the terms in correct order of a logical sequence.
(i) More white moths, Industrialisation, More black moths, Lichens on trees, Lichens disappear
(ii) Skillful man, Cro-Magnon man, Erect man, Neanderthal man, *Homo sapiens* (who first evolved in the course of evolution)

Ans. (i) Lichens on trees, More white moths, Industrialisation, Lichens disappear, More black moths
(ii) Skillful man, Erect man, Neanderthal man, Cro-Magnon man, *Homo sapiens*

9. State the main function of the following.
(i) Opposable thumb
(ii) Binocular vision

Ans. (i) The opposable thumb enables the hand for better grasping power.
(ii) Binocular vision helps in depth perception and distance estimation.

10. Mention one difference between each of the following pairs on the basis of what is given in the bracket.
(i) Lamarckism and Darwinism (definition).
(ii) Inherited traits and Acquired traits (general features)

Ans. (i) Difference between Lamarckism and Darwinism is as follows

Lamarckism	Darwinism
New individuals are formed due to the inheritance of acquired characters.	New individuals are formed by the accumulation of variations.

(ii) Difference between inherited traits and acquired traits is as follows

Inherited traits	Acquired traits
These are obtained from the parents.	These are developed during the life of an individual.

11. Give biological/technical terms for the following.
   (i) Organs present in reduced form and do not perform any function.
   (ii) Struggle of living forms against the environmental conditions.
   (iii) The term proposed for future man.

Ans. (i) Vestigial organs
   (ii) Environmental struggle
   (iii) *Homo futuris*

12. Briefly explain the following terms.
   (i) Evolutionary biology
   (ii) Survival of the fittest
   (iii) Fossil

Ans. (i) Evolutionary biology is the study of history of lifeforms on Earth.
   (ii) The ability to survive and to reproduce in their respective environment is termed as survival of the fittest.
   (iii) Fossils are the remnants and impressions of the lifeforms that lived in the remote past.

13. Answer the following questions briefly.
   (i) Mention the name of postulates stated by Lamarck through which an organism acquires new characters.
   (ii) What was Lamarck's explanation for long neck of giraffe?
   (iii) Name a vestigial organ found in horse.
   (iv) What is fitness according to Darwin?
   (v) Name the scientist who also came to similar conclusion as Darwin. Where did he work?
   (vi) Mention the two key concepts of Darwinism.

Ans. (i) The name of postulates stated by Lamarck through which an organism acquires new characters are
   (a) Use and disuse of organs.
   (b) Inheritance of acquired characters.
   (ii) According to Lamarckism, long neck and high forelimbs of giraffe were well-developed due to their stretching for obtaining foliage (leaves, etc.) from the trees when ground vegetation became sparse.
   (iii) Splint bones in the hindlimbs are vestigial in horse.
   (iv) The fitness according to Darwin refers ultimately to reproductive fitness.
   (v) Alfred Wallace. He worked in Malay Archepelago.
   (vi) The two key concepts of Darwinism are
   (a) Branching descent
   (b) Natural selection

2 Marks Questions

14. What does the inheritance of acquired characters mean? Who gave this idea?

Ans. Inheritance of acquired characters means organs used more extensively would enlarge and become more efficient and such changed characteristics (acquired traits) would be transmitted to the offsprings. This idea was the central theme of Lamarckism and was given by Lamarck.

15. Which traits are important for evolution?

Ans. Inherited traits are important for evolution because these traits are transferred from generation to generation. Accumulation of inherited traits of variations for several generations can give rise to new species. While retention of inherited traits of similarities for generations maintain integrity of existing species.

16. Explain Darwin's concept of natural selection.

Ans. According to Darwin's concept of natural selection, the organisms, which are provided with favourable variations would survive because they are fittest to face their surrounding, while the organisms, which are unfit for surrounding variations are destroyed.

17. Which theory of evolution can best explain the process of organic evolution?

Ans. The theory of natural selection or Darwinism is an important theory for explaining the process of organic evolution.
Natural selection provides better adaptability to the organisms as it wipes out unfit or less adaptive organisms and thus, helpful for better survival.

18. Who among the *Dryopithecus* and *Ramapithecus* was more man like ?

Ans. *Ramapithecus* was more man like. They walked erect on their hindlegs, ate hard nuts and seeds like modern man and had jaws and teeth similar to humans. They arose from *Dryopithecus*, which was considered to be a common ancestor of man and apes.

Dryopithecus was more ape like and had same length of arms and legs.

19. Try to trace the various components of human evolution (hint : brain size and function, skeletal structure, dietary preference, etc).

Ans. With time, the brain size increased quite significantly. Skeletal structures has changed from ape like, i.e. from a projecting jaw to broad forehead, a well-developed chin, developed and the semi-erect posture provided the ability to walk on their two hindlimbs.

3 Marks Questions

20. Describe Lamarck's theory of evolution.

Ans. Lamarck's theory It is known as theory of inheritance of acquired characters.

According to this theory, organisms undergo certain changes to adapt themselves to the environment. These characters acquired by an organism during its lifetime, are passed on to the progeny, e.g. the long neck of giraffe was explained by Lamarck, the ancestors of giraffe had short neck who used to graze on grass. Due to change in environment, these areas became arid and the vegetation was gradually replaced by tall trees outcome of these animals they had to stretch their necks constantly to eat the leaves on the upper branches of the trees.

21. Name the ancestors of man based on the features given below

(i) Human like meat eater with 800-1100cc brain, lived in Java.

(ii) More human with brain size 1450 cc, lived in Central Asia, used hides and buried their dead.

(iii) Human like, vegetarian, with brain capacity between 700 cc and 800 cc.

Ans. (i) *Homo erectus* (ii) Neanderthal man

(iii) *Homo habilis*

22. (i) When and where did neanderthal man live?

(ii) What was his brain capacity?

(iii) Mention the advancements he showed over *Homo erectus*.

Ans. (i) Neanderthal man lived in near East and Central Asia, between 1,00,000- 40,000 years before.

(ii) His brain capacity was 1450 cc.

(iii) He used hides to protect the body. He buried the dead. His brain size was more (1450 cc) than that of *Homo erectus* which was 800-1100cc.

Section-II [5 Marks]

Structured Questions

1. Lamarckism is the first theory of evolution. It is also known as theory of inheritance of acquired characters. This theory was criticised by many evolutionary biologists.

(i) Who gave the theory of inheritance of acquired characters?

(ii) In which book, this theory was given?

(iii) Write the main essence of his theory.

(iv) What are the three postulates of this theory?

(v) Why his theory was criticised?

Ans. (i) Jean Baptiste de Lamarck gave the theory of inheritance of acquired character.

(ii) *Philosophie Zoologique'*

(iii) The main essence of this theory is that the environment keeps changing and creates new needs. Organisms acquire new habits (involving use and disuse of certain body structures) to meet these new needs. Useful organs modify and enlarge and disused organs get reduced and gradually disappear. These acquired changes are inherited and give rise to new species.

(iv) The three postulates of Lamarckism are

(a) Use and disuse of organs.

(b) Effect of environment and new needs.

(c) Inheritance of acquired characters.

(v) Lamarck's theory was criticised because acquired characters are not inherited. Weismann showed that even after cutting the tails of white mice continuously for 22 generations, a tail-less mouse was never born. Thus, the idea of inheritance of acquired characters was not found to be true.

2. Refer to the given diagram and answer the questions that follows.

(a) (b)

(i) Which evolutionary phenomenon is shown in figure?

(ii) Which type of moths were abundant before industrial revolution?

(iii) How tree trunks used to appear before industrialisation and what was its significance?

(iv) Why dark-coloured moths survived in post-industrialisation period?

(v) Mention the scientific name of given organism.

Ans. (i) Industrial melanism is shown in figure.

(ii) In England, before industrial revolution, there were more white-winged or dull-grey moths on the tree trunks than the dark-winged or melanic moths.

(iii) Before industrialisation, there used to be a thick growth of the white-coloured lichens on the tree trunks. Thus, tree trunks used to appear white in colour. Due to this, the white-winged moths survived better whereas the dark-coloured moths were easily spotted and picked up by their predators.

(iv) During post-industrialisation period, the trunks became dark with the industrial smoke and soot. Under this condition, white-winged moths did not survive as predators could easily spot them, while dark-winged or melanic moths survived better.

(v) *Biston betularia*

3. Given below are two stages in the evolution of man. Study them and answer the questions that follows. (2019)

A B

(i) Identify *Australopithecus* and neanderthal man from the above pictures.
(ii) Mention two characteristic features each for the two stages.
(iii) Who proposed the theory of 'natural selection'?
(iv) Name the organism used as an example to explain 'industrial melanism.'
(v) Give two examples of vestigial organs in humans.

Ans. (i) *A*- Neanderthal man
B- *Australopithecus*

(ii) Characteristic features of *Australopithecus* are
- Erect posture and omnivorous diet
- Cranial capacity volume (brain size) was 500-700 cc.

Characteristic features of neanderthal man are
- Cranial capacity of neanderthal man was 1300-1600cc, average 1450cc.
- They used to kill the large animals by group attack and used knives to butcher.

(iii) Charles R Darwin postulated the theory of natural selection. He postulated the 'theory of origin of species' by natural selection.
(iv) *Biston betularia* (peppered moth) is used as an example to explain 'industrial melanism'.
(v) Two examples of vestigial organs in human are
- **Wisdom teeth** The third pair of molars are vestigial in humans
- **Vermiform appendix** The presence of non-functional appendix in man indicates that the ancestors of man had a diet rich in cellulose.

4. *Homo sapiens* belongs to the order-Primata of class–Mammalia. They originated from ape like ancestors after undergoing several changes.
(i) Name the primates that lived about 15 million years ago.
(ii) List their characteristic features of primates asked in (i).
(iii) Where was the first man like animal found?
(iv) Write the order in which neanderthals, *Homo habilis* and *Homo erectus* appeared on the Earth. State the brain capacity of each one of them.
(v) When did modern *Homo sapiens* appear on this planet?

Ans. (i) *Dryopithecus* and *Ramapithecus* are the primates that lived about 15 million years ago.
(ii) Their characteristic features are
(a) They were hairy.
(b) They walked like gorillas and chimpanzees.
(c) *Ramapithecus* was more man like while *Dryopithecus* was more ape like.
(iii) The first man like animal was found in East African grasslands.
(iv) *Homo habilis*, *Homo erectus* and neanderthals had brain capacities of 700-800 cc, 800-1100 cc and 1450 cc, respectively.
(v) The modern *Homo sapiens* first appeared about 11000 years ago in the region around the Caspian and Mediterranean sea.

Chapter Assessment

Section-I

1 Mark Questions

1. Name the following.
   (i) Origin of species by gradual modification.
   (ii) The organs that have ceased to be of any use to the possessor but still persists generation after generation in a reduced form.
   (iii) The slow and continuous process whereby complex forms of life have emerged from simpler forms.

2. Correct and rewrite the following statements by changing the underlined words.
   (i) <u>*Homo erectus*</u> lived during old stone age which is also called Palaeolithic age.
   (ii) <u>*Homo sapiens*</u> was the earliest man like primate.

3. Match the following columns.

	Column I		Column II
A.	Lamarckism	1.	Industrial melanism
B.	Darwinism	2.	Opposable thumb
C.	Dexterity	3.	Long neck in giraffe

4. Choose the correct answer from the four options given below.

(i) Darwin in his 'natural selection theory' did not believe in any role of which one of the following in organic evolution?
(a) Parasites and predators as natural enemies
(b) Survival of the fittest
(c) Struggle for existence
(d) Discontinuous variations

(ii) The name *Homo sapiens* can be assigned to
(a) Java man
(b) Peking man
(c) Shivalik man
(d) Cro-Magnon man

(iii) *Australopithecus* is also known as Southern ape, because it had
(a) man like characters
(b) ape like characters
(c) Both (a) and (b)
(d) monkey like characters

5. Fill in the blanks by using suitable words.
   (i) According to Darwin, organic evolution is due to .... and .... competitions.
   (ii) Natural selection operates when nature selects for ....
   (iii) Cro-Magnon lived during .... age.

6. Choose the odd one out from the following terms given below and name the catcegory to which other three belong.

   Direct effect of environment, Overproduction, Use and disuse of organs, Inheritance of acquired character

7. Mention one difference between each of the following pairs on the basis of what is given in the bracket
   (i) *Australopithecus* and Cro-Magnon (chin)
   (ii) *Homo* erectus and *Homo sapiens sapiens* (cranial capacity)

8. Briefly explain the following terms.
   (i) Interspecific struggle
   (ii) Evolution

9. Answer the following questions briefly.
   (i) What was the Lamarck's idea of acquisition of new characters?
   (ii) Name any two vestigial organs in humans.
   (iii) Give an example of branching descent.

2 Marks Questions

10. Explain survival of the fittest proposed by Darwin.
11. Differentiate the terms 'orthognathous and prognathous' face.
12. Give any two characteristics of *Homo habilis*.

3 Marks Questions

13. Natural selection is directional and variations are directionless. Comment.
14. Compare Lamarck and Darwin's theory.
15. Write the cranial cavity volume of different hominoids mentioned below.
    (i) Java man
    (ii) The first ape man
    (iii) *Homo habilis*

16. Mention any three characteristics of Neanderthal man that lived in near East and Central Asia.
17. Name the first human like hominid. Mention his food habit and brain capacity.

Section-II

[5 Marks]

Structured Question

18. Given below are the few structures of human body. Observe them carefully and answer the questions that follows.

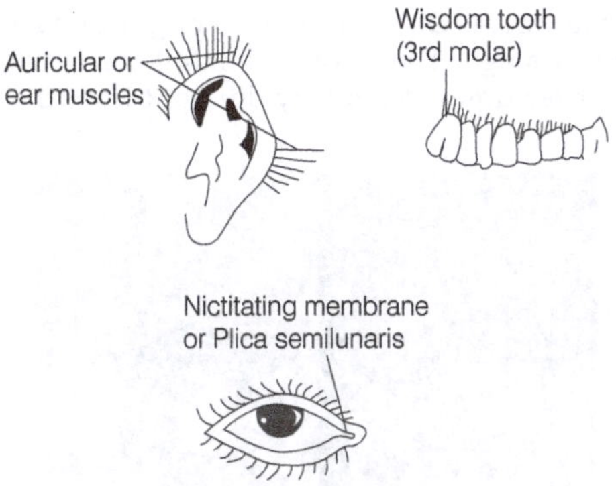

(i) What do these structures called?
(ii) Give any two characteristics of these structures.
(iii) How many of such organs are found in human body?
(iv) What is the function of wisdom tooth?
(v) What explanation of these structures was given by Lamarck?

For explanations scan the given QR Code

Olympiad Section

Brain Teasing Questions asked in Previous Olympiads

1 A small population of monkeys from Africa (Old world) are thought to have drifted to South America (new world) on natural rafts about 40 million years ago. There were no monkeys in the new world. On reaching South America, these monkeys bred and over time looked very different from the monkeys in Africa. They formed new species. **[IJSO Dubai, 2021]**

1. Old world monkeys 2. New world monkeys

Arrange the evolutionary processes that would lead to the formation of the new species.

(a) Migration → Adaptation → Natural selection
(b) Genetic drift → Natural Selection → Adaptation
(c) Natural selection → Adaptation → Genetic drift
(d) Adaptation → Genetic drift → Natural selection

2 A phylogenetic tree is a diagram that depicts the lines of evolutionary descent of different species from a common ancestor. In the phylogenetic trees shown below, the evolutionary descent of three organisms, humans (1), whale (2) and sharks (3) is depicted.

Which of the following phylogenetic trees correctly represents the relationship between these three organisms? **[IJSO Dubai, 2021]**

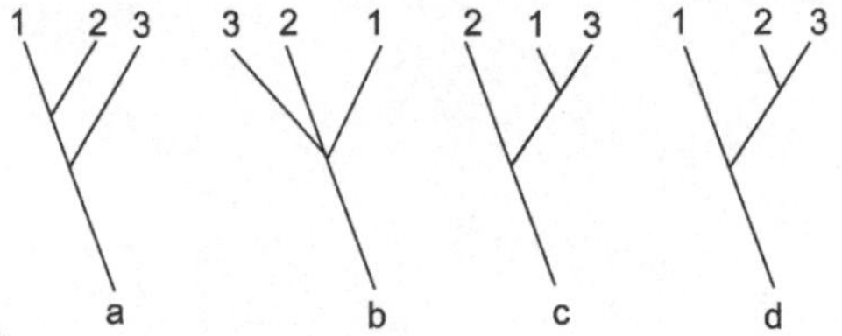

3 According to Darwin's theory, the more closely related two different organisms are **[IJSO Durban, South Africa 2011]**

(a) the more similar their habitats
(b) the less similar their DNA sequence
(c) the more recently they shared a common ancestor
(d) the more similar they are in size

Answers

1. (b) **2.** (a) **3.** (c)

**These questions may or may not be asked in the examination, have been given just for additional practice required for olympiads, scholarship exams etc. For detailed explanations refer Page No. 247.*

CHAPTER

14

Pollution

Chapter Inside

• Pollution • Types of Pollution • Greenhouse Effect • Global Warming • Ozone Layer Depletion

Pollution

The undesirable change in physical, chemical or biological characteristics of environment which directly or indirectly affect human beings is called pollution. It is due to addition of any unwanted substance to the environment that may adversely affect or deteriorates the different forms of life on Earth. Any substance, whether chemical or physical that causes pollution is called **pollutant**.

Classification of pollutants on the basis of their existence can be done as follows

(i) **Quantitative pollutants** These are the components which become pollutants when their concentration reaches beyond a threshold value, e.g. CO, CO_2, NO_2, etc.

Non-quantitative pollutants These substances do not occur in nature, but are produced through human activities, e.g. DDT and other pesticides.

(ii) **Primary pollutants** are those emitted from natural or anthropogenic sources directly into the atmosphere.

Secondary pollutants are formed by the physical or chemical interaction between the primary pollutants.

(iii) Pollutants can also be categorised as **biodegradable** or **non-biodegradable** (discussed later on).

Types of Pollution

Pollution is of following five types

1. Air pollution
2. Water pollution
3. Soil pollution
4. Noise pollution
5. Radioactive pollution

1. Air Pollution

The presence of any material or gas in the air in such a concentration that degrades the quality of air and could be harmful for living as well as non-living beings is called air pollution. It occurs due to undesirable changes in the physical, chemical or biological characteristics of air.

Air pollutants are of following two main types

(i) **Particulate pollutants** These are harmful particles such as dust particles, metallic particles, smoke, particles from mining, stone drilling, wearing of rubber tyres, etc., which remain suspended in the air.

(ii) **Gaseous pollutants** These are harmful gases such as CO_2, H_2S, CO, SO_2, NO_2, etc., that are given out from the emission of different sources.

Sources of Air Pollution

Air pollution can be caused by **natural sources** like ash from volcanic eruptions, fumes from forest fires, dust from storms, pollens, and **man-made sources** like excessive use of automobiles, garbage, industries, brick kilns, use of leaded petrol, thermal plants, etc.

Some of the man-made sources of air pollution are described below

(i) **Vehicular air pollution** All the vehicles which run on petrol and diesel, liberate harmful **gaseous pollutants** mainly CO_2, NO_2, SO_2 and CO. Besides this, dust and rubber particles released from the wearing of rubber tyres of automobiles also cause vehicular pollution.

(ii) **Industrial air pollution** Various small scale industries (like pottery, carpet weaving units, etc.) to large scale industries (such as textiles, automobiles manufacturing units, sugar and food industries, oil refineries, stone drilling coal and metal mines, etc.) expel out gaseous and **particulate pollutants** that are responsible for air pollution. The chief industrial gaseous pollutants are CO_2, SO_2, CO and oxides of nitrogen.

(iii) **Burning garbage** It is the garbage from homes and kitchen wastes which includes items such as vegetable and fruit peels, polythene bags, etc. These wastes are either used in making manures for agricultural purposes or burnt in enclosures. On burning garbage, harmful gases such as CO and CO_2, etc., are released which causes particulate air pollution. Dioxin is a harmful pollutant and a carcinogen released by garbage burning.

(iv) **Brick kilns** These are fire-heated enclosures used for making bricks that are further used in construction purposes. The wastes and smoke produced by these enclosures include large quantity of ash and broken pieces of bricks, which cause air pollution.

Smog

The smoke from vehicles, industries, fire, etc., contains oxides of nitrogen that combine with other air pollutants and the drops of fog. This leads to the formation of smog. It results in visibility problems and if inhaled, it causes respiratory problems like coughing and asthma.

Photochemical smog was first reported in Los Angeles in 1946. It contains secondary pollutants, e.g. O_3, PAN, etc.

Effects of Air Pollution

Harmful effects of air pollution depend on concentration of pollutants, duration of exposure to the pollutants and the types of pollutants

(i) In plants, it causes fruit damage, leaf damage, chlorosis, necrosis, mottled spots on leaves, less yield of crops and premature death of plants, etc.

(ii) In humans, it causes respiratory ailments like asthma, hay fever, allergic diseases, cancer and genetic mutations.

(iii) Carbon monoxide (CO) released as pollutant can combine with haemoglobin thus, preventing the supply of O_2 to the cells and cause death due to asphyxiation because it leads to damage of the brain.

(iv) Burning of fossil fuels, exhausts from the automobiles, etc., release SO_2 and NO_2 in the atmosphere. These gases are oxidised to form sulphuric acid and nitric acid in the air. They get dissolved with the rainwater (pH = 6) falling on the Earth and forms the **acid rain** (pH = 3-4).

Control Measures of Air Pollution

The government of India passed the Air Prevention and Control of Pollution Act in the year 1981. It was meant for the preservation of good air quality.
To control air pollution, several ways have been devised. Some of these are as follows

(i) Compulsory use of electrostatic precipitators, scrubbers, catalytic converters and filters in automobiles and industries.

(ii) Establishing the industrial areas away from residential occupancy.

(iii) Use of various unconventional sources of energy like CNG, hydropower, wind, Sun, etc.

(iv) Ban on crackers during festivals, functions, etc.

(v) Maximum use of public transport, start initrating car-pooling, prefering walk or cycle for short distances, etc.

(vi) To control high level of air pollution in Delhi, the entire fleet of public transport were converted to run on **CNG** (Compressed Natural Gas). Also, the use of unleaded petrol was encouraged.

Note
- In CNG, methane is stored at high pressure of about 20-25 MPa, usually in cylindrical or spherical shapes.
- Hybrid vehicle technology produces vehicles which can run on dual mode like petrol and CNG. It reduces consumption of fossil fuels and thus, environmental pollution.

(vii) Engines should be switched off when traffic light signals stop. They help in reducing vehicular noise as well as air pollution.

Euro/Bharat Stage : Standard for Vehicles to Reduce Air Pollution

Bharat stage or Euro norms are emission standards instituted by the government of India to regulate and check the pollutant levels emitted from automobiles that use combustion engines.

The main goal of this standard is to reduce sulphur and nitrogen oxides from the automobile exhausts. Any motor vehicle running on the road has to follow emission norms in order to reduce pollution.

These standards are based on European regulations and these were first introduced in 2000 and have been upgraded since then as BS-II, BS-III and now BS-IV. The BS numbers are based of European emission norms *viz.* Euro 4, Euro 5, Euro 6, etc.

Table Showing the Latest Mass Emission Standards in India

Types of Vehicle	Norms	Cities of Implementation
4 Wheelers	Bharat Stage III	Throughout the country since October, 2010
4 Wheelers	Bharat Stage IV	13 Mega cities (Delhi and NCR, Mumbai, Kolkata, Chennai, Bengaluru, Surat, Kanpur, Agra, Lucknow and Sholapur) since April, 2010 and it has been enforced to entire country since April 2017.
3 Wheelers	Bharat Stage III	Throughout the country since October, 2010
2 Wheelers	Bharat Stage III	Throughout the country since October, 2010

In 2016, the Central Pollution Control Board of Indian government announced that the country would skip the BS-V norms altogether and adopt BS-VI norms by 2020.

Acid Rain

It is the form of precipitation of acid in the form of snow, rain, etc. Acid rain is caused by emissions of sulphur dioxide and nitrogen oxide which react with water molecules in the atmosphere, to produce acids. The problem of acid rain is not a new one but the nature of problem has changed from being local for towns and cities to being an international issue.

Acid rain causes many harmful effects that can show impact for a very long period of time.

Harmful Effects of Acid Rain

(i) Acid rain is harmful to the environment as it damages the fish and other aquatic life by increasing acidity of water bodies.

(ii) It damages the vegetation by killing the useful soil microbial community.

(iii) Acid in the rain reacts with the calcium of statues, sculpture and ancient monuments and damages them (e.g. damage to Taj Mahal).

(iv) Acid rain damages the aerial parts of the plants and also acidifies the soil. It leads to the production of free radicals, decreases in photosynthesis and its productivity.

Check Your LEARNING...

1 Give few examples of gaseous pollutants causing air pollution.
2 Mention the harmful effect of smog.
3 Name the gaseous pollutants involved in asphyxiation.
4 What is the main goal of Bharat stage emission standard?
5 Name the acids present in acid rain.

2. Water Pollution

Water is said to be polluted when its quality gets degraded due to the addition of various inorganic, organic, biological and radiological substances which make it unfit and hazardous to human and all other living organisms.

Sources of Water Pollution

Domestic waste, sewage, soaps and detergents, run-off from agricultural fields having fertilisers and pesticides, industrial wastes, wastes from animal sheds and slaughter houses, oil spills, etc., all constitute the sources of water pollution.

Some of them are discussed below

(i) **Sewage** The liquid waste released out from domestic activities is called sewage. It includes toilet waste, kitchen and other household wasteswater. In order to renew water, it is necessary to remove dirt from it and release clean water into the nearby water bodies and rivers. For this purpose, many big cities have sewage treatment plants.

Small cities and rural areas do not have such facilities and they discharge sewage waste directly into a nearby water body such as rivers and lakes thereby, polluting them. This results in pollution of water at major level.

(ii) **Household detergents** Detergents or soaps used for household purposes, like washing clothes, utensils and for bathing, when released directly in water bodies, cause water pollution.

(iii) **Industrial wastes** Water released both by small scale and large scale industries contains various types of chemical pollutants and other wastes which is collectively called **effluent**.
These industries discharge dirty water directly into the rivers, lakes, etc., and cause water pollution.

(iv) **Oil spill** These are the accidental discharge of petroleum and their products by oil refineries, overturned oil tanks, offshore oil mining into seas, oceans and estuaries. Oil spreads rapidly over the water surface and form a thin layer called **oil stick**. This cuts off the interaction between the air and water. Due to oil pollution, many aquatic lifeforms are killed.

(v) **Thermal pollution** Industries like oil refineries, nuclear power plants and other thermal power plants use water for cooling their machinery. They release hot water into the nearby streams. The water released by industries is 8-10°C warmer than the normal water of streams. Also, the warm water contains less amount of oxygen as compared to normal water.
Due to this temperature change, the aquatic life get affected.

(vi) **Agricultural Run-off** The run-off from agricultural land is polluted with pesticides and fertilisers. It enters the water sources by seeping through the soil to groundwater or enter the streams as surface run-off.

Note Some people in India follow the practice of disposing off dead bodies into sacred rivers like **Ganga**. Such practices cause water pollution.

Effects of Water Pollution

The various effects of water pollution are given below

(i) Sewage, fertiliser and agricultural run-off contain organic materials. When discharged into water, these increases the growth of algae, which causes the depletion of oxygen levels. The low oxygen levels in water result in the death of aquatic animals.

(ii) Industrial chemicals and agricultural pesticides that end up in aquatic environments can accumulate in fishes which are later eaten by humans. Fishes are easily poisoned with metals that are also later consumed by humans. **Minamata disease** in Japan was caused due to mercury poisoning from fungicides which reached fish and then humans. Mercury has been found to cause weakened muscles, interfere with the development of the nervous system in foetus and young children.

(iii) **Eutrophication** It is the natural ageing of lake by the nutrient enrichment of its water. Due to introduction of nutrients such as nitrogen and phosphorus, there is growth of aquatic organisms.
Slowly and steadily as the fertility of the lake increases, organic matter remains begin to deposit in the lake. Over the centuries, the organic debris piles up, lake becomes shallower, turns marshy and eventually dries up to form land.

(iv) **Infectious diseases** Consumption of polluted water causes many diseases like typhoid, cholera, dysentery, etc., in humans.

Control Measures of Water Pollution

To control the level of water pollution, following steps must be undertaken

(i) Industrial waste should be processed for the removal of toxic constituents before being dumped in the water bodies.

(ii) Proper sanitation facilities should be provided. This will reduce the pollution of water due to excretory products.

(iii) If the hot water generated by the industries is collected at common place, allowed to cool and then discharged in water bodies, it will not affect the breeding capacity of aquatic organisms.

(iv) The Government of India passed Water (Prevention and Control of Water Pollution) Act, 1974 to safeguard the water resources from pollution and contamination.

(v) Sewage treatment should be setup in populated areas and septic tank in houses help to control water pollution by sewage and wastewater.

Check Your LEARNING...

1 Name two sources of water pollution.
2 What is sewage? How does it pollute natural water bodies?
3 Why agricultural run-offs are the main cause of water pollution in villages?
4 In which year, the Water Act was introduced?

3. Soil Pollution

Any undesirable change in the soil profile that affects its productivity is called soil pollution. It reduces the fertility of the soil and the diversity of organisms that live in it.

Sources of Soil Pollution

The source of soil pollution are wastes generated and accumulated from different sources. Waste constitutes any unwanted substances generated or released from industries, agriculture, household, etc. These are classified as follows

(i) **Biodegradable wastes** These substances can be degraded by microbial action into harmless and non-toxic substances. Some of them are
- Domestic and kitchen wastes like vegetable scraps, peel of fruits, grains, paper packaging, etc.
- Agricultural wastes like animal wastes, leaves, hay, etc.

(ii) **Non-biodegradable wastes** These substances cannot be degraded by microbial action. They persist as such for a long time and accumulate in the environment, which results in pollution.

Some major sources of soil pollution are as follows.
- **Urban and domestic wastes** Solid wastes produced from our homes, shops, restaurant, etc., include plastic bottles, polythene bags, bulbs, kitchen wastes, etc. These wastes are collected and disposed off by kabadiwalas and municipal workers, who dispose the wastes in nearby areas and cause pollution.
- **Industrial wastes** Various industries release solid wastes in addition to gaseous air pollutants and other chemicals. The solid wastes from industries is thrown out in the form of metallic ash, fly ash chemical residues, etc., which get settled on the surface of soil, thus polluting it.
- **Biomedical wastes** Wastes produced by hospitals, clinics, laboratories, etc., are also the major causes of soil pollution. Numerous items such as syringes, needles, unused or discarded tablets, research material, wound dressings, etc., are discarded and disposed off carelessly in the municipal garbage due to which soil gets polluted.
- **Chemical fertilisers** used for increasing crop yield are proved to be harmful in excess amount. They wash away from crop fields and drain into the nearby river and lake. Hence, they affect the aquatic life present in these water bodies.
- **Pesticides** Such as DDT (Dichloro diphenyl trichloroethane) which are used to kill pests and other insects in agricultural farms and fields, also act as major source of soil pollution. These chemicals reach the living beings such as humans and animals through the food grown in such soils and thus, get concentrated in food chains at various levels (**biomagnification**).

Effects of Soil Pollution

There are following effects of soil pollution or biological magnification

(i) Soil pollution may lead to loss of soil fertility.

(ii) Accumulation of pesticides is increasing in concentration in the body of living beings through food chain.

(iii) Increased concentration of DDT in birds affects calcium metabolism in them due to which their egg shells become thin and break before maturity.

Chemical Pollutants Present in the Soil and their Effects

Chemicals	Effects
Lead and mercury	Severe brain damage
Arsenic	Skin damage
Molybdenum	Abnormality in bones, diarrhoea, gout, etc.
Chromium	Respiratory distress, lung cancer, etc.

Control Measures of Soil Pollution

Soil pollution can be controlled by adopting the following measures

(i) **Burning** or **incineration** of solid wastes in a well-designed furnace.

(ii) **Sanitary landfills** are the areas used for solid wastes disposal in a trench or depression which are covered with layer of soil.

(iii) The natural vegetation cover and forest land should be protected. These are threatened because of industrialisation and urbanisation.

(iv) Agricultural pesticides and fertilisers should be used in a judicious way. **Organic farming** should be adopted as the new way of farming. This will decrease the dependence on chemicals like fertilisers, pesticides, etc., and help in reduction of pollution.

(v) Cropping techniques such as crop rotation, contour ploughing should be followed to improve soil fertility.

(vi) Soil pollution can be reduced by recycling the waste such as plastic bags, bottles, glasswares, metal containers, etc., instead of dumping these anywhere.

4. Noise Pollution

Noise is an undesirable high level of sound. Noise pollution is defined as the unwanted sound, which is released into the environment and disturbs the living system. A normal person can hear 20 dB sound and feels discomfort with sound of or above 85 dB.

Causes of Noise Pollution

The major sources of noise pollution are as follows

(i) Use of loudspeakers, music systems during social gathering, festivals, political gatherings, etc.
(ii) Industrial establishment, loud noise from machines, etc., especially near residential areas.
(iii) Increased motor vehicles on road, air planes, jets, etc., create lots of noise.
(iv) Construction work, drilling, demolition, etc.
(v) Burning of crackers during celebrations.

Effects of Noise Pollution

The general effects of noise pollution are as follows

(i) Sound level higher than 150 dB may damage eardrums and may permanently impair the hearing ability of humans.
(ii) Psychological disorders (anxiety and stress).
(iii) Hearing disability in humans.
(iv) Auditory impairment, i.e. whistling and buzzing in ears cause headache.
(v) Lowers efficiency of work.
(vi) It interferes with communication.
(vii) Disturbs sleep, leads to nervous irritability and insomnia.

Control Measures of Noise Pollution

The noise pollution can be controlled by the following measures

(i) Use of sound absorbent material in buildings.
(ii) Muffling or suppressing noise can be done by planting more trees.
(iii) Creating horn-free zones around hospitals and schools.
(iv) Sticking to the permissible sound level of crackers and loudspeakers.
(v) Framing laws to enforce particular timing for playing music dj, loudspeakers, etc.
(vi) Silencers can be fitted to automobiles and industrial goods.

Check Your LEARNING...

1 Name two sources of soil pollution.
2 Chemical fertilisers add nutrition to the soil. So, how do they cause soil pollution?
3 Define biological magnification.
4 Name two chemical pollutants of soil.
5 What is the cause of whistling and buzzing in ears?

5. Radioactive Pollution

Contamination of air, water and soil with radioactive substances is called radioactive pollution. The radioactive elements, e.g. uranium, radium, etc., emit protons, electrons, X-rays and gamma rays as radiations. This property is called **radioactivity**.

Sources of Radioactive Pollution

The chief sources of radiation are as follows

(i) Leakage of radioactive materials from power plants.
(ii) Unsafe disposal methods of radioactive wastes.
(iii) X-rays and radioactive rays.
(iv) Spent fuel reprocessing plants.
(v) Research laboratories.
(vi) Natural or man-made radiations.
(vii) Nuclear fall outs.
(viii) Terrestrial radiations from radioisotopes present in the Earth.
(ix) Cosmic rays from space.

Effects of Radioactive Pollution

When radiation passes through different living organisms the following problems might occur

(i) Radiation splits the molecules of the tissues into ions and free-radicals and causes mutation by breaking DNA (Deoxyribonucleic Acid) molecules in the nucleus.
(ii) Radiation in bone marrow may cause leukemia.
(iii) Radiation causes skin burns which may lead to skin cancer.
(iv) Radiation expoure in pelvic regions of pregnant ladies cause damage to the foetus.
(v) Change in blood composition, nausea, vomiting, fatigue, etc., might occur.

- In 1986, in Ukraine, the Chernobyl disaster was the worst nuclear accident.
- Bhopal gas tragedy occurred on 2nd December, 1984, due to the leakage of methyl isocyanate from union carbide plant, M.P.
- In March 2011, in Japan, nuclear plant explosion caused the radiation pollution of iodine 53. It causes thyroid cancer, haemorrhaging, etc.
- In 2010, in Delhi, radioactive waste cobalt 60 somehow reached the market streets in Delhi from a research centre. Several exposed people suffered and few died.

Control Measures of Radiation Pollution

Nuclear waste management could be achieved by following means

(i) Disposal method should be safe and harmless. It has been recommended that nuclear waste before disposal should be pre-treated and buried about 500 m deep below the Earth's crust in suitably shielded containers. However, this method of disposal is also facing criticism. Disposal can be done by putting the waste in polar ice sheets or deep ocean floors.

(ii) Preventive measures should be taken to maintain the level of radiation within permissible limits.

(iii) Regular checking of nuclear reactors to check for any source of leakage should be done.

(iv) Care should be taken to check man-made radiation pollution at source.

(v) Nuclear tests should be banned.

(vi) Leakages from nuclear reactor, careless handling transport and use of radioactive fuels must be stopped.

(vii) Regular monitoring and quantitative analysis should be done in risk areas.

Swachh Bharat Abhiyan : A National Campaign for Clean India

'A clean India would be the best tribute, we Indians could pay to Mahatama Gandhi on his 150th birth anniversary in 2019.' This was quoted by our Prime Minister Shri Narendra Modi before launching the 'Swachh Bharat Abhiyan' officially on 2nd October 2014 at Rajghat, New Delhi. This campaign is a significant drive for undertaking cleaning of cities, towns and villages of India.

The objectives of this campaign are as follows

- Elimination of open defecation to make an Open Defecation Free (ODF) India and construction of in house and commercial toilets.
- Cleaning the streets, roads and infrastructure of our country's towns and cities.
- Efficient management and disposal systems to be developed for solid and liquid wastes.

Check Your LEARNING...

1 Define radioactivity.
2 How do X-rays damage the body cells?
3 Name two radioactive elements which emit X-rays.
4 Name two sources of radioactive pollution.
5 At what depth should nuclear waste be buried?

Greenhouse Effect

Greenhouses are glass houses which are used to grow plants during cold weather. The glass panel in these houses permit the sunlight to enter but does not allow the heat to escape from it. Thus, it results in warming the area.

The greenhouse effect is a naturally occurring phenomenon that is responsible for heating Earth's surface and atmosphere. Certain gases such as carbon dioxide (CO_2) and methane (CH_4) get accumulated in the atmosphere, thus prevent the escape of heat (Infrared or IR radiations) and cause warming of air. These gases are known as the **greenhouse gases.**

Without the effect of greenhouse, the average temperature on the surface of the Earth would have been around −18°C rather than the present average temperature of 15°C.

Global Warming

The rise in temperature of Earth due to higher emission of greenhouse gases is called global warming. The composition of different greenhouse gases is 60% carbon dioxide (CO_2), 20% methane (CH_4), 6% nitrous oxide (N_2O) and 14% Chlorofluorocarbons (CFCs).

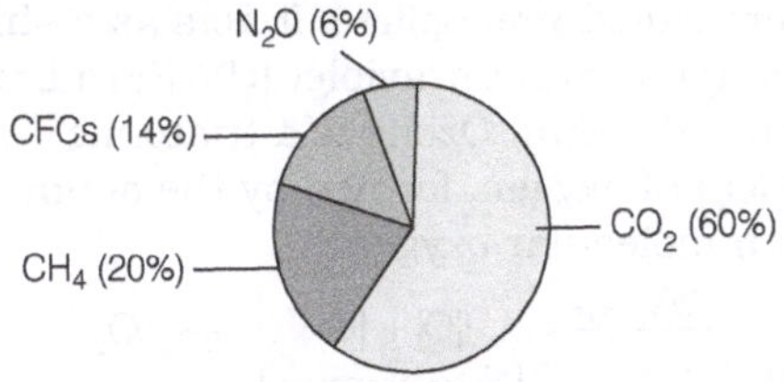

Relative contribution of various greenhouse gases to total global warming

Causes of Global Warming

The main causes of global warming are as follows

(i) Carbon dioxide emission is the most important cause of global warming which is released by burning fuels, respiration, etc.

(ii) Less utilisation of CO_2 during photosynthesis due to decrease in the vegetation and deforestation.

(iii) High levels of greenhouse gases (CO_2, CFCs, etc.) in the atmosphere. All these gases allow the heat waves to reach Earth, but prevent their escape and thus, the Earth becomes warm.

Effects of Global Warming

Various effects of global warming are as follows

(i) Earth temperature has increased by 0.6°C in last three decades. This causes change in precipitation patterns.

(ii) Global warming could cause melting of ice caps. It would raise the water level of sea and many global cities would be at risk of getting submerged in water.

(iii) The high temperature results in increased weed growth, eruption of diseases and pests that could decrease crop productivity.

(iv) Decline in food production and fishery resources.

Control of Global Warming

Global warming can be controlled by taking following measures.

(i) Cutting down the excessive use of fossil fuels.

(ii) Improving energy efficiency.

(iii) Reducing deforestation.

(iv) Planting trees and population control.

Ozone Layer Depletion

Ozone is found in the upper part of the atmosphere called **stratosphere**. It acts as a shield in absorbing harmful ultraviolet (UV-B) radiations coming from the Sun. Ozone is a triatomic molecule (O_3) of oxygen, formed by the action of UV-rays on molecular oxygen.

$$\underset{\text{(Molecular oxygen)}}{O_2} \xrightarrow{\text{UV rays}} \underset{\text{[Nascent oxygen]}}{[O] + [O]} \longrightarrow O_2$$

$$+ [O] \xrightarrow{\text{UV rays}} \underset{\text{(Ozone)}}{O_3}$$

Ozone layer depletion is simply the wearing out (reduction) of ozone in the stratosphere. Various gaseous compounds like CFCs (used as refrigerants), styrofoam, freon gas from aerosol sprays, etc., cause ozone depletion when released into the environment. This happens in the following ways

(i) CFCs are discharged in the lower part of atmosphere. From there, they move upward towards the stratosphere.

(ii) In stratosphere, UV-rays act on them and release Cl^- atoms.

(iii) Cl^- degrades ozone releasing molecular oxygen, i.e. O_3 into O_2 and O.

(iv) Cl^- atoms are not consumed in the reaction. Hence, once CFCs are added to the stratosphere, they have permanent and continuous effects on ozone levels.

Ozone Hole

Ozone depletion is particularly marked over the Antarctica region. This leads to the formation of a large area of thinned ozone layer, known as ozone hole. If the ozone layer gets depleted continuously, it would not prevent the entry of UV-rays reaching the Earth.

UV-rays cause harmful effects like

(i) UV-B damages DNA and causes mutation.

(ii) Damage to the skin cells and ageing.

(iii) Inflammation of the cornea, i.e. snow blindness due to high dose of UV-B.

(iv) Cataract (a disease of blurred vision) and cancer.

Control of Ozone Depletion

Ozone depletion needs to be controlled right away. The most appropriate control can be achieved by the restriction of CFCs releasing or chlorine substances. We should also avoid the use of dangerous nitrous oxide, that is one of the harmful gases causing ozone depletion.

International Ozone Day is observed on 16th September every year.

Check Your LEARNING...

1 Name the radiations absorbed by greenhouse gases.

2 What is the present average temperature of Earth?

3 What proportion of CH_4 and N_2O is found in greenhouse gases?

4 Which component of CFCs is involved in degrading ozone?

5 How ozone layer is formed?

QUiCK Revision

- **Pollution** is any undesirable change in physical, chemical or biological characteristics of air, land, water and soil.
- **Pollutants** are chemical or biological substances that deteriorate our natural environment.
- Any undesirable change in the physical, chemical and biological characteristics of air that causes adverse effects on living things is called **air pollution**. It is mainly caused by combustion of fossil fuels, automobiles, etc.
- **Air pollution** causes fruit damage, leaf damage, chlorosis, etc., in plants. Carbon monoxide combines with haemoglobin and reduces the oxygen carrying capacity of blood.
- **Acid rain** is caused by oxides of sulphur and nitrogen. The pH of acid rain is less than 5.65.
- **Electrostatic precipitator** can remove over 99% particulate matter present in the exhaust from a thermal power plant.
- **Water pollution** is the contamination of water bodies due to the changes in physical, chemical and biological properties of water that affect the living beings adversely. Sources of water pollution are of two types, i.e. natural sources, anthropogenic or man-made sources. Domestic sewage, industrial waste and agricultural run-off are the main sources of water pollution.
- **Thermal pollution** is warming of an aquatic ecosystem to the point, where desirable organisms are adversely affected. It is caused by the water released from thermal power plants, oil refineries, etc.
- **Eutrophication** refers to the ageing of a lake by nutrient enrichment of its water. Nutrients rich in phosphates and nitrogen promote algal growth. Organic matter in water acts as a food source and promotes growth of planktonic algae, called **algal bloom.** It imparts a distinct colour to the water bodies and causes deterioration of the water quality, fish mortality, etc.
- **Biomagnification** is the increase in concentration of the toxic substance at successive trophic level in the food chain. It is the indicator of water pollution.
- **Soil pollution** is the alternation in soil quality caused by the removal or addition of substance. It is of two types, i.e. negative and positive soil pollution. Soil pollution can be reduced by incineration and pyrolysis.
- **Noise pollution** is caused by loud disturbing sounds dumped into the ambient atmosphere. Sound level more than 80 dB causes noise pollution. The intensity of sound in normal conversation is 30-60 dB. Hatching of birds is disturbed due to noise pollution.
- **Radioactive pollution** is physical pollution of air, water and soil due to radioactive materials. Some elements such as radium 224, uranium 235, thorium 232, etc., naturally emit radiations.
- **Radioactive wastes** are released from radioactivity emission of α-particles, β-particles or γ-rays from nucleides of their elements. Radiation causes mutations very frequently and also increases the chances of cancer.
- **Greenhouse effect** is the increase in global temperature mainly due to CO_2 concentration. Greenhouse gases like CO_2, CH_4, CFCs, etc., are produced by various human activities.
- **Global warming** is the gradual increase in average temperature of surface of the Earth as a result of increased concentration of greenhouse gases.
- **Ozone** is found in the stratosphere. It is continuously formed by the action of UV-rays on molecular oxygen.
- **Ozone layer depletion** is caused by the action of chlorine released from chlorofluorocarbons on ozone. Ozone hole is particularly marked over Antarctica region.

Chapter Practice

Section-I

1 Mark Questions

1. Name the following.
   (i) Name the pollutants that cannot be broken down to simple and harmless forms. [2016]
   (ii) Name the non-biodegradable pesticide. [2013]
   (iii) The vehicular standard for controlling air pollution. [2017]
   (iv) One gaseous compound which depletes the ozone layer. [2019]

Ans. (i) Non-biodegradable
(ii) DDT
(iii) Bharat Stage Emission Standard
(iv) Chlorofluorocarbon

2. Correct and rewrite the following statements by changing the underlined words.
   (i) Agricultural waste is a type of non-biodegradable waste.
   (ii) Particles of dust, mining, stone drilling, etc, constitutes gaseous pollution.
   (iii) Incineration are the places where wastes are dumped in a ground depression.
   (iv) Water pollution can be reduced by incineration and pyrolysis.
   (v) CNG is mainly responsible for the formation of acid rain.

Ans. (i) Agricultural waste is a type of biodegradable waste.
(ii) Particles of dust, mining, stone drilling, etc., constitutes particulate pollution.
(iii) Sanitary landfills are the places where wastes are dumped in a ground depression.
(iv) Soil pollution can be reduced by incineration and pyrolysis.
(v) SO_2 and NO_2 is mainly responsible for the formation of acid rain.

3. Give biological reasons for the following.
   (i) Cutting of trees should be discouraged. [2017]
   (ii) Carbon monoxide is dangerous when inhaled. [2019, 14]
   (iii) Acid rain is harmful to the environment. [2019]

Ans. (i) Cutting of trees should be discouraged because plants utilise atmospheric CO_2 during photosynthesis and release O_2 which help in maintaining the balance of O_2 and CO_2 in environment and is also helpful in reducing pollution.
(ii) Carbon monoxide is dangerous when inhaled because it has great affinity with haemoglobin due to which, it gets mixed with haemoglobin almost 300 times more than oxygen. Thus, it cuts off the supply of oxygen to body tissues, which can cause death due to asphyxiation.
(iii) Acid rain is harmful to the environment in many ways which are as follows
- It damages the fish and other aquatic life by increasing acidity of water.
- It damages the vegetation by killing the useful soil microbial community.
- Acid in the rain reacts with the calcium of statues, sculptures and ancient monuments and damages them, e.g. damage to Taj Mahal.

4. (i) Match the following columns.

Column I	Column II
A. Biomagnification	1. Ageing of lake
B. Eutrophication	2. Reduction of soil pollution
C. Pyrolysis	3. Increased concentration of toxins at successive trophic level.

(ii) Match the following columns.

Column I	Column II
A. Ozone	1. Bad ozone
B. Greenhouse effect	2. Rise in sea level
C. CO_2, CH_4 and CFCs	3. Protective shield around atmosphere
D. Ozone present in troposphere	4. Global warming
	5. Greenhouse gases

Ans. (i) A-3, B-1, C-2
(ii) A-3, B-4, C-5, D-1

5. Choose the correct answer from the four options given below.
   (i) The unfavourable alteration in environment due to human activities is termed as
   (a) ecological disturbance (b) catastrophe
   (c) ecological degradation (d) pollution

Ans. (d)

(ii) Which one of the following is non-biodegradable? [2018]
(a) DDT (b) Vegetable peel
(c) Cardboard (d) Bark of trees

Ans. (a)

(iii) Compressed Natural Gas is
(a) propane (b) methane
(c) ethane (d) butane

Ans. (b)

(iv) In the textbook, you came across Chernobyl disasters associated with accidental leakage of radioactive wastes. In India, we had Bhopal gas tragedy. It is associated with which of the following?

(a) CO_2 (b) Methyl isocyanate
(c) CFCs (d) Methyl cyanate

Ans. (b)

(v) Which one of the following is a biodegradable waste? [2023]

(a) Metal cans (b) E-waste (c) Plastic (d) Flowers

Ans. (d)

(vi) Which one of the following is a greenhouse gas?

(a) Oxygen (b) Methane
(c) Sulphur dioxide (d) Nitrogen [2018]

Ans. (b)

(vii) The primary source of chlorofluorocarbons is [2017]

(a) vehicular emissions (b) industrial effluents
(c) domestic sewage (d) refrigeration equipments

Ans. (d)

6. (A) Fill in the blanks by using suitable words.

(i) A non-degradable pollutant is ....

(ii) The acid rain is caused by the oxides of .... and ....

(iii) Drinking water coming from a polluted source causes disease like .... and ....

(iv) A value more than .... decibel leads to noise pollution.

(v) .... causes corrosion of the marble or brick surface. [2015]

(B) Complete the sentences by inserting correct word in the blanks.

(i) If there was no greenhouse effect, the average temperature of the Earth's surface would be ....

(ii) CO_2, CH_4, N_2O and CFCs are called greenhouse gases because they absorb and emit ....

Ans. (A) (i) plastic (ii) sulphur, nitrogen
(iii) cholera, dysentery (iv) 85
(v) Acid rain
(B) (i) $-18°C$ (ii) IR rays

7. Choose the odd one out from the following terms given below and name the category to which the other three belong.

(i) Detergents, Sewage, X-rays, Oil spills [2018, 17]

(ii) Sewage, Newspaper, Styrofoam, Hay [2016]

(iii) Polythene bag, Crop residue, Animal waste, Decaying vegetables [2019]

(iv) Used bandages, Pesticides, Face masks, Syringes [2023]

(v) Dust, Smoke, Carbon monoxide, Effluents [2023]

Ans. (i) **Odd term** is X-rays.
Rest three are the sources of water pollution.

(ii) **Odd term** is styrofoam.
Rest three are biodegradable pollutants.

(iii) **Odd term** is polythene bag.
Rest three are biodegradable wastes.

(iv) **Odd term** Pesticides
Category Other glands medical waste hormones.

(v) **Odd term** Effluents
Category Others are industrial air pollutants.

8. Expand the following biological abbreviations.

(i) CNG (ii) BS (iii) ODF (iv) CFC

Ans. (i) Compressed Natural Gas
(ii) Bharat Stage
(iii) Open Defecation Free
(iv) Chlorofluorocarbons

9. State the main function of the following.

(i) Chemical fertilisers
(ii) Ozone
(iii) Chlorofluorocarbons

Ans. (i) Chemical fertilisers help to increase the yield of crops.
(ii) Ozone prevents UV rays to reach the Earth.
(iii) Chlorofluorocarbons are used in refrigeration purpose and act as ozone depleting substances.

10. Mention one difference between each of the following pairs on the basis of what is given in the bracket.

(i) Biodegradable and Non-biodegradable waste (chemical nature)
(ii) Smoke and Smog (composition)

Ans. (i) Difference between biodegradable and non-biodegradable waste is as follows

Biodegradable wastes	Non-biodegradable wastes
These are organic waste that can be broken down by microorganisms into harmless and non-toxic substances.	These are substances that cannot be broken down by microorganisms.

(ii) Difference between smoke and smog is as follows

Smoke	Smog
It is composed of gaseous pollutants like CO_2, SO_2 CO and particulate pollutants like dust.	It is composed of smoke and small drops of fog.

11. Give biological/technical terms for the following.

(i) The process causing an undesirable change in the environment. [2016]

(ii) A mixture of smoke and fog.

(iii) The component which grows abundantly in organic matter rich lake.

(iv) The type of waste generated in hospitals and pathological laboratories. [2017]

Ans. (i) Pollution
(ii) Smog
(iii) Algal bloom
(iv) Biomedical wastes

12. Briefly explain the following terms.
(i) Biomedical waste [2014]
(ii) Electrostatic precipitator
(iii) Photochemical smog

Ans. (i) Biomedical wastes consist of the waste produced by hospitals, i.e. wastes containing dressing, amputated body parts, used surgical instruments, etc. These spread diseases if left unmanaged.
(ii) Electrostatic precipitators are the devices that can remove 99% particulate matter present in the exhaust which is released from industries.
(iii) The photochemical smog contains secondary pollutants like O_3, PAN, etc.

13. Answer the following questions briefly.
(i) Air is called as 'breath of life'. Why?
(ii) Give one example of water pollutant. [2014]
(iii) Mention any three causes of soil pollution. [2017]
(iv) Is it true that carpets and curtains/drapes placed on the floor or wall surfaces can reduce noise level? Explain briefly.
(v) Mention any two objectives of 'Swachh Bharat Abhiyan'. [2019]
(vi) Why use of CFC is banned in many countries? [2014]
(vii) Name any two greenhouse gases present on Earth alongwith their percentage contribution in greenhouse effect.

Ans. (i) Air is called as 'breath of life' because it contains oxygen, which is required by all living organisms for respiration.
(ii) Domestic sewage is an example of water pollutant.
(iii) Three main causes of soil pollution are
- Industrial wastes.
- Domestic wastes like plastic, urban and commercial wastes.
- Fertilisers and pesticides such as DDT and agricultural wastes.

(iv) Yes, it is true. This is because they act as muffling device and absorb sounds at moderate level.
(v) The objectives of Swachh Bharat Abhiyan campaign are as follows
- Elimination of open defecation and construction of in-house and commercial toilets.
- Cleaning the streets, roads and infrastructure of our country's towns and cities.

(vi) Chlorofluorocarbons (CFCs) are banned in many countries because they are one of the major causes for ozone layer depletion.
(vii) Carbon dioxide (CO_2)-60% and methane (CH_4)-20%.

2 Marks Questions

14. State any two harmful effects of acid rain.

Ans. Two harmful effects of acid rain are as
(i) Acid rain increases acidity in the soil and destroys forests and crops.
(ii) It corrodes fences, buildings, monuments, bridges and statues.

15. Excessive use of fertilisers in agricultural fields reduces the yield of crops. Justify the statement. [2023]

Ans. The excessive use of fertilisers in agricultural fields can actually have a negative impact on crop yields in the long run. This is because excessive fertiliser use can lead to a number of problems, including
- Overuse of nitrogen-based fertilisers can cause the soil to become more acidic, which can ultimately reduce the soil's ability to support healthy plant growth.
- Overuse of a particular type of fertiliser can lead to imbalances in soil nutrients, which can cause some nutrients to become unavailable to the plant, while others are present in excess. This can lead to stunted growth and reduced yields.

16. Explain the cause of algal bloom in a water body. How does it affect an ecosystem?

Ans. Algal bloom is caused by the enrichment of nutrients in the water body, especially by the presence of phosphorus and nitrogen.
It affects the ecosystem in following ways
(i) Deterioration of water quality.
(ii) Death of aquatic organisms.

17. What are the sources of radioactive waste?

Ans. Sources of radioactive waste are as follows
(i) Accidental leakage of nuclear material or radiations from nuclear power plants.
(ii) Improper disposal of nuclear or radioactive waste.

18. Define ozone hole. When is the International Ozone Day observed?

Ans. Ozone hole is the thinning of ozone layer due to increased use of CFCs. International Ozone Day is observed on 16th September every year.

3 Marks Questions

19. Explain why smog formation occurs in cold weather.

Ans. The combustion of fossil fuels increases the amount of suspended particles such as unburnt carbon particles (i.e. hydrocarbons) in air. Presence of high levels of these pollutants cause visibility to be lowered, especially in cold weather when water also condenses out of air. This is known as smog and it is a visible indication of air pollution.

20. Water pollution is a major problem in our country. State three major factors which lead to water pollution.

Ans. Three major factors which lead to water pollution are

(i) **Industrial waste** Effluent of industries contains large quantities of harmful chemicals and acids that are discharged into water bodies (rivers and lakes) and pollute them.

(ii) **Fertilisers and pesticides** These are excessively used in fields to increase production. These are washed away by water into water bodies and thus, pollute them.

(iii) **Sewage** Organic wastes contributing as domestic and commercial sewage are discharged into water bodies which decreases the quality of water.

21. The figure shows some human activities which affect the environment.

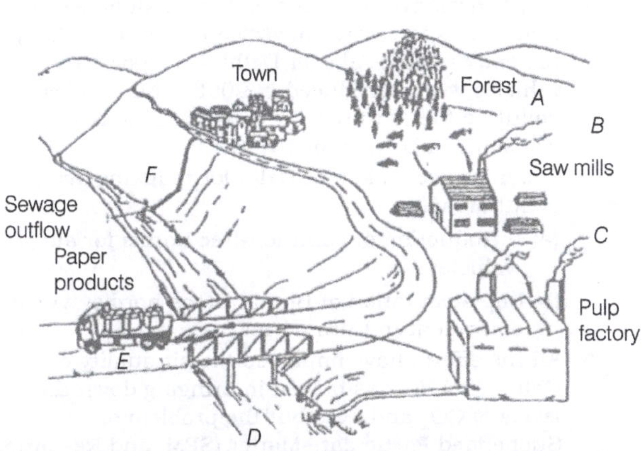

(i) Explain the harmful effects of these activities.

(ii) Suggest ways in which the harmful effects of such activities might be overcome.

Ans. (i) Deforestation at (*A*) can lead to soil erosion and floods. The part of soil that is washed into rivers and seas reduces the clarity of water and reduces photosynthesis by water plants. Deforestation can also lead to desertification.

The saw mills (*B*) and pulp factory (*C*) cause air pollution from the smoke given off. The pulp factory also throws out waste products into the river (*D*) thus causing water pollution. At (*E*), the smoke given out by the lorry is a further a source of air pollution.

The carbon monoxide and other substances are harmful to animals in high concentrations. The sewage discharge at (*F*) into the river by the town causes water pollution. The bacteria in the sewage use oxygen in the water and cause fishes and other organisms in the river to die.

(ii) The harmful effects might be overcome by preventing the cutting down of forests, treating sewage and reducing the smoke from factories and vehicles by using less harmful fuels.

22. Name any one greenhouse gas and its possible source of production on a large scale. What are its harmful effects?

Ans. The common greenhouse gases are CO_2, CH_4, CFCs, oxide of nitrogen (N O), water vapour and O_3. **Source** The level of CO_2 (a greenhouse gas) is increasing due to large scale deforestation, change in land use, unlimited burning of fossil fuels and rising population.

Harmful effect Rise in CO_2 level leads to absorption of heat rays thus causing an increase in temperature of the atmospheres, i.e. global warming. CO_2 is estimated to contribute around 60% towards greenhouse effect.

23. Carbon dioxide is necessary for plants. Why do we consider it as a pollutant?

Ans. Carbon dioxide gas is necessary for plants to perform photosynthesis. But it is also a greenhouse gas.

So, upto certain concentration (approx. 350 ppm) in atmosphere, it is considered as ideal raw material for photosynthesis as well as essential for keeping the Earth warm. But, when concentration of CO_2 rises from certain level, it becomes a pollutant.

24. List any three human activities, which lead to release of carbon dioxide content of air.

Ans. The human activities, which would lead to an increase in the CO_2 content of air are

(i) **Respiration** is the natural way to release CO_2 by plants and animals both. It is balanced by the release of oxygen by plants. So, it is not harmful for the environment.

(ii) **Deforestation** increases the level of CO_2 in the environment. Trees carryout photosynthesis and convert CO_2 into organic compounds such as glucose, starch, etc. In their absence, CO_2 cannot be utilised.

(iii) **Combustion** of fuels leads to increase in CO_2 level in the atmosphere. Fuels are burnt to carry out activities like cooking, transportation and in industrial processes.

25. The figure shows greenhouse effect. Observe it carefully and answer the questions that follow.

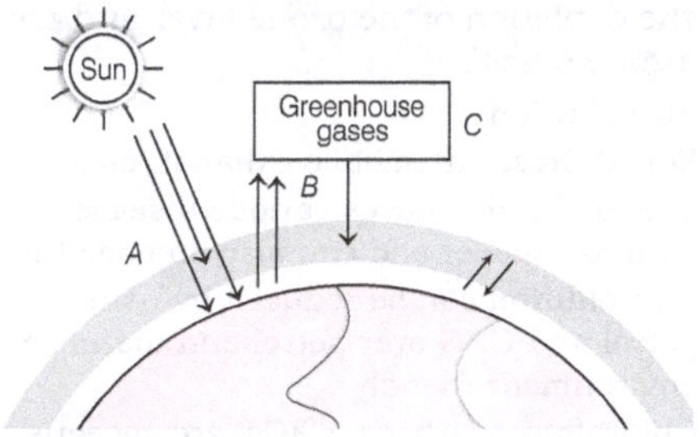

(i) What happens to *A* as it travels to Earth?

(ii) Describe *C* and its effect.

Ans. (i) Half of the incident radiations (*A*) fall on the Earth surface and heat it and some portion of it is reflected back.

(ii) Greenhouse gases absorb long wave (infrared) radiation from the Earth and emit it again towards the Earth. The cycle continues till the Earth's surface has no long wave radiation to emit.

26. Refrigerants are considered to be necessity in modern living, but are said to be responsible for ozone hole detected in Antarctica. Justify.

Ans. Refrigerants contain Chlorofluorocarbons (CFCs), the substances that do not degrade easily and travel up to the stratosphere. In the stratosphere, UV-rays act on them and a chlorine atom is released.

These chlorine atoms act as catalyst and degrade ozone. Chlorine atoms are recycled in this reaction so, they keep on damaging ozone layer, leading to creation of ozone hole as formed over Antarctica. Thus, besides being a necessity, refrigerants are responsible for ozone hole.

Section-II [3/5 Marks]

1. Given below is the representation of a type of pollution. Study the picture and answer the questions that follows.

(i) Name the type of pollution shown in the picture.
(ii) Name one source of this pollution.
(iii) How does this pollution affect human health?
(iv) Write one measure to reduce this pollution.
(v) State one gaseous compound that leads to the depletion of the ozone layer and creates 'ozone holes'. [2018]

Ans. (i) Air pollution
(ii) Forest fires, automobile exhaust, etc.
(iii) This pollution causes various diseases such as asthma, cancer and can also damage the CNS.
(iv) Air pollution can be reduced by using unleaded petrol and CNG over petrol and diesel as it is environment friendly.
(v) Chlorofluorocarbons (CFCs) are gaseous compounds responsible for the depletion of ozone layer and create ozone holes.

2. The metro cities in India are worst affected by poor air quality. Multiple policies have been declared and implemented by city authority with a hope of improving air quality and to attain ambient air quality standard.
(i) Mention the major causes of air pollution in metro cities.
(ii) What is particulate pollution?
(iii) When does the use of CNG was encouraged by Delhi government?
(iv) Mention the initiatives taken in Delhi for reducing air pollution.
(v) Has air quality improved in Delhi?

Ans. (i) Causes of air pollution in metro cities are as follows
(a) Effluents from thermal plants, smelters and other industries.
(b) Emission from automobiles exhaust.
(c) Smoke from forest fires, volcanic eruptions, etc.
(d) Use of leaded petrol.
(ii) Particulate pollution constitutes particles such as those of dust, smoke, mining, stone drilling, etc.
(iii) As per directives of Supreme Court, all buses of Delhi transport were converted to run on CNG by the end of 2002. All over Delhi, CNG powered vehicles were introduced in 2006. CNG is a less polluting fuel. At present, most of the public transport in Delhi runs *via.* CNG.
(iv) The initiatives taken in Delhi for reducing air pollution are
(a) Introduction of pollution-free norms for all vehicles.
(b) Implementation of Bharat Stage norms, which is equivalent to Euro norms.
(v) All the efforts have improved the air quality of Delhi. As CNG has helped in bringing down the levels of CO_2 and SO_2, but the problem of Suspended Particulate Matter (SPM) and Respirable Suspended Particulate Matter (RSPM) is yet to be overcome.

3. Study the picture given below and answer the following questions. [2019]

(i) Identify the type of pollution.
(ii) Name one pollutant that causes the above pollution.
(iii) Mention the impact of this pollution on human health.
(iv) State one measure to contol this pollution.
(v) What is a pollutant ? Explain the term.

Ans. (i) Water pollution
(ii) Sewage or industrial waste.
(iii) Effects of water pollution on human health are as
- Pollution of water may cause many water borne diseases such as typhoid, dysentery, etc.
- Aquatic animals and sea birds may be killed due to oil spills. Oil does not dissolve in water and it

forms layer on water which prevents the oxygenation of sea water, which affects the aquatic organisms.

- Discharge of excessive nutrients through sewage into the static water leads to death of aquatic life. The organic matter increases growth of algae that consumes a lot of O_2. This decreases the O_2 and cause problem for water organisms. This phenomenon is known as **eutrophication**. It refers to the natural ageing of lake by the nutrient enrichment of its water.

(iv) Water pollution can be controlled by introducing sewage treatment plants.

(v) Pollutants are the agents that cause pollution and bring undesirable changes in the environment.

4. Given is a representation of a kind of pollution. Study the same and answer the questions that follow **[2017]**

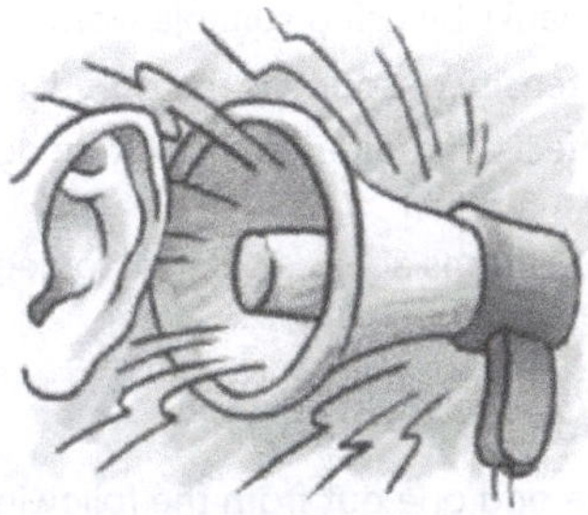

(i) Name the kind of pollution.
(ii) List any three common sources of this pollution.
(iii) Mention three harmful effects of this pollution on human health.
(iv) Explain the term 'pollutant'.
(v) Name two soil pollutants.

Ans. (i) Noise pollution

(ii) The three common sources of noise pollution are
(a) Trains (b) Loudspeakers
(c) Jet crafts

(iii) The three harmful effects of noise pollution on human health are as follows
(a) Nervous irritability
(b) Damaged eardrum
(c) Interferes with the concentration and thoughts

(iv) Refer to Ans. 3 (v)

(v) Two soil pollutants are
(a) Pesticides like DDT.
(b) Biomedical wastes like syringes, needles, etc.

5. The diagram given below depicts the climate change on planet Earth.

Answer the following questions. **[2023]**

(i) Name the climatic phenomenon for the increase in Earth's temperature.
(ii) Mention one reason for this warming.
(iii) What measures can be taken to prevent this climate change?

Ans. (i) Global warming

(ii) Due to the increase in concentration of greenhouse gases such as
- Carbon dioxide.
- Methane.
- Nitrous oxide.

(iii) Measures to prevent this climate change are
- Stop deforestation and promote afforestation.
- Reduce air pollution caused due to vehicles and various industries.

Chapter Assessment

Section-I

1 Mark Questions

1. Name the following.
   (i) The disease caused due to mercury poisoning from fungicides in Japan.
   (ii) A radioactive substance that caused serious damage in Delhi in 2010.
   (iii) Unit of energy present in X-rays.
   (iv) Air pollutants contributed by aeroplanes.
2. Correct ard rewrite the following statements by changing the underlined words.
   (i) The phenomenon by which certain pollutants accumulate in the body tissues in increasing concentration is called <u>eutrophication</u>.
   (ii) The Montreal Protocol aims at control of <u>carbon dioxide emission</u>.
3. Give biological reasons for the following.
   (i) Warm water acts as a pollutant.
   (ii) Oil spill adversely affects the aquatic life.
4. Match the following collumns.

Column I		Column II	
A.	Agricultural pollutant	1.	Uranium
B.	Biodegradable pollutant	2.	Vegetable waste
C.	Radioactive pollutant	3.	Pesticides
D.	Water pollutant	4.	Sewage

5. Choose the correct answer from the four options given below.
   (i) Non-biodegradable pollutants are created by
   (a) nature
   (b) excessive use of resources
   (c) humans
   (d) natural disasters
   (ii) Which air pollutant could cause rain to be acidic?
   (a) Dust particles from cement factories
   (b) Insecticides from crop sprays
   (c) Smoke from wood fires
   (d) Sulphur dioxide from coal-fired power stations
   (iii) Ozone is present in abundance in this layer, which gets heated up as the incoming radiations are absorbed by ozone.
   (a) Mesosphere (b) Troposphere
   (c) Stratosphere (d) Thermosphere
   (iv) CFCs are not recommended to be used in refrigerators because they
   (a) increase temperature (b) deplete ozone
   (c) affect environment (d) affect human body
6. Fill in the blanks by using suitable words.
   (i) The intensity of sound is measured in ....
   (ii) The effects of radioactive pollution depend on .... of the material.
   (iii) The Cl^- atoms act as a catalyst to degrade ozone and release molecular ....
   (iv) Ozone depletion is caused by .... exhaust from jet emission.
7. Choose the odd one out from the following terms given below and name the category to which other three belong.
   Sulphur dioxide, Carbon monoxide, Oxygen, Nitrogen dioxide
8. Expand the following biological abbreviations.
   (i) IR radiations
   (ii) DDT
9. Mention one difference between each of the following pair on the basis of what is given in the bracket.
   Primary pollutant and Secondary Pollutant (origin)
10. Briefly explain the term incineration.

2 Marks Questions

11. How do agricultural practices contributes to water pollution?
12. What are the various constituents of domestic sewage?

3 Marks Questions

13. What measures an individual could take to reduce environmental pollution?
14. Discuss the effects of sewage discharge in river.

Section-II

[5 Marks]

Structured Question

15. Observe the figure given below and answer the questions that follow.

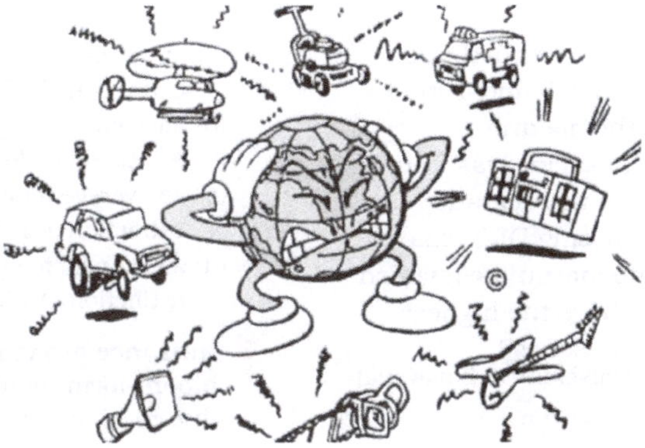

(i) What is represented by the given figure?

(ii) List any two causes of this demonstration.

(iii) Give two effects on us, of the given scenerio.

(iv) Suggest atleast two control measures for the same.

For explanations scan the given QR Code

Olympiad Section*

Brain Teasing Questions asked in Previous Olympiads

1 The pesticide Dichlorodiphenyl Trichloroethane (DDT) was widely used between 1940 and 1960 to kill mosquitoes that transmit the malaria pathogen. Though useful, the pesticide was found to be persistent, meaning it does not degrade easily in the environment. Supposing DDT was sprayed on grasses to eradicate mosquitoes, which organisms in the food web will have the highest concentration of DDT within its tissues? **[IJSO 2018, University of Botswana]**

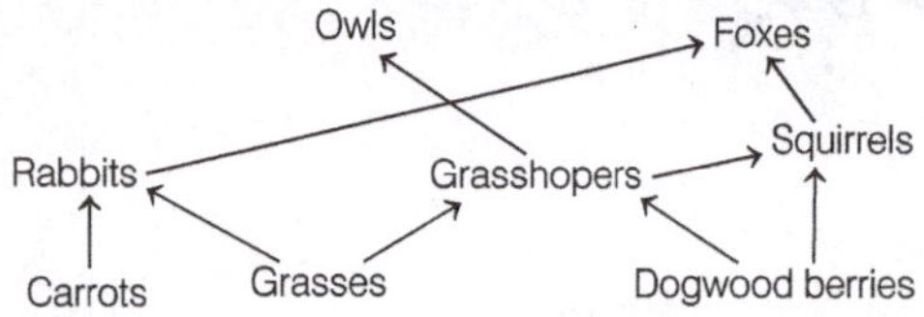

(a) Rabbits (b) Owls (c) Squirrels (d) Foxes

2 Examine the two graphs (figures A and B) which were provided by the Department of Environmental Affairs in South Africa. The graphs show the average temperature increase during the period 1975 to 2010 and related species decline in South Africa. **[IJSO 2011, Durban South Africa]**

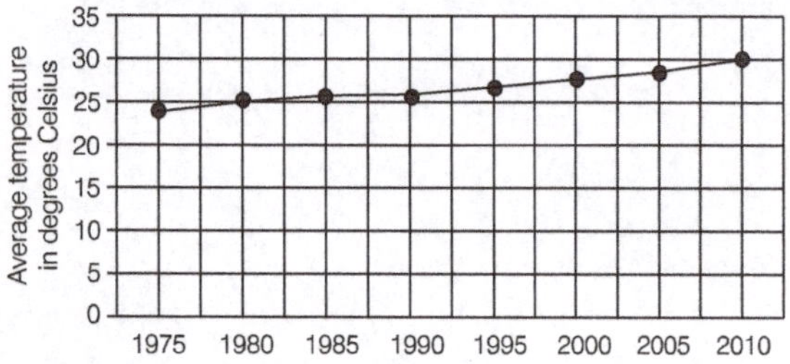

Fig. A

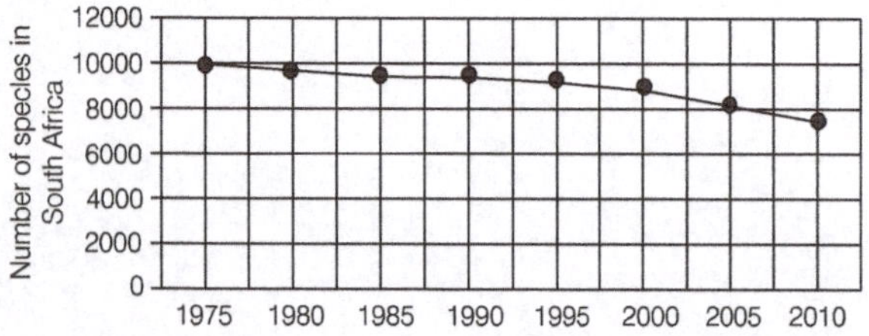

Fig. B

It can be deduced that during the period 1995 to 2005.

(a) an average temperature increase of 10°C resulted in extinction of 2000 species
(b) an average temperature increase of 2°C resulted in extinction of 3000 species
(c) an average temperature increase of 5°C resulted in extinction of 2000 species
(d) an average temperature increase of 2°C resulted in extinction of 1000 species

3 Nuisance growth of aquatic plants and bloom-forming algae in natural water is generally due to high concentrations of

(a) carbon (b) sulphur
(c) calcium (d) phosphorus

4 The diagram shows a tropical forest before and after clearing for agricultural use.

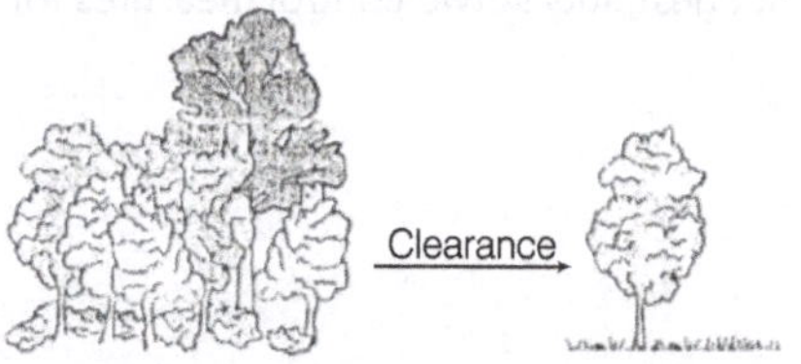

Which of the effects of deforestation causes soil erosion?

(a) Less photosynthesis occurs
(b) Rainfall is reduced
(c) Roots of trees die
(d) Salt concentration in the soil decreases

5 The concentration of Polychlorinated Biphenyls (PCB, an organochloride contaminant) in many fish populations has been declining, since a ban on their production was instituted in the late 1970s. PCBs remain a potential problem, however, because they are lipophilic and are known to biomagnify. Based on this knowledge, what type of fish is expected to be safest for human consumption?

(a) Piscivorous fish species (i.e. which eat other fish).
(b) Benthivorous fish species (i.e. which eat invertebrates on the lake bottom)
(c) Small (young) fish
(d) Fish species with high fat content

Answers

1. (d) **2.** (d) **3.** (d) **4.** (c) **5.** (c)

These questions may or may not be asked in the examination, have been given just for additional practice required for olympiads, scholarship exams etc. For detailed explanations refer Page No. 247.

Explanations to Olympiad Section

Chapter 1. Cell Cycle, Cell Division and Structure of Chromosome

1. (c) The metaphase stage in a cell cycle shows highly condensed chromosomes. Allele is a gene that is found at a particular site on a homologous chromosome. Nucleosome is a basic unit of chromosome that consists of histone octamer and 200 base pair DNA. Bacteria have circular DNA that lack histone protein.

2. (c) Given that there are 110 Guanine and 110 Thymine bases in a double-stranded DNA.

Number of Thymine = Number of Adenine (As T pairs with A *via* hydrogen bonds)

110 (T) = 110 (A)

Similarly,

Number of Guanine = Number of Cytosine (As G pairs with C)

110 (G) = 110 (C)

∴ Total number of bases will be 440.

3. (b) A spindle poison is a poison that interrupts the cell division by affecting the spindles. Colchicine inhibits the microtubule organisation and orientation of spindle fibres that is essential for mitosis. Since, there is no formation of spindle fibres, there will be no arrangement of chromosomes.

Chapter 2. Genetics

1. (b) The cross made will be as shown

Seeds (Round) RR × Seeds (Wrinkled) rr

↓

Rr — Self-pollination F_1 progeny-Round seeds

RR Rr Rr (300) rr (100) — F_2 progeny

A gene has two alleles R (dominant) and r (recessive). In a diploid cell, p and q represents the frequency of allele R and allele r respectively.

Frequencies of all the allele can be calculated using the expression - $p + q = 1$.

Total seeds produced = 400

No. of plants with wrinkled seeds are = 100

So, frequency of plant with wrinkled is,

$$q^2 = \frac{100}{400}$$

(here q^2 = frequency of individuals with homozygous recessive alleles (rr))

$$q = \sqrt{\frac{100}{400}} = \frac{1}{2} = 0.5$$

$$p + q = 1$$

$$p = 1 - q = 1 - 0.5 = 0.5$$

% of p = 50%

2. (d) Given in question,

Black fur (B)is dominant to brown fur (b).

Long tails (T) are dominant to short tails (t).

The cross will be as follows

Parents: Bb Tt × BBtt

Gametes: (BT) (Bt) (bT) (bt) × (Bt)

On crossing

	BT	Bt	bT	bt
Bt	BBTt Black fur + Long tail	BBtt Black fur + Short tail	BbTt Black fur + Long tail	Bbtt Black fur + Short tail

For the phenotype to be black fur, both homozygous and heterozygous conditions are considered, i.e. both BBtt and Bbtt will yield progeny with black fur and short tail.

Fraction of progeny of crosses having black fur and short tail.

$$= \frac{\text{No. of phenotypes showing black fur and short tail}}{\text{Total no. of results}}$$

$$= \frac{2}{4} = \frac{1}{2}$$

3. (c)

4. (c) Given that the woman is a carrier for both haemophilia and colour blindness, will thus have a genotype $X^{ch}X$ where c and h denote genes for both colour blindness and haemophilia respectively, on one X-chromosome. When this woman marries a man with a normal phenotype for both the traits so, their 50% of the sons will be haemophilic and colourblind and 50% will be normal. This can be shown as

Parents: $X^{ch}X$ (Genotype of woman) carrier for both traits × XY Normal male

↓

Gametes: (X^{ch}) (X) (X) (Y)

On crossing, F_1-generation will have the below genotype

♂ \ ♀	X^{ch}	X
X	$X^{ch}X$ (Carrier daughter)	XX (Normal daughter)
Y	$X^{ch}Y$ (Colourblind and haemophilic son)	XY (Normal son)

Thus, there are 50% affected sons and 50% normal.

5. (a) A pure dwarf variety of *Pisum sativum* (pea plant) is denoted by tt.

When this variety is treated with gibberellic acid, it becomes tall. Progeny obtained on crossing it with a pure tall plant (TT) will give 100% tall plants as F_1 progeny as shown

TT (Pure tall)	×	tt (Pure dwarf + GA_3 treated)	Parents
	↓		
	Tt (Heterozygous dominant, tall (All plants))		F_1-generation

This result is obtained because GA_3 applied to the dwarf variety only increases the length of the plant and does not cause any changes in the genetic make up of the individual.

6. (d)

Chapter 3. Absorption by Roots

1. (a) When a cell is placed in a hypotonic solution, it generally ends up gaining water from the outside environment leading to stiffening and regaining shape or bursting as seen in solutions *A* and *C*.

But when a cell is placed in hypertonic solution, the cell shrinks as the concentration of solute outside the cell is higher as compared to that inside it. Thus, leading to exosmosis as seen in solutions *B* and *D*.

Thus, option (a) is correct.

2. (b) When a cell is turgid, its wall is stretched under pressure from inside. This pressure of the cell contents on the cell wall is called turgor pressure and is balanced out by the pressure exerted by the cell wall on the cell contents, i.e. wall pressure. This counter balancing of both pressures lead the cell to a balanced state with no net movement of water to and from the cell.

3. (b) Diffusion involves free movement of molecules of a substance from a region of their high concentration to that of their low concentration when they are in direct contact.

4. (d)

Chapter 4. Transpiration in Plants

1. (a) A–3, B–4, C–1, D–2

Osmosis is the movement of solvent molecules (water molecules) from a region of higher concentration to that of lower concentration across a semipermeable membrane.

Guttation is the process by which the sap escapes. In other words, it is the exudation of drops of xylem sap on the tips or margins of leaves of certain vascular plants.

Apoplast is the space outside the plasma membrane within which materials diffuse freely.

Symplast is the space within the plasma membrane in which water and low molecular weight solute can diffuse freely.

2. (b) It is because of the positive pressure generated in roots due to transpiration that maintains water continuity and water is pulled up the column.

3. (a) Guttation is the loss of water from the tips of leaves mainly as vapour. Roots develop positive pressure due to the active absorption of nutrients from soil as a result of which water is pushed out of the xylem of roots in the leaves and thus, lead to guttation.

4. (d) As stated, cobalt chloride paper changes colour from blue to pink when it comes in contact with moisture. So, the observation given for plant V is correct because

In case V, the paper attached with leaves coated with vaseline will not turn pink however paper in stem area will show colour change. Rest observations can be corrected as

In case I, the cobalt chloride paper will show change in colour due to lenticular transpiration in the stem region. Since, the leaves have been coated with vaseline jelly; thus, no transpiration will occur.

Similarly, in case II, the paper at the stem area will not show any change in colour since it is coated but leaf area will turn pink as stomatal transpiration occurs. In case III, since, no area of the plant is coated, paper in both stem and leaf region will turn pink. Paper attached to a herbaceous plant with stem coated with vaseline as in case IV, will not turn pink (due to absence of lenticular transpiration). However, paper in leaf area (uncoated) will show colour change from blue to pink.

In case VI, both stem and leaves of herbaceous plant will change colour from blue to pink.

Chapter 5. Photosynthesis

1. (d) During the light hours, algae carryout photosynthesis and release oxygen.

2. (d) Statements II and IV are correct.

Maize is a C_4 plant that can fix CO_2 twice in the process of photosynthesis by PEPcarboxylase and the enzyme RuBisCO. They can fix CO_2 at very low concentrations due to the enzyme PEP carboxylase.

3. (c) Intermembranous proteins allow ATP and ADP to pass through them freely. The ATP synthase molecule requires ADP and Pi in order to produce ATP. Thus, these ADP molecules are made available to the ATP synthase by random movements.

4. (d) A plant given homochromatic light will show maximum rate of photosynthesis in red (*B*) light. Higher the rate of photosynthesis, more will be the O_2 bubbles evolved. Similarly, blue (*C*) light shows a comparatively lower rate of photosynthesis.

Least rate is shown in the presence of green (*D*) light as green light is poorly absorbed by chlorophyll.

5. (b) Cacti close their stomata during the day as an adaptive strategy to prevent water loss. They take up CO_2 during the night through the stomata and store it in their photosynthesising cells as an intermediate. When again the sunlight is available, they photosynthesise using the stored CO_2.

Chapter 6. Chemical Coordination in Plants

1. (a) Auxin moves to the darker side of the plant, causing the cells there to grow larger than the cells on the lighter side of the plant. This produces bending of the plant stem tip in the direction of the light.

2. (d) The observations in I and IV are correct as

In I, both the light source have same intensity thus the plant will grow toward them. Similarly in IV, the light intensity is more in right thus the plant will bend towards right side.

3. (d)
4. (d) The experiment proved that some photosensitive substance responds to light near the shoot apex/coleoptile and the growth response is generated few millimetres below the perceiving area. This happens due to auxin accumulation in a direction opposite to the illuminated area. Elongation of cells in auxin region results in the growth of coleoptile towards light.

   So, the correct option is (d), the light signal is perceived of the tip of coleoptile, but the growth response occurs a few millimetres below the tip.

Chapter 7. Circulatory System

1. (c) As per the given data, the blood of Landsteiner is agglutinated with almost all of his colleagues except Dr. St., whose blood is similar to that of Landsteiner only. It means Landsteiner's blood, serum contains abtibodies against both the antigens A and B. Such blood group is represented as 'O'.
2. (d) In the given situation, Alka will continue to bleed for sometime because while sucking blood, leeches release an anticoagulant called heparin. It prevents blood clotting so that blood keeps on flowing.

   Also, they release an anesthetic at the attachment site of the host to prevent the host from recognising the attack.

   Thus, Alka would not feel pain after leech detaches from her leg.
3. (a) Since the cross-sectional area of the arteriole is reduced, the velocity of the blood flowing through it would be higher than the surrounding area. Blood pressure rises when the arteries are blocked and the blood can no longer flow freely. Increased blood pressure occurs in response to heart effort to supply enough oxygen and nutrients to body tissues.

Chapter 8. Excretory System

1. (a) In comparison to type A and type B nephrons, the urine produced by a type B nephron is likely to be more concentrated because in the nephron of type B, the loop of Henle is longer and is extended deeper into the renal medulla. The longer the loop and the deeper it extends into the renal medulla, the greater the concentrating power of the nephron. This type of nephron is observed in desert dwellers such as the kangaroo rat which produce the most hypertonic urine.
2. (b) Difffusion of water through skin (do not mix up with sweating) is not influenced by body activity and must be constant. Strenuous activity will result in extra air inhalation (breathing), causing extra water loss by lung ventilation. This must be process I. Meanwhile this extra water loss will result in reduction of urine production (process III).
3. (b)

Chapter 9. Nervous System and Sense Organs

1. (a) As chicken will develop eyes according to red light (highest wavelength value) hence when goggles are removed other light will be focused before the retina. Myopia, also known as near sightedness and short sightedness, is an eye disorder where light focuses in front of instead of, on the retina. Therefore, concave lens will be required to correct the vision of chicken.
2. (d) Fovea is the region on the retina where the image is perceived and formed in normal circumstances.
3. (a) The membrane of neurons contains $Na^+ - K^+$ pump which allows the movement of these ions which in turn excites the membrane and leads to the generation of impulse. Increased number of $Na^+$and K^+channels would increase the excitability of a patch of neuronal cell membrane.
4. (d) There are numerous sensory neurons in our lips which are more sensitive to temperature or touch as compared to other organs. Upon stimulation, these neurons get activated all at once and send signal to CNS.
5. (c) Statements I and III are correct with respect to motor neurons.
6. (a) The correct flow that represent the process is

   Light → Cornea → Aqueous humour →Pupil → Lens → Vitreous humour → Retina → Action potentials in neurons → Optic nerve → Brain
7. (d) Cornea is devoid of blood supply, i.e. an avascular structure. Therefore, the transplantation of cornea is likely to be more successful as compared to other transplantation.

Chapter 10. Endocrine System

1. (c) The given graph indicates the level of insulin. After consuming meal (as indicated by the downward arrow) any carbohydrates consumed are broken down into glucose and passed into bloodstream. This rise in glucose level is detected by the pancreas which secretes insulin to counter attack the increased level.
2. (c) Individuals with diabetes are prescribed a low glycemic index as foods with low glycemic index increase the glucose level in the body gradually, whereas foods with high glycemic index, raise the glucose level at a faster rate which proves to be harmful for the individual.
3. (c) Protease are a group of enzymes that break the long chain like molecules of proteins into shorter fragments (peptides). Since, pituitary gland produces hormones like ACTH, FSH, etc., which are made up of peptides or proteins, they get broken down due to the action of protease.
4. (c) Extra glucose (from diabetic mother) enters through the placenta into baby's blood which results in higher glucose level. This stimulates the baby's pancreas to produce more insulin to counter excess sugar from mother. Thus, the baby born to a diabetic mother sometimes show signs of hypoglycaemia for sometime just after birth.
5. (b)

Chapter 11. Reproductive System

1. (d) Corpus luteum secretes a large amount of progesterone in order to maintain endometrium lining whereas decreased LH and FSH levels indicate luteal or secretory phase.
2. (b)
3. (c) In the given graph, *A* and *B* are FSH and LH, respectively. The secretion of both LH and FSH attain peak level during ovulation.
4. (d) Although spermatozoa are said to be mature when they leave the epididymis, their activity is held in check by multiple inhibitory factors secreted by the genital duct epithelia. Therefore, when they are first expelled in the semen, they are unable to perform fertilisation of the ovum. However, on coming in contact with the fluids of the female genital tract, multiple changes occur that activate the sperm for the final processes of fertilisation. The secretions of the female genital tract remove coating substances deposited on the surface of the sperms particularly those on the acrosome. Thus, the receptor sites on the acrosome are exposed and sperm becomes active to penetrate the egg.
5. (b) Luteinizing Hormone (LH) triggers ovulation in human females. If LH is inhibited, release of ovum is further prevented.

Chapter 12. Population and Its Control

1. (b) The *Plasmodium* carrying mosquito will still survive because they are not bird predator. But the monkey of species Y are not immune to *Plasmodium*. Thus, they will fall sick and die which will result in the increase mortality of species Y.
2. (c) As reflected in given graph, no method provide 100% contraception, thus, statements in options (a), (b) and (d) are incorrect as
   Douche method is not effective in preventing pregnancy and in rhythm method, contraceptive success rate is 70-75%. The only correct statement is in option (c), i.e. 98% pregnancies can be prevented by using hormone pills.
3. (b)
4. (c)

Chapter 13. Human Evolution

1. (b) Migration refers to gene flow from one population to another. Genetic drift is the change in the frequency of an existing gene variant in a population due to random chance. The founding population of monkeys showed genetic drift and not migration since no gene flow could occur because of the absence of monkey populations in S. America. Hence option (a) is wrong. Option (b) is correct because the founding population formed by genetic drift was acted upon by natural selection over generations which led to their adaptation to the new habitat. Natural selection or adaptation will occur only after migration or genetic drift brings about an alteration in allelic/gene frequencies hence options (c) and (d) are wrong.
2. (a) Option (c) and (d) are wrong because the shark is very different from whales or humans, since it is a fish while the latter two are mammals. Option (b) is wrong because it shows that all three, i.e. sharks, humans and whales have diversifled from a common ancestor. Option (a) is correct because it shows that whales and humans share a more recent common ancestry then they do with sharks.
3. (c) According to the Darwin's concept of branching of descent, two closely related different organisms are those having a common ancestor.

Chapter 14. Pollution

1. (d) Fox would have highest concentration of DDT because it derives nutrition from more than one food chain so the pesticide reaches it through biomagnification maximally.
2. (d) As per the given graphs, gradual increase in temperature occurs every year and number of species declines with it. In the year 1995-2005, about 2°C increase in temperature lead to decrease in about 1000 species (froms 9000 to 8000 species).
3. (d)
4. (c) The roots of the plants keep the soil particles intact and prevent them from seeping away with strong wind, rain water, etc. Due to deforestation, roots of trees would not longer be available and it will result in soil erosion.
5. (c) Heavy metals and pesticides enter the food chain and get accumulated in each trophic level through biomagnification. Therefore, the organism at lower trophic level would have lesser concentration. Therefore, the small (young) fish will be safest for human consumption.

Internal Assessment of Practical Work

Plant Life

Experiment 1

Aim

To study, observe and draw the various stages of mitosis from the prepared permanent slides.

Materials Required

Permanent slides of various stages of mitosis, compound microscope, paper, pencil, etc.

Theory

Somatic growth in plants and animals takes place by the increase in the number of cells. A cell divides mitotically to form two daughter cells wherein, the number of chromosomes remains the same (i.e. unchanged) as in the mother cell. In plants, such divisions rapidly take place in meristematic tissues of root and shoot apex, where the stages of mitosis can be easily observed. Mitosis is completed in two stages

1. **Karyokinesis** (Division of nucleus)
   - Prophase — Appearance of chromosomes.
   - Metaphase — Spindle formation and arrangement of chromosomes at equator.
   - Anaphase — Movement of daughter chromosomes towards poles.
   - Telophase — Formation of daughter nuclei.
2. **Cytokinesis** Division of cytoplasm to form two daughter cells.

Procedure

(i) Place the permanent slide on the stage of a compound microscope.

(ii) Observe the slide initially under lower magnification (10× objective) to locate the dividing cells.

(iii) Now, observe it under higher magnification (40 × objective) to examine different stages of mitosis.

(iv) Observe all the slides in the same way.

Observations

Under lower magnification, rectangular cells with pink nucleus are seen scattered. Most of the cells were in interphase. Under higher magnification, different stages become distinct which can be described as follows

Interphase

(i) It is a non-dividing phase of the cell cycle between two successive cell divisions.

(ii) The cells are mostly rectangular, oval or even circular in shape.

(iii) Nuclear envelope is distinct.

(iv) The nucleus is homogeneous, situated almost at centre and looks granular.

(v) Chromatin fibres appear in the form of an interconnected network within the nucleus.

(vi) Nucleolus is also observed inside the nucleus.

Stages of Mitosis

1. Prophase

(i) Nucleus is enlarged and occupies most of the cell volume. Intact nuclear outline is seen.

(ii) Chromatin (seen as homogeneous material in the nucleus at interphase) gets condensed and appears as long thread-like structures called **chromosomes**.

(iii) Nuclear membrane starts disappearing.

(iv) Nucleoli may or may not be visible. Nucleolus gradually disappears by the end of prophase.

2. Metaphase

(i) Chromosomes become shorter or thicker and hence, become distinct and clearly visible under the compound microscope.

(ii) Nuclear membrane completely disappears.

(iii) Chromosomes orient themselves at the equator with their centromeres arranged on an equatorial line forming **metaphase plate**. The two chromatids face the opposite poles which can be seen by changing the resolution of microscope.

(iv) A **bipolar spindle** is made up of fine spindle fibres, appears in the cell in this phase.

(v) In animal cells, **astral rays** appear around the centriole pairs at opposite poles. These aid in spindle formation and orientation by accumulation of microtubules.

(vi) Series of spindle fibres attach the centromeres to the opposite poles. The points of attachment are known as **kinetochores.**

(vii) Nucleolus is not observed during metaphase.

3. Anaphase

(i) The two sister chromatids of each chromosome separate from the centromere and move towards the opposite poles.

(ii) Chromatids separate due to splitting of the centromere. Each chromatid now represents a separate chromosome having its own centromere.

(iii) The daughter chromosomes (separated chromatids) appear in V, J, L and I shapes, depending upon the position of centromere on the chromosomes.

(iv) Anaphase is designated as early, mid and late, depending on the position of moving chromosomes with respect to the opposite poles.

4. Telophase

(i) Chromosomes reach the opposite poles, lose their individuality and look like a mass of chromatin again.

(ii) Nuclear membrane reappears to form the nuclei of two future daughter cells.

(iii) Nucleolus gets reconstituted.

(iv) Two daughter nuclei formed at the two poles of a cell, are similar to the parent nucleus both quantitatively and qualitatively.

Cytokinesis

It is commonly known as division of the cytoplasm of parent cell into two daughter cells.

A furrow appears on the periphery and deepens toward the centre, which finally splits the cells into two daughter cells. Cytokinesis in plant cells is different from animal cells due to the presence of a rigid cell wall.

(i) **In plant cells** The division of cytoplasm occurs by cell plate or phragmoplast formation. The cell plate extends from the centre to the periphery and forms two daughter cells.

(ii) **In animal cells** Cytokinesis occurs by the infolding or invagination of plasma membrane.

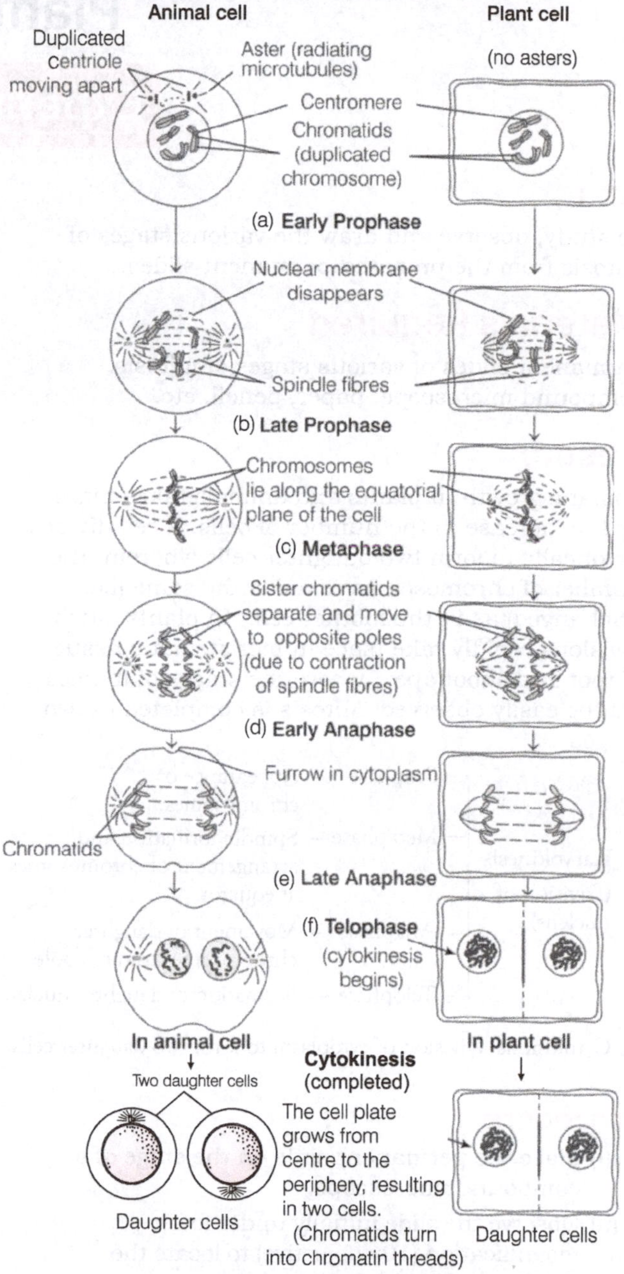

Different stages of mitosis

Precautions

(i) Observe all the slides carefully.

(ii) Handle the permanent slides with care.

(iii) First take observations under low power of objective then at higher magnification of microscope.

Viva-Voce

1. Identify and define the cell division process which helps in regeneration.

Ans. Mitotic cell division results in the formation of identical daughter cells. It helps in regeneration by forming new cells and replacing the older ones.

2. Name the chemical which inhibits cell division at metaphase stage.

Ans. Colchicine

3. At which stage of mitotic cell division are the chromosomes most distinctly visible?

Ans. Metaphase

4. Chromatids are pulled towards opposite poles at anaphase. How?

Ans. Through contraction of spindle fibres.

5. From where do the spindle fibres originate?

Ans. Spindle fibres in animal cells originate from centrioles whereas in plants, they develop from the cytoplasm.

6. If a cell has 6 chromosomes, what will be the number of chromosomes in daughter cells if it divides by mitosis and meiosis?

Ans. By mitotic division, the number of chromosomes will remain 6. By meiotic division, the number will be reduced to 3.

7. In a plant, which parts will divide by mitotic division?

Ans. Mitotic division occurs in the growing region of the plant such as meristematic tissues of root and shoot apex.

8. The spindle fibres attach to the centromere at which point?

Ans. Spindle fibres attach to the centromere by kinetochore.

9. Nucleolus and nuclear membrane reappear in which phase?

Ans. Telophase

10. Division of cytoplasm differs in animal and plant cells in what ways?

Ans. In animal cells, cytoplasm division occurs by cell furrowing while in plant cells, cytoplasmic division occurs by cell plate method.

Experiment 2(a)

Aim

To demonstrate the process of diffusion in the laboratory.

Materials Required

Beaker, water, a few tablets of potassium permanganate.

Theory

Diffusion is the process by which the molecules of a substance, i.e. solute, gas, liquid, solvent, etc., move from a region of higher concentration to a region of lower concentration.

The movement occurs when both the regions are in contact with each other.

Procedure

(i) Take a beaker and fill it up with water.

(ii) Drop a tablet of potassium permanganate in it.

(iii) Leave the setup undisturbed for an hour and observe the changes.

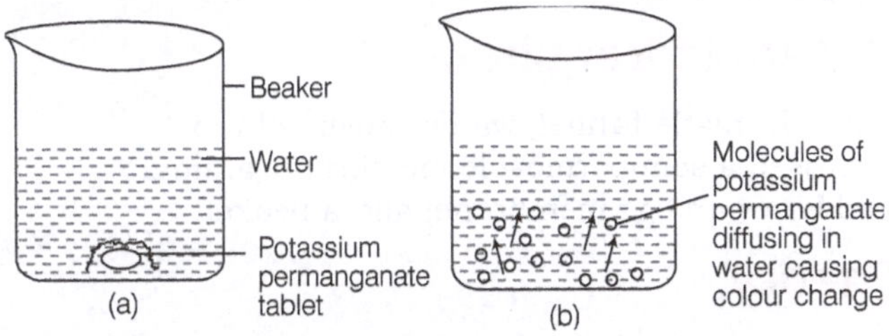

Experimental setup to demonstrate the process of diffusion

Observation

The colour of water turns pink after some time.

Conclusion

The molecules of solid potassium permanganate diffuse in water because of its lower concentration in it.

But after some time, when the equilibrium is reached, the water in the beaker turns homogeneously pink.

Precautions

(i) Clean water should be used.

(ii) Do not swallow or smell the potassium permanganate tablet.

(iii) Leave the setup undisturbed for some time.

Viva-Voce

1. Can diffusion occurs in all types of media?

Ans. Yes, diffusion can occur in any medium.

2. Give any two factors that affect the rate of diffusion.

Ans. Two factors that affect the rate of diffusion are as

(i) Concentration gradient (ii) Temperature

3. Diffusion is an active process or passive transport.

Ans. Diffusion is passive transportation of materials from its higher concentration to lower concentration area in a medium.

4. List an example of diffusion from your day to day life.

Ans. The fragrance of an incense stick placed in one corner of a room spreads all over the room. This is because the molecules of the gas diffuse in the whole room.

5. Is osmosis a type of diffusion process?

Ans. Yes, it is the special type of diffusion process in which the movement of water molecules occur from the region of higher concentration to a lower concentration through a semipermeable membrane.

6. Diffusion is a mode of transportation of water in plants. Why is there a need of water in plants?

Ans. Plants require water to carryout various processes of photosynthesis. Water also helps in the transport of various other materials throughout the plant.

7. Diffusion is considered as a very important phenomenon in plants. Comment.

Ans. Apart from transport of gases, diffusion is the only means of transport of gases in plants. Thus, it is considered as a very important phenomenon in plants.

Experiment 2(b)

Aim

To demonstrate osmosis by an experimental setup in laboratory.

Materials Required

A stand, thistle funnel, water, sugar solution (sucrose), a semipermeable membrane (animal bladder or an egg membrane) and a beaker.

Theory

Osmosis can be defined as the net movement of water molecules or solvent molecules through a differentially permeable or semipermeable membrane from the region of low solute concentration to the region of high solute concentration till a state of equilibrium is reached. Osmosis depends on the **permeability** of the separating membrane. Permeability is the ability of a membrane to allow the passage of gases, liquids and liquid dissolved substances through it.

The membrane that allows passage of all types of substances through it is called **permeable membrane**, while the membrane that allows passage of only certain molecules or ions through it is called **semipermeable membrane.**

Types of Osmosis

Osmosis is of two types

(i) **Endosmosis** When the cell is placed in a hypotonic solution (i.e. osmotic potential is lower than cell sap), the solvent or water moves inside the cell. It is called endosmosis.
During endosmosis, the cells swell up due to the entry of water and become **turgid.**

(ii) **Exosmosis** When the cell is placed in a hypertonic solution (i.e. osmotic potential is higher than cell sap), the outward flow of water or solvent takes place. It is called exosmosis. During exosmosis, the cells tend to shrink and become **flaccid.**

Procedure

(i) Take a thistle funnel and tie its mouth with a semipermeable membrane.

(ii) Fix the thistle funnel to a stand in the inverted form.

(iii) Take a beaker filled with water and keep it at the base of the stand.

(iv) Insert the thistle funnel into the beaker.

(v) Pour sugar solution into the stem of inverted thistle funnel.

(vi) Mark the initial level of sugar solution and leave the apparatus undisturbed for a few hours.

(vii) After few hours, mark the final level of sugar solution.

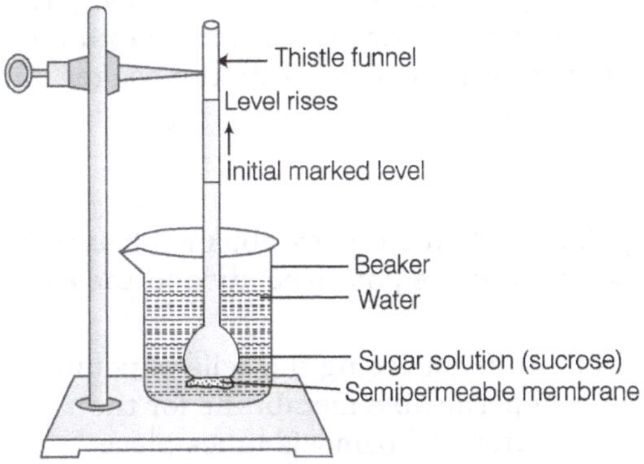

Experimental setup to demonstrate process of osmosis

Observation

The level of the sucrose solution will rise in the funnel stem.

Conclusion

The water moves into the stem of thistle funnel through the semipermeable membrane. It will continue to move untill an equilibrium state is achieved.

Precautions

(i) The semipermeable membrane used in experimental setup should be intact.

(ii) Note the initial level of sugar solution carefully.

Viva-Voce

1. Define osmosis.

Ans. It is the movement of water molecules from their higher concentration to lower concentration through a semipermeable membrane.

2. How is osmosis different from diffusion?

Ans. Osmosis involves movement of water across a semipermeable membrane. It occurs only in liquid medium. In diffusion, particles moves from region of higher concentration to the region of lower concentration. It does not require water for the movement of particles.

3. Osmosis is a special kind of diffusion, in which water diffuses across the cell membrane. List the factors on which the rate and direction of osmosis depend upon.

Ans. (i) Pressure (ii) Concentration gradient

4. Enumerate the importance of osmosis in plants.

Ans. Importance of osmosis in plants are as

(i) It helps in maintaining turigidity of the cells.

(ii) It affects absorption of water by the roots.

5. What is meant by permeability?

Ans. Permeability is the ability of a membrane to allow the passage of gases, liquids and liquid dissolved substances through it.

6. Give difference between hypotonic and hypertonic solutions.

Ans. The solution whose osmotic potential is lower than that of the cell sap is called **hypotonic solution,** while the solution whose osmotic potential is higher than that of the cell sap is called **hypertonic solution**.

7. What do you mean by osmotic pressure?

Ans. The pressure which has to be applied to prevent the flow of pure water into concentrated solution under ideal osmotic condition is called osmotic pressure.

8. Define the following terms

(i) Exosmosis (ii) Endosmosis

Ans. (i) **Exosmosis** The outward movement of water from the cell when kept in a hypertonic solution is called exosmosis.

(ii) **Endosmosis** The inward movement of water inside the cell when kept in a hypotonic solution is called endosmosis.

Experiment 2(c)

Aim

To study the process of osmosis by potato osmoscope or osmometer.

Materials Required

A fresh big potato, peeler or scooper, 10-20% sugar solution (or conc. salt solution), petridish, blade, beaker, water and pins or needles marked with ink (waterproof).

Theory

The living cells contain an osmotically active cell sap, which is surrounded by semipermeable membrane called **tonoplast** over the vacuole and plasma membrane over the protoplast.

Thus, living cells show osmosis when placed in water or solutions having concentration lower than cell sap.

Reverse osmosis is the expulsion of pure water from solution through a semipermeable membrane under the influence of external pressure, higher than the osmotic pressure of solution.

Procedure

(i) Cut the potato into two equal halves with blade. Peel off the outer skin of potato and shape the two halves into squares to give it a flat and even base.

(ii) Make a square or circular-shaped cavity in the centre of the potato by scooping the soft parenchyma with the help of a peeler or scooper. The cavity prepared by scooping should have minimum thickness at the bottom.

(iii) Place the potato on its flat cut end in a petridish, half-filled with water in such a way that 2/3rd of the potato is dipped in water.

(iv) Fill half the cavity of the potato with 10-20% sugar solution and mark the level of sugar solution inside the cavity with the help of a pin or dissecting needle. This prepared apparatus works as an osmoscope or osmometer.

(v) Leave this osmometer undisturbed for about 2-3 hours.

(vi) Observe the level of sugar solution.

(vii) Repeat this experiment using water in potato cavity and sugar solution in petridish.

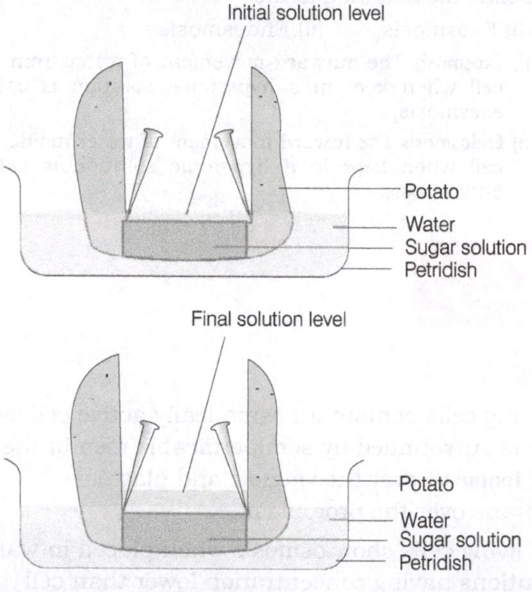

Demonstration of osmosis by potato osmometer or osmoscope

Observation

The level of sugar solution in the potato cavity (which acted as an osmometer or osmoscope) rises after some time due to the entry of water from the beaker into as a result of endosmosis.

Conclusion

A water potential gradient is established between sucrose solution in the potato cavity and the external water.

The cell membrane enclosing the cells of potato acts as a selectively permeable membrane for the movement of water and osmosis takes place successfully.

Precautions

(i) The potato cavity should be deep enough to keep only a thin layer of tissues at the base.

(ii) The potato block should be flat at the lower end to keep it stable in the petridish.

(iii) Sugar solution should be highly concentrated, as compared to the cell sap of potato cells for osmosis to take place.

Viva-Voce

1. Why do we use potato for making an osmometer or osmoscope?

Ans. Potato is an easily available living material and can be handled easily, therefore it is used as an osmometer or osmoscope.

2. Why is potato peeled off while making it as an osmometer?

Ans. The skin of potato is thick and makes it impermeable for water to move across it. Therefore, it must be peeled off before making it as an osmometer.

3. What will happen if we use boiled potato for making an osmometer?

Ans. If we use boiled potato for making an osmometer, the living cells of potato will be killed by boiling and osmosis cannot be demonstrated.

4. Can we use salt solution instead of sugar solution to demonstrate the process of osmosis?

Ans. Yes, salt solution can also be used instead of sugar solution but it must be concentrated.

5. Why only living cells can act as an osmometer?

Ans. Since, living cells contain an osmotically active cell sap and are surrounded by semipermeable membrane, they can be used to act as osmometer. Dead cells do not have active cell sap.

Experiment 2(d)

Aim
To demonstrate that roots of a plant absorb water.

Materials Required
Two test tubes, water, oil, a young small herbaceous plant with intact roots.

Theory
Plants absorb water through their roots. The root hairs contain cell sap which has higher concentration of salts compared with the outside water.

The difference between these two media triggers osmosis and the water present outside the cell starts diffusing into the root hairs.

The upward movement of water is facilitated by the root pressure developed in xylem tissues.

Procedure
(i) Take two clean test tubes and fill them with water. Label them as A and B.

(ii) In test tube A, the young plant with intact roots is inserted carefully.

(iii) Add a few drops of oil in test tube A to prevent the loss of water by evaporation.

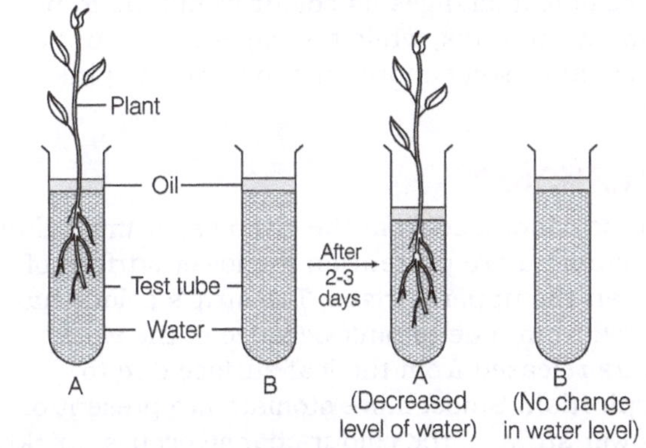

Experimental setup to demonstrate that plant roots absorb water

(iv) Prepare a similar setup in test tube B but without the plant.

(v) Mark the level of water in both the tubes.

(vi) Leave the setup undisturbed for few hours or a day.

Observation
The level of the water in test tube A declines from the marked level. In test tube B, no change is observed.

Conclusion
The decrease in the level of water in test tube A occurs because the water is being absorbed by the roots of the plant.

Precautions
(i) A healthy and fresh plant should be selected.

(ii) Mark the level of water in both the tubes for accurate observations.

Viva-Voce

1. Identify the process which causes lose of water from plants.

Ans. Transpiration removes water in the form of vapour from aerial parts of plant.

2. Which part of leaf aids the transpiration process?

Ans. Stomata

3. What is the purpose behind adding oil in the test tubes?

Ans. Oil cuts off the exchange between the surfaces and inhibits evaporation of water.

4. Identify the part of plants that absorbs water.

Ans. The root hairs present in roots absorb water from the soil.

5. Name the tissue responsible for upward movement of water.

Ans. Xylem

Experiment 3(a)

Aim
To demonstrate the process of transpiration using a bell jar.

For complete experiment refer to page no. 56.

Experiment 3(b)

Aim

To demonstrate the unequal transpiration in a dorsiventral leaf using cobalt chloride paper.

Materials Required

A potted plant, cobalt chloride ($CoCl_2$) solution, filter paper, glass slides, rubber bands, hot plate, blotting sheet, clip, vaseline and a desiccator.

Theory

Transpiration is the loss of water in the form of vapour from the aerial parts of a plant.

It mainly occurs through the minute pores on the surface of leaves called **stomata**. It occurs mostly during daytime when temperature is comparatively high and stomata are open.

About 85% of transpiration takes place through stomata and is called **stomatal transpiration**. The number of stomata present on the two surfaces of the leaves differ in most of the plants. Some amount of water is also lost through cuticles and this type of transpiration is called **cuticular transpiration**.

The rate of transpiration from the two surfaces of a leaf can be studied by comparing the loss of water vapour from the two surfaces of the leaf.

Transpiration can be easily demonstrated by cobalt chloride paper test. Cobalt chloride is blue coloured in anhydrous (dry) form but turns pink, when it comes in contact with water. This property of cobalt chloride is used to demonstrate that water is lost during transpiration.

Procedure

(i) In 100 mL of water, dissolve 5 g of cobalt chloride to prepare a 5% solution of cobalt chloride.

(ii) Take a filter paper and cut thin uniform strips and dip these strips in $CoCl_2$ solution.

(iii) Now, dry the filter paper strip on hot plate or oven but take care that strips should not get burned or charred. These anhydrous cobalt chloride coated strips will appear blue in colour.

(iv) Store these cobalt chloride coated strips in a desiccator.

(v) Select a leaf of a potted plant and blot the leaf dry from both the sides with the help of blotting sheets.

(vi) Keep one dry cobalt chloride paper strip on the upper surface of leaf and another strip of cobalt chloride paper on the lower surface of leaf.

(vii) Now secure them with the help of two slides and clips as shown below.

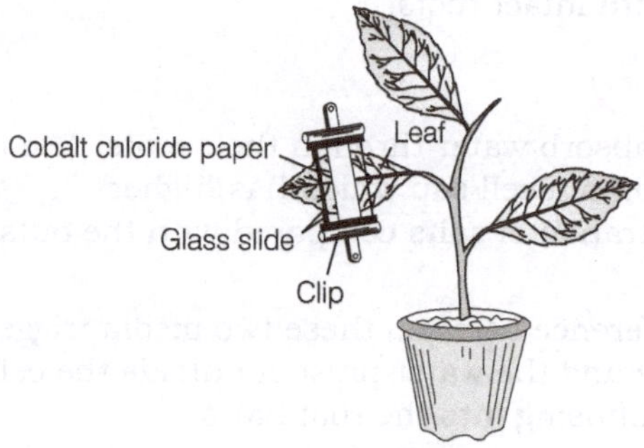

Demonstration of the rate of transpiration (loss of water) by cobalt chloride method

(viii) Apply vaseline around the slide's edges to make it airtight.

(ix) Now, place the potted plant in sunlight.

(x) Keep observing after every 2 minutes till the strips turn blue to pink.

Observation

It is observed that the strip fixed to the lower surface of leaf changes its colour from blue to pink, within few minutes, while the paper on the upper surface takes some more time to turn into pink colour.

Conclusion

It can be concluded from the given experiment that more stomata are present on the lower surface of leaf than the upper surface. The strip's colour has changed from blue to pink because of the water vapours released from the leaf surface due to transpiration. Since, more stomata are present on the lower surface, the colour change occurs quickly in the strip attached to lower surface.

Precautions

(i) The potted plant should be healthy and watered

(ii) The strips dipped in cobalt chloride should be dried completely.

(iii) Do not handle the dried strips with wet hands or place on wet surface.

(iv) Cover the strips completely with the glass slides. The clips should be fixed tightly to hold the strips.

Viva-Voce

1. What is transpiration?

Ans. The phenomenon of loss of water in the form of vapours from aerial parts of leaf.

2. State the part of leaf through which maximum transpiration occurs.

Ans. Stomata

3. From which surface of leaf, do you think that the rate of transpiration is less and why?

Ans. The rate of transpiration is reduced in the upper surface of leaf. This is so because the number of stomata is less on the upper surface of leaf as compared to the lower surface.

4. Name the factors that can affect the rate of transpiration.

Ans. Factors affecting transpiration rate are
(i) humidity (ii) light
(iii) temperature (iv) wind

5. What is the purpose of transpiration process in plants?

Ans. Transpiration helps in keeping the plant cool and in absorption of water by the roots through transpirational pull.

6. Why do we use the paper strips dipped in $CoCl_2$ solution in this experiment?

Ans. The strips dipped in $CoCl_2$ changes colour, i.e. it is blue when dry and turns pink when wet.

Experiment 3(c)

Aim

To demonstrate the uptake of water and the rate of transpiration using Ganong's potometer.

Materials Required

A twig from a plant like *Coleus*, Ganong's potometer, water, beaker, a colouring dye (eosin).

Theory

Transpiration is the loss of water from aerial parts of plants like leaves, shoot, etc. It occurs at an increasing rate during the daytime. However at night, this rate is checked by closing of stomata. The transpirational pull is a force that pulls up the absorbed water and minerals to the top of trees. This pull is strong enough to resist the gravitational force and allows narrow xylem channels to uptake the water.

Potometers are the instruments used to measure the rate of transpiration in a cut twig under laboratory conditions in a plant.

The Ganong's potometer comprises a glass tube, which is bent twice and a glass cylinder having a wide mouth. A capillary tube is inserted in a horizontal glass bar attached to a reservoir.

The broad mouthed glass cylinder is present towards the front end of the entire setup. The opening of the cylinder is attached with a single rubber cork. The newly cut twig for the experiment is placed *via* this hole in the rubber cork.

The horizontal rod has a bent end containing a nozzle mouth. This bent side is placed in a beaker that consists of coloured water.

As we move towards the front end of the rod, a vertically placed reservoir is present that is attached with the horizontal rod in which water is accumulated.

A stop cork is present at the bottom of reservoir to enable or stop the flow of water from reservoir to horizontal rod. The entire apparatus is mounted on a flat surface like the table with the help of a stand.

Procedure

(i) Select a twig from a plant and cut it out with a sharp knife.

(ii) Fix the shoot at the upper end of the graduated capillary tube of the apparatus through a rubber cork.

(iii) Fill the entire apparatus with the water. A few drop of eosin oil is added to water to make it coloured.

(iv) One end of the tube is made to dip in the beaker filled with coloured water (pink, if eosin is used).

(v) An air bubble is allowed to enter the horizontal capillary tube by lifting the bent capillary tube above the coloured water containing beaker. The air bubble has to be kept at the zero reading of the horizontal bar.

(vi) The reservoir in the apparatus helps to bring air bubble to its original position. This can be done by releasing some more water into the capillary tube by opening the stop cock.

(vii) Observe the apparatus without any disturbance.

(viii) The capillary tube is graduated and will give an idea about the volume of water lost at the end of the experimental observation.

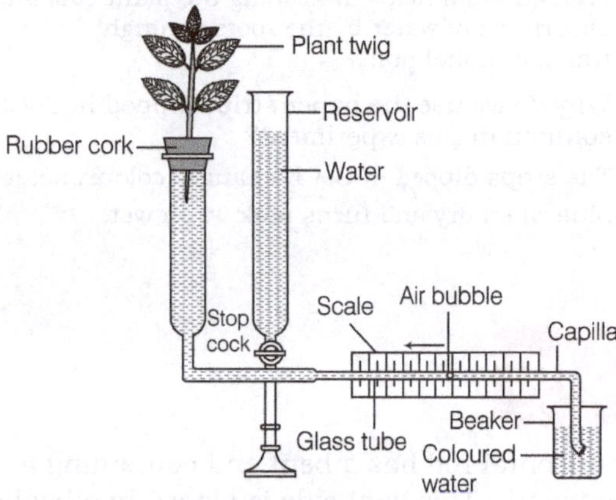

Ganong's potometer

Observation

When the process of transpiration starts in the twig, the bubble will move forward or the coloured water rises in the tube. This happens because of the suction force generated by transpiration which pulls the coloured water up from the beaker. The transpiration rate is calculated by taking the distance covered by the air bubble in a certain time. Several readings are noted by repeatedly adjusting the air bubble to zero. The average of these reading gives the transpiration rate.

Conclusion

Transpiration is occurring from the leaves of a twig which results in absorption of water by the roots. The absorbed water then moves upto the leaves *via* the stem.

Precautions

(i) The apparatus should be filled with water.

(ii) Make sure no air spaces are present.

(iii) Introduce the bubble carefully into the apparatus.

Viva-Voce

1. What is the purpose of using coloured water in this experiment setup?

Ans. The coloured water can be easily seen moving through the apparatus.

2. How is the transpiration rate checked at night?

Ans. At night, the stomatal opening closes which checks the rate of water loss.

3. Name any antitranspirants you know.

Ans. ABA and wax.

4. Desert plants have modified themselves in certain ways to check the rate of transpiration to avoid water loss. List some of these modifications.

Ans. Some of these modifications are as

(i) Thick cuticle (ii) Sunken stomata

(iii) Reduction of leaves to spines

5. What is the limitation of using Ganong's potometer?

Ans. The placing of bubble in the capillary tube is difficult, thus making apparatus less effective.

Experiment 4 (a)

Aim

To experimentally show that light is necessary for photosynthesis.

Materials Required

A healthy potted green plant, black paper strips, glass slides, alcohol, beaker, water bath, burner or spirit lamp, tripod stand, rubber band, iodine solution, petridish, paper clips.

Theory

Plants prepare their food by the process of photosynthesis. This process utilises the light, CO_2 and water along with chlorophyll pigment. Light from the Sun provides energy for this process. Light is converted into chemical energy by the photosynthetic pigments of the plant.

Procedure

(i) A healthy green plant is selected for the experiment.

(ii) The potted plant is kept in a dark place for 1-2 days. This leads to destarching of the leaves of plant.

(iii) After destarching the leaves, cover few leaves by uniform strips of black paper in the middle.

(iv) The paper strips can be attached using paper clips or by glass slides bound together with rubber bands.

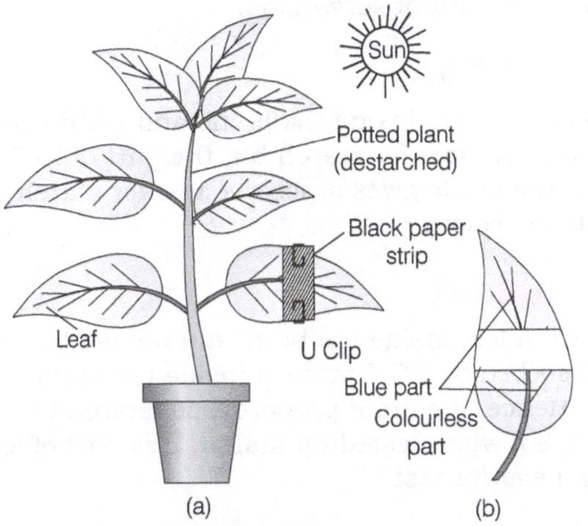

Experimental setup to show that light is necessary for photosynthesis

(v) The plant is placed in sunlight for few hours or a day.

(vi) After the stipulated time, remove the experimental leaf and remove the black paper strips.

(vii) The experimental leaf is boiled in beaker containing alcohol kept in a water bath, maintained at about 60°C.

(viii) The leaf is boiled until it becomes colourless. The leaf is taken out and washed with water. Put it in a clean petridish.

(ix) Add a few drops of iodine solution to petridish and observe the changes occurring in exposed and covered part of the leaf.

Observations

(i) The portion of the leaf kept covered with black strips of paper does not turn blue-black on the addition of iodine.

(ii) The colour of uncovered portion of leaf changes into blue-black in the presence of iodine.

Conclusion

In the covered portion of leaf, photosynthesis did not occur. Starch, the end product of photosynthetic reaction was absent in this portion.
Iodine gives blue-black colour only in the presence of starch. Since, there was no starch in the covered portion of leaf, no colour change was observed unlike in the exposed portion of leaf.

Precautions

(i) The plant should be properly destarched.

(ii) Black paper strips should be carefully clipped so that no sunlight reaches the leaf surface.

(iii) Boiling in alcohol should be done in a water bath. Alcohol is inflammable, it will catch fire if boiled directly.

(iv) Leaf should be washed after boiling in alcohol.

Viva-Voce

1. Define photosynthesis.

Ans. The process by which green plants make food using sunlight, CO_2 and water in the presence of chlorophyll pigment.

2. Identify the cellular organelle which performs photosynthesis.

Ans. Chloroplast

3. Black paper strips of paper should be carefully fixed on leaf. Why?

Ans. Black paper inhibits the light from reaching the leaf surface. It should be fixed properly on leaf to block the path of light.

4. What is the role of light energy in the photosynthesis?

Ans. Light energy is converted into chemical energy during photosynthesis.

5. Name the first product of photosynthesis.

Ans. Glucose is the first product of photosynthesis.

Experiment 4 (b)

Aim

To show that carbon dioxide is essential for photosynthesis.

Materials Required

A green plant, potassium hydroxide (KOH), glass bottle, split cork, iodine, alcohol, spirit lamp, tripod stand, test tube, a water bath, petridish.

Theory

Carbon dioxide is one of the raw materials required for photosynthesis. It is taken up by the plants from the atmosphere.

Procedure

(i) Place the healthy green plant chosen for experiment in a dark place for 24 hours to destarch it.

Note Destarching is important in all these experiments because if starch is already present in the leaves it will give positive test with iodine and experiment will not yield accurate result.

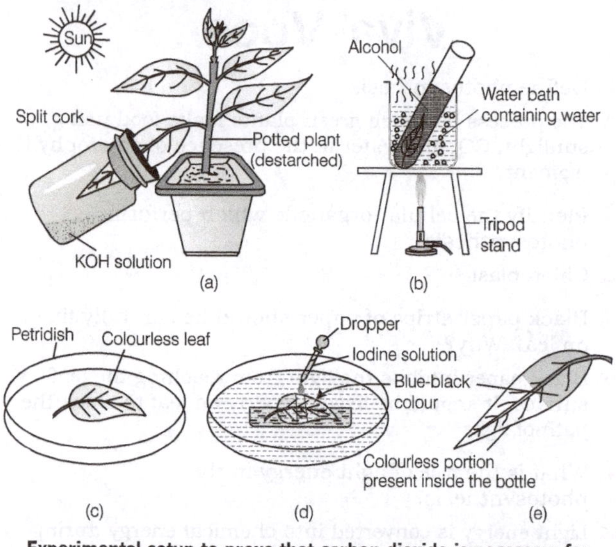

Experimental setup to prove that carbon dioxide is necessary for photosynthesis

(ii) Take a wide mouthed corked bottle and add potassium hydroxide (KOH) in it. The cork of the bottle is split in the middle.

(iii) One of the leaves is inserted about half of its length through the split cork into the bottle.

(iv) Place the whole apparatus in light for about 8 hours.

(v) Remove the leaf from the bottle after 8 hours and test it for the presence of starch.

(vi) Boil the leaf in an alcohol contained in a test tube, which is kept in a water bath. Boiled the leaf till it is completely decolourised.

(vii) Remove the leaf from alcohol solution, wash it with water and place it in a clean petridish.

(viii) Add a few drops of iodine on the leaf.

(ix) Record your observations.

Observation

Portion of the leaf inside the bottle and within cork gives negative test for starch but the part of leaf outside the bottle gives a positive test for starch (blue-black colour).

Conclusion

The part of leaf inside the bottle did not get CO_2 as it was absorbed by KOH present inside the glass bottle. Hence, it cannot prepare food (starch in plants). So, when tested for starch, this part of leaf gives a negative test.

Precautions

(i) Completely destarch the plant.

(ii) Use freshly prepared KOH solution.

(iii) The glass bottle should be airtight.

Viva-Voce

1. Plants synthesise food by photosynthesis in which form?

Ans. Starch

2. It is necessary to completely destarch a plant before the experiment. Why?

Ans. Destarching is done to make sure that the starch present in plant is completely used up.

3. What is the role of KOH in this experiment?

Ans. KOH absorbs the CO_2 present in the bottle.

4. Give any one significance of photosynthesis.

Ans. Photosynthesis indirectly supplies the food to all the heterotrophs through plants.

5. What will happen when CO_2 availability to plant is less?

Ans. The rate of photosynthesis will decline.

Experiment 4(c)

Aim

To show that chlorophyll is necessary for photosynthesis.

Materials Required

A potted plant with variegated leaves (*Coleus/ Croton*), iodine solution, alcohol, petridish, tripod stand, burner, beaker, water bath.

Theory

Chlorophyll is the green coloured pigment present in leaves. It converts the light energy of the sun to the chemical energy during photosynthesis.

Procedure

(i) Take a healthy potted plant with variegated leaves (having different colour zones, i.e. green and non-green areas).

(ii) First, destarch the leaves by keeping them in the dark room for about 2-3 days.
Then restarch them by keeping the plant in the sun.

(iii) After few hours, pluck one leaf. Draw the outline of green and non-green areas of leaf on the paper and mark the green and non-green parts.

(iv) Now, test the leaf for starch with iodine solution.

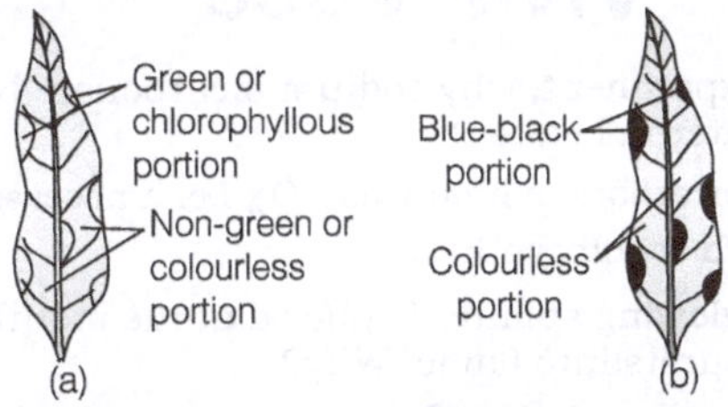

Experiment to show that chlorophyll is essential for photosynthesis: (a) Variegated leaf before experiment, (b) Variegated leaf after treatment with iodine solution

Observation

The areas of leaf which were green will turn into blue-black colour.

Conclusion

The green plants of the leaves have chlorophyll so they carryout photosynthesis and thus, make starch. Starch gives blue-black colour with iodine. Therefore, this experiment proves that photosynthesis can take place only in the presence of chlorophyll.

Precautions

(i) Destarch the plant completely.

(ii) Draw the outline of leaves carefully.

Viva-Voce

1. If we keep a potted plant in dark for a very long time, what is likely to happen?

Ans. Leaves will likely to become pale due to the decomposition of chlorophyll and plant may die later on.

2. What steps will be taken to decolourise the leaf in this experiment?

Ans. The leaf should be boiled in alcohol solution, kept in a water bath until it is colourless.

3. How is variegated leaf different from a normal leaf?

Ans. Variegated leaf has different colour zones, i.e. green and non-green zones.

4. Why is chlorophyll necessary for photosynthesis?

Ans. Chlorophyll pigment traps solar energy and converts it into chemical energy by the process of photosynthesis.

5. Write a balanced chemical equation for photosynthesis in plants.

Ans. $6CO_2 + 12H_2O \xrightarrow[\text{Chlorophyll}]{\text{Sunlight}} C_6H_{12}O_6 + 6H_2O + 6O_2$

Experiment 4 (d)

Aim

To show that oxygen is evolved during photosynthesis.

Materials Required

An aquatic plant stem/twig (e.g. *Hydrilla*), water, beaker, glass funnel, splinter, matchbox, test tubes, sodium bicarbonate.

Theory

The process of photosynthesis is used by plants to prepare their food. It requires the presence of light, CO_2 and water and releases oxygen in the process. The overall equation of this reaction is

$$\underset{\text{(Carbon dioxide)}}{6CO_2} + \underset{\text{(Water)}}{12H_2O} \xrightarrow[\text{Chlorophyll}]{\text{Sunlight}} \underset{\text{(Glucose)}}{C_6H_{12}O_6} + \underset{\text{(Water)}}{6H_2O} + \underset{\text{(Oxygen)}}{6O_2}$$

In plants, photosynthesis takes place in organelles called **chloroplast**.

Procedure

(i) Place any aquatic plant twig in a glass funnel.

(ii) Place the glass funnel in inverted position in a beaker containing water.

(iii) Ensure that the water in beaker is above the level of stem of the inverted funnel.

(iv) Add a pinch of sodium bicarbonate to the water in the beaker to produce carbon dioxide in the setup.

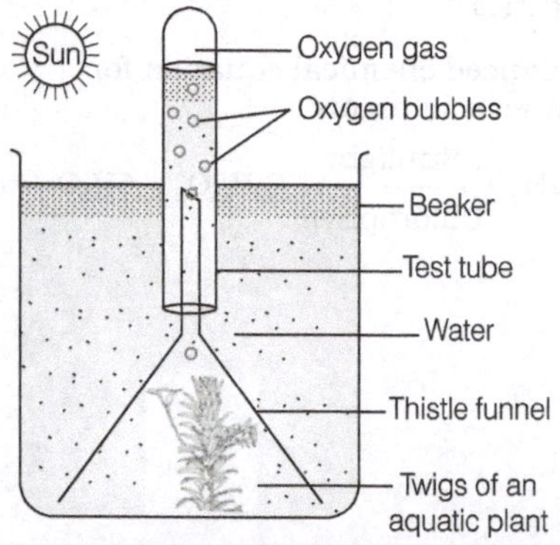

Demonstration of the liberation of oxygen in photosynthesis by an aquatic plant

(v) Now take a test tube full of water and invert it over the stem of the funnel. Allow the setup to stand in the sunlight for about few hours.

Observation

After a few hours, you will observe the presence of bubbles in the inverted test tube, which will get collected in the form of gas in the test tube.

The test tube will completely lose its water contents. A glowing splinter is introduced in the test tube, it will burst into flames. This demonstrates that oxygen (O_2) is liberated as a byproduct in photosynthesis.

Conclusion

On testing, it is confirmed that the gas is oxygen. The liberated gas is evolved due to the breakdown of water in the presence of water.

Precautions

(i) Ensure that the aquatic plant stem (e.g. *Hydrilla*) is completely submerged in water.

(ii) Remove the empty test tube carefully by placing your thumb at its mouth to prevent escape of gas.

(iii) Maintain distance while inserting the splinter into the test tube.

Viva-Voce

1. In this experiment, why sodium bicarbonate is added to the water in beaker?

Ans. Sodium bicarbonate produces CO_2, i.e. a necessary raw material for photosynthesis.

2. When a glowing splinter is placed at the mouth of test tube, it bursts into flame. Why?

Ans. The splinter bursts into flame because oxygen is present in the tube which supports burning.

3. Why is aquatic plant used in this experiment?

Ans. An aquatic plant can perform photosynthesis in water.

4. The oxygen released from photosynthetic reactions comes from splitting of water or CO_2?

Ans. The oxygen released comes from splitting up of water molecules.

Animal Life

Experiment 1(a)

Aim

To study the internal structure of human heart using chart or model.

Materials Required

A model or chart of the human heart.

Procedure

(i) Observe the model and chart given by the teacher carefully. Note down the important features.

(ii) Carefully observe the labelling and location of the parts of heart.

(iii) Draw a well-labelled diagram of heart in your notebook along with comments.

Observations

Heart is the main pumping organ found in the thoracic cavity in human beings, i.e. between the two lungs and above the diaphragm. It is made up of cardiac muscles having unique features like automatic contraction and does not get fatigued.

External Structure

It is about the size of our closed fist, i.e. 12 cm in length and 9 cm in width. It is protected by a double membranous covering known as **pericardium**. The space between the two pericardial membranes is filled with **pericardial fluid**, which protects the heart from any mechanical injury and shocks. It also helps in reducing friction.

Human heart is comprised of four main chambers, i.e. two relatively small upper chambers called **auricles** (sing. auricle) and two larger lower chambers called **ventricles** (sing ventricle). The right atrium is slightly larger than the left atrium. Both these atria are meant to receive blood from different body parts.

Internal Structure

Internally, the chambers of heart, i.e. two auricles (atria) and two ventricles are separated by different septa and valves. The chambers of heart are discussed below

1. **Auricles** (Atria) These are the upper two thin-walled and smaller chambers. They serve to receive the blood, therefore are called **receiving chambers** (right atrium and left atrium). Both the right and the left atria are separated by a thin, muscular wall known as **interatrial septum**.

   (i) **Right atrium** This right chamber deals with only **impure** (deoxygenated) blood. It receives impure blood from various parts of the body through two major veins, i.e. superior and inferior vena cava. It also receives blood from the walls of the heart itself (through a coronary sinus).

   (ii) **Left atrium** This chamber is meant to deal with only **pure** (oxygenated) blood. It receives pure blood from lungs through two **pulmonary veins** (i.e. one from the each lung).

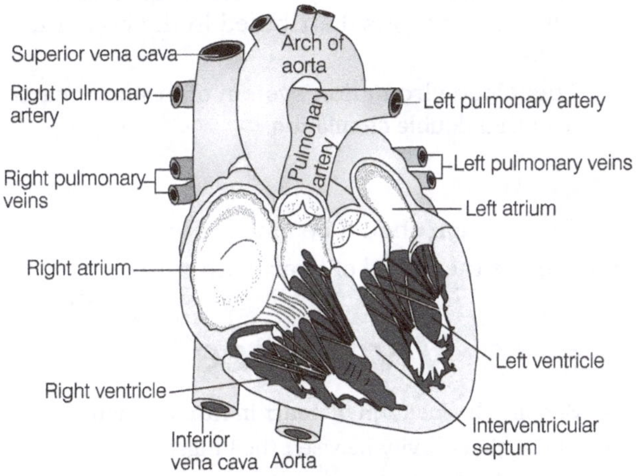

Internal structure of human heart

2. **Ventricles** These are lower two chambers of the heart that pump the blood away from the heart. These functions as **pumping chambers**. Both the right and the left ventricles are separated by the **inter-ventricular septum**. The atrium and the ventricle of the same side are also separated by another septum, a thick fibrous tissue called **Atrio-Ventricular septum** (i.e. AV septum).

   (i) **Right ventricle** It receives impure blood from right atrium and pumps blood into

pulmonary artery, which further takes this blood to lungs for purification.

(ii) **Left ventricle** It receives pure (oxygenated) blood from left atrium and pumps its pure blood to **aorta** (largest artery in the pathway), which in turn takes this blood to whole body and organs.

Functioning of the Human Heart

(i) The heart beats 72 times per minute. The beating of heart corresponds to the contraction and relaxation of the chamber of heart.

(ii) Blood circulation is the result of the rhythmic movement of the heart.

(iii) Heartbeat originates at the SA node.

(iv) A complete separation of the oxygenated and deoxygenated blood is observed in human heart.

(v) Vena cava brings the deoxygenated blood to the heart and pours it into right auricle. From here, the blood goes into the right ventricle. The blood then passes to lungs for oxygenation *via* pulmonary arteries.

(vi) The oxygenated blood is brought by pulmonary veins to left auricle. From here, it goes to left ventricle and gets distributed in the body *via* aorta.

This blood circulation system of human heart is called **double circulation**.

Precautions

(i) Observation should be made carefully.

(ii) Handle the model of heart with care.

Viva-Voce

1. Specify the location of heart in human beings.

Ans. In the chest cavity between the lungs.

2. What type of circulation system is found in humans?

Ans. Closed circulatory system. In this, the blood flows through a closed network of vessels.

3. The initiation and maintenance of the rhythmic activity of heart is function of which part of heart ?

Ans. Sino-atrial node. It is also known as the pacemaker of heart.

4. The walls of ventricles are found to be thicker than those of auricles. Why?

Ans. The ventricles pump the oxygenated blood with great pressure to long distance from the heart.

5. Why are valves present in heart and veins?

Ans. Valves are present in heart and veins to ensure that blood does not flow backward in their respective source chambers.

6. Name the protective covering of the heart.

Ans. Pericardium is the protective covering of the heart.

7. State the exact location of the tricuspid valve.

Ans. Tricuspid valve is found between the right auricle and right ventricle.

8. All veins carry deoxygenated blood. Do you agree?

Ans. No, pulmonary vein is an exception because it carries oxygenated blood from lungs to left atrium.

9. Differentiate between the bicuspid valve and tricuspid valve (function).

Ans. The difference between bicuspid valve and tricuspid valve are as follows

Bicuspid valve	Tricuspid valve
It guards the opening when blood rushes from left auricle into left ventricle.	It guards the opening when blood rushes from right atrium to right ventricle.

10. Write the functions of two upper chambers of human heart.

Ans. The functions of two upper chambers, i.e. left atrium and right atrium of human heart are given below

(i) Left atrium receives oxygenated blood from pulmonary vein.

(ii) Right atrium receives deoxygenated blood from vena cava.

11. State the correct location of pulmonary semilunar valve.

Ans. Pulmonary semilunar valve is located at the base of the pulmonary trunk.

Experiment 1(b)

Aim

To study the structure of human urinary system using chart or model.

Materials Required

A model or chart of the human urinary system.

Procedure

(i) Observe the model or chart given by the teacher carefully. Note down the salient features of the system.

(ii) Carefully observe the labelling and location of various parts.

(iii) Draw a well-labelled diagram of urinary system in your notebook along with comments about the system.

Observations

Urinary system in humans consists of a pair of kidneys, a pair of ureters, urinary bladder and urethra.

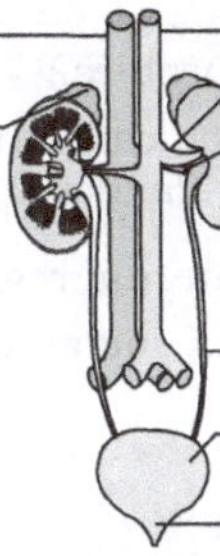

Urinary system in human

Kidneys

These are two bean-shaped structures, located on either sides of the backbone in the abdominal cavity. Kidneys are located below the diaphragm on the left and right sides and are protected by the last two ribs.

Right kidney is slightly lower than left kidney because liver takes much space of right side and pushes it down.

External Structure of Kidney

Each kidney is about 10 cm long, 6 cm wide and 3.5 cm thick. The outer surface of kidney is convex and the inner surface is concave.

At the inner concave surface, a notch-type structure called **hilum** is present, through which the supply of blood occurs, i.e. renal artery and renal vein, pass in and out of the kidneys along with ureter and nerve supply of the kidney. The kidney is bounded externally by a thin sheet of white fibrous tissue called **renal capsule**.

Internal Structure of Kidney

Internally, each kidney is made up of two main regions, i.e. **outer cortex** and **inner medulla**. The cortex is the outer darker region which is dotted in appearance. The **nephrons** are highly coiled in this region.

The medulla is composed of finely stripped substance being arranged in several conical projections called **renal** or **medullary pyramids.**

Apex of each renal pyramid projects inwards towards the pelvis.

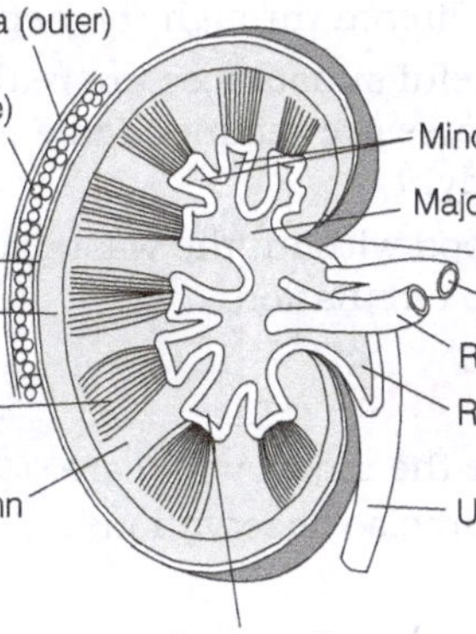

Longitudinal section of a kidney

Each kidney is composed of enormous number of microscopic tubules called **nephrons** or **renal tubules**, or **uriniferous tubules**, which are the functional units of the kidney.

Ureters

These are the paired tubular structures arising from the pelvis of each kidney. The upper half of the ureter is located in the abdomen and lower half is located in the pelvic area. The tube has thick walls comprised of a fibrous, a muscular and mucus coat, which are able to contract. The urine produced in the kidneys constantly flows through these ureters and collects into the urinary bladder. The valves present in the ureters prevent the backflow of urine during the contraction of bladder.

Urinary Bladder

It is a thin-walled and pear-shaped sac which is meant to store the urine temporarily. It is located in the lower abdominal area of body near the pelvic bones.

The urine enters the bladder *via* ureters and exits *via* urethra.

Urethra

It is a membranous tube through which urine emptied from bladder is conduced to the exterior.

The **urethral sphincters** keep the urethra closed and open it only at the time of urination.

Its main function is to excrete waste product out of the body.

Functioning of the Human Urinary System

(i) The nephrons present in kidney act as filters. The blood carrying waste reaches the kidney and is filtered through the nephrons.

(ii) The useful substances are reabsorbed while the wastes are retained to be passed out of the body.

(iii) The blood without the waste is then returned back to circulation.

Precautions

(i) Handle the model with care.

(ii) Make precise observations.

Viva-Voce

1. Where does the kidneys are located?

Ans. They are present in the abdominal cavity on either sides of the vertebral column.

2. What is the shape and weight of a kidney?

Ans. It is bean-shaped and its weighs about 120-170 g.

3. Name the components of the human urinary system.

Ans. The human urinary system consists of a pair of kidney, a pair of ureter, a urinary bladder and a urethra.

4. What is the process of urine formation called?

Ans. Uropoiesis

5. Name the structural and functional unit of kidneys.

Ans. Nephron

6. What is the excretory product of reptiles?

Ans. Uric acid

7. Name the two components of nephron that together form Malpighian body or renal corpuscle.

Ans. Glomerulus and Bowman's capsule.

8. Which blood vessel will carry the filtered blood away from the kidneys?

Ans. The renal vein.

9. Give the name of the reservoir of urine in the body.

Ans. Urinary bladder.

10. What is the role of ureters?

Ans. These are ducts which carry the urine from the kidneys towards the urinary bladder.

11. What are the two internal regions of kidney?

Ans. It has an outer cortex and an inner medulla.

Experiment 1 (c)

Aim

To study the structure of human brain using chart or model.

Materials Required

A model or chart of the human brain.

Theory

Brain along with the spinal cord constitutes the Central Nervous System (CNS). It is the integrating and commanding centre of the nervous system.

The brain is the central information processing unit in our body.

It controls many activities, few of them are

(i) The voluntary and involuntary movements.

(ii) Maintenance of body balance.

(iii) Thermoregulation, hunger and thirst.

(iv) Regulation of vision, speech, memory, intelligence, etc.

Procedure

(i) Observe the model and chart of brain carefully and note down its features.

(ii) Draw a well-labelled diagram of brain along with comments in your notebook.

Observations

Brain

The brain is the anterior most part of the central nervous system. It is the central information processing organ which acts as the 'command and control system'of all body activities. It is located in the cranium (cranial cavity) of the skull. Its weighs about 1.4 kgs. It is made up of approximately 86 billion neurons.

Protective Covering of the Brain

Inside the skull, the brain is protected by meninges. The meninges are continuous with the spinal cord and consists of three layers as follows

(i) **Duramater** Tough fibrous outermost covering.

(ii) **Arachnoid mater** Middle, very thin and delicate layer.

(iii) **Piamater** Innermost very thin, tough and highly vascular.

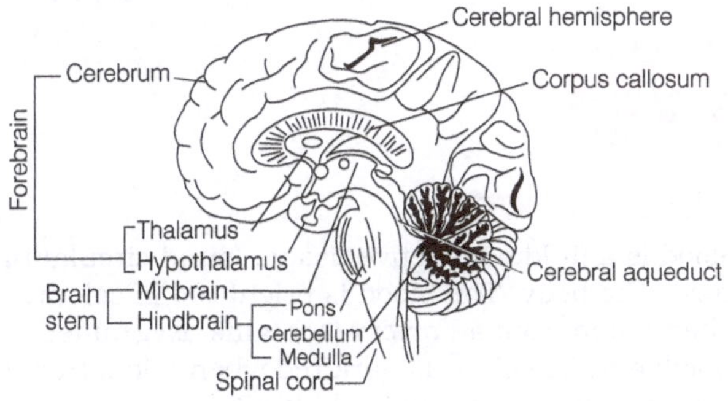

Diagram showing sagittal section of the human brain

Parts of Brain

Human brain is divisible into three main parts

(i) Forebrain

It is the largest part of the brain. It is divided into olfactory lobe, cerebrum and diencephalon. All of these are discussed below

(a) **Olfactory lobes** These are paired lobes and functionally related with sense of smell.

(b) **Cerebrum** It is the largest, most complex and most developed part of the human brain. Hence, it is considered as the **seat of intelligence**.

It is divided into two main parts (halves) known as **cerebral hemispheres**. Each cerebral hemisphere is hollow from interior and has two regions, i.e. **outer cortex** and **inner medulla**.

The outer (cortex) portion is greyish in colour containing all the cell bodies of the neuron. It is also known as **grey matter**. The large grooves formed by the layers of grey matter are called **gyri** and the small folds in it are called **sulci**.

The inner (medulla) portion is composed **white matter**, which mainly consists of axons of the neurons. The two cerebral hemispheres are interconnected by a sheet of fibres known as **corpus callosum**. It is meant to transfer information from one cerebral hemisphere to the another.

Cerebrum enables us to think, invent, plan, memorise, reason, logic, etc. It mainly controls all the voluntary actions. It also contains subconscious mind where past experiences are stored.

(c) **Diencephalon** It consists of two major parts, i.e. **thalamus** (a major coordinating centre for sensory and motor signalling) and **hypothalamus** (mainly controls body temperature, urge for eating, drinking, anger, pleasure and actions of pituitary gland).

(ii) Midbrain

It is located in between the **thalamus/hypothalamus** of forebrain and **pons** of hindbrain. It is the small tubular part (about 2cm long) of brain, which helps to relay information for vision and hearing.

The medulla oblongata, the pons and the midbrain form **brain stem**.

(iii) Hindbrain

It further consists of following three main parts

(a) **Cerebellum** It is situated at the base, under the cerebrum of forebrain. It is also known as **little brain**.

It is composed of outer cortex and inner medulla consisting of grey and white matter, respectively. It has no convolutions but has numerous furrows. It coordinates the muscular activity and maintains the balance of the body.

(b) **Pons** It is located below the cerebellum and is responsible for carrying impulses from cerebellum to cerebrum. It also helps in regulation of breathing movements.

(c) **Medulla oblongata** It is the lowermost portion of the hindbrain situated at the base of the skull. It continues behind as the spinal cord.

Its main function is to control the activities ofinternal organs like respiration, gastric secretions, beating of heart, peristaltic movements, etc.

Precautions

(i) Observe the models and charts carefully.

(ii) Handle the models with care.

Viva-Voce

1. Give the name of the central information processing organ of our body.

Ans. Brain

2. Identify the main parts of the brain.

Ans. Cerebrum, cerebellum and medulla oblongata.

3. Which is the largest and most complex part of the brain?

Ans. Cerebrum

4. Any injury occurring to the medulla most often results in death. Comment.

Ans. The medulla oblongata controls vital activities like beating of heart, respiration, etc. Thus, any injury occurring to the medulla most often result in death.

5. Name the structural and functional unit of the brain.

Ans. Neuron (nerve cell).

6. Name the part of the brain associated with memory.

Ans. Cerebrum is the part of brain associated with the memory.

7. Give the exact location and function of the meninges.

Ans. Meninges are located as the covering of brain and spinal cord. Its function is to provide protection to the brain and spinal cord.

8. What is grey matter?

Ans. It is the outer portion of the cerebrum which contains cell bodies of neuron.

9. State the exact location of corpus callosum.

Ans. It is found between the two lobes of cerebrum called cerebral hemispheres.

10. What is corpus callosum?

Ans. It is a band of fibres which joins the two cerebral hemispheres.

Experiment 2

Aim

To identify different types of blood cells under a microscope.

Materials Required

Permanent slides of blood smear, microscope, a chart showing the type of blood cells.

Theory

Blood is a fluid connective tissue comprising of plasma and other cellular elements.

The other cellular elements are blood corpuscles of different types which form about 45% of the blood.

Procedure

(i) Take the permanent slide and wipe it with a dry tissue.

(ii) Fix the slide on the stage under the low power objective lens of microscope. Make your observations.

(iii) Change the power of objective lens to higher magnification and record your observation.

(iv) Draw a well-labelled diagram in your notebook with few characteristics.

Observations

Blood is a fluid connective tissue, found circulating inside the body. The blood is bright red in colour, when taken from an artery (contains oxygenated blood) and its colour is dark red when taken from a vein (contains deoxygenated blood).

Its pH is 7.3-7.5, i.e. slightly alkaline in nature. The amount of blood present in an average adult human is 4-6 litres.

The blood corpuscles are the cellular elements of the blood constituting about 45% of the blood. These include erythrocytes **(RBCs)**, leucocytes **(WBCs)** and thrombocytes **(platelets)**.

The following types of blood cells can be observed in the blood smear.

(i) **Erythrocytes** (RBCs) They are the most abundant type of cells found in the blood. RBCs are biconcave disc-like structures. Sometimes, due to an abnormality (mutation), RBCs become fragile and sickle-shaped. This condition is called **sickle-cell anaemia.** Erythrocytes are extremely small in size (about 7 μm), due to which they move easily through the capillaries in the body. Humans have 4-6 million/mm^3 RBC in blood.

The average lifespan of a mature RBC is only 120 days, after which it gets destroyed in the spleen (graveyard of RBCs).

Function The major function of RBCs is to transport respiratory gases to the tissues.

(ii) **Leucocytes** (WBCs) These are the most active and motile constituents of blood. They differ from RBCs as they are nucleated (have nucleus) and lack the coloured pigment haemoglobin.

WBCs are irregular in shape and are generally short-lived, i.e. only 12-14 days. They comprise 5000-9000 cells/mm^3 of human blood.

Different Types of White Blood Cells (Leucocytes) after Staining

Two major categories of WBCs	Cell type	Distinguishing features	Functions
Granular	Neutrophils (62%)	Nucleus with 3-4 lobes. Granules stain with neutral dyes.	Engulf bacteria (phagocytosis)
	Eosinophils (2-3%) count increases during allergic reactions	Nucleus with 2 lobes. Granules stain dark red with eosin (acid dye).	Engulf bacteria. Secrete antitoxins, that are associated with allergy.
	Basophils (0.4%)	Nucleus large indistinctly lobed. Granules stain with basic dyes, i.e. methylene blue.	Release chemicals (such as histamine) for inflammation which dilate blood vessels.
Agranular	Lymphocytes (30%)	Smallest type of WBC. Single large nucleus.	Produce antibodies
	Monocytes (5.3%)	Large kidney-shaped nucleus. Transform into macrophages at the site of infection.	Ingest germ

Functions The major function of leucocytes is to act in defence mechanism for body. They have the ability of phagocytosis or engulfing the foreign particles, e.g. neutrophils. Some types of WBCs help in reducing inflammation caused by injury or trauma (e.g. monocytes, neutrophils). WBCs also produce antibodies that provide immunity and help in killing foreign particles, e.g. lymphocytes.

(iii) **Thrombocytes** (Blood platelets) They are minute, oval or round and nucleated structures found floating in the blood.

They are 200000-400000/mm^3 in blood. Their lifespan is about 3-5 days after which they get destroyed in the spleen along with RBCs.

Function Their main function is to help in clotting or coagulation of blood.

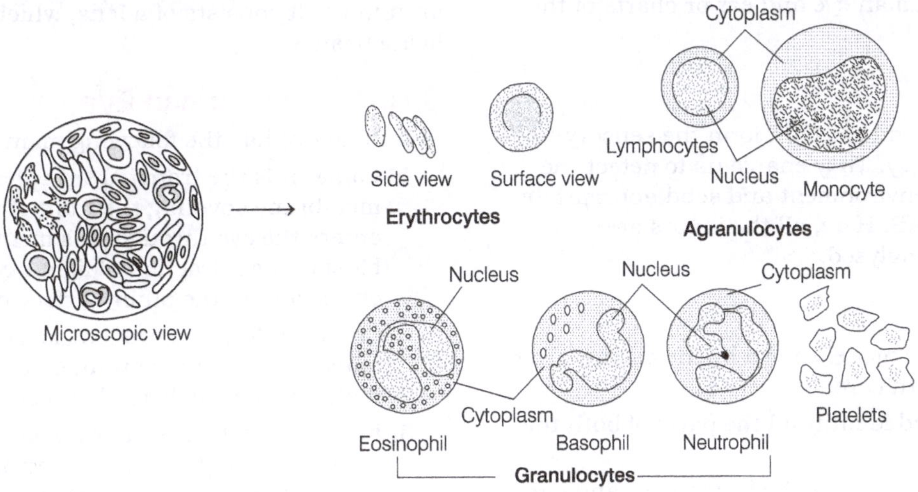

Types of blood corpuscles

Precautions

(i) Handle the slide carefully.

(ii) Wipe the surface of slide softly with dry tissue.

(iii) First, observation should be made in low power followed by high power objective.

Viva-Voce

1. Define blood.

Ans. Blood is a fluid connective tissue present in our body and is responsible for circulation.

2. Identify the components found in blood.

Ans. Plasma and formed elements (i.e. RBC, WBC and platelets).

3. What should be the normal leucocyte count in humans?

Ans. 5000-9000 mm^3 of blood.

4. Which blood cells boost the immune system of our body?

Ans. White blood cells.

5. Give any two functions of blood.

Ans. Two functions of blood are as

(i) Helps in transportation of respiratory gases.

(ii) Maintains pH, water and ionic balance of the body.

6. A reduction in platelet count is observed in an individual during blood test. What possible problem will he suffer from?

Ans. A reduction in platelet count leads to clotting disorder which will cause excessive blood loss at the time of an injury.

7. All the allergic responses in our body are attributed to which cells?

Ans. Eosinophils

8. Mention the function of RBCs in our body.

Ans. RBCs help in oxygen transport with the help of respiratory pigment, i.e. haemoglobin.

9. What will happen if the RBC count declines from the normal level?

Ans. The condition occurring due to fall in RBC number is called anaemia.

10. Do RBCs have a nucleus?

Ans. No, they do not have a nucleus.

Experiment 3

Aim

To study the structure of human eye and ear using model and charts.

Materials Required

Models of the human eye and ear or charts of the same.

Theory

The human eye and ear both form the sensory organs in our body. They enable us to detect the changes in the environment and send appropriate signals to the CNS. Here, all the inputs are processed and analysed.

Procedure

(i) Observe the model shown by the teacher from all sides with care.

(ii) Observe and identify all the parts of both the organs.

(iii) Draw the diagram of the human eye and ear with correct labelling. Take help from the charts shown.

Observations

The Human Eye

The human eye is one of the most valuable and sensitive sense organs in the human body. It enables us to see the wonderful world and colour around us. It consists of a lens, which is made up of living tissues.

Structure of Human Eye

A human eye has the following main parts

1. **Cornea** It is the transparent spherical membrane covering the front of the eye. Light enters the eye through this membrane. Most of the refraction of light rays entering the eye occurs at the outer surface of the cornea.
2. **Crystalline lens** The eye lens is a convex lens made up of a transparent, soft and flexible material like a jelly made up of proteins.
3. **Iris** It is a dark muscular diaphragm between the **cornea** and the **lens**. It controls the size of the **pupil**. It is the colour of the iris that we call colour of the eye.

4. **Pupil** It is a small hole between the **iris** through which light enters the eye. In dim light, it opens up completely due to expansion of iris muscles, but in bright light, it becomes very small due to the contraction of iris muscles.
5. **Ciliary muscles** They hold the lens in position and help in modifying the curvature of the lens.
6. **Retina** It is the light-sensitive surface of eye on which the image is formed. It contains light-sensitive cells, i.e., **rods** and **cones.** Rod cells respond to the bright light and cones respond to the dim light. Their number is around 125 million. Number of rod cells is greater than number of cone cells. These cells generate signals which are transmitted to the brain through optic nerves.

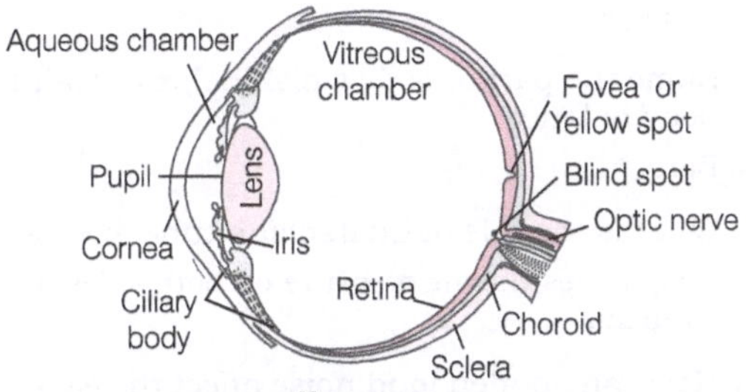

Human eye

7. **Optic nerve** It transmits visual information from the **retina** to the **brain.**
8. **Sclera** It is an opaque, fibrous, protective and an outer layer of an eye containing **collagen** and **elastic fibre**. It is also known as **white of the eye**.
9. **Blind spot** It is the point at which the optic nerve leaves the eye. It contains no rods and cones, so an image formed at this point is not sent to the brain.
10. **Aqueous humour** Behind the cornea, we have a space filled with a transparent liquid called the aqueous humour and behind this, there is a crystalline lens which helps to refract light to be focussed on retina and maintains intraocular pressure.
11. **Vitreous humour** The space between eye lens and retina is filled with another liquid called vitreous humour.

Working of the Eye

The light rays reflected from the object enter the eye through the cornea and are converged by the lens. An inverted image forms on the retina. Photoreceptor cells are activated, nerve impulses are generated and get transmitted to the cerebrum *via* optic nerve. This leads to the formation of an upright image on retina.

The Human Ear

Human ear is concerned with two functions, sensory functions such as hearing and maintenance of body balance.

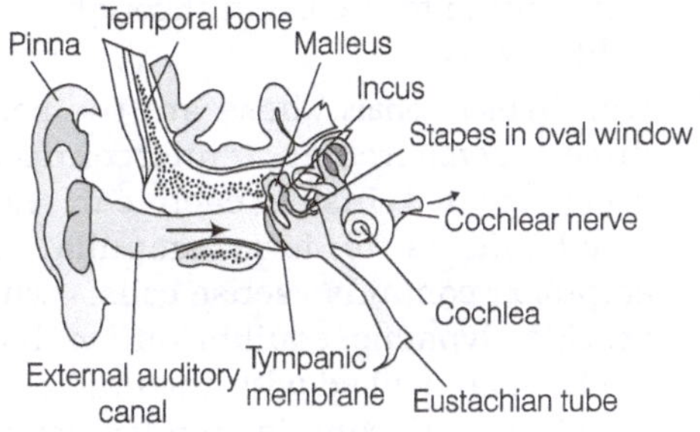

Human ear

This organ receives sound waves during hearing. The ear analyses these sound waves for examining the pitch, intensity, quality and direction.

Structure of Ear

Each ear is divided into three main divisions as follows

1. **Outer** (External) **ear** This portion of ear mainly consists of **pinna** and **auditory canal** leading to the eardrum.
2. **Middle ear** This portion of the ear contains three ossicles or bones called **malleus** (hammer), **incus** (anvil) and **stapes** (stirrup), which are attached to each other in chain-like fashion. One end of hammer is attached to the eardrum **(tympanic membrane)** and the other free end is attached to the oval window of inner ear.

   It opens into the **Eustachian tube**, which connects with the pharynx and maintains the pressure on each sides of the eardrum. An infection in throat may also lead to ear infections due to this connection.
3. **Innerear** This portion of ear consists of a **labyrinth**, i.e. fluid-filled chambers within the temporal bone of the skull. The fluid within the chambers of membranous labyrinth is called **endolymph**. The membranous labyrinth is divided into two main parts

   (i) **Cochlea** It is a coiled portion of the labyrinth and has around two and half turns. Its inner winding cavity is divided into three parallel canals separated by membranes. Out of these, the middle canal contains area, which has auditory sense cells called **organ of Corti**. An extracellular fluid called **'perilymph'** is found within the cochlea containing hair cells. The impulses from the cochlea of the ear are transmitted to the brain through **auditory nerve.**

(ii) **Semicircular canals** These are the set of three semicircular, interconnected tubes located inside each ear. Each canal widens to form ampulla. The ampulla contains sense cells, which provide dynamic equilibrium to body. Each canal is filled with the fluid called **endolymph** and contains motion sensory cells within the fluid.

Working of the Ear

Pinna (of outer ear) collects the sound waves from the surroundings. These waves pass through the ear canal (auditory canal) and fall on the eardrum (tympanum) or tympanic membrane. The **eardrum** starts vibrating back and forth rapidly.

These vibrations are amplified several times by the three bones in the middle ear and then passed to the liquid (endolymph) in the cochlea. Due to this, the liquid in the cochlea begins to vibrate and the pressure variations are turned into electrical signals by the cochlea.

These electrical signals are carried by auditory nerve to the brain and the brain interprets them as sound and we get the sensation of hearing.

Viva-Voce

1. Name the covering that maintains the shape of the eyeball.

Ans. Sclera

2. Identify the type of vision in human eye.

Ans. Binocular vision.

3. Name the light sensitive layer present in the eye.

Ans. Retina

4. List any two defects of vision.

Ans. Cataract and myopia.

5. An individual's eyesight was lost in an accident without any damage to eye. What could be the reason for loss of sight?

Ans. The region concerned with sight is cerebrum so, the reason for the loss of sight could be that the cerebrum is damaged.

6. Name the part of body which helps in maintenance of body balance.

Ans. Ears

7. What is the role of Eustachian tube in ears?

Ans. It equalises the air pressure on both sides of the eardrum.

8. How can sudden loud noise affect the ears?

Ans. Loud noise can cause damage to the eardrum causing loss of sound.

9. Identify the nerve carrying impulse from cochlea to cerebrum.

Ans. Auditory nerve

10. What is the role of waxy substance present in our ears?

Ans. The waxy substance, i.e. earwax traps dust particles and other foreign substances entering the ear.

Experiment 4

Aim

To identify and locate endocrine glands (adrenal, pancreas, thyroid, pituitary) using model or chart.

Materials Required

A model or chart of the human endocrine system.

Theory

The endocrine system is a special kind of coordination and integration system provided to all the cells for continuous cellular functioning.

Endocrine glands are ductless glands. This system employs hormones that are released directly into the blood from various glands present in our body.

Procedure

(i) Study the model and charts carefully to see the location and structure of endocrine glands.

(ii) Draw labelled diagram with specific comments on endocrine glands studied in your notebook.

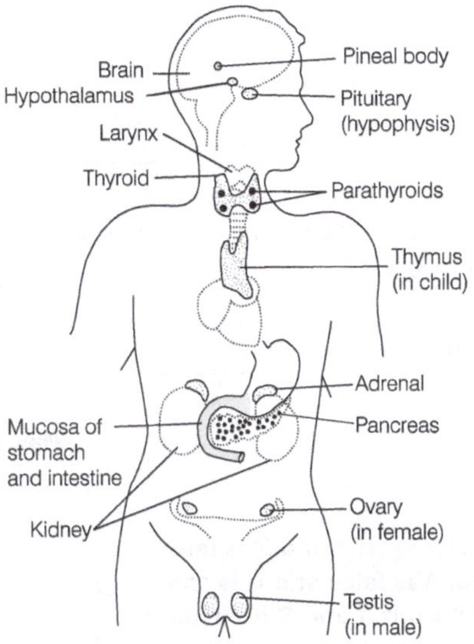

Human endocrine system

Observations

1. Pituitary Gland

(i) The smallest endocrine gland found attached to the base of the midbrain.

(ii) It is also called **master gland** as it controls the secretion from other endocrine glands in the body.

2. Adrenal Glands

(i) These are paired glands located just above the anterior part of each kidney.

(ii) Adrenal glands are conical yellowish bodies formed by two type of tissues

(a) Cortex (b) Medulla

(iii) Adrenal gland secretions are considered as emergency hormones.

3. Pancreas

(i) It is a composite gland that acts both as the exocrine and endocrine glands.

(ii) It lies just below the stomach, in the loop of duodenum.

(iii) An irregular shape elongated gland. It secretes insulin and glucagon. These hormones regulate the level of sugar in the blood.

4. Thyroid Gland

(i) It is the largest endocrine gland.

(ii) It is a bilobed butterfly-shaped gland located below the larynx surrounding its front.

(iii) It secretes thyroxine hormone which regulates the
rate of growth and metabolism in our body.

Precautions

(i) Handle the model with care.

(ii) Observe the structure of each gland carefully.

Viva-Voce

1. Define endocrine glands.

Ans. The ductless glands which pour their secretions directly into the blood.

2. What is the advantage of endocrine system over neural system?

Ans. Endocrine system provides networking to each cell for continuous cellular functioning. Nerve cells do not reach every cell of the body.

3. Pituitary gland is called as the master gland. Why?

Ans. It controls the secretion of hormones from other glands.

4. A person heard a gun shot nearby. Which gland will be secreting hormones during this condition?

Ans. The anxiety and fear of the person result in the secretion of hormones from adrenal gland.

5. What happens whenever there is under or over secretion of hormones in the body?

Ans. Certain abnormalities arise specifically associated with hyper or hyposecretion of hormone.

6. Name a composite gland present in our body.

Ans. Pancreas

7. Name the condition occurring due to hyposecretion of insulin.

Ans. Diabetes mellitus.

8. Thyroid is considered as an important hormone in our body. Why?

Ans. The hormone released by thyroid affects the growth and metabolism in a person.

9. Some people are gifted with good height while others are short. Give reason.

Ans. The growth hormone released by pituitary gland affects the growth of a person. Hyposecretion results in stunted growth while hypersecretion leads to gigantism.

SAMPLE QUESTION PAPER 1

A HIGHLY SIMULATED Sample Question Paper for ICSE Class X

Biology (Unsolved)

General Instructions

1. You will not be allowed to write during the first **15** minutes. This time is to be spent in reading the question paper.
2. The time given at the head of this paper is the time allowed for writing the answers.
3. **Section A** is compulsory. Attempt **any four** questions from **Section B**.
4. The intended marks for questions or part of questions are given in brackets [].

Time : 2 Hrs **Max. Marks : 80**

Section-A [40 Marks]

*(Attempt **all** questions from this section)*

1. Select the correct answers to the questions from the given options. (Do not copy the question. Write the correct answer only). [15]

(i) **Assertion** (A) A person having 'AB' blood group is known as a universal donor.

Reason (R) A person with AB blood group has both A and B antigens, but no antibodies in the plasma.

(a) A is true and R is false
(b) A is false and R is true
(c) Both A and R are true
(d) Both A and R are false

(ii) The average ratio of male to female individuals based on XX and XY type of sex-determination, in a human population is

(a) 3 : 1 (b) 1 : 3 (c) 1 : 4 (d) 1 : 1

(iii) During ventricular systole, the atrioventricular valves .....(*P*)..... and semilunar valves .....(*Q*)..... .

(a) *P*-Close, *Q*- Open
(b) *P*-Close, *Q*- Close
(c) *P*-Open, *Q*- Close
(d) *P*-Open, *Q*- Open

(iv) **Assertion** (A) The dark reaction of photosynthesis occurs in the thylakoids of the chloroplast.

Reason (R) The dark reaction does not require light energy but needs ATP and NADPH produced during the light reaction.

(a) A is true and R is false
(b) A is false and R is true
(c) Both A and R are true
(d) Both A and R are false

(v) Darwin proposed the theory of origin of species by

(a) hybridisation (b) mutation
(c) natural selection (d) acquired characters

(vi) Riya tried to match the stages of mitosis with their important events. She tabulated the pairs as follows.

Stages of Mitosis	Important Event
P	Chromosomes align at the cell's equatorial plane.
Q	Sister chromatids are pulled apart to opposite poles.

Identify the correct pair of joints.

(a) *P* - Metaphase, *Q* - Anaphase
(b) *P* - Prophase, *Q* - Anaphase
(c) *P* - Telophase, *Q* - Metaphase
(d) *P* - Metaphase, *Q* - Telophase

(vii) Ramesh inserted a hairpin into his right ear to remove wax. He felt a sudden sharp pain with loss of hearing. This was due to

(a) rupture of eardrum
(b) rupture of vestibule
(c) rupture of cornea
(d) rupture of pinna

(viii) The loss of turgor pressure of guard cells results in .... of stomata

(a) increasing (b) decreasing
(c) opening (d) closing

(ix) **Assertion** (A) Transpiration helps in cooling the plant.

Reason (R) As water evaporates from the surface of the leaves, it releases latent heat, reducing the temperature of the plant.

(a) A is true and R is false
(b) A is false and R is true
(c) Both A and R are true
(d) Both A and R are false

(x) Which out of these can solubilise chlorophyll?

(a) NaCl
(b) Methylated spirit and alcohol
(c) Sugar solution
(d) Iodine solution

(xi) **Assertion** (A) Auxin is responsible for apical dominance.

Reason (R) Auxin can induce fruit formation without fertilisation in fruit like apples.

(a) A is true and R is false
(b) A is false and R is true
(c) Both A and R are true
(d) Both A and R are false

(xii) Extraordinary decrease in the number of leucocytes is called

(a) leucopenia (b) leukemia
(c) myopia (d) embolism

(xiii) The passage of white blood corpuscles through unruptured wall of blood vessels is known as

(a) diapedesis (b) haemopoiesis
(c) phagocytosis (d) cyclosis

(xiv) In which part of the female reproductive system, implantation of zygote takes place.

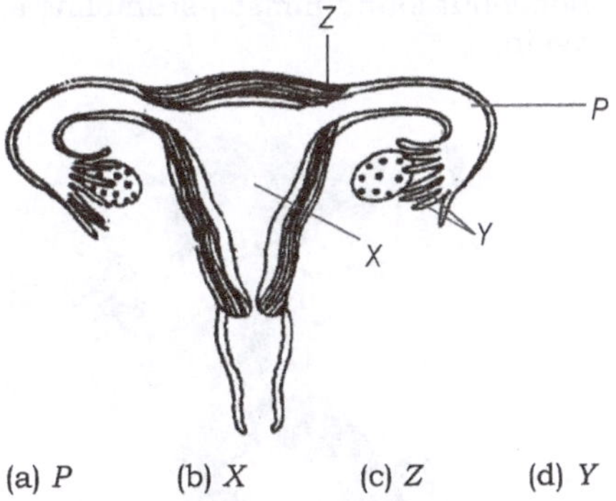

(a) *P* (b) *X* (c) *Z* (d) *Y*

(xv) A biology teacher asked her students to give two sources of air pollution.

Karan : Brick kilns and burning garbage

Arjun : Oil spills and vehicles

Sita : Sewage and chemical

Gita : Biomedical waste and radioactive rays

Who were correct?

(a) Karan and Arjun (b) Only Karan
(c) Sita and Gita (d) Arjun and Gita

2. (i) Name the following. [5]

(a) Part of the brain responsible for maintaining posture and balance of the body.
(b) Visible indication of air pollution, in which high levels of suspended particles cause the visibility to be lowered.
(c) Part of female reproductive system, in which the zygote gets implanted.
(d) The cell division, which is also known as equational division.
(e) The first ape man.

(ii) Arrange and rewrite the terms in each group in the correct order so as to be in a logical sequence beginning with the term that is underlined. [5]

(a) <u>Initial growth</u>, Increase in size, Cell division, Chromosome replication
(b) <u>Cortex</u>, Endodermis, Xylem vessels, Pericycle
(c) <u>Cuticle</u>, Palisade tissue, Upper epidermis, Spongy parenchyma
(d) <u>Injured tissue</u>, Prothrombinase, Thromboplastin, Prothrombin
(e) <u>Eyeball</u>, Retina, Sclerotic, Choroids.

(iii) Given below is a structure of nephron. Match the structures marked (*A*) to (*E*) with their correct functions. [5]

Structure of nephron	Functions
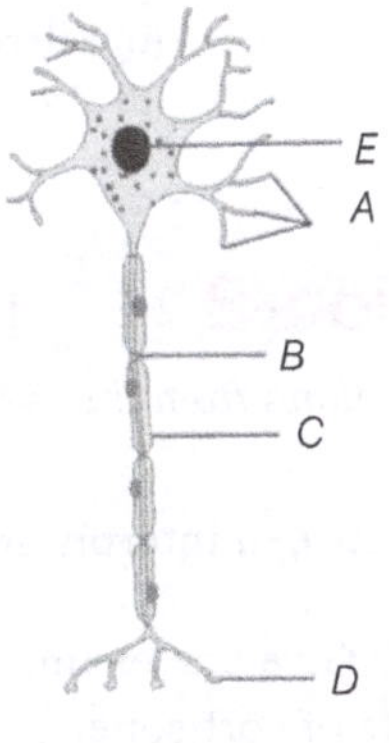	1. Provides insulation
	2. Controls the cell's activities, including growth, metabolism, and protein synthesis.
	3. Transmit signals to other neurons.
	4. Receive signals from other neurons.
	5. Transmit impulses away from the cell body.

(iv) Read the explanation given below and name the structure. [5]

(a) Name the gland located in front of the neck region, just below the larynx.
(b) The part of brain associated with memory.
(c) Thin, flattened membrane-bound sac found within the chloroplast.
(d) Name the endocrine cells found in the pancreas that secrete hormones.
(e) Name the part of the human brain concerned with the coordinates muscular activity.

(v) Given below is the structure of human sperm. Read the information below the diagram and fill in the blanks.

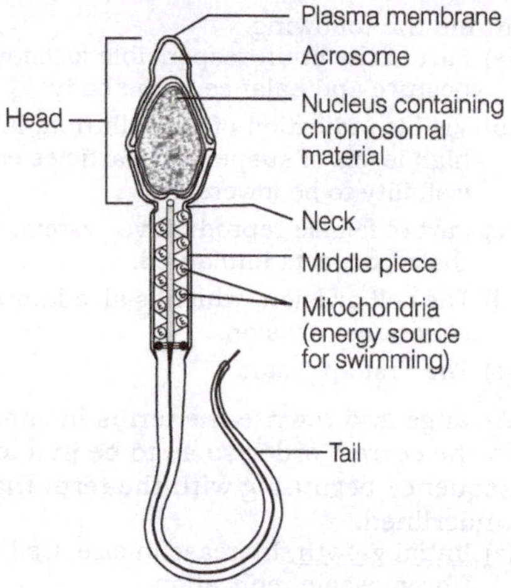

A mature sperm cell or spermatozoa is a microscopic, tadpole-shaped structure of about 2-5 mm in diameter and 60 mm long. It comprises of three main parts.

The head of sperm is composed of a large nucleus and a small cap-like structure known as .....(a)....., which secretes .....(b)..... enzymes. The neck consists of funnel-shaped basal body and a pair of .....(c)..... lying at the right angle to each other. Middle piece is cylindrical in shape and is known as ....(d).... of the sperm cell because it possesses .....(e)..... . [5]

(a) Cowper's gland (b) Stirrup
(c) Stroma (d) Uterus
(e) Ciliary body

Section-B [40 Marks]

*(Attempt **any four** questions from this section.)*

3. (i) Define gene. [1]
(ii) Give differences between interphase and M-phase. [2]
(iii) What is mutation? Give one example. [2]
(iv) List any two effects of cortisone. [2]
(v) Study the diagram given below and answer the questions that follow. [3]

(a) Name the tropic movement shown in the figure.
(b) What is stimulus for this movement?
(c) Which hormone is responsible for tropic movement?

4. (i) Expand the abbreviation HDN. [1]
(ii) Name two hormones secreted by pancreas. [2]
(iii) 'Poverty and population both affect each other'. Explain this statement by giving any two suitable reasons. [2]
(iv) What are the long terms benefits of the Swachh Bharat Abhiyan? [2]
(v) Given below is a diagram representing the structure of of an ovum surrounded by a few sperm cells. Study the diagram and answer the questions that follows. [3]

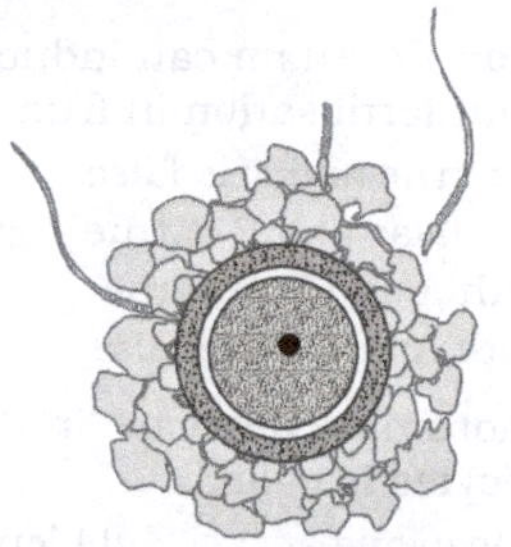

(a) Where does fertilisation normally take place?
(b) Mention the chromosome number in egg and zygote in humans.
(c) What is the main function of corona radiata?

5. (i) Define defibrinated blood. [1]
(ii) What are the significances of transpiration? [2]
(iii) State two functions of pericardial fluid. [2]
(iv) After consuming alcohol, Rohan tried to walk home but found himself stumbling again and again. [2]

(a) Which part of the brain is responsible for Rohan's movement?
(b) Discuss other functions of the part involved in Rohan's movement.

(v) Draw a neat labelled diagram to show the internal view of testis. [3]

6. (i) Define population explosion. [1]
(ii) Differentiate between growth curve and growth rate. [2]
(iii) What are anticoagulants? Also given with a suitable example. [2]
(iv) Leaf of a green plant is called a food factory. Explain. [2]
(v) Draw a neat, labelled diagram of a Malpighian capsule. [3]

7. (i) Explain hypophyseal portal system. [1]
(ii) We should switch off the engines of our automobiles, while waiting at the traffic signal. Give two reasons. [2]
(iii) Mention two functions of abscisic acid. [2]
(iv) What are the differences between guttation and bleeding? [2]
(v) Draw neat labelled diagram showing the vertical section of a leaf. [3]

8. (i) Define filial generation. [1]
(ii) Potato cubes when kept in water become turgid but when kept in sugar solution become flaccid. Give reason. [2]
(iii) Differentiate between haemoglobin and haemocyanin. [2]
(iv) Give two measures to minimise the biomedical wastes. [2]
(v) **Sorabh** visits a park where he notices that the plants growing in areas with direct sunlight appear much greener and healthier compared to those growing in shaded areas. [3]

(a) What could be the reason for the difference in growth between the plants as observed by sorabh?
(b) What improvements might Sorabh notice if the shaded plants were moved to areas with more sunlight?
(c) What other factors, besides sunlight, could affect the growth and colour of the plants in the park?

SAMPLE QUESTION PAPER 2

A HIGHLY SIMULATED Sample Question Paper for ICSE Class X

Biology (Unsolved)

General Instructions

1. You will not be allowed to write during the first **15** minutes. This time is to be spent in reading the question paper.
2. The time given at the head of this paper is the time allowed for writing the answers.
3. **Section A** is compulsory. Attempt **any four** questions from **Section B.**
4. The intended marks for questions or part of questions are given in brackets [ ].

Time : 2 Hrs **Max. Marks : 80**

Section-A [40 Marks]

*(Attempt **all** questions from this section)*

1. Select the correct answers to the questions from the given options. (Do not copy the questions. Write the correct answer only). **[15]**

(i) A biology teacher asked her students to give two examples of vestigial organs in the human body.

Rahav said: Wisdom teeth and pinna

Sunita said: Body hair and large intestine

Rohan said: Vermiform appendix and wisdom teeth

Abhay said: Pinna and ossicles

Who were correct?

(a) Abhay and Sunita
(b) Sunita and Rohan
(c) Raghav and Rohan
(d) Abhay and Raghav

(ii) The cellular elements found in highest number in blood are

(a) RBCs (b) lymphocytes
(c) eosinophils (d) basophils

(iii) During menstrual cycle, the production of LH is high during .....(*P*)..... phase and progesterone is during .....(*Q*)..... phase.

(a) *P* - Follicular; *Q* - Luteal
(b) *P* - Menstrual; *Q* - Luteal
(c) *P* - Ovulatory; *Q* - Follicular
(d) *P* - Luteal; *Q* - Ovulatory

(iv) When a haemophilic male is mated with a heterozygous haemophilic female, what proportion of offspring will be haemophilic in each sex?

(a) 50% of males will be haemophilic and 50% of females will be haemophilic
(b) 50% of males will be haemophilic and 50% of females will be carriers
(c) 100% of males will be haemophilic and 50% of females will be haemophilic
(d) 100% of males will be haemophilic and 50% of females will be carriers

(v) Transpiration is highest during which season?

(a) Summer (b) Winter
(c) Rainy (d) None of these

(vi) Production of food rises by

(a) geometrical progression
(b) arithmetic progression
(c) Both (a) and (b)
(d) None of the above

(vii) When the level fo thyroxine concentration exceeds the normal level in blood then it

(a) inhibits the secretion of TRH by anterior pituitary gland
(b) inhibits the secretion of TSH from the hypothalamus
(c) inhibits the secretion of TRH by hypothalamus
(d) stimulate the scretion of TSH from pituitary gland

(viii) Jyoti tried to match common eye defects with their respective characteristics. She tabulated the pairs as follows.

Eye defects	Characteristics
P	Eye is unable to focus horizontal and vertical lines
Q	Corrected by concave lens

Identify the correct pair of hormones.
(a) *P*- Cataract, *Q*- Hypermetropia
(b) *P*- Astigmatism, *Q*- Myopia
(c) *P*- Hypermetropia, *Q*- Presbyopia
(d) *P*- Myopia, *Q*- Astigmatism

(ix) Choose the correct function of the hormone secreted by *X*.

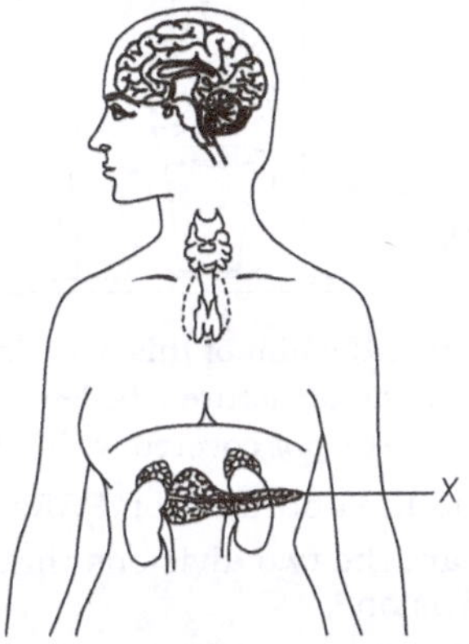

(a) Acts on melanocytes and regulate the pigmentation of skin.
(b) Stimulates glycogenolysis, which results in an increased blood glucose.
(c) Regulate the growth of mammary glands and stimulate the production of milk in them.
(d) Stimulate the reabsorption of water and electrolytes by distal tubules.

(x) **Assertion** (A) The left ventricle has thicker walls than the right ventricle.
Reason (R) The left ventricle pumps blood to the lungs, which requires greater force.
(a) A is true and R is false
(b) A is false and R is true
(c) Both A and R are true
(d) Both A and R are false

(xi) **Assertion** (A) Cytokinins cause quicker growth in conifers.
Reason (R) Cytokinins are used to obtain economically important seeds.
(a) A is true and R is false
(b) A is false and R is true
(c) Both A and R are true
(d) Both A and R are false

(xii) **Assertion** (A) Oxygen is released during the light reaction of photosynthesis.
Reason (R) Oxygen is produced when water is split during the light reaction, not during the dark reaction.
(a) A is true and R is false
(b) A is false and R is true
(c) Both A and R are true
(d) Both A and R are false

(xiii) Opening and closing of stomata based on
(a) sodium ion exchange theory
(b) potassium ion exchange theory
(c) magnesium ion exchange theory
(d) calcium ion exchange theory

(xiv) Imbibition is a phenomenon by which the living or dead plant cells absorb water by
(a) surface attraction
(b) ascent of sap
(c) root hairs
(d) All of the above

(xv) **Assertion** (A) Mitosis is responsible for growth, repair and asexual reproduction in organisms.
Reason (R) Mitosis ensures the production of genetically identical cells, maintaining the consistency of the organism's genetic material.
(a) A is true and R is false
(b) A is false and R is true
(c) Both A and R are true
(d) Both A and R are false

2. (i) Name the following. [5]
(a) A natural phenomenon that becomes harmful due to the pollution.
(b) Pouch-like structure of pigmented skin arising from the lower abdominal wall.
(c) Phase which is considered to be reversal of prophase.
(d) Spot found at the lateral side of the yellow spot.
(e) The liquid part of the blood.

(ii) Correct and rewrite the following statements by changing the biological term that is underlined for each statements. [5]
(a) Henle's loop is the U-shaped region of nephron existing in the <u>cortex region</u> of the kidney.
(b) <u>Eyes</u> are responsible for maintaining balance of the body.
(c) Sperms contain <u>diploid</u> chromosomes.
(d) The <u>first molars</u> are vestigial in humans.
(e) Astigmatism is corrected by using <u>concave</u> lenses.

(iii) Given below is the diagram, showing a section of human brain. Read the information below the diagram and fill in the blanks.

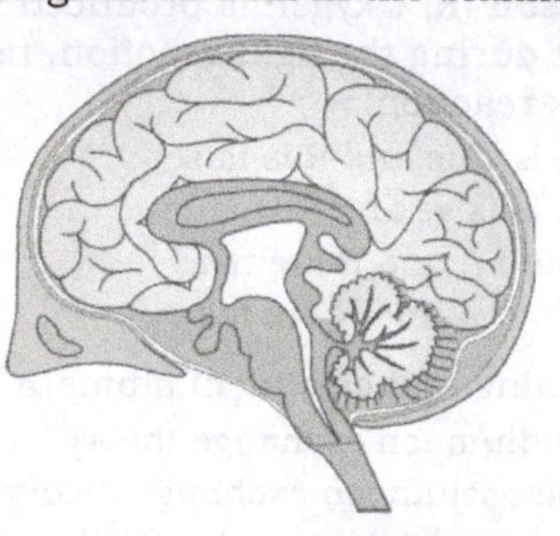

The brain is the central information processing organ of our body and acts as the 'command and control system' of all body activities. It is anterior most part of the central neural system, which is located in the cranium of the skull.

Human brain is divided into .....(a)....., ...(b)..... and hindbrain. .....(c)..... is the largest part of the brain and is divided into olfactory lobe, ...(d)..... and cerebrum. Cerebrum is considered as the seat of intelligence and is divided into two main parts known as .....(e)...... **[5]**

(iv) Given below is a structure of nephron. Match the structures marked (*A*) to (*E*) with their correct functions. **[5]**

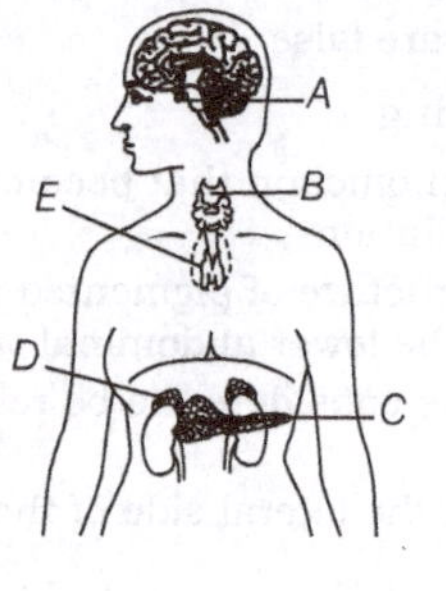

Human endocrine system	Functions
	1. Control blood glucose level.
	2. Control sugar metabolism, salt concentration, stress or strain and sexual activities.
	3. Stimulate other endocrine glands to produce their specific hormones.
	4. Regulate and maintain basal metabolic rate.
	5. Produce hormone that help in immune system function.

(v) Read the explanation given below and name the structure. **[5]**

(a) Gland found surrounding the urethra of human male.

(b) Cell formed by fusion of gametes.

(c) Duct found between the urinary bladder and urethra of human male.

(d) Ear ossicle, which is attached to the tympanum.

(e) Structure that protects the base of a nail.

Section-B [40 Marks]

(*Attempt **any four** questions from this section*)

3. (i) Define autochory. **[1]**

(ii) Give differences between cuticular transpiration and lenticular transpiration. **[2]**

(iii) What is tropism? Give one example. **[2]**

(iv) State two modern applications of genetics. **[2]**

(v) Study the diagram given below and answer the questions that follows. **[3]**

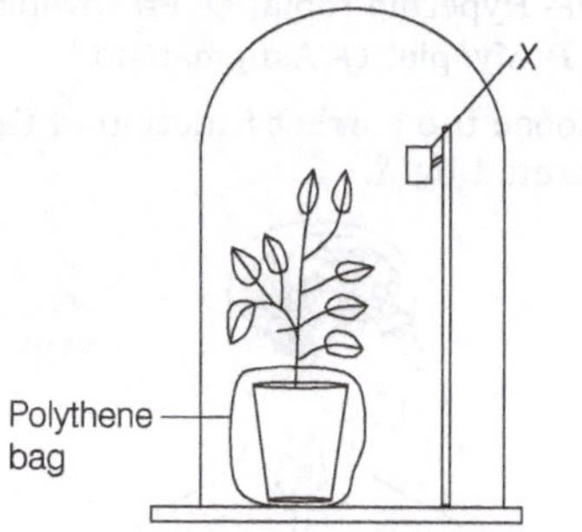

(a) What is the aim of this experiment?

(b) Name the structure labelled as *X*.

(c) Why is the pot covered with a polythene bag?

4. (i) Expand the abbreviation PGRs. **[1]**

(ii) What are the two divisions that follow during cell division? **[2]**

(iii) Rapidly growing industries favoured population rise. Explain by giving suitable reasons. **[2]**

(iv) Mention two main steps of photochemical phase of photosynthesis. **[2]**

(v) Draw a diagram of the nucleus of a cell, having chromosome number 6, as it would appear in the metaphase stage of mitosis and label the following parts. **[3]**

(a) Aster rays

(b) Achromatic spindle

(c) Chromatid

5. (i) Define osmoregulation. **[1]**

(ii) What is the significance of spleen? **[2]**

(iii) Sohan was watching the display of firework in the sky.

(a) Name the transparent part of eye that covers the coloured part.

(b) Trace the path of light rays using the following terms:

Retina, Iris, Lens, Aqueous chamber, Vitreous chamber. [2]

(iv) Which gland secretes vasopressin? What is its effect on body? [2]

(v) Draw a neat and labelled diagram of human sperm. [3]

6. (i) Define nucleosomes. [1]

(ii) Differentiate between cobalt chloride paper and goats bladder. [2]

(iii) State the function of motor neuron and draw the path of reflex arc. [2]

(iv) In a certain species of animals black fur (B) is dominant over brown fur (b). Predict a genotype and phenotype of the offspring when both parents are B or have heterozygous black fur. [2]

(v) While hiking up a steep trail, Rina began to feel lightheaded and noticed her heart pounding faster than usual. As she climbed higher, her breathing became laboured and she started to sweat heavily. Her guide, familiar with the challenges of high altitudes, advised her to take a break. After resting for a few minutes, Rina felt more energised and resumed her hike, though she still felt mildly winded. [3]

(a) Why did Rina's heart race and her breathing become shallow during the hike?

(b) How did resting help her feel better and why did she still feel slightly out of breath afterward?

(c) What is the physiological process behind Rina's condition at higher altitudes and how does the body adapt to such conditions over time?

7. (i) Explain squint. [1]

(ii) Give reason for education plays an important role in population control. [2]

(iii) Mention function of prostate gland and bulbourethral glands. [2]

(iv) What are the differences between hemizygous and heterozygous? [2]

(v) Draw neat and labelled diagram showing the oxygen diffuses into the tissue fluid around cells. [3]

8. (i) Define global warming. [1]

(ii) Light reaction is also called the photochemical phase. [2]

(iii) Differentiate between amphimixis and asexual reproduction. [2]

(iv) Write two main effects of soil pollution. [2]

(v) The diagram given below depicting a tropic movement in plants. Answer the questions that follows. [3]

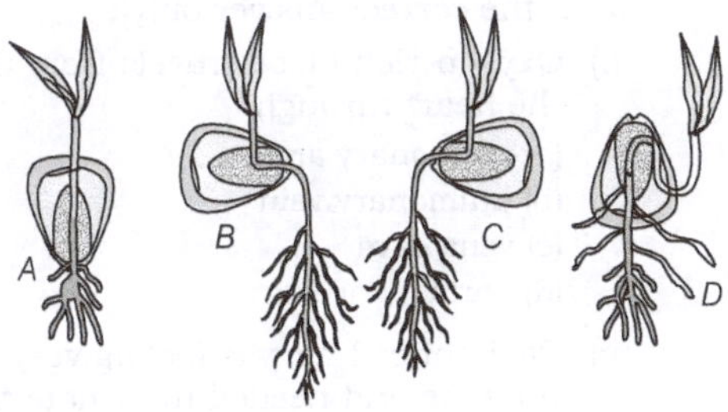

(a) Which type of tropic movement is shown in the given image?

(b) What is common in *A, B, C* and *D*?

(c) State the effect of auxins and abscisic acid on senescence.

SAMPLE QUESTION PAPER 3

A HIGHLY SIMULATED Sample Question Paper for ICSE Class X

Biology (Unsolved)

General Instructions

1. You will not be allowed to write during the first **15** minutes. This time is to be spent in reading the question paper.
2. The time given at the head of this paper is the time allowed for writing the answers.
3. **Section A** is compulsory. Attempt **any four** questions from **Section B**.
4. The intended marks for questions or part of questions are given in brackets [ ].

Time : 2 Hrs **Max. Marks : 80**

Section-A [40 Marks]

*(Attempt **all** questions from this section)*

1. Select the correct answers to the questions from the given options. (Do not copy the questions write the correct answer only). [15]

(i) Oxygen-rich blood travels from the lungs to the heart through
(a) pulmonary artery
(b) pulmonary vein
(c) vena cava
(d) aorta

(ii) Ravi noticed he was feeling very thirsty all the time and needed to urinate frequently, even at night. His doctor diagnosed him with a condition related to the Antidiuretic Hormone (ADH). Ravi's symptoms might be due to
(a) excessive release of ADH causing water retention
(b) deficiency of ADH leading to excessive urine output
(c) high ADH causing low blood pressure
(d) low ADH causing increased water reabsorption in kidneys.

(iii) **Assertion** (A) Sperm cells have a tail-like structure called a flagellum.

Reason (R) The flagellum helps the sperm to swim towards the egg for fertilisation.
(a) A is true and R is false
(b) A is false and R is true
(c) Both A and R are true
(d) Both A and R are false

(iv) The type of barrier method to control population which can be fitted deep in the vagina on the mouth of the uterus is
(a) condom
(b) spermicidal agents
(c) intrauterine devices
(d) diaphragms

(v) **Assertion** (A) A high birth rate contributes to rapid population growth.

Reason (R) A high birth rate results in a decrease in the fertility rate of a population.
(a) A is true and R is false
(b) A is false and R is true
(c) Both A and R are true
(d) Both A and R are false

(vi) During photosynthesis, plants produce ....(*P*)....... by converting ....(*Q*)....... into glucose using sunlight.
(a) *P*- glucose, *Q*- carbon dioxide
(b) *P*- oxygen, *Q*- nitrogen
(c) *P*- water, *Q*- oxygen
(d) *P*- carbon dioxide, *Q*- glucose

(vii) Priyanka tried to match the components of blood with their respective functions. She tabulated the following pairs.

Components	Their Functions
P	Produces antibodies as part of the immune response.
Q	Initiates the coagulation cascade to stop bleeding.

Choose the correct option.
(a) *P* - Erythrocytes, *Q* - Thrombocytes
(b) *P* - Leukocytes, *Q* - Platelets
(c) *P* - Plasma, *Q* - Erythrocytes
(d) *P* - Thrombocytes, *Q* - Leukocytes

(viii) Water absorption through roots can be increased by keeping the potted plants
(a) in the shade
(b) in dim light
(c) under the fan
(d) covered with a polythene bag

(ix) Which one of the following has cytoplasm but not nucleus?
(a) Xylem vessel (b) Sieve tube
(c) Tracheid (d) Companion cell

(x) **Assertion** (A) The hormone responsible for stimulating uterine contractions during childbirth is often referred to as the birth hormone.

Reason (R) This hormone also regulates blood pressure and electrolyte balance in the females.
(a) A is true and R is false
(b) A is false and R is true
(c) Both A and R are true
(d) Both A and R are false

(xi) The directional movement or orientation of a plant part in response to light is termed as
(a) chemotropism (b) phototropism
(c) thigmotaxis (d) photoperiodism

(xii) Mr. Sharma asked his students about the metaphase stage of cell division.

Riya said: During metaphase, chromosomes align at the cell's equatorial plane.

Amit said: Metaphase is the phase where DNA replication occurs.

Sneha said: In metaphase, spindle fibres attach to the centromeres of chromosomes.

Kunal said: Metaphase is the phase where the cell membrane divides.

Who gave the correct answer? Choose the correct option given below.
(a) Riya and Sneha both
(b) Amit
(c) Kunal
(d) Riya and Kunal both

(xiii) The information source for making proteins in the cell is
(a) chromosome (b) DNA
(c) enzyme (d) nucleus

(xiv) When we enter a cinema hall, we cannot see properly for a short time. This is because
(a) pupil does not open
(b) pupil does not close
(c) adjustment of the size of pupil takes sometimes
(d) None of the above

(xv) **Assertion** (A) E-waste contains hazardous substances that can harm the environment.

Reason (R) E-waste contains toxic metals like lead mercury, and cadmium, which can contaminate soil and water.
(a) A is true and R is false
(b) A is false and R is true
(c) Both A and R are true
(d) Both A and R are false

2. (i) Name the following. [5]
(a) Part of the chloroplast where dark reaction occurs.
(b) Organ in man concerned with maintaining water balance in the body.
(c) Nerve which transmits impulses from the eye to the brain.
(d) Smallest blood vessel.
(e) Chemical used to test starch.

(ii) Give the biological/technical term for the following. [5]
(a) Excess of glucose in blood.
(b) Cell division that does not involve nuclear changes.
(c) Transmission of characters from one generation to another.
(d) Genetic makeup of an individual.
(e) Carries impulses towards the brain and spinal cord.

(iii) Given below is a human excretory system. Match the structures marked *A* to *E* with their correct functions. [5]

Human Excretory System	Functions
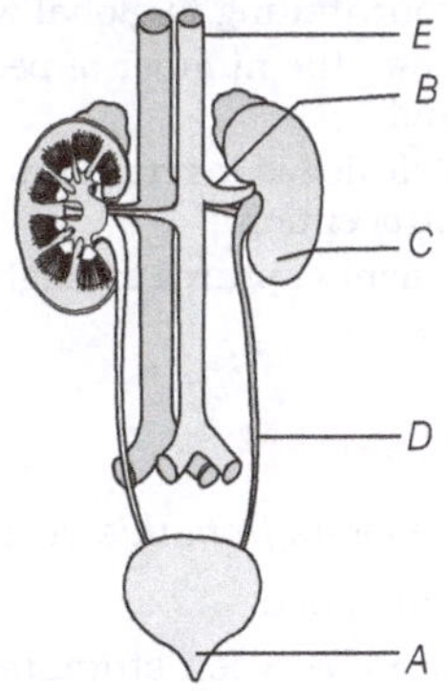	1. **Ureter:** Carries urine from the kidneys to the urinary bladder.
	2. **Dorsal Aorta:** Distributes oxygenated blood from the heart to the lower regions of the body.
	3. **Renal Artery:** Supplies oxygen-rich blood to the kidneys for filtration.
	4. **Posterior Vena Cava:** Filters blood to remove waste products and excess substances, producing urine.
	5. **Urethra:** Transports urine from the bladder to the outside of the body during urination.

(iv) Fill in the blanks.

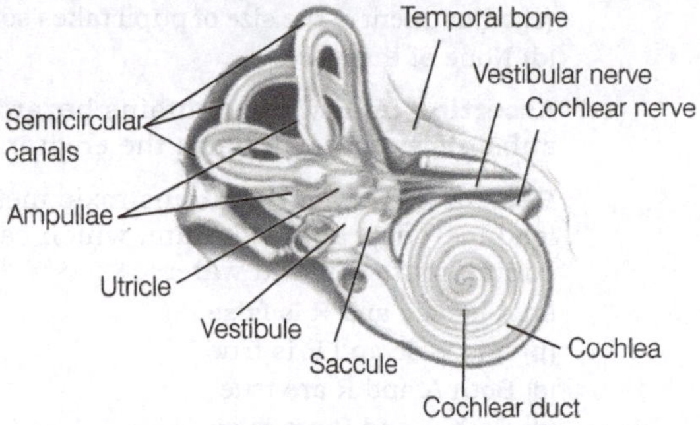

Sense organs are specialised structures that help organisms perceive and respond to their environment. The five primary sense organs are the eyes, ears, nose, tongue and skin, each responsible for detecting specific stimuli like light, sound, smell, taste and touch.

The ear is a vital sense organ responsible for .....(i)..... and .....(ii)..... . It consists of three main parts: the outer ear, middle ear and inner ear. The outer ear collects .....(iii)..... and directs them through the ear canal to the eardrum. Vibrations from the eardrum pass through the middle ear's small bones (ossicles) to the inner ear. The inner ear contains the .....(iv)....., which converts .....(v)..... into electrical signals sent to the brain *via* the auditory nerve. The ear's complex structure ensures accurate hearing and balance, playing a critical role in daily activities and overall well-being. [5]

(v) Read the explanation given below and name the structure. [5]

(a) Gland produces sperm and testosterone in males.

(b) Layer of gases traps heat in the earth's atmosphere, contributing to global warming.

(c) This metric shows the number of people per unit area of land.

(d) This T-shaped device is inserted into the uterus for contraception.

(e) This green pigment captures sunlight for photosynthesis.

Section-B [40 Marks]

*(Attempt **any four** questions from this section)*

3. (i) Define passive transport. [1]

(ii) Give two differences between stomatal and cuticular transpiration. [2]

(iii) What is chemotropism? Give one example. [2]

(iv) Which theory of evolution can best explain the process of organic evolution? [2]

(v) Draw a labelled diagram of section of a leaf. [3]

4. (i) Expand the abbreviation NADP. [1]

(ii) Name the complex structure consisting DNA strand and a core of histone. [2]

(iii) It is better to transplant seedlings in a flower-bed in the evening and not in the morning.
Explain by giving suitable reason. [2]

(iv) Mention how water content affects the rate of transpiration. [2]

(v) Study the diagram given below which represents a stage during the mitotic cell division and answer the questions that follows. [3]

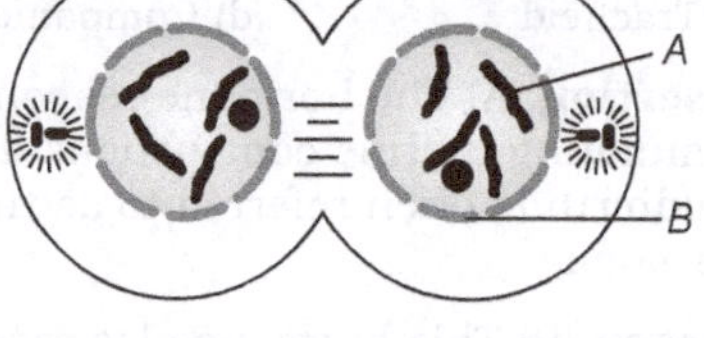

(a) Identify the stage giving suitable reasons.

(b) Name the parts labelled *A* and *B*.

(c) What is the technical term for the division of nucleus?

5. (i) Define exocrine gland. [1]

(ii) What is the significance of Rh-factor in pregnancy? [2]

(iii) State the functions of aqueous humour. [2]

(iv) Which gland secretes insulin? What will be its effect on sugar level in blood, if the secretion is insufficient. [2]

(v) Draw a well-labelled diagram of nephron. [3]

6. (i) Define aster. [1]

(ii) Differentiate between pure breed and hybrid. [2]

(iii) State the functions of parasympathetic nervous system with suitable example. [2]

(iv) The gender of a child depends on father. Explain. [2]

(v) Manvi is sitting at her study desk, concentrating on solving a complex math problem. She is using a pen to write down calculations, analysing the steps carefully, and occasionally pausing to think deeply. [3]

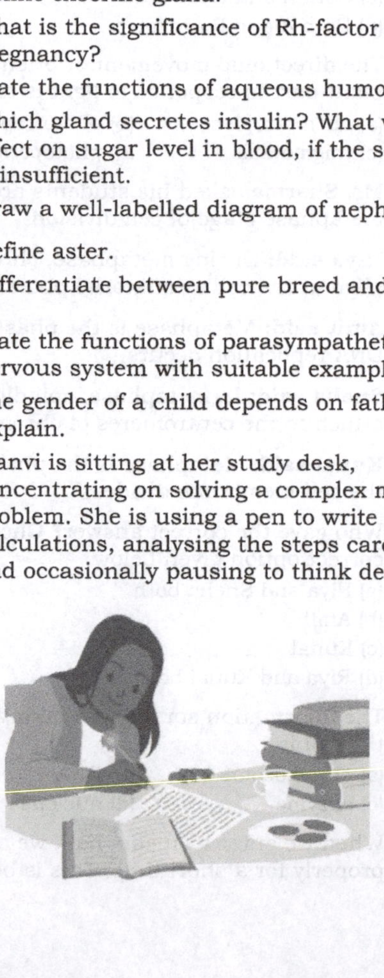

(a) Which part of Manvi's brain is primarily involved in problem-solving and decision-making, while she works on the math problems?

(b) Apart from problem-solving, write two other important functions of this part of the brain.

(c) Which involuntary actions controlled by the medulla oblongata help Manvi to maintain her breathing and heart rate, while focusing on her math problems?

7. (i) Explain presbyopia. Also mention how it can be corrected. [1]

(ii) Give two reasons for dying of fishes near a sea shore. [2]

(iii) Mention two functions of ovaries. [2]

(iv) What are the differences between the cytokinesis in animal cell and plant cell? [2]

(v) Draw a flowchart explaining the mechanism of blood clotting. [3]

8. (i) Define secondary pollutants. [1]

(ii) Green leaves are thin and broad. Explain. [2]

(iii) Differentiate between amnion and placenta. [2]

(iv) Mention two harmful effects of pollution on human health. [2]

(v) Study the experimental setup carefully and answer the questions that follows. [3]

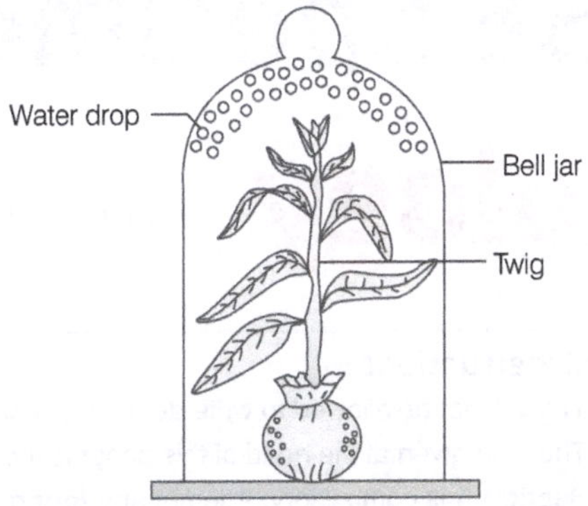

(a) Explain the process that is being studied.

(b) Why is the pot showing water drops after sometime?

(c) Mention the advantages of this process to the plant.

LATEST
ICSE Specimen PAPER
Biology (Fully Solved)

General Instructions
1. You will not be allowed to write during the first **15** minutes. This time is to be spent in reading the question paper.
2. The time given at the head of this paper is the time allowed for writing the answers.
3. **Section A** is compulsory. Attempt **any four** questions from **Section B**.
4. The intended marks for questions or part of questions are given in brackets [].

Time : 2 Hrs **Max. Marks : 80**

Section-A [40 Marks]

*(Attempt **all** questions from this section)*

1. Choose the correct answer to the questions from the given options.
(Do not copy the questions, write the correct answer only.) [15]

(i) The loops of Henle lie in • *Recall* [1]
(a) renal cortex (b) renal medulla
(c) renal pelvis (d) renal artery

(ii) The antiseptic present in tears • *Recall* [1]
(a) iodine (b) hydrogen peroxide
(c) lysozyme (d) lysosome

(iii) **Assertion** (A) The foetus respires but does not breathe.
Reason (R) The maternal blood supplies oxygen to the foetus through placenta. • *Analysis* [1]
(a) A is true and R is false
(b) A is false and R is true
(c) Both A and R are true
(d) Both A and R are false

(iv) During ventricular systole, the atrioventricular valves (*P*) and semilunar valves (*Q*) • *Application* [1]
(a) *P*-close, *Q* - open (b) *P*-close, *Q* - close
(c) *P*-open, *Q* - close (d) P-open, *Q* - open

(v) The two cerebral hemispheres are joined by a sheet of fibres called • *Recall* [1]
(a) pons (b) corpus luteum
(c) hypothalamus (d) corpus callosum

(vi) The onset of menstruation in a human female is called • *Recall* [1]
(a) menopause (b) menarche
(c) ovulation (d) oogenesis

(vii) **Assertion** (A) Rods and cones are photoreceptors in the sclera of eyeball.
Reason (R) Rods are sensitive to dim light. • *Application* [1]
(a) A is true and R is false
(b) A is false and R is true
(c) Both A and R are true
(d) Both A and R are false

(viii) Priya tried to match the hormones with their effect on the human body. She tabulated the pairs as follows: • *Understanding and Application* [1]

Hormones	Effect on the body
P	Stimulates conversion of glycogen to glucose
Q	Reabsorption of water by the nephrons.

Identify the correct pair of hormones.
(a) *P*-Insulin, *Q*-Glycogen
(b) *P*-Adrenaline, *Q*-Oxytocin
(c) *P*-Glucagon, *Q*-Vasopressin
(d) *P*-Vasopressin, *Q*-Adrenalin

(ix) While studying the stages in the evolution of man, a well-developed chin is observed in • *Recall* [1]
(a) *Homo habilis* (b) *Homo erectus*
(c) *Homo sapiens* (d) *Australopithecus*

(x) A pair of corresponding chromosomes of the same shape, size and one from each parent is called • *Recall* [1]
(a) autosomes
(b) allosomes
(c) analogous chromosomes
(d) homologous chromosomes

(xi) **Assertion** (A) We urinate more in summer.

Reason (R) Sweat glands are more active in summer. • *Understanding* [1]

(a) A is true and R is false
(b) A is false and R is true
(c) Both A and R are true
(d) Both A and R are false

(xii) Rahul inserted a hairpin into his right ear to remove ear wax. He felt a sudden sharp pain with loss of hearing. This was due to

(a) Rupture of eardrum • *Analysis* [1]
(b) Rupture of vestibule
(c) Rupture of cornea
(d) Rupture of pinna

(xiii) **Assertion** (A) All food chains begin with herbivores.

Reason (R) Green plants are heterotrophs.

(a) A is true and R is false • *Application* [1]
(b) A is false and R is true
(c) Both A and R are true
(d) Both A and R are false

(xiv) A biology teacher asked her students to give two examples of vestigial organs in the human body.

Raj said: Wisdom teeth and Pinna

Sonu said: Body hair and large intestine

Lata said: Vermiform appendix and wisdom teeth

Abhay said: Pinna and Ossicles

Who were correct? • *Recall and Understanding* [1]

(a) Abhay and Sonu (b) Sonu and Lata
(c) Raj and Lata (d) Abhay and Raj

(xv) During a practical exam, a plant cell in a particular solution was placed under a compound microscope. Students were told to observe the cell and name the tonicity of the solution and mention the process that occurred in the cell. • *Analysis and Application* [1]

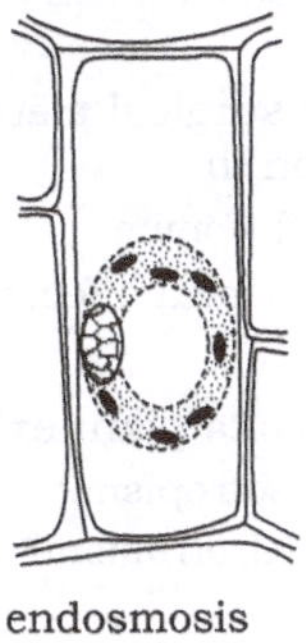

(a) Isotonic, endosmosis
(b) Hypotonic, active transport
(c) Hypertonic, endosmosis
(d) Hypertonic, exosmosis

2. (i) Name the following [5]

(a) The basic units of heredity. • *Recall*
(b) The undesirable change in the environment leading to its deterioration • *Understanding*
(c) The structure that connects placenta and the human foetus. • *Analysis*
(d) The statistical study of human population. • *Recall*
(e) The nitrogenous base that pairs with adenine. • *Understanding*

(ii) Given below is the transverse section of the spinal cord. Read the information below the diagram and fill in the blanks: • *Recall and Application* [5]

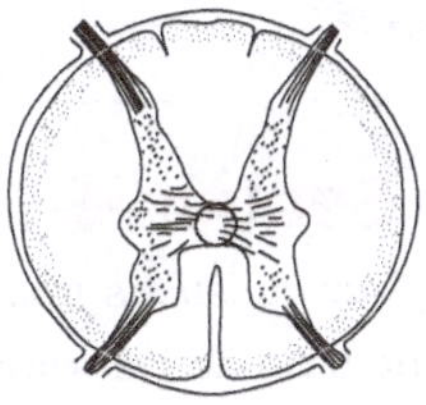

The spinal cord extends from the medulla oblongata of the brain and runs down through the whole length of the vertebral column. The spinal cord is covered by the meninges. It conducts impulses from the skin and muscles to the brain. It also conducts impulses from the brain to the muscles of the trunk and limbs.

The spinal cord is a part of the (a)......... nervous system. The grey matter in the picture given above consists of (b)......... the white matter consists of (c)......... The spinal cord is concerned with the (d)......... actions below the neck. (e)......... is the bony structure that protects the spinal cord.

(iii) Arrange and rewrite the terms in each group in the correct order so as to be in a logical sequence beginning with the term that is underlined. • *Analysis* [5]

(a) Apical meristem, Positive phototropism, <u>Auxins</u>, Cell elongation.
(b) Urethra, Urinary bladder, Ureter, <u>Kidney</u>.
(c) <u>Auditory canal</u>, Organ of corti, Stapes, Malleus.
(d) Cell membrane, <u>Chromatin fibres</u>, Cell wall, Cytoplasm.
(e) Lungs, Right auricle, <u>Inferior vena cava</u>, Pulmonary artery.

(iv) Read the explanations given below and name the structure: • *Understanding* [5]

(a) Food conducting tissue in vascular plants.
(b) A cell formed by the fusion of gametes.
(c) The smallest blood vessels in the human body.
(d) A tubular passage that connects the pharynx and the middle ear.

(e) The openings on the barks of trees through which transpiration occurs.

(v) Given below is a cross section of the human eye. Match the structures marked (*a*) to (*e*) with their correct functions: • *Analysis* [5]

Cross section of Human Eye	Functions
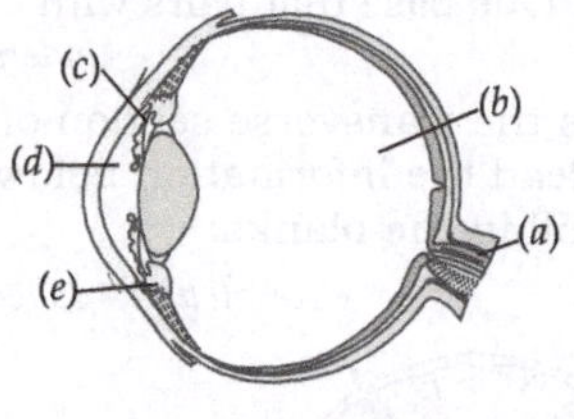	1. Protects retina
	2. Regulates the size of the pupil
	3. Alters the shape of the lens
	4. Keeps the lens moist
	5. Transmits nerve impulses to brain

Section-B [40 Marks]

(Attempt ***any four*** *questions from this section)*

3. (i) Explain the term active transport. • *Recall* [1]

(ii) Name the structures through which transpiration and guttation occur in a plant. • *Understanding* [2]

(iii) How does the rate of transpiration differ when there is
(a) high temperature?
(b) high humidity? • *Analysis* [2]

(iv) Write the overall chemical equation for photosynthesis. • *Recall* [2]

(v) Sam observed a slide containing the lower epidermis of a leaf under a microscope. A number of tiny openings between the epidermal cells were present as shown below in the diagram: • *Application* [3]

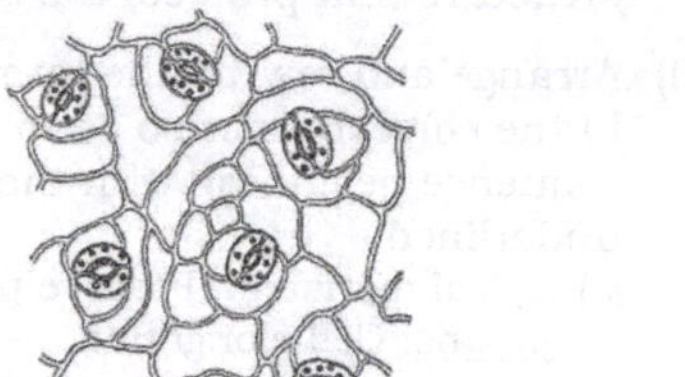

(a) What are these tiny openings called?
(b) Name the cells that regulate the opening and closing of these structures.
(c) Which ion is responsible for the opening and closing of these openings?

4. (i) Why is adrenaline called the 'Emergency Hormone'? • *Understanding* [1]

(ii) Expand the abbreviation ADH. Give one example of a diuretic substance. • *Recall* [2]

(iii) Mention the significance of the following minerals
(a) Iodine in our food.
(b) Magnesium in green plants. • *Application* [2]

(iv) State two objectives of Swachh Bharat Abhiyan. • *Recall* [2]

(v) Draw a neat and labelled diagram of a root hair. • *Recall* [3]

5. (i) Mention one characteristic of roots for absorbing water from the soil. • *Understanding* [1]

(ii) What is parthenocarpy? Give one example. • *Recall* [2]

(iii) State the difference between micturition and parturition. • *Recall* [2]

(iv) Write any two functions of lymph. • *Understanding* [2]

(v) Study the picture given below and answer the questions: • *Analysis and Application* [3]

(a) How does water get polluted?
(b) What is the effect of water pollution on human life?
(c) Mention one control measure to stop the pollution of water bodies.

6. (i) State Mendel's law of segregation. • *Recall* [1]

(ii) What are tropic hormones? Give one example. • *Understanding* [2]

(iii) Differentiate between the terms phenotype and genotype. • *Understanding* [2]

(iv) What is the significance of testes being placed in scrotal sacs? • *Analysis* [2]

(v) Draw a neat and labelled diagram of a human sperm. • *Understanding, Creative and Skill* [3]

7. (i) What is the scientific name of the pea plant that Mendel used for his experiments? • *Recall* [1]

(ii) Mention the surgical methods of contraception in
(a) men (b) women • *Understanding* [2]

(iii) Name two harmful effects of noise pollution. • *Application* [2]

(iv) Which parts of a plant exhibit
(a) negative geotropism?
(b) positive hydrotropism? • *Analysis* [2]

(v) Kathak is an Indian classical dance which involves a lot of spinning by the dancers. The learners of this dance experience dizziness in the beginning while spinning.
• *Analysis and Application* [3]

(a) Name the part of the membranous labyrinth responsible for this dizziness.
(b) Give a suitable reason for your answer.
(c) Mention the nerve that carries the impulse for dizziness to the brain.

8. (i) How does transpiration help in the uptake of water from the soil? • *Application* [1]

(ii) Given below are two statements which are incorrect. Rewrite the correct statements.
(a) Fresh water fish when placed in hypertonic salt solution absorb water and burst.
(b) Seminiferous tubules secrete testosterone.
• *Analysis* [2]

(iii) During mitosis, what is the position of chromatids in
(a) Metaphase? (b) Anaphase? • *Recall* [2]

(iv) Chris was watching the display of fireworks in the sky. • *Application* [2]
(a) Trace the path of the light rays using the following terms: Fovea, Lens, Conjunctiva, Pupil, Cornea
(b) Name the nerve that carries the impulse for vision to the brain.

(v) Draw a neat and labelled diagram of a Malpighian body. • *Recall* [3]

Answers

Section-A

1. (i) (b) renal medulla
(ii) (c) Lysozyme
(iii) (c) Both A and R are true.
(iv) (a) *P*-close, *Q*-open
(v) (d) Corpus callosum
(vi) (b) Menarche
(vii) (b) A is false and R is true. A can be corrected as Photoreceptors (rods and cones) are specialised light-detecting cells on the retina, at the back of eyes
(viii) (c) *P*-Glucagon, *Q*- Vasopressin.
(ix) (c) *Homo sapiens*
(x) (d) Homologous chromosomes
(xi) (b) A is false and R is true. A can be corrected as We urinate more in winter. Due to more perspiration in summer, there is more water loss from the body.
(xii) (a) rupture of eardrum
(xiii) (d) Both A and R are false. These can be corrected as
- All food chains start with a producer.
- Green plants are autotrophs.

(xiv) (c) Raj and Lata
(xv) (d) Hypertonic, Exosmosis

2. (i) (a) Genes
(b) Pollution
(c) Umbilical Cord
(d) Demography
(e) Thymine (T)
(ii) (a) central
(b) cytons/nerve cell bodies
(c) Axons/nerve cell fibres
(d) reflex
(e) Vertebral column
(iii) (a) Auxins, Apical meristem, Cell elongation, Positive phototropism.
(b) Kidney, Ureter, Urinary bladder, Urethra.
(c) Auditory canal, Malleus, Stapes, Organ of Corti.
(d) Chromatin fibres, Cytoplasm, Cell membrane, Cell wall.
(e) Inferior vena cava, Right auricle, Pulmonary artery, Lungs.
(iv) (a) Phloem
(b) Zygote
(c) Capillaries
(d) Eustachian tube
(e) Lenticels
(v) (a) 5 (b) 1 (c) 2 (d) 4 (e) 3

Section-B

3. (i) Active transport is the movement of salt or ions across a cell membrane from lower to higher concentration by the use of energy.
(ii) Transpiration in plants occurs through stomata, lenticels and cuticle, while guttation occurs through hydathodes.
(iii) (a) The rate of transpiration increases when there is high temperature.
(b) The rate of transpiration decreases in the case of high humidity.
(iv) Photosynthesis is a physiological process in which living plant cells that contain chlorophyll, synthesise food in the form of glucose and starch from CO_2 and water, using light energy.
Overall reaction of photosynthesis can be summarised as follows

$$\underset{\text{Carbon dioxide}}{6CO_2} + \underset{\text{Water}}{12H_2O} \xrightarrow[\text{Chlorophyll}]{\text{Sunlight}} \underset{\text{Sugar}}{C_6H_{12}O_6} + \underset{\text{Water}}{6H_2O} + \underset{\text{Oxygen}}{6O_2} \uparrow \text{ (By product)}$$

(v) (a) These tiny openings are called as stomata.
(b) Guard cells regulate the opening and closing of the stomata.
(c) K^+ /potassium ions are responsible for the opening and closing of the stomata.

4. (i) Adrenaline is called as the 'Emergency Hormone' because it is secreted under conditions of stress like anger, fear, excitement. It prepares the body to face the emergency situation.
(ii) ADH stands for Antidiuretic Hormone. One example of a diuretic substance is alcohol.
(iii) (a) For synthesis of thyroxine by thyroid gland.
(b) For synthesis of chlorophyll.
(iv) The two objectives of Swachh Bharat Abhiyan are as follows
- To clean streets, roads, cities and towns.
- To eliminate open defecation by constructing toilets.

(v) Diagram of a root hair.

5. (i) One characteristic of roots for absorbing water from soil is the presence of root hairs. Root hairs increase the surface area of a root, enhancing its ability to absorb water and nutrients from the soil.

(ii) Parthenocarpy is the development of fruits without fertilisation of the ovules, resulting in seedless fruits. One example of parthenocarpy is banana.

(iii) Differences between micturition and parturition are as follows

Micturition	Parturition
Expulsion of urine from the urinary bladder.	It is the expulsion of fully developed foetus from the uterus at the end of gestation.
Involves urinary system.	Involves the reproductive system.
Removal of waste products in the form of urine.	Delivery of a baby from the mother's womb.

(iv) The function of lymph are as follows

Transport of nutrient and waste - Lymph help to transport nutrients, oxygen and hormones to cells through out the body and removes metabolic waste products and toxins from tissues.

Immune function - Lymph plays a crucial role in the immune system by transporting white blood cells, especially lymphocytes, which help to fight infections.

(v) (a) Water pollution occurs through various means including sewage, waste water, industrial effluents, oil spills and agricultural run off.

(b) Water pollution has significant impact on human life, including health risks from waterborne diseases such as diarrhoea, cholera, typhoid and reduced access to clean drinking water.

(c) Implementing strict sewage treatment regulations and ensuring proper waste water management, to prevent untreated sewage from being discharged into water bodies are crucial measures to stop water pollution.

6. (i) Law of segregation states that the alleles do not show any blending and both the characters are recovered as such in the F_2 generation. The factors or alleles of a pair segregate from each other in a way that a gamete receives only one of the two factors.

(ii) Tropic hormones are hormones that regulate the function of other endocrine glands by stimulating their growth and secretion of hormones. These hormones are typically produced by the pituitary gland and act on target glands else where in the body.

One example of tropic hormone is thyroid-stimulating hormone (TSH), which is produced by the anterior pituitary gland.

(iii) Differences between genotype and phenotype are as follows

Genotype	Phenotype
Genetic makeup of an organism.	Observable physical traits.
Complete set of gene an organism carries.	Physical expression influenced by genes and environment.
Example : TT, tt	Example : tall and dwarf

(iv) The scrotal sac allow testes to be positioned outside the body, maintaining their temperature at about 2-2.5°C lower than the internal body temperature. This cooler environment is crucial for optimal sperm production (spermatogenesis) and ensure sperm quality and viability, thereby supporting male reproductive functions.

(v) Diagram of human sperm.

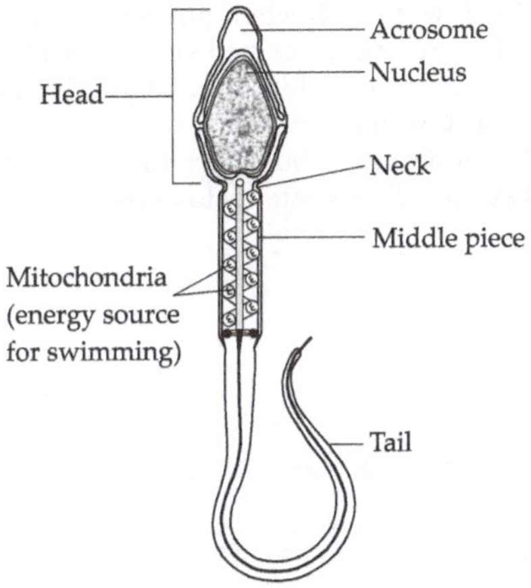

7. (i) The scientific name of pea plant that Mendel used for his experiment is *Pisum sativum.*

(ii) (a) The surgical method of contraception in men is vasectomy. In vasectomy, a small part of the vas deferens is cut and tied up through a small incision in the scrotum.

(b) The surgical method of contraception in female is tubectomy. In tubectomy, a small part of Fallopian tube is cut or tied up through small incision in the abdomen or vagina.

(iii) The two harmful effects of noise pollution are as follows

- Prolonged exposure to loud noises can damage the eardrums and may permanently impair the hearing ability of humans.
- Chronic noise exposure can lead to increased stress levels which can elevate blood pressure and the risk of heart diseases.

(iv) (a) The part of a plant that exhibit negative geotropism is shoot. Negative geotropism refers to the growth of the plant part in the direction away from the force of gravity.

(b) The part of a plant that exhibit positive hydrotropism is the root. Positive hydrotropism refers to the growth response of plant towards water.

(v) (a) Semicircular canals.

(b) The semicircular canals in the inner ear detect rotational movements of the head *via* fluid movement and hair cell.
When these canals signal rapid head motion to the brain, it can cause sensation of dizziness due to sensory inputs.

(c) Vestibular nerve carries the impulse for dizziness to the brain.

8. (i) Transpiration creates a negative pressure in the leaves as water evaporates, pulling water up from the roots through the xylem. This process facilitates the continuous uptake of water and nutrients from the soil.

(ii) (a) Fresh water fish when placed in hypertonic salt solution lose water and shrink. While, marine fish when placed in hypotonic salt solution absorb water and burst.

(b) Seminiferous tubules produce sperms while, Leydig cells secrete testosterone.

(iii) (a) During metaphase of mitosis, chromatids are aligned at the cell's equatorial plane, also known as the metaphase plate. This alignment ensures that each daughter cell receive an identical set of chromosome when chromatids are separated during anaphase.

(b) During anaphase of mitosis, the sister chromatids are separated and pulled towards the opposite poles of the cell. This movement is facilitated by the shortening of the spindle fibres attached to chromatids centromere.

(iv) (a) Conjunctiva, Cornea, Pupil, Lens, Fovea.

(b) Optic nerve carries the impulse for vision to the brain.

(v) Diagram of Malpighian body

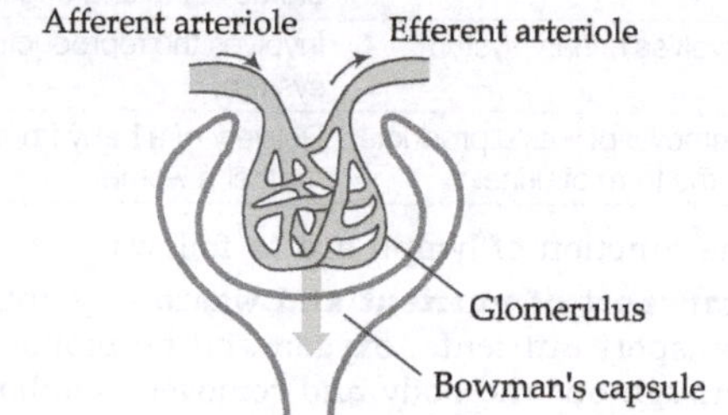

ICSE Examination Paper 2024

Biology

General Instructions

1. You will not be allowed to write during the first **15** minutes. This time is to be spent in reading the question paper.
2. The time given at the head of this paper is the time allowed for writing the answers.
3. **Section A** is compulsory. Attempt **any four** questions from **Section B**.
4. The intended marks for questions or part of questions are given in brackets [].

Time : 2 Hrs **Max. Marks : 80**

Section-A [40 Marks]

(Attempt **all** *questions from this section)*

1. Select the correct answers to the questions from the given options. [15]

(Do not copy the question, write the correct answer only)

(i) Duplicated chromosomes are joined at a point termed
(a) centrosome (b) centromere
(c) centriole (d) chromatid

(ii) The process of conversion of ADP to ATP during photosynthesis is called
(a) photolysis
(b) phagocytosis
(c) photophosphorylation
(d) polymerisation

(iii) The process in which water is lost from the margins of strawberry leaves is
(a) osmosis (b) imbibition
(c) diffusion (d) guttation

(iv) The hormone that affects urination is
(a) adrenaline (b) vasopressin
(c) oestrogen (d) thyroxine

(v) Which one of the following helps in the opening of stomata?
(a) Cobalt ions
(b) Potassium ions
(c) Magnesium ions
(d) Aluminium ions

(vi) A zygote which has Y-chromosome inherited from the father will develop into a
(a) will depend on the chromosome inherited form the mother
(b) girl
(c) either boy or a girl
(d) boy

(vii) The ear ossicle that transports sound vibrations to the inner ear
(a) stapes (b) malleus
(c) incus (d) cochlea

(viii) If a person has a heart attack, what must be done immediately?
P. Loosen his/her clothing
Q. Make him/her lie down in an airy room
R. Rush him/her to the hospital
S. Engage him/her in a conversation
(a) P and Q (b) P and S
(c) R and S (d) P, Q and R

(ix) Adjusting the focal length of the eye lens to view objects at different distances is done by
(a) cornea (b) iris
(c) ciliary muscles (d) sclera

(x) Four friends P, Q, R and S were discussing the examples of genetic disorders. The examples they quoted were as follows
P. Colour blindness and malaria
Q. Albinism and cholera
R. Haemophilia and colour blindness
S. Haemophilia and albinism

Who gave the correct examples?

(a) P and Q (b) R and S

(c) P and R (d) Q and S

(xi) Osmosis takes place when there is

(a) a freely permeable membrane

(b) a cell wall

(c) a selectively permeable membrane

(d) an impermeable membrane

(xii) A male gorilla has 48 chromosomes in each of its body cells. How many chromosomes will each of the sperms have?

(a) 24 (b) 48

(c) 12 (d) 16

(xiii) **Assertion** (A) Sympathetic nervous system prepares the body for violent action against abnormal conditions.

Reason (R) Sympathetic nervous system accelerates heartbeat.

Which of the following is correct?

(a) Both A and R are true

(b) A is true, R is false

(c) A is false but R is true

(d) Both A and R are false

(xiv) Birth rate is the number of live births per thousand persons in

(a) 1 year

(b) 2 years

(c) 10 years

(d) 20 years

(xv) Industrial Melanism was observed in

(a) mice

(b) peppered moth

(c) house flies

(d) crow

2. (i) Name the following:

(a) Unicellular outgrowths from the epidermis of roots.

(b) A defect in our eyes, in which some parts of the object are in focus while the other parts are blurred.

(c) The tropic movement of plant parts in response to chemicals.

(d) The main nitrogenous waste formed in the body.

(e) The process of attachment of fertilised ovum to the wall of uterus.

(ii) Arrange and rewrite the terms in each group in the correct order to be in a logical sequence beginning with the term that is underlined: [5]

(a) *Australopithecus*, Cro-Magnon, *Homo erectus*, Neanderthal man.

(b) Pupil, Aqueous humour, Retina, Vitreous humour.

(c) Effector, Receptor, Motor neuron, Sensory neuron.

(d) Loop of Henle, Distal Convoluted tubule, Bowman's Capsule, Proximal convoluted tubule.

(e) Water vapour, Soil water, Leaves, Ascent of sap

(iii) Study the diagram given below and fill in the blanks with suitable words. [5]

In order to prove that carbon dioxide is necessary for **(a)**.......... a potted plant is placed in dark for 48 hours to **(b)** .... the leaves. A part of a leaf is inserted into a conical flask containing potassium hydroxide solution. This is to absorb **(c)** .... from the flask. The plant is then placed in sunlight for a few hours. The experimental leaf is tested for starch. The part of the leaf that was inside the conical flask turns **(d)** .... whereas the part of the leaf outside turns **(e)**......... in colour.

(iv) Choose the odd one out from the following terms and name the category to which the others belong . [5]

(a) Prothrombin, Thrombin, Fibrinogen, Albumin

(b) Tonsils, Glomerulus, Spleen, Lymph nodes

(c) Neutrophils, Basophils, Monocytes, Eosinophils

(d) Leaves, Styrofoam, Grass, Cow Dung

(e) Pulmonary artery, Renal artery, Coronary artery, Hepatic artery

(v) Match the items given in Column I with most appropriate ones in Column II and rewrite the corret matching pairs : [5]

	Column I	Column II
(a)	Leydig cells	1. Lack of thyroxine in children
(b)	Stoma	2. 12 pairs
(c)	Ova	3. Testosterone
(d)	Cranial nerve	4. Diffusion of respiratory gases
(e)	Cretinism	5. Haploid cells
		6. 31 pairs
		7. Diploid cells

Section-B [40 Marks]

(Attempt **any four** questions from this section.)

3. (i) Expand the abbreviation - NADP. [1]

(ii) Mention two adaptations in roots for absorption of water from the soil. [2]

(iii) Differentiate between Afferent arteriole and efferent arteriole (diameter). [2]

(iv) Give two examples of water pollutants. [2]

(v) Ali has some pea plants in his garden which need a support to grow as seen in the picture given below. [3]

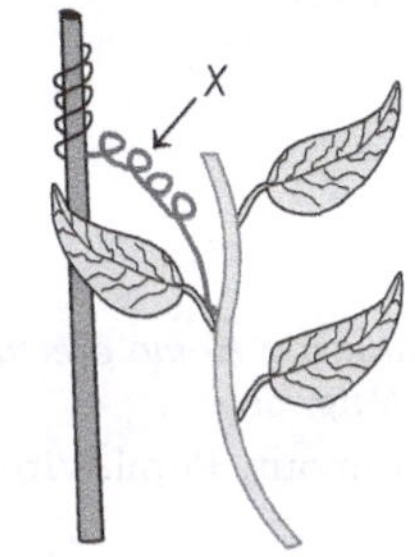

(a) Name the phenomenon depicted by the shoot in the given figure.

(b) Define the above phenomenon.

(c) Write the name of the part marked *X*.

4. (i) Give the biological term for the surgical method of contraception in human females. [1]

(ii) State two harmful effects of acid rain on the environment. [2]

(iii) Mention two advantages of transpiration. [2]

(iv) Write any two objectives of Swachh Bharat Abhiyan. [2]

(v) Mohan is fond of playing basketball. His concentration is on shooting the ball into the opponent s basket as given in the picture. [3]

(a) Which part of the brain helps Mohan to concentrate in putting the ball into the basket?

(b) Name the sense organ that helps to gauge the distance between the ball and the basket.

(c) Name the part of the brain that co-ordinates all the voluntary muscles of his body.

5. (i) Name the type of nerve which has the fibres of both sensory and motor neurons. [1]

(ii) Differentiate between *Australopithecus* and Modern man based on body hair. [2]

(iii) "Birth rate in India is very high. " Mention two reasons in support of the statement. [2]

(iv) Give the exact location of [2]

(a) Pericardium

(b) Bicuspid valve

(v) Given below is a schematic representation of the inheritance of the shape of seeds of garden pea Answer the questions that follows: [3]

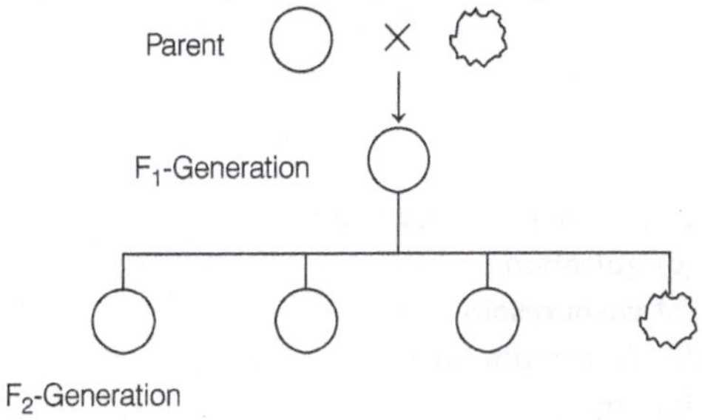

(a) Which is the dominant and recessive allele of the trait ?

(b) What does the ratio 3 : 1 in the F_2-generation represent?

(c) State Mendel 's law of dominance.

6. (i) Define the term-Diapedesis. [1]

(ii) Distinguish between Diabetes mellitus and Diabetes insipidus (endocrine gland concerned). [2]

(iii) Carbon monoxide is dangerous when inhaled in excess. Comment on the statement. [2]

(iv) The diagram given below shows a section of the human ovary. [2]

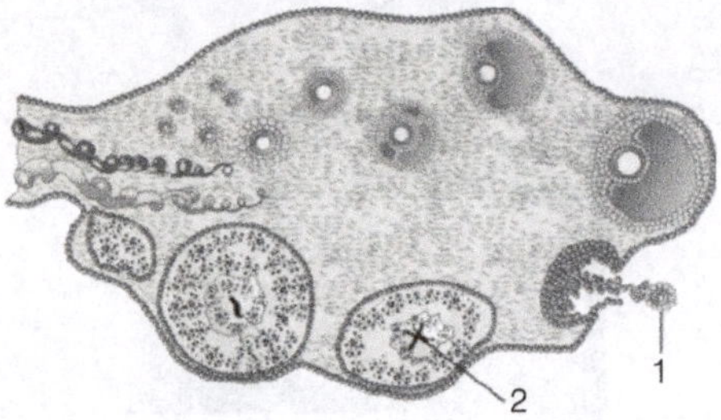

(a) Name the process for the release of the part labelled 1.

(b) Write the name of the structure marked 2.

(v) Draw a neat, labelled diagram of a chloroplast. [3]

7. (i) Define the term hormone. [1]

(ii) Which parts of the ear are responsible for [2]

(a) static equilibrium?

(b) dynamic equilibrium?

(iii) Mention two structural differences between an artery and a vein. [2]

(iv) Write any two limitations of using a Ganong's Potometer to demonstrate the uptake of water. [2]

(v) A teacher drew the diagram of heart on the blackboard and told the students to copy it in their note books. Mahesh couldn't see the diagram clearly as it appeared blurred to him. [3]

(a) Name the defect of the eye Mahesh is suffering from.

(b) Where is the image formed in this defect?

(c) Mahesh consults an eye doctor and is prescribed suitable lenses to correct the defect. Which type of lens do his spectacles have?

8. (i) Define the term ultrafiltration. [1]

(ii) Name the mineral elements required for [2]

(a) clotting blood

(b) synthesis of thyroxine

(iii) Mention two harmful effects of nose pollution. [2]

(iv) Why are RBCs efficient in their functions though they lack nucleus and mitochondria? [2]

(v) The diagram given below represents a stage in mitosis. [3]

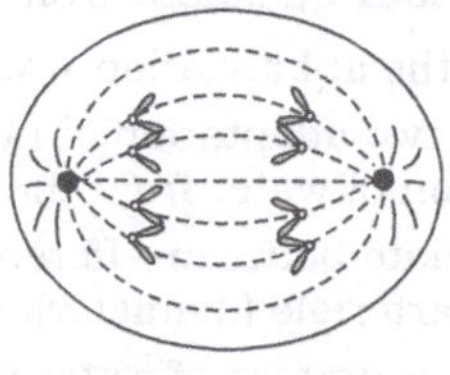

(a) Identify the stage given above.

(b) Give one reason to support your answer in (a).

(c) Mention the number of chromosomes given in the diagram.

Answers

1. (i) (b) centromere

(ii) (c) photophosphorylation

(iii) (d) guttation

(iv) (b) vasopressin

(v) (b) Potassium ions

(vi) (d) boy

(vii) (a) stapes

(viii) (d) P, Q and R

(ix) (c) ciliary muscles

(x) (b) R and S

(xi) (c) a selectively permeable membrane

(xii) (a) 24

(xiii) (a) Both A and R are true

(xiv) (a) 1 year

(xv) (b) peppered moth

2. (i) (a) Root hair

(b) Astigmatism

(c) Chemotropism

(d) Urea

(e) Implantation

(ii) (a) *Australopithecus*, *Homo erectus*, Neanderthal man, Cro-Magnon.

(b) Aqueous humour, Pupil, Vitreous humour, Retina.

(c) Receptor, Sensory neuron, Motor Neuron, Effector.

(d) Bowman's Capsule, Proximal convoluted tubule, Loop of Henle, Distal convoluted tubule.

(e) Soil water, Ascent of Sap, Leaves, Water vapour.

(iii) (a) Photosynthesis (b) Destarch

(c) Carbon dioxide (d) Colourless

(e) Bluish-black

(iv) (a) **Odd term** : Albumin

Category : Others are blood clotting factors.

(b) **Odd term** : Glomerulus

Category : Others are lymphatic organs.

(c) **Odd term** : Monocytes

Category : Others are granulocytes.

(d) **Odd term** : Styrofoam

Category : Others are biodegradable wastes

(e) **Odd term** : Coronary artery

Category : Others supply blood to various organs.

(v)

	Column I		Column II
(a)	Leydig cells	3.	Testosterone
(b)	Stoma	4.	Diffusion of respiratory gases
(c)	Ova	5.	Haploid cells
(d)	Cranial nerve	2.	12 pairs
(e)	Cretinism	1.	Lack of thyroxine in children

3. (i) NADP stands for Nicotinamide Adenine Dinucleotide Phosphate.

(ii) (a) The root hair represents a large surface area in contact with the soil particles.

(b) The root hair can penetrate between soil particles.

(iii) (a) Afferent arterioles deliver blood to the glomerulus of the nephron and efferent arterioles carry blood away from the glomerulus.

(b) The average diameter of afferent arteriole is much larger than efferent arteriole due to which blood pressure in the efferent arteriole is higher than the blood pressure in the afferent arteriole.

(iv) Examples of water pollutants are:

Chemical wastes, heavy metals, pollutants from live stock operations, sewage, industrial wastes, etc. (Any two).

(v) (a) Thigmotropism

(b) Thigmotropism can be defined as the movement of plant part in response to stimulus of contact.

(c) Stem tendril.

4. (i) Tubectomy

(ii) Harmful effects of acid rain on the environment are:

(a) Acid rain water accumulates in river causing death of aquatic life.

(b) It damages the buildings and monuments made up of stones and metals.

(c) It causes damage to crops. (Any two)

(iii) The advantages of transpiration are as follows:

(a) The absorption of water and ascent of sap to various parts of the plant body is mostly due to transpiration. Transpiration pull is responsible for mass movement of water and solutes in upward direction.

(b) Plants receive solar energy in very large amounts for the synthesis of carbohydrates. If there is no dissipation of energy, the temperature of leaf surface would rise to a lethal level in less than two minutes. Transpiration plays an important role here. It helps in dissipation of this excess energy by evaporating water from the leaf surface and thus, helps in keeping the plant cool.

(c) Transpiration helps in removing excess of water.

(d) Development of mechanical tissues, growth of root system, increasing mineral and sugar content of fruits and development of resistance are other beneficial effects of transpiration. (Any two)

(iv) Objectives of Swachh Bharat Abhiyan are:

- To eliminate open defecation through the construction of household-owned toilets.
- To establish an accountable mechanism of monitoring toilet use.
- To spread cleanliness awareness among people and strengthening the cleanliness systems in all areas.
- To achieve efficient solid and liquid waste management systems. (Any two)

(v) (a) Cerebrum helps Mohan to concentrate in putting the ball into the basket.

(b) Eyes help to gauge the distance between the ball and the basket.

(c) Cerebellum is the part of the brain that co-ordinates all the voluntary muscles of the body.

5. (i) Mixed nerves have the fibres of both sensory and motor neurons.

(ii) Difference between *Australopithecus* and Modern man on the basis of body hair:

Australopithecus	Modern man
Their body is covered with hair.	They have highly reduced body hair.

(iii) "Birth rate in India is very high" due to the following reasons:

(a) **Illiteracy**: Most of the rural population which forms the bulk of our society are still illiterate, ignorant and superstitious. They also do not know the functioning of the human reproductive system.

(b) **Traditional beliefs**: Among the people from lower strata of society, children are regarded as a gift of God and a sign of prosperity. Therefore, they make no effort to avoid pregnancy.

(c) **Mortality rate**: Due to high infant mortality rate in our country, people from the economically weaker section think it safer to produce more children so that at least some may survive.

(d) **Desire for a male child**: Most Indian families still hold the view that a male child is essential for keeping up the name of the family. Further, a male child is usually a great help to the aged parents.

These two reasons often contribute to getting several children before getting one son or sometimes not even that. (Any two)

(iv) (a) Pericardium is a double layered protective covering of heart.

(b) Bicuspid valve is located between the left atrium and left ventricle.

(v) (a) Dominant allele is R. Recessive allele is r.

(b) The ratio 3 : 1 in the F_2-generation represents the phenotypic ratio, i.e. that 3-plants have round seeds and 1-plant has wrinkled seeds.

(c) Mendel's law of Dominance: In a single individual, when two different alleles of a unit factor or gene responsible for a single character are present, then one allele is dominant over the other.

6. (i) Diapedesis is the process in which white blood cells come out of the blood vessels into the surrounding area in case of injuries.

(ii) Differences between Diabetes mellitus and Diabetes insipidus (endocrine gland concerned) are

Diabetes mellitus	Diabetes insipidus
It is the disorder associated with pancreas.	It is the disorder associated with posterior lobe of pituitary gland.
It is caused due to the deficiency of insulin hormone.	It is caused due to deficiency of vasopressin hormone.

(iii) Carbon monoxide is a poisonous gas. It is produced due to incomplete combustion of fuels such as petrol and diesel. It reduces the oxygen-carrying capacity of haemoglobin in our blood.

In the presence of carbon monoxide, instead of binding with oxygen, haemoglobin combines with carbon monoxide as it has more affinity for carbon monoxide resulting in the formation of carboxyhaemoglobin which is more stable than oxyhaemoglobin (formed when oxygen combines with haemoglobin). It causes headache, nausea, dizziness and may even result in death of the person.

(iv) (a) The process is called ovulation.

(b) The structure marked 2 is corpus luteum.

(v)

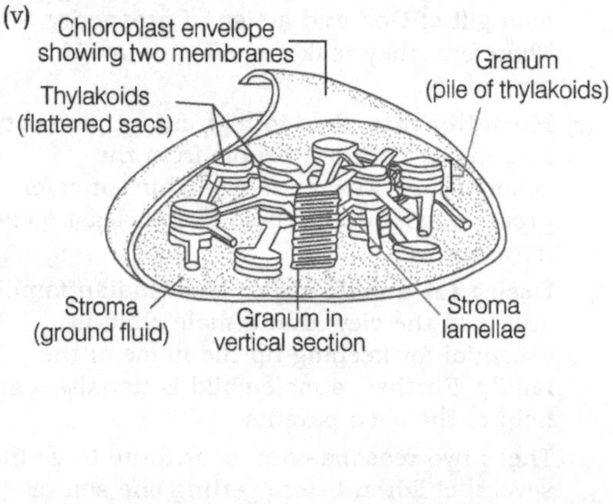

7. (i) Hormones are chemical compounds which are synthesised at places away from where they act and simply diffuse to the area of action.

(ii) (a) Utriculus and sacculus (b) Semicircular canals

(iii) Differences between arteries and veins are:

	Arteries	Veins
(a)	These are usually deep seated.	These are usually superficial.
(b)	Internal valves are absent.	Internal valves are present to prevent back flow of blood.
(c)	These carry blood away from the heart.	These carry blood towards the heart.
(d)	Thick walled, strong and muscular.	Comparatively thin walled and less muscular.
(e)	Flow of blood is very fast with jerks.	Flow of blood is slow without jerks. (Any two)

(iv) Two using a limitations of Ganong's potometer are as folows

(a) Thes twig does not remain alive for a long time.

(b) It is very difficult to introduce the bubble.

(v) (a) Myopia

(b) The image is forms before retina (and not on the retina).

(c) His spectacles have concave or diverging lens which is used to correct this defect

8. (i) The filtration of blood in glomerulus part of a nephron under high pressure is called ultrafiltration.

(ii) (a) Calcium (b) Iodine

(iii) Harmful effects of noise pollution are:

(a) It interferes in communication.

(b) It interrupts concentration of thought and disturbs peace of mind.

(c) It lowers efficiency of work.

(d) It disturbs sleep and leads to nervous irritability. (Any two)

(iv) Mature erythrocytes lack nucleus and mitochondria so as to make space for haemoglobin. Hence more oxygen can be bind with haemoglobin molecules. Mitochondria are absent so that oxygen is not utilised by the erythrocytes and all the oxygen is transported to the target organs.

(v) (a) Anaphase

(b) During anaphase the centromere of each chromosome splits into two, resulting into two sister chromatids. It leads to the migration of daughter chromosomes towards respective poles.

(c) 8

ICSE Examination Paper 2025

Biology

General Instructions

1. You will not be allowed to write during the first **15** minutes. This time is to be spent in reading the question paper.
2. The time given at the head of this paper is the time allowed for writing the answers.
3. **Section A** is compulsory. Attempt **any four** questions from **Section B**.
4. The intended marks for questions or part of questions are given in brackets [].

Time : 2 Hrs **Max. Marks : 80**

Section-A [40 Marks]

*(Attempt **all** questions from this section)*

1. Select the correct answers to the questions from the given options. [15]

(Do not copy the question, write the correct answer only)

(i) The number of live births per thousand people per year is called
(a) mortality
(b) population density
(c) population growth rate
(d) natality

(ii) The structure that lies at the junction of the choroid and the iris and is itself a part .of the choroid is called
(a) ciliary body (b) suspensory ligament
(c) pupil (d) lens

(iii) **Assertion** (A) Seminal vesicles pour an alkaline secretion into the semen as it passes through the ureter.

Reason (R) The female vagina is acidic and needs to be neutralised for sperm survival.
(a) A is true and R is false.
(b) A is false and R is true.
(c) Both A and R are true.
(d) Both A and R are false.

(iv) The hormone that induces vigorous contractions of the uterus in a pregnant mother is
(a) oestrogen (b) prolactin
(c) oxytocin (d) progesterone

(v) A scientist wanted to conduct a genetic experiment on mice. He cut the tails of all the mice and made them reproduce. What will be the phenotype of the offsprings?
(a) All the offsprings will be tailless.
(b) There will be a mix of tailed and tailless offsprings.
(c) All the offsprings will have tails.
(d) Tail of the offsprings cannot be predicted.

(vi) **Assertion** (A) A turgid plant cell is in a balanced state.

Reason (R) In a turgid cell, turgor pressure and wall pressure are equal and in the same direction.
(a) A is true and R is false.
(b) A is false and R is true.
(c) Both A and R are true.
(d) Both A and R are false.

(vii) The optimum temperature for photosynthesis is
(a) 10 - 15 °C (b) 60 - 65 °C
(c) 40 - 45 °C (d) 25 - 35 °C

(viii) Ajay and Vijay are siblings. Ajay can roll his tongue while Vijay cannot.

What is the genotype of their parents?
(a) Both the parents are homozygous dominant.
(b) Both the parents are homozygous recessive.
(c) One parent is homozygous dominant, and the other is homozygous recessive.
(d) Both the parents are heterozygous dominant.

(ix) **Assertion** (A) Deficiency of antidiuretic hormone causes an increase in urination.

Reason (R) Antidiuretic hormone acts on the kidney to reabsorb water from the kidney tubules.

(a) A is true and R is false.
(b) A is false and R is true.
(c) Both A and R are true.
(d) Both A and R are false.

(x) A phase of cell division where the spindle fibres disappear is

(a) telophase (b) prophase
(c) metaphase (d) anaphase

(xi) **Assertion** (A) Arachnoid layer helps in speeding up the transmission of nerve impulses along the axons.

Reason (R) Axon endings at the synapse secrete acetylene.

(a) A is true and R is false.
(b) A is false and R is true.
(c) Both A and R are true.
(d) Both A and R are false.

(xii) Many nuclear power plants are constructed near water sources. They use water for cooling their machinery and release it back into the water stream. Identify the kind of pollution caused

(a) radiation pollution (b) water pollution
(c) industrial pollution (d) thermal pollution

(xiii)

Owls are nocturnal animals. They are active at night and hunt small animals for food. Owls have large eyes and can see well at night. This is due to

(a) cones and rhodopsin
(b) rods and iodopsin
(c) rods and rhodopsin
(d) cones and iodopsin

(xiv) Sunil tried to match the tropic movements in plants with the stimulus they respond to. The tabulation is given below:

	Tropism	Stimulus
P	Thigmotropism	Touch
Q	Geotropism	Water
R	Chemotropism	Chemicals
S	Phototropism	Gravity

Identify the correct pair.

(a) P and R (b) Q and S
(c) R and S (d) P and R

(xv) Observe the following picture, identify the defect and the cause of the defect.

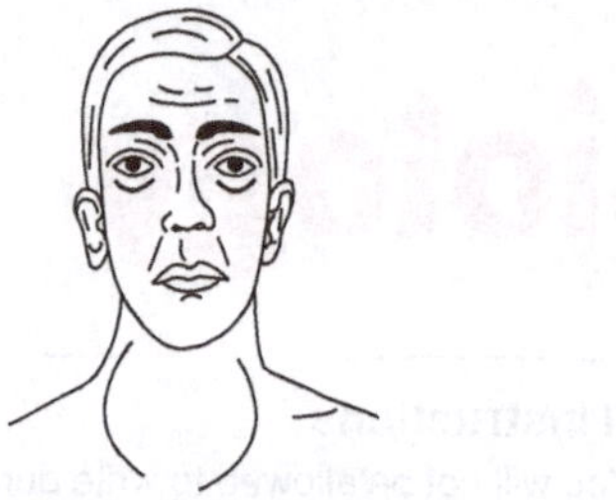

(a) Simple goitre, under secretion of thyroxine.
(b) Ex-ophthalmic goitre, over secretion of thyroxine.
(c) Simple goitre, over secretion of thyroxine.
(d) Ex-ophthalmic goitre, under secretion of thyroxine.

2. (i) Name the following: [5]

(a) The fully developed part of the ovary containing a mature ovum.
(b) A waxy layer on the upper epidermis of leaves meant to reduce transpiration.
(c) The ear ossicle which opens into the oval window of cochlea.
(d) The physiological process which is the starting point of all food chains.
(e) An insect which is a classic example of natural selection due to industrial melanism.

(ii) Given below is the diagram of a human heart. Read the information below the diagram and fill in the blanks: [5]

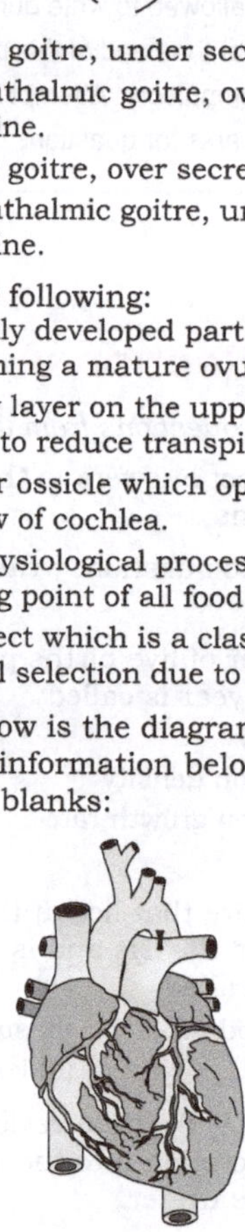

The human heart pumps blood throughout the body. It is the size of a large fist. The heart is located between the lungs in the thoracic cavity. It has four chambers. The heart functions all through the lifespan of a person and is responsible for the survival of the person.

The heart is enclosed by a membrane called (a) .... The ventricles give rise to two large blood vessels called (b) .... and (c) .... The flaps of the cuspid valves are kept in position by (d) .... (e) ....

arteries supply oxygenated blood to the walls of the heart.

(iii) Arrange the terms in each group in the correct order. Write them in a logical sequence beginning with the term that is underlined. [5]

(a) Palisade cells, Cuticle, Upper epidermis, Spongy cells.

(b) Hepatic portal vein, Stomach, Hepatic vein, Liver.

(c) Cyton, Dendrites, Synaptic cleft, Axon endings.

(d) Insulin release, High blood sugar, Lowers blood sugar, Stimulates glucose uptake from blood.

(e) Sperm duct, Seminiferous tubule, Epididymis, Efferent ducts.

(iv) Read the explanations given below and name the structures. [5]

Example The tubules which produce sperms.

Answer Seminiferous tubules

(a) The canal through which the testes descend down into the scrotum just before the birth of a male baby.

(b) The part of the brain that regulates the peristaltic movement of the alimentary canal.

(c) A structure that collects the soundwaves and conducts them through the external auditory canal.

(d) The point of attachment of two chromatids of a chromosome.

(e) Regulation of the opening and closing of stomata.

(v) Given below is an outline of the human body showing the important endocrine glands. Match the glands marked (a) to (e) with their correct functions. [5]

Example (*f*) 6. Secretes testosterone.

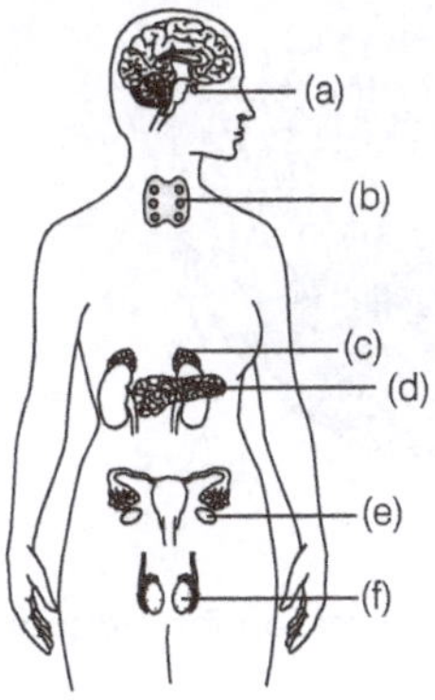

Endocrine glands	Functions
	1. Prepares the body to face stress.
	2. Secretes tropic hormones
	3. Secretes oestrogens
	4. Maintains blood sugar level
	5. Regulates basal metabolism
	6. Secretes testosterone.

Section-B [40 Marks]

(*Attempt **any four** questions from this section.*)

3. (i) Write the overall chemical equation for photosynthesis. [1]

(ii) Ramesh is a farmer who has a vineyard and cultivates grapes. To improve the shape of the grapes and make them elongated he sprays particular phytohormone at the time of fruiting. [2]

(a) Name the phytohormone that Ramesh sprays on the plant at the time of fruiting.

(b) These grapes are said to be seedless. What is the technical term for the formation of such fruits?

(iii) Mention the two pairs of nitrogenous bases that are present in a DNA strand and pair with each other by hydrogen bonds. [2]

(iv) State any two disadvantages of living close to an airport. [2]

(v) Draw a neat, labelled diagram of an animal cell showing metaphase with four chromosomes. [3]

4. (i) What is the structure of DNA as proposed by Watson and Crick? [1]

(ii) Name the white blood cells that

(a) show phagocytosis.

(b) produce antibodies. [2]

(iii) Complete the food chain by mentioning the names of the organisms in (c) and (d): [2]

(a) (b)

(iv) State any two harmful effects of acid rain. [2]

(v) Given below is a picture of a tree. Mention the scientific phenomena occurring in the parts labelled (a), (b) and (c). [3]

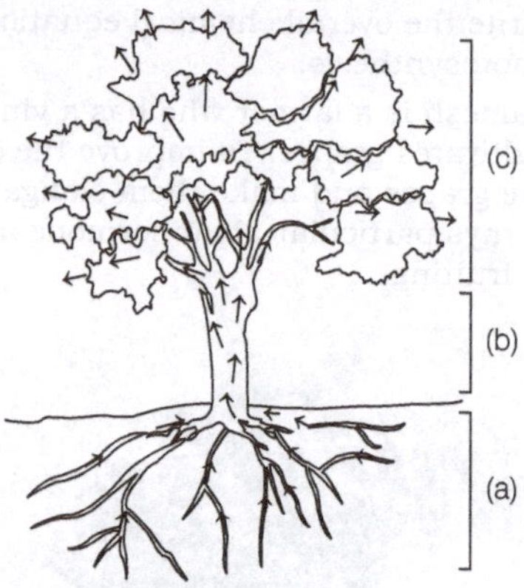

5. (i) What is micturition? Explain. [1]

(ii) What are biomedical wastes? Give an example. [2]

(iii) Differentiate between the functions of urethra and uterus. [2]

(iv) Rachna is an expert gymnast on the balance beam. She has been vigorously practising for the Olympic games. Lately, she has been experiencing dizziness and losing her balance during the practise sessions. [2]

(a) Which part of the membranous labyrinth is responsible for maintaining the body balance on the beam?

(b) Which type of balance is maintained by the structure mentioned in (a)?

(v) Draw a neat, labelled diagram to show that oxygen is released during photosynthesis. [3]

6. (i) Where are hydathodes located?. [1]

(ii) What are vestigial organs? Give one example of a vestigial structure in the human mouth. [2]

(iii) Ahmed had a severe throat infection. After a few days he developed an earache too. What could be the reason for the pain in his ears? Explain. [2]

(iv) Mr. Sharma is a 76 years old man. His vision was gradually becoming blurred. He consulted an eye doctor and it was diagnosed as cataract. [2]

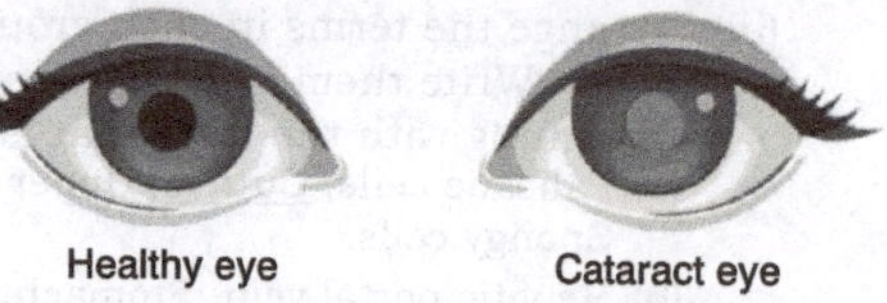

(a) Which part of the eye does cataract affect?

(b) Why does the vision become blurred?

(v) Given below is the diagram of a plasmolysed cortical cell of a root. [3]

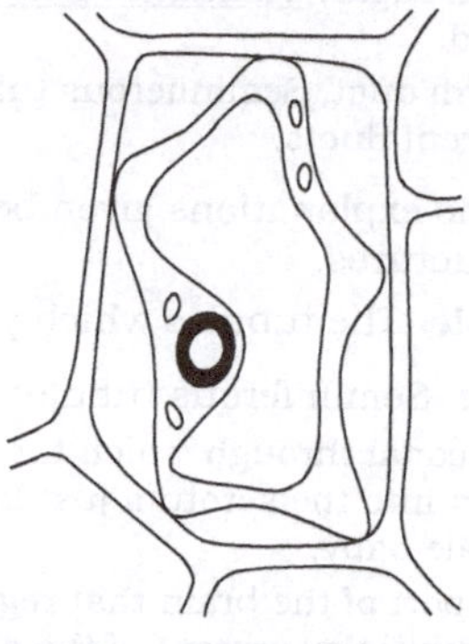

Copy the diagram and label the following parts in the diagram.

(a) Cytoplasm

(b) Hypertonic solution

(c) Plasma membrane

7. (i) Define the term allele. [1]

(ii) In the last century, the human population has increased tremendously. Death rate has reduced and life expectancy has increased. This rapid growth has placed significant pressure on resources. Global cooperation is needed for environmental preservation. [2]

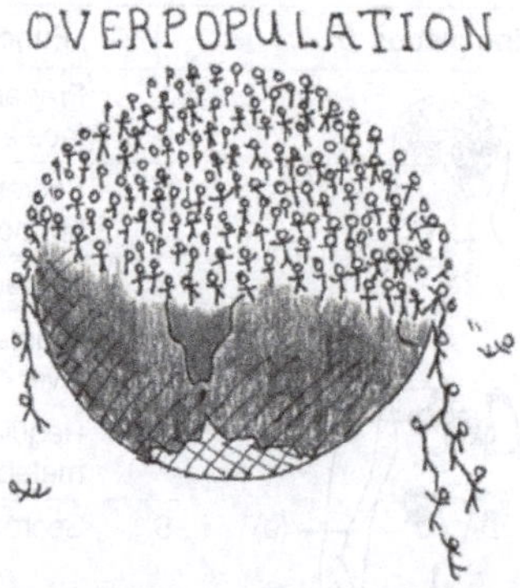

(a) Mention any one reason for reduction in the death rate.

(b) Name any one resource that is under pressure due to population explosion.

(iii) Mention any two functions of amniotic fluid. [2]

(iv) Expand the following abbreviations. [2]
(a) CFC
(b) CNG

(v) Vineet's day begins with a cup of piping hot coffee. Caffeine is a stimulant present in coffee which increases the circulation of adrenaline in the body. Vineet feels refreshed, alert and focussed. [3]

(a) Name the organ that is stimulated by caffeine which makes Vineet alert and focussed.
(b) Give the collective term for the protective membranes of the organ mentioned in (a).
(c) Which part of the autonomic nervous system increases the secretion of adrenaline?

8. (i) Explain the term excretion. [1]
(ii) State the difference between nephron and neuron. [2]
(iii) Mention any two objectives of Swachh Bharat Abhiyan. [2]
(iv) Give any two characteristic features of a Cro-Magnon man. [2]
(v) A farmer cultivates a unique species of tomato plants. The two traits selected for breeding were: Colour of the fruits and height of the plants. The farmer initially crosses a homozygous tall planf bearing red fruits (TTRR) with a dwarf plant bearing yellow fruits (ttrr) and the genotype of all the offsprings of the F_1-generation was TtRr. Next, he crosses two F_1-generation plants (TtRr). [3]

(a) Explain the phenotype of the offsprings of the F_1-generation obtained from the initial cross.
(b) Mention the phenotypic ratio of the F_2-generation offsprings.
(c) State Mendel's law of independent assortment.

Answers

1. (i) (d) Natality
   (ii) (a) Ciliary body
   (iii) (b) A is false and R is true. The seminal vesicles do secrete an alkaline fluid rich in fructose, but semen does not pass through the ureter. The ureter is the tube that carries urine from the kidneys to the bladder in males.
   (iv) (c) Oxytocin
   (v) (c) All the offsprings will have tails . This is because the length of a tail in mice is determined by genes, not by acquired traits.
   (vi) (c) Both A and R are true
   (vii) (d) 25- 35 °C
   (viii) (d) Both parents are heterozygous dominant
   (ix) (c) Both A and R are true
   (x) (a) Telophase
   (xi) (d) Both A and R are false . The arachnoid layer is one of the three meninges (protective coverings of the brain and spinal cord), but it does not play a direct role in nerve impulse transmission. And the correct neurotransmitter is acetylcholine (ACh), not "acetylene".
   (xii) (d) Thermal pollution
   (xiii) (c) Rods and rhodopsin
   (xiv) (a) *P* and *R*
   (xv) (b) Exophthalmic goiter, over secretion of thyroxine.

2. (i) (a) Graafian follicle (b) Cuticle
   (c) Stapes (d) Photosynthesis
   (e) Peppered Moth (*Biston Betularia*)
   (ii) (a) Pericardium
   (b) Pulmonary artery and Aorta
   (c) Chordae tendineae
   (d) Coronary
   (iii) (a) Cuticle, upper epidermis, Palisade cells, Spongy cells
   (b) Stomach, hepatic portal vein, liver, hepatic vein.
   (c) Dendrites, cyton (cell body), axon endings, and finally, the synaptic cleft.
   (d) High blood sugar, stimulates glucose uptake from blood, Insulin release, lowers blood glucose sugar.
   (e) Seminiferous tubules, Efferent duct , Epididymis, Sperm duct (Vas deferens)
   (iv) (a) Inguinal canal
   (b) Medulla oblongata
   (c) Pinna
   (d) Centromere
   (e) Guard cells
   (v) a- 2, b- 5, c -1 , d- 4, e- 3

3. (i) $6CO_2 + 6H_2O + \text{Light} + \text{Energy} \rightarrow C_6H_{12}O_6 + 6O_2$
   (ii) (a) Gibberellin
   (b) Parthenocarpic fruits
   (iii) Adenine and Thymine
   (iv) Two disdvantages are :
   (a) Airports generate constant loud noise from aircraft takeoff, landing, and taxiing.
   (b) expose residents to air pollution affecting health and overall well-being.
   (v)

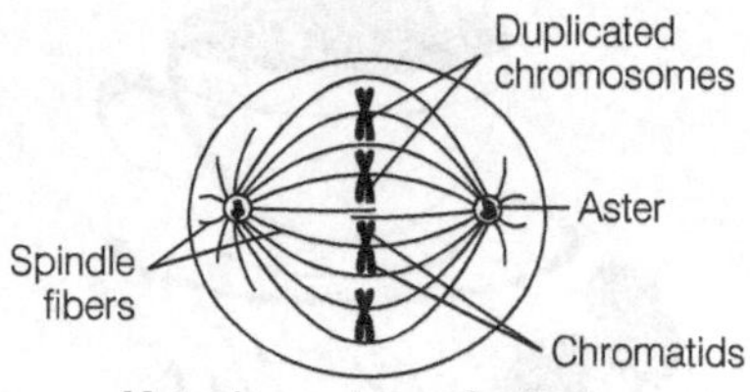

Metaphase stage of mitosis

4. (i) Double helical structure of DNA
   (ii) (a) Macrophage
   (b) B-lymphocytes
   (iii) (c) Eagle
   (d) Snake
   (iv) Harmful effects of Acid rain are
   (a) It damages the fish and other aquatic life.
   (b) It also damages the vegetation by killing the useful soil community
   (v) (a) Absorption of water and minerals from soil
   (b) Ascent of sap
   (c) Transpiration

5. (i) The process of expelling out of urine is known as micturition. This process is done under the impulse of nervous system.
   (ii) The wastes produced by the hospitals, clinics, laboratories are known as biomedical wastes. These are the major causes of soil pollution. For, e.g. Wound dressings.
   (iii) Urethra- Transports urine (and semen in males) out of the body
   Uterus- Supports fetal development during pregnancy
   (iv) (a) Semicircular canal
   (b) Static balance
   (v)

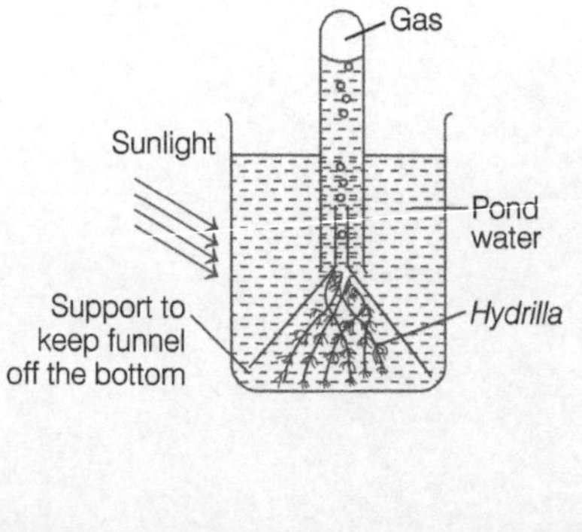

6. (i) At the tips and margins of leaves

(ii) The organs that are present in reduced for and do not perform any function in the body are called vestigial organs. For eg, The third pair of molars are the vestigial organ present in the mouth of the human. These are known as wisdom tooth.

(iii) The malleus (or hammer) of the middle ear on its one end is attached to the eardrum and other free end is attached to the oval window of the inner ear. It opens into Eustachian tube that connects with the pharynx and maintains the pressure on each sides of the ear drum. This is the reason, an infection in the throat may lead to the ear infections due to this connection.

(iv) (a) Cataract affects the lens of the eye

(b) The vision becomes blurred because the crystalline lens of the eye becomes milky or cludy due to the growth of a membrane over it.

(v)

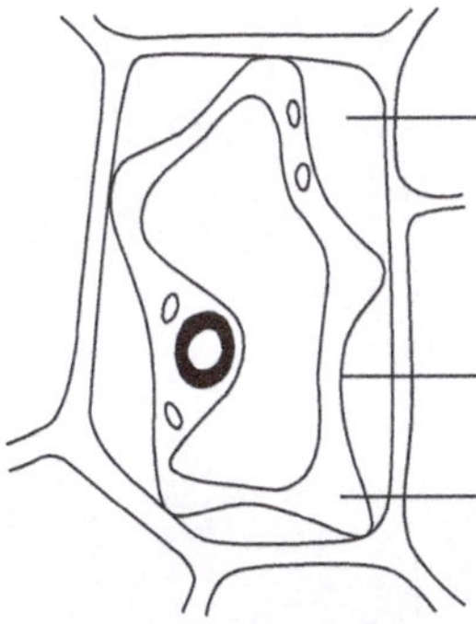

7. (i) Alleles are the alternative forms or varieties of gene in a particular gene pair.

(ii) (a) The one reason for the reduction in death rate is improved medical facilities

(b) Food resources as increased population may lead to shortage of food supply.

(iii) Amniotic fluid perform following functions:

(a) It provides an aqueous environment in which the embryo is protected from shocks and keep even pressure all around the embryo.

(b) It also restricts foetal movements and prevents sticking foetus to the amnion.

(iv) (a) CFC- Chloroflurocarbon

(b) CNG- Compressed Natural gas

(v) (a) Brain

(b) Meninges.

(c) The sympathetic nervous system (SNS) of the autonomic nervous system (ANS) increases the secretion of adrenaline.

8. (i) The process of removal of harmful metabolic waste products from the body is called excretion.

(ii) **Nephron**- The structural and functional unit of the kidney, responsible for filtration and urine formation.

Neuron- The structural and functional unit of the nervous system, responsible for transmitting nerve impulses.

(iii) Two objectives of Swachh Bharat Abhiyan are :

(a) To Eliminate open defecation

(b) To improve waste management & cleanliness

(iv) Two major features of Cro- Magnon man are:

(a) Broact and arched forehead

(b) Strong jaws

(v) (a) The phenotype of F_1 generation obtained by the initial cross is Tall red (TtRr)

(b) The phenotypic ration of F_2 generation is – 9:3:3:1

(c) The law of Independent assortment states that when two pairs of contrasting traits or characters are combined in a hybrid, segregation of one pair of character is independent of the other pair of character at the time of gamete formation.